Allianz and the German Insurance Business, 1933–1945

Gerald Feldman's history of the internationally prominent insurance corporation Allianz in the Nazi era is based largely on new or previously unavailable archival sources, making this a more accurate account of Allianz and the men who directed its business than was ever before possible. Feldman takes the reader through varied cases of collaboration and conflict with the Nazi regime with fairness and a commitment to informed analysis, touching on issues of damages in the Pogrom of 1938, insuring facilities used in concentration camps, and the problems of denazification and restitution. The broader issues examined in this study – when cooperation with Nazi policies was compulsory and when it was complicit; the way in which profit, ideology, and opportunism played a role in corporate decision making; and the question of how Jewish insurance assets were expropriated – are particularly relevant today given the ongoing international debate about restitution for Holocaust survivors. This book joins a growing body of scholarship based on free access to the records of German corporations in the Nazi era.

Gerald D. Feldman is Professor of History and Director of the Institute of European Studies at the University of California at Berkeley. His book, *The Great Disorder* (Oxford, 1993), received the DAAD Book Prize of the Association of German Studies and the Book Prize of the Conference Group for Central European History of the American Historical Association. He was an invited expert at the London Gold Conference in December 1997 and at the U.S. Conference on Holocaust Assets (Washington, DC) in December 1998. He serves on the Historical Commission of Deutsche Bank and is Chairman of the Historical Commission of Bank Austria.

Allianz and the German Insurance Business, 1933–1945

GERALD D. FELDMAN

University of California, Berkeley

CAMBRIDGE
UNIVERSITY PRESS

PUBLISHED BY THE PRESS SYNDICATE OF THE UNIVERSITY OF CAMBRIDGE
The Pitt Building, Trumpington Street, Cambridge, United Kingdom

CAMBRIDGE UNIVERSITY PRESS
The Edinburgh Building, Cambridge CB2 2RU, UK
40 West 20th Street, New York, NY 10011-4211, USA
10 Stamford Road, Oakleigh, VIC 3166, Australia
Ruiz de Alarcón 13, 28014 Madrid, Spain
Dock House, The Waterfront, Cape Town 8001, South Africa

http://www.cambridge.org

First published 2001

Printed in the United States of America

Typeface Sabon 10/12 pt.   *System* AMS-TEX   [FH]

A catalog record for this book is available from the British Library.

Library of Congress Cataloging in Publication Data
Feldman, Gerald D.
Allianz and the German insurance business, 1933–1945 / Gerald D. Feldman.
p.   cm.
Includes bibliographical references and index.
ISBN 0-521-80929-0
1. Allianz Versicherungs AG (Germany) – History – 20th century.   2. Insurance
companies – Germany – History – 20th century.   I. Title.

HD8619.Z9 A584   2001
368'.006'543 – dc21   2001035667

ISBN 0 521 80929 0 hardback

Contents

Contents

Preface

In the spring of 1997, the Board of Management of the Allianz AG commissioned me to write this history of Allianz in the National Socialist period and to do so as an independent historian accountable only for the completion of the study according to the standards of my profession. The immediate reasons for their decision to promote such a study at that time were very clear. On the one hand, Allianz – along with a number of other German and European insurance companies – was charged in class actions in United States courts with failure to properly discharge their obligations toward Jewish policyholders. Allianz thus had the problem of explaining what had happened to the policies of its Jewish customers, and this involved explaining not only how Jewish assets were expropriated by the National Socialist regime but also the postwar restitution policies. On the other hand, Allianz found itself confronted with press reports[1] about insuring SS-owned factories in the concentration camps, among them factories in Auschwitz. The revelations inevitably lent new importance and significance to what had previously been known but unappreciated or neglected. One example is that of Kurt Schmitt, the general director of Allianz between 1921 and 1933, who had been Hitler's second Reich Economics Minister in 1933–1934 and regularly appeared in an SS uniform while in office. Another example concerns an Allianz director, Eduard Hilgard, who had led the Reich Group for Insurance between 1934 and 1945 and had also participated in the infamous meeting of November 12, 1938, summoned by Hermann Göring in the Reich Air Ministry following the Pogrom unleashed against the Jews on November 9. Exactly what all this added up to was impossible to say, at least for the ideologically unpredisposed, since there was no adequately researched and accurate account of the Allianz in the Third Reich. An understanding of Allianz's history during that period was unlikely to emerge by simply stumbling from one unpleasant and damaging press revelation to another. Also, the adoption of a bunker mentality (as was attempted by some firms and concerns inside and outside Germany) was not deemed an acceptable solution by those managing Allianz. In practical terms, one cannot defend or explain a historical record if one does not know what is in that record. The company's situation was like that of a number of other concerns and firms taking a similar posture who have sought the help

---

[1] See "Das 'Wagnis Auschwitz'," *Der Spiegel*, Heft 23 (June 1997), pp. 50–63.

of historians practiced in the fields of economic and business history and with knowledge of the period and conditions under which businessmen operated between 1933 and 1945.

The significance of this revolutionary situation in the status of business history – and of the relationship between some enterprises and historians – deserves some brief comment and reflection here in order to place this book in its context. Until recently, historians like myself with an interest in economic and business history have formed a small and somewhat isolated group in the profession. Historians, like most intellectuals, have often taken a somewhat dim view of the object of our interests – namely, business – which they have treated either with intellectual disdain or with profound suspicion and even hostility. Prior to the end of the Cold War, the subject of business history, especially in Germany, was caught up in ideological debates about the purported responsibility of business for bringing Hitler to power and the question of whether the Nazi regime could be viewed as an instrument of big business. Neither of these positions can be seriously maintained today, but the question of what the actual relationship was between big business and National Socialism has only been made more pressing and important by now being considered and answered in different terms. Indeed, the role of business is more important than ever before, and it still remains for practitioners of business history to assert – and for general historians to recognize – the centrality of the modern corporation and the business community to our understanding of the modern world.

However, much of the suspicion aimed at business history, as well as its neglect, must be laid at the door of the business community itself. The old response of German business to liberal and left-wing critics was that business was a victim of National Socialist anticapitalism and totalitarianism – a simplistic explanation of a complex relationship that was implausible from the start. It was left unproven because closed business archives and inaccessible archives in the communist East acted as a barrier to serious historical investigation. Previously, with very few exceptions, industrial firms commissioned journalists or historians to write celebratory volumes on the occasion of some major anniversary, and very often the most important contribution of the volumes thus produced were the pictures. The authors of such works certainly were not invited to deal with the darker sides of company histories and were often discouraged from doing so. At the same time, independent historians had a difficult time getting firms to open their archives about matters pertaining to even the nineteenth century, let alone the National Socialist period. Indeed, many important companies did not even have an archive. Also, serious business and economic historians were unwilling to subject themselves to censorship or to engage in self-censorship. Only a few enterprises were prepared to permit scholars unfettered use of their documentary materials or to encourage serious business histories. Therefore, the present situation – in which one enterprise after another has been establishing archives, opening their archives to historians, and supplying them with substantial resources and assistance to facilitate dredging up details of their history during the

National Socialist period – constitutes a major breakthrough for business historians and for the field of business history.[2] One should, of course, guard against euphoria. There is no guarantee that the present "boom" will not turn to "bust," and that the increased interest in business history will not be mostly confined to the Third Reich, or that its practitioners will not be marginalized once again. Also, it is always possible that archives will be closed and that companies will return to the production of slick anniversary volumes lacking in serious content. Nevertheless, it is my hope that the lessons learned from recent experience include these two: ignorance is not bliss; and the promotion of critical business history is a public responsibility and a wise policy as well. The business community can only benefit from a sober appreciation of its own history. At the same time, it is essential that historians pay more attention to business history as a crucial area of general history in the modern age, since they do, after all, have some responsibility to their students and the general public to explain the real world in which we live.

This said, the author of such a study faces certain serious methodological and practical problems that deserve mention. Scholars producing a study in political, diplomatic, or cultural history have the benefit of a substantial body of literature in their fields upon which they can rely for background and for the definition of the questions they seek to answer. Ideally, the work now being done on the business history of the Third Reich should be done in the context of business biographies, general literature on the role of business in modern German history, and a well-developed general business history literature of carefully researched and sophisticated corporate histories based on open archives and written by independent historians. For the reasons already stated, this is not how things are. This is especially true of the insurance business, which (in contrast to banking or iron and steel) suffers particularly from a dearth of modern historical literature dealing with the industry as a whole and with individual enterprises. There are, to be sure, some useful works at hand, but a study such as this – which concentrates on a particular period and on certain special issues – must suffer from the absence of a well-developed secondary literature.[3]

---

[2] The Deutsche Bank pioneered such studies and then continued after the business history of the Third Reich became a public issue. See Lothar Gall et al., *The Deutsche Bank 1870–1995* (London, 1995), and Jonathan Steinberg, *The Deutsche Bank and Its Gold Transactions during the Second World War* (Munich, 1999). Other illustrations are in Johannes Bähr, *Der Goldhandel der Dresdner Bank im Zweiten Weltkrieg. Ein Bericht des Hannah-Arendt-Instituts* (Leipzig, 1999). See also Hans Mommsen & Manfred Grieger, *Das Volkswagenwerk und seine Arbeiter im Dritten Reich* (Düsseldorf, 1996); Werner Lotz, *Die Deutsche Reichspost 1933–1945. Eine politische Verwaltungsgeschichte, Bd. 1: 1933–1939* (Berlin, 1999); and Gerd R. Ueberschär, *Die Deutsche Reichspost 1933–1945. Eine politische Verwaltungsgeschichte, Bd. 2: 1939–1945* (Berlin, 1999).

[3] Ludwig Arps, *Auf sicheren Pfeilern. Deutsche Versicherungswirtschaft vor 1914* (Göttingen, 1965), and Ludwig Arps, *Durch unruhige Zeiten. Deutsche Versicherungswirtschaft seit 1914, Bd. 1: Erster Weltkrieg und Inflation, Bd. 2: Von den zwanziger Jahren zum Zweiten Weltkrieg* (Karlsruhe, 1970 & 1976). See also Eckhard Wandel, *Banken und Versicherungen im 19. und 20. Jahrhundert* [Enzyklopädie Deutscher Geschichte, Bd. 45] (Munich, 1998).

There are some scholars in the field of business history who would view this
as a fatal barrier to a satisfactory study and would indeed go so far as to argue
that one can properly deal with the history of Allianz (or any other company)
only in the context of a corporate history based on subordination of their accounts to questions of "the internal economic logic of entrepreneurial action."[4]
In its most extreme form, business historians taking this position would argue
that business history is, in effect, a subordinate field of economics and economic
history and that the analysis and judgment of business behavior can only take
place once it has been analyzed from an economic perspective. In this view, the
writing of histories of firms in the Third Reich should wait upon the production
of their economic histories, since "[w]ithout the prior appropriate analysis of
the real conditions under which businessmen act, all premature assessment ...
easily takes on the odor of cheap moralizing."[5]
There is a strong tendency in Germany for methodological debates to take
on a doctrinal character in which positions are inflexibly defended and maintained at the expense of common sense. This is not the place for such exercises.
The amount of information at our disposal is always imperfect, and it would
be absurd for those working on business history in the Third Reich to enter
into a state of suspended animation and wait upon the analyses of those seeking to unravel the "economic logic" of the concerns in question before coming
to judgment about various aspects of their histories. And while it is instructive
and important to study business history from a purely economic perspective,
it is no less important to examine the political and moral economy of entrepreneurial behavior – as this study seeks to do. Furthermore, as will be shown
throughout this book, the individuals running Allianz and the insurance industry
were compelled to conduct their business in the context of a regime that powerfully influenced or increasingly dictated decisions about investments, products
and markets, and industrial relations in ways that to a substantial degree did
not conform to any "economic logic" previously known to them. Finally, "economic logic" does not exist independently of business ethics and basic moral
standards. National Socialism challenged all of these qualities of what one
can consider appropriate business (or even human) behavior; it is quite legitimate, indeed necessary, to approach business history from these perspectives.
Hence this study, while holding fast to traditional methods of historical analysis
and certainly eschewing armchair anticapitalism, seeks to arrive at some clear

---

[4] "[D]ie innere ökonomische Logik unternehmerischen Handelns"; Toni Pierenkemper, "Was kann
eine moderne Unternehmensgeschichte leisten? Und was sollte sie tunlichst vermeiden," *Zeitschrift
für Unternehmensgeschichte* 44/1 (1999), pp. 15–31, quote on p. 20; Manfred Pohl, "Zwischen
Weihrauch und Wissenschaft? Zum Standort der modernen Unternehmensgeschichte. Eine Replik auf Toni Pierenkemper," ibid., 44/2 (1999), pp. 150–63; Toni Pierenkemper, "Sechs Thesen
zum gegenwärtigen Stand der deutschen Unternehmensgeschichtsschreibung. Eine Entgegnung
auf Manfred Pohl," ibid., 45/2 (2000), pp. 158–66.
[5] "Ohne eine vorausgehende, sachgerechte Analyse der realen Handlungsbedingungen der Unternehmer gerät alles vorschnelle Bewerten m.E. sehr leicht in den Ruch wohlfeilen Moralisierens."
Pierenkemper in ibid., 44/1, p. 31.

conclusions that contain moral judgments about business behavior under National Socialism.

This study relies heavily on primary source material, which might at first sight seem surprising in view of the almost total destruction of the Allianz archive in wartime bombing raids. In fact, the most difficult and frustrating research problem faced in completing this study was that most of the original Allianz archive – and especially the papers of its board of management – were destroyed in bombing raids during the war. This has imposed severe constraints on subjects about which I would have wished to say more. For example, the inability to discuss middle management and to present information about the political activities and party membership of Allianz employees has been a constant disappointment. In many cases, I was forced to depend heavily on postwar interrogations and denazification proceedings. Obviously, such materials must be used with caution, and yet they were often the only sources at my disposal. The remnant of the original Allianz materials, however substantial and significant in many respects, is what Allianz employees managed to take with them for whatever reason, or what has been found at other companies or branches in the concern, or in the private possession of the families of former Allianz managers. The papers of Kurt Schmitt, for example, have proven an invaluable source for this study. These materials have been gathered together to form the core of the Allianz archive, but the bulk of the materials used in this study came from public and private archives and collections to be found not only in Germany but also in places stretching from Paris to Moscow and from Milan to Tallinn. The management of Allianz not only supported but also encouraged me and my research team to go wherever we felt significant material might be found.

Although a list of the archives visited by myself and my research team will be found at the end of this book, certain aspects of our research effort deserve special mention. One of the major reasons it has been possible to secure so much archival material about Allianz and insurers generally is that insurance was a regulated industry subject to the control of the Reich Supervisory Office for Insurance, and this authority was subordinate to the Reich Economics Ministry. The papers of the Reich Supervisory Office at the German Federal Archives were a tremendously rich source for this study. An especially critical source were the papers of the Reich Economics Ministry dealing with banking and insurance. As it turned out, this enormous collection was to be found in the so-called Special Archive in Moscow, and it has played a major role not only in this study but also in the work of colleagues investigating the banking history of the Third Reich and other important questions related to Holocaust assets. We take special pride in the fact that we were among the first to use these papers systematically for the business history of the Third Reich and so helped to inform the research of our colleagues who worked there subsequently.[6]

---

[6] Barbara Eggenkämper, Marian Rappl, & Anna Reichel, "Der Bestand Reichswirtschaftsministerium im 'Zentrum für die Aufbewahrung historisch-dokumentarischer Sammlungen' ('Sonderarchiv') in Moskau," ibid., 43 (1998), pp. 227–36.

There are two other important archival collections that deserve special mention at this point because of their relation to the content of this study. These include the documents of the Munich Reinsurance Company (Münchener Rückversicherungs-Gesellschaft AG or Münchener Rück). As we shall see, "Munich Re" and Allianz were closely related both by formal contract and in their activities during this period. The Munich Re collections made a substantive contribution to this study at practically every point. Of similar importance for the writing of this book were the papers of the Reich Association for Private Insurance and the Reich Group for Insurance in the archive of the present-day Association of German Insurers. Allianz was the largest and most dominant concern in the German insurance business and played an especially active role in the major organizations of the industry. This does not mean that the history of the other German insurance companies can be dismissed as more or less miniature histories of Allianz. On the contrary, it will be very important to have histories of those companies – all of which have their own peculiar characteristics and interests – if we are ever to attain a satisfactory understanding of the insurance business. Nevertheless, as noted earlier, the German insurance business was government regulated and, especially during the National Socialist period, had to deal with the government in a collective manner. This was done through the Reich Association for Private Insurance and the Reich Group for Insurance, created in 1934, both of which were led by an Allianz manager and dominated to a significant extent by Allianz and Munich Re managers. In this respect, this is not only a history of Allianz during the Third Reich but also of the politics of the private insurance business in that period.

It has been gratifying to have had access to so many archives within and outside Germany, and this testifies to the new openness about the history of the National Socialist period and the problems of Holocaust assets. It is also necessary to record, however, that certain archives remained unavailable to us. In the case of the Polish government archives in Wroclaw (Breslau), the papers of the Allianz branch in that city became unavailable when the archive flooded in 1997. Many precious materials were in need of restoration, and the papers of interest for this study were unavailable in time for the completion of this work. One can only hope that these documents will be in condition to be evaluated at some future date. Despite many requests, we were repeatedly denied access to the archives of the Powszechny Zakład Ubezpieczeń S.A. (PZU), successor company to the previously nationalized Polish insurance organization and which we believe to have papers of liquidated German insurers that had operated in Poland. We were constantly told that the archives were being "reorganized." It strains my credulity to believe that some accommodation could not have been made for research pertaining to this project. Certainly the account of Allianz activities in occupied Poland would have benefited from access to these materials.

One may hope that such archival sources are opened at a future date, and one may be certain that some new documents and information will turn up over the years. Nevertheless, I am reasonably confident that this book presents a full and accurate account of the history of Allianz and its daughter companies in the National Socialist period. There will, of course, always be differences of interpretation, and from this perspective no historical work can be definitive. One of the conditions of my undertaking this project was that the documents I used be made available to other researchers so as to satisfy the scholarly requirements of replication and falsification – as well as to open the doors to further research. I have tried to provide enough evidence to enable other interpretations of the difficult questions dealt with in the text.

The organization of this book is designed to illuminate the most important aspects of the relationship between Allianz and National Socialism. The first chapter tries at once to provide essential background on the history and organization of Allianz, especially in the Weimar Republic, and to deal with the important contacts between leaders of Allianz and National Socialists – primarily Hermann Göring – prior to 1933. The next three chapters deal with the relationship of Allianz and the insurance industry organizations with the regime in the prewar period. Thus, Chapter 2 discusses the initial adaptation of Allianz to the regime and the appointment and policies of Allianz's general director, Kurt Schmitt, as Reich Economics Minister. Chapter 3 examines the extent of Nazification within the concern and especially its policies toward Jewish employees and its role in "Aryanizations." Chapter 4 explores Eduard Hilgard's role as leader of the Reich Group for Insurance, the politics of the insurance business and its internal conflicts, and the struggle between Nazi leaders of the publicly chartered insurance companies and leadership of the private insurance industry.

The next two chapters are more topical in character and focus on events and issues of both historical and current significance. Chapter 5 is concerned with the role of the insurance industry in dealing with the problems created by the Pogrom of November 1938 – a sorry story at once dramatic and complicated – in which problems of liability and business ethics are explored in depth. Chapter 6 deals with the question of the expropriation of Jewish insurance assets, which is obviously the issue of greatest concern in the recent lawsuits against Allianz and other insurers. Its purpose is to explain the various processes by which Jews lost their assets between 1933 and 1945 and to describe the behavior of Allianz toward its Jewish customers. It is worth noting here that the purpose of my work has never been to discover unpaid Jewish insurance policies, which is the task of auditors, but rather to treat the problem historically.

The two subsequent chapters take up various issues of importance to the history of the concern between 1938 and 1945. Chapter 7 deals with the role of Allianz in Germany's prewar expansion into Austria and Czechoslovakia and its continued struggles with the publicly chartered companies. Chapter 8 discusses the expansion of Allianz in the West and the East in German-controlled Europe, its implication in various business operations connected with the crimes of the regime, and its efforts to stay afloat as Germany headed toward defeat. The final chapter of the book examines two themes of the post-1945 period: the denazification at Allianz and the restitution of Jewish assets between 1945 and 1960.

I think it important to conclude this portion of the preface by returning directly to the question of my position as a historian commissioned to undertake this work. At no time during the entire course of this project has the management of Allianz sought in any way to influence my findings or interpretations. Because of the complexity of the insurance business, I have turned to various persons in the concern for technical information, and I have also pressed for clarifications where further information was needed. Such information was always supplied generously and patiently. Furthermore, the management of Allianz gave me every conceivable assistance in my research. It graciously accepted the fact that the study could not be finished in the time originally expected and would not be as short as initially desired, and it also extended the contracts of my research team when this proved necessary.

In short, Allianz's management did everything possible to facilitate my work. At the beginning of the project, it was agreed that my study would be submitted to a group of historians chosen by me to review what I had written and make criticisms and suggestions. Such a meeting was held in May 2000 with eight historians.[7] The work had not been finished at that time, but chapters were sent out to some of these historians subsequently, and the entire manuscript has been vetted by readers. The historians involved reviewed my manuscript at the same time as the management of Allianz received it, so that the findings were made known simultaneously. The comments and questions of the colleagues who read the manuscript have been extremely valuable and have contributed to the final product in many positive ways. The manuscript has never been vetted by Allianz. Needless to say, the sole responsibility for this book rests with myself.

This does not conclude the question of my independence, however, since various persons have challenged the idea that a historian paid to produce such a work can truly be independent. I must confess that I find this attitude a curious one. All professional experts are paid for their services and are expected to provide clients with full, accurate information and unbiased judgments, for which they are professionally accountable. Manifestly, some professional experts are paid to argue a case as best as their expertise and the available evidence permit. In the case of a historian, it is unethical to accept compensation to argue a case, and it would be unethical for a client to ask him or her to do so. I see no reason, however, why historians should not be compensated for their work as independent scholars – especially when their expertise has been built up over a long professional life – or why reasonable compensation will make them less honest. More importantly, I can imagine no sum worth my personal and scholarly reputation, and I think that the colleagues I work with in this field feel the same way. There are always those ready to criticize a historian committed to the free market system who is working on such a topic. Yet part of that commitment is to be highly critical of those businessmen who – through whatever combination

---

[7] The historians, aside from members of my research team, were Johannes Bähr, Avraham Barkai, Ingo Böhle, Harold James, Stefan Karlen, Hans Mommsen, Dieter F. Stiefel, and Dieter Ziegler.

of political short-sightedness, opportunism, and sheer greed – nearly destroyed German capitalism and had co-responsibility for the wreckage experienced by concerns like Allianz in 1945. Finally, I think it worth noting that I am a Jew, and that there have been many times when I have found working on this book depressing and even intolerable. I took this assignment in part because I believed it was high time that I actually researched and not merely taught the history of the Third Reich. I do not regret having done so, but the research and writing of this book have been anything but conducive to the softening of my views and judgments. There are a number of ways to write such a history, and every historian will do it somewhat differently. Whether I have done so fairly and successfully, and whether this book has done anything but let the historical chips fall where they may, is for the reader to decide.

This book owes a great deal to the labor, support, and engagement of many persons. It is no exaggeration to say that this study could have been neither undertaken nor completed without the tireless and enthusiastic efforts of the research team organized by the head of the Center for Corporate History of Allianz AG, Barbara Eggenkämper. She not only led the team but was a major participant in its work and, indeed, in every aspect of this project. I wish to express my appreciation for the rare combination of historical sensibility, organizational and managerial skill, good sense, and cheerfulness she displayed in the course of our work together. I would like to thank Stefan Laube, Anna Reichel, and Stephan Wendehorst for their excellent work surveying and collecting archival materials during the research phase of this project, as well as my assistants at Berkeley: Drew Keeling, for his work at the U.S. National Archives, and Sean McMeekin for helping to prepare the English version of the manuscript. Evelyn Zegenhagen assisted me with my research in Poland and catalogued a substantial portion of the archival materials used in this study. She helped me in numerous other ways during my stays in Berlin and Berkeley; she applied her historical training most effectively to work her way into the very difficult subject matter of this study and went well beyond the call of duty in assisting me. Gerd Modert and Marian Rappl have worked on this project from its inception to its conclusion, and Stefan Pretzlik joined the team for its final three years. All three researched in archives throughout Europe and catalogued the many complicated documents. With their keen sense of detail and wide knowledge of the subject, they painstakingly went through the preparation of the manuscript and helped to edit the German and English versions of the book. They contributed enormously to save me from errors both major and minor and to improve on its clarity and fluidity. Working with these talented young German historians has been both a personal pleasure and an intellectually gratifying experience.

This work was supported by the management of Allianz AG in ways that were more than material. I am grateful to Henning Schulte-Noelle for his friendly reception and expressions of support, and I am especially indebted to Herbert Hansmeyer for his active interest and encouragement of my work, our interesting conversations about problems of corporate culture and other issues, from which I learned a great deal, and his gracious hospitality during my visits to Munich. Emilio Galli-Zugaro was enthusiastic and forthcoming in a host of ways, and it was a pleasure to work with him. They all made it possible for me to tap various offices at Allianz AG for information and technical assistance, and they strove to open research opportunities outside Allianz AG that would otherwise have been difficult or impossible to come by. I wish to express a special word of thanks to Walter Neiss of Allianz Lebensversicherungs-AG for clarifying important technical issues connected with life insurance and also to their company for allowing access to files. The importance of the Münchener Rückversicherungs-Gesellschaft AG files has already been noted, and I am most grateful to its management for their cooperation. The head of Corporate Communications of Allianz Elementar Versicherungs-AG in Vienna, Marita Roloff, was most forthcoming during my visit to Vienna and also provided me with the benefit of her historical expertise.

I profited in significant ways from access to other private archives and persons related to or connected with their leadership. In Germany, the archive of the Hamburg-Mannheimer Versicherungs-Gruppe provided valuable material, as did the AXA Colonia Konzern AG. Roland Knebusch, the grandson of Johannes Tiedke, who was general director of Alte Leipziger Versicherung AG, gave me access to important documents and also offered his hospitality and a memorable evening of discussion. Volker Weiß of Alte Leipziger was kind enough to supplement this documentation. The archival materials in the Gesamtverband der deutschen Versicherungswirtschaft were of exceptional importance to this study, and I would like to thank Gabriele Hoffmann, Gloria Neuhaus, and Jörg Fischer for their gracious assistance. In Switzerland, I received access to the rich materials in the archive of the Schweizerische Rückversicherungs-Gesellschaft and wish to express my gratitude to those who made this possible. I would like to thank Peter Spaelti and Silvia Balsiger-Signer of the Winterthur Lebensversicherung for their assistance and Heinz Fehlmann for making available correspondence between his father Heinrich Fehlmann and Kurt Schmitt. An important and fascinating source was the papers of Arnoldo Frigessi di Rattalma in the Banca Commerciale Italiana in Milan; the bank's archivist Francesca Pino informed me of their existence, and I am extremely grateful to her and to the donor, Adolfo Frigessi. I would also like to thank Giulio Baseggio and his colleagues at the Riunione Adriatica di Sicurtá S.p.A. for their hospitality and assistance.

The papers of Kurt Schmitt constitute one of the most important sources for this study, and I am very much in debt to his granddaughter, Vera Krainer, for inviting me to the family home in Tiefenbrunn, searching for them with me, and turning them over to the Center for Corporate History of Allianz AG. The generosity of the Krainer family and their appreciation of the importance of making these papers available for historical study was a memorable moment in my research. I would also like to express my appreciation to Hermann Niemöller for sharing with me his memories of Kurt Schmitt and the Schmitt family and for providing some valuable documentation. Two smaller but very useful sets of personal papers were those of Eduard Hilgard and Hans Heß, and I would like to thank Hilgard's grandson, Herbert Schneidler, and the family of Hans Heß for their willingness to have the papers copied and placed in the Allianz archive.

The research team and I worked in a host of public archives, and we are grateful for all the assistance received from the archivists and staffs of these institutions. It would be impossible to mention every archive and every person who helped us here, but we would like to express a special note of gratitude to Andrej W. Doronin for all the aid he gave us during our visit to the "Special Archive" in Moscow as well as to Roman A. Matwejew, who patiently pored over the Russian catalogues with us and translated them volume by volume into German. We also wish to record our special appreciation to the hard-pressed staff of the Bundesarchiv in Berlin, which was so forthcoming whenever we descended on the archive.

I benefited greatly from the comments and suggestions of the historians who attended the symposium to discuss my manuscript, and I thank them for their interest and diligence. I would like to add a special word of thanks to Ralf Banken, Ingo Böhle, Stefan Karlen, Andrea H. Schneider, and Dieter F. Stiefel for providing important documents and information arising from their own work and to Peter Hayes and Dieter Ziegler for reading the final version of the manuscript in full.

Even peripatetic scholars like myself need institutional bases during their journeys, and I have been extremely fortunate in this respect. I spent 1997/98 at the Wissenschaftszentrum Berlin, which was generous in providing me not only with facilities but also with a great deal of intellectual companionship. I would like to thank Meinolf Dierkes for bringing me there and its former President Friedhelm Neidhardt and his colleagues for doing everything possible to make my stay so productive. In 1998/99, I had the good fortune to be awarded a Berlin Prize Fellowship to the newly created American Academy in Berlin. It was exhilarating to participate in the birth of so significant a new institution. The Academy proved a wonderful venue to continue my work and also to begin presenting some of the fruits of my research and my ideas to the stimulating intellectual community in Berlin. I am grateful to Academy Director Gary Smith and his able, helpful, and gracious staff for providing such splendid working conditions. I am most appreciative of the understanding shown by the History Department of the University of California at Berkeley and by the university itself for its willingness to permit me so protracted a stay in Berlin.

This study is appearing in both German and English, and I owe a great deal to my editors and their staffs. Working with Ernst-Peter Wieckenberg of the Verlag C. H. Beck over the past decade is one of the most treasured experiences of my professional life. He is a cherished friend as well as a remarkable editor. From the beginning, he has supported this study with unabated enthusiasm and throughout he has afforded me encouragement in too many ways to mention. Frank Smith of Cambridge University Press has long shown interest in my work in general and in this project in particular, and it is a privilege and pleasure to do this book with him. I am extremely grateful to him and to the staff at Cambridge University Press for facilitating the publication of this study in every conceivable way. I would like to add a special word of thanks to Matt Darnell, whose copyediting has improved this book in many ways.

My wife, Norma von Ragenfeld-Feldman, is a never-ending source of strength and inspiration, and her devotion to me and involvement in this project during a period of much personal loss and sadness have been extraordinary. I have been very fortunate.

This book is dedicated to the memory of the Jewish employees of Allianz. Sadly, we do not have a complete record of all of them. As shall be related in the course of this book, some were murdered while others were fortunate enough to survive. They all, however, suffered isolation from and rejection by the society in which they had peacefully lived and productively labored and thus, in one form or another, shared the bitter experience of being cast out.

Abbreviations

a. G.	auf Gegenseitigkeit (mutual)
AM	Amtsgericht München, Registratur S
AN	Archives Nationales, Paris
APL	Archiwum Państwowe w Łodzi (State Archive Lodz)
APP	Archiwum Państwowe w Poznaniu (State Archive Poznan)
AVV	Allgemeiner Verband der Versicherungsangestellten (General Association of Insurance Employees)
AXA	AXA Colonia Konzern AG, Historisches Archiv
AZLB	Allianz Lebensversicherungs-AG, Archiv Berlin
AZ Wien	Allianz Elementar Versicherungs-AG, Archiv (Vienna)
BAB	Bundesarchiv Berlin
BAK	Bundesarchiv Koblenz
BAR	Schweizerisches Bundesarchiv (Bern)
BCI	Banca Commerciale Italiana, Archivo (Milan)
BEG	Bundesentschädigungsgesetz (Federal Restitution Law)
BGBl	Bundesgesetzblatt (Federal Official Legislative Journal)
Bl.	Blatt (folio)
CABR	Ministerie van Justitie, Centraal Archief Bijzondere Rechtspleging (Ministry of Justice, Central Archive for Special Legal Questions)
CREH	Centre de Recherches et d'Etudes Historiques de la Seconde Guerre Mondiale (Center of Research for Historical Studies of the Second World War)
DAF	Deutsche Arbeitsfront (German Labor Front)
DAW	Deutsche Ausrüstungswerke GmbH
DINTA	Deutsches Institut für Technische Arbeitsschulung (German Institute for Technical Labor Training)
DNVP	Deutschnationale Volkspartei (German National People's Party)
Favag	Frankfurter Allgemeine Versicherungs-AG
FHA	Firmenhistorisches Archiv der Allianz AG (Center for Corporate History of the Allianz AG)
GDV	Gesamtverband der deutschen Versicherungswirtschaft e.V. (General Association of the German Insurance Industry), Archiv

Gestapo	Geheime Staatspolizei
GM	Goldmark
HADB	Historisches Archiv der Deutschen Bank
HessHStA	Hessisches Hauptstaatsarchiv
HM	Hamburg-Mannheimer Versicherungs-Gruppe, Unternehmensarchiv
Hptm.	Hauptmann (captain)
HTO	Haupttreuhandstelle Ost (Head Trusteeship Bureau East)
IfZ	Institut für Zeitgeschichte
IG Farben	Interessengemeinschaft Farbenindustrie AG
JRSO	Jewish Restitution Successor Organization
KZ	Konzentrationslager (concentration camp)
MdF	Ministère des Finances, Office des Séquestres (Sequestration Archive)
MR	Münchener Rückversicherungs-Gesellschaft AG (Munich Reinsurance Company – Munich Re) Historisches Archiv
NA	U.S. National Archives
NL	Nachlaß (personal papers)
NSBO	Nationalsozialistische Betriebszellen-Organisation (National Socialist Factory Cell Organization)
NSDAP	Nationalsozialistische Deutsche Arbeiterpartei (National Socialist German Labor Party)
OMGUS	Office of Military Government, United States
ÖstA-AdR	Österreichisches Staatsarchiv - Archiv der Republik
ÖVAG	Österreichische Versicherungs-AG
Pg.	Parteigenosse (Party comrade)
RAA	Reichsaufsichtsamt für Privatversicherung (Reich Supervisory Office for Insurance)
RAS	Riunione Adriatica di Securtà
RFM	Reichsfinanzministerium (Reich Finance Ministry)
RGBl	Reichsgesetzblatt (Reich Official Legislative Journal)
RIOD	Rijksinstituut voor Orlogsdocumentatie
RJM	Reichsjustizministerium (Reich Justice Ministry)
RM	Reichsmark
RWM	Reichswirtschaftsministerium (Reich Economics Ministry)
SA	Sturmabteilung der NSDAP (storm troopers)
SD	Sicherheitsdienst der SS (security service of the SS)
SM	Centr Chranenijsa Istoriko-Dokumental'nych Kollekcii [Zentrum für die Aufbewahrung historisch-dokumentarischer Sammlungen – "Sonderarchiv Moskau"] (Special Archive, Moscow)
SR	Schweizerische Rückversicherungs-Gesellschaft (Swiss Reinsurance Company – Swiss Re), Archiv
SS	Schutzstaffel der NSDAP

VAG   Versicherungsaufsichtsgesetz (Insurance Supervisory Law)
WGÄ   Wiedergutmachungsämter von Berlin (Restitution Offices, Berlin)
WGB   Wiedergutmachungsbehörde Bayern (Restitution Authority,
           Bavaria)
ZN   Zweigniederlassung (branch)

Photo Credits

1

The Allianz Concern and Its Leaders, 1918–1933

ONE of the most extraordinary aspects of modern Germany is that so many of its greatest enterprises have managed to survive the misadventures of its political history. Of the five political systems that have held sway on German soil since 1870, four have suffered an ignominious demise, and a goodly number of the street names that were identified with those regimes have disappeared with them. Not so with a host of German companies and corporations founded in the nineteenth century. Siemens, Krupp, Thyssen, Bosch, Degussa, Deutsche Bank, Dresdner Bank, and the MAN are still with us; though changing modes of production and globalization are creating fusions of and transformations in these companies that may more profoundly affect their futures than two world wars, they still have kept their identification as German companies with a continuous tradition for a remarkably long period of time. This also holds true for many of the leading enterprises in the German insurance field, one of the most neglected areas of German business history despite its lengthy development over time and extraordinary importance to the German economy. It holds true also for the largest among the leading insurance companies and the subject of this book, the Allianz.[1]

As indicated in the Preface, this study cannot and is not intended to remedy the absence of full historical accounts that might do justice to Allianz and the important branch of the German economy in which it is embedded, although one may hope that other historians will be encouraged to address happier periods in the growth and development of Allianz and the German insurance business. Here the concentration must be on those elements in the history of Allianz – and those problems in the private German insurance industry – that are relevant for understanding the policies and practices of their leaders between 1933 and 1945 and their efforts to cope with the legacy of National Socialism after 1945. The most important of these elements were shaped and formed during the years following Germany's defeat in 1918, and it is necessary to begin this study with a

---

[1] Allianz's name has changed often over the years. Founded in 1890 as the Allianz Versicherungs-Aktien-Gesellschaft (Allianz Insurance Corporation), it was renamed the Allianz und Stuttgarter Verein Versicherungs-Aktien-Gesellschaft (Allianz and Stuttgart Association Insurance Corporation) in 1927; in 1940 it returned to the old name Allianz Versicherungs-Aktiengesellschaft. In this study, the short designation "Allianz" will be employed.

brief survey of the key relevant developments in Allianz's history that make intelligible its mode of adaptation to the Third Reich and subsequent recovery.

BUILDING THE CONCERN

The Allianz Insurance Corporation was founded in 1890 in Berlin as a joint stock company with a capital of 4 million marks. It was initially licensed to provide transportation and accident insurance, as well as reinsurance in the fields of life, accident, fire, and transportation. In reality, it was a daughter company of the Munich Reinsurance Co. (Munich Re, founded in 1880), whose driving personalities – General Director Carl Thieme (1844–1924) and banker Wilhelm Finck (1848–1924), the chairman of the supervisory board – decided to enter the direct insurance business in Berlin in order to gain speedy approval of a concession from the Prussian government and access to the North German and national markets. Another Munich Re director, Paul von der Nahmer (1858–1921), joined the board of directors of Allianz in 1894, thus intensifying the union between the two companies and providing Allianz with excellent banking connections and the benefits of von der Nahmer's international experience. He became sole chairman of the board of directors in 1904. The choice of the Reich eagle as Allianz's logo, with the Munich Kindl and the Berlin Bear in the left and right bottom corners, pointed to the original and new location of the enterprise, although the specificity of these particularist elements was eliminated in 1923 when the logo was transformed to reflect at once the unity and the multiplicity of an expanded company. The new logo showed a single mother eagle encompassing three smaller eagles, and while the contours of the logo were to become "softer" and more appealing by the mid-1970s, the basic symbolism was retained after 1923.[2]

Initially concentrating on accident and transport insurance, particularly of valuables and gold, Allianz rapidly expanded its fields of endeavor. It pioneered machine insurance, took up break-in and theft insurance, and entered the liability insurance field. By the end of the 1890s, Allianz was also engaged in a considerable amount of foreign business – primarily in France, but also in Switzerland and Belgium, whose large banks took their insurance from Allianz. At the same time, Allianz participated in a variety of risk-sharing agreements

---

[2] For the logo as well as other important information on the history of the concern, see Peter Borscheid, *100 Jahre Allianz* (Munich, 1990), esp. pp. 96, 410. Much can also be learned from the extremely informative unpublished study by Director Rudolf Hensel, written in 1930, "40 Jahre Allianz. Ein Stück deutscher Versicherungsgeschichte," FHA, AZ 1.3/1. See also Wilhelm Kisch, *Fünfzig Jahre Allianz. Ein Beitrag zur Geschichte der Deutschen Privatversicherung* (Munich, 1940) and Ludwig Arps, *Wechselvolle Zeiten. 75 Jahre Allianz Versicherung 1890–1965* (Munich, 1965). The best general study of the German insurance business is Ludwig Arps, *Auf sicheren Pfeilern*; see also Arps, *Durch unruhige Zeiten*. The background details presented here are based on these works. See also the brief and not very satisfactory treatment in Wandel, *Banken und Versicherungen*, Ch. 4.

with other direct insurers and also further developed its reinsurance activities. This was accompanied by the onset of what was to be a long history of expansion through the acquisition of other companies which either could no longer afford to stay in operation or found it advantageous to come under Allianz's wings. In 1905, for example, it took over Fides Insurance Company, which had pioneered break-in insurance. In the same year, the Allianz entered the fire insurance field just in time to sustain 300,000 marks in losses in the San Francisco earthquake of 1906, which was a small amount compared to the losses of 46 million marks suffered by German insurers as a whole and of more than 14 million marks lost by Munich Re. The San Francisco earthquake was an important test of the strength of the German insurance business, and it was one from which Munich Re (which was especially hard hit) and Allianz emerged very successfully and learned important lessons about premium levels and risk sharing. By 1914, Allianz was collecting 50 million marks in premiums, 30 million of it from transport insurance, and ranked first among Germany's direct insurers in property insurance. It accounted for 2.3% of the German insurance industry's 2 billion marks in premiums in 1913 and collected 2% of the industry's 500 million marks in premiums from foreign business. The First World War disrupted these promising prospects, causing a significant reduction in both domestic and foreign business. On the one hand, the company's international business suffered a severe setback, for obvious reasons. On the other, military call-ups and other wartime problems limited advertising and insurance sales activities. As the war went on and morale and physical plant deteriorated, claims increased despite rising premiums, especially for burglary and theft and also in the relatively lucrative transportation insurance field. Inflation at once increased personnel and other costs and reduced returns on long-term policies. Allianz did, however, enter some important new fields during the war, one of which was flight insurance. The most significant field was automobile insurance, when Allianz joined with Munich Re and Imperial Automobile Club to found Kraft Insurance Corporation in April 1918. However, one could have mixed feelings at best about the newest form of insurance introduced after the Revolution of 1918: civil commotion insurance. It did, to be sure, yield 35 million marks in premiums in 1920, but it also involved claims in the millions for burned-down breweries and plundered warehouses. Nevertheless, the rising star at Allianz, Director Kurt Schmitt (1886–1950), had entered into the new branch with considerable enthusiasm and optimism, albeit with an insistence on high premiums and an unwillingness to remain in the cartel of civil commotion insurance providers when he came to the conclusion that their premiums were too low.[3]

Calculated expansionism and genuine business creativity and energy were to be the hallmarks of Schmitt's leadership of Allianz after he assumed the general directorship upon von der Nahmer's death in April 1921, a position he retained

[3] See his correspondence with Kisskalt in 1919–1920 and the Aktennote of Nov. 10, 1920, MR, G 1/17.

until his resignation to become Reich Economics Minister in June 1933.[4] These qualities were to continue to characterize his subsequent leadership of Munich Re so long as one could find some room for their expression between 1935 and 1945. Schmitt, whose father was a family doctor and whose mother came of prosperous peasant stock, grew up in the Rhenish Palatinate before his family moved to Munich when he was 16. Despite a somewhat indifferent education in the rural schools of the Palatinate, he managed to make it through the Maxgymnasium in Munich and went on in 1905 to study law at the University of Munich. His chief enthusiasm at the beginning of his study seems to have been his activities in the Corps Franconia, to which his father had belonged, and the repair of damage done to his nose in the course of duelling – which he pursued as a sport rather than as a quest for "satisfaction" – was so successful that it was said to have improved his already quite handsome looks. He remained an enthusiastic corps brother throughout his life, although he was to become highly critical of duelling. Gradually, he also became a more serious student, a cause undoubtedly promoted by a year of military service and his marriage to a friend of his sister, Marguerite Wengler, in 1909. In that year he finished his doctorate, writing a dissertation on a subject dealing with commercial law, an interest that reflected his decision to pursue a business career. Government service was a good stepping stone to the higher reaches of the business world, however, and so he went to work in the Bavarian Interior Ministry under Staatsrat Gustav von Kahr, who was later to achieve considerable political notoriety as the reactionary State Commissar of Bavaria in the early 1920s and as one whose policies made it possible for extreme right-wing groups, among them the National Socialists, to find Bavaria so hospitable.

Schmitt successfully completed his civil service examination in 1912, did some work for a law firm, and sought a position in a bank or the Foreign Office in Berlin. A man of modest means, however, he could not afford the low pay and high costs that he found in Berlin and thus returned to Munich, where a friend recommended him to General Director Carl von Thieme of Munich Re. After a successful interview with Thieme's right-hand man and later successor, Wilhelm Kisskalt, who was impressed by Schmitt's creative energy, Schmitt was hired in June 1913 for 200 marks a month and given the task of working out the conditions for machine insurance. This was an underdeveloped field and also, for Schmitt at least, a very boring one. He was soon rescued when Kisskalt recommended him to Gustav Knote, director of the Munich branch of Allianz between 1919 and 1932. The latter needed a jurist, and Schmitt seized upon the opportunity, thus "entering into the service of a corporation in which I was to work and enjoy the most beautiful years of my life."[5]

---

[4] There is a good sketch of Schmitt in Arps, *Wechselvolle Zeiten,* pp. 73–7, and in Ludwig Arps, "Kurt Schmitt und Hans Heß" in Ludwig Arps, *Deutsche Versicherungsunternehmer* (Karlsruhe, 1968), pp. 165–79. He also left behind an important collection of personal papers; see FHA, NL 1.

[5] This is based on Schmitt's own account in a small memoir he wrote about his career prior to 1914, kindly placed at my disposal by Hermann Niemöller and to be found in FHA, NL 1/163, quotation p. 17.

Schmitt immediately demonstrated the managerial vision and style that was to bring him such rapid success. Assigned to the liability insurance section, Schmitt had little difficulty performing the immense amount of paperwork connected with the incoming claims yet – in seeming contrast to the 25 other men working in the office – became thoroughly dissatisfied with the bureaucratic and clumsy manner in which claims were handled and the extent to which they ended up in court. In Schmitt's view, another way had to be found based on a broader perspective: "I confronted the economic, commercial, and social tasks with respect to the company, the insured, and those who had suffered damages, in short, the economic significance and interconnections involved."[6] On his own initiative, Schmitt decided that personal intervention and the arrangement of acceptable settlements – on the basis of a careful study of the materials – between the insured and those making claims against them would save time and resources and produce better results. While this irritated his section head no end, the success of Schmitt's methods could not be denied, and he was appointed head of the section on August 1, 1913. Schmitt's willingness to take the initiative, cut through red tape and legalisms, and settle claims through direct and unbureaucratic intervention served him well and was typical of his approach to problems. He was now in a position to implement his method by establishing a staff of regulators to engage in the settlement of liability cases. This brought him into contact with the insurance agents themselves and the company organization, and he soon began to give lectures on the importance of liability insurance as well as on the regulation of cases. The reduction of court cases received grateful recognition in Berlin and led to the prospect of Schmitt's appointment as Knote's deputy and to his engagement in the settlement of large claims in Norway.

These promising developments were interrupted by the First World War. A reserve officer, Schmitt was called up immediately but had the good luck to suffer a minor wound that was repeatedly infected so that he could not be sent back. As a result, Allianz, which was laboring under severe personnel shortages, was able to reclaim him from the front, first to Munich and then to Berlin, where the death of the head of the accident division led to his appointment as the director in charge and thus to the board of directors. He soon became the right-hand man of von der Nahmer, who was suffering from an incurable cancer, and his appointment as general director in 1921 was no surprise, despite his young age of 34, and was warmly supported by Kisskalt before the board of supervisors.[7]

Schmitt's achievements as general director of Allianz, as well as his subsequent engagement in the insurance business, owed much to two men whom he brought into the company at this time, with whom he collaborated intimately, and who were fated to attain the height of their careers in the Third Reich: Hans Heß

---

[6] Ibid., pp. 17f.

[7] See Wilhelm Kisskalt's unpublished "Erinnerungen an die Münchener Rück" (Garmisch, 1953), pp. 14–15, FHA.

Dr. Kurt Schmitt (1886–1950), general director of Allianz 1921–1933, about 1925.

(1881–1957) and Eduard Hilgard (1884–1982).[8] Heß was the son of an insurance inspector in Leipzig, where he attended both Gymnasium and university and received his law degree in 1909. He followed in the footsteps of his father, first working for the Accident Association in Magdeburg and then going to work for the Swiss Winterthur firm, first as their general agent in Thuringia and Saxony and then as district director for the same area. He seems to have received his job with Winterthur as the consequence of a dispute with the company involving the accidental death of his father, and it was not the last time that people were to be impressed with his stubborn and forthright personality. Schmitt became aware of his talents and brought him into Allianz as a deputy director in

---

[8] On Heß, see Arps, *Wechselvolle Zeiten,* pp. 107–10, as well as Heß's small collection of papers, FHA, NL 3. There is no really satisfactory discussion of Hilgard in the secondary literature, but his personal papers and memoirs are quite valuable; see FHA, NL 2.

1918. Heß was above all an organization man, and he was largely responsible for building up the branch organization of Allianz and unifying the company by (among other things) holding regular meetings of its representatives. The first of these was held in 1919, the same year in which Heß founded the company newspaper: *Allianz-Zeitung*. Heß was an "insurance man" through and through, and he played a decisive role in defining the company culture by cultivating identification with the company and a sense of "family." An avid sportsman, he was largely responsible for the promotion of sports in the company, the building of an Allianz stadium in Berlin-Mariendorf (which was graced by Karl Moebius's statue of the Spear Thrower and was the site of company "Olympics"), and the development of sports facilities at various branches of the concern. At the same time, he promoted a spirit of friendly but rigorous competition to increase "production" among the company representatives, with a model of the Spear Thrower awarded to the most successful branch of the company each year. "Papa Heß," as he became known, was much respected in the company both for his talents and his integrity, and he was precisely the organizational talent needed to give structure and unity to the mass of acquisitions that took place under Schmitt's restless guidance. Heß and Schmitt rapidly became close friends and worked well together in shaping the expanding concern.

In certain very important respects, however, Schmitt was to be even more dependent on Hilgard, who had known Schmitt since his youth as they grew up only a few kilometers from one another. They had only casual contact then but saw one another more regularly in Munich, where Hilgard did his training for state service at the time Schmitt was completing his studies. Hilgard intended to have a civil service career and, after serving in the war, went to work in the peace treaty section of the Reich Finance Ministry and participated in some of the more important immediate postwar diplomatic negotiations. Among them was the Spa Conference of July 1920, where the very diplomatic Hilgard strongly disapproved of the rude and tactless behavior of the German industrialist Hugo Stinnes. Hilgard seemed to have enjoyed everything about his government work but the pay, which was causing him and his wife increasing difficulties in those inflationary times. Thus, when unexpectedly called by Schmitt at the end of 1920 and asked if he were willing to make a change of career, Hilgard accepted the invitation to have an interview with Schmitt, Heß, and von der Nahmer; he subsequently accepted the position of deputy director and the attractive salary that came with it. As Hilgard was well aware, his decision involved something of a social comedown, not only because of the continued high status enjoyed by members of the ministerial bureaucracy but also because, as his in-laws made sure to remind him, the insurance field had a much lower status than banking at that time. Indeed, von der Nahmer appeared to have shared these attitudes. He tended mainly to the financial aspects of the company, continued to think of himself as a banker, and scarcely socialized with colleagues from the insurance business. Schmitt was well aware of the low esteem in which the insurance business was held, and it galled him. Hilgard later recalled the impression made on him by a conversation with Schmitt on this subject in which the latter found

Dr. Hans Heß (1881–1957), general director of Allianz 1933–1948, about 1940.

this attitude "all the more unjustified because he was utterly convinced by the high tasks of the insurance field and the ethic which it expressed. This idea became fixed in me at that time and never left me, thank God, during my entire career with the Allianz."[9] They both agreed that it was one of their tasks to change public attitudes toward the significance and value of the insurance business and that, toward this end, the insurance industry needed a much greater public presence. For his part, Hilgard was to stress the importance of becoming more active in Berlin society as a means of raising the status of the insurance

---

[9] Eduard Hilgard, "Mein Leben in der Allianz" (unpublished ms., ca. 1970), FHA, NL 2/7, pp. 12–13.

business. This willingness to engage in social and public activity was to become one of the strong links between the two men; Heß, who seemed anxious to keep up with Schmitt, likewise demonstrated a willingness to participate in such activities. Not only did Hilgard (who valued external trappings) encourage Schmitt and Heß to wear tailor-made suits and thus cut better figures in public, he also led the way in becoming very active in the Club of Berlin, a gathering place for the city's leading businessmen.

Hilgard's preoccupation with such matters became possible only because of the very special position he assumed upon the death of von der Nahmer in March 1921. Initially, he had been assigned to the liability insurance department under Director Clemens Maiholzer, and he found it just as boring as Schmitt had found machine insurance. Schmitt's appointment as general director, however, put an end to Hilgard's growing nostalgia for the civil service, since Schmitt took him away from Maiholzer, lodged him in an office next to his own, and turned him into a kind of general secretary – with a host of interesting and variegated tasks of great importance for which he was eminently suited. On the one hand, Schmitt increasingly used Hilgard to represent himself in the employers' association and in the Reich Association for Private Insurance, so that Hilgard came to play a growing role in the various associations, an activity that promoted his public role but that did not contribute much to his becoming truly versed in the technicalities of the insurance business. On the other hand, Schmitt used Hilgard as a sounding board for his ideas, something he apparently needed despite his decisiveness. Hilgard was his right-hand man and negotiator in the stormy expansion of Allianz that took place under Schmitt's leadership. For Hilgard, of course, this was a rather extraordinary advancement within a matter of a few months, and the fact that Hilgard now accompanied Schmitt to supervisory board meetings (along with Heß) and had such a close relationship to the general director was probably rather difficult for the older directors to swallow. Heß was apparently not disturbed by Hilgard's position, but it is interesting to note that Schmitt's advancement of Hilgard puzzled the latter, whose reflections (more than forty years later) provide some interesting insights into the personalities and characters of these three key individuals in the history of Allianz:

I have often asked myself what was basically the reason for this way of acting on the part of Schmitt. I do not believe that in the short period between my entrance into Allianz and the first meeting of the supervisory board Schmitt could have formed a reliable impression of my abilities. I believe much more that Schmitt, with the good feeling that he often, albeit not always, had for people, very quickly intuited that he could make a true friend and collaborator out of me. Perhaps he already at that time had an unconscious feeling for the fact that his deputy, Dr. Heß, with whom he would be bound in a strong friendship for decades, was basically a stronger personality than he himself, and he may have therefore wished to have a man at his side upon whom he could depend and with whom he could also discuss especially confidential things at such times as he did not want to turn to his official deputy.[10]

---

[10] Ibid., p. 21.

Indeed, even before von der Nahmer's death, Schmitt had treated his succession to the General Directorship as a certainty and had revealed to Hilgard a series of bold projects, so that

> it was already at that time completely obvious to Schmitt that he would not only bring Allianz to the leading position among German insurance companies, but that he – and this seemed to me in view of the hapless situation of Germany especially noteworthy – at that time already had the firm intention of capturing large portions of the world market for the Allianz.[11]

Fundamental to the great period of expansion now to begin – and, indeed, to the history of Allianz throughout the period discussed in this book – is Allianz's intimate relationship with Munich Re. On April 15, 1921, Allianz and Munich Re concluded a joint contract aimed at restructuring and deepening the relationship between the two companies. It was signed only a few days before von der Nahmer's death and was the work of him and Thieme, who was to retire that year and be replaced by Kisskalt. Thus 1921 was an important year of contractual as well as personnel changes. The contract was to run through December 31, 1970, and it was subject to automatic renewal for another half century if neither of the parties objected. Munich Re's capital participation in Allianz was set at 25%. The general director of each of the companies was to have a seat on the supervisory board of the other, and at least three of the supervisory board members of each of the firms were to serve in common on the supervisory board of both companies. Munich Re agreed not to establish any daughter companies in insurance branches in which Allianz was active, and such daughter companies of Munich Re as already existed would be transferred to Allianz in order to promote the concentration of Allianz's activities. Allianz agreed to restrict itself to direct business and Munich Re to indirect business; Allianz agreed to give half of its reinsurance business and all of its excess-loss reinsurance business (i.e., coverage for liability and other forms of insurance for damages that exceeded normally anticipated risk or whose risk could not be easily calculated because of the newness of the insurance involved) to Munich Re. The obligation to cede business to Allianz was to extend to any new mergers or participations on the part of Allianz, while Munich Re agreed to pay for half of such cessions. Munich Re also agreed to participate in the amount of 50% in the foundation by Allianz of new companies, capital share participations, and security accounts.[12] What all this meant is that Allianz and Munich Re were to work ever more closely in the future, and that the latter was committed to supporting the former in its efforts to achieve economies of scope and scale through a policy of expansion, concern building, and organizational rationalization.

[11] Ibid., p. 11.
[12] This is based on the discussion in Martin Herzog, "Was Dokumente erzählen können – Zur Geschichte der Münchener Rück," VII Bde. (Munich, 1986–1992), unpublished ms., FHA, here Bd. IV, pp. 756–9.

Allianz, of course, was by no means unique in its policies of concentration and concern building, which were general characteristics of the Weimar economy during the inflationary period 1918–1923 and then in the period of stabilization between 1924 and 1929–1930. Finance man that he was, von der Nahmer had provided well for Allianz during the war, investing as little as possible in war bonds while storing up foreign exchange wherever he could. Many smaller firms were not so lucky and had unmanageable debts that were payable only in foreign exchange. These "Valuta debts," as they were called, were a source of much bad blood between the Swiss and the Germans during and after the inflation, but Allianz was relatively untouched by the problem; indeed, even at some cost to itself, Allianz cultivated its good relations with Schweizerische National-Versicherungs-Gesellschaft in Basel, in which both Munich Re and Allianz held substantial shares. In 1920, Allianz took over the Schweizer National's German engagements while the latter took over Allianz's Swiss engagements. However, the difficulties experienced by other, less fortunate, German companies encouraged them to surrender their independence or simply sell out to the larger firms in the business. Thus, already by 1921 Allianz had entered two new branches of insurance by acquiring the important Hermes Kreditversicherungs-Bank-AG and Brandenburger Spiegelglas-Versicherungs-AG; it also took over Globus Versicherungs-AG and acquired via fusion two fire insurance companies, Badische Feuerversicherungs-Bank and Securitas Feuer-Versicherungs-AG.

In the following year, Allianz began calling itself a *concern,* that is, it had become a conglomeration of companies with a central headquarters in Berlin. This was coincident with no less important a development: the entry of Allianz into the life insurance field. Allianz had initially sought to enter this field through a working partnership or community of interest with another company, the Friedrich Wilhelm, but this had not worked out. Schmitt and his colleagues in Munich Re decided the time was ripe to make the most of their developing organizational capacities and form their own Allianz Lebensversicherungsbank-AG in Berlin with a capital of 20 million marks.[13] Hilgard, whose work in the Finance Ministry had brought him into contact not only with the leading Berlin banks but also with bankers (e.g., Max Warburg) throughout Germany, was especially useful in the task of gathering a formidable collection of banks and bankers for the supervisory board.[14] Schmitt successfully appealed to them with the argument that

the moment is especially favorable for the founding of an Allianz Lebensversicherungs-bank because, in contrast to early times, the competitive capacity of a young corporation

[13] The Allianz Lebensversicherungsbank AG (Allianz Life Insurance Bank Corporation) was renamed the Allianz und Stuttgarter Lebensversicherungsbank AG (Allianz and Stuttgart Life Insurance Bank Corporation) in 1927 and in 1940 was renamed the Allianz Lebensversicherungs-AG (Allianz Life Insurance Corporation). In this study, the shortened name "Allianz Leben" will be used.

[14] Hilgard, "Leben," FHA, NL 2/7, pp. 25–6.

against older ones is to be deemed extraordinarily favorable. As is known, all German life insurance companies are suffering under the huge costs of their old insurance stock, whose average value, based on prewar circumstances, is much too small in relationship to today's costs. To this must be added that it is just the old and large life insurance companies which have to bear substantial engagements in foreign currencies because of their international business, especially because of the fact that their reserves for such business were not in the relevant currency but rather in Reich marks.[15]

The entry of so potentially powerful a new company into the field caused understandable fear and resentment, not only because of the competition for customers but also because it was likely to attract agents and representatives away from other companies. The hostility became evident quite early and took on ugly forms. In July 1922, Deputy Director Franz Rinsler of Allianz Leben assured Munich Re that it would show special consideration in dealing with the life insurance companies with which Munich Re did business but also asked that the courtesy be returned, since one of the leading managers of the Arminia Insurance Co. was trying to compete by characterizing Allianz Leben "as a pronouncedly Jewish company."[16] It is possible that this was more a reference to the bankers on the supervisory board of Allianz Leben than to its employees, but it is significant that there was such an undertone in certain circles in the insurance business and that anti-Semitic sentiments could be instrumentalized in this manner at so early a date. The Allianz leadership found such behavior both unfair and inappropriate, and this seems to have held true for Munich Re as well.[17]

Whatever the case, Arminia was shortly to be relieved of the need to exercise itself about such matters when it was swallowed up by Allianz Leben in 1923. In a final burst of inflation-period concentration that year, Allianz also took over Providentia Frankfurter Versicherungs-Gesellschaft and Deutsche Phönix Versicherungs AG, both in Frankfurt am Main, the Wilhelma Allgemeine Versicherungs AG in Magdeburg, and Freia Bremen-Hannoversche Lebensversicherungs Bank AG in Berlin. It also acquired Union (Allgemeine Deutsche Hagel-Versicherungs-Gesellschaft) in Weimar. These were all well-known companies, and their acquisition required much tactical skill, attention to often

---

[15] Anlage zum Schreiben Schmitt vom 12. Jan. 1922, MR, A 3.4/6.

[16] Rinsler an Münchener Rück, 5. Juli 1922, MR, A 3.4/6.

[17] It is always difficult to tell how much anti-Semitic sentiment there was in the business world and how effective such propaganda might be with the public at large. That virulent anti-Semitism greatly increased during and after World War I is indisputable. Another interesting illustration in the insurance business was a letter of June 14, 1923, from V. Mittermann of the Austrian Großdeutsche Volkspartei to Rudolf Schmidt of Munich Re. Mittermann complained that he had taken out a policy with the Austrian Janus company, which he thought had "an Aryan foundation," only to find that it had a Jew on its administrative board representing Munich Re. Schmidt replied on June 18, assuring Mittermann that Janus (Allgemeine Versicherungsanstalt a. G. in Wien) was indeed an "Aryan institute" and that it was the Munich Re alone that was exercising its right to name a member of the board and that Janus had not the "slightest influence" in this regard. For the correspondence, see MR, A 1/30.

unpredictable market opportunities that suddenly arose, and shrewd negotiation on the part of Schmitt. He sometimes failed to attain his goal, as in the case of Colonia Kölnische Feuer- und Kölnische Unfall-Versicherungs-AG, whose acquisition Schmitt thought would constitute a "happy addition"[18] but was blocked by Colonia supervisory board members friendly to Aachener und Münchener Feuerversicherungs-Gesellschaft and Vaterländische und Rhenania Vereinigte Versicherungs-Gesellschaften AG. An especially important acquisition, accomplished jointly by Allianz and Munich Re, was Bayerische Versicherungsbank AG in Munich, which was sold by Bayerische Hypotheken- und-Wechsel-Bank despite its sound condition and substantial supply of foreign exchange. In the course of this burst of expansionism, Allianz also acquired some very experienced and promising personnel, the most important of whom were Rudolf Schloeßmann (1880–1945) and Maximilian Eichbaum (1881–1958), both extraordinarily intelligent and talented insurance men from the Wilhelma. Eichbaum, a Jew, remained as head of Wilhelma, while Schloeßmann was made general director of Allianz Leben and joined Schmitt, Heß, and Hilgard to form a quartet of directors that was to dominate the affairs of Allianz in the years to come. Schloeßmann's tactical skills and winning ways were to prove instrumental in settling organizational battles with Heß that arose primarily from Schloeßmann's singular concentration on life insurance.[19]

The security of life insurance assets and investments were matters of great concern in these years. Inflation and then hyperinflation led to a combination of increasing policyholder underinsurance and rising costs for insurers. By 1922–1923, old policies were worthless, and efforts to keep up with inflation through the revision of premiums and values on policies proved hopeless. The cost of collecting premiums exceeded the value of the premiums themselves. Increasingly, the only secure policy was one denominated or pegged to gold or secure foreign exchanges – above all, the dollar – and such policies only were permitted in 1923. With the stabilization in 1923–1924, the value of paper mark assets simply disappeared, and the revaluation laws passed in 1925 provided for up to a 15% revaluation of life insurance policies, depending on the real value of the coverage available for old policies. This complicated arrangement, which was meant to help "Old Savers," bore fruit only for inflation victims in the early 1930s. The entire experience undermined the sense of "equity and good faith" in German society and did its share to subvert business morality as well as conjure up a dread of inflation that significantly influenced business attitudes.[20]

In the inflationary struggle for survival, Allianz emerged as one of the small number of insurance groups that came out at the top of the heap – along with Aachener und Münchener, Frankfurter Allgemeine Versicherungs-AG (Favag),

---

[18] See Schmitt to Mosler, April 9, 1923, BAB, 80 Ba 2/P 5784.
[19] On Schloeßmann, see Arps, *Wechselvolle Zeiten,* pp. 125–7, and Hilgard, "Leben," FHA, NL 2/7, pp. 44–5.
[20] See Ludwig Arps, *Durch unruhige Zeiten,* Bd. 1, Kap. 7–8, Bd. 2, Kap. 1.

Dr. Rudolf Schloeßmann (1880–1945), chairman of the board of Allianz Leben 1923–1944, about 1940.

Magdeburger Feuerversicherungs-Gesellschaft, Vaterländische, and Nordstern Allgemeine Versicherungs-AG. The coming years were to show that the Darwinian struggle was by no means over but that Allianz was a winner in the concentration movement. This certainly was not due to mere luck or clever speculation. Allianz was a remarkably well-run and impressively managed enterprise. During the inflation, for example, the sum of its reserves denominated in paper values grew enormously, but the financial management of the firm cleverly booked its substantial holdings of foreign currencies at prewar exchange rates. Therefore, beneath the paper mark cover was a tidy sum of real values that remained once the paper marks had disappeared. Also, the concern enjoyed the largest holdings in real estate of any German insurance company. Nevertheless, in contrast to its closest competitor (Favag), Allianz resisted the temptation to overcapitalize. Where Favag set its capital at 20 million gold marks but collected only 40 million in premiums in 1924, Allianz, which collected 80 million in premiums that year, set its capital worth at a modest 30 million Reichsmark (RM) for Allianz and 6 million for Allianz Leben. At the same time, Allianz managed to increase its income from premiums by 30 million marks over 1913 totals, despite the fact that the competition for business was extraordinarily keen. Indeed, Allianz pursued a policy of charging relatively high premiums while counting on its capacity to provide more comprehensive forms of protection and better service.

The evolution of Schmitt's policies with respect to the currency denomination of policies sold by Allianz was characterized by the quest for maximum solidity and reliable coverage for the company's obligations. Thus, in February 1924, when the success of currency reform was still a matter of uncertainty, Schmitt instructed that agencies working for Allianz concentrate on selling as many policies in foreign currency as possible. As the security of the Reichsmark became more certain a year later, however, Schmitt began to press for policies denominated in Reichsmark. This soon became the dominant currency for nearly all branches of insurance, although many life insurance policies continued to be taken out in foreign currencies. In such instances, however, the premiums also had to be paid in foreign currency so that the policies could have genuine backing in the currencies in question. Schmitt was a sharp opponent of issuing policies denominated in gold marks or in fine gold, because sufficient numbers of dollars were not available to provide genuine coverage for them. Nevertheless, many companies continued to draw up such policies, accepting RM premiums and using RM as backing. Schmitt felt very strongly that such practices were dangerous and urged the bankers on his supervisory board to persuade other insurance companies with whom they were associated to abandon them. It would appear, however, that other companies did not take this advice, with the result that the Allianz concern ended up with many such policies in its portfolio as a result of mergers and acquisitions in the late 1920s.[21]

As was the case throughout the financial sector after the inflation, Allianz engaged in large-scale staff reductions now that the immense amount of paperwork entailed by inflation could be reduced. Most important, however, was cost cutting in the effort to increase profitability. Schmitt continuously complained that not enough was being done to reduce costs while increasing production, and both he and Heß worked assiduously to make organizational improvements, provide production incentives while avoiding risky engagements, and create better training programs so as to maintain high-level performance and ensure good personnel in the future. In addition to their commitment to solid financial practices and organizational strength, Schmitt and Heß were anxious to create company loyalty and identification – what Schmitt called the "Allianz spirit." This "was to be understood not only as a healthy optimism, but also with respect to the technical aspect as a striving for the best training and constant promotion of our

---

[21] 2. erweiterte Vorstandssitzung am 26./27. Feb. 1924, 5. erweiterte Vorstandssitzung am 17./18. Feb. 1925, FHA, S 17.2/4; Aktenvermerk Mosler, 11. Dez. 1924, BAB, 80 Ba 2/P 5784.

knowledge.... The goal must be the greatest possible development of our operations, which after a few years must be without competition."[22] The importance attached to the *Allianz-Zeitung,* to the establishment of a friendly atmosphere, and to sports and social activities were all reflections of this desire to induce Allianz workers to back Schmitt's ambitions.

Indeed, such mechanisms of integration were of great importance as Allianz braced itself for and then engaged in another wave of expansion. In 1926, the Frankfurter Phönix and Providentia, the Wilhelma, and other recent acquisitions were fused with Allianz and integrated into the branches of the concern where they were located, although Schmitt allowed continued use of the mentioned names because of their fine reputations. The way was thus prepared for the greatest fusion in the history of the German insurance business, that between Allianz and Stuttgarter Verein in October 1927.

The two concerns had almost merged in 1922, when the predecessor company of Stuttgarter Verein (Allgemeiner Deutscher Versicherungsverein) backed out of the already prepared contract, despite its foreign exchange debts, and sought to maintain its independence. Initially a mutual insurance organization of three insurance associations, it took the path of incorporation in 1923, forming two joint stock companies: Stuttgarter Verein Versicherungs-AG, which concentrated on accident and liability insurance, and Stuttgart-Lübeck Lebens-versicherungs-Aktien-Gesellschaft. The new companies managed to resolve their financial difficulties, and the projected association with Allianz appeared to be dead.

However, the idea was revived in the spring of 1927 when Director Schloeßmann encountered Adolf Kimmel (head of Stuttgart-Lübecker) at a conference in London and persuaded the latter to entertain consolidation proposals from Allianz. Schmitt immediately seized upon the opportunity and began discussions with the head of the Stuttgarter concern, Max Georgii (1855–1934). The negotiations were extremely difficult. The Stuttgarter concern was in no way in distress, and there was no immediate reason for fusion. Some of the Stuttgarter directors opposed the move, and the City of Stuttgart was especially hostile to having so important a concern move to Berlin. Thus, all kinds of concessions had to be made. Allianz had to promise that the headquarters of the life insurance business – as well as those of accident and liability insurance – would be moved to Stuttgart. The relocation of accident and liability insurance was especially inconvenient. Also, a larger number than desired of Stuttgarter directors had to be taken on board the consolidated company. The name of the new company was a major issue, and the final decision was to call it the Allianz und Stuttgarter Verein Versicherungs-AG. Schmitt's willingness to make these concessions was crucial to the success of the effort, but Georgii (who was to become chairman of the supervisory board of the consolidated companies) later admitted to Hilgard that the most decisive factor was Schmitt's persistence and

---

[22] 3. erweiterte Vorstandssitzung am 17./18. Juni 1924, FHA, S 17.2/4, p. 11.

persuasive powers. Be that as it may, what the involved companies described as the most "significant" consolidation in the history of the German insurance industry was approved by the various supervisory boards in early November 1928, thereby creating the Allianz und Stuttgarter Verein Versicherungs-AG, with Allianz now doubling its share capital from 30 to 60 million RM, as well as the Allianz und Stuttgarter Lebensversicherungsbank AG, with Allianz Leben increasing its share capital from 6 to 20 million RM. The new concern clearly was the largest in Germany. At the end of 1928, Schmitt could boast of 1.6 billion RM in life insurance alone, followed by 17 publicly chartered institutions with 1 billion, Victoria zu Berlin Allgemeine Versicherungs-AG with 950 million, the Gerling concern with 550 million, and Favag with 470 million. At the same time, thanks to the mergers, staffing could be reduced to 90% of 1927 levels. The concern was also increasing its foreign business and was especially pleased with the results of Spanish Plus Ultra Company, the majority of whose shares it had acquired in 1926.[23]

The consolidation of 1928 must be viewed in the context of the wave of big mergers, fusions, and consolidations that took place in other economic sectors in the second half of the 1920s, among which were the creation of IG Farben in 1925, Vereinigte Stahlwerke in 1926, and Deutsche Bank and Disconto-Gesellschaft in 1929. The last-named banking consolidation bears particularly interesting similarities to that of the Allianz–Stuttgarter Verein merger of the previous year.[24] The period between 1924 and 1933 was characterized not only by a massive concentration movement but also by ugly financial scandals, and one of these – the collapse of Favag in 1929 – brought about the last large acquisition from which Allianz was to profit in this period. Its significance for the insurance business paralleled that of the collapse of Darmstädter und Nationalbank (Danat-Bank) of July 1931, which was a direct consequence of the failure of the Nordwolle textile company due to financial irregularities on the part of its management. The deeper causes of these and other business scandals lay in the economic and financial conditions of the Weimar Republic that followed the loss of capital in the war, misdirection of capital during and after the inflation, dependence on short-term loans from abroad, and inadequacy of supervision by government agencies and supervisory boards. Socioeconomic issues in the Weimar Republic were highly politicized. Government expenditure at all levels, social insurance, wage levels, and the policies of public and private enterprises were all subjects of bitter debate and controversy. At the same time, the economy was highly dependent on short-term foreign loans and vulnerable to shocks, so that scandals like

---

[23] On the fusion, in addition to the standard studies, see Hilgard, "Leben," FHA, NL 2/7, pp. 61–3. See also "Zusammenschluss," prepared for the Aufsichtsrat in October 1928, and Aktenvermerk Mosler, 11. Dez. 1928, BAB, 80 Ba 2/P 5784.

[24] See Gerald D. Feldman, "The Deutsche Bank from the First World War to the World Economic Crisis, 1914–1933," in Lothar Gall et al., *The Deutsche Bank 1870–1995* (London, 1995), pp. 130–276, here pp. 230–40.

those mentioned and other untoward economic events threatened to undermine confidence in the economy both at home and abroad. The Favag affair, coming as it did on the cusp of the Great Depression, was not only a trauma for the insurance industry but also a major national and international event and one of those occurrences that helped to undermine support for and belief in the economic liberal order during the coming years of depression. Business behavior in the Third Reich must be understood against the background of such occurrences and their underlying causes, and it is necessary therefore to dwell somewhat on the Favag scandal and the role of Allianz in it.[25]

Both the rise and fall of Favag had much to do with its general director since 1897, Paul Dumcke, who was regarded as one of the giants of the German insurance business.[26] He had built up the company before the war through communities of interest with various reinsurance companies and then by fusion with Preußische Rückversicherungs-AG, which was renamed Helios Allgemeine Rückversicherungs-AG and expanded into multibranch direct insurance as well. War and inflation provided Dumcke with the opportunity to expand still further. Foreign business was particularly important, since Favag's engagements in Southeast Europe and in Switzerland and its extensive international transportation insurance activities provided the company with the hard currency needed to take advantage of inflation and expand at home. Favag took under its wing the whole (or substantial portions of) Karlsruher Lebensversicherungs-Bank AG, Vereinigte Berlinische und Preußische Lebensversicherungs-AG, and the Hammonia (Allgemeine Versicherungs-AG), Hamburg. Thus, by the end of the 1920s it was second only to Allianz in the German composite insurance business and was a major national and international player in both direct insurance and reinsurance. At its shareholder meeting on June 18, 1929, the directors reported an increase in premiums of 14 million RM over the previous year, assets amounting to 73.8 million RM, a net profit just short of 3.1 million RM, and a 12.5% dividend totaling 2.3 million RM.[27]

Despite this seemingly happy state of affairs, rumors were rife about peculiarities in the financial management of the company. The Favag supervisory board and the important bankers who sat on it were aware of these rumors, but they

---

[25] On these more general aspects and for a fuller treatment, see ibid. and Gerald D. Feldman, "Insurance Company Collapses in the World Economic Crisis: The Frankfurter Allgemeine Versicherungs-AG (Favag) and the Austrian Phönix," in Harold James (ed.), *The Interwar Depression in an International Context* (Munich, 2001).

[26] The roots of the company go back to 1865, when it concentrated on glass insurance. It then moved into transportation insurance and was called Frankfurter Transport- und Glasversicherungs-Gesellschaft until its takeover of Frankfurter Lebensversicherungs-AG in 1911 led to its change of name to Frankfurter Allgemeine Versicherungs AG. See Arps, *Durch unruhige Zeiten,* Bd. 1, pp. 424–7.

[27] Bericht der in der General-Versammlung vom 30. Sept. 1929 gewählten Revisions-Kommission der Frankfurter Allgemeinen Versicherungs-Aktien-Gesellschaft zu Frankfurt am Main, p. 17, FHA, B 2/601.

chose to accept the optimistic statements of Dumcke and his directors and to do nothing. It should come as no surprise that Kurt Schmitt considered Favag a potentially promising acquisition; it was a major competitor and had a good organization. He was very aware of its overcapitalization in 1924 and purportedly remarked that "in five years we will also have the Frankfurter and, if we want, the 'Vaterländische' also."[28] Schmitt was aware that Favag had been doing business with a considerable amount of borrowed money and had told Dumcke that he considered this a mistaken policy, profitable or not, but he also thought Dumcke hard to replace and thus bided his time. However, Dumcke died unexpectedly from an operation on February 12, 1929, and was laid to rest with songs of praise for his contributions to the insurance business. This freed Schmitt to broach the subject of an Allianz–Favag collaboration in a conversation with Director Siegmund Bodenheimer of Danat-Bank, a Favag supervisory board member. This seemed all the more opportune since the leading personage in the concern, Director Philipp Becker, was a "finance man" rather than an "insurance man," and none of the "insurance men" were of Dumcke's alleged caliber. There were reports of conflicts among the directors, and one of the Favag directors had actually approached Director Hans Heß of Allianz in 1928 and suggested a merger and the buying out of contracts of some leading Favag directors. There were also rumors going around about the investments of these directors. Schmitt pointed out that a careful audit of Favag's finances would be required before any consolidation could take place. Bodenheimer thanked Schmitt for the suggestion but responded that "he knows the situation exactly, and that the financial business of the Frankfurter has run profitably. Even if the banks are not in agreement with all the engagements, there is still no doubt that the Frankfurter was a first-class corporation that is making good earnings and progressing. He saw no place for a collaboration with Allianz at the moment."[29]

This was quite optimistic given the rumors that had been circulating, and the passivity of Bodenheimer and other bankers on the Favag supervisory board is no less remarkable in the face of the newspaper articles that began to appear in the *Frankfurter Zeitung* in the spring of 1929. These articles were the work of Artur Lauinger, a pioneer in investigative journalism who had a special interest in insurance questions. He had good relations with Allianz and Munich Re leaders, although there is not the slightest reason to believe that he was deliberately serving their interests. A diligent reader of company reports and balance sheets and a careful observer of shareholder meetings, Lauinger was also a regular visitor at the Frankfurt exchanges and had heard all sorts of rumors about banking activities by Favag through Südwestdeutsche Bank AG. Lauinger had

[28] Reported by Hensel in "40 Jahre Allianz," FHA, AZ 1.3/1, p. 298. Hensel's is a very sober history, so that this report of Schmitt's long-term ambitions deserves credence. Vaterländische also collapsed in 1929, but Hensel points out that Allianz was too preoccupied with Favag to take over yet another company. It was acquired by Nordstern.

[29] Aktennotiz Schmitt, 26. Nov. 1929, BAB, 80 Ba 2/P 5785.

been shown discount bills with Dumcke's signature that he deemed very dubious. For Lauinger, however, the more important question was whether an insurance company had any business discounting bills of the type shown to him and engaging in banking business of this kind.

Lauinger visited Dumcke shortly before the latter's death and insisted on knowing more about Favag's activities in the guarantee and lending fields. Dumcke referred him to Finance Director Becker, whom Lauinger met with sometime in late March or early April 1929. He found Becker as reluctant to provide concrete information as the late Dumcke, whereupon Lauinger told him that he considered the credit operations of Favag totally inappropriate for an insurance company and, moreover, that he intended to openly attack Favag if he were not provided with accurate balances and if a halt was not put to the credit operations in question. Becker then promised to gather the information and to keep Lauinger abreast of developments, but Lauinger soon launched a press campaign against Favag's way of doing business. Also, Lauinger began informing members of the Favag supervisory board and the Reich Supervisory Office for Insurance of serious problems at Favag.

It is important to realize that since 1901 the private insurance business had been subject to national government regulation under the Reich Insurance Law (VAG). This law had created the Reich Supervisory Office for Insurance (RAA), which was charged with the tasks of licensing insurance companies after investigating their trustworthiness, making sure that the coverage for life insurance policies was administered separately from other assets and was securely invested, and making sure that insurance companies complied with the business plan they had regularly to submit in order to receive and retain their business licenses. Only the RAA could permit an insurance company to declare bankruptcy. As was the case in licensing, so in the case of bankruptcy: a courtlike procedure was employed involving the use of experts from outside the RAA. In short, the RAA was there to protect consumer and public interests and prevent abusive practices by insurance companies. In the case of Favag, however, inflation-period legislation and RAA inattentiveness played no small role in the collapse. On the one hand, the VAG had been revised in July 1923 to allow investments in real estate and participations in companies, and Favag had made extensive use of the latter. On the other hand, the RAA was understaffed and unduly trustful. This manifested itself in a willingness to accept minimal reporting and mere satisfaction of the technical requirements connected with the actual insurance business, an inclination to overlook financial engagements inappropriate for an insurance company, and a failure to follow up on activities that it did protest.[30]

---

[30] On the VAG and RAA, see the useful summary of its history in André Botur, *Privatversicherung im Dritten Reich. Zur Schadensabwicklung nach der Reichskristallnacht unter dem Einfluß nationalsozialistischer Rassen- und Versicherungspolitik* [Berliner Juristische Universitätsschriften. Zivilrecht, Bd. 6] (Berlin, 1995), pp. 17–20. See also the RAA's report to the RWM of June 6, 1930, BAK, B 280/13273. The most important source of information on the RAA's activities and

Insofar as the Favag supervisory board is concerned, the chief problem lay (as so often the case with such scandals) in the blind confidence placed in the directors and the failure to demand information even in the face of considerable suspicion that all was not well with its financial management. German supervisory boards were composed of persons who were not personally responsible for their failures as supervisors and whose organizations were not responsible, either. The supervisory board of Favag did take some action in May by setting up an auditing committee, but the Favag directors continued to maintain that the company was sound and provided the required information only slowly and reluctantly. Finally, however, enough facts were out to make impossible any further unwillingness on the part of the supervisory board to at least discuss the problem. Sometime in the summer of 1929, Lauinger was summoned home from vacation for a special meeting of the supervisory board of Favag, which was in a state of despair over the mounting evidence of irregularities in its balances. Lauinger advised them to demand an accurate balance and to determine who was responsible for the losses – advice for which the bankers on the board showed little enthusiasm because they feared that Favag would close its accounts with banks that pressed them too hard and give its business to competing banks instead. Needless to say, the supervisory board members were also rather nervous about revelations that would make matters worse and cast a shadow over their performance as supervisors. The trouble was that the RAA was also responding to the news it was getting from Lauinger and began to launch an investigation of its own.[31] On August 17, Favag announced the cessation of payment to its creditors. Three days later, Allianz took over its direct insurance business, thus guaranteeing that policyholders would be protected. However, the satisfaction of other creditors (both national and international) was to become the subject of tedious negotiations as well as civil lawsuits, some of which dragged on into the mid-1930s. The criminal trials of the leading directors lasted into 1932, when they received jail sentences and fines. The Favag affair was thus of a piece with the other bankruptcies and scandals of the Depression period and with public perceptions that there was something rotten in the world of capitalism.

Once the scandal had broken, it very soon became manifest that the Favag gold mark opening balance was 5 million gold marks in excess of what it should have been, thanks to Dumcke's desire to increase the company's prestige and attractiveness to investors. The chief beneficiary of Dumcke's folly, Kurt Schmitt – who

on court decisions connected with the insurance business is the *Veröffentlichungen des Reichsaufsichtsamts für Privatversicherung* (Leipzig, 1901ff.).

[31] Artur Lauinger, *Das öffentliche Gewissen. Erfahrungen und Erlebnisse eines Redakteurs der Frankfurter Zeitung* (Frankfurt a.M., 1958), pp. 18–22. Lauinger's account telescopes some of the events between late 1928 and August 1929; he leaves the impression that his interviews with Dumcke and Becker and the supervisory board meeting took place within a short space of time, which could not have been possible because Dumcke died in February. Fortunately, a memorandum of Munich Re General Director Wilhelm Kisskalt of January 25, 1930, who spoke with Lauinger in April 1929 about the interview with Becker, helps clarify the sequence of events. The memorandum is in BAB, 80 Ba 2/P 5785.

later attributed Allianz's survival in the Depression to the modesty of its 1924 gold mark opening balance and the purposefulness of its expansion policy explained as follows: "The excessively high demands on the capital resources of the company necessarily arose from the exaggerated conversion to gold of the Frankfurter Allgemeine. The decision to enter into dangerous financial engagements also arose from the effort to master these difficulties, which in the last analysis led to the collapse of the Frankfurter."[32] Even as Schmitt and his concern took over the best and most profitable parts of Favag's business, he warned against excessive optimism and risky engagements. Favag had collapsed because of a spectacular mix of bad decisions in the field of indirect insurance, banking activities inappropriate for an insurance company, an inorganic concern structure, and conflation of the concern's interests with the personal enterprises of the directors. In the process Favag had accumulated very high debts – including short-term debts in Switzerland, England, and the Netherlands – for the financing of long-term projects. German supervisory institutions, both governmental and private, had obviously failed to do their job. Schmitt was quite aware that all this had created a danger of international distrust of the German financial insurance business and the German economy in general. As he somewhat cynically (but still hopefully) told his board of directors:

One cannot deny that the events at the "Frankfurter" have led to a general crisis of confidence in the private insurance business; but it is to be hoped that this crisis will be overcome soon. In working against a migration of business, especially of life insurance to foreign companies, it is useful to point out that collapses similar to the "Frankfurter" are not unknown in America and England.[33]

It is important to note that there had been some genuine national and international resistance against Allianz's self-interested but salutary intervention in the Favag affair. As mentioned previously, Schmitt had broached the possibility of fusion with Allianz in his talks with Bodenheimer, and other discussions had taken place at a time when the problems of the company had not been revealed. Even after they were, the basic insurance business remained very attractive, which explains the rapidity of Schmitt's intervention. It was attractive to others as well, especially the group of insurance companies connected with Director Johannes Nordhoff of the Berlinische Feuer-Versicherungs-Anstalt. The latter was closely allied to the Schweizerische Rückversicherungs-Gesellschaft (Swiss Re) in Zurich, which was a competitor of the Allianz-associated Munich Re. It was anxious to expand its operations in Germany, not by acquiring portions of the Favag itself (from which it expected more "surprises") but rather by gaining control of two old, solid, and well-respected companies in the Favag concern: Karlsruher Lebensversicherungsbank-AG in Karlsruhe and Vereinigte Berlinische und Preußische Lebensversicherungs AG in Berlin. Nordhoff complained to his friends in the Disconto-Gesellschaft that the Allianz takeover would upset the

---

[32] Vorstandssitzung am 5. und 6. Nov. 1929, FHA, p. 4, S 17.2/4.
[33] Ibid., p. 5.

balance in the insurance business and would also bring about a further economic concentration in Berlin at the expense of Frankfurt and South Germany.[34]

Yet another scheme was urged by the Victoria Versicherungs-Gesellschaft, and supported by Jakob Goldschmidt of the Danat-Bank, that would involve joint action on the part of all the large German insurance companies to deal with the problem. In the last analysis, however, the leading banks represented on the Favag supervisory board found the Allianz takeover most acceptable and welcome despite the power shift that it entailed. On the one hand, the alternatives were all being proposed in August 1929, while the full scope of the disaster was gradually coming into focus – for example, that the "silent reserves" of Favag were really its own shares that it had bought and were being held in the portfolios of companies in the concern. On the other hand, Allianz had the distinct advantage of operating in all the various insurance fields in which Favag operated, had a superior apparatus and organization for dealing with the Favag policies, and was willing to put up guarantees for these immediately while negotiating over the final purchase price. Time was of the essence if a widening crisis were to be averted and unwelcome interventions by the State avoided. As the bankers concluded:

Finally, in view of the fact that it is impossible in the time available to wait for the coming together of the big insurance companies, which would take a very long time, and that one under no circumstances should allow the Reich Supervisory Agency for Private Insurance to mix in, it was decided to ask Herr Dr. Schmitt and Hilgard from the Allianz as well as Dr. Herzfelder of the Hermes Kreditversicherungsbank-AG to discuss the matter with us.[35]

Furthermore, Allianz had considerable influence with the Reich Supervisory Agency, thus making its role even more advantageous.

Indeed, the RAA had to approve the contracts between Allianz and Favag; it did so on August 20, 1929, and thus immediately alienated a substantial (and the most intact and lucrative) portion of Favag's business without even summoning a meeting of its shareholders. Furthermore, the RAA thereby issued an effective ban on payment to other creditors until the price Allianz would pay could be decided and until the assets and liabilities of the rump Favag could be determined. It fell within the powers of the RAA to give primary protection to the policyholders, but these actions also involved a bypassing of the interests of shareholders and other creditors that the RAA could only justify with the argument that the value of Allianz's acquisition would diminish if insurance business turned elsewhere and that this would not be in the interest of anyone. Although Allianz certainly stood to gain substantially and could determine what it would and would not take over, it was willing to pay some heed to South German sensibilities as well as

---

[34] Aktenvermerk Frank (Disconto), 16. Aug. 1929, and other relevant correspondence in HADB, S236; Schweizer-Rück-Ausschuß-Sitzungen, August 1929, SR, Ausschuß-Sitzungen, Bd. 10.

[35] Sitzung der Berliner Hauptbeteiligten des Bankkonsortiums, 17. Aug. 1929, HADB, S245. Hermes was a part of the Allianz concern, and Emil Herzfelder was a specialist in credit insurance.

to anxieties about its increased power. Thus, Favag would be neither formally annexed nor allowed to disappear; rather, it would be reestablished (albeit as a company within the Allianz concern) as Neue Frankfurter Allgemeine Versicherungs AG. Also, the major insurance companies in the Favag concern – the Hammonia (which was taken over jointly by Allianz and Munich Re), Karlsruher Leben, and Vereinigte Berlinische und Preußische Lebensversicherungs-AG – were to retain their formal independence and not be externally designated as belonging to Allianz. Nevertheless, despite a general recognition that Allianz (and particularly Schmitt) had acted to prevent the Favag collapse from turning into a major disaster for the German insurance business and the German economy, there was also considerable feeling, not only in the German insurance circles but also on the part of Swiss Re, that Allianz had taken whatever was worth taking.[36]

There was also a great deal of sentiment at home and abroad that Allianz, which paid Favag 36,897,301 RM for the assets it acquired, had paid too little for the advantages received.[37] The view of Allianz, of course, was that it had prevented a catastrophe for the German insurance industry and for the German economy in general. Both arguments were probably correct, and the debate was highly relevant to the second and far less soluble aspect of the Favag collapse: paying off as much as possible of the domestic and international debts the concern had contracted. These amounted to 63.9 million RM to domestic creditors and 35.6 million RM to foreign creditors.[38] The obvious solution was to form a standstill syndicate of the creditors while the banking committee of the Favag supervisory board provided some guarantees and time was taken to determine Favag's actual status and what Allianz was willing to pay Favag for its acquisitions. Some of Favag's foreign creditors proved unwilling to agree and thought that the German banks on the supervisory board should pick up the bill. The situation was worrisome to Economics Minister Curtius, who summoned Directors Oscar Wassermann of Deutsche Bank and Jakob Goldschmidt of Danat-Bank and told them "the banks must make large payments to prevent a cessation of payment by Favag. The German economy cannot bear a collapse." They all agreed, however, that the Reichsbank had to intervene and assist, and they went to see Reichsbank President Hjalmar Schacht toward this end. Schacht, however, refused to do any such thing and also warned against the Reich Supervisory Agency issuing a payment ban "because the outside world would view this as demonstrating the possibility of intervention from above with respect to the fulfillment of payment obligations.... intervention from above would create fear

---

[36] Aktenvermerk Moesler, 19. Aug. 1929, HABD, S236, and Vorstandssitzung am 5. und 6. Nov. 1929, FHA, S 17.2/4. Little credence seems to have been given to the charges of the indicted directors that Allianz had been plotting to take over Favag all along and had even been responsible for the Lauinger articles. See the responses by Schmitt, Heß, Hilgard, and Kisskalt and their valuable accounts of their dealings with Favag in BAB, 80 Ba 2/P 5785. For the Reich Supervisory Agency decision and justification of its actions, see its formal decision of Nov. 16, 1929, in the Protokol über die Gläubigerversammlung, 15. Jan. 1930, pp. 1–2, HABD, S244.

[37] See Favag an das Finanzamt Frankfurt am Main, 17. Dez. 1932, BAK, B 280/13283.

[38] Favag an Waller, 27. Aug. 1929, HABD, S234.

that the same could also happen with respect to the numerous municipal credits taken abroad."[39] The great vulnerability created by the private and public borrowing in Germany was thus apparent. The reality of the Favag case, however, was that a Reich Supervisory Agency payment ban had been created under the terms of the grant of permission to Allianz to take over the direct insurance business of Favag. This automatically protected policyholders. The RAA also mandated a payment ban for what remained of the Favag until its financial status was established and until Allianz and the Favag settled on what the former would pay the latter for the assets it had taken over. Schacht apparently raised no objections to this. Also, the Favag bankers seem to have used his good offices and influence to bring recalcitrant English banks into accepting the standstill arrangement.[40]

At the end of a rather dragged-out process, the creditors of Favag received between 20% and 40% of their due. It should come as no surprise that representatives of the creditors bitterly resented the way in which the banks on the Favag supervisory board had behaved between August 1929 and when they finally met in mid-January 1930:

The first thing that the administration did in the "protection" of the interests of the creditors was to take the most valuable assets which this enterprise had as its basis and sell them to Allianz. They should have been all the more cautious in doing so since the Allianz concern is one in which the majority of the administration banks are just as much represented as in the Favag concern. Represented in Allianz are: Deutsche Bank, Disconto-Gesellschaft, Darmstädter Bank, Commerz- und Privatbank. One had, without setting a purchase price first, shifted over this valuable set of assets from a concern that was in distress to a concern that was not and one had removed what had previously been the most dangerous competitor of the firm that was not in distress and turned it into the single most decisive insurance concern in Germany.... One had more or less skimmed the cream off the cake and left behind an unpalatable, spoiled dough for the creditors, without there being any security as to what is still to be saved from the Allianz concern for the creditors of the Favag concern.[41]

This was probably a self-interested exaggeration under the circumstances. From a longer-term perspective, the solution to the Favag crisis must be understood in terms of the need, in Jakob Goldschmidt's words, "to permit the curtain to fall over the matter so agitating for the public."[42] Whatever the aftershocks in the law courts, the agreements made between Favag and Allianz and between the Favag banking committee and the creditor committee in February 1930 laid the basic issues to rest and permitted the liquidation of Favag with some satisfaction of the creditors.[43] It was an immense triumph for Kurt Schmitt, Hilgard (who played a prominent role in the negotiations), and Allianz, whose top leaders'

[39] Aktenvermerk Moesler, 1. Nov. 1929, HABD, S239.
[40] See Moesler to Schacht, Sept. 4, 1929, HADB, S238.
[41] Justizrat Heilbrunn at the Creditors meeting on Jan. 15, 1930, HADB, S245.
[42] Aktennotiz vom 30. Jan. 1930, HADB, S241.
[43] The agreements are to be found in HADB, S233.

initiative and whose sheer strength had made it possible to provide the surest and most speedily implementable alternative to bankruptcy. This solution is in sharp contrast to that involving the failure of Danat-Bank in July 1931 (under, to be sure, much worse economic and financial conditions). The major banks refused or failed to come to the aid of Danat; the government had to step in and take over Danat-Bank and later Dresdner Bank, while the banking system itself was subjected to much more rigorous controls and much more serious attacks.

THE ALLIANZ CONCERN IN THE 1930S: STRUCTURE, ORGANIZATION, AND PERSONNEL

In May 1930, less than a year after it had acquired the insurance business of Favag and founded Neue Frankfurter, the Allianz concern celebrated its fortieth anniversary. Appropriately enough, it returned to its Munich roots. The supervisory board meetings and the formal anniversary celebration and dinner for the leadership of the concern took place in the elegant facilities of Munich Re. The members of the various supervisory boards, their counterparts in the regional committees for the branches of the concern, and the managing boards and directors of the various companies and branches in the concern added up to a few hundred persons. They heard Kisskalt, Schmitt, and Georgii give speeches on the history of the concern, discuss contemporary issues of economic policy, and expound on the role of the insurance business and Allianz in the past, present, and future.[44]

The festivities were not limited to such high personages, however. The Allianz close-of-the-business-year national meeting, which rotated between Berlin, Stuttgart, and Munich, was also held in the Bavarian capital on May 27–28 and brought together some five hundred "Allianzers" from branches, field offices, and district offices of the company along with prize winners of various competitions and older employees in all pay categories. The host Allianz organization for these members of the "Allianz family" was Bayerische Versicherungsbank and its General Director, Wilhelm Arendts. They, too, were treated to an anniversary celebration at which five hundred persons were in attendance in the Festival Hall of the Munich City Hall. One of the high points of this occasion was the award of the Spear Thrower to Alfred Wiedemann, head of the Dresden branch and later general director of Neue Frankfurter, which was conceded with grace and good humor in self-composed verse by the previous year's winner and one of the stars of the concern with a seemingly bright future, Director Maximilian Eichbaum of the Magdeburger branch. Prizes were also awarded to ten section heads (for different types of insurance offered by the concern), while sixteen insurance officials working in the field also received various prizes.

---

[44] Bericht Moesler, 27. Mai 1930, BAB, 80 Ba 2/P 5787.

Rudolf Schloeßmann, Hans Heß, Eduard Hilgard, and Kurt Schmitt (from right to left) at an excursion on the occasion of the end-of-the-fiscal-year conference (1930), May 15, 1931.

While Allianz thus honored the achievements of its employees, the latter's representatives also chose to celebrate their concern's birthday. Zech, chairman of the Berlin factory council and a representative of the Social Democratic Central Association of German Employees, presented Schmitt with a congratulatory card containing the signatures of every employee in the Berlin offices. Schmitt received these and other gifts of the Allianz councils with his usual grace and charm. In his speech, he emphasized the progress that had been made in the struggle against overspecialization in various branches of insurance, the creation of branches and offices that were better rooted in local conditions, the importance of providing good customer service at low cost, and the need to train new generations of insurance agents and provide opportunities for promotion within the concern. All in all, it seems to have been a high-spirited event, undoubtedly made all the more jovial by the Bierabend in the Löwenbräukeller that followed the formal celebration and the excursion into the mountains on the following day.[45]

The celebrations of May 1930 revealed the Allianz corporate culture at a critical juncture in its history and, indeed, in German history. With its acquisition of

[45] "Abschlußtagung am 27. und 28. Mai 1930," *Allianz-Zeitung* 12 (1930), pp. 128–34.

Favag, Allianz attained a plateau in its expansion that was to last until 1938 and faced the crucial tasks of digestion and organization. This was well reflected in Schmitt's remark that a strong bond of friendship needed to be created among companies and persons who had been in sharp competition with one another for many years and now found themselves parts of Allianz. At the same time, the events just described took place in the early stages of what was to become the Great Depression and all the economic and political catastrophes that came in its wake. Thus, the May 1930 celebrations mark a convenient point from which to consider the structure and character of the Allianz concern and its personnel in the 1930s.

It is essential to understand how the concern was organized and conducted its business if one is to discuss its subsequent history sensibly. Yet this is a somewhat frustrating undertaking because of the wartime destruction of internal correspondence and other relevant materials that might have provided more intimate insights into the management practices, relationships among central headquarters and branches and daughter companies, and personnel problems that are so important to a full business history. Here one is highly dependent on the concern's self-presentation in published and unpublished histories and in its yearly business reports. Needless to say, these sources are intended to present the concern in the best possible light and offer a somewhat static and rosy picture of a very complicated and dynamic enterprise. Nevertheless, an effort will be made to breathe some life into the available material.

As Chart I shows, Allianz was a complex organization consisting of a central headquarters in Berlin, a number of companies devoted to special types of insurance, and regional branch headquarters in various cities, a few of which were intimately related to important Allianz-controlled companies that nevertheless maintained a measure of individual identity. There were also companies not formally integrated into the concern but in which controlling interest had been acquired in various proportions by Allianz, Stuttgarter Verein, Allianz Leben, and Munich Re in the wake of the Favag collapse. It should be noted that Karlsruher Leben (which had a community interest with Hammonia) and Vereinigte Berlinische und Preußische Lebensversicherungs-AG were allowed to function independently, while Hammonia and Neue Frankfurter were under the technical control of the concern. Hermes, whose controlling shares were held by Allianz and Munich Re, operated independently because of the special nature of credit insurance.

There was manifestly some duplication in the insurance products sold by the individual companies and corporations in the concern. Allianz Leben and Karlsruher Leben both sold life insurance, while Hammonia, Allianz, and Neue Frankfurter all marketed property insurance. There was certainly some regulation of competition within Allianz, and the entire concern benefitted from maintaining the names, connections, and good will established by the old companies that had entered its fold. Allianz did provide a substantial amount of their capital and also provided reinsurance or excess risk reinsurance. This participation reflected

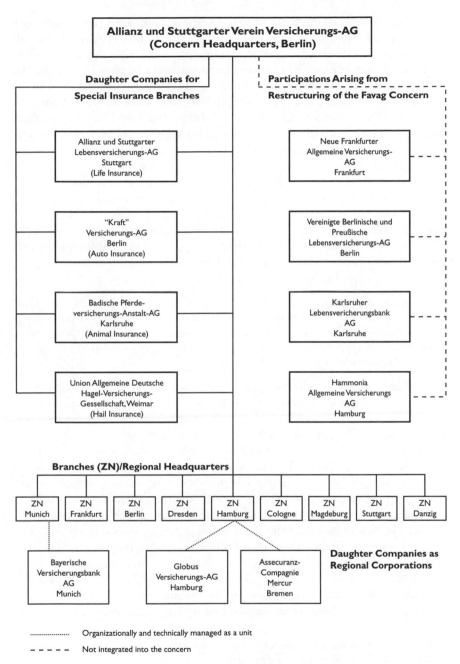

Chart I. Organization of the Allianz Concern in 1931. *Source:* Allianz Business Report (1931).

the wider purposes of this form of concentration: to broaden the "community of those at risk," create a healthy mix of risks, improve the capacity for risk calculation, and establish a broader and more secure coverage and guarantee of policies. At the same time, the greater the concern, the larger was the potential pool of experience and experienced personnel upon which it could draw, and the stronger was the incentive and opportunity for fruitful rationalization and cost reduction. The history of the concern had shown and would continue to show that the companies brought into its community of interest almost inevitably were gradually absorbed into its fold and lost their autonomy, thus reflecting a policy of friendly takeovers and friendly absorptions over the years.[46]

Not only was the Allianz concern by far the largest and most important exponent of the private corporate insurance business (as opposed to the publicly chartered insurance societies and the mutuals) in Germany, it was also the leading and unabashed advocate of concentration in the insurance business. Those who spoke for Allianz, headed by Schmitt, rejected charges that the concern reflected "trustification" of the insurance business or some kind of monopoly. As one of its directors and historians, Rudolf Hensel, wrote in 1930:

Our Allianz, which only unites a sixth of the German insurance business in its entire concern, is unfortunately very far away from such a monopoly position – I expressly say unfortunately, for a further consolidation (it does not have to occur through us) would make insurance cheaper through the elimination of uneconomic companies and the savings of cost thereby brought about.[47]

Thus Hensel vigorously defended Allianz's expansion and also welcomed expansion by its big competitors, such as Victoria, Nordstern, and Aachener und Münchener. The alternative to such concern building would have been cartels in the various insurance branches, and the experience with cartels in fire insurance and in other areas had not been satisfactory. Most of the cartels had collapsed after the war and inflation. The reason in insurance (as well as in other fields of business) was that cartels were unstable in times of monetary unrest and unsatisfactory in periods of capital shortage. Individual firms had a strong tendency to break ranks in order to gain some immediate advantage, thus breaking up the cartel. The conditions under which the Weimar economy operated from beginning to end were such that they favored the principle: "to they that have shall be given."[48] Large concerns offering a wide range of insurance products appeared to be a more satisfactory way of attaining sensible levels of risk management and sensible premiums within major portions of the industry and thus in the industry as a whole. Therefore, competition among large concerns did not exclude

---

[46] These processes of absorption are demonstrated in illuminating detail in Hensel, "40 Jahre Allianz," FHA, AZ 1.3/1, pp. 127–216 and 259–98.

[47] Ibid., p. 274.

[48] See Alfred D. Chandler, *Scale and Scope. The Dynamics of Industrial Capitalism* (Cambridge, 1990), Ch. 13; for a good discussion of these processes in the insurance industry itself, see Arps, *Durch unruhige Zeiten*, Bd. 1, Kap. 11.

collaboration and the need to moderate ambition. Further acquisitions after the Favag affair would have given Allianz digestive problems and bad publicity both. This was demonstrated in May 1931, for example, when Nordstern appeared to be in difficulty. Schmitt expressed a willingness to purchase a block of Nordstern shares and then helped that company with its organizational problems and in improving its performance in the transportation insurance field. He insisted, however, that the purchase be kept a secret since "a takeover by fusion cannot come into question during the next decade."[49]

Of course, one might argue that Schmitt and Hensel could afford to be generous to their competitors in the private insurance business, since the other concerns had a long way to catch up. In 1928, Allianz collected 178 million RM in premiums on all forms of property insurance. Adding the 30 million RM in premiums collected by Favag's successor, Neue Frankfurter, yields a total of approximately 208 million RM in 1929–1930. The next-ranking concern, Nordstern und Vaterländische, collected 70 million RM in premiums, while Albingia Versicherungs-AG and Victoria Feuer-Versicherungs-AG collected 37 and 34 million RM, respectively. In considering the growth and economic power of Allianz, therefore, it is important to take into account both the relative position in the private insurance business and what this meant in absolute earnings. In 1930, the concern collected over 20% of the entire premium income of the private insurance business in eight out of fourteen insurance categories: life (20.5%), liability (28%), accident (26.2%), break-in and theft (29.4%), guarantee and credit (53.4%), glass (21%), machines (97.2%), and water damage (36.7%). At the same time, it was also collecting a great deal more money. In 1924, Allianz collected 108 million RM (10.2%) of the 1.1 billion RM in premiums collected by all German private insurance companies. In 1929, its percentage rose to 13.1% after collecting 340 million RM out of a total of 2.5 billion RM in premiums. Similarly, Allianz Leben collected 1.6 billion RM (15.6%) of the 10.2 billion RM collected by 55 life insurance companies in 1927; in 1930, it collected 3 billion RM (18.7%) of the 16 billion RM in premiums collected by 53 companies.[50] Allianz Leben was not, however, the only life insurance company in the Allianz concern. Hence there could be no question that Allianz was far ahead as the leader in the German private insurance business.

The effectiveness of Allianz, and indeed of any concern, ultimately depended on the talents and skills of its leadership and personnel and on the balance between centralization and decentralization in its organization. One of the chief charges made against concerns of this type, after all, was that their structure and organization were opaque and that they were overly bureaucratized, so that their costs and premiums were unnecessarily high. This is not the place to investigate such questions, except to note that the available records indicate that

---

[49] Aktenvermerk Moesler, 20. Mai 1931, BAB, 80 Ba 2/P 5784.
[50] See the appendices in Hensel, "40 Jahre Allianz," FHA, AZ1.3/1, and *Allianz-Zeitung* 12 (1930), p. 99.

the concern benefitted from a hard-nosed, cost-conscious management and obviously had a high degree of success in increasing its market share. The evidence suggests also (as already noted with reference to "Papa Heß") that Allianz leadership succeeded in maintaining a high level of employee morale and loyalty and that it was aware of the need to work hard at keeping its customers and probably attained a reasonable measure of customer satisfaction.

One of the most important tasks of the concern leadership was to create a healthy balance between centralization and decentralization.[51] As might be expected, the managing board in Berlin determined the general lines of policy: the branches of insurance to be developed, insurance policy conditions, premiums to be charged, acquisitions, investments, legal questions, personnel policies, relations with government authorities, membership in and relationship to business associations, and general bookkeeping and accounting. It thus combined administrative and monitoring functions. In the former case, for example, the board managed the pension and health care funds and other provisions designed to benefit the employees; in the latter case, it exercised oversight with respect to the development of the various branches of insurance within the entire concern. An especially important function of central headquarters was management of Allianz's substantial assets in cash, securities, shares, and real estate. There was, to be sure, a certain amount of decentralization even at the top of the company, since life, accident, and liability insurance were handled in Stuttgart. Nevertheless, the basic management of the concern was centralized in Berlin.

Allianz branches in various key cities and regions had already been created by Heß in 1919. The decision to introduce a higher and more formal degree of decentralization was taken in 1928.[52] By this time, the concern had consummated fourteen mergers, and management decided to set up nine regional headquarters (Landesdirektionen) at the geographical branches contained in the organization chart. By and large, these corresponded to the old big branches (or Zweigniederlassungen, ZN) but now they became major administrative units for large geographical areas. Each of the regional headquarters did the equivalent business of a medium-sized insurance company (20–25 million RM in premiums per year) and each had an organizational structure that more or less paralleled that of the central office in Berlin.

Each of the various regional headquarters was provided with what was tantamount to its own supervisory board in the form of a regional committee (Landesausschuß) composed of prominent businessmen and public figures from the region encompassed by the headquarters. Thus, in 1930, Allianz had not only a supervisory board of some 30 prominent bankers and businessmen but also a network of over 80 such persons in the various regional committees throughout Germany. The significance of Allianz's supervisory boards (and of the like

---

[51] There is an excellent discussion of the organization of the concern in Kisch, *Fünfzig Jahre Allianz*, pp. 103–20.

[52] See Aktenvermerk Moesler, 11. Dez. 1928, BAB, 80 Ba 2/P 5787.

organs connected with its geographical branches) did not lie in their putative supervisory functions. As Hilgard noted with respect to his first experience with a supervisory board meeting in 1921, "I was already struck at this first meeting that the supervisory board, on which sat the top men of the German banking business, indicated very little interest in the material under discussion and were exclusively interested in the size of the dividend to be expected, upon which depended the amount of their supervisory board royalty."[53] Such attitudes had led to the Favag's demise, but Allianz was a different company with different leaders, and the 16% dividend given in 1930 was a proper reflection of the company's successes. Schmitt made a point of identifying the branches where the company was not doing well and indicating areas where he felt costs were unacceptable. One of the novelties of the business report for 1930 was that it provided detail beyond the call of duty with respect to the company's share and security investments.[54] In the wake of the Favag scandal, Schmitt undoubtedly wished to set a standard and be a model of transparency. This all probably was quite reassuring to the supervisory board and regional land committees, but their real importance was in the business connections they established and the business they brought in for Allianz at the national, regional, and local levels.

The work of selling insurance remained with the field organization itself, and much of this was done at the level below the regional headquarters, which had organizational units under them in the form of branch field offices (Filialdirektionen) and district field offices (Bezirksdirektionen). The former – of which there were up to five, depending on the size of the regional headquarters and the amount of business involved – were smaller versions of the regional headquarters and had bookkeeping responsibilities; thus they were involved in the technical administration of their policies and also had personnel appointed to deal with the various branches of insurance. The district offices – between two and twelve per Landesdirektion – were exclusively concerned with the propaganda and personnel involved in the selling of insurance. At the head of each stood a district director, who oversaw the work of a number of district inspectors charged with the operation of smaller districts. Although some insurance companies (and even Allianz, at times) used general insurance agencies run by independent agents who worked on a commission basis at this level, Allianz had pursued a policy of replacing such agents with salaried employees of its own whose task it was to find, train, and control suitable insurance salesmen in the various branches of insurance sold in the district. The actual insurance sales force was a combination of salaried persons working solely for Allianz (only 2,334 in 1939), independent full-time salespersons who made their living from commissions, and men and women who sold insurance part-time in an effort to supplement their income. The exact number of such part-time salespersons is uncertain because part-time work was not registered in the Allianz statistics

[53] Hilgard, "Leben," FHA, NL 2/7, p. 23.
[54] Bericht Moesler, 27. Mai 1930, BAB, 80 Ba 2/P 5787.

examined and, indeed, is not available for Germany as a whole (since part-time work was not included in the national occupational census). The number of independent salespersons in Germany, whether full- or part-time, was estimated at 50,000 in 1939. The part-time salespersons often serviced a variety of companies, and they unquestionably played a vital role for the entire industry. Insofar as it was possible, Allianz sought salespersons that would sell Allianz products exclusively. In any case, it was very important that sales personnel be honest, be attentive to the needs of their clients, and engage in fair competition. This was not always the case, and the reputation of insurance salespersons often suffered as a result.[55]

Inspectors and subinspectors therefore performed the crucial function of oversight, since it was at this level that the company often dealt directly with its customers. The task of these company officials, like that of the over 300 company employees charged with handling claims, was an especially delicate one. It is thus not surprising that the concern devoted considerable attention to the training of personnel. On the one hand, it had a substantial apprentice program so as to provide future insurance professionals with training from an early age on. On the other, special effort was made to hone the skills of those employed as inspectors. Not only did they receive an 8–10-week training course, they also were required to work closely with a more experienced inspector for a substantial period of time before operating on their own. Furthermore, the entire staff of inspectors at a given branch met weekly on a Sunday or Monday evening to receive the latest directives from the home office, listen to lectures on current issues, and exchange experiences. As noted earlier, the concern also ran a variety of competitions, and it was a special honor to be a member of the "million club" – that is, to have sold a million RM in insurance. As Table A shows,[56] the core companies in the Allianz concern underwent a considerable growth of personnel between the end of the inflation and 1938, and it is remarkable that the number of employees increased even during the Great Depression. Moreover, the reported staffing levels, especially in the so-called field service, does not include those selling insurance for commissions. Yet the increase in personnel was actually quite modest, given the extraordinary growth of the concern over these years. This may be explained by the fact that Allianz systematically sought to rationalize its operations, both technically and organizationally, and seems to have been reasonably successful in doing so.

The role of technological rationalization was already evident with the introduction of the typewriter, telephone, and copying devices after the First World War and also involved the increasing use of female employees for secretarial and clerical tasks. Rationalization and deskilling through the use of office machinery inevitably led to a downgrading of the males, who had previously performed many of these tasks by hand and who considered themselves to be "officials."

---

[55] Hensel, "40 Jahre Allianz," FHA, AZ 1.3/1, pp. 68, 225–30.
[56] Kisch, *Fünfzig Jahre Allianz,* p. 208.

Table A. *Employees at Allianz, 1924–1938*

Year	Home Office Employees Property Insurance	Life Insurance	Total	Field Service Employees	Total
1924	3,660	291	3,951	1,818	5,769
1925	3,164	339	3,503	757	4,260
1926	2,983	370	3,353	460	3,813
1927	4,040	680	4,720	546	5,266
1928	4,342	786	5,128	672	5,800
1929	5,699	1,753	7,452	1,005	8,457
1930	5,590	2,285	7,875	1,205	9,080
1931	5,606	2,933	8,538	1,412	9,950
1932	5,881	3,179	9,060	1,373	10,433
1933	6,236	3,445	9,681	1,669	11,350
1934	6,544	3,466	10,010	1,828	11,838
1935	6,940	3,514	10,454	2,345	12,799
1936	7,098	3,479	10,577	2,725	13,302
1937	7,377	3,457	10,834	2,819	13,653
1938	7,345	3,465	10,810	2,701	13,511

The technical changes of greatest importance in insurance, however, were the introduction of automatic addressing machines (the so-called Adrema process) and of the Hollerith punchcard system, which permitted the mechanical calculation of premiums, production of policies, and record keeping. Much of the push for such mechanization came from the introduction in 1926 of the ASS (Allianz Spar- und Sterbekasse) – inexpensive, low-value insurance policies that combined life and burial insurance and whose necessarily lower profit margins made cost cutting particularly desirable. It was important, however, not to overdo the degree of mechanization. The Hollerith machines were lodged in the mathematical section of the concern and hardly achieved the broad use they were to enjoy after the Second World War (not to mention the later computers). American insurance companies apparently made much greater use of office machinery. The American model was very much in the vogue, but even though Director Rudolf Hensel journeyed to the United States in 1927 and recounted his experiences in the *Allianz-Zeitung*, this side of American rationalization was slow to develop.[57]

[57] See Barbara Eggenkämper, "Die Vision vom 'aktenlosen Büro'. Von der Lochkarte zum Computer," in Burkhart Lauterbach (ed.), *Großstadtmenschen. Die Welt der Angestellten* (Frankfurt a.M., 1995), pp. 229–48. More generally, see Mary Nolan, *Visions of Modernity. American Business and the Modernization of Germany* (Oxford & New York, 1994). For Hensel's trip to the United States see *Allianz-Zeitung 1927–1929* and Rudolf Hensel, *Amerika. Aus Tagebuchblättern einer Reise* (Berlin, 1928).

Indeed, as the leadership in Berlin pointed out in November 1929, the success of rationalization measures aimed at simplifying procedures, as important as they were, had limited success compared to large-scale organizational measures recently implemented: the closing of the large branches in Breslau, Hannover, Karlsruhe, and Stettin as well as the shutting down of other smaller operations and the transfer of their business to the remaining large branches. Hence, plans were being made to undertake further consolidations – for example, of the organization of Stuttgarter Verein and of Allianz offices in Württemberg and Baden. The shifting of business (and the related greater administrative responsibilities) to the regional headquarters was accompanied by a strong pressure to reduce costs and the establishment of maximum costs for each branch of the business. For example, the acceptable cost quotient for break-in and burglary insurance was set at 50%, of which 40% was allowed to the regional headquarters and 10% to the general headquarters in Berlin.[58]

The constant pressure to cut costs and increase efficiency meant that Allianz's management had a considerable incentive to maintain the morale and loyalty of its regular employees. Director Hensel not only praised American rationalization methods but also the American system of "welfare capitalism"; he argued (in his unpublished history of Allianz in 1930) that the concern not only attained American standards in the size of its operations but also measured up to its American counterparts in what it did for employees.[59] One of the most important benefits was providing a subsidized meal in the canteens of its Berlin and other major urban branch offices. This made it possible for employees to avoid traveling long distances home to take the main meal of the day and, needless to say, obviated an excessively long mealtime break. Because of its size, Allianz had its own sickness insurance fund, which was typical of such large business organizations. Much less typical, however, was the Allianz pension fund, established in 1924 after the old pension fund had been wiped out in the inflation and Allianz took over its obligations in order to prevent its employees from losing those assets. The new organization was based on the principle of self-administration by the employees themselves, and all regular employees of the concern were entitled to join if they were between the ages of 20 and 50 (in the case of men) or between 20 and 40 (for women). The fund had 3.2 million RM in assets at the end of 1929, and it was set up to care for the needs of employees and their survivors after retirement or in case of disability. Employees contributed 6% of their yearly income, although the maximum income for such purposes was 10,000 RM, while Allianz contributed slightly under double the employee payment. Members (of which there were 3,766 in 1929–1930) received only half their pension under the government insurance program for white-collar employees if they opted to join the Allianz plan also. In such cases, that half of the government pension to which they were entitled came out of the Allianz pension fund. Hence, the purpose was to make it possible to receive a larger pension by joining

[58] 15. erweiterte Vorstandssitzung am 5. und 6. Nov. 1929, FHA, S 17.2/4, pp. 20–4.
[59] Hensel, "40 Jahre Allianz," FHA, AZ 1.3/1, pp. 217–24.

the Allianz plan. Pensions started at 30% of income after four years, increased by 2% per year thereafter, and could reach a maximum of 70%, with the surviving spouse receiving half the pension upon the death of the employee. Allianz also provided monies to assist widows and orphans and to pay for funeral costs.

An important element in the corporate culture of Allianz was its emphasis on the physical well-being of its employees. Thus, by 1930, the concern had three vacation homes for employees who did not have the means to pay for a family vacation. The homes were located in Bad Harzburg, Aidenbach near Passau, and on the island of Rügen; rooms were made available at a modest cost. Most important, however, was the concern's emphasis on sports, an interest that reflected a more general trend in Germany at this time to try to correct the alleged ill consequences of urban living and desk work. The first Allianz Sports Club was founded in Dresden in 1922. In 1925, the Sportverein Allianz-Konzern e.V. was founded, centered in Berlin and with local branches at other major Allianz outposts. It boasted 600 members by the end of 1929 and offered a wide range of sport facilities and activities – especially in Berlin, where it had a large indoor sports facility, a boat house in Köpenick, and (as a gift to the employees in honor of the concern's fortieth anniversary in 1930) a large stadium that held 1,000 spectators and substantial facilities for family recreation in Berlin-Mariendorf. The high point of these activities was the Allianz "Olympics" held every fall and attended religiously by the managing board, where teams and athletes from the branches of the concern competed for prizes.

In his otherwise very sober account of the concern, Hensel waxes rapturous in expressing the ideological side of the Allianz sports program: "Movement, light, air, water are the greatest healing factors in the struggle with the damages of civilization." Sports drove away "beer bellies, alcoholic fogginess, and cigarette poison." Sports also had positive political and social consequences by "teaching comradeship and a sense of community and is in our divisive age almost the only area in which the members of the various 'estates,' 'classes,' and 'parties' can find themselves as equal members of a single and great people's community." Last but not least, sports in his view promoted the kind of energy and spirit that Germany needed to compete in world markets; from this perspective, "the health of the people is economic capital."[60]

Left-wing critics like Siegfried Kracauer treated such programs – whether they were company vacation homes, company sports organizations, or even company newspapers – as so much eyewash designed to cover up rather than transcend class differences, to veil the proletarianization of the white-collar workers and many of the firm officials, and to distract attention from the processes of deskilling and exploitation connected with rationalization.[61] Translating American techniques of corporate welfare capitalism into German equivalents certainly had

[60] Ibid., p. 221.
[61] This was the position taken by Siegfried Kracauer in *Die Angestellten. Aus dem neuesten Deutschland* (Frankfurt a.M., 1930), reprinted as *Die Angestellten. Eine Schrift vom Ende der Weimarer Republik* (Allensbach & Bonn, 1959). See especially his comments on the role of sports, pp. 66–74.

its limitations. Businessmen like Hensel were well aware that conditions in the United States were very different, since there was scarcely any collective bargaining and no social security system across the Atlantic. Also, many of the practices of Allianz and other concerns reflected a home-grown German interest in technocratic approaches to employer–labor relations that favored company unions (Werksgemeinschaften).[62] Nevertheless, there is no evidence of a strong anti-union posture at Allianz and no real evidence that the corporate culture of the concern had sinister manipulative purposes.

In the absence of much concrete information that would enable one to study the collective bargaining negotiations in the insurance business over time and to examine the discussions between the Allianz factory councils and the management, it is difficult to form a definitive judgment. It is important to note that white-collar workers were splintered among several trade unions: the Socialist Central Association of White-Collar Employees, the moderate bourgeois Unified Association of White-Collar Worker Unions, the right-wing German National Retail Clerks Union, and the bourgeois but politically neutral General Association of Insurance Employees (AVV).[63]

The last-named union, which concentrated specifically on the insurance field, did not rule out strikes but appeared most committed to direct settlement with employers and seemed to have had a substantial following. It is revealing that the factory councils at the branches in Frankfurt, Hamburg, and Cologne, as well as the majority of employees in Hannover, supported the 1927 collective agreement between the AVV and the insurance industry employer organization and protested when the Central Association of White-Collar Employees, the Unified Association of White-Collar Worker Unions, and the German National Retail Clerks Union rejected the proposed agreement and called for binding arbitration by the Labor Ministry. These other unions were accused of taking such steps purely for purposes of agitation. As in most important sectors of the economy, labor disputes in the insurance industry were settled by binding arbitration in the Weimar Republic, so such militance was of limited consequence. In 1929 these unions pressed even harder for a salary increase and binding arbitration in their favor, and they made remarkably good use of Schmitt's speeches on how well the insurance business had been doing since 1925. In fact, the insurance industry employers justified their resistance to a salary increase by arguing that they had to show solidarity with their less fortunate colleagues in the rest of the economy. In the end, employees received a 3% increase.[64] Whatever the case, the general impression is one of relatively decent relations between management and employees at Allianz.

---

[62] The most important of these advocates was the German Institute for Technical Labor Training, concerning which useful information is scattered in Nolan, *Visions of Modernity*. Its supporters, however, came by and large from industry.

[63] On these unions, see Hans Speier, *German White-Collar Workers and the Rise of Hitler* (New Haven & London, 1988), esp. Chs. 12–14.

[64] On the 1927 and 1929 wage contract negotiations, see the documents in BAB, R 4101/2582 and 2583.

THE POLITICS OF THE INSURANCE BUSINESS

Successful as Allianz may have been, the private insurance industry did not escape entirely unscathed from the Favag affair, even as it managed to avoid massive state intervention and an excess of public criticism. The leaders of Allianz played a dominant role in industry politics, and interest-group politics and general politics were becoming more and more intertwined in the final years of the Weimar Republic. The Favag affair demonstrated that government supervision of insurance had been inadequate, and the RAA began working toward a reform of the VAG almost immediately after the Favag revelations in August 1929. Schmitt himself thought that such reform was necessary, since Favag had not been alone in failing to take the necessary "step backwards" when setting up its gold mark opening balance in 1924 and then not making the necessary corrections because of competition within the industry. Many companies were prepared to do anything to maintain their dividend levels. In Schmitt's view, "the situation of the entire German insurance business with respect to profitability must be described as extraordinarily troublesome," and the RAA "has not, at least in the last years, troubled itself about maintaining the health of insurance industry, but on the contrary has made business more difficult by concessions to the insured." What Schmitt had in mind were the small companies charging low premiums that he considered unfair competition because they did not cover costs and risk sufficiently. This was in sharp contrast to the RAA's Swiss counterpart, which forced companies to demonstrate they could make do with lower premiums than those charged by larger companies.[65]

Schmitt certainly was no friend of excess government intervention or regulation, and his advocacy of a greater role for the RAA and a reform of the law must be understood in the context of his strong support for a strong Reich Association for Private Insurance. The origins of this industry association go back to 1911. Originally combining the employer association and branch associations, the former was separated from the latter in 1919 so that the Reich Association could devote itself exclusively to defending and representing the general interests of the industry. Schmitt and Hilgard were very anxious to strengthen the Reich Association as much as possible in order to increase its influence with the RAA and also with the public in general, so as to fight more effectively against critics and opponents of private insurance. Schmitt was deputy chairman of the Reich Association and, by 1929, one of its most powerful voices; likewise, Allianz was one of its most influential members. Schmitt and Hilgard tried everything possible to upgrade the prestige and effectiveness of the Reich Association, and it was at Hilgard's suggestion that Schmitt wooed away the highly respected Berlin Stock Exchange Commissar Geheimrat Heinrich Lippert to serve as executive director of the Reich Association.[66]

---

[65] Niederschrift über die Sitzung des Ständigen Ausschusses am 11. Dez. 1929, pp. 8–9, GDV, RS/24.
[66] Hilgard, "Leben," FHA, NL 2/7, pp. 52–3.

In the aftermath of the Favag affair and the impending VAG reforms designed to increase the supervisory powers and role of the RAA, Schmitt pushed through organizational reforms in the Reich Association that were designed to increase its effectiveness. Indeed, the Favag affair and its aftermath demonstrate Schmitt's conception of how business–government relations were supposed to work. Just as the RAA's ability to prevent Favag from declaring bankruptcy was an essential power that enabled Allianz to take over its policies and secure the interests of the insured and insurers against other creditors and interests, so its increased oversight capacity would act as a barrier to further bankruptcies caused by inappropriate investment policies or faulty business plans – thereby giving the Reich Association the leverage it needed to induce member organizations and companies to fall into line. As Schmitt put it:

It is one of the tasks of the Reich Association, through a detailed presentation of the situation, to influence the supervisory office to view the maintenance of the health of the insurance industry as an important part of its tasks. I am not arguing that the Reich Association should set itself the task of intervening in individual branches; the individual tasks should rather be reserved to the individual branch associations as before. But it is necessary to create the mentality and mood which is necessary in the branch associations so that they can overcome difficulties and constraints which show up at the branch level.[67]

Thus, Schmitt was a strong opponent of invasive legislation, preferring state regulators to work hand-in-hand with business organizations. He was being perfectly consistent when he later argued against detailed banking legislation after the banking crisis: "Banking supervision ... [and] supervision of the insurance business must work economically together in an effective way with the branch representatives to bar and prevent abuses. The development of scandals is usually noted at the right time in informed circles."[68]

The new VAG promulgated on June 6, 1931, reflected the collaboration between the Reich Association and the RAA, and it is significant that it was one of the few pieces of economic legislation of the 1930–1933 period that was not the product of a decree but instead of the normal legislative process. The major new features of the law addressed themselves to the Favag experience. The types of assets that could be used as primary reserve for policies were severely restricted, and the RAA reserved the right to ban investment of non–primary reserve funds in assets that had nothing to do with the insurance business. Most importantly, all insurance companies covered by the law were required to have their balances certified by an independent auditor approved by the RAA, and the disposition over primary reserve assets required the approval of an independent trustee approved by the RAA. Finally, where before the RAA had been simply entitled to undertake an on-site audit of insurance companies every five years,

[67] Niederschrift über die Sitzung des Ständigen Ausschusses am 11. Dez. 1929, p. 9, GDV, RS/24.
[68] Sitzung des Ausschusses II des Wirtschaftsbeirats am 11. Nov. 1931, *Akten der Reichskanzlei. Weimarer Republik. Die Kabinette Brüning I und II, bearbeitet von Tilman Koops, Bd. 3: 10. Okt. 1931 bis 30. Mai 1932* (Boppard am Rhein, 1990), p. 1952.

this review was now mandatory. This was, indeed, a vast increase of the over-sight powers and capacities of the RAA, but the Reich Association successfully fought back consumer demands for placing transport and reinsurance under the RAA. The Association argued that these branches were not suitable for such control and used its chief supporter in the Reichstag, People's Party Deputy Paul Moldenhauer, to drive through a compromise under which supervision could be extended to uncovered branches if the Reich Economics Ministry and the Reichs-rat agreed to do so. Both were expected to be friendlier to business interests than the Reichstag.[69] In general, therefore, the new legislation was a political success for the insurance industry and was based on the type of business–government collaboration advocated by Schmitt.

Indeed, the insurance business faced important political problems and chal-lenges in the Weimar Republic, and Schmitt was anxious to upgrade the qual-ity and visibility of the Reich Association. Thus, with the strong support of Kisskalt, in 1926 he successfully proposed that the general meetings of the Reich Association be modeled after those of the Central Association of German Banks and Bankers, so that – alongside the internal discussions – general reports and speeches of broader interest would be given "in order to direct public interest toward the private insurance business." Also, representatives of the press and high officials were to be invited. In his capacity as general director of Allianz, Schmitt was very active in cultivating the press for both economic and political purposes. In 1925, at the recommendation of Dresdner Bank's Herbert Gut-mann (who sat on the supervisory board of Allianz), the company employed Baron Edgar von Uexküll, a once rich but now impecunious Baltic nobleman who had served as an adjutant in the Russian embassy in Berlin. Gutmann recommended Uexküll for his excellent contacts and not for his understanding of the insurance business, which was initially nonexistent. Not quite knowing what to do with him, Hilgard sent Uexküll to Heß's organization section; after a short stint as an acquisition agent, Uexküll engaged in what is today known as public relations and persuaded his superiors that what was needed was a press office to cultivate the media. As it turned out, he had superb contacts with the German press, especially such noted Jewish publishers as Theodor Wolff and Georg Bernhard, and was naturally gifted as a public relations man. He was thus made head of a newly created press section and organized frequent press breakfasts or luncheons in the Kaiserhof Hotel at which Schmitt and Hil-gard regularly joined him. These turned out to be extremely popular events, and Schmitt's open and honest reporting on the state of the insurance busi-ness and other economic matters made him and his press meetings extremely popular.[70]

---

[69] Niederschrift über die Sitzung des Allgemeinen Präsidial-Ausschusses am 18. März 1931, pp. 2–4, GDV, RS/10.

[70] See Niederschrift über die Sitzung des Ständigen Ausschusses am 13. April 1926, GDV, RS/24, pp. 35f., quotation p. 35; Hilgard, "Leben," FHA, NL 2/7, pp. 67–9; Interrogation of Baron Edgar Uexküll, June 9, 1947, NA, RG 260, OMGUS, FINAD, 2/57/4.

The goal of creating a good image for Allianz was of no small significance as the concern expanded. Thus, at the end of 1928, Schmitt invited leading parliamentarians and press representatives to tour the offices of Allianz and also hear him speak on the important role played by Allianz in helping reconstruct Germany's capital stock and long-term investments – not only by investing in real estate and shares but also by increasing its holdings of mortgages, now that inflationary anxieties could be set aside. He stressed the significance of insurance to a modern economy and noted that Germany was finally catching up with the United States and England in this respect. It was now in a position to bear the high risks of flight and auto insurance. At the same time, he emphasized that his expanded enterprise in no way represented a trustification of the German insurance business, since it held only 12.2% of the private insurance industry's premium income and 16.7% of its capital and reserves.[71]

Schmitt also used this and other similar exercises in public relations and press cultivation to stake out a position in the most serious conflict involving the private insurance industry after World War I: its struggle with publicly chartered insurance societies. This is not to be confused with the industry's brief struggle against socialization. While there had been some talk of socializing the insurance business shortly after the Revolution of November 1918, such plans were buried (along with all the other socialization plans) at this time. The idea of socialization actually went back to the prewar period – when it was advocated by the "professorial socialist," Adolph Wagner – and much of the enthusiasm for socialization during and after the war was fiscal in character and aimed at an insurance monopoly that could serve state finances. The Socialists were themselves divided on the issue and had no clear idea of what they wanted to do. The end result was the introduction of an insurance tax that irritated companies and consumers alike but effectively ended the socialization debate for the rest of the Weimar Republic. Its primary effect was to mobilize the industry and encourage the development of the Reich Association.[72]

The chartered insurance societies, like the private companies, were no friends of an insurance monopoly or of socialization. Originally created before the war to insure real estate, they were territorially based insurance societies organized on the principle of mutuality, that is, participation of insurers and insured in gains but also in coverage of losses. A monopoly would necessarily be antithetical to these characteristics, whereas socialization would turn all their agents into civil servants and reduce their incomes. After the war, the chartered societies began expanding their fields of activity and were soon competing with the private companies in nearly every field of insurance. Like the savings banks, which also began expanding into other fields of banking in this period, these societies were often linked to municipal and state governments, which encouraged and guaranteed their activities. They had the strong support of advocates of compulsory fire and property insurance and were looked upon with favor by the Social

---

[71] Börsen-Kurier vom 8. Dez. 1928, GDV, 8-020 P1/Kurt Schmitt.
[72] See the good discussion in Arps, *Durch unruhige Zeiten,* Bd. 1, Kap. 6.

Democrats as a form of "socialization" that was linked to increased municipal and government activity in the economy. They also enjoyed support in conservative (especially agrarian) circles as well as from regionalist-minded conservatives in Bavaria and elsewhere.[73]

The aggressiveness of the chartered society agents in trying to win customers away from private insurers – together with the countermeasures employed by the private insurance agents – led to a considerable amount of ugly and costly competition. At the same time, the situation in the insurance industry was part of a larger struggle on the part of the private sector of the economy against what became known as "cold socialization": the growing involvement of the public sector in a host of financial, commercial, and industrial activities; and the increasing competition for capital between the private and public sectors.[74] Thus, not only were municipal authorities competing with the private construction business by engaging in actual housing construction, but the mortgages were being financed by municipal savings banks and insured by chartered insurance societies. On November 10, 1926, the various peak associations of the business community, including the Reich Association for Private Insurance, joined together at a protest meeting in Berlin to attack "cold socialization." Hilgard was given the task of speaking for the private insurers, and he launched a sharp attack on the publicly chartered companies for expanding into new areas and above all for having unfair advantages in their competition with the private insurers. Not only were they free of the corporation tax, tax on assets, stamp taxes, and other fees, but they also were spared RAA supervision. They were favored by the public authorities, who not only recommended them but often mandated their use – as, for example, with school student accident insurance in certain places. Local governments had actually recapitalized some of the societies after the inflation, guaranteed their policies, and allowed them to charge premiums that were economically unjustifiable and violated sound business practices. Public authorities gave the impression that such unwarranted low premiums were a public good but actually were subsidizing the chartered societies at the expense of the taxpayer. Hilgard warned in dire tones that the private insurance business would be ruined by such unfair competition, that its employees would be thrown out of work, and that the increasing amounts of foreign exchange gained through private insurance business abroad would be lost to the national economy.[75]

Hilgard's attack infuriated the chartered society associations, who not only denied the charges but also launched counterattacks of their own, claiming especially that private insurance agents were themselves engaging in underbidding and were claiming that the chartered company agents were Social Democrats. At

---

[73] Ibid., Bd. 2, Kap. 1.
[74] See Carl Böhret, *Aktionen gegen die "kalte Sozialisierung" 1926–1930. Ein Beitrag zum Wirken ökonomischer Einflußverbände in der Weimarer Republik* [Schriften zur Wirtschafts- und Sozialgeschichte 3] (Berlin, 1966).
[75] Beilage zu Heft 11 der *Allianz-Zeitung* 8 (1926) and other related materials in BAB, R 3101/17049.

the same time, the chartered associations insisted that they wanted to cooperate with the private insurers for the common good, that the attacks on them were bound to revive the dormant socialization discussion, and that Hilgard's ferocious assault threatened to make a peaceful solution impossible. Typical of the mood was the decision of the chief reinsurance organization of the chartered societies, the Deutscher Gemeinnütziger Rückversicherungs-Verband, to break relations with Munich Re. Director Friedrich Baumgarte found it totally implausible that Hilgard could have made such a speech unless it represented the views of Allianz and Munich Re; this contention Kisskalt flatly denied, claiming that Hilgard was not speaking for the concerns but rather as the appointed spokesman for the Reich Association. The distinction was more convenient than convincing, but this was by no means the last time it would play a role: it involved a useful division of labor between Hilgard, who was often to be sent to the front line, and the other Allianz leaders, who could decide how to act later. In this case, Hilgard had fired a shot across the bow of the chartered insurance societies but, as Kisskalt pointed out, a peaceful settlement was bound to be the end result of such conflicts.[76]

This was, indeed, the goal of Hilgard as well, who feared that a court case would develop out of the charges and countercharges. There was also the danger that complaining about publicly chartered companies charging excessively low premiums would backfire, since the public was naturally disposed to lower premiums. He appealed to the Reich Economics Ministry (RWM) to mediate. The matter was taken over by Ministerial Director Hans Schäffer, one of the great economic talents in the government at this time,[77] who decided to follow Hilgard's suggestion because he did not want the entire idea of insurance to be damaged by an open conflict between the two kinds of companies. While not formally exercising control over the publicly chartered companies, the RWM nevertheless had responsibility for the general economic welfare. Also, it tended to be favorably disposed to private enterprise. Although Hilgard was speaking for the industry and not the concerns with whom it was connected, it was precisely the leadership of Allianz and Munich Re – Schmitt, Hilgard, and Kisskalt – who negotiated for the private insurers in the discussions that began in early March 1927 and thereby demonstrated the powerful position their concerns had in the Association. Hilgard and Schmitt excused the sharpness of their attack by pressure from below (i.e., the insurance agents) as well as by the need for the private sector to show solidarity; there was no intention to question the integrity of the chartered societies. Nevertheless, they then catalogued what they considered to be special privileges enjoyed by the chartered societies and called for an end to their abuse in competition with the private companies. For their part, the chartered companies claimed they had been victimized by unfair attacks and demanded that the Reich Association disavow Hilgard's remarks.

---

[76] Baumgarte an Thieme, 20. Dez. 1926, Kisskalt an Baumgarte, 29. Dez. 1926, MR, A 3.15/29.
[77] See the rather inadequate biography by Eckhard Wandel, *Hans Schäffer. Steuermann in wirtschaftlichen und politischen Krisen* (Stuttgart, 1974).

A major source of difficulty was the claim – sometimes contained in the very names of the chartered societies – that they were "gemeinnützig," that is, non-profit organizations serving the public interest. The private companies claimed they were also effectively nonprofit, since most of their profits were returned to their customers, and were even more adamant that they were serving the public interest. Whatever the case, an agreement was reached that Hilgard's words and intent had been "misunderstood"; an armistice was called while a subcommittee representing the two sides hammered out a compromise and developed mechanisms for the adjudication and mediation of their differences. This was finally achieved in July 1927, although special arrangements had to be made for Bavaria and some chartered societies and private companies. Johannes Tiedke, the general director of Alte Leipziger, was particularly hostile to the chartered societies and refused (as was often the case with this rather crusty and independent personage) to compromise. In truth, the agreement did not prove terribly effective, as demonstrated by another meeting in the RWM in November 1930: now it was the chartered societies who protested the behavior of private company agents and of Tiedke, while Schmitt warned that throwing Tiedke out of the Reich Association would make him even more obstreperous. Significantly, the RAA supported private insurers in their continued protest that chartered societies were unfairly laying claim to a monopoly on "Gemeinnützigkeit." Once again, a decision was made to try to avoid an open battle and to rein in both sides, but this was no easy matter in the depressed and highly competitive conditions of the early 1930s.[78]

Kurt Schmitt, who became chairman and thus leading spokesman of the Reich Association for Private Insurance at the end of 1931, never tired of pointing out that the insurance business was weathering the economic crisis rather well compared to other business sectors. Allianz was doing particularly well under the circumstances. He attributed this success to the long-range character of insurance policies, the care with which the industry invested its money, and the need for every kind of insurance even in bad times. Because of the need to back up its policies with proper coverage, the insurance industry was not dependent on short-term foreign money but was rather a granter of credits itself and thus did not suffer from the liquidity problems facing other economic sectors. Thus, whereas many sectors had as much as a 50% reduction of business in 1931, the insurance sector dropped only between 5% and 10%. Schmitt was certainly concerned about premature termination of policies, which reflected the growing impoverishment of many Germans, and he felt that it was worth the extra administrative cost to maintain existing policies and bring in new business. In his frequent public statements to the press and in radio addresses, Schmitt sought to present an upbeat message and to promote confidence in Germany's business leadership. He was very critical of the dragging on of trials in connection with various business scandals, as was occurring in the Favag and other cases, and he

---

[78] See the negotiations of March 4, 1927, the agreements of July 1, 1927, and the negotiations of November 28, 1930, in BAB, R 3101/17049. See also the diary entry for March 4, 1927, in Hans Schäffer, Tagebücher, Leo Baeck Institute, New York, Hans Schäffer Papers.

emphasized the probity of Germany's business community. A similar tone was taken in the business reports of Allianz, and it reflected the attitude expressed at meetings of the Allianz directors. Thus, on October 25, 1932, at the last such meeting held before the National Socialists came to power, note was taken of a general reduction of pessimism and improvement of business conditions even as continued economic uncertainty required an ongoing policy of caution.[79]

These public pronouncements were free of partisan political commentary and criticism despite the profound political unrest and political violence of these years. Indeed, such restraint characterized Allianz as well as the Reich Association, distinguishing it from the more vociferous criticisms to be found in public commentary put out by great industrial firms and by the Reich Association of German Industry. Insofar as Allianz and its leaders (as well as the industry) concerned themselves with political issues, such engagement appeared limited to those areas directly affecting their interests.

Typical of such interest-group politics was the reaction of the insurance business to the introduction of exchange controls following the banking crisis of July 1931. Designed to prevent the further flight of capital that had played a major role in bringing on the banking crisis, the measure effectively took Germany off the gold standard. However, in contrast to the British departure from gold in September 1931, the Germans sought to maintain the value of the Reichsmark by persisting in deflationary policies at home. Nevertheless, the new exchange control regime was a severe departure from liberal economic trade policies, and it was one that had dangerous implications for the insurance industry. Quite aside from the fact that there were a number of foreign insurers operating in Germany that could be affected by the measures, the entire reinsurance business was international in character and domestic German insurance companies also operated abroad. Allianz, for example, was substantially increasing its foreign business at this time. On the one hand, it had opened or was opening agencies or insurance marketing connections for varieties of insurance – not only in the major European countries but also, for example, in Palestine, Cyprus, Iraq, the British and Dutch Indies, China, Siam, and Ceylon. On the other hand, it was increasing or acquiring shares in foreign insurance companies, most notably Bore Insurance Company in Stockholm and the South African Liberal Life Ltd. In almost all cases, Allianz required the approval of the RAA for such engagements because they involved a change in the business plan, but the introduction of exchange controls meant that they also needed permission to secure the foreign exchange necessary to carry on these operations. Finally, as noted earlier, there were numerous policies denominated in foreign currencies, and the payment both of premiums and of policy proceeds were now subject to exchange controls.[80]

[79] 20. erweiterte Vorstandssitzung am 25. Okt. 1931, FHA, S 17.2/4. There is a good collection of Schmitt's press interviews and radio talks in GDV, 8-020 P1/Kurt Schmitt, and in BAK, B 280/14321. See also the Geschäftsberichte of Allianz for 1930–1933 in FHA.

[80] See the correspondence in BAK, B 280/12253, Bl. 2–76, and BAK, B 280/12257, Bl. 1–53. See also the Allianz Geschäftsbericht for 1931, pp. 7, 12, and for 1932, p. 44, FHA.

The ensuing years-long preoccupation with the endless stream of decrees and regulations connected with foreign exchange is a monument to the stupidities and inefficiencies of the illiberal trade policies and governmental regulation that came to characterize this era. Beginning with the issuance of the first decrees and then throughout the coming years, the insurance business made extraordinary and often remarkably successful efforts to establish a special place for itself in the foreign exchange control regime. This was possible only through constant effort. The system placed a high premium on close and good contacts with the relevant government authorities and made this a central consideration in all political calculations. Thus, even though the initial decrees explicitly protected insurance contracts, supervision was placed in the hands of the RAA, which was empowered to evaluate foreign exchange operations in great detail. In early August 1931, the Reich Association leadership (accompanied by Kisskalt) appeared on the doorstep of the government authorities with complaints that the industry was not being protected enough from the complicated requirements and with warnings that its domestic and foreign business was being threatened. The result of such efforts was a series of exemptions, but these could only be achieved with the promise that the industry demonstrate extreme discipline in moving capital, that it show profitability in its international business, and that it apply the utmost restraint in its foreign exchange requests. All of this, in turn, placed a premium on discipline within the industry itself and greatly strengthened the hand of the Reich Association. Thus, when Lippert reported the results of these negotiations with the government to the full assembly of the Reich Association on November 26, 1931, Schmitt immediately followed by warning his colleagues to follow the regulations as precisely as possible and to avoid doing anything that might make the precarious foreign exchange situation of the Reich even worse. He pointed to the difficult position of the savings banks in July 1931, which had placed their monies at the disposal of municipalities that, like the insurance companies, had made long-term investments, primarily in mortgages. The savings banks, like the insurance companies, had never anticipated a run. The situation of the savings banks had improved thanks to government intervention, while the insurance companies had been spared and enjoyed large reserves. For Schmitt, this was their opportunity to reinforce their position, so that "hopefully one will later be able to point out with pride that the German life insurance has proven itself in the greatest crisis as the largest continually functioning reserve of the German people."[81]

As Schmitt well knew and was by no means shy about saying, the same could not be said for the German social insurance system, whose total deficit he estimated to be 18–22 billion RM and whose yearly deficit he estimated to be 1.2–1.4 billion RM. Schmitt had provided these figures confidentially to the Allianz supervisory board in May 1931 in connection with his request that the

---

[81] Sitzungsbericht über die 2. Ordentliche Hauptversammlung des Reichsverbandes der Privatversicherung am 26. Nov. 1931, GDV, RS/3, p. 12; for the various decrees and discussions, see GDV, RS/2 and 3.

Allianz business report for 1930 indicate, which it subsequently did, that the social insurance system was in trouble and that a reconstruction plan was essential. He pointed out that it was politically impossible to reveal the full extent of the deficit and noted that, whereas Allianz had thirty insurance mathematicians at its disposal, the entire social security system had only five such persons. It was necessary to raise contributions and reduce payments if the system were to survive.[82]

If Schmitt felt called upon to take such a measure, it was because he had become something of a public figure who was well-informed and very concerned about such matters. This undoubtedly was due to his press conferences and other public relations activities as well as to his decisiveness and success in the Favag affair. He thus enjoyed considerable authority, and given the desperate efforts of the dying Republic's final governments to secure the active participation of leading businessmen, Schmitt appeared to be a natural candidate for a high ministerial position. Chancellor Brüning was one of the many high government personages with whom Schmitt had contact because of his central role in the Reich Association and other business organizations. In 1931, Brüning invited Schmitt and Professor Hermann Warmbold, an IG Farben director, to discuss the economic situation with the intention of inviting one of them to take the post of economics minister. Schmitt turned down the idea, because of "my lack of membership in any political party and my lack of interest in leaving the Allianz in favor of a political post."[83] Brüning, in any case, seemed to prefer Warmbold, who was an economic statistician of high repute. In the same year, Brüning commissioned the private banker Hans Arnhold, who had some business dealings with Schmitt, to ask the latter if he would not serve as finance minister. Again, Schmitt refused, responding to Arnhold's overture by saying that "it is too early." Trying later to explain his decisions to Arnhold, who had fled Germany and was living in New York when they resumed contact in 1948, Schmitt claimed that "it was not because of my political position, but rather out of lack of desire to leave my beautiful Allianz to go into politics, but in general also because of the justified feeling at that time, that the activity would have stood on weak and short-term legs given the constitution of the parties and their short-sighted egotistical fight among themselves."[84]

This disdain for political parties and partisan political conflict certainly was no novelty among leading German businessmen, and Schmitt was not the only business leader to turn down a high post for the reasons he gave. Nevertheless, he

[82] Aktenvermerk Moesler, 12. Mai 1931, BAB, 80 Ba 2/P 5787, and Allianz Geschäftsbericht 1930, p. 7, FHA.

[83] Interrogation of Kurt Schmitt, July 8, 1947, NA, RG 260, OMGUS, FINAD, 2/58/3. See also Schmitt's testimony at Nuremberg in his interrogation by Robert W. Kempner, Aug. 1, 1946, AM, Spruchkammerakten Dr. Kurt Schmitt, Akten der Spruchkammer Starnberg, Teil I, Dokument 38.

[84] Arnhold to Schmitt, March 25, 1948, and Schmitt to Arnhold, April 1, 1948, FHA, NL 1/16. For a published version of this exchange, see Gerald D. Feldman, "Existenzkämpfe," in *Der Tagesspiegel*, 6. Nov. 1998, Sonderbeilage über die American Academy Berlin, p. 5.

was willing to lend his services as an adviser to the government, and in October 1931 he accepted an appointment to serve on the newly created Economic Advisory Council. This council was established at the outset of Heinrich Brüning's second Cabinet, and the Chancellor attached great importance to its assigned role in helping to work out the details of his deflationary program of reducing not only wages and salaries but also prices and interest rates.[85] It proved less significant than Brüning had hoped.

Although certainly worried about the economic situation, Schmitt's basic stance was that ultimately the economy had to cure itself and to avoid excessive state intervention. Naturally, he placed great emphasis on deficit reduction at all levels of government and on maintaining the stability of the currency. Although he could not deny the need for emergency measures, he was especially concerned about the inclination to reduce interest rates by decree, seeing in such measures a loss of nerve that would create greater uncertainty and insecurity in the population. This stance was hardly surprising for an insurance business executive, since lower interest rates would reduce both the return on insurance assets and on the mortgages that constituted an important component of insurance company reserves. Arguing that premiums inevitably adjusted to price levels in any case, Schmitt insisted the situation would even be worse if lower premiums were mandated. In short, he was insistent that one could not relieve debtors without creating insecurity among creditors and that the result would be artificial regulations trying to square the circle. Indeed, Schmitt – in alliance with the powerful lignite industrialist Paul Silverberg – preferred to see the Reichsbank lower its discount rates and to have a measure of subsidization of the heavily indebted agricultural sector and expansion of credit to spark the economy, a policy opposed by the Reichsbank and by more conservative members of the Advisory Council. The end result of all these deliberations was the Fourth Emergency Decree issued at the beginning of December 1931, which sought to lower prices and interest rates and created a new office of price commissar, filled by the former mayor of Leipzig, Carl Goerdeler. The decree, however, also pushed wages and salaries back to 1927 levels. The basic goal was to complete the process of deflation and prepare the way for an upswing. Schmitt certainly believed this possible, but when he met with his colleagues on the Reich Association, the emphasis was above all on cost reduction – that is, the reduction of wages and salaries.[86]

The Economic Advisory Council was presided over by Reich President Paul von Hindenburg, and Schmitt's performance seemed to have pleased the old man, who had a liking for veterans who cut a good figure and conveyed a confident and

---

[85] On the Economic Advisory Council, see Brüning's remarks at the Cabinet meeting of Oct. 10, 1931, in *Akten der Reichskanzlei. Weimarer Republik. Die Kabinette Brüning I und II, bearbeitet von Tilman Koops, Bd. 3: 10. Okt. 1931 bis 30. Mai 1932* (Boppard am Rhein, 1990), pp. 1823–4, as well as the first meetings of Oct. 29–30, 1931, ibid., pp. 1860–72, 1881–90.

[86] Ibid., pp. 1884–5, and the meeting of Nov. 11, 1931, ibid., pp. 1948–58. For his general evaluation of the Emergency Decree and his views on the need to cut costs, see his remarks at the Sitzungsbericht über die 2. Ordentliche Hauptversammlung des Reichsverbandes der Privatversicherung am 26. Nov. 1931, pp. 7–8, GDV, RS/3.

optimistic message. This may have had something to do with Schmitt's name coming up high on the list of potential finance ministers when Franz von Papen was forming his new government in June 1932. Be that as it may, Schmitt met von Papen for the first time at this juncture and was offered the ministership, which Schmitt refused, telling his interrogators in 1947, "I considered his government could not be long lived as it possessed too narrow a base among the parties. No government could hope successfully to carry on for a long period with the Socialists, Communists, Nazis and a portion of the Center Party in opposition."[87]

Thus, Schmitt had turned down Brüning because one could not rule with the political parties, and now he turned down von Papen because one could not rule without them. The common denominator, aside from the fact that he was loathe to leave his job at Allianz, was a belief that he could not be an effective minister under existing conditions. These were perfectly rational perceptions for a man with no political experience and interests, and Schmitt's preference for playing the economic policy expert to the unstable authoritarian regimes ruling Germany is understandable. Nevertheless, Schmitt was well aware of the great hardships created by the depression and the deflationary policies he advocated. He fretted over the high unemployment and worried about political violence, especially from the left. There is no evidence that he had any formal political affiliation during the final years of the Republic, and the increasingly authoritarian character of the Brüning and von Papen regimes and their dependence on emergency decrees obviated the need for party affiliation in his contacts with the government. Like most business leaders, he urged contact with all the political parties and seems to have had decent relations with Social Democrats as well. Indeed, insofar as direct participation in a politicized organization is concerned, there is only his somewhat mysterious decision to join the Stahlhelm (a right-wing veterans' organization) sometime in 1931 and to leave it sometime in 1932.[88] Nevertheless, Schmitt did have very close (albeit private) contacts with the leaders of one political party: the National Socialists.

SCHMITT, GÖRING, AND HITLER

Tracing the relationships among businessmen and political leaders and parties is never an easy matter, but it is especially difficult when the party in question is a radical totalitarian political movement. Before the National Socialists (NSDAP) came to power, it was not politic for businessmen to have openly close relations

---

[87] Interrogation of Schmitt, July 8, 1947, NA, RG 260, OMGUS, FINAD, 2/58/3. On von Papen's offer, see the press clippings in GDV, 8-020 P1/Kurt Schmitt, especially the clipping from "Die Versicherung" (Wien), June 2, 1932, and also the press clippings in FHA, NL 1/47.

[88] On his Stahlhelm affiliation, see the Fragebogen vom 4. Aug. 1937, BAB, ehem. BDC, SSO Dr. Kurt Schmitt (*7.10.1886). On Schmitt's contacts with representatives of other parties, including the SPD, see the statement of the Allianz lawyer in 1933, Carl Wolff, dated April 20, 1946, AM, Spruchkammerakten Dr. Kurt Schmitt, Akten der Spruchkammer Starnberg, 6. Teil, Dokument 30.

with them, and only a few mavericks like Fritz Thyssen and Emil Kirdorf were prepared to openly identify themselves with the NSDAP. Once Hitler was installed in office, it was difficult if not impossible for businessmen *not* to have contacts and relations with at least some elements in the political leadership, but then it becomes very difficult for historians to distinguish between what was said and done for tactical or opportunistic reasons and what was the product of conviction. The investigation of societies in which people do not speak or write freely and are loathe to set down their thoughts or records of their conversations presents grave problems. It is much easier to study businessmen in the Weimar Republic than in the Third Reich. Finally, businessmen – and, indeed, all persons who had been engaged with the regime – did not feel a pent-up urge to recount their experiences once the regime was gone, especially if they were being interrogated by Allied officers or were being denazified. In fact, most persons involved felt a desperate need to reconstruct their memories so as to make them more bearable to their own self-esteem. They had no desire to dwell on the horrors of the regime and preferred to concentrate on their present hardships. In short, a study such as this faces massive problems of critical analysis of the sources, made all the more difficult by the Allied bombers who succeeded in destroying the buildings and records at Allianz headquarters in Berlin. The exercise in historical reconstruction and judgment that now begins with Kurt Schmitt's and Allianz's relationship to the National Socialists is one for which I take full responsibility.

After 1945, Schmitt (and others who spoke for him) sought to portray his relation with the National Socialist leader and Reichstag Deputy Hermann Göring in the aforementioned context of general contact with all the non-Communist political parties in order to protect company and industry interests. In one of his interrogations in July 1947, Schmitt claimed that he first met Göring in 1932 at a small dinner party given by Walter Eggerss, a director of Allianz who specialized in the fire insurance field, and claimed never to have met Hitler prior to his coming to power. He stated that perhaps four or five persons were present at the meeting with Göring, Hilgard possibly being one of them.[89] The latter's account in his unpublished memoirs was somewhat different.[90] According to Hilgard, Schmitt and he were concerned about the rise of the NSDAP and felt it important to keep abreast of developments in the party and try to influence its economic policies. The most promising person in this connection appeared to be Göring, whose views were thought to be closest to those of the business community. When they learned that Eggerss had a personal connection with Göring, they asked him to arrange a meeting. According to Hilgard, this first meeting took place in the fall of 1932 in a private room at the Restaurant Hiller, located on the Unter den Linden in Berlin. Hilgard remembered it as being a two-hour meeting that left a rather unsatisfactory impression. Göring spoke in glowing terms about Hitler's goals, gave vague assurances that business had nothing to fear from the Nazis, who were anxious to promote private initiative, and tried to

---

[89] Interrogation of Schmitt, July 8, 1947, NA, RG 260, OMGUS, FINAD, 2/58/2–7.
[90] For the discussion that follows, see Hilgard, "Leben," FHA, NL 2/7, pp. 86–90.

calm their fears with respect to the Jewish question. According to Göring, Nazi intentions were to prevent more foreign Jews, especially from the East, from entering Germany and to gradually remove Jews from public offices. They would, however, remain free to pursue their economic activities.

Hilgard claimed that Göring's performance only increased his own mistrust in the NSDAP, but that the meeting had the important result of leading to a meeting with Hitler himself. The initiative came from Göring, who was apparently very impressed with Schmitt, and was seconded by *Berliner Börsenzeitung* editor Walther Funk, a prominent journalist who had gone over to the NSDAP and was anxious to bring business leaders into the fold. Thus, in November or December 1932, Göring and Funk accompanied Schmitt and Hilgard to a meeting at the Hotel Kaiserhof, where Hitler held court at this time. Hilgard, for whom clothes made the man, was repulsed by Hitler's unkempt appearance and his inelegant double-breasted dark blue suit, and he claims to have found it hard to shake Hitler's hand on this and the two or three other occasions when they met in subsequent years. Matters were not improved by the ninety-minute lecture to which they were subjected, Hitler arguing that the NSDAP was the only barrier remaining against the Communists and that it was therefore important to give his party support and money. Hitler did not appear to be in a mood for discussion, and the meeting ended after a few questions and cursory answers.

According to Hilgard's account, he and Schmitt went away with the feeling that Hitler's coming to power was not in Germany's interest but also that it was important "not to remain on the sidelines in the near future but to seek contact with the leading men of the NSDAP and in this way to gain influence over the way things developed."[91] Göring was in hot pursuit in any case, and followed up the meeting with an invitation to lunch in his home in the Kaiserstraße, where they were joined by his later adjutant Paul Körner. What most interested Göring, of course, was a large contribution to the Party, but he also pressed Schmitt to join the Party and promised to arrange the matter. Schmitt demurred and the matter was left hanging, but Hilgard knew that Schmitt, who had a tendency to seek out the positive in everyone, found Göring quite charming – especially in comparison with Hitler.

There are obviously substantial differences between Hilgard's account, written in the 1960s after Schmitt was dead, and Schmitt's statements at his 1947 interrogation. Whereas both agree that the meeting with Göring took place in 1932 and that Eggerss was the contact man, Schmitt denied that he had ever met Hitler before the latter took power. Hilgard's memoirs thus contradict Schmitt's testimony by claiming that there had been such a meeting with Hitler and at least one other meeting with Göring. Then again, however, Hilgard himself had told a somewhat different story when he was interrogated on July 14, 1947 (i.e., at the same time as Schmitt). In that interrogation, he never mentioned a meeting with Hitler and spoke of only one meeting with Göring in the summer, not the fall, of 1932. He claimed there that during one of the Allianz press conferences he had asked Emil Helfferich – brother of the late Karl Helfferich (a German National People's Party deputy) and a businessman from Hamburg – if the NSDAP had any exceptional personalities, to which Helfferich replied by naming Göring as the ablest representative of the Party despite his terrible character. Hilgard then suggested to Schmitt that they make contact with Göring, which they did through Eggerss. According to this account, Göring came two hours late to the Restaurant Hiller, asked for support against the Communists, indicated an intention to drive the Jews from public life, but did not make any specific requests for propaganda and financial support. While admitting that both he and Schmitt were impressed with Göring as a coming man, Hilgard nevertheless claimed to have never met with him again before the seizure of power. Yet we have seen that Hilgard's own memoirs belie this statement.[92]

It is, of course, in no way surprising that Schmitt and Hilgard were anxious to hide or forget contacts with Hitler before 1933 and, more generally, to date their contacts with Göring and the Nazis to as near the end of the Weimar Republic as possible. The trouble with both accounts, however, is that they are refuted by the interrogation of the man who did indeed bring them together with Göring – namely, Walter Eggerss, who on August 17, 1947, gave a precise and detailed account of what happened that in no way flattered himself or anyone else.[93]

Eggerss had met Göring for the first time at the home of Georg Emil von Stauß of the Deutsche Bank in October 1930. Stauß was a member of the German People's Party but was one of the first major businessmen to try to forge a link with the National Socialists in the flush of their great victory in the Reichstag elections of September 1930, and he regularly invited major Nazis to his home. Göring was one of the dozen or so persons present at the dinner in question, and Eggerss spoke with him privately for about an hour, primarily about Hitler's idea of setting up an "economic senate" of leading experts to advise him. Fritz Thyssen, one of the few industrialist enthusiasts for Hitler, had agreed to serve. While it was expected that those who served would support the goals of the Party, membership was not required. Eggerss suggested that it would be important to have an insurance industry leader on such a body and recommended that he meet Schmitt. Eggerss, who had a very favorable impression of Göring and who was convinced that "sooner or later the Nazis were certain to come to power," spoke to Schmitt on the next day and pointed out that "it would be clever tactics on our part to cultivate the acquaintanceship of leading Nazi personalities at an earlier rather than at a later date so as to win thereby a voice in the shaping of the economic program of the Party." Schmitt agreed with this analysis, and what then followed was a meeting at Restaurant Hiller in the last days of October or the first days of November 1930 between Eggerss, Schmitt, and Göring.

---

[92] Interrogation of Eduard Hilgard, July 14, 1947, NA, RG 260, OMGUS, FINAD, 2/57/4.

[93] The account and quotations that follow are based on this interrogation of the just-retired Walter Eggerss on August 17, 1947, NA, RG 260, OMGUS, FINAD, 2/56/10.

During the two-hour luncheon, Göring apparently so impressed and over-whelmed the two men that "he won us over completely to the political program of the Nazi Party." Göring

spoke of the Jews ... and expressed the view that they ought to be permitted to live peace-fully in Germany but that the right to vote should be withdrawn from them and that they should not be permitted to hold public office or to participate in the professions or to hold positions which would place them in authority over Germans.

Eggerss admitted that "Dr. Schmitt and myself shared these views at the time and hence Göring's statement struck us both as very reasonable." Furthermore, this was by no means the only meeting; Eggerss stated that Schmitt, Göring, and Eggerss held some eight to ten meetings at two- or three-week intervals at Restaurant Hiller between October 1930 and March 1931. Eggerss remembered two other persons being present at individual meetings as well. One was the later Reichsstatthalter of Bavaria and Schmitt's former regimental commander, Franz Xaver Ritter von Epp. The other was Eduard Hilgard, who was at one of the luncheons in early 1931.

Schmitt apparently expressed great admiration for Göring. Thus, after one of the lunches in the fall of 1930, Schmitt told Eggerss: "If I did not hold my present position of the first rank in the German economy, I could readily conceive that I would gladly play a role in this movement." For the same reason of his role as a leading business executive and public figure, Schmitt did not want to join the projected economic senate and proposed that Eggerss enter it instead "and re-main in the foreground but that he would stand behind me in the background." The senate never came into being, but Göring continued to enjoy eating and drinking at Allianz's expense – the lunches ran between 180 and 200 RM for three persons – although Eggerss admitted that "we found it quite amusing to indulge his appetite." Schmitt also seemed willing to indulge Göring's rather ex-pensive lifestyle. When Göring complained that he was finding it hard to meet expenses, Schmitt told Eggerss that Göring "has good political ideas and we must help him. I will get the Allianz Insurance Company to send him a check for RM 5,000." Eggerss considered Schmitt a man of his word and was certain the check was sent.

There are many reasons to give more credence to Eggerss's account than to either Schmitt's or Hilgard's. First of all, Eggerss's explanation of how he came to contact Göring is consistent with what is known about the banker Stauß.[94] Second, Eggerss was no longer in Berlin after April 1931, when he was trans-ferred to the board of directors of Neue Frankfurter. He stayed there until 1934, took a leave of absence to work with Kessler of the Reich Economic Chamber,

---

[94] See Feldman, "Deutsche Bank," p. 249; Harold James, "The Deutsche Bank and the Dictatorship, 1933–1945," in Lothar Gall et al., *The Deutsche Bank, 1870–1995* (London, 1995), pp. 277–356, here pp. 308–18; and Henry A. Turner, Jr., *German Big Business and the Rise of Hitler* (Oxford & New York, 1985), pp. 142–4.

and then returned to Allianz in the fall of 1934 and stayed on until May 1947. Eggerss became a member of the NSDAP in the spring of 1933 but then voluntarily withdrew from the party in October 1935. His testimony, it is important to note, was given after his retirement. Therefore, it is obvious that Eggerss introduced Schmitt and Hilgard to Göring before he left for Frankfurt in the spring of 1931. All this does not mean that Schmitt and Hilgard did not meet with Göring after April 1931 and in 1932. Indeed, Eggerss specifically states that the meetings continued and that his role as liaison was taken over by Director Walter Boehm, later director of the Allianz branch in Dresden encompassing Saxony and Silesia. Thus, Schmitt had many meetings with Göring, and Hilgard attended at least at one before the meetings he describes in his memoirs.

In fact, this was well attested to by others who worked with Schmitt, both later and at the time. Thus, in his interrogation in 1947, Baron Uexküll was much less precise than Eggerss but quite definitive about the relationship, saying that Schmitt met Göring

about 1931 and as a result became an enthusiastic Nazi. He lunched frequently with Göring during 1931/1932 at Hiller's Restaurant on Unter den Linden. During 1932 Dr. Schmitt met Hitler at the Kaiserhof Hotel at Berlin and spoke to me afterward about it in glowing terms. Dr. Schmitt was also on excellent terms with Walther Funk, who was devoting his full energies toward the winning over to the Nazi cause of leading figures in industry and finance.[95]

Similarly, on August 17, 1932, Reich Association Executive Director Lippert responded to reports of complaints made to General Director Stieringer of the National Allgemeine Versicherungs-AG in Stettin that the insurance industry was failing to have sufficient contact with the NSDAP leadership, suggesting that those to whom Stieringer had spoken were not in contact with the Party leadership since "it is known to me that the chairman of the Reich Association, General Director Dr. Schmitt has already often conferred with leading representatives of the National Socialist Party. Herr Dr. Schmitt has also even reported about this at various times in meetings."[96] Finally, what Eggerss and Uexküll described concerning Schmitt's enthusiasm for Göring and Hitler is completely consistent with Schmitt's unreflective, very personal, and impulsive approach to politics before and after January 30, 1933.

In fact, Schmitt's first meeting with Hitler did not take place in November 1932, as Hilgard claims in his memoirs, but rather on February 3, 1931. The source of this information is Oscar Wagener, Hitler's economic adviser at this time and a leading figure in the Sturmabteilung (SA). Wagener was in the radical wing of the Party and was no friend of industry; though his views were quite eccentric, there is no reason to question the reliability of postwar reconstructions from his diary. Indeed, what he describes fits in quite well with the

[95] Interrogation of Baron Edgar Uexküll, June 9, 1947, NA, RG 260, OMGUS, FINAD, 2/57/4.
[96] Lippert to Stieringer, Aug. 17, 1932, NA, RG 260, OMGUS, FINAD, 2/58/2–7.

impulsiveness of Schmitt in his dealings with the Nazis at this time. The encounter took place just when Hitler had made the Kaiserhof, which was across
the street from the central offices of Allianz, his Berlin headquarters with the
purpose of having quarters satisfactory enough to meet the high and mighty. At
this time, Hitler and his closest advisers were concerned about the danger of a
right-wing reactionary putsch that would set loose left-wing violence and create a civil war that would tear the NSDAP apart. In their view, only an armed
SA could challenge the army and stop the Socialists and Communists. This required substantial sums of money, and Wagener proposed they consult with the
journalist Walther Funk. The latter produced a number of industrialists for discussions of this problem, which was to be posed naturally as an effort to counter
a revolt from the left, not the right. The first of the businessmen produced by
Funk were Kurt Schmitt and the head of the Allianz supervisory board, August
von Finck of the Bavarian private banking house of Merck, Finck & Co. Hitler
laid out the position in a half-hour talk, which was followed by a discussion in
which both Schmitt and von Finck indicated considerable pessimism with respect to the unemployment problem and their feeling that left-wing unrest was
inevitable. After showing them out, Funk came back with the news that Allianz
would provide 5 million RM for the arming of the SA in the event of left-wing
unrest. Since the eventuality never arose, the promise was never tested, but this
was yet another demonstration of Schmitt's predisposition toward the Nazis before 1933.[97]

Indeed, there is no evidence that Allianz gave any money to the National Socialist Party or made more than a modest contribution to Göring's lunchtime
contentment and high living. It is notable, however, that Allianz carried an ad-
vertisement in the *Völkischer Beobachter* as early as June 3, 1930 (and then again
on November 11, 1930), despite its numerous attacks on Jewish banks – and their
role in the Favag affair – and critical articles on insurance company profits. It
was rare for large concerns to advertise there until 1932. Nevertheless, this can
easily be attributed to aggressive marketing rather than ideological sympathy.
In contrast to Stauß, whose open support for National Socialist participation
in the government caused embarrassment for Deutsche Bank and loss of Jewish
customers, Schmitt's contacts were private and discreet; he studiously avoided
partisan political statements. Whereas Eggerss seemed to share Schmitt's enthusiasm for National Socialism, there is no evidence that Hilgard felt the same way
or that any other leading directors at Allianz or its affiliated companies were
involved. What, then, was the meaning and the content of Schmitt's National
Socialist enthusiasm?

---

[97] Henry A. Turner, Jr. (ed.), *Hitler aus nächster Nähe. Aufzeichnungen eines Vertrauten 1929–
1932* (Frankfurt a.M., 1978), pp. 368–74, and Turner, *German Big Business*, pp. 149–50. Unfortunately, this is the only source available on this encounter and the 5 million RM mentioned is extremely sizeable for this period. Also, on the basis of this source it is hard to tell how seriously Kurt
Schmitt took his offer and whether he was thinking of Allianz alone or of other companies as well.

Allianz and Allianz Leben advertised in the Nazi paper *Völkischer Beobachter* as early as June 3, 1930 ("travel carefree") and November 11, 1930 ("whether you earn 3,000 RM or 30,000 RM a year").

Although Schmitt was reluctant to reveal to his postwar interrogators the amount of contact he had with Göring and Hitler before 1933, he did try to put down his thoughts and remembrances at various points, and these are useful in understanding his mentality. He confessed that prior to 1933 he had scarcely concerned himself with the actual content of the National Socialist program beyond reading headlines in the papers and various placards. He had never read more than a small fraction of Hitler's *Mein Kampf.* In the critical period at the end of 1932, he did listen to speeches by von Papen and Hitler and, like most of those with whom he consorted in educated and wealthy circles, was impressed by the difference between the rhetoric of the two men. While put off by Hitler's speeches, he was surprised by how Hitler's following had grown and noted that, in the propaganda struggle with the Communists, it was not the Social Democratic Party and other parties but rather the Nazis that held the field. Indeed, Schmitt argued that, in the industrial areas and the Ruhr, anxiety about a left block led by the Communists was very great; the NSDAP skillfully played upon the need to cleanse public life, recognize achievement, protect private property, save the Mittelstand, and the like. Added to this was the failure of the parliamentary system in Germany. There were too many parties and there was too much partisan politics. This was in sharp contrast to England (for which Schmitt had great admiration), where the number of parties were small and the governmental transitions smooth. The National Socialist claim to be "above" parties was particularly appealing in this context, and Schmitt considered especially promising its advocacy of the right to work and its pledge to end the demoralization of youth.

Needless to say, these are not terribly original or interesting explanations in themselves. They reflected the thought of a person who paid little attention to politics and whose anxiety about the existing situation – above all, the threat of Communism – and distaste for politics had rendered him oblivious to the moral differences between one kind of political party and another. Schmitt, in fact, was a perfect illustration of the antidemocratic political culture of important segments of the business community inherited from the old Empire and carried on into the Weimar Republic. In contrast to many more conservative business-men who were attracted to Franz von Papen's authoritarian and conservative program, Schmitt, who did not come from any old establishment and had risen on the strength of his own talents, was probably for such reasons more ready to place his trust in a "modern" and "dynamic" movement. Whatever the case, his political sense and understanding were pathetically underdeveloped, which was truly remarkable in an otherwise so talented businessman and negotiator.

Even more depressing, however, was his understanding of and attitude toward the "Jewish question," which found expression in his acceptance of Göring's description of National Socialist plans to fundamentally reverse Jewish emanci-pation and in effect drive the Jews from public life. His postwar reflections are especially revealing and deserve extensive quotation:

I was no anti-Semite. I had a number of personal and business friends, who were Jews. In part, I did not know, but in any case it hardly interested me if they were persons I found agreeable. On the other side, there was in Berlin a type of Jew that was not only thoroughly disagreeable to people like us but also to their own upright co-confessionals. They were loud, frivolous and presumptuous beyond all measure. Along with it they had the unpleasant characteristic of systematically only drawing Jews into their circle. This type was very strongly represented in the legal profession. When I think back to the Favag trial and the unheard of manner in which I was treated in the hearing like a person ac-cused, then I can only today be thankful to the presiding judge and the state attorney that I was spared having to defend myself. There were also very unpleasant types of this kind in economic life .... Such a person was, for example, Sobernheim of the Commerzbank, whom I knew particularly well from the Favag trial and of whom I have the most unpleas-ant remembrance. Such people rode roughshod over the interests of other people with cold-bloodedness and cynicism .... It is certainly false to generalize such phenomena. There are Christians who are second to none in what has been described, and there are Jews who I have always only admired for their fineness and selflessness in thought which they combined with the greatest possible capacity and feeling of responsibility.

This, then, was the context in which Schmitt viewed the plans for the Jews expressed by Göring before and immediately after the seizure of power:

I must honestly say, that I had no reservations about this line, for it cannot objectively be contested that in our public and intellectual life, beginning with the Reichstag, in the press, and also in many scientific faculties, in the legal field and above all in the Berlin banking business, the Jews had too strong and too loud and also an unhealthy influence. A certain pushing of them back and holding them to great modesty can only be desired and good. Many a Jewish friend has confirmed this as his own view.[98]

---

[98] Schmitt, "Erinnerungen," FHA, NL 1/133, pp. 22f.

Manifestly, neither Schmitt's politics nor his views on the "Jewish question" were unique to himself, and he was right in saying that there were Jews who felt that they were bringing some of the criticism upon themselves.[99] Nevertheless, Schmitt was not just any person but rather the general director of Germany's leading insurance company and a public figure of great importance. He was going to learn a thing or two during the coming years, but not, alas, as much as one could hope given his post-1945 reflections. At the same time, however, it is important to recognize that the responsibility for the evils that he and his organization were to experience and perpetrate during the coming years lay to an important extent in the fact that he (and others like him) shared a political culture and an anti-Semitic posture that made the coming and installation of the Third Reich possible.

[99] See for example the proposal of Georg Solmssen, a director of the Deutsche Bank, to Göring that a Jewish National Council be founded to examine the charges against Jews and organize the expulsion of those who were considered harmful or who were otherwise undesirable. See James, "Deutsche Bank," p. 296.

2

Allianz, Kurt Schmitt, and the Third Reich, 1933–1934

DISORDER AND DELUSION: AN ECONOMICS MINISTER FOR THE THIRD REICH

THE RELATIONS between Allianz executives and the National Socialists appear to have been limited to a very few persons at the top of the concern, and there is no record of how many of the concern's personnel were sympathetic to the Nazis or involved with them. Schmitt's dealings with Göring and Hitler had been private, and Allianz apparently banned partisan political activity or the wearing or carrying of party uniforms, insignia, and the like at work before January 30, 1933, and for as long as it could afterward.[1] The only evidence found so far of official favor to the Party came from Munich, where Barerstraße 15, a building owned by Allianz, was used on November 30, 1930, for a meeting of the SA leadership. The NSDAP later owned the building and probably was already renting offices there.[2] There is also very little information available about National Socialist activities within the company. It certainly had its National Socialist factory cell organization (NSBO), as did many other leading insurance companies and banks in Berlin and elsewhere. Thus, the National Socialist *Angriff* reported in December 1930 that the factory cell had held its monthly meeting at which a Party comrade (Pg.) Pfister gave a "convincing" talk on the financial program of the Party that allegedly resulted in new memberships. The next month, Pfister held forth on "What Will 1931 Bring?" The Party also agitated at meetings of its branch group, where Pg. Körner, who came from Allianz, spoke on "Why National Socialist Factory Cells?"[3]

---

[1] See the remarks of Hilgard at the 21. erweiterte Vorstandssitzung am 10. Mai 1933, p. 12, FHA, S 17.2/4.

[2] Lagebericht der Polizeidirektor München, 4. Dez. 1930, Bayerisches Hauptstaatsarchiv, MA 101235/3. The building in question was Barerstraße 15, which had formerly been the administration building of Deutsche Lebensversicherungsbank Arminia. It was sold to the NSDAP in 1934 because it formed part of the NSDAP Party quarter of the city. See Geschäftsberichte für 1933, p. 23, and 1934, p. 23. See also Andreas Werner, *SA und NSDAP. SA "Wehrverband," "Parteitruppe" oder "Revolutionsarmee"? Studien zur Geschichte der SA und der NSDAP 1920–1933*, Phil. Diss. (Erlangen, 1964), pp. 503–11. For the SA meeting, see BAB, Sammlung Schumacher/403.

[3] *Der Angriff*, Jan. 3, 1931, March 9, 1931, Nov. 3, 1931, Nov. 22, 1931, Dec. 22, 1931, Feb. 2, 1932. There is a problem in identifying the Körner in question. Two Wilhelm Körners worked for

Despite its efforts, the NSBO apparently had only limited success, as evidenced by the factory council elections at Allianz of March 16, 1933. These elections took place after Hitler became chancellor and after the Reichstag fire and decrees of February 27–28 that effectively established the dictatorship and unleashed all the suppression and terror that followed. The factory council elections also took place after the Reichstag election of March 5, which gave a majority to the so-called Government of National Resurrection. Nevertheless, the Socialist-oriented Central Association of Employees received five seats; the National Socialist list, four seats; and the General Association of Insurance Employees, one seat.[4] These results provided National Socialist critics of the big insurance companies with a welcome opportunity to make their case that the "internal operation of the companies is strongly Jewish and Marxist," and that "such red companies must be put in check."[5]

They had no grounds for fear. On March 30, the new Allianz factory council met to hold its constitutive meeting, which was supposed to elect a chairman and plant committee. By this time, the Enabling Act of March 21 had also been passed by the Reichstag, but this had been done under a mantle of promises of law and order and that there would be no "individual actions." Exactly how little such promises meant was demonstrated at the beginning of the Allianz factory council meeting, when fifteen uniformed SA and SS men came into the back entrance of the Allianz Berlin headquarters on the Mauerstraße, where they were met by the Allianz NSBO members. The SA and SS men then took control of all entrances and exits to the building and the telephone. The SA men and some NSBO officials betook themselves to an anteroom whose door opened upon the factory council room, where the meeting had just begun. At this point the NSBO official, Hans Lange, read a written declaration announcing that a commissarial factory council was being established for Allianz "until a final legal regulation was put in place by the Reich government" and that "the elected members of the Marxist-oriented Central Association of White-Collar Employees were immediately to declare their resignations in writing on forms that had already been specially prepared." When Zech, the chairman who was also the senior member of the council and a member of the union in question, asked by whose authority the action was being taken, he was informed that there would be no discussion and that the resignations were to be submitted unconditionally. A similar

Allianz in this period, and both were acting directors of the machine section of the concern. The first retired in 1934; the second became an acting director in 1937. For reasons that will become clear later in this study, it is most likely the second Körner.

[4] The report in the *Vossische Zeitung*, 17. März 1933, on the Allianz election of March 16, BAK, B 280/1432, Bl. 174, gives the National Socialists only one seat and is not accurate. See the figures given in Allgemeiner Verband der Versicherungsangestellten an Reichsarbeitsminister Seldte, 30. März 1933, BAB, R 3101/17078.

[5] Carl Gerlach an das Reichsministerium des Innern, 18. April 1933, BAB, R 3101/17069. The writer was an insurance adviser who identified himself as a Pg. and also complained about the huge salaries of the insurance executives and the lack of professionalism among insurance salesmen.

demand was made of Georg Kreutzinger, who represented the General Association of Insurance Employees (AVV), even though he protested that he was not a Marxist or even politically engaged. Under the impress of the SA and NSBO men in the next room, however, the resignations were tendered. Additionally, Zech was told to give a declaration that he had no factory council documents in his personal possession and to surrender all the council's documents in its offices. These were then formally declared sequestered. The key to the rooms was taken, and the rooms were declared sealed. Finally, the names of the commissarial factory council were posted in order to inform the employees of the existence and membership of the new council that had seized office in the manner described.[6]

The General Association of Insurance Employees complained in a letter to the Labor Minister that this violated the promises of the government, but they had even more to protest with respect to the NSBO and SA actions at Allianz Leben. The factory council there had been elected on November 30, 1932, because the NSBO representatives had resigned from the council elected in June. The council that took over consisted of four representatives of the General Association, two from the Central Association of White-Collar Employees, two from the NSBO, and one each from the centrist General Association of Employees and the German National Retail Clerks Association, which was close to the Nazis. In this case, the council was meeting under the chairmanship of Max Scholber of the General Insurance Employees Association on March 30, 1933, when the door was forcibly opened by NSBO member Bruno Rycerz. The council members were then summoned individually to sign their resignation forms, which they all did "because the danger existed of arrest by the two SA men standing by." There followed the installation of another commissarial factory council. Once again the General Association protested the "individual action" and this all the more because it, like the Central Association, claimed to be nonpolitical and nonpartisan – as if the NSBO and SA should consider these special virtues.[7] The usefulness of appealing to the government in such an instance was well illustrated by the reaction of Reich Economics Minister Alfred Hugenberg, who argued that "since such interventions only create an actual condition but not a legal condition the RWM ought initially to refrain from taking special measures."[8] The actions in question were in fact anything but "individual" and were part of a pattern of factory council takeovers by the NSBO and SA throughout the country. Indeed, the new government was paving the way for the eventual destruction of the trade union movement by issuing a law on April 4 suspending all factory council elections still scheduled to be held, retroactively legalizing the

---

[6] Allgemeiner Verband der Versicherungsangestellten an Reichsarbeitsminister Seldte, 30. März 1933, BAB, R 3101/17078.
[7] Allgemeiner Verband der Versicherungsangestellten an Reichsarbeitsminister Seldte, 31. März 1933, ibid.
[8] Vermerk (undated), ibid.

takeover of factory councils, and giving employers the right to dismiss workers who behaved in a way hostile to the State.[9]

Allianz had never, of course, been a "red" company, but all the evidence suggests it was not run by fire-eating employers either. Max Scholber, the ousted Social Democratic chairman of the factory council who was to return to that position after 1945, had constant dealings with Hilgard, who represented both the management of Allianz and the insurance industry employers. Scholber had nothing but praise for the social policies of Allianz, and he gave credit to Hilgard for constantly promoting them. Obviously their politics were different, but their relation seems to have been based on mutual respect. While Hilgard does not seem to have lifted a finger to prevent the removal of the duly elected factory council by the NSBO, he absolutely refused to accede to the demand that Scholber be fired, and as the latter – who apparently remained at Allianz and resumed his old position as head of the factory council after the war – testified in 1947, "Herr Hilgard told me in a last conversation (1933) that his door remained open to me as before."[10]

While Hilgard maintained his reserve toward the National Socialists and continued his old personnel practices as best he could, others were less willing to remain aloof from the new order coming into being. August von Finck and Kurt Schmitt, for example, were among those invited to attend a meeting of big business leaders at the home of Göring on February 20, 1933 (i.e., before the March election) at which Hitler would allegedly explain his economic policies. Hitler greeted each of those present and gave a ninety-minute speech, promising among other things that the forthcoming election would be the last. Hjalmar Schacht called on the business community to make a 3-million RM contribution to the cause. Von Finck claims to have slipped out before being called upon personally to contribute and, given his reputation for stinginess, this may well have been the case; but he was to make up for this lapse later. As for Schmitt, he later reported that Schacht visited him at his office the next day and Schmitt agreed to make a donation of RM 10,000 to the election campaign, and that Munich Re would pay one third of that amount.[11]

It was a sign of the changing situation that Schmitt decided to identify with the new regime and express support for it publicly. Sometime in the spring of 1933 he joined the National Socialist Party and became member Nr. 2651252. He was later to claim that he applied for admission to the Party only when he became economics minister at the end of June and was accepted in August. His Party

[9] See *Akten der Reichskanzlei. Regierung Hitler 1933–1938*, hrsg. *von Konrad Repgen & Hans Booms, bearb. von Karl-Heinz Minuth, Teil I: 1933/34*, Bd. 1: 30. Januar bis 31. August 1933 (Boppard am Rhein, 1983), I, pp. 254–5, 274–5, 279–80, 334–6.

[10] Erklärung Max Scholber, 22. April 1947, FHA/NL 2/1.

[11] Interrogation of August von Finck, Sept. 22, 1947, NA, RG 260, OMGUS, FINAD, 2/57/4; interrogation of Kurt Schmitt, July 8, 1947, ibid., 2/58/3. More generally, see Turner, *Big Business*, pp. 329–32.

book did indeed give August 25, 1933, as the date of his entry into the Party, but this was probably because he had requested a Party membership book; his membership card gives August 1, 1933, as the date of his entry. Other documents in his Party file give April 1 and May 1 as the date of his entry into the Party.[12] In any case, Schmitt joined the Party at least two months before he was appointed to a government position. It is thus in no way surprising that Schmitt also decided to express support of the new regime openly on the occasion of Hitler's birthday on April 20, 1933. The *Völkischer Beobachter* reported that the entire office closed down at 14:30 "to celebrate the birthday of our Leader Adolf Hitler" and that, after NSBO members had assembled before the Allianz offices and marched in closed ranks to the festival hall, they entered the latter to marching music provided by the Allianz orchestra. Furthermore, General Director Schmitt and other directors joined the celebration and, after "Party Comrade Körner held the impressive celebration speech," Schmitt took the floor and "emphasized that now our people can face a better and happier future." This was followed by the singing of the German national anthem.[13]

Needless to say, such celebrations had not been held for previous chancellors of Germany, and it was not long before the new political commitment became company policy. This became clear on May 10, 1933, when the Allianz concern held one of its periodic expanded management meetings. These meetings, which had been held since the currency reform and stabilization of 1924, provided an opportunity for the top management in Berlin to update their colleagues in the various companies and major branches of the concern regarding the state of business in the overall concern as well as in the multitude of insurance branches in which Allianz provided services, to lay down the basic lines of policy, and to discuss current issues. After making his usual report on business conditions, which basically had not changed much since they last met in October 1932, Schmitt turned to the political situation, which of course had changed dramatically. Schmitt announced that a positive attitude was in order:

Until now the "Allianz" has practiced a self-evident reserve with respect to the political development, since politics in general ought have nothing to do with business operations. Naturally this does not mean that no influence should be exercised over important decisions in economic policy. In particular, today's conception of the state fundamentally

[12] Thus, in the questionnaire for the SS he filled out in August 1937, he was asked to give his party number and date of entry "according to the Party book" and gave Aug. 25, 1933, as the date, BAB, ehem. BDC, SSO Dr. Kurt Schmitt (*7.10.1886). The Kurt Schmitt Party file in BAB, ehem. BDC, PK Dr. Kurt Schmitt (*7.10.1886) contains various documents of relevance: a letter from the Gauleitung of Hessen-Nassau of April 17, 1942; a political report of Sep. 16, 1942; a report of the Auslands Organisation of July 7, 1943, which give May 1, 1933 as his date of entry; a letter to the Gauleitung Berlin and a political report of April 26, 1939, which date his entry into the Party as April 1, 1933; and a membership file card that contains as the entry date August 1, 1933; BAB, ehem. BDC, NSDAP-Mitgliederkartei Dr. Kurt Schmitt (*7.10.1886).

[13] *Völkischer Beobachter*, 25. April 1933, p. 3.

means that a different position must be taken, now that party differences in the previous sense no longer exist and what matters is to represent common German interests. It would be false today to withdraw from collaboration in the building up of our Fatherland, and one can only desire that especially the leading men of our company everywhere in the Reich make available their energies and capabilities for positive collaboration so that inexperienced elements do not play the defining role in decision making. If, as in the past, the insurance industry fulfills its tasks, then there is no danger of socialization since the government has committed itself to a free economy.[14]

The message was not only for the managers, however. On May 19, Allianz celebrated the conclusion of its business year by opening a new building in Cologne. As the *Allianz-Zeitung* described in almost euphoric terms, Schmitt took the speaker's podium before his "soldiers" while they awaited his words in "breathless silence."

If previously the view was correct, so he [Schmitt] declared, that we do not occupy ourselves with pure political matters, then a change has now taken place. Not, that we should now begin to politicize – for we are here to work in our profession – but rather that the entire German people is politicized through the national resurrection and everyone must work together so that the goal of a people inflamed by its ideals can be attained.[15]

What, however, did it mean to take a "different position" and to engage in "positive collaboration" with the new regime? After celebrating a "Day of National Labor" on May 1, the National Socialists smashed the trade union movement and seized all assets of the non–National Socialist organizations on May 2. At Allianz, of course, the factory councils had already been "coordinated," but the usurpers could now claim full legitimacy. Hilgard reported to the Allianz directors at the May 10 meeting that relations with the new councils in Berlin and elsewhere were good, but warned against granting them greater responsibilities than those defined in the Factory Councils Law. At the same time, however, he admitted that the ban on wearing party pins and symbols at work could not be implemented under existing conditions, although he thought it advisable to let the regulation stand for the time being.

The situation was quite touchy, as demonstrated by a meeting of the Allianz employees in late May or June 1933 at which a representative of the newly created German Labor Front (DAF) gave a fiery nationalist speech, which was followed by the singing of the Horst Wessel song. The Party members present gave the National Socialist salute during the singing. When the directors present abstained from this exercise, they were called upon to join in by the factory council leaders and then were subjected to threatening catcalls when they refused to do so. Schmitt saved the day, and Hilgard was full of admiration for the way Schmitt – totally unprepared and visibly upset – nevertheless pulled himself together and

[14] 21. erweiterte Vorstandssitzung am 10. Mai 1933, FHA, S. 17.2/4.
[15] *Allianz-Zeitung* 15 (1933), p. 160.

spoke to the throng about the importance of maintaining the dignity of the concern and its leaders.[16]

Nevertheless, Schmitt was rather more enthusiastic and active than his colleagues in pandering to the new order at this time. Not only was he prominently on display at the aforementioned Hitler birthday festivities, he also catered to the "socialistic" side of the regime while playing the public defender of employer interests with the new rulers as well. Thus, Schmitt was instrumental in summoning a meeting of the Berlin insurance industry employers on April 28 and proposing that all employers give a bonus to employees in honor of May Day. Apparently the agreement was secured, but it was a violation of the statutes of the insurance industry employer association to decide labor questions in another insurance association. One executive, who claimed to stand on the side of the "national movement," openly criticized the action, suggesting that "apparently there was a company which wanted to gain 'special credit' under the changed political constellation."[17] Be that as it may, Allianz gave a 40% monthly pay bonus to its employees in honor of the Day of National Labor, as did Nordstern; other companies gave 30% or 20%.[18] This was followed, however, by yet another Schmitt sociopolitical initiative that put him into the limelight – namely, a visit to Reich Propaganda Minister Joseph Goebbels on May 4 to discuss work creation and the future of employer–employee relations. The press reported that Goebbels assured Schmitt that the new regime would also be protective of the merchant and employer who "decided to engage in positive collaboration in the new political and social tasks."[19]

Schmitt was in fact taking a series of initiatives, not all of them supportive of the Nazis. Notwithstanding his own anti-Semitic feelings toward certain types of Jews and his sympathy with some of the anti-Jewish measures being taken by the regime,[20] he thoroughly and consistently disapproved of the attacks on Jewish business colleagues and the already visible efforts to drive them from German business life. He did have close personal relations with some Jewish businessmen, particularly the banker Otto Jeidels of Berliner Handelsgesellschaft; he got on very well with former Undersecretary Hans Schäffer in the Finance Ministry and was on excellent terms with the journalist Artur Lauinger of the *Frankfurter Zeitung*.

The campaign against Jews in the first months of the National Socialist regime was in fact a terrible shock. April 1933 marked a major turning away from Jewish emancipation and the start of a process that would begin with progressive

---

[16] Since the DAF was founded on May 10, 1933, and Schmitt left Allianz on June 30, the event described by Hilgard must have occurred between these dates; see Hilgard, "Leben," FHA, NL 2/7, pp. 96–7.

[17] Director Tosberg an Generaldirektor Tiedtke, 22. Mai 1933, HM, E0002-00005/2.

[18] Deutschnationaler Handlungsgehilfenverband, Rundschreiben, 2. Mai 1933, BAB, NS 6 VI/13500, Bl. 114.

[19] *Berliner Börsen-Zeitung*, 5. Mai 1933, BAK, B 280/12237.

[20] Schmitt, "Erinnerungen," FHA, NL 1/133, pp. 22–3.

exclusion and end in extermination. The month began with an organized nationwide boycott of Jewish businesses, allegedly in response to Jewish-organized foreign protests against the new regime's treatment of the Jews. This was followed by legislation. The Law for the Restoration of the Professional Civil Service of April 7 mandated that all non-Aryans – defined as those who had one parent or grandparent who was Jewish – be excluded from the civil service. Another law of April 11 excluded Jews from the legal profession. In both cases, however, exemptions were made for Jews who had done military service or had been in the civil service or had been practicing before 1914. Legislation was also passed on April 22 limiting the institutions in which Jewish physicians could practice, and restrictions were imposed on April 25 limiting the number of Jews who could attend universities. These measures were accompanied by a variety of local SA, NSBO, and NSDAP initiatives that excluded Jews from public facilities. No less portentous than the aforementioned organized boycott and legal measures, however, were the "spontaneous" efforts to drive Jews from employment by putting pressures on businesses to eliminate their Jewish employees and to designate as "non-German" those companies with Jewish directors, supervisory board members, or personnel. There was a growing fear that Jews would simply be eliminated from German economic life.[21]

Schmitt's opposition to such economic discrimination against the Jews must have been known to these men. It was therefore natural that he should be among those contacted when the Hamburg banker Max Warburg and his colleague Carl Melchior – along with General Director Emil Herzfelder of Victoria Insurance Co., banker Rudolf Loeb of the banking house of Mendelssohn & Co., and Hans Schäffer – launched an effort to fight economic exclusion while trying to meet the Nazis half-way by encouraging young Jews to shift out of urban and professional activities and move into agriculture and other forms of manual labor. The Gentile businessmen involved (in addition to Schmitt) were Carl Bosch of BASF, Gustav Krupp of Bohlen und Halbach, Carl Friedrich von Siemens, and Albert Vögler of Vereinigte Stahlwerke. Actually, Schmitt did not attend either of the two meetings held by the group – the first on May 23 and the second on June 28, 1933 – but was kept informed. He was thus less a member of this circle than an important figure who encouraged their work and to whom they felt they could turn. The program developed by the group, which they planned to set down in a memorandum, at once sought to stop the anti-Jewish economic measures and promote an occupational redirection of Jews. It called for the ending of the boycott in the provinces as well as Berlin, the support of enterprises trying to keep their Jewish employees by business organizations, and the elimination of discriminatory clauses in public contracts that were being used to strengthen the boycott and promote the firing of Jewish employees. They were particularly

---

[21] Saul Friedlander, *Nazi Germany and the Jews. Volume 1: The Years of Persecution, 1933–1939* (New York, 1997), pp. 20–39; Peter Longerich, *Politik der Vernichtung. Eine Gesamtdarstellung der nationalsozialistischen Judenverfolgung* (Munich & Zürich, 1998), Ch. I.

concerned about preventing an "organic" reconstruction of the economy (according to occupations) that would also involve an exclusion of Jews.[22]

It is important to recognize that the insurance business was also under strong pressure to fire its Jewish employees, particularly those in key positions. Thus, Kurt Daluege, a Party member since 1922 and a member of the SS who was to take over the Prussian Police in April and become head of Himmler's Order Police in 1936,[23] forwarded a denunciation to the RAA claiming that Victoria Insurance Company was "Jewified" and corrupt. The response of Kissel (head of the RAA), which he sent through the Reich Economics Ministry, was to point out that while it was certainly true that, relatively speaking, there were quite a few Jews at Victoria, the RAA could not simply dismiss directors and employees who had legal contracts.[24] This was not, in the end, going to save the jobs of Jewish employees and directors at Victoria – Herzfelder, who had become general director in 1932, was to flee Germany in 1935 – and there were more effective means of pressuring companies at the disposal of the National Socialists. Nevertheless, so early an intervention by so sinister and powerful a personage as Daluege was indicative of the kind of pressure already being exercised early in the regime on both government agencies and firms.

However, the chief demands to dismiss Jewish supervisory board members, directors, and employees came at this time less from government agencies or management than from below. A good illustration was Hamburger-Mannheimer Versicherungs AG, a majority share of which was actually owned by a Swedish firm, Svea. As General Director Hermann Hitzler reported on April 7, 1933, the "Jewish question" (the quotation marks were Hitzler's) had become "acute" far earlier than he had anticipated. The insurance companies would obviously not be spared, "especially [as] our company finds itself in the critical crossfire, since we work especially strongly with middle class and civil service circles and it is precisely these strata of the population that have adapted to the new order and are ready to support the government in all its intentions, even in very specific ones, most consequentially." To be sure, there had been a measure of anti-Semitism that was widespread during the previous few years, but it had little practical significance. Now, however, the matter had taken on serious dimensions – not only because of measures against Jews in civil service and professions but also because the boycott of Jewish businesses had led to the resignation of Jewish supervisory board members from large department stores (like Karstadt and Tietz) and major concerns like the AEG. This became apparent in the manner in which the company's insurance agents were being compelled to declare that their

[22] Schäffer Tagebuch, 23. Mai 1933, IfZ, ED 93, pp. 47–9. More generally, see Peter Hayes, "Big Business and 'Aryanization' in Germany, 1933–1939," *Jahrbuch für Antisemitismusforschung* 3 (1992), pp. 254–81, esp. pp. 257–9, 275.

[23] On Daluege, see Wolfgang Benz et al., *Enzyklopädie des Nationalsozialismus* (Munich, 1997), p. 829.

[24] Kissel to RWM, April 13, 1933, BAB, R 3101/17024.

company was not "Jewish" and had no Jewish directors or supervisory board members. Hitzler had suggested to the agents that they answer such questions to the best of their knowledge without contacting the home office, but ultimately this would not work. What made the matter worse was that there were insurance companies that were truly "free of Jews" and could thus gain a competitive advantage. Hamburg-Mannheimer, however, had a number of Jews on its supervisory board, including the politician Erich Koch-Weser and Erich Warburg, the son of Max Warburg. The entire situation was very "painful" since the company itself would never have thought of treating Warburg as if he were a burden. Yet when Hitzler asked the views of the Svea leadership, their response was unequivocal: "that the Svea in no case considers the continuation of Herr Warburg to be correct if his remaining involves an impairment of business."[25] Evidently, opportunistic conformity was not a vice limited to Germans, and it was not long before the supervisory board was "Judenfrei" through the anticipatory or "suggested" withdrawal of its Jewish members.

As Hitzler correctly noted, there were some firms that had few or no Jewish supervisory board or management board members. Allianz did have some Jewish bankers on its supervisory board, most notably Hans Fürstenberg of Berliner Handelsgesellschaft, who worked closely with Schmitt. There is no record of the Berlin concern itself having Jewish managing board directors. Nevertheless, the concern was not free of the pressures experienced by other insurance companies because it did have some Jewish directors among its member companies. Neue Frankfurter was an early case in point, where the Jewish director of the Frankfurt branch of Allianz, James Freudenburg, also served as a member of the Neue Frankfurter board of directors. That this had become a problem was evident from a letter written to Director Carl Gehrke by Director Robert Röse on April 21, 1933:

As a result of the political transformation we have repeatedly had to defend ourselves against the complaint that we are Jewish-oriented. The loss of the Youth-Care contract is, along with a substantial lower premium bid by the "Düsseldorfer Lloyd," probably to be attributed to the fact that it was claimed by an interested party that there was a Jewish influence on our company. Unfortunately, because I was not aware of this, I could not contradict it in time. For the same reason we almost lost the insurance contract for the higher and public schools of the Free State of Hessen. It will interest you in this connection that Herr Dr. Freudenburg has announced his resignation from the board of our company.

There was also some new business to be reported by Röse since the political regime change: "On the other side, we have also done business with the National Socialist Party, and it is anticipated that through Herr Busch in Düsseldorf, a deal of truly considerable dimensions will be concluded."[26] Freudenburg did in

[25] Hitzler to Sandorf, April 7, 1933, HM, A0002-00003/4.
[26] Röse to Gehrke, April 21, 1945, FHA, B 2.4.5/145.

fact leave the Neue Frankfurter board, although he attended board meetings during 1933 as a "guest."[27]

These, then, were the conditions that had led to the initiative of Warburg and his colleagues to find a way of protecting Jews already employed in economic life while preparing the way for the pursuit of more "diverse" occupations by coming generations. It was indicative of how little Schmitt understood the National Socialism toward which he professed such enthusiasm that he was prepared to promote such efforts. The goal of the Nazis, after all, was to get rid of the Jews, not to have them till Germany's sacred soil. In contrast, Schmitt's vision of National Socialism mainly involved the creation of a political environment in which the economy could recover. At a meeting of Germany's most important business leaders with Hitler on May 29, 1933, concerning work creation, Schmitt continued to make his usual argument that recovery ultimately depended on private initiative and not the State. What was needed was the reconstruction of purchasing power, as demonstrated by the fact that insurance policies purchased by individuals were averaging no more than 1,000 RM; increased purchasing power would be possible only if people were economically active. To achieve this, it was necessary "to throw the great spark of work creation into the economy. And that is home ownership, road construction, automobiles." Schmitt was thus a believer in the idea that the economy could recover only if it were "ignited," after which it would continue under its own power. Crucial to success, however, was a climate of legal security and confidence that one could invest and make a profit, and now "we have, thank God, a State in which one does not have to be concerned that another policy will be pursued in six weeks."[28]

Given this alleged policy stability, it was somewhat ironic that National Socialist Germany's first economic minister, Alfred Hugenberg (the German Nationalist Party leader) was proving inadequate to his task, irritating Hitler and Göring with his opposition to their efforts against unemployment and – by his performance at the World Economic Conference – giving Germany and the world an impression of uncertainty and inadequacy in the managing of Germany's economic affairs.[29] Schmitt was to be his replacement. As with his contacts with National Socialist leaders before January 30, his post-1945 explanations of his behavior need to be compared with other testimony and with the evidence available from 1933. Let us begin with Schmitt's post-1945 explanation to the denazification authorities of his decision to enter into Hitler's Cabinet, which was based on an exposé dated June 1, 1945.[30] According to Schmitt, Göring had

---

[27] See the meetings of Sept. 22 and Nov. 29, 1933, in FHA, B 2.3.1/2.

[28] Besprechung mit Industriellen über Arbeitsbeschaffung am 29. Mai 1933, BAB, R 43 II/536, Bl. 118–21. On Schmitt's "initial spark" concept, see Dan P. Silverman, *Hitler's Economy. Nazi Work Creation Programs, 1933–1936* (Cambridge, Mass., 1998), pp. 221–2.

[29] On Hugenberg, see Willi Boelcke, *Die deutsche Wirtschaft 1930–1945. Interna des Reichswirtschaftsministeriums* (Düsseldorf, 1983), pp. 58–65.

[30] The discussion and quotations that follow are based on Schmitt's exposé written for his denazification procedure, June 1, 1945. See AM, Spruchkammerakten Dr. Kurt Schmitt, Akten des Generalanklägers, Teil II, also to be found in FHA, NL 1/73–76.

suggested in the course of their meetings after the March 1933 elections that he would be a good economics minister. Schmitt claims to have visited Göring two or three times in the latter's capacity as Minister-President of Prussia for the purpose of using Göring's influence to stop SA and party actions against businesses and businessmen. In one case, Schmitt gained the release of a Bohemian sugar industrialist, Ernst von Janotta, whom the Nazis were attempting to intimidate by holding him in jail. Göring's willingness to act on Schmitt's requests gave the latter the feeling that Göring wanted to prevent actions against the business community and maintain law and order.

On June 28, 1933, Göring summoned Schmitt and formally offered him the post of economics minister, something that Schmitt claims not to have expected despite Göring's previous hints. Schmitt's initial response was that he did not have any political experience, had only been engaged with one sector of the economy, and above all feared "as a nonmember of the Party [sic!] and former general director of the largest insurance company, that I would not be able to have my way, which seemed most urgent in view of the many interventions by party agencies." Göring responded by pointing out that if German businessmen refused to participate, "then they ought not wonder and complain when the dogmatic persons in the party determine the fate of the economy. The Reich Chancellor and he would like to have at the head of the Economics Ministry a person who has been successfully active in business practice. His own and the Reich Chancellor's support would guarantee my authority."

Schmitt asked for an opportunity to think the matter over and claims to have found the decision very difficult, since he had no political ambitions and enjoyed his present work. However, he also felt that the fate of Germany now lay in the hands of the National Socialists, who had an absolute majority in the Reichstag. That this majority had been attained by exclusion of the opposition and by terror did not, apparently, disturb him. In any case, he believed this was an opportunity to ensure that the German economy would continue to have private enterprise as its basis and that foreign trade, which he considered in dire need of support, could be strengthened. He evidently also felt that he could do something about the Jewish situation.[31]

Ironically, it was because of his summons to Göring that Schmitt was compelled to miss a meeting of the group Warburg had assembled on the problems of the Jews, which he had planned to attend and which had produced a memorandum outlining their program. However, the group did not know where to send the document or whether it was wise to send it at all. Schmitt, when informing them of the reasons for his nonattendance, suggested that the time was probably not right to submit such a document because "things have once again become much worse"; he also indicated that if negotiations on taking over the RWM came to a positive result then "things will be better," since Schmitt intended to secure "certain commitments" as part of his price for taking on the new job.[32]

[31] Ibid.
[32] Schäffer Tagebuch, 28. Juni 1933, IfZ, ED 93, p. 66.

Thus, in considering Göring's offer, Schmitt claimed he had to ask himself the question: "In the case of my refusal would the German economy not be shaken in its foundations by inexperienced party doctrinaires and the confidence of the outside world be placed at risk?"

Göring summoned Schmitt once again on June 29 and told him that various Party agencies had tried the previous evening to prevent Schmitt's appointment, but that Göring had forcefully come down on Schmitt's side. Schmitt felt he had no choice: "Filled with a sense of responsibility, I set aside my reservations and considered it my duty toward my own country as well as toward the world to take over the Ministry and thereby prevent a sliding into radicalism." Göring then took Schmitt to Hitler, who confirmed that he did not want a dogmatic Party man in the job and promised to help Schmitt in every way to run the economy in an independent manner. On June 30, 1933, Schmitt was appointed minister of economics by Hindenburg. He alleged that it was only then that he applied for membership in the National Socialist Party and was accepted in August. As we have shown, he was already a member of the Party and, indeed, was greeted as such by a reception committee of National Socialists (headed by Lossau, the NSBO leader in the Ministry) and a maid of honor with a bouquet of flowers. They expressed gratitude that at last a National Socialist was in charge of the Ministry.[33]

As with his accounts of pre-1933 contacts with Göring and Hitler, Schmitt's post-1945 account of his decision to take the position of economics minister reflects his tendency to date compromising contacts and actions – especially his joining the Party – later than they actually occurred. Nevertheless, his explanation in his denazification proceedings of his decision to become economics minister was precise and detailed and, as far as it goes, confirmed by other reliable sources. One of these is his successor as general director of Allianz, Hans Heß, who detested the National Socialists, never joined the Party (no small matter for a man in his position), and was to prove his hostility to the regime in deed as well as word. His friendship with Schmitt was extremely close, and the two men discussed business and political affairs regularly both before and after Schmitt took office. Heß may have been the only one among Schmitt's close friends and associates who strongly advised him against taking the Ministry position – not only because he disliked the National Socialist leaders but also because, as he wrote to Schmitt in November 1945, "I instinctively felt that you would fit with these people like fire and water."[34] Nevertheless, Heß was convinced that Schmitt took the position out of idealism and a desire to serve his Fatherland and that it was a "sacrifice." This view was shared by Hilgard, a shrewd man who had also warned Schmitt that he would have a hard time working with the people around Hitler. Apparently, the strongest proponent

---

[33] Report on the Investigation of Dr. Kurt Schmitt, NA, RG 260, OMGUS, AG, 1948/120/2. See Boelcke, *Deutsche Wirtschaft*, pp. 66–7.
[34] Heß to Schmitt, Nov. 8, 1945, FHA, NL 1/20.

(among his colleagues) of Schmitt's taking the office was August von Finck, who – according to Hilgard – was anxious for business to have a strong voice in the new regime and also felt it would be helpful to Allianz and to his bank. Munich Re General Director Wilhelm Kisskalt also spoke of Schmitt's "sacrifice" and later admitted that he and others were guilty of urging Schmitt to accept the position for the benefit of the German economy. Schmitt's family was quite divided. Frau Schmitt opposed the National Socialists for religious reasons and did not want her husband to become minister, while their eldest son Günther was very ambitious for his father and urged him to accept the offer.[35]

Most impressive, however, was the testimony of the banker Otto Jeidels of Berliner Handelsgesellschaft, who wrote on behalf of Schmitt in September 1946 from San Francisco, where he had become vice-president of the Bank of America.[36] Jeidels (who was Jewish) and Schmitt had become good friends before 1933 and continued their business and personal relationship until Jeidels went into exile in 1938; it then resumed between 1945 and Jeidels's death in 1947. Schmitt regularly took long public walks in the Tiergarten with Jeidels even after becoming economics minister, and it is hard to imagine that this went unnoticed. According to Jeidels, Schmitt had already been warning his banking and business friends before 1933 to be prepared for the National Socialists taking a dangerous direction. Jeidels claimed that Schmitt had been outraged by the National Socialist government even if he was "realist enough" to recognize its strength. Schmitt expressed frequent concern to Jeidels about the violent behavior that accompanied the National Socialist seizure of power in early 1933, but he also argued that "it had at least come into existence constitutionally in form" and that its existence was a reality requiring that "one had to exercise influence over it through a certain measure of collaboration." Thus, "it was extraordinarily difficult for Kurt Schmitt to accept Hitler's call, and he also spoke to me at that time about his positive considerations, about his conscience pangs, and about his personal problem as to a friend in whom he had confidence." In Jeidel's view, Schmitt – who stood at the peak of his business career – had nothing whatever to gain from taking the office and was indeed making a sacrifice in the hope that Hitler would respond to it by supporting him. Schmitt told Jeidels that he even hoped he could eliminate the Party's anti-Semitism, or at least tone it down. Jeidels was less sanguine, but he does not seem in any way to have tried to dissuade Schmitt from taking the position and remained deeply respectful of his good and honorable intentions.

In his own self-defense, Schmitt made a particular point of noting that this positive view of his decision was shared not only by his friends and colleagues but also by the press at home and abroad. The *London Times* viewed his appointment as "the unmistakable sign of the desire to get back to solid grounds

---

[35] Kisskalt to Schmitt, Jan. 18, 1946, FHA, NL 1/74, and Hilgard, "Leben," FHA, NL 2/7, 89–91.
[36] Otto Jeidels, Erklärung betreffend Herrn Dr. Kurt Schmitt, 4. Sept. 1946, FHA, NL 1/74.

in economics," while the *Basler Nachrichten* positively commented on the fact that whereas his undersecretary in the Ministry (Gottfried Feder) and the new agriculture minister (Walther Darré) were identified as Party members, Schmitt was in no way so described. In Germany, the *Deutsche Allgemeine Zeitung* celebrated Schmitt's achievements at Allianz and made a special point of noting that he came from a business that was particularly supportive of savers and of building capital, so that one could expect him to support the interests of such persons: "Schmitt's name guarantees therefore that there will be no experiments at the expense of the saver, shareholder, and bondholder."[37] Schmitt undoubtedly was very pleased by this response in the international press and by similarly worded letters of congratulation he received from home and abroad. A good illustration was the note from his close friend Heinrich Fehlmann from Schweizerische Unfall Versicherungs-Gesellschaft in Winterthur, who was aware of the previous ministership offers made to Schmitt. Fehlmann was especially happy that Schmitt came from the insurance business and was thus internationally oriented.[38]

This was, of course, precisely the reaction Hitler and Göring were seeking when they appointed Schmitt as economics minister. Gaining the support (or at least the passivity) of the business community was essential to the consolidation of National Socialist power, and they needed to keep the Party radicals in line with respect to the economic sector. Göring had told Schmitt the absolute truth when he claimed on June 29 that radicals in the Party opposed his appointment. His information was based on an intelligence report giving an account of an entire series of conversations held within a network of party radicals who supported an anticapitalist "second revolution" and were anxious to have Otto Wagener (SA Chief of Staff, head of the economic policy office of the NSDAP, and, since April, Reich Commissar for the Economy) replace Hugenberg. Wagener had been prepared in 1931 to take 5 million RM from Allianz if it were needed to arm the SA, but he always argued that the goal of the Party had to be a new socialism that would replace the "egoistic spirit of profit of the individual person with common striving in the interest of the community." What Schmitt and his ilk wanted, in Wagener's eyes, was "to earn money, money, filthy money."[39] Wagener's supporters were well informed that not he but rather Schmitt, Ludwig Grauert (the reactionary fellow traveler of the Nazis and executive director of the northwest group of the Association of German Iron and Steel Industrialists), and Walther Funk (the economic journalist who had worked so hard to bring industrialists and Nazis together) were Göring's candidates for the Hugenberg succession. Not one of these was an "Old Fighter" or a tried and true National Socialist in the eyes of Wagener's supporters, the most active of which was a retired Captain Gustav Wolff. As the intelligence agent reported:

[37] *London Times,* Aug. 1, 1933, FHA NL 1/68; *Basler Nachrichten,* 30. Juni 1933, and *Deutsche Allgemeine Zeitung,* 2. Juli 1933, FHA NL 1/48.
[38] Fehlmann to Schmitt, June 30, 1933, FHA, NL 1/1.
[39] Quoted in Turner (ed.), *Hitler aus nächster Nähe,* pp. 373–4.

Captain Wolff speaks with Gauleiter Terboven and tries to influence him that he should support a 100% National Socialist, namely Dr. Wagener, since Göring and Goebbels had the intention, with the help of Dr. Schacht, to push through Director Schmidt [sic] of Allianz, one of the March fallen,[40] a typical liberal and representative of the capitalist world view. The Führer wants to do Dr. Schacht a favor at the moment and name Schmidt [sic] economics minister. The circle around Dr. Wagener, without the knowledge of Dr. Wagener, wants to have Wagener as economics minister. All the Gauleiter in the East and the territory of Dr. v. Gregory are storming the Führer about this. Röhm has already gone to bat for Dr. Wagener twice. Everyone that knows Schmidt [sic] rejects him. Terboven should join this movement. Terboven answers that he does not to be sure know Schmidt [sic], but that the Führer from his high position has a better overview concerning this than all the others.[41]

Such efforts to mobilize Nazi radicals and Old Fighters (like the Nazi businessman and Governor of Saxony Martin Mutschmann) or Nazified organizations (like the Chamber of Commerce in Königsberg) were stopped dead in their tracks by Göring. Hitler may in fact have planned to appoint Wagener, since he summoned him to the Reich Chancellory on the evening of June 28. Göring got there first, however, and Wagener was forced to wait in the antechamber while Göring showed Hitler the intelligence reports concerning the efforts of those in Wagener's circle to organize a campaign against Schmitt. Göring apparently persuaded Hitler that Wagener was the wrong man for the job. Hitler was infuriated with Wagener and personally called him in, telling Wagener that he had intended to make him economics minister but was now dismissing him instead. The four men from Wagener's office involved in the action against Schmitt were thrown out of the Party because "they have tried to rob the Führer of his freedom to take necessary decisions by sending telegrams and making calls to Gauleiter, chambers of commerce, and industrialists."[42] It was a severe punishment for men like these who lived for the Party and movement, and they spent a year and a half appealing for reinstatement and confessing the error of their ways before finally being taken back into the fold through a pardon by Hitler in February 1935.[43] The lesson was clear: Hitler knew best, and those who "worked toward the Führer" would get their reward while those who did not would be cast down.[44]

---

[40] A reference to those who joined the Party after March 1933.

[41] Nachrichtenamt an Ministerpräsident, 28. Juni 1933, BAB, ehem. BDC, OPG Gustav Wolff (*20.11.1876), Bl. 7–9. I would like to thank Ralf Pauli, Munich, for bringing this material to my attention.

[42] Parteiausschluß auf Befehl des Führers für Hauptmann Dr. Ernst Zunker, Hauptmann Willy Marwitz, Hauptmann Hermann Cordemann, Hauptmann Gustav Wolff, Ende Juni/Anfang Juli 1933, ibid., Bl. 3–6.

[43] See the correspondence between September 1933 and February 5, 1935 (ibid.). See also Turner, *Hitler aus nächster Nähe*, pp. iii, 482–3.

[44] This was the revealing phrase used by Werner Wilikens of the Prussian Agricultural Ministry; it is a central point, and I believe a valid one, in the interpretation of the regime. Ian Kershaw, *Hitler. 1889–1936. Hubris* (New York & London, 1999), pp. 529–31.

The episode also sheds some light on fundamental problems in the interpretation Schmitt and his defenders gave to his decision to head the Economics Ministry. Göring and Hitler knew what they were doing when they picked Schmitt, a basically decent but ambitious, vain, and politically naïve man who would in his own way "work toward the Führer" whether he wanted to or not. Schmitt was an optimist by nature. Though he claimed he was making a great sacrifice to prevent the radicals in the Party from having their way, he deluded himself into believing that he was on the road to victory for his ideas and that the new leaders were genuinely ready to support him. Hence there was another side to the coin of his anxieties about the new regime – and he could hardly be oblivious to its violent nature – namely, a measure of enthusiasm and willingness to believe that all would be well. As Kisskalt, who himself had joined the NSDAP on May 1, 1933,[45] wrote to a Swedish colleague:

The taking over of the Reich Economics Ministry is thought neither from the side of Herr Dr. Schmitt nor from the side of the Reich Chancellor as a passing matter. On the contrary, we hope that he will remain 10 to 20 years in this post. Fortunately, we do not live any longer in a democratic State in which the fate of the Cabinet is dependent on changing majorities.

It was certainly a great sacrifice for Schmitt to leave Allianz, just as things were settling down after the Favag acquisitions, and to take up the heavy burdens of public office; but, as Kisskalt reported, Schmitt

is thoroughly confident about this and, just as in his speech yesterday to the business leaders, so also in detailed private conversations with me, he has given expression to his absolute optimism with respect to a favorable development and his continually increasing admiration for the great statesmanlike qualities of the Reich Chancellor Hitler. We can therefore look into the future with the greatest confidence and always console ourselves with respect to the Allianz that if the Reich Economics Ministry was otherwise occupied this could in certain circumstances be a misfortune for the entire German economy.[46]

The political scientist Karl W. Deutsch once described the 1930s as "a period of cognitive catastrophes,"[47] and Kisskalt and Schmitt offered an exceptionally fine illustration of what Deutsch meant by the term. Such cognitive catastrophes, however, are no less subject to criticism than business failures. There was nothing in past experience, including the most recent, to suggest that Schmitt would not actually become what he apparently thought he would – namely, the

---

[45] BAB, ehem. BDC, PK Dr. Wilhelm Kisskalt (*24.8.1873).

[46] Kisskalt an Generaldirektor Adolf Jochnick, 14. Juli 1933, MR, D/5. Hilgard, in his memoirs, also noted that Schmitt expected to hold the office for a long time; see Hilgard, "Leben," FHA, NL 2/7, p. 91.

[47] See his discussion in Martin Broszat et al. (eds.), *Deutschlands Weg in die Diktatur* (Berlin, 1983), p. 324. For a fuller treatment of the theme, see Gerald D. Feldman, "Politische Kultur und Wirtschaft in der Weimarer Zeit," *Zeitschrift für Unternehmensgeschichte* 43 (1998), pp. 3–18.

general director of the German economy – for a decade or longer. His willingness to entertain such fantasies reflected a deficit of political culture, also shared
by Kisskalt and many other German businessmen, who were willing to convince
themselves that Hitler had "statesmanlike qualities." The alacrity with which
they welcomed the end of parliamentary democracy and put themselves at the
disposal of a person whom they had previously perceived to be a political dem-
agogue – in the expectation that they could use his dictatorial powers to run
the economy according to their lights – reflected a posture toward politics that
helps explain why the National Socialists would find it so easy to "coordinate"
the business community. Schmitt had no qualms whatever about describing his
path to National Socialism in 1933. Thus, no less important an economic journal than the *Deutsche Volkswirt* reported, after Schmitt took office, that

when advising the Brüning government, he [Schmitt] came to the realization that there
was no possibility in a parliamentary democracy to translate economic insight into fruitful reality. From this time on he strengthened his connections to the National Socialist
movement that he had taken up quite early and whose leader he recognized as the man to
overcome an obsolete political system. Today the road is open for the economic minister
to realize many of his basic ideas for the reordering of German economic life.[48]

Schmitt had thus been doing a rather good job of self-coordination for some
time, and he was continuing the process of his own volition. He did not have
to join the Party when he did. Hilgard, who had been a member of the German People's Party, did not join at this time, and Heß never did join. Schmitt
wanted to have it both ways, to appear as the nonpartisan and expert economic
adviser to the government but also to become part of the movement itself – for
the simple reason that he believed that Hitler had produced the kind of regime
in which he could realize his ideas. Once that step was taken, worse ones could
and did follow. Thus, when Himmler in September 1933 offered to do him the
honor of appointing him an SS-Oberführer with the right to wear an SS uniform,
Schmitt accepted the offer. There can be no question about the fact that he had
a peculiar penchant for wearing the uniform on public occasions, that he cut an
impressive figure in it, and that it pleased his vanity. As Baron Uexküll later put
it: "Dr. Schmitt who was a handsome and physically impressive man frequently
wore his SS uniform when traveling. The uniform showed him off particularly
well and he attracted in it considerable attention."[49] There is some plausibility
to Schmitt's later excuse that the SS did not play the role in 1933 that it was to
play later and that it appeared quite "nonpolitical" in comparison to Röhm's SA,
but the SS was certainly not the Rotary Club and the uniform was not exactly a
business suit.

---

[48] *Der Deutsche Volkswirt,* 7. Juli 1933, FHA, NL 1/48, along with other articles dealing with
Schmitt's appointment.
[49] Interrogation of Baron Edgar Uexküll, June 9, 1947, NA, RG 260, OMGUS, FINAD, 2/57/4. See
Himmler to Schmitt, Sept. 18, 1933, BAB, ehem. BDC, SSO Dr. Kurt Schmitt (*7.10.1886). On
Schmitt's enthusiasm for the uniform, see Hilgard, "Leben," FHA, NL 2/7, p. 93.

Finally, it is also important to note certain limits to Schmitt's "sacrifice," which were revealed in the course of his denazification proceedings after the war and which are also relevant to understanding his mentality. Unlike Wagener, Schmitt did not find money "filthy." Schmitt had built up a considerable and well-earned fortune in his labors for Allianz. His income in the early 1930s was 630,000 RM a year, and his taxable assets totaled 1.49 million RM. Half his income went to taxes, a quarter to investment, and another quarter to consumption. Thus, his ministerial position would have involved a considerable change in lifestyle because he had a house in Dahlem that cost 20,000 RM a year, a hunting domain in Bavaria which he leased for 15,000 RM a year, and an agricultural estate in Bavaria, Tiefenbrunn, that cost 20,000 RM a year. He also kept up life insurance policies to the tune of 25,000 RM in annual premiums. Entry into the civil service meant a reduction of his yearly income to 20%–25% of what it had been, even with Allianz's generous pension plan. In his opinion, this would have been a "monstrous sacrifice," especially in view of the fourteen mergers over which he had presided, his role in building up the concern more generally, and the surrender of his satisfying position in order to serve the German economy on the basis of assurances given by Hitler and Göring. Thus, Schmitt asked and received of Allianz a "respectable recognition" for his services in the form of 1,000–1,200 Allianz shares valued at RM 400,000. The alternative would have been a doubling of his pension, a solution he eschewed. As he explained in 1946, that would have involved a continuous burden for the company. Ironically, the RAA was unconvinced and complained about the arrangement, to no avail. Schmitt thought it important to note as well that he refused to accept the government housing available to him and actually did not want to take his government salary. He had to accept the latter for income tax reasons, but he then donated what remained after taxes to charitable causes. In this fashion he intended, as he explained with his breathtaking political naïveté, "to maintain my complete financial independence of the State and those who held power."[50]

THE SCHMITT INTERMEZZO: REORGANIZING FOR THE THIRD REICH

Schmitt was to pay a high price for the "cognitive catastrophe" of believing he could be an effective economics minister in the new regime, and the year he spent actively heading the Ministry was to prove a personal nightmare. Business was now linked to politics as never before, and the internecine conflicts that plagued Schmitt's efforts to run the economy provide a useful context for dealing with the problems faced by Allianz and the insurance industry in this period. The industrial leaders in this sector, as in all others, had to respond to the demands

---

[50] Aktennote über mein Einkommen vor der Ministerzeit, 1. April 1946, AM, Spruchkammerakten Dr. Kurt Schmitt, Akten der Spruchkammer Starnberg, 2. Teil, Bl. 201–3c; and Hilgard, "Leben," FHA, NL 2/7, p. 91.

and challenges set by the dictatorial regime. Schmitt had chosen to do so by becoming part of the regime itself and by identifying with what he thought were its positive features in order to serve the German economy as a whole. The alternative would have been to remain aloof politically, deal with the situation as best one could, and try to conduct business as usual.

Even this posture, however, required making complicated arrangements, as was evident in the distribution of responsibility at the highest levels of Allianz after Schmitt's departure. Hans Heß succeeded Schmitt as general director of Allianz. This constituted a political problem; though Heß was deeply respected for his capacities as an organizer and insurance man, his distaste for the Nazis was well known to his colleagues. Thus, as Uexküll later testified, "it was agreed that Eduard Hilgard would represent the Allianz in its relations with government and Party officials and that Dr. Heß would attend strictly to the internal administration of the Allianz."[51] This is not to say that Heß did not have National Socialist friends. For example, he had a close relationship with Wolf H. Count von Helldorf, the Nazi police president in Potsdam and (after 1935) Berlin, whom Heß had previously employed in the industry section of Allianz.[52] Helldorf was a notorious SA leader and anti-Semitic rowdy who had spent a great deal of time violating the law before becoming an alleged law enforcer, and it is hard to see how Heß could consort with him. What seems to have bound them together was their enthusiasm for horses and card playing, and both were members of the Club of Berlin. Apparently they agreed to disagree on politics. As for the role assigned to Hilgard, it is important to remember that Hilgard had already been used by Schmitt in all issues dealing with employee relations and had often been asked to represent Schmitt in the various associations. He was smooth, self-assured, diplomatic, and a talented political infighter. Hilgard was well equipped by his previous government career and experience to take on the public functions assigned to him. The new leaders of Allianz intended to run the concern "in the old sense and spirit," and Schmitt remained a presence in the concern since he continued to be consulted on important questions.[53]

Indeed, Hilgard was far better equipped than Schmitt, who found himself not only in the unfamiliar world of government bureaucracy but also trying to maneuver in the evolving National Socialist polycracy with its multiple and competing power centers.[54] That Hitler had been prepared to appoint Wagener

---

51 Interrogation of Baron Edgar Uexküll, June 9, 1947, NA, RG 260, OMGUS, FINAD, 2/57/4.
52 Ibid. See Dirk Walter, *Antisemitische Kriminalität und Gewalt. Judenfeindschaft in der Weimarer Republik* (Bonn, 1999), pp. 211–18, 313–15.
53 Report by General Director Bebler of the Swiss Re on his discussions with Hilgard and Heß, Sept. 6, 1933, SR, Feuer 11.
54 For the interpretation of National Socialism as a polycratic state, see especially Martin Broszat, *Der Staat Hitlers. Grundlegung und Entwicklung seiner inneren Verfassung* (Munich, 1975); for a critical discussion, see Klaus Hildebrand, "Monokratie oder Polykratie? Hitlers Herrschaft und das Dritte Reich," in Gerhard Hirschfeld & Lothar Kettenacker (eds.), *Der "Führerstaat": Mythos und Politik. Studien zur Struktur und Politik des Dritten Reiches* (Stuttgart, 1981), pp. 73–97.

(before Göring persuaded Hitler to appoint Schmitt) as economics minister was indicative of Hitler's fundamental lack of interest in the basic issues of economic policy, let alone rational modes of governance. Schmitt was given as undersecretary none other than Gottfried Feder, the man who had written the Nazi Party Program.[55] The Program, with its attack on "interest slavery" and other absurdities, was a far cry from any of the economic principles Schmitt had taken office to defend. Feder, however, was a spent force (albeit an irritating one), in conflict with many of his fellow Old Fighters and in desperate need of the job and salary to take care of his family and pay off his debts. His appointment reflected the fact that Schmitt, as once remarked, was a "National Socialist greenhorn"[56] who required the kind of help with Party matters that the other RWM civil servants were in no position to give. The real problems came from the host of NSBO, SA, and Party leaders throughout the country who were trying to implement their notions of how the economy should be run, and above all from the Nazi empire builders in high places like Joseph Goebbels, who simply took over the directing of economic propaganda, exhibitions, and fairs. Most dangerous were Robert Ley (leader of the German Labor Front) and Walter Richard Darré (of the Reich Food Estate), who was also Reich Food and Agricultural Minister. The former wanted to take the entire economy under his wing with a thoroughgoing organization of the economy according to "occupational estates." The latter, a blood and soil fanatic, treated all agricultural issues as belonging to his personal fiefdom. Schmitt found all of this most irrational, especially since he was firmly convinced that the economy needed a period of peace and quiet. At the same time, Schmitt found it difficult to see Hitler and, despite all the latter's promises, to push through his programs.[57]

By early September, Schmitt was feeling some discomfiture in his own ministry. Thus, when Hans Schäffer – who at this time acted as a go-between for the Wallenbergs (important Swedish bankers with close ties to Germany) and other Swedish business interests – wished to convey information to Schmitt, he was told to see Hilgard instead. Hilgard expressed Schmitt's regrets that he could not see him in the Ministry, to which Schäffer responded by saying that he realized that Schmitt "feels controlled there." Hilgard confirmed that this was indeed the case.[58] Schäffer did see Schmitt shortly afterward, undoubtedly outside the Ministry, where Schmitt responded somewhat helplessly to Schäffer's complaints about plans for an estate system and the treatment of Jews in department stores

[55] Albrecht Tyrell, "Gottfried Feder – Der gescheiterte Programmatiker," in Ronald Smelser & Rainer Zitelmann (eds.), *Die braune Elite I. 22 biographische Skizzen* (Darmstadt, 1989), pp. 28–40.

[56] Herbert Rolf Fritzsche an Schmitt, 31. Aug. 1948, FHA, NL 1/16.

[57] See Boelcke, *Deutsche Wirtschaft*, pp. 68–76; Schmitt's account of his tenure in the RWM of June 1, 1945, AM, Spruchkammerakten Dr. Kurt Schmitt, Akten des Generalanklägers, Teil II, pp. 3–13; Hilgard, "Leben," FHA, NL 2/7, pp. 92–3. On Ley and his ambitions, see Ronald Smelser, *Robert Ley. Hitler's Labor Front Leader* (Oxford, New York, & Hamburg, 1988), esp. Chs. 5–6.

[58] Schäffer Tagebuch, 4. Sept. 1933, IfZ, ED 93, Bl. 83.

Kurt Schmitt (2nd row, 1st on left) wearing the uniform of an SS-Oberführers at the May Day celebrations 1934 at the Tempelhofer Feld in Berlin. Next to Schmitt on the right are Richard Walter Darré (Minister for Food and Agriculture) and (front row, from the left) Rudolf Heß, Hermann Göring, Adolf Hitler, Joseph Goebbels, Max Amann (President of the Reich Press Chamber), Vice Chancellor Franz von Papen, Minister of the Interior Wilhelm Frick, and Labor Minister Franz Seldte.

like Karstadt. As Schäffer reported, Schmitt "complains that the individual businessmen do not have any courage. He is the only one who occasionally expresses his opinion."[59]

This assessment was curiously at odds with conversations between General Director Emil Bebler (of Swiss Re), Heß, and Hilgard on September 6 in Berlin. Hilgard was "extraordinarily confident with respect to future developments." Regarding the dangers to private enterprise, Hilgard thought matters very much under control:

For the private economy, which appeared strongly endangered in the first period of the Revolution, there are no more grounds for fear today. Dr. Schmitt has the reins firmly in his hands in this respect. He has known how to push through his views relentlessly

---

[59] Schäffer Tagebuch, 15. Juli 1933, Schäffer Papers, Leo Baeck Institute (New York). Schäffer saw Schmitt yet again on January 13, 1934; see his letter to Schmitt of Jan. 13, 1934, and accompanying material on the anti-Jewish boycott, AM, Spruchkammerakten Dr. Kurt Schmitt, Akten der Spruchkammer Starnberg, 6. Teil.

in the Ministry. Hitler has great confidence in him. The influence of State Secretary Dr. Feder, who dominated things in the Reich Economics Ministry with his unclear ideas during Hugenberg's time, is today completely pushed back. "Feder eats out of Schmitt's hand," Hilgard remarked. Since he is one of Hitler's oldest Party comrades and is very well known and regarded in National Socialist circles, Schmitt uses him as a valued collaborator.[60]

These contradictory assessments of Schmitt's situation undoubtedly reflected the genuine ambiguity of these early months of his tenure in office. On balance, however, Schmitt was in a difficult situation – and so was the Allianz concern and the insurance industry as a whole. Political considerations often took precedence over economic ones. The ambitious Nazi leaders at the top of the regime were jockeying for position, and Schmitt was constantly having to take into account their plans and programs, many of which made no sense at all to him. There were constant complaints about Nazi "initiatives" from below. At the same time, all kinds of schemes were being hatched for the reorganization of the economy or its various key sectors, which made the economy's future a matter of concern and anxiety. Fundamentally, the leaders of the insurance industry (and, indeed, of most of German industry) would have been quite content to retain the organizational status quo, but this had become a dangerous proposition; if one did not participate proactively in the reorganization mania, one was likely to end up being reorganized by Germany's new political bosses. Also, many of the new schemes for organizing the economy had profound implications for the conduct of the private insurance industry itself. It is not surprising, then, that all eyes in the private insurance business turned to Schmitt – who was, after all, their man. Heß and Hilgard were, of course, quite aware that an excessively visible reliance on Schmitt could backfire, and they instructed the regional headquarters of the concern *not* to turn to Schmitt for help in dealing with the special business interests of Allianz and also to handle problems with Party interference in their affairs through direct negotiation with local and regional Party leaders.[61] Insofar as some problems affected interests of the industry as a whole, however, reliance was increasingly placed on the insurance industry's organizations, where Allianz directors played a decisive leadership role. The history of Allianz in the National Socialist period is therefore intimately bound up with the history of the organizations it dominated.

Of course, some priorities of the new regime simply had to be accepted. Although Schmitt was strongly opposed to unproductive work as a means of fighting unemployment, employment policies at Allianz did not really change during his tenure in office. At the last meeting of the directors over which he presided on May 10, 1933, Schmitt opposed personnel reduction as a means to combat

---

[60] Report by General Director Bebler of the Swiss Re on his discussions with Hilgard and Heß, Sept. 6, 1933, SR, Feuer 11.
[61] 22. erweiterte Vorstandssitzung am 8. Sept. 1933, FHA, S 17.2/4.

rising costs due to diminishing premiums. Not only had administrative work increased, but also he viewed it as a mistake to release trained workers at a time when the economy was expected to improve. Moreover, dismissals would run counter to the goals of the government. When the directors met again on September 8 under Heß's chairmanship, premiums had continued to decline while costs had gone up; still, Heß noted that "since appropriate countermeasures through personnel savings which are in and of themselves possible, are out of the question at this time in view of the desire of the government to fight unemployment as quickly and effectively as possible, one will have to accept this development."[62] Even so, Heß instructed his directors to resist "unreasonable demands" to hire more personnel by pointing out that in July 1933 Allianz already had 4.6% more officials in the home office and 10% more in the field than it had in July 1932. Yet such injunctions seem to have been of limited effect, since Heß reported new hires at the meeting of May 4, 1934, despite diminishing premiums and higher administrative costs. Some of the additional personnel had been necessary because of the conversion of non–RM-denominated policies into RM-denominated policies, but people had also been hired simply to prevent a further increase of unemployment. In fact, the cost of the work creation effort had made it impossible to reduce premiums, which might otherwise have been reduced by 10%. The pressure exerted by the new regime obviously had its special qualities, but the economy still failed to "ignite" in the way Schmitt had hoped.[63]

There was pressure not only to hire but also to fire, and here both Schmitt and the insurance business generally were locked in conflict with Nazi officials and Party activists at various levels who tried to reduce unemployment by driving out "double earners," that is, persons holding two jobs and female members of families who were earning money in addition to the principal male breadwinner. Both Schmitt and Labor Minister Franz Seldte fought such interventions, which were often inconsistent with one another and of dubious or nonexistent legality. The actions taken against double earners were also quite destructive of government intentions, since many families were utterly dependent on more than one earner and since double earners were often precisely the individuals whose energy and initiative one wished to encourage.[64] For the insurance industry, the matter was of particular importance because working as an insurance agent or salesperson was often a secondary occupation. The insurance industry counted on a large network of persons at the local level who made a practice of informing their friends, neighbors, and clients of the availability of various kinds of insurance and then receiving a commission for their roles in either selling such insurance or acting as intermediaries

---

[62] See ibid. for this and the other such meetings discussed here.
[63] See Gerald D. Feldman, "Industrialists, Bankers and the Problem of Unemployment in the Weimar Republic," *Central European History* 25 (1992), pp. 76–96.
[64] See the valuable discussion in Silverman, *Hitler's Economy*, pp. 207–9.

in the selling of policies. For example, real estate agents, movers, jewelers, and veterinarians played an important role in informing their customers of relevant insurance and in helping to sell policies. Heß and his colleagues were anxious that "their indispensable and economically important activity be permitted again."[65] Allianz, along with the Reich Association, appealed to both the Reich Office for Labor Exchanges and Unemployment Insurance and to the RWM for relief from these pressures, and decrees prohibiting some of the Nazi excesses were duly issued. The ministries had hoped to issue regulations dealing with the problem but rapidly discovered that government regulatory efforts would do more harm than good in so complex an area. Therefore, orders were issued between September and November 1933 that left the question to individual employers and heads of government agencies, and it was made clear that dismissals were to occur only in extreme cases of disproportionate earnings.[66]

One significant area where tensions between Nazi organizational efforts and insurance business interests were closely linked was agriculture. On September 13, 1933, Darré had set up his Reich Food Estate (Reichsnährstand) and then expanded it in such a way that, by the early months of 1934, it encompassed portions of the crafts connected with food (e.g., butchers and bakers) and also those who marketed and sold food. On the one hand, this removed agriculture and the food trades from the RWM's purview. On the other, it separated them from the regular organizations of industry and commerce and created an encapsulated agrarian sector that well reflected the blood-and-soil fantasies of Darré and his colleagues. The most important expression of their ideology was the Law on Hereditary Entailment (Erbhofgesetz) of September 29, 1933, which removed 55% of Germany's agricultural land from the market to provide the security of tenure and protection from foreclosure due to indebtedness.[67]

While Schmitt and the business community were helpless to contain the agrarian empire being established by Darré and his cronies, the private insurance industry was interested in the new agrarian leaders as clients and in selling as much insurance as they could to farmers under the new conditions. Indeed, Allianz had a special interest in the question because it had an agreement with the chief agrarian organization, the Landbund, under which the latter recommended Allianz for insurance. Thus, at the end of August 1933, the Allianz concern sought to cement its relations to agriculture by inviting Staatsrat

---

[65] 22. erweiterte Vorstandssitzung am 8. Sept. 1933, FHA, S 17.2/4. See also Heinrich Köbel, "Der nebenberufliche Vertreter im Versicherungsgewerbe," *Neumanns Zeitschrift für Versicherungswesen* 56 (1933), pp. 832–3.

[66] Niederschrift über die Sitzung des Allgemeinen Präsidialausschusses des Reichsverbandes der Privatversicherung, 19. Sept. 1933, GDV, RS/24, p. 7. See also the Rundschreiben of the Reichsverband of Nov. 21 and Dec. 9, 1933, FHA, S 17.7/61.

[67] See John E. Farquharson, *The Plough and the Swastika. The NSDAP and Agriculture in Germany 1928–1945* (London & Beverly Hills, 1976), esp. Ch. 8, and Gustavo Corni & Horst Gies, *Brot. Butter. Kanonen. Die Ernährungswirtschaft unter der Diktatur Hitlers* (Berlin, 1997), esp. Ch. 2.

Wilhelm Meinberg (Darré's right-hand man) and the Bavarian agrarian leader State Secretary Georg Luber to join the supervisory boards of, respectively, Allianz and Bayerische Versicherungsbank.[68] Private insurers fretted over the danger that they might be prevented from collecting overdue premiums from the peasants benefiting from the entailment law, and they were especially disturbed by some farmers who felt they no longer needed to take out liability insurance and were indeed free of their obligations under such insurance. Still, private insurers were anxious to take advantage of the law and persuade peasants to take out life insurance, since mortgages could no longer secure provision for old age.[69]

The campaign to sell life insurance to peasants using such arguments was sharply criticized by the strong opponents of private life insurance in the agrarian sector. The effort to create a special agrarian estate was accompanied by an attempt on the part of the Regeno-Raiffeisen-Versicherungsgesellschaften – which had been set up in collaboration with the Reich Association of Agricultural Cooperatives – to monopolize the sale of insurance to peasants and farmers. It began to claim that Hitler stood behind insurance by occupation and that the regime supported a monopoly of insurance in agriculture by those companies set up specially to serve agriculture. Indeed, Darré had actually encouraged the peasants and farmers to give their business to the Regeno-Raiffeisen-Gesellschaften. Thanks to protests from the Reich Association of Private Insurers, this formal endorsement was revoked by the fall of 1933, although not quite to the satisfaction of the Association. Hilgard also negotiated an agreement with the leadership of the Regeno-Raiffeisen-Gesellschaften in November under which the latter disavowed any pretension to having a monopoly in agriculture.[70]

In fact, by early 1934 the Association found that the agreements reached only a few months earlier with Staatsrat Meinberg were not being kept and that some of the peasant leaders were not paying any attention to them, either. The supporters

---

[68] Announcement in the *Deutsche Allgemeine Zeitung*, 24. Aug. 1933, BAB, B 280/1432, Bl. 186. On Meinberg and Luber, see Corni & Gies, *Brot*, pp. 190ff., 181ff. Neither lived up to expectations. Luber was dismissed for corruption at the end of 1933, while Meinberg ended up quarrelling with Darré and went into industry in 1938. On the question of unpaid premiums and the complicated solution to this issue in 1936, see the Tagesordnung für die ordentliche Hauptversammlung des Reichsverbandes der Privatversicherung am 17. Nov. 1933, Anlage 4: Landwirtschaftliche Schutzmaßnahmen (Vollstreckungsschutz), S. 6–7, GDV, RS/5, and Tagesordnung für die Hauptversammlung des Reichsverbandes der Privatversicherung, 13. Feb. 1936, Anlage 10, p. 18, GDV, RS/14.

[69] *Deutschland-Berichte der Sozialdemokratischen Partei Deutschlands (Sopade) 1934–1940*, (1934), (Frankfurt a.M., 1980), p. 52. On the liability insurance issue, see the Bericht über die Ausschußsitzung des Unfall- und Haftpflicht-Versicherungs-Verbandes am 12. Dez. 1933, FHA, AZ 7.1/8.

[70] Sitzung des Allgemeinen Präsidialausschusses des Reichsverbandes am 19. Sept. 1933, p. 7, GDV, RS/12; Niederschrift über die gemeinsame Sitzung des Hauptausschusses und des Allgemeinen Präsidialausschusses des Reichsverbandes am 16. Nov. 1933, pp. 8–9, GDV, RS/13; Rundschreiben des Reichsverbandes vom 13. November 1933, FHA, AZ 5.1/3. On the Regeno-Versicherungsgesellschaft, see Arps, *Durch unruhige Zeiten*, Bd. 1, pp. 430–1.

Brochure of Allianz Leben on the Law on Hereditary Entailment, advertising life insurance (1939).

of separate insurance for farmers insisted that they were not getting the kind of capital investment they needed in light of the premiums they were paying to the insurance companies. This, indeed, was an important motive for all proponents of occupational insurance: that the investment of the insurers should go exclusively to the group being insured. Director Schloeßmann and other leaders of the life insurance business protested that they actually invested disproportionately *more* in mortgages and agricultural securities than they received in policies from the agricultural sector. Indeed, Allianz Leben did a special calculation to prove that, while its premium income from agriculture was 4.5%–5% of its business, its investment was about 6%–7%. As far as the private insurers were concerned, however, such calculations really were not to the point. They argued that juxtaposition of premiums and capital investment was absurd because the truly relevant comparison was between premiums and claims paid.[71] Ultimately, matters were "settled" by direct negotiations between Schmitt and Darré, who in March 1934 came up with a joint statement that the creation of monopoly-like credit institutes and occupation-based insurance enterprises was "undesirable" and that banks and insurance companies should take into account the special needs of the sectors with which they were dealing. However, the Reich Association did not seem particularly sanguine about the enforceability of this agreement, commenting that much more was needed to eliminate the unbearable aspects of the existing situation and so make the agreement a reality. Nevertheless, the cultivation of Meinberg by Allianz seemed to have worked: in early May, after numerous negotiations with him, Director Koenig was able to report that the Reich Food Estate had taken over the old agreement with the Reichslandbund to recommend Allianz for insurance purposes. This 40-year-old agreement was annulled at the end of 1935 because the Reich Supervisory Board had placed a ban on such arrangements, but Allianz made a special point of emphasizing that this in no way detracted from its good relations with the Reich Food Estate and that Meinberg's presence on the supervisory board was not affected.[72]

A much greater threat – both to Schmitt's conception of economic organization and to the private insurance business – was Ley's German Labor Front. Ley had begun a campaign to bring employers into the DAF, which was to rest on four pillars: the employers, salaried employees, workers, and free professions. These were then to be divided regionally by district (Gau) and also by branch. As Hilgard – who had taken Schmitt's place in the Reich Association and who had negotiated on its behalf with Ley and Wilhelm Keppler (Hitler's economic adviser in the Reich Chancellory) – worriedly noted, there was the danger that "through a premature entry into the Labor Front, the corporatist task could be prematurely settled, which would contradict the tendency of the Reich government, especially the Reich Economics Ministry."[73] The entire matter was very muddy, which is not surprising given the utter absurdity of trying to base a modern industrial society on corporatist principles and the empire-building that characterized the new Nazi regime, but Hilgard felt that they had to express a basic willingness to join. At the same time, he urged collaboration between the private insurance companies and the banks, which were also affected, as well as development of an employer position and strategy. It would be necessary, for example, to clarify the future of the Reich Association and the employer

---

[71] Niederschrift über die Sitzung des Allgemeinen Präsidialausschusses, 8. März 1934, pp. 2–5, GDV, RS/13; for the Allianz position, see the Rundschreiben of March 23, 1934, in FHA, S 17.7/61.

[72] For the agreement between Darré and Schmitt, see the Reichsverband Rundschreiben of March 5, 1934, GDV, RS/5. For the Allianz agreement with Meinberg, see the 23. erweiterte Vorstandssitzung am 4. Mai 1934, FHA, S 17.2/4. On the cancellation of the policy, see the Allianz Rundschreiben of 23. Dez. 1935 and the lengthy explanation sent out to the various branches, FHA, AZ 5.1/4.

[73] Niederschrift über die Sitzung des Allgemeinen Präsidialausschusses des Reichsverbandes der Privatversicherung am 19. Sept. 1933, p. 4, GDV, RS/24.

association. Indeed, given the elimination of trade unions, there seemed to be no further need for an employer association.

As in the case of the new order in agriculture – only far more so with respect to the new organization of labor – competition within the insurance business itself constituted a great threat to private insurance interests. The DAF had become a substantial participant in the insurance business overnight by acquiring the old trade union insurance organizations: Deutscher Versicherungs-Konzern, which had its headquarters in Berlin and had been run by the Christian unions; the Hamburg-based Deutscher Ring, which had been run by the German National Retail Clerks Association; and Volksfürsorge, also based in Hamburg, which was connected with the Socialist unions. The private insurance companies might have tried to purchase these assets, but the DAF had every intention of turning them into economic enterprises of its own and to begin competing with the private and the publicly chartered insurance organizations for market share. There was considerable anxiety that any new organization of the economy would operate in a way that favored DAF enterprises and might produce a socialization of the insurance industry itself. That is, the private insurance industry had to confront not only the old publicly chartered companies but also the old trade union insurance enterprises now associated with the politically formidable DAF.

Relations between the private and the union insurance organizations, especially Deutscher Ring, were anything but pleasant. Allianz and the Cologne-based Concordia had sued Deutscher Ring for advertising itself as the only insurance organization that understood its national and social mission and whose insured were not the victims of "dividend-addicted directors and shareholders." Most distressing was the claim of a Nazi insurance agent working for Deutscher Ring that "Allianz is a Jewish company or a mainstay of Jewish high finance."[74] Allianz won the cases alleging unfair competition and defamation that it brought against the Deutscher Ring and the insurance agent involved. Court orders of June 28 and July 7, 1933, required that the charge against Allianz be withdrawn; that the man who made it publicly declare that it was unfounded; and that the Deutscher Ring cease its unfair competition through invidious claims about its "mission" in its business reports.

Nevertheless, this hardly solved the general problem, which in fact intensified as discussions moved forward about reordering the economy along occupational lines. Even Nazis were complaining. In August, Fritz Sauckel (Reich District Governor of Thuringia) sent the RWM protests from an Old Fighter from the Gothaer Lebenversicherungsbank a. G. about the manner in which various Party members, the NSBO, and other agencies were recommending and favoring

---

[74] Rundschreiben Allianz, 25. Juli 1933, FHA S 17.20/167, and "Allianz und Stuttgarter Leben und Concordia gegen Deutscher Ring," *Neumanns Zeitschrift für Versicherungswesen* 56 (1933), pp. 589–90.

various insurance companies, among them those associated with the DAF. The insurance man in question reported that the concept of occupational organization was leading people to think that the entire insurance industry could be organized according to occupational principles and even be given a monopoly. This was very dangerous in his view, which was shared by the private insurance industry in general:

One must strongly warn against such an organization of insurance. There are great dangers in the gathering of different occupational groups each in their own companies, which are especially to be found in the absence of a sufficient mixing of risks and in the mixing of capital investments. Further to be considered is that an organization of life insurance according to occupational estates, which would grant a monopoly position to individual companies, must lead to the exclusion of a healthy competition that will serve progress.[75]

He noted that Italy had experimented with nationalizing its insurance industry but that Mussolini decided to reprivatize, with the result that the Italian industry was enjoying a big upswing. The Reich District Governor was in complete agreement with these points and went on to note that General Director Hans Ullrich of the Gothaer, himself long associated with the NSDAP and a Party member, was asking for a direct discussion with Economics Minister Schmitt about the problem.

The complaints continued through the fall of 1933 and the first months of 1934. The Reich Association struggled against tendencies to encapsulate agrarian insurance under one company and also expressed worries that the craftsmen would be organized along occupational lines for insurance purposes. What was particularly galling was the use of the Swastika and Party symbols (as well as of Hitler's name and particularly Nazi slogans like "the common good before personal good") to suggest that some types of insurance or certain companies were favored by the regime.[76] It is certainly no surprise that Schmitt was profoundly irritated by all this, as were the other RWM officials – above all Ministerial Councilor Bernard, who was in charge of the desk dealing with insurance questions. At the end of September, he issued a press release pointing out that the mixing of the Party with business interests was not allowed and that no one had the right to claim they were acting in the name of the NSDAP in trying to win insurance customers.[77]

Such injunctions seem not to have had much effect on the Deutscher Ring and Volksfürsorge, whose autumn campaigns repeatedly stressed their relationship to the Labor Front. This led to renewed protests against such advertising practices, not only from the private insurance leaders but also from their NSBO activists. In

---

[75] Reichsstatthalter in Thüringen an Reichswirtschaftsminister, 19. Aug. 1933, und Anlage, BAB, R 3101/17057, Bl. 25– 6.
[76] Reichsverband an den Reichswirtschaftsminister, 12. Sept. 1933, ibid., Bl. 30–7.
[77] Aktennotiz, 30. Sept. 1933, ibid., Bl. 69.

November, the NSBO steward at Allianz, Bruno Rycerz, and the chairman of the Workers Council, Hans Lange, joined with their counterparts from Aachener und Münchener, Friedrich-Wilhelm Lebensversicherungs-AG, and Victoria to protest the competitive practices of the DAF insurance companies.[78] Especially interesting in this vein was a long complaint to Pg. Haid of the Deutsche Ring from Hans Goebbels (brother of Propaganda Minister Joseph Goebbels), who was head of the publicly chartered Provinzial-Feuerversicherungsanstalt der Rheinprovinz. He, too, warned against an overemphasis on exclusive occupation insurance companies, but he particularly protested that the "coordinated" former trade union insurance companies seemed to forget the true purpose of "coordination." It certainly was not "to experience a new rendition of the war of all against all under the imprimatur of our sacred fighting symbol!"[79]

This by no means meant that the private and the publicly chartered companies had buried the hatchet, but the most immediate threat certainly came from the DAF. It was producing major conflicts with the RWM, where various insurance companies and Schmitt were protesting DAF interference in the health insurance area.[80] Finally, an agreement was reached between the Reich Association and the DAF insurance organizations in mid-February 1934; the former promised not to advertise against the latter by calling them "Marxist," and the latter agreed not to advertise themselves as DAF insurance organizations and to engage in fair competition.[81] Whether this was really the end of the conflict or only the first skirmish in the struggle with the DAF companies remained to be seen, but the competition faced by the private insurance industry had broadened in a very dangerous way owing to the Nazi seizure of power.

The various "treaties" that were concluded with reference to insurance in agriculture and relations between private insurers and DAF organizations in the early winter of 1934 were a reflection of more general treaties – between Schmitt, on the one hand, and Darré and Ley, on the other – concerning the organization of the economy, and they were symptomatic of the odd way in which government affairs were now being conducted. Schmitt and Seldte were anxious to prevent the DAF from becoming either a super trade union or a vehicle for structuring the economy along corporatist lines. They seemed on the road to achieving their goal when they signed (in late November 1933) an agreement with Ley, who was becoming very nervous about the radicals in his ranks and especially in the NSBO. Ley accepted the notion that the DAF was to function as a mass

---

[78] See their letter to the Wirtschaftspolitisches Amt of the NSDAP of Nov. 4, 1933, as well as Werner Lenz an Schmitt, 25. Nov. 1933, and the various appended documents, ibid., Bl. 129–30, 180–205.

[79] Hans Goebbels an den Verbandsvorsteher Pg. Haid, 15. Nov. 1933, ibid., Bl. 203–5.

[80] See the Niederschrift über die gemeinsame Sitzung des Hauptausschusses und des Allgemeinen Präsidialausschusses des Reichsverbandes, 16. Nov. 1933, GDV, RS/24, pp. 12–16, and the correspondence of Director George von Bruchhausen of Deutsche-Kranken-Versicherungs-AG of Aug.–Sept. 1933, HM, E0002-00005/2.

[81] Rundschreiben Reichsverband, 13. Feb. 1934 with appendices, BAB, R 3101/17052, Bl. 230–2.

organization for the purposes of educating and guiding the workers, rather than as a great union. Employers and workers alike were to be urged to join, and this explains Hilgard's rather tentative readiness to state that insurance industry employers were willing to join the DAF.[82]

Schmitt and Seldte continued working together to constraint and constrict the activities of the DAF. At the beginning of December 1933, Schmitt presented a proposal designed to relegate the DAF to the function of a corporate body charged with primarily "educational" functions, precluding its involvement in wage questions. He also hoped to bar it from owning economic enterprises and thereby prevent the DAF's expanding into an overwhelming factor in the economy. Labor questions – to be formally legislated in the "Law for the Ordering of National Labor" presented to the cabinet a few days later and then promulgated on January 20, 1934 – were to be handled on an individual enterprise basis, with the employers as "plant leaders" and with appointed steward's councils assuming the task of employee representation in each enterprise. Appointed labor trustees were to function as arbitrators in the event of disputes that could not be settled on the spot. The DAF was assigned the fundamental task of replacing class conflict with a sense of community and gaining acceptance for the leadership principle in business enterprises.[83]

Schmitt was not successful in his effort to place the DAF in a position where it had a clear legal status – it was not to have such a status throughout the regime's history – and he also failed to bar it from the insurance business and other economic activities. However, just as Schmitt was able to ally with Seldte to prevent the DAF from functioning as a union, so he was able to ally with Finance Minister Schwerin von Krosigk to mobilize criticism of the high dues and other financial demands on workers being made by the DAF.[84] Finally, and most importantly, Schmitt was able to bury proposals for an occupational or "estate" organization of the economy once and for all, except in agriculture, by securing Cabinet acceptance in late February 1934 of his own law for the "organic" organization of the economy. The Law for the Preparation of the Organic Structuring of the German Economy was officially promulgated on March 13, 1934. Its fundamental purposes, aside from preempting other options and ensuring a key position for the RWM in determining German economic organization and policy, was to rationalize the organization of the economy by replacing or supplementing the existing associational structure of peak associations and

[82] Smelser, *Robert Ley*, pp. 147–8. Hilgard's position paralleled that of the other business organization leaders.

[83] See Schmitt's presentation to the Cabinet meeting of Dec. 1, 1933, Karl-Heinz Minuth (Bearb.), *Akten der Reichskanzlei. Die Regierung Hitler 1933–1938. Teil 1: 1933/1934*, 2 Bd. (Boppard am Rhein, 1983), 2, pp. 992–5. On the Gesetz zur Ordnung der nationalen Arbeit, see Cabinet meeting of Jan. 12, 1934, ibid., pp. 1070–3, and RGBl, 1934, I, p. 25. See also Tim Mason, *Sozialpolitik im Dritten Reich. Arbeiterklasse und Volksgemeinschaft* (Opladen, 1977), pp. 117–23.

[84] Smelser, *Robert Ley*, pp. 220–2.

interest-group organizations with Reich Groups for the various branches of the economy, organizing them on the basis of the "Führer principle" and thereby creating organizations that would prove adequate for the transmission of aims formed by the State.[85]

The new law was the outcome of yet another power struggle in the regime and was the latest "treaty" between Schmitt and Ley. Thus, on March 21, 1934, Hilgard sent members of the Reich Association for Private Insurance an interview given by Schmitt to the editor of the DAF newspaper *Der Deutsche,* in which Schmitt spelled out the significance of the new law in providing the basis for a unified economic policy under the guidance of leaders that he was summoning to head the new Reich Groups. He characterized the law as "a bold attempt to form a synthesis between the free play of forces and the national socialist principle of 'community interest before self-interest.'" Schmitt explicitly rejected the notion that the law created "estates" in the economy, pointing to the Reich Food Estate as an illustration of what he was *not* doing. Similarly, he made clear that the DAF was not to conduct union activities and that Germany no longer had either trade unions or employer organizations. The DAF's purpose was rather to create a "community of labor," and it was toward this end that the new economic organizations and the DAF were to collaborate. The text of Schmitt's interview was accompanied by one of those typically ecstatic exchanges of telegrams designed to suggest a unity of intention (and to veil the intense differences) among the new leaders. Ley, who sent the telegram to Schmitt on March 20, praised the law and expressed complete accord with the Schmitt interview, both of which he had just read on his return from two weeks abroad. Ley saw the arrangement between the new economic organization and the DAF as an illustration of how the liberal age and Marxist class struggle had been overcome and as a demonstration that "Germany is the first and only land in the world to have eliminated the nation-subverting ideas of the French Revolution of 1789." While no match for Ley as a rambling purveyor of National Socialist discourse, Schmitt showed that he was not without promise when it came to linguistic adaptation by joyously responding that the "heartfelt and manly solidarity of the leaders is the precondition and deepest guarantee for the success of the National Socialist people's community."[86]

Not everyone in the business community was equally enthusiastic about Schmitt's organizational measures. Reichsbank President Schacht thought the entire legislation was nonsense and likely to do more harm than good, as he made a point of telling Hilgard after replacing Schmitt as economics minister. But Hilgard saw the matter differently and considered the legislation a

---

[85] Cabinet meeting of Feb. 27, 1934, *Akten der Reichskanzlei, Regierung Hitler 1933–1938,* Teil I, Bd. 2, pp. 1169–70. For the law, see RGBl, 1934, I, S. 185–6. On the Reich Groups and this reorganization, see Boelcke, *Deutsche Wirtschaft,* pp. 95–100.

[86] For these documents, see Hilgard an die dem Reichsverband angeschlossenen Fachverbände und Verbandsgesellschaften, 21. März 1934, GDV, RS/5.

masterstroke on the part of Schmitt designed to preempt DAF efforts to gain control over the economy. Schmitt's cause had, to be sure, been well served by Ley himself, whose confused presentation of ideas alarmed those with whom he spoke; so that even party leaders like Rudiger Graf von der Goltz, whom Schmitt asked to take over the leadership of the industrial economy organizations, felt that something had to be done.[87] Schacht was not a man to extol the achievements of others, and Hilgard probably was right in viewing Schmitt's preemptive strike as something of a triumph – especially since the DAF was far from neutralized and was actually in the process of building a substantial empire with its leisure time organization "Strength through Joy" and other social programs. This said, however, Schmitt's actions in the interest of the business community did create mechanisms that made state intervention in economic affairs far easier than they had been under the more diffuse prior organization.

Insurance was to be one of the eleven Reich groups to be established under the new arrangement, and Hilgard was soon to become its "Führer." To their credit, the leaders of the Reich Association did not seem to take their potential roles as "Führer" with too much seriousness. Reich Association Managing Director Heinrich Lippert treated the whole matter as a change of terminology, suggesting that the chairman become a "Führer" with a narrow council of "Führer" corresponding to the present Präsidium and an expanded committee of "Führer" corresponding to the existing main committee. There were then to be "Führer" for the organizations for the branches of insurance, which would presumably have counterpart structures. In short, their basic character as self-governing bodies would continue. Lippert's proposal was made in early March 1934, but Hilgard warned against voting on anything until Schmitt's intentions were clear. He then proceeded, however, to propose a structure – with a "Führer" at the top and a group of "Führer" rings – that did not deviate much from the Lippert proposal. Although there was general consensus that Hilgard be the "Führer" of the Reich Association, Hilgard urged that all "Führer" be subject to a yearly vote of confidence.[88]

Matters were not necessarily to be so simple and convenient, however. This the Presidial Committee of the Reich Association discovered in their discussion with another "Führer," Rudolf Lencer, who on March 8, 1934, was given the charge of establishing and leading the projected Reich Company Community for Banking and Insurance of the DAF. Lencer, a bank official and enthusiastic National Socialist who was a significant figure in the DAF, gave a speech at a rally held on February 27, 1934, in which he contended not only that the employer associations should disappear (now that the trade unions were gone) but also that the Reich Association would gradually disappear as well and be replaced by the DAF company group. Hilgard thought it wise to learn more about

---

[87] Hilgard, "Leben," FHA, NL 2/7, pp. 92–6.
[88] Niederschrift über die Sitzung des Allgemeinen Präsidialauschusses, 8. März 1934, pp. 7–10, GDV, RS/13.

Reich Economics Minister Schmitt giving a speech about the reorganization of the German economy to senior representatives of political and economic management in the conference hall of the Reich Economic Council, March 13, 1934. Next to him are Undersecretaries Gottfried Feder and Hans Posse (wearing glasses).

Lencer's plans, which Lencer – arriving so late to the meeting that many insurance managers had already left – described in extraordinarily confusing but very discomfiting terms. Naturally there was the usual verbiage about the "educative" functions of the DAF (i.e., its allegedly crucial role in infusing National Socialist ideas into the factories and offices of Germany), but the substantive point seemed to be that the DAF had plans to abscond with the idea of forming Reich Groups by establishing such groups for itself in the form of its company groups, which would effectively organize the entire economy. Thus, the DAF would have a branch group devoted to insurance and composed of private insurance, the publicly chartered companies, and social insurance. Most importantly, Lencer sketched a scheme under which both social and economic matters would come under its control. Thus, questions of basic wage and working conditions would be discussed in the company groups, and the labor trustee would be called in only as an agency of last resort. Similarly, in response to a question by Allianz director Walter Eggerss – who was clearly alarmed at the prospect of DAF interference in anything – Lencer recognized that the technical side of the insurance business needed expertise in the initial phase; however, he went on to suggest that the DAF and economic organizations would first work parallel to one another but would then grow together in one organization. Thus, the "educative" function now appeared to be merely a transitory phase during which DAF officials would learn to interfere in every aspect of the insurance business. Lencer also implied that he would end up being the "Führer" of them all: the person in charge of assuring that both social and economic policies fulfilled the goals of the DAF.[89]

Although the questions raised by the insurance executives demonstrated that they found Lencer confusing and inconsistent, Hilgard was careful to treat him with studied politeness and to express warm support for the high tasks and functions of the DAF. Privately, he detested Lencer, whom he considered "a prototype of the young guard of the Party. He sought to compensate for his inadequate general education with a considerable amount of arrogance and thoughtless unreliability."[90] For Hilgard, as for Schmitt and others, the rambling ambitions of Ley and his cronies were prime evidence favoring anticipatory self-organization by the business community in ways that would at once conform to the expectations of Germany's new rulers and preserve the fundamental structures they had built up over the years. Thus, when Schmitt asked Hilgard to assume the position of leader of the new Reich Group for Insurance, the latter, as he frankly admitted,

hardly gave any thought to the question of whether I should accept or not. Far more, it was self-evident that I should place myself at his disposal, since I had the feeling that I could satisfy the tasks of the position and could administer it to the benefit of the private insurance business. I therefore undertook the job in good spirits and never had any

---

[89] Ibid., pp. 11–17.
[90] Hilgard, "Leben," FHA, NL 2/7, p. 96.

thought that this activity would later be interpreted as work in the service of the NSDAP. Such a view was all the more distant from me since I was personally completely opposed to Hitler and his Party, and I actually viewed the summons to be leader of the Reich Group for Insurance as a chance, at least in our area, to be able to fight against encroachments by the Party.[91]

Nevertheless, Party membership was a prerequisite for his new position, and Hilgard applied for membership in February 1934. At the time, the Party had issued a ban on new memberships, but an exception was made in Hilgard's case at the request of the Reich Party Leadership. Hilgard later claimed he never requested a Party book nor knew his number.[92]

As leader of the Reich Group for Insurance, Hilgard was on the front line of his industry's relations with the government as well as on the front line of relations between his industry and the outside world. He no longer represented the private insurance business alone. When the Reich Group was formally established on June 20, 1934, Hilgard surrendered his position as chairman of the Reich Association for Private Insurance to General Director Christian Oertel of Colonia in Cologne. At the same time, a second and parallel group within the industry was placed in the Reich Group under his leadership – namely, those old competitors of the private insurance business, the publicly chartered insurance organizations. Professor Paul Riebesell, a noted insurance mathematician and general director of the Hamburger Feuerkasse, was made leader of this group. As Hilgard rapidly discovered, however, the real powers in the publicly chartered insurance business were two dangerous Nazis: Franz Schwede-Coburg, who was made Gauleiter and Governor of Pommerania in 1934, and Hans Goebbels. The former was a genuine Old Fighter, who led the SA in Coburg as early as 1922 and became mayor of the city in 1931 before being elevated to Gauleiter. Radical and (as it was to turn out) murderous, Schwede-Coburg took a special interest in publicly chartered insurance for ideological reasons and became active in its organizations.[93] Hans Goebbels was also a fanatical Nazi who had made a career as head of the Provinzial-Feuerversicherungsanstalt der Rheinprovinz and enjoyed access to his more famous brother and the radical circles around him. Hilgard apparently earned their enmity very early on when, at an introductory meeting with leadership of the publicly chartered group, where Riebesell had introduced him and Hilgard had given one of his conciliatory and politically correct speeches, Schwede-Coburg and Goebbels cornered him. Schwede-Coburg told him that his remarks were all well and good but that they would judge him

---

[91] Ibid., pp. 93–4.
[92] See his Fragebogen, undated, FHA, NL 2/3, and BAB, ehem. BDC, PK Walter Gladisch (*2.1.1882).
[93] See the articles celebrating his 50th birthday in *Deutsche öffentlich-rechtliche Versicherung*, 1. März 1938, and *Völkischer Beobachter*, 5. März 1938, GDV, 0-012/2. For an enthusiastic but useful account of his career, see Herbert Gaede, *Schwede-Coburg. Ein Lebensbild des Gauleiters und Oberpräsidenten von Pommern* (Berlin, 1939). See also Hermann Weiß (ed.), *Biographisches Lexikon zum Dritten Reich* (Frankfurt a.M., 1998), p. 424.

by his adherence to the will of the Party. Hilgard's response was that he was legally subordinate to the Reich Economics Minister and intended to follow the latter's directions.[94]

The trouble was that Hilgard's friend and Reich Economics Minister Schmitt was in less and less of a condition to give directions to anyone, and his public career was coming to a very unhappy end. He had grave difficulties dealing with the polycratic competition and settling matters with Darré and Ley. He also had to keep the lid on Feder, who had periodic bursts of energy during which he tried to make policy; this irritated the other RWM officials and inevitably led to quarreling in the Ministry. Schmitt finally managed to place Feder in charge of land settlement policy, which was one of Feder's old interests, but he remained a thorn in the side of the ministerial bureaucracy. For example, when RWM Press Officer Herbert Rolf Fritzsche prevented Feder from placing a racist article on behalf of the Ministry in the press, Schmitt had to come to Fritzsche's defense.[95]

This episode was indicative of Schmitt's most important problem: the extent to which his views on key questions differed from those of both the Nazi leadership and the most powerful elements in the Party's rank and file. The tendency to openly discriminate against the Jews in economic affairs was an especially sore point. Schmitt made no secret of the fact that he viewed the economy as a kind of sanctuary for Jews from the "Aryan paragraphs" and that there was "no Jewish question in the economy." Thus, to at least some extent, he kept his promise to his Jewish business colleagues and made the acceptance of this policy by Hitler and Göring one of the conditions for his taking office. Yet the limits of Schmitt's influence, and also of his commitment, were apparent from the outset. Thus, at the Cabinet discussion of the granting of public contracts on July 14, 1933, Rudolf Heß (deputy leader of the NSDAP) announced that the boycott against Jewish enterprises was being lifted but also declared that public agencies would themselves find the means to end their connections with Jewish enterprises. On July 19, Schmitt issued guidelines emphasizing the primacy of work creation in the giving of contracts. Conditions being equal, preference was to be shown to "Aryan" firms, but Schmitt warned against creating insecurity and unrest by yielding to unwarranted pressures from those seeking to serve their own interests by pursuing the racial origins of shareholders and supervisory board members of companies seeking contracts. Schmitt thus had no objections to discrimination against Jewish enterprises per se and indeed declared it the goal of German economic policy "to push back Jewish influence in the economy" and to promote the transformation of Jewish into non-Jewish firms. He objected, however, to denying formerly Jewish firms public contracts, as was the policy of the Postal Ministry – and especially to explicitly giving the Jewish (or formerly Jewish) character of a firm as the reason for its exclusion from contracts. Schmitt feared that this would lead to reprisals abroad and to loss of jobs at home. He

[94] Hilgard, "Leben," FHA, NL 2/7, pp. 94–5.
[95] Herbert Rolf Fritzsche an Schmitt, 31. Aug. 1948, FHA, NL 1/16.

renewed this summons to moderation on September 5, noting that firms and government agencies were being flooded with inquiries about whether various companies were truly German-owned or -controlled.[96] On September 27, 1933, he issued yet another pronouncement:

I do not consider a distinction between Aryan and non-Aryan or pure Aryan firms in the economy and especially when engaging in business relations to be implementable. Such a distinction with the purpose of boycotting non-Aryan firms must necessary lead to serious disturbances of the economic reconstruction, since unfavorable effects on the labor market through reductions of operations by the firms affected by the boycott and negative consequences for the suppliers of these firms and their workers would be unavoidable.[97]

In mid-December 1933, Schmitt sent around a circular to the state governments and chambers of commerce warning against any disturbing of Christmas business by "special actions" against "non-Aryan" businesses and department stores designed to prevent them from showing Christmas displays or selling Christmas articles and Christmas tree ornaments.[98] If these were not ringing cries for tolerance and decency – and in fact masked Schmitt's willingness to support active measures to reduce the role of Jews in public life – they were nevertheless received at home and abroad as a substantial self-limitation by the regime on its anti-Semitic program. They led not only to criticism but also to outright noncompliance and even open defiance by Gauleiter and other Nazi leaders. The Gauleiter of the Palatinate Josef Bürckel, for example, bluntly stated that "the utterances of some big-name Nazis don't mean a thing to old Nazis like us."[99]

---

[96] Cabinet meeting of July 14, 1933, *Akten der Reichskanzlei Regierung Hitler 1933–1938*, Teil I, p. 677. Schmitt's "Richtlinien über die Vergebung öffentlicher Aufträge" of July 19, 1933, as well as his subsequent statement of Sept. 5, 1933, are printed in the *Ministerialblatt für die Preußische innere Verwaltung* 94 (1933), Teil I, Bd. 1, pp. 983–5, 1279. The problems faced by Schmitt are well illustrated by the anti-Semitic policies of the Post Office leadership, discussed in Lotz, *Deutsche Reichspost*, pp. 208–9. The evidence for Schmitt's support for the basic policy of reducing Jewish economic influence and his desire to avoid making discriminatory practices public is to be found in the minutes of a meeting on November 13, 1933, of various ministries in the RWM at which Schmitt, Finance Minister Schwerin von Krosigk, and Post Minister Freiherr von Eltz-Rübenach were personally present; the issue of giving contracts to foreign companies was also discussed, with Schmitt taking a moderate line here, too. See "Vermerk über die Chefbesprechung am 13. November 1933 über Auftragsvergebung der Reichspost," BAB, R 4701/22057, Bl. 8–11.

[97] RWM to the German Chamber of Industry and Commerce, with copy to the state governments, 8. Sept. 1933, BAB, R 4701/22056. In general, see his postwar "Judenpolitik während meiner Ministerzeit," FHA, NL 1/77, which quotes the policy statement in question. In his postwar self-defense, Schmitt never referred to an official document but rather to the publication of the statement in an article entitled "Kein Arierparagraph in der Wirtschaft" in the "8-Uhr Abendblatt," 27. Sept. 1933. The article is to be found among the exhibits in his denazification trial, AM, Spruchkammerakten Dr. Kurt Schmitt, Akten der Spruchkammer Starnberg, 1. Teil.

[98] See "Keine Störungen des Weihnachtsgeschäfts. Eine Anordnung des Reichswirtschaftsministers," *Deutsche Allgemeine Zeitung*, 16. Jan. 1933, ibid.

[99] For both the press and the Nazi reactions, see Schmitt's "Judenpolitik während meiner Ministerzeit," FHA, NL 1/77.

The Nazi press simply did not report Schmitt's instructions on Jewish business, omitted portions of his speeches dealing with such issues, or consigned his policy statements to the back pages.[100] Indeed, the Social Democrats in exile in Prague took note of Schmitt's problems, reporting that the Nazi left "are raising a storm against Reich Economics Minister Schmitt, his capitalist course, and his moderate position on the Jewish question" and that such protests against Schmitt were not a matter of single individuals but rather of the mass of Nazi supporters.[101]

Schmitt's efforts did, to some extent, protect Allianz from attacks for having Jewish employees or Jewish shareholders. Thus, when the Breslau NSDAP spread reports that Allianz was not a pure German firm, Hilgard complained to State Secretary Feder. The latter not only confirmed that Allianz was "a pure German enterprise in the sense of the NSDAP" but went out to point out that "our Führer would most certainly not have summoned the general director of this significant corporation to become Reich Economics Minister if there existed even the slightest doubt as to the pure German stance of your corporation with respect to its business." Feder authorized Hilgard to make use of this testimonial in its advertising and assured Hilgard that the Breslau Party office would be appropriately instructed.[102] Allianz did indeed make use of this letter by publishing it immediately in the *Allianz-Zeitung,* and it was not without positive consequence. Thus, when the Mayor of Osterode wrote to the RAA asking whether Jewish capital did not play an important role in Neue Frankfurter, in which case he intended to change the insurer of the local schools, Neue Frankfurter's reaction was to point out that the company was largely under the control of Allianz and make reference to the Feder letter. The RAA not only responded to the mayor by repeating the company's remarks verbatim but also reminded him that the economics minister had instructed that "the distinction between Aryans and non-Aryans [be] set aside in the economy."[103]

Although Hitler had given Schmitt his verbal support on this issue on economic grounds, Hitler himself did nothing to rein in his followers regarding their anti-Semitic practices. Schmitt's relations with Hitler seemed agreeable enough, the latter visiting Schmitt's Bavarian estate Tiefenbrunn on April 5, 1934. Family photos were taken of Hitler and Hitler's photographer Heinrich Hoffmann with the Schmitt family. It seems to have been a pleasant enough occasion, although Schmitt's efforts to discuss his Ministry problems proved disappointing. By this time, however, Schmitt was deeply distressed about his situation.[104]

---

[100] It is interesting that the Reich Association took note of this problem in an internal file: "Notiz. Berücksichtigung der Kundgebungen des Reichswirtschaftsministers im Völkischen Beobachter," 24. Okt. 1933, GDV, 8-020 P1/Kurt Schmitt.

[101] Deutschland-Berichte der Sozialdemokratischen Partei Deutschlands, 1934, p. 20.

[102] Feder an Hilgard, 24. Juli 1933, BAK, B 280/12237, Bl. 54.

[103] *Allianz-Zeitung* 15 (1933), p. 214. RAA an den Bürgermeister in Osterode, 5. Juni 1934, and related correspondence, BAK, B 280/13206, Bl. 58–61.

[104] For the photos, see FHA, NL 1/174, 179, 182. On the visit, see Interrogation of Schmitt, July 9, 1947, NA, RG 260, OMGUS, FINAD, 2/58/3.

Hitler and Schmitt at Schmitt's estate Tiefenbrunn, April 5, 1934.

The acid test of Schmitt's performance as minister, after all, was his success in mastering the unemployment problem and reducing the trade deficit; his failure in both respects and inability to push through his policies weighed more and more on his spirits. He was also very concerned about improving Germany's external relations and had a highly successful visit to England in December 1933, where he met the political and economic leaders, got on very well with Stanley Baldwin, and received favorable press as a German with whom one could do business.[105] Similarly, despite considerable tensions between Germany and the United States, the American Ambassador Joseph E. Dodd (who considered Schmitt a "most loyal Hitlerite") found his speeches on economic policy

---

[105] See the material in FHA, NL 1/65.

"statesmanlike" and even "courageous in opposition to some Nazi policies," albeit "conservative."[106]

He was indeed conservative, and while willing to spend money productively in order to promote employment, he was sharply critical of unproductive expenditure (especially for Party and military purposes) and of excessive expenditure on the Autobahns and other such projects instead of infrastructural and industrial constructions that were likely to have a longer-term payoff. Schmitt was particularly hostile to Hitler's policy of stockpiling chemicals and in other sectors potentially important for rearmament, regarding this as an uneconomic and wasteful approach to Germany's economic problems. He also opposed giving the German people the impression that some "wonder" was going to occur instead of giving them the sober news that they faced a hard upward economic struggle. While never particularly close to Reichsbank President Hjalmar Schacht, he nevertheless thought him an ally with respect to these questions when the two men agreed to visit Hitler at Obersalzberg in March 1934 to decide on future economic policy. Hitler was prepared to support Schmitt on all issues but one – military expenditure, which he viewed as the most "productive" expenditure of all because it was the only way Germany could overcome the disabilities created by Versailles and its inferior situation in the world. This meeting provided to be a "turning point" for Schmitt, not only because of Hitler's obvious insistence on military expenditure but also because Schacht immediately expressed agreement with Hitler, going so far as to say he was prepared to ruin the currency if necessary in order to achieve rearmament. Schmitt was horrified by so extreme a statement coming from Schacht, not to mention what it suggested about Schacht's character, and while he was cautious enough at Schacht's postwar trial to say simply that he was disappointed that Schacht had not withheld comment until they could discuss the issue, Schmitt's account in his private reminiscences did report Schacht's pandering response to Hitler.[107]

Schmitt now felt utterly trapped; while he soldiered on, he poured out his daily grievances over conditions at the Ministry to Heß. He also became increasingly indiscreet. In a conversation with Ambassador Dodd on June 1, Schmitt rhetorically asked how one could make a trade treaty with the United States when German policy toward Jews and others produced such hostility. As Dodd noted: "I have never seen a German statesman so much distressed, and I was quite sympathetic when he again and again referred to the folly of Hitler's policy."[108] Apparently, the final straw for Schmitt came when Dodd and a number of American bankers who had given credits to the Saxon State Bank complained about

---

[106] See William E. Dodd, Jr., & Martha Dodd, *Ambassador Dodd's Diary, 1933–1938* (London, 1942), entries for July 14, 1933 (p. 26), January 31, 1934 (p. 89).

[107] Zeugenaussage Schmitts in dem Spruchkammerverfahren gegen Hjalmar Schacht, 22. April 1947 und 4. Aug. 1948, FHA, NL 1/77. The private comments on Schacht are to be found in FHA, NL 1/14. For the effect on the meeting at the Obersalzberg, see Schmitt to Heß, Nov. 26, 1945, FHA, NL 1/20.

[108] Dodd, *Diary* (June 1, 1934), p. 116. See also the entries for June 13, 15, and 23 (pp. 121–2, 126).

the arrest of the president of Saxon State Bank, Carl Degenhardt, and a number of other Saxon bankers by the Gauleiter of Saxony Martin Mutschmann on the basis of denunciations. Mutschmann rejected Schmitt's plea on the grounds that Schmitt was too new a member of the Party; when Schmitt went to Hitler, the latter handled the issue in a very dilatory manner. Degenhardt and the others were finally released after a month in custody, but the entire episode – along with the other strains to which he was subjected – seem finally to have broken Schmitt down, and he collapsed after giving a speech on June 28. Heß had been with him shortly beforehand in the Tiergarten, and he noted that Schmitt did not want to put on another of his obligatory and increasingly frustrating speaking engagements and actually became so agitated that he turned pale and threw up. Although the basic cause of the collapse was a heart problem, there can be little question that the constant stress to which he had been subject played no small role in his condition.[109]

It was a timely collapse, not only because it paved the way for Schmitt's resignation but also because he thereby missed the grim events of two days later: the Blood Purge of June 30, 1934, when Hitler, Himmler, and Goering moved against the SA and instigated the murder of Röhm and other SA leaders as well as other opponents. Hitler, who paid the recuperating Schmitt a personal visit at his Berlin home on July 2, expressed sympathy with Schmitt's plight but also "stated that he too was suffering in consequence of the attempted putsch launched by some of his closest collaborators."[110] Initially, Schmitt took a six-month leave because Hitler asked him to stay on as economics minister. Schmitt, who was also visited by Dodd, told the Ambassador that he wanted to resign but felt it was his duty to stay on. Dodd, however, had the impression that Schmitt feared being murdered if he resigned.[111] Subsequently, Schmitt was able to persuade Hitler that his health would not permit his continuation in office, and he was able to resign effective January 30, 1935. Hitler parted from Schmitt with a handshake and expressed the hope that they would be friends. He gave Schmitt a standing invitation to come to lunch at the Chancellory without going through official channels.[112] Thus, Schmitt emerged from his high office a *persona grata,* rather than the corpse that Dodd and perhaps Schmitt himself had feared he might soon become. Schacht, who took over as commissarial economics minister, effectively inherited Schmitt's position and its problems. Schmitt had always felt that Schacht was more "robust," and Schacht did survive his tenure as commissarial minister (and, indeed, the Third Reich) in much better physical and psychological condition than Schmitt.

[109] Boelcke, *Deutsche Wirtschaft,* pp. 68–9; Heß to Schmitt, Nov. 8, 1945, FHA, NL 1/20; and Schmitt exposé of June 1, 1945, AM, Spruchkammerakten Dr. Kurt Schmitt, Akten des Generalanklägers, Teil II, pp. 11–12.
[110] Interrogation of Schmitt, July 9, 1947, NA, RG 260, OMGUS, FINAD, 2/58/3.
[111] Dodd, *Diary,* July 4, 1934 (p. 129).
[112] Interrogation of Schmitt, July 9, 1947, NA, RG 260, OMGUS, FINAD, 2/58/3.

As for Schmitt himself, he was overjoyed to leave office and (after recuperating for six months) return to Allianz in February 1935. He could not, of course, resume his old job, but he was well placed to influence the fate of his old concern by his appointment as chairman of the supervisory board of Allianz Leben and deputy chairman of the supervisory board of Allianz. Schmitt had no intention of resting on his laurels but instead anticipated using his positions, as Emil Bebler reported after a visit to Schmitt in Berlin, "to again win decisive influence on the leadership and fate of the 'Allianz' companies. He is thinking of structuring his position in a manner analogous to that of a delegate in Switzerland. He has his own office at 'Allianz.' He does not simply want to visit 'Allianz' daily but as before be exclusively active on behalf of the company."[113]

Nevertheless, Germany was not Switzerland, and Schmitt's position was formally an advisory one. The less lucrative but also less binding connection to Allianz encouraged him to take advantage of invitations to diversify his interests and employ his restored energies. Thus, in 1935, Schmitt took on the chairmanship of the supervisory boards of AEG and Deutsche Continental Gas-Gesellschaft (Dessauer Gas). Significantly, his appointment to both companies was strongly promoted by Hans Fürstenberg and Otto Jeidels of Berliner Handelsgesellschaft, the dominant bank in their supervisory boards. The two companies were in bad odor with the Nazis. The AEG, whose General Director Hermann Bücher was a friend of Schmitt's, was viewed as a "Jewish" company because of the Jewish founder of the company, Emil Rathenau, his son Walther Rathenau (who served as Germany's Foreign Minister before being assassinated by right-wing killers in 1922), and the Jewish General Director Felix Deutsch. The company had experienced considerable financial difficulties in the Weimar period. Bücher was anxious to promote its recovery and improve its position for government contracts. As for Dessauer Gas, it had been rocked by a financial scandal connected with its General Director Bruno Heck, who went to jail and was replaced by Ministerial Director Eduard Schalfejew.[114]

As an ex-minister with good contacts in high places, Schmitt was a political asset not only to Allianz but also to these corporations. His disappointments as economics minister by no means changed his attitude toward working with the regime for the good of the business community. Apparently wishing to maintain contact, he took up Hitler's invitation to lunch three or four times prior to the 1938 Munich Crisis, after which the luncheons ceased. While he found that the luncheons – involving as they did some ten or fifteen people – did not provide much opportunity to talk directly with Hitler about anything serious, his attendance did place him in a special category of persons. Furthermore, his SS connections intensified after he left office. While Schmitt had offered to resign from his honorary SS position when he left office, Himmler would not consider

---

[113] Bebler report, July 11, 1935, SR, Feuer 11.
[114] See his statement of June 1, 1945, FHA, NL 1/73, and Fürstenberg to von Stauß, May 11, 1935, BAB, R 8119 F/P 496, Bl. 213–15.

it; indeed, Himmler promoted Schmitt to the rank of Brigadeführer shortly afterward. About the same time, Schmitt became a member of Himmler's "circle of friends" through Fritz Kranefuss. The model for the Himmler Circle was the so-called Keppler Circle, a group of businessmen organized (by Hitler's economic adviser, Wilhelm Keppler, before the seizure of power) to provide economic ideas to the Party and support the Nazis. Kranefuss was Keppler's nephew and had been his aide, but he now struck out on his own in the service of Himmler with a similar circle. At the behest of Himmler, Kranefuss had issued a number of invitations to Schmitt to attend meetings of the Circle, and eventually Schmitt did show up at one of them. He also took advantage of his connection with Kranefuss to try to stop the SS publication *Das Schwarze Korps* from regularly attacking Allianz. Kranefuss obliged Schmitt, but then suggested that Schmitt (and the companies with which he was involved) should make a contribution to the Circle in return. Schmitt felt it was only reasonable to do so in light of present and potential future services, but he soon discovered that what he thought would be a one-time contribution for 1935 turned out to be an annual request made by the Circle's treasurer, the Cologne banker Kurt von Schröder. Thus, until 1941–1942, Allianz and AEG provided the Himmler Circle with 12,000–15,000 RM yearly; Munich Re gave 6,000 RM a year and Dessauer Gas provided 6,000–8,000 RM a year.[115]

It was not long, however, before the restive Schmitt was able to return to a full-time general directorship in the insurance business, thanks to the retirement of Kisskalt from his post at Munich Re in late 1937. Given the close relationship between Munich Re and Allianz (which was to become even closer), this appointment increased Schmitt's engagement with both concerns. Heß was active in promoting Schmitt's appointment in negotiations with von Finck and Kisskalt, but he also felt that Schmitt should adhere to a standing principle that he himself had introduced: that concern directors and certainly the general director should dedicate themselves exclusively to their jobs and should not hold supervisory posts in other large concerns. Schmitt, however, made his continuation as supervisory board chairman in AEG and Dessauer a precondition of his taking the general directorship of Munich Re; to Heß's irritation, he later entered the supervisory board of Löwenbräu brewery and then joined (and became head of) Süddeutsche Zucker AG, whose headquarters were located in his native Palatinate. When Schmitt tried to palliate Heß by informing the latter of his decision – recounting how many offers he had turned down and assuring Heß that he had a special interest in the sugar business – Heß could not refrain from reiterating his principled objections and calling for a formal abrogation of the principle that Schmitt had broken, even though Heß had no intention of taking advantage of

---

[115] See Interrogation of Schmitt, July 9, 1947, NA, RG 260, OMGUS, FINAD, 2/58/3, which discusses the luncheons with Hitler and these other matters. On Kranefuss, see the references in Turner, *Big Business*, pp. 244, 257, 432 n68; on the Himmler Circle, see Reinhard Vogelsang, *Der Freundeskreis Himmler* (Göttingen, 1972).

it. Schmitt's response was to claim that the principle in question applied only to banks, since it was important for Allianz not to favor one bank over the other. Yet this claim rings rather hollow, and Schmitt's second argument appears more to the point:

My entry into some large enterprises as chairman of the supervisory board had its cause in my special situation as former Reich Economics Minister and my temporary departure from the insurance business. It would have been both personally and objectively false for me to give up this so important and strong position, for there can be no doubt about the fact that my important influence also with respect to Munich Re and Allianz, is not only based on my earlier ministerial position and the personal connections tied to it but above all on my present influence with large enterprises.[116]

Schmitt had certainly lost whatever political ambitions he may have had. It is noteworthy that he turned down the offer of the very important Ambassadorship to Great Britain in 1936, suggested to him by von Ribbentrop and formally offered by Hitler himself, and that he later refused requests by Himmler and Göring that he go back to the Economics Ministry after Schacht was forced to resign in early 1937. In both cases he pleaded health as the reason.[117] What all this suggested, however, is that he felt healthiest doing what he knew how to do best; he intended to capitalize on his political connections and expand his power and influence in the world of business. Whatever his bad experiences and disappointments as one of Nazi Germany's rulers, he was not going to let them interfere with his ambitions.

---

[116] Schmitt to Heß, July 15, 1940; see also Schmitt to Heß, June 26, 1940, and Heß to Schmitt, July 1, 1940, FHA, NL 1/161.
[117] See Interrogation of Schmitt, July 15, 1947, NA, RG 260, OMGUS, FINAD, 2/58/3.

3

Adaptation and Aryanization

THE EXTENT AND LIMITS OF NAZIFICATION AT ALLIANZ

THE ALLIANZ concern fared quite well during the years before the Second World War. The new regime did create certain novel difficulties and demands, and these intensified once the Four-Year Plan for German rearmament was launched in late 1936 and the radicalization of its domestic and foreign policies accelerated. Nevertheless, the necessary adaptations were made with reasonable success. It is useful to remember that the German business community – thanks to war, revolution, inflation, and depression – had ceased to have the experience of engaging in "normal" business activity for a sustained period of time since 1914 and had reached the point where even the appearance of normality was welcome. The Nazi regime had the advantage over its predecessors of being able to stamp out the old rebelliousness of the businessmen through its dictatorial practices. Some of the atmosphere of these years was captured trenchantly in 1936 by a well-known and well-connected Jewish industrialist who had fled to Turkey and there encountered some of the major German industrial leaders with whom he had worked over the years: "The industrial and personal manner of operating of all these gentlemen has hardly changed from what it was before. One hardly speaks of politics, and one always has the feeling that they also actually do not know anything and also do not at all want to know anything."[1]

This was indeed to the point, as leading businessmen concentrated primarily on business. In 1938, Allianz collected 204,599,046 RM in premiums, thus substantially exceeding the 196,226,938 RM collected in 1930 (the previous best year in the concern's history) and showing the extent of recovery that had taken place since its worst year, 1933, when total collected premiums were 145,670,886 RM. The same pattern holds for Allianz Leben, which collected 212,470,280 RM in 1938, thus also exceeding its previous best year of 1930

---

[1] Max von der Porten to Hans Schäffer, June 28, 1936, Schäffer Papers, Leo Baeck Institute (New York), Box II, Folder 2, O-Z, 1936. The industrialists to whom Porten was referring were Albert Vögler, Peter Klöckner, and Wolfgang Reuter.

(when it collected 151,009,019 RM) and demonstrating the substantial recovery from the 128,809,515 RM collected in 1933. There had been improvements in all types of policies provided by Allianz, but the biggest increases (as in 1937) were in automobile insurance, reflecting the regime's emphasis on motorization, and in industrial fire insurance, which was a consequence of the massive increase in economic activity. Whereas in the early years of the regime Allianz had noted diminished profits due to the need to hire and retain redundant employees, by 1938 the pressure to employ more persons had been replaced with an emphasis on rationalization, especially through the introduction of more machinery. The total size of the combined "retinue," as the employees and workers were now archaically called, had been reduced at Allianz and Allianz Leben for the first time in years, from 13,653 to 13,511 (i.e., by 1%). The trends of 1938 continued into 1939, and Allianz had high hopes of massive cost and personnel reduction through the development, in cooperation with Siemens, of a booking and registration machine that would permit two employees to do the work of 200.[2]

Manifestly, it made more economic sense for Allianz (or any other company) to cut costs by rationalization than to lose money by hiring or retaining redundant employees, but both policies were dictated by the regime's political decisions and the manner in which it defined both the economic situation and appropriate responses to it. It was precisely National Socialism's capacity to marshal private initiative and enterprise – and even to encourage forms of inventiveness and creativity useful to the regime – that explains so much of the system's success. The difference made by the regime lay in its exclusive power to define the societal (above all, racial) goals toward which members of the "national community" were to work and, once the regime had stabilized, to determine the imperialist international goals it was bent on realizing.

At the same time, National Socialism also made itself felt on the level of everyday life by rewarding those who employed National Socialist language and ritualistic behavior in the conduct of their daily affairs and by requiring that activities be conducted in such contexts. While true believers had no trouble meeting these requirements, those who were not (and those who were skeptical) were necessarily driven on the path to various degrees of inner corruption by constantly having to behave in the required manner in order to protect and promote their interests. The more they internalized such behavior, the less it mattered in a practical sense whether or not they believed what they were saying and doing. Their political correctness required "correct" language as well, which in turn further reinforced the requisite "correct" political behavior. This was especially evident in the case of Eduard Hilgard, who as factory leader of Allianz and as leader of the Reich Group for

---

[2] Geschäftsbericht 1933, p. 52, and Geschäftsbericht 1938, pp. 7–11, FHA; Kisch, *Fünfzig Jahre Allianz*, p. 134, 165, 208; Aktenvermerk Moesler, 5. Mai 1939, BAB, 80 Ba 2/P 5787.

Insurance became a master of the Lingua Tertii Imperii (Language of the Third Reich).[3]

Hilgard's position as factory leader was made much easier by the end of collective bargaining, which relieved him and his colleagues of a good deal of tedious negotiation and simplified their industrial relations work. As Hilgard noted at the director's meeting of May 1934, the steward's councils had the sole function of advising management; but the final decisions lay with the plant leader and, "in contrast to the old factory council, the steward's council has no independent functions." The new councils were not even allowed to meet without the plant leader being present, although a meeting had to be summoned if at least half the steward's council asked for one.[4]

Nevertheless, this was no simple restoration of pre-1918 authoritarianism in labor relations, since neither simple obedience to employers nor paternalism was deemed sufficient. The DAF and its leaders were serious about promoting a new sense of "community" in enterprises and wanted to assure the workers that the new regime was looking out for the welfare of employees and not simply serving the interests of management. In the case of Allianz, it is difficult to tell how much the measures taken by Allianz reflected its long-standing modern managerial policies and how much they involved pandering to the DAF. Although some of the actions taken by Schmitt in May 1933 with respect to employee bonuses and work creation obviously were politically motivated, there was considerable continuity with past practices in the social policies of the concern. Thus, in May 1934, the concern established a Dr. Schmitt–Dr. Heß Foundation to provide assistance to Allianz insurance salesmen who got into financial difficulty through no fault of their own; the concern also provided substantial sums for its sport clubs, vacation homes, canteens, pensions, and other company welfare programs.[5] It is interesting that Allianz did not make significant mention of its social programs in its business reports until the Propaganda Ministry and the DAF began in early 1937 to pressure insurance companies to say more about their social programs in their business reports. Allianz complied by publishing an extensive social report within its business report for 1936, which came out in June 1937. The report mentioned that the company was exceeding the salaries stated in the existing scales, and it also noted the Christmas bonus amounting to 60% of a month's pay, a special bonus for the end of the fiscal year, the special benefits provided to war-disabled individuals, and the increased vacation time it had introduced. Allianz duly noted improvements made in recent years – its collaboration with the DAF's "Strength through Joy" program (intended to organize and control leisure and recreational activities for Germany's labor force), training programs for youth, and instruction for future mothers – and much stress was placed on how old were many of the social welfare benefits

---

[3] Viktor Klemperer, *LTI. Notizbuch eines Philologen* (Leipzig, 1975).
[4] See Hilgard's remarks at the 23. erweiterte Vorstandssitzung am 4. Mai 1934, FHA, S 17.2/4.
[5] Ibid.

(especially the sports programs, but also the pension benefits) provided by the company.[6]

However, the important thing was to please the Nazis, a rather costly and trying affair. When the concern directors met in October 1935, for example, they seem to have decided to show some resistance to Nazi social demands. Thus, Hilgard, Heß, and Schmitt all agreed that it was impossible to hire more personnel to improve employment. They were also concerned about rising costs because of increasing taxes and what they termed (with quotations inserted by the authors of the meeting's minutes) "voluntary expenditures." The situation had certainly improved since the early days of the regime, when companies were exposed to wild and unpredictable demands of various kinds by the SA, SS, and other Nazi organizations and agencies for what was often tantamount to protection money. Donations to Nazi causes had now been organized and regularized in the Adolf Hitler Donation of the German Business Community. Nazi agencies and organizations were formally barred from solicitations of companies that contributed to the Hitler Donation, and Allianz had actually used its certificate of contribution to the Hitler Donation to refuse further donations to the SS Group East in September 1933.[7] Added to the Hitler donation, however, were various donations made through the private insurance group of the Reich Group for Insurance; there were also "winter help" donations, which all employees made to assist the poor and which were usually collected by payroll deduction.[8] There is good evidence, however, that neither the government nor the enterprises were able to free themselves from pressures for other donations, since the Curatorium for the Adolf Hitler Donation had to send out a circular in May 1937 warning firms against making other donations and thereby finding it difficult or impossible to contribute to the Hitler Donation.[9]

Indeed, the insurance industry made substantial donations to the House of German Art in Munich, and the lead in the support of this pet project of Hitler's was taken by August von Finck, chairman of the supervisory boards of both Allianz and Munich Re. Exactly how fanatical a Nazi von Finck was is a contested issue that will be discussed later in connection with his wartime performance, but he was definitely anxious to cultivate the National Socialists from the very beginning of the regime, if not earlier. His importance in Bavarian business circles, as well as in the banking industry, made him a logical choice to head the Curatorium of the House of German Art. Von Finck was to prove a champion fundraiser, collecting 12 million RM between the laying of the cornerstone of

[6] For the pressure to include social reports in the business reports, see the Sitzung des Beirats der Wirtschaftsgruppe Privatversicherung, 11. März 1937, pp. 16–21, GDV, RS/14. For the first Social Report of Allianz, see Geschäftsbericht 1936, pp. 13–16, FHA.

[7] Sitzung des Allgemeinen Präsidialausschusses des Reichsverbandes der Privatversicherung, 19. Sept. 1933, p. 10, GDV, RS/12.

[8] See the Rundschreiben of May 5, 1933, June 12, 1933, July 21 and 27, 1933, and Sept. 17, 1934, in FHA, S 17.7/61; the Rundschreiben of Sept. 10 and Oct. 3, 1935, in ibid./62.

[9] Rundschreiben vom 8. Mai 1937, ibid./63.

the building in October 1933 and its grand opening in 1937, and then collecting another 8 million RM between 1939 and 1942 for a second structure intended by Hitler for the display of architectural designs (because of the war, it was never built). At Hilgard's instigation, the Reich Association for Private Insurance provided 300,000 RM in 1933. Von Finck sat to the right of Hitler at the banquet to celebrate the laying of the cornerstone and at subsequent gala events connected with the museum, and he frequently accompanied Hitler when the latter visited the museum. In these activities, he worked closely with the Gauleiter of Munich, Adolf Wagner, to whose pet charities and causes he and other prominent businessmen (among them insurance executives of the Allianz concern) gave substantial donations.[10]

Munich Re was especially engaged in the House of German Art events, and used the occasion of the cornerstone laying in 1933 to invite no fewer than 76 foreign business leaders for the purpose of providing them with a more favorable view of the new Germany. They were given choice seats at the theatre and other events, especially those where they could gain a more favorable impression of Hitler than they had received from their newspapers. The Munich Re leadership felt that their guests came away with a more positive view of the Nazi regime. It reported approvingly, for example, of one Swedish insurance executive and city council member who had not only attended the festivities in Munich but had also taken advantage of his stay to tour a concentration camp. He then wrote articles asserting that conditions were not as bad as had been claimed, and he also reported favorably on the trial of the Communists accused of burning down the Reichstag.[11]

Even where one could escape courting the new regime with cash payments – apparently quite difficult in Munich, the "Capital City of the Movement," which was under the sway of the especially rapacious Gauleiter Adolf Wagner – one still courted it with demonstrations of ideological loyalty. The DAF was an especially money-hungry organization (which caused much complaining among employees) whose financial demands Allianz also sought to resist as best it could. At the October 1935 meeting of the directors, Hilgard made it clear that he wanted everyone in the concern (including the leading officials) to join the DAF, but he also declined to make any contributions to the financing of "Strength through Joy" tourist trips because expenditures on Allianz holiday homes "has already reached the limits of the bearable."[12] Hilgard was thus anxious to display his enthusiasm for the DAF but to keep its costs within reason. This policy was demonstrated

---

[10] See the interrogation of August von Finck of Sept. 23 and 25, 1947, NA, RG 260, OMGUS, FINAD, 2/57/4, and the acknowledgment of the Reichsverband donation of Jan. 4, 1934, in GDV, RS/5.

[11] Bericht über die Einladungen ausländischer Gäste zum "Tag der Deutschen Kunst" durch die Münchener Rückversicherungs-Gesellschaft und Auswirkungen dieser Besuche, Okt. 1933, MR, B 3/3.

[12] 26. erweiterte Vorstandssitzung am 29. Okt. 1935, FHA, S 17.2/4.

on February 3, 1936, when 3,000 Berlin employees of Allianz assembled in the Kroll Opera House for a "comradely evening" to celebrate that – "finally," as the *Völkischer Beobachter* remarked[13] – the entire staff of the Allianz concern in Berlin had joined the DAF. DAF leader Robert Ley himself graced the meeting with his presence, and Hilgard's speech on the occasion stressed that the success of bringing everyone into the fold was more than a matter of the concern's re-cruitment effort: "We see in it the united manifestation of the will of our firm to bear witness to the Führer and his work, and believe that there is no better way to celebrate the anniversary of the transfer of power to National Socialism than through the manifestation of this will." Since this was the first time Ley had vis-ited a private insurance company, Hilgard made a special point of reciting all the social benefits and expenditures Allianz provided its employees. Nevertheless – and typical of the speeches Hilgard gave during these years – he also stressed the importance of maintaining the enterprise's profitability and competitiveness. The task of the "true plant leader in the National Socialist State" was not to make himself popular at the expense of the viability of the concern, but rather to serve the community and make social expenditure possible by remaining fi-nancially strong and competitive.[14]

This effort to cast principles of private enterprise into the mold of National Socialist rhetoric and thereby drive home a political point in no way deterred Ley from suggesting that other things counted more than profit and making his own political points. Unlike the Allianz newspaper, the *Völkischer Beobachter* reported Ley as saying that the "Strength through Joy" movement, which he de-fined as a great idealistic venture, depended on supplementary funds of at least 200–300 million RM but had received only a small portion in the past two years and was likely to receive nothing in the current year.[15] The point could hardly have been lost on Hilgard. Ley, caught up as usual in the spell of National So-cialist rhetoric, responded more generally to Hilgard's report by defining two worlds: one, "that of the present, the German, Nordic, productive people who have found their realization in National Socialism, and the other, that of the past, in which all the elements of decomposition express themselves." He went on to argue that it was indeed false to treat idealism and economy as being in opposi-tion since "we National Socialists have demonstrated in three years that there is only one economy, one reality: it is faith and nothing else!" National Socialists were certainly flexible; Hitler himself had declared at the Nuremberg Party rally that the essence of their economic doctrine was to have no doctrine whatever. What counted was performance. This was as true in insurance as anywhere else and, as Ley pointedly remarked: "If the private companies perform more than

---

[13] *Völkischer Beobachter,* 5. Feb. 1936, pp. 1–2. It is interesting to note that while Allianz was men-tioned in the caption showing Ley speaking to the assemblage, the article refers only to "an" insurance company.
[14] *Allianz-Zeitung* 18 (1936), pp. 47–9.
[15] *Völkischer Beobachter,* 5. Feb. 1936, p. 2.

the public, then the private ones are the right way. But if the public companies perform more, then the public ones are the right way. Show what you can do!"[16]

Most of the performance that interested Ley, however, had little to do with profitability or work efficiency but rather with worker mobilization and ideological indoctrination – as well as empire building of the DAF. Employers and workers were expected to devote not only money but also time and energy to the new order. At Allianz, adaptation to donating employer and worker time to regime celebrations, announcements, and events was already evident in March 1934, when the Propaganda Ministry ordered all working places in the Reich to participate in the March 21 Great Fighting Day, slated to open the Labor Struggle that would be introduced by Hitler himself at the construction site of the Autobahn running from Munich to the Austrian border. The management not only set aside an hour of the regular working day to hear Hitler's speech but also instructed the various branches of the concern to purchase the necessary sound equipment and radios, since renting them for such occasions (which could be expected to repeat themselves) would be very expensive.[17] This was indeed a sound and necessary investment, because there were to be numerous occasions when work would cease and both employers and employees would be expected to listen in common to speeches and pronouncements. Even more important were the plant roll calls, organized demonstrations, and celebrations, as well as other events during and outside the working day where attendance was expected. Bayerische Versicherungsbank, for example, held no less than three such events in the spring of 1938 in connection with the annexation of Austria. The demonstration on April 6 before the plebiscite of April 10 (aimed at securing public acclamation of the Anschluß) was attended by everyone in the company, from General Director Arendts to the youngest apprentice. Arendts, who had joined the Party on May 1, 1933, gave an enthusiastic speech, while the DAF representatives emphasized the importance of voting positively in the "election."[18] The Allianz orchestra was regularly featured at the November 9, January 30, May Day, and other National Socialist occasions, both festive and solemn, in Berlin. So were leading directors, not only Hilgard but also his deputy Paul Lux, a member of the Party, and Director Georg König. Choral speaking and singing were an important part of such events.[19] At Allianz Leben in Stuttgart, Directors Arno Eberhard, Hans Parthier, and Alwin Dietz – all identified as members of the Party – assembled on December 31, 1937, to celebrate the past year, look forward to 1938, and listen as plant steward Willi Haag (who had begun his career in insurance back in 1913 and was a veteran Party and SA man who had founded the NSBO cell in Stuttgart in 1931) expressed his appreciation

[16] Ibid.
[17] Rundschreiben der Verwaltungsabteilung an die Zweigniederlassungen, 14. März 1934, FHA, S 17.6/8.
[18] *Allianz-Adler*, May 1938, pp. 17–18, FHA, B 3.6/2.
[19] The *Allianz-Adler* is filled with such reports, e.g., Feb. 1939, pp. 12–13, ibid.

to management for the day's festivities. Eberhard himself, in a speech filled with military imagery, emphasized the need for solidarity between the internal and external service in the company and celebrated Hitler and his works.[20] Such plant roll-call meetings were held every month at Neue Frankfurter, and one had to admit that it was no easy task to make them equally interesting and stimulating. Thus, Neue Frankfurter was praised by the DAF in 1939 for its imaginative approach in proposing a kind of "question and answer game" in which Party comrade and Director Alfred Wiedemann would stand at the microphone (with his fellow comrade and plant steward Finzer and his DAF colleague Simon) and respond to questions about company matters and problems of concern to the "retinue." Although questions from the audience were planned, time proved too short for the projected question-and-answer period to take place. The focus was on bread-and-butter issues, like rumors that there would be no yearly bonus or organizational questions in the automobile insurance sector.[21] Critical comments or thinking that went beyond such matters obviously were not in order. As the Socialist underground reported of one Berlin insurance company: "Any sort of critical conversation is impossible in this company, although the employees in part were very active before the revolution. There is so little collegiality that no one trusts the other a bit, and anyone who at some time said a word too many speedily strives to wipe away the bad impression."[22] What employees and managers actually thought of all the aforementioned roll calls and meetings mattered little. Attendance was compulsory, and the courts ruled that unexcused absence was sufficient reason for immediate dismissal.[23]

The goal of Ley was to create a community of labor with a new identity using the omnipresent Swastika, rituals, and activities at the workplace – the "second home" of employees. The intention was to "educate" employees to accept a new value system. An important element in this process for Ley and the DAF was the creation of uniformed plant brigades of young male workers over 18 who would serve a vanguard function in the factories and plants in carrying out DAF goals. The effort to create such brigades began in 1935 and was viewed with some suspicion by other high Nazi authorities. They viewed (and not without reason) the program and Ley's other bursts of organizational energy as efforts to build up his DAF empire with yet another uniformed troop as well as costly enterprises aimed, like the "Strength through Joy" program, at securing popular support and participation. At the Berlin offices of Allianz, the local DAF leadership in November 1936 recruited some SA men and other volunteers to set about organizing

[20] *Allianz-Adler*, Feb. 1938, pp. 8–9, ibid. On Haag, see ibid., April 1938, p. 18. Eberhard applied for membership in the Party on May 1, 1933, and formally become a member in 1935. See his denazification proceeding before the Spruchkammer in Stuttgart, Oct. 21, 1946, Staatsarchiv Ludwigsburg, E902/20, AZ 17/8068.

[21] *Allianz-Adler*, April 1939, p. 11, FHA, B 3.6/2.

[22] Deutschland-Berichte der Sozialdemokratischer Partei Deutschlands 1937, p. 820.

[23] *Allianz-Adler*, Dec. 1938, p. 8, Feb. 1939, p. 11, FHA, B 3.6/2.

Wilhelm Arendts, general director of Bayerische Versicherungsbank, making a speech to the headquarters staff in Munich, March 13, 1939: "The plant community of the kind we need must be formed out of the good will of each individual member. Each person must be consumed with the consciousness that 'this is my plant'." Note the company brigade behind the lectern.

a brigade. Following a roll-call meeting in March 1937 at which Director Lux announced Allianz's support of the effort and the program was explained to the "retinue," 80 employees joined the 55 that had already signed up. Thanks to further organizing work at various solemn ceremonies – one of them, in celebration of the summer solstice, a public display of the brigade's capacities in marching, choral singing, and choral speaking at a craftsmen's congress in Berlin – the membership rose to 172. This paved the way, "at long last," for the "marching out" of the brigade on Saturday, January 22, 1938, in Berlin-Zehlendorf, where it put on a display of its marching skills and the talents of its mouth-harmonica band. Bayerische Versicherungsbank also had a very active and visible brigade of 144 men, which included its own marching band and a conductor who produced a special march, "Comrades Are We." The *Allianz-Adler*,[24] a DAF newspaper that first appeared in January 1937 intending to report on activities of "plant communities" throughout the Allianz concern (but totally separate from the concern's *Allianz-Zeitung*), made no bones about the military character of the brigade.

---

[24] The *Allianz-Adler* is to be found in FHA, B 3.6/2–3.

In contrast to other efforts to create special bodies of workers like the guilds, the Christian organizations, and the political trade unions, the brigades would be successful precisely because they were uniformed. Military forms were most "natural" for Germans, and the brigade was "the visible expression of the activists marching together, the disciplined Socialist front in the plants." On the one hand, the brigades were intended to replace the NSBO and assume its previous functions plus new ones. On the other hand, they were part of an effort by Ley to link up with the SA, which had been cast into the shadows after the Röhm purge. Thus, SA men played an important role in organizing the brigade in Allianz's Berlin offices and, in Stuttgart, the Allianz brigade joined with other brigades and the local SA to celebrate January 30, 1938, by inducting 500 persons (presumably from the brigades) into the SA. While the more grandiose hopes Ley placed in the brigades were to be disappointed as they remained restricted to the plant level, they were nevertheless a prominent presence in Allianz's self-presentations during these years and seem to have attracted some of the younger male employees.[25]

Furthermore, the brigades were expected to play a leading role in connection with other programs launched by Ley that kept Allianz managers and employees busy during these years: the Performance Competition of German Factories, the Reich Skills Competition, and various DAF prizes culminating in being designated an NS Model Factory. One of Ley's major goals was to have the DAF take over vocational training; one of his chief inspirations was Professor Karl Arnhold, who had organized the German Institute for Technical Labor Training (Dinta) during the Weimar Republic and was a major proponent of the anti–trade union plant community concept favored by many industrialists. Arnhold strongly supported a more militaristic organization of the labor force and favored a combination of technical and ideological training – just the sort of thing Ley believed. The Dinta, along with Arnhold (who joined the Party), was absorbed into the DAF, and it was Arnhold who cooked up the various individual skills competitions, a sort of Olympics for works, and competition among plants for recognition as models of National Socialist organization. These programs were an important accompaniment to the Four-Year Plan launched in 1936, but they also provided the DAF with a mechanism by which to investigate and evaluate practically every aspect of the competing enterprises: productivity; relations between employers and employed; social policies and welfare measures; and, of course, the ideological disposition of management and "retinue."[26] Promoted with a vast amount of advertising, it was impossible for a concern so prominent as Allianz not to take part, although business and various government ministries and agencies worked to temper some of the more excessive ambitions of Ley in

---

[25] On the brigades, see Smelser, *Robert Ley,* pp. 204–7, and *Allianz-Adler,* April 1938, pp. 11–13, FHA, B 3.6/2. For the Bavarian brigade, see the publication celebrating the new building of the Bayerische Versicherungsbank, "Dies Haus ist Euer Haus! Unser Betriebsjahr 1938," pp. 52–3, FHA B 3.6/4.

[26] Smelser, *Robert Ley,* pp. 191–7.

connection with these programs. Allianz, with its long-standing emphasis on corporate welfare programs, sports, good working conditions, vacation homes, pensions, and the like, had a good foundation for scoring well in such competition. It is not impossible that even Heß, otherwise cold to National Socialist ideology, may have respected some of Arnhold's ideas, and it is significant that a picture of Heß standing alongside Arnhold – the latter in Party uniform with a Swastika armband – was chosen for the volume of photos accompanying the Allianz fiftieth anniversary volume. It most certainly would not have appeared without Heß's approval.[27]

Allianz's participation in these competitions, which began in 1937, was politically important, especially given its conflicts with the DAF and the publicly chartered insurance companies. Thus, considerable notice was taken of the number of Allianz personnel throughout Germany who competed with varying degrees of success in the Reich Skills Competition.[28] In 1939, Allianz boasted two victors at the Reich level, fourteen at the Gau (regional) level, and a substantial number at the district level. Especially important, however, was the success of the various branches of Allianz in the Performance Competition of German Factories. In 1939, seven Allianz branches or offices qualified for the lowest level of prize, the Gau Diploma for outstanding performance, while another eight received honorary mention and yet another for its support of the "Strength through Joy" and its training program. In 1941, the Frankfurt branch and Bayerische Versicherungsbank, as well as branches or offices in Danzig, Halle, Cologne, and Nuremberg, had received the Gau Diploma three times, while the Augsburg office was a four-time winner.[29]

The competition for these diplomas was keen, and they were not given without a thorough investigation of conditions at the branch's offices. Happily, the reports on the Cologne branch survived; they provide an interesting picture of conditions at the branch and also at Allianz more generally. Although the concern was deconcentrated, many of the basic policies toward labor were uniform throughout the company. The Cologne branch did have the advantage of one of the most modern buildings in the Rhineland; it had been opened in 1933 and by 1941 was considered by the DAF to be a serious candidate for the status of a Model Plant. It employed 640 persons (200 of them women) and its plant leader was Director Otto Würz, who was a Party member. Indeed, the Cologne branch had 115 Party members in its ranks, along with 19 members of the Hitler Youth and 23 members of the League of German Girls. DAF membership was required for employment, and the brigade consisted of 22 men. Hence the Cologne branch was politically a very correct place, but it was also praised for being a good place to work. Special provision was made for female employees, especially if they

[27] See *Allianz-Zeitung*, 1937, p. 225, and *50 Jahre Allianz. Eine Chronik in Bildern* (Berlin, 1940), p. 68.
[28] *Allianz-Adler*, April 1938, p. 10, May 1938, pp. 12–13, FHA, B 3.6/2.
[29] Geschäftsbericht 1940, p. 14, FHA, and *Allianz-Adler*, May–June 1941, p. 1, FHA, B 3.6/2.

New building of Allianz branch in Cologne on Kaiser-Wilhelm-Ring 31, opened May 1933.

became pregnant. The apprentice training program met DAF standards, and young workers were given an opportunity for both schooling and sports within working hours. The pay and bonus arrangements were in conformity with the rest of the concern, and employees had access to the five vacation homes maintained by the company. The DAF officials were especially impressed with the modern, well-lit, clean, and comfortable work facilities, the new and modern canteen used by 90% of the staff, the spaces allocated for sports, the growing library and its regular use by the "retinue," the attention given to health, the facilities for rest and relaxation, the vacation program, and the participation in "Strength through Joy" programs. Labor relations were deemed excellent. It was, in other words, precisely the sort of workplace that the DAF sought to promote, and one has the sense that the Cologne branch – like Allianz itself – found it relatively easy to adapt many of the practices and policies it had already been pursuing to the special demands of the DAF; they were simply poured into a National Socialist mold, and this apparently was not a difficult task.[30]

How deep nazification went is a more difficult – indeed, impossible – question to answer, and undoubtedly the degrees of commitment to the regime varied

[30] For the reports by and on the Cologne branch of 1938 and 1941, see BAB, NS 5 IV/260, Bl. 1–19.

from individual to individual and also at different times between 1933 and 1945. If Cologne were to be taken as a measure then the number of Party members among employees was significant, but there is no evidence that it was typical in this regard. Certainly there were enough genuine National Socialists employed at Allianz to ensure that the proper "spirit" and "attitude" were maintained by the mass of their colleagues. It is reasonable to suppose that, as in the case of Hilgard, Party membership among the directors was often opportunistic and involved little personal conviction. Among the so-called plant leaders (e.g., Hilgard, Lux, Arendts, and Würz) it was a virtual requirement. After the war, Arendts, who had been a member of the Bavarian People's Party and was a practicing Catholic, admitted that he had joined the Party in 1933 partially in the hope that it would take an evolutionary path but also because it appeared advisable as the general director of a major enterprise in the "Capital City of the Movement." To all external appearances, Arendts seemed to have transformed himself into a devoted National Socialist, was a member of several Nazi organizations in addition to the Party, and was known to deliver National Socialist speeches on public occasions. Indeed, the Bavarian Minister of Justice in 1933–1934 (and later head of the Generalgouvernement in Poland), Hans Frank, had asked Arendts to be a founding member and treasurer of the Academy for German Law in 1933, just as he had asked Kisskalt to serve as head of the Academy's committee on shareholder law and von Finck to serve as chairman of the committee on banks and stock exchanges. Arendts was not a jurist and was obviously chosen for his business connections to help Frank in his fundraising. At the same time, however, Arendts developed something of a reputation for protecting political opponents of Nazism and even Jews, half-Jews, and persons related to Jews. He was plagued by a particularly fanatical Nazi cell, which actually complained to (Gauleiter of Munich) Adolf Wagner in late 1938 or 1939 that Arendts and his family were devout Catholics with Jewish relations who protected political undesirables while sending Party loyalists in management to other posts. They lamented the protection that he seemed to enjoy from Hans Frank. As later developments were to show, there were good reasons to be suspicious of Arendt's devotion to National Socialism, but Arendts was stunningly successful in appearing "brown on the outside" while remaining "black on the inside."[31]

Heß's situation was simpler by comparison. Although general director, he had deliberately refused the plant leadership (which he left to Hilgard and Lux)

---

[31] It was a measure of Arendts's success that Frank chose to appoint him an honorary member of the economic law group of the NS Lawyer's League. See Lasch to Mönckmeier, June 5, 1939, in Arendts's Party file, BAB, ehem. BDC, PK Wilhelm Arendts (*6.2.1883). A full investigation of Arendts's political performance was undertaken after the war, and the undated attack against him by the Nazi cell in his company, as well as the defense of his behavior by the factory council after the war and by others protected by him, can be found in AM, Spruchkammerakten Wilhelm Arendts. On the appointments of Kisskalt and von Finck, see the interrogation of von Finck of Sept. 25, 1947, in NA, RG 260, OMGUS, FINAD, 2/57/4.

so as to continue avoiding Party membership. While he could not manage to escape membership in the DAF, which Allianz managers and employees joined as a body, he managed never to attend a roll call, which certainly must have been noticed. Indeed, he deliberately abstained from leading the Allianz directors and employees to the May Day 1934 celebration at the Tempelhof Airport, as had been demanded of the concern heads in Berlin. He studiously limited his speeches to company events, where he was often surrounded by Swastikas but did little or nothing to identify himself with them. He apparently enjoyed an authority and popularity, even among the National Socialists at Allianz, that protected his exposed position and enabled him to let Schmitt, Hilgard, and others do the saluting, parading, singing, and delivering of pandering speeches.[32]

Others could not always afford these luxuries, especially once they had made the decision to join the Party and wanted to move forward with their careers. One could feel belated distaste but not act upon it. This was illustrated by Hans Goudefroy, who was one day to be Heß's successor. Goudefroy, who came of modest circumstances and had struggled considerably to secure his legal education, joined the Party on May 1, 1933, primarily because he was planning to become a judge at the time and knew he would not be accepted otherwise. He later claimed he felt comfortable in his decision because Hitler had been appointed by Hindenburg and was committed to fighting unemployment. He rapidly became disaffected, however, owing to Party interference in judicial matters. He decided to accept a job with the legal division of Allianz in 1934 and, once hired permanently, gave up his plans for a judicial career. He soon became head of the legal division and a member of the board of directors in 1938. Heß had taken early notice of Goudefroy and found him to be talented, dedicated, and personable, which undoubtedly played no small role in Goudefroy's rapid rise. Heß seems to have been especially impressed with Goudefroy's willingness to buck Party pressures in legal issues affecting the concern. Thus, when the Party tried to collect the accident insurance of Gregor Strasser and SA-Obergruppenführer Karl Ernst (two victims of the Röhm purge) in the name of their survivors, Goudefroy refused on the grounds that they were subjects of an execution, not an accident. He did so despite warnings that as a member he stood under the jurisdiction of the Party and of the Nazi Lawyer's Organization as well. In other cases he also resisted pressures from high Party officials. Apparently, Goudefroy was so incensed by Nazi attitudes toward the law that he wanted to resign from the Party in 1935, but Heß, who feared that Goudefroy would also announce his reasons, warned him that such a step would be damaging to both himself and the concern. As a result, Goudefroy remained in the Party but was to have difficulties during the war with the Gestapo and other Nazi agencies because of his protection of politically suspect persons and employees with Jewish spouses – although, as

---

[32] See Heß's exposé, "Meine politische Einstellung, in Sondernheit [sic] zum Nationalsozialismus," Aug. 5, 1945, FHA S 17.13/165, and his Fragebogen of Feb. 2, 1946, FHA, NL 3/6.

demonstrated in Chapter 5, he was not always as fastidious about legal niceties as was later claimed.[33]

It is important to recognize that Goudefroy's efforts were not made at the expense of Allianz's otherwise quite satisfactory relations with the Party and the State. In fact, Allianz cultivated its relations with the Party, which proved to be a source of considerable business from early on in the regime. Despite the aggravation caused by Schwede-Coburg, Hans Goebbels, and those of their cronies desiring to socialize the insurance business, the reality was that 70% of the Party's insurance business was done with the private companies, 25% with the publicly chartered societies, and 5% with the DAF companies. Allianz received the lion's share of this business, which consisted mainly of group insurance – that is, an insurance contract made directly with an organization or company that entitled its members to participate in an insurance plan involving fixed rates and benefits. The Allianz contract providing life and burial insurance with the National Socialist Teachers' League brought in 2.5–3 million RM in premiums annually between 1934 and 1945. A similar important group insurance policy was with the Reich Lawyers' League, which paid 2 million RM in annual premiums during the same period. Allianz also provided accident insurance for the National Socialist Women's Organization between 1936 and 1945. This policy, half of which was later divided with the publicly chartered societies, brought in 300,000 RM per year, and Allianz remained the leader of the consortium. Allianz provided insurance for the National Socialist organization for the care of war victims. Although other major private insurers (e.g., Agrippina and Gerling) also had significant contracts with Party organizations, Allianz normally received preference whenever some policy had to be concluded quickly; it also had some lucrative small contracts with the Party that brought in 80,000–120,000 RM per year between 1936 and 1945. It insured the Party congresses, for example, and the machines in Party buildings. This, in any case, was the information provided by Georg Amend (head of the NSDAP insurance office and, after October 1939, president of the RAA) at his interrogations after the war. While Amend was no great friend of the private insurers and may have been attempting to place them in as bad a light as possible, Allianz's group insurance policies with at least some of the organizations mentioned can be verified from other sources. As early as August 1933, for example, Allianz sent an obviously celebratory circular to its branches informing them about its recent contracts with "national organizations." Topping the list was the collective life insurance policy developed with the National Socialist Reich Association of German War Victims, headed by Hans Oberlindober, which had at least 800,000 members. Allianz did have to share some, with 15% of this business going to Deutscher Ring and another 15% to Karlsruher Leben, but then the latter company was in

---

[33] The most important information on Goudefroy is in his denazification file, Staatsarchiv Hamburg, 221-11/F 17350. See especially the letters of Hans Heß of Aug. 6, 1945, and Sept. 10, 1946, as well as Goudefroy's own statement of Nov. 10, 1945.

the Allianz group. Similarly, the circular noted the conclusion of various policies with the Fraternal League of German Police Officials in Berlin, which will be discussed shortly.[34]

Indeed, there can be no question that the number and significance of group policies increased dramatically in 1933 and then between 1933 and 1938. Thus, the number of new insurance certificates increased from 180,000 in 1932 to 1,572,000 in 1933; the number of new certificates was 728,000 in 1934 and 583,000 in 1935. In 1933 there was an actual decline in large life policies (concluded with individuals in the amount of 2,000 RM or more with a yearly premium) and an increase in small policies (less than 2,000 RM and based on a monthly premium) of 43,000, and increases in such individual policies amounted to 51,751 for 1934 and 62,343 for 1935. Therefore, the increase in insurance certificates was obviously a result of (and was, in fact, attributed to) group policies in the Allianz business reports. These group policies were calculated according to the number of "risks" – that is, persons certified to be entitled to benefits under the policies – and the total number of such persons increased from 308,039 at the end of 1932 to 2,739,697 at the end of 1938. Although group policies were also contracted with industrial enterprises, those with National Socialist organizations involved a few hundred thousand persons and thus were quite significant.[35]

According to Amend, Schmitt had played an important role in negotiating these contracts. Amend first met Schmitt in 1933 at the offices of his father-in-law (NSDAP treasurer Franz Xaver Schwarz), who told Amend to favor Allianz in the Party's insurance business. This led to frequent meetings between Schmitt and Amend about such contracts. Manifestly, Schmitt's early support of and ties to the Party had proven very useful indeed. Amend also claimed that Schmitt had procured the National Socialist Lawyers' League contract through connections with Hans Frank, who headed the organization. Schmitt, in his postwar interrogations, could not remember any significant contact with Frank and suggested that General Director Arendts was the more likely contact with Frank.[36] This is quite plausible given the appointment of Arendts as treasurer of the Academy for German Law when it was founded in June 1933. Needless to say, lower-placed persons could also serve Allianz well in gaining contracts. Thus, Amend remembered that one of the general agents in Frankfurt or Wiesbaden had good connections with Oberlindober, head of the National Socialist organization of war victims.

Nevertheless, Amend certainly was on target when he claimed that Schmitt's connections with Reich Master of the Forests and Reich Master of the Hunt

[34] Interrogation of Georg Amend, July 2, 1947, NA, RG 260, OMGUS, FINAD, 2/56/2. The Allianz contracts with the NS-Lehrerbund and the NS-Rechtswahrerbund are mentioned in a letter from the RAA to the RWM of July 10, 1936, SM, 1458/1/172/Bl. 52–4. On the contracts with the NS-Kriegsopferversorgung, which dated from Dec. 13, 1933, see BAK, B280/1519. For the circular of August 15, 1933, see FHA, AZ 5.1/3.

[35] *Allianz Leben*, Geschäftsberichte, 1932–1935, FHA; Kisch, *Fünfzig Jahre Allianz*, p. 163.

[36] Interrogation of Kurt Schmitt, July 15, 1947, NA, RG 260, OMGUS, FINAD, 2/58/3.

Hermann Göring played no small role in securing an Allianz monopoly, worth some half million RM a year, on the obligatory hunting liability insurance introduced at the turn of 1936–1937. Göring was unhappy about the competition among private insurance companies for this business, the high rates being charged, and the complexities involved in the settlement of liability issues by a variety of companies. His solution was to create a new publicly chartered liability corporation solely for hunters that would impose a single premium with the granting of licenses. The Economics Ministry was unhappy with this solution and engaged Schmitt to persuade Göring to find an alternative. Schmitt, in a series of memoranda and negotiations, argued that it was a mistake to deprive the private insurance industry of income in this manner, given its importance to the financing of the recently launched Four-Year Plan. Most importantly, however, Schmitt warned that the creation of a new organization to regulate complicated problems – where the private companies already had experience – would be costly and cumbersome. Göring apparently found these arguments persuasive, but only on condition that one concern (namely, Allianz) assume full responsibility for the regulatory activity and establish the necessary apparatus at its headquarters. This put Schmitt in a pleasant but awkward position, since there were complaints from other firms and insurance agents that they were being cut out, but ultimately Schmitt was able to persuade the Association of Private Accident and Liability Insurers that the alternative was to have the private insurance business cut out altogether; Schmitt promised the continuation of existing contracts on the basis of a uniform premium in return for its administrative services. It is doubtful that everyone was satisfied but in the end there was considerable gratitude to Schmitt for using his connections and for the power and organization of Allianz's newly created "Obligatory Hunting Liability Insurance Bureau for German Hunters" to serve the interests of the private insurance business.[37]

Schmitt also took a direct role in negotiating yet another group policy of great importance to the National Socialist leadership – namely, the Fraternal League of German Police Officials. The organization had been founded after the dissolution of the old police unions in 1933. Göring, as Minister President of Prussia, had decided to purge rather than disband the Prussian police, once considered a strong support of the vanished Republic, and he and Police General Kurt Daluege were anxious to instill a National Socialist spirit and a sense of comradeship in the police force. The Fraternal League was viewed as the best mechanism for doing so, and the provision of low-cost insurance and other social benefits was considered an important instrument in the service of this cause. Allianz was

---

[37] The lengthy negotiations are to be found in SM, 1458/1/263. See especially Schmitt's memos and notes to Göring of Dec. 11 and 18, 1936 (Bl. 35–44) and Göring to Schmitt, Jan. 1, 1937. See also the documents in BAK, B 280/12352. See also the Sitzungsbericht über die ordentliche Hauptversammlung des Reichsverbandes der Privatversicherung am 12. März 1937, GDV, 205-3, pp. 31–2, and the Allianz Rundschreiben of 9. März 1937, FHA, AZ 7.1/9.

ideally positioned for this purpose, not only because of the personal connections of its leaders but also because it was such a strong concern. In August of 1933, the Fraternal League concluded five-year group insurance policies with Allianz and Allianz Leben amounting to 300 million RM in coverage. The police and their wives were covered under these policies for death, accident, theft, fire, and liability at a particularly low single rate for the combined policy. Calculation of the life insurance component was based on term insurance rather than the higher costs entailed in capital coverage insurance. The basic obligatory insurance was 600 RM for men and 400 RM for wives and widows, but members had the option of taking out multiple insurance up to three times the basic amount. The terms of the police group insurance had been personally negotiated with Schmitt, who (as one of the officials of the Fraternal League reported) "as general director in the Allianz concern had a great interest in the conclusion of an insurance agreement for the benefit of the police." Indeed, it was anticipated that Schmitt would retain an interest in continuation of the contract.[38]

However, the contract with the Fraternal League faced two serious challenges. The first came in 1934, when it seemed that Interior Minister Frick wished to integrate the police into the Civil Service League, which would have led to the dissolution of the Fraternal League and the raising of insurance rates for the policy by 100%. This caused considerable unrest among the police because of the popularity of the Fraternal League and its insurance program, but the danger was averted by the insistence of Daluege that police retain their independence and their organizations and that all state police forces be included in the group insurance agreement. At the end of 1936, Himmler (who had taken charge of the police throughout Germany) and Daluege ordered that the uniformed Order Police join the Fraternal League in the new year. This, of course, added substantially to the number of those falling under the group insurance policy.[39]

The second challenge to the group contract of the Fraternal League came from the RAA, which disapproved of term policies as being risky because members of the group insurance inevitably included older persons with each renewal of the contract; the RAA also considered these policies a form of unfair competition. Thus, in 1934 it required special RAA permission for the renewal of such policies and also issued guidelines that would have required a substantial increase

[38] Polizeioberst Dillenburger an Admiral von Levetzow, 14. Feb. 1934, AZLB, Akte "Kameradschaftsbund Deutscher Polizeibeamten, 187/1955, Originalvertrag, Ordner I." The materials in these files as well as in SM 1458/1/72 provide a detailed picture of the evolution, problems, and character of this group contract.

[39] In addition to the letter of Dillenburger of Feb. 14, 1934 (cited previously), and the various testimonials from police organizations connected with it, see also the projected draft by the Minister of the Interior attempting to integrate police and civil servants and the Aktennotiz of Sept. 5, 1934, in which Daluege insisted that the police retain their Fraternal League. On the Order Police, see Fraternal League to Allianz Leben, Dec. 21, 1936, with copy of Daluege's order to the Order Police of Dec. 19, 1936, ibid.

of premiums. This regulation was a severe threat to the Fraternal League contract, which was to expire in 1938. It was an important and lucrative contract, and its continuation meant a great deal both to the Fraternal League and Allianz. The number of persons covered under the basic policy, which had been 187,219 in 1933, had risen to 252,869 in 1936 – 128,590 men, 115,045 women, and 9,234 widows. The number of those who had taken out multiple insurance had increased by 37,406, from 111,889 in 1933 to 149,295 in 1936. The combined premiums had been 1.5 million RM in 1933 and were 3.6 million RM in 1936. In the latter year, 3.1 million RM had been paid in death benefits. Saving the contract, therefore, was worth the effort put into it.[40]

The Allianz Leben directors Schloeßmann and Werner Krause joined forces with Major Bäcker of the Fraternal League as early as August 1936 to ward off this danger. Allianz was planning to approach the RWM about the problem, and Bäcker intended to send a memorandum to Daluege and Himmler stressing the unrest that would be caused by a change of the contract. Bäcker thought it important that Allianz hold back with its inquiries at the RWM and promised confidentially to supply Allianz with his own petition, with the purpose of having Schmitt contact Himmler and stress the importance of the contract to the SS leader. This collusion between Allianz and the Fraternal League proved quite effective and went so far as to involve collaboration in reviewing and revising the draft of Himmler's letter to the RWM of February 1, 1937. Allianz, for example, advised providing less problematic detail than that contained in the original draft. In any case, Himmler stood behind the arguments of Allianz and the Fraternal League that the death rates among the police were very low while recruitment of younger men was increasing. At the same time, Himmler noted that the police could not afford long-term policy premiums. Himmler considered it essential for economic reasons and for reasons of State that the policies be renewed, and he asked that the RAA guidelines not be imposed in this instance. Indeed, Party authorities were pointing out to the RAA just at this time (in the spring of 1938), in connection with other insurance contracts, that the RAA was not always sufficiently sensitive to "National Socialist needs"; they received assurances from Ministerial Director Kurt Lange that the RAA had every intention of basing its decision on National Socialist principles. Insofar as the Fraternal League contract was concerned, the RAA informed Allianz Leben on April 21, 1937 that, "in view of the reasons of State put forward by the Reich SS leader and chief of the German police," it accepted the extension of the contract between Allianz and the Fraternal League. The history of the group insurance of the Fraternal League and its prolongation well illustrates the business relations between Allianz and the regime and the importance of Schmitt's contacts with the SS.[41]

---

[40] See the exposé by Krause of Feb. 23, 1937, ibid.
[41] Aktennote Besprechung vom 6. Aug. 1936, correspondence about drafts of the Himmler letter, Oct. 1–5, 1936; RAA an Allianz, 21. April 1937, ibid. Also, see Köhler to Lange, May 6, 1938,

ALLIANZ, ITS JEWISH EMPLOYEES, AND ARYANIZATION

An important test of Allianz's adaptation to National Socialism was, of course, the "Jewish question" as it evolved between 1933 and 1939. The problems of Allianz and its Jewish customers will be examined in Chapters 4 and 5; Allianz's treatment of its Jewish employees and its role in Aryanization of Jewish property present distinct problems that are the subject of this section.

Allianz's treatment of its Jewish employees, the full number of which is indeterminable, suggests that Schmitt's notion of there being no Jewish question in the economy seems to have been shared by the top leadership of the concern and maintained for as long as possible. It was a losing battle, but it was fought with some honor and attention to elementary decency. This was especially true with respect to the treatment of the two Jewish directors in the concern, James Freudenburg (director of the Frankfurt branch) and Maximilian Eichbaum (director of the Magdeburg branch). Having already departed from the board of Neue Frankfurter at the end of 1933, Freudenburg apparently found the situation at the Frankfurt branch, where he remained as director, so uncomfortable that he decided to resign at the end of 1934, a year before his contract formally ran out. Freudenburg did so while reserving his contractual rights, and Allianz chose to handle his entitlements unbureaucratically and give him his full salary for 1935 so that his pension would then start in 1936. Given the circumstances, the parting went beyond decency and politeness. Thus, the letter accepting his resignation (because of the "existing circumstances"), signed by Heß and Koenig, concluded:

We gladly use this opportunity to give you our honest and heartfelt thanks for the services which you have performed in so outstanding a measure for our corporation in your long years of activity. Your name will remain unforgotten in our corporation. Throughout the entire period, we have not only seen in you the prudent and experienced head of our branches in Stuttgart and Frankfurt a.M.; we have above all valued you as a person and are bound to you through bonds of friendship well beyond the confines of business relations. It is therefore our honest wish that, after your official departure from the service of our corporation, you will remain not only professionally but also personally associated with us.[42]

Freudenburg, obviously touched by the letter, responded gratefully, pointing out that "I leave your service with a heavy heart. I have been an Allianz man with my entire soul and will remain one to the end of my life."[43] Needless to say, Freudenburg had not departed from Allianz voluntarily.

and Lange's reply of May 19, 1938, SM, 1458/1/72, Bl. 275–6; on the police insurance question, see Himmler to RWM, Feb. 1 1937, ibid., Bl. 151–5, and Allianz's exposé concerning the policies of Feb. 27, 1937, ibid., Bl. 77–160.

42 Allianz an Direktor Freudenburg, 3. Dez. 1934, FHA, B 2.4.5/134.

43 Freudenburg an den Vorstand der Allianz (z.Hd. Herrn Dr. Heß), 11. Dez. 1934, Ibid.

Freudenburg's life ended at the age of 68 in Auschwitz, from whence, on January 10, 1944, he was reported dead of "debilitas corporis et senilis enteritis acuta,"[44] the cynical terminology used to cover up what most certainly was death either by gassing or caused by the general conditions and mistreatment at Auschwitz. As his wife Erika (who was not Jewish) told an Allianz official working at the pension office in Frankfurt – who had asked after her husband in June 1943 – Freudenburg had been summoned to the Gestapo and had not returned, but the Gestapo refused to tell her his whereabouts. After the news of his death, she collected her widow's pension. While he was still alive they had received his regular pension, although he had assigned it to her for safety's sake in 1940. Apparently, Freudenburg had realized the advisability of such security even though the top executives at Allianz had faithfully resisted pressures to cease paying or curtail such pensions – following a ruling by the Reich Court of July 12, 1939, that it was "unfair" for an employer to pay pensions to persons dismissed for racial reasons after the exclusion of Jews from economic life ordered on November 12, 1938. The DAF sought to interpret the ruling as being relevant also to persons who had been dismissed or had resigned for such reasons before November 12, 1938, and Director Lux in Berlin was repeatedly asked by the plant committee at the head office whether the concern should not terminate pension payments to Jewish pensioners. Lux, however, took the position that the few Jewish pensioners in question, among them Freudenburg, had paid into the fund and thus had a claim. As he informed the man who was Freudenburg's successor in Frankfurt, General Director Alfred Wiedemann, the legal obligation to pensioners who had paid into such funds was not obliterated by their having to retire because of race, and he wanted Wiedemann to be aware of this position should the question of Freudenburg's pension come up.[45] This was, in any case, the position Wiedemann took in dealing with the DAF leadership in Frankfurt. The Allianz management, therefore, was intent to watch over Freudenburg's pension interests even if he chose to take some measures of his own to protect them.

The fate of Director Eichbaum was a much happier one than that of Freudenburg, and his treatment also speaks well for the Allianz leadership – and especially for General Director Heß and Kurt Schmitt. As Eichbaum pointed out in 1947 in a very moving letter to Heß, with whom he apparently had a strong personal friendship, it was largely because of Heß's protection that he was able to remain head of the Magdeburg office until the fall of 1935. When Eichbaum's continuation became untenable, Heß and his wife personally travelled to Magdeburg to help organize his future. He initially worked at the head office in Berlin, and his name came up both before and after his departure for Berlin in connection with possible attempts to gain control of Allgemeine Versicherungs-Gesellschaft Phönix (Elementar-Phönix) in Austria. This was the non–life insurance part of

---

[44] Reichsvereinigung der Juden in Deutschland an Erika Freudenburg, 22. Jan. 1944, ibid.
[45] Lux to Wiedemann, Oct. 5, 1939, ibid. The court judgments and interpretations are also contained in this file.

James Freudenburg and his wife Erika in Marienbad, April 31, 1929.

the Phönix insurance company in Austria, which was already in visible financial difficulty, and Kisskalt of Munich Re apparently looked to Allianz to take over the non–life insurance portions of the company. In a discussion with Heß, Hilgard, and Schloeßmann, the idea was rejected by Allianz leaders because of the anticipated difficulties with Lebensversicherungs-Gesellschaft Phönix (Phönix Life) and the unlikelihood that the German government would allow use of foreign exchange for this purpose. As Kisskalt noted, however, "this is regrettable for one reason, namely because Allianz in the person of Herr Eichbaum would without doubt have at hand an outstandingly suitable head of Phönix, since Herr Eichbaum is having increasingly difficulties with his work in Magdeburg."[46] Eichbaum, like Freudenburg, was very much an "Allianz man" and was not prepared to depart Germany unless he could somehow remain part of the concern. The problem was solved in 1937 when he was sent to represent Allianz at the South African Liberal Insurance Company, which Allianz had acquired in 1932. Most striking, however, is Eichbaum's praise for Heß's open expressions

[46] Aktennote, 1. Juni 1935, MR, A 2.13/46.

of friendship and respect, which – as Eichbaum knew altogether too well from the behavior of others – demonstrated a rare courage:

For as long as we were in Germany, we were able to openly visit with you and you with us, and indeed more than before. Also on the professional public scene, for example at the anniversary of the Bayerische [Lebensversicherungsbank] and the end of fiscal year conference in Munich in May 1935, you insisted on my participation and praised me publicly – a risky thing to do![47]

In contrast to Freudenburg, who was nearing retirement age, Eichbaum could continue to be of service to the concern abroad. This was an increasingly tricky business. Eichbaum was sent to South Africa thanks to an agreement between Kurt Schmitt and Economics Minister Schacht, and this was viewed as useful in promoting Germany's colonial ambitions. The attitude toward the employment of Jews abroad toughened up under Schacht's successor, Funk, in part because of the radicalization of policies toward the Jews and in part because of the tightening of foreign exchange controls. Thus, in September 1938, the RWM required that continued employment of Jews abroad (and payment to them) be subjected to careful scrutiny and agreement on the part of the relevant agencies and that companies make every effort to terminate all contracts with Jews as rapidly as possible.[48] The employment of Eichbaum, ostensibly in a special category, nevertheless produced minor and major problems. Among the former was that Schmitt was hounded in 1939 by a disgruntled insurance regulator and his wife, who charged that the concern was showing an insufficient understanding of the Jewish "intriguing" by sending Jews like Eichbaum as representatives to South Africa and paying them "fantastic settlements."[49] Much more significant, however, was that the RWM began raising questions about the status of South African Liberal and whether it was bringing in foreign exchange. The underlying reason for this concern was pressure from the Party in connection with Eichbaum, and officials at the ministry privately told Allianz executives they did not think Eichbaum could be retained. Nevertheless, Eichbaum continued on actively – indeed, too actively for some of his South African colleagues, who were not free of anti-Semitism, either – and this led to pleas by the Berlin directors that Eichbaum stay in the background as much as possible. While Eichbaum was greatly admired for his competence by Schmitt and Heß, his forceful personality seemed to have irritated others, and this made him something of a target.[50] As Uexküll reported to Hilgard and Lux in June 1939, Eichbaum was very much in the foreground as far as Julius Streicher's anti-Semitic *Der Stürmer* was concerned. Although

[47] Eichbaum to Heß, Johannesburg, June 28, 1947, FHA, NL 3/6.
[48] RWM an die Reichsstelle für den Außenhandel, 13. Sept. 1938, betr. Abbau jüdischer Auslandsvertreter, BAB, R 3101/9040, Bl. 1–2.
[49] Erna Liedtke to Schmitt, Dec. 28, 1939, and other related correspondence, FHA, NL 1/10.
[50] Hilgard disliked him and felt that he failed to win the sympathies of his co-workers; see Hilgard, "Leben," FHA, NL 2/7, p. 51.

the *Stürmer* people sometimes made arrangements with the RWM to be silent about Jews working for German companies abroad, Eichbaum was held to be "one of the most typical Jews, who must and would be rendered harmless." *Der Stürmer* had been pursuing the matter for some time, had even sent inquiries to Reich Leader Martin Bormann at the Party chancellory, and wanted proof that Eichbaum was bringing in foreign exchange or was useful in some other way to the German economy. It was now threatening to publish articles; since the *Stürmer* was considered a semiofficial organ of the government in all Jewish questions, Eichbaum's position became very tenuous indeed. It was highly unlikely that Gauleiter Ernst Bohle, head of the foreign bureau of the NSDAP and who watched over such matters, would be helpful in defending Eichbaum's position any longer.[51] The outbreak of the war terminated this discussion, however, since Allianz no longer directly controlled the company. Eichbaum set himself up as an insurance consultant and had considerable success. When invited by Schmitt to return to Germany and help rebuild Allianz after the war, he admitted that he was attracted by the prospect "to be able to work again in the circle of men who have proven themselves to be friends through the entire time," but concluded that he "could not recover and cleanse himself from the poison of the last thirteen years" and chose to stay in South Africa until his death in 1950.[52]

We know a great deal less about the number and fate of other Jewish employees of the Allianz concern. It is a measure of the pressure placed upon Allianz that the legal department felt it important to answer attacks against it for still employing Jewish lawyers by explaining that these were by and large old cases to which such lawyers had previously been assigned. Also, in liability cases involving Jewish customers, the concern felt it necessary to heed the wishes of their clients and employ lawyers they trusted, especially since "Aryan lawyers cannot and do not want to take over the representation of non-Aryan policyholders."[53] The available evidence suggests that the Allianz concern retained Jewish employees for as long as it could. This is hardly surprising, given the attitudes of Heß and Schmitt. There is a cryptic mention of the "Aryan question ... the present legal conditions and the shortly to be expected legal regulation"[54] at the October 1935 meeting of the concern directors – that is, shortly after the announcement of the Nuremberg Laws in September defining who was an Aryan and who was not. A year later, however, the SS publication *Das Schwarze Korps* carried a lengthy article sharply critical of Neue Frankfurter and Allianz. The former was accused of giving well-paying jobs to Democrats and Social Democrats who had held positions in the Weimar period as well as employing a full Jew (Martin Bruck) as head of its Breslau branch and a Romanian Jew (Joseph Rittberg) as

[51] Uexküll to Hilgard and Lux, June 20, 1939, Lux to Schmitt, Nov. 30, 1939, and Aktennote, 10. Juli 1939, FHA, S 17.14/83.
[52] Eichbaum an Schmitt, 1. Sept. und 15. Dez. 1946, FHA, NL 1/14.
[53] Rundschreiben der Allianz vom 9. Okt. 1935, FHA, AZ 5.1/4.
[54] 26. erweiterte Vorstandssitzung am 29. Okt. 1935, FHA, S 17.2/4, p. 5.

NAME u. VORNAME	Austritt Eintritt	Abteilung Geburtsdat.	Stichtag	verh	Geburtsdat. d. Kinder	Bemerkungen
118. Hill, Friedel	31.12.1936	Orga.				Heirat
119. Lippmann, Hans	15.11.1936	Unfall-Zfh				Gez. Verw. Erfurt
120. Siegel, Otto	15.11.36	Kraft-Zfh				
121. Oberle, Hilde	31.12.36	B.J.				Heirat
122. Langendörfer, Margarete	31.12.36	L.S.Kapaukainne				"
123. Haas, Anna	31.12.36	H.-Shd.				"
124. Lindenthal, Lilly	31.12.36	Prüder.				"
125. Merkel, Hedwig	31.12.36	"				Jdg. (Jüdin)
126. Friedländer, Ilse	22.11.36	Büro-z-Hd				Jdg. (Jüdin)
127. Willms, Rudolf	20.11.36	Waren				vers. B.V. Köln
128. Hauf, Max	31.12.36	Leifer				pensioniert
129. Jans, Pauline	12.12.36	Putzfrau				Aushilfe
130. Baer, Willi	31.12.36	Kraft				Jdg. (Jude)
131. Holzapfel, Nathan	30.12.36	Qual.				† 30.12.36
132. Hohmann, Josef	3.12.36	Kraft				Militär

List of Neue Frankfurter employees leaving the company, including dates of resignation, the departments concerned, and reasons for leaving. In the cases of Hedwig Merkel, Ilse Friedländer, and Willi Baer, the words "Jüdin" and "Jude" are recorded as grounds for dismissal.

an inspector in its Dresden branch. Neue Frankfurter was not alone in hiring and retaining such persons, and *Das Schwarze Korps* suggested that "certain other firms not upset themselves about the 'Frankfurter' but rather look to themselves a bit in order to spare us these efforts, which are always felt to be 'an interference with business.' This is not directed against the 20 employed Jews at 'Allianz,' but only against the corporation that apparently cannot separate itself from them."[55] The appearance of this article led RAA to have a discussion with Director Goudefroy, and the result was "a series of dismissals" aimed at satisfying these criticisms.[56] Exactly how many persons were involved is impossible to say, but a good indication of the pressures at this time is the record of employment terminations of Neue Frankfurter, which explicitly records four cases of persons departing the company because they were Jewish: one in late November 1936, two on December 31, and another on January 31, 1937.[57]

[55] "Heimstätten für abgetakelte Bonzen," *Das Schwarze Korps,* 19. Nov. 1936, BAB, B 280/13206, Bl. 95.
[56] See the marginal notations of various RAA officials, ibid.
[57] Verzeichnis der ausgeschiedenen Angestellten der Neuen Frankfurter, FHA S17.8/19. Needless to say, other terminations recorded in the book may also have been for racial reasons, but the reasons given in these cases are specific.

An especially good indication of the influence of the *Schwarze Korps* was the termination (effective March 31, 1937) of one of those singled out, Martin Bruck, who had built up and headed the Breslau branch of Neue Frankfurter since 1931. Bruck, whose contract ran until 1940, ceased to exercise any managerial duties at the beginning of the year and negotiated a settlement that he hoped would enable him to join his son and brother in Brazil. The evidence suggests that General Director Wiedemann and Director Röse were willing to help him – both with respect to the financial settlement and with a strong letter of recommendation – although efforts to keep him in the pension fund were to no avail because Director Alfred Haase of Allianz felt it impolitic. The recommendation was of special concern to Bruck, who wanted to continue his career, and he was taken aback when he received a rather laconic and cool certification of his work for Allianz. After he complained to Röse, however, Bruck received a much more detailed letter that described his virtues and capacities; it demonstrated that his leadership of the large Breslau office had been exceptional and thus made obvious that his departure, which was described as the product of "mutual agreement," was a genuine loss.[58]

Hence, it obviously required some pressure and threats of negative publicity to induce the management of Allianz to dismiss Jewish employees. At the same time, however, employees in significant positions could hardly escape the realities of the situation. Such an individual was Hans Gerson (a section head of Hermes), who had joined the company in 1925, when he also joined the pension fund. Born in 1894, Gerson had volunteered for military service in 1914, served four years, was wounded, and left the army an officer. He had also performed various patriotic acts during the French occupation of the Ruhr. Nevertheless, he anticipated being let go but wanted to ease his situation as much as possible, since he was married and had a very small child. The dilemma was that, even though he was the most senior person in the pension fund, he would qualify only after attaining the age of 45 and after fifteen years of membership – that is, in 1940. Although Allianz made exceptions to this rule by predating membership in the fund when recruiting persons who had paid into a fund elsewhere, Gerson petitioned in February 1937 for exceptional consideration on the grounds that he was not responsible for his anticipated separation and that Hermes had no economic reason to let him go, either. Yet in this case – as in other cases of separation from non-Aryan employees – the Allianz pension fund refused to make an exception to its rules and would only pay back his contributions. It would seem, however, that Gerson anticipated a negative reply but wanted to have it in writing because he had connections (through his father) with persons in banking and industry who were prepared to help him out if he could demonstrate his non-entitlement to a pension. There is no record available as to when Gerson actually left the concern or his subsequent fate, but he clearly recognized that

---

[58] The correspondence on the Bruck case, which runs between Dec. 2/3, 1936, and Aug. 23, 1937, is to be found in FHA, B 2.5.1/7a.

his days with Allianz were numbered irrespective of his record and his services to Hermes.[59]

The company initially displayed considerable reluctance to terminate its relationship with Jewish salespersons and agents. A telling example was provided by a Frankfurt insurance agent named Hans Grünebaum, who had worked for the Stuttgart branch of Allianz and for Neue Frankfurter since 1929. In 1933, Allianz extended the contract for five years and then prolonged the contract again in June 1936 until the end of August 1941. They were clearly intent on maintaining the relationship, but Grünebaum's continued service for Allianz inevitably attracted the attention of the authorities, becoming the subject of unpleasant newspaper articles and, finally, a letter from the Gauleiter's office expressing astonishment that Allianz continued to employ a Jewish agent in this manner. At this point the pressure was too great, and Allianz terminated the contract in early June 1938. Apparently, Grünebaum, who subsequently emigrated to the United States, negotiated directly with General Director Heß; an agreement was reached that he receive his full annual commission of 35,000 RM – that is, to the end of 1939.[60]

A central argument for retaining Jews as insurance agents was that their employment was necessary to service the needs of Jewish customers. Thus, at a meeting of the branch heads of Neue Frankfurter in late June 1937, General Director Wiedemann declared that

insofar as the Aryan question with reference to the sales representatives is concerned, we stand in agreement with the authoritative bodies of the Labor Front and the industrial economy that, in view of the maintenance of Jewish business, in taking the position that so long as all the operating corporations in Germany have not realized the Aryan principle, the dismissal of non-Aryan sales representatives can only lead to substantial damage to business that is neither in the interest of the corporation nor in the public interest.[61]

By 1938, however, these arguments were becoming less and less effective in the face of the organized effort to reform the external service of the insurance business and "cleanse" it of undesirable elements. As in so many other areas dealing with the relations between business and the State in these years, the policies of Allianz and other insurance companies were pre-empted by policies of the regime – as promoted, mediated, or transmitted by the Economic Group for Private Insurance and the Reich Insurance Group. As we shall later see, Hilgard (as leader of the Reich group) had agreed to the appointment of Andreas Braß, a

[59] See the Aktennote of 17. Feb. 1937, Gerson an die Allianz-Versorgungskasse, 20. Feb. 1937, and Allianz-Versorgungskasse an Hans Gerson, 23. Feb. 1937, FHA, O 1.4.2/6.

[60] On this case, which will receive further discussion in Chapter 9, see BAK, B 215/Fall Nr. 1401; see also Allianz an die Allianz Pensionsverwaltung, 27. Juli 1951, in FHA, O 1.4.2/9, and HessHStA Wiesbaden, Wiedergutmachungsakten, Ffm-6516 (Harry Gray).

[61] Niederschrift über die Tagung der Geschäftsleiter am 28. und 29. Juni 1937 in Frankfurt a.M., p. 9, FHA, S 17.3/121.

dedicated Nazi, to head the Economic Group for Private Insurance. Anti-Semitic as he was, Braß was still willing to tolerate the employment of Jewish agents to take care of Jewish customers, a position he first enunciated in March 1937 and then repeated on a number of occasions. In 1938, however, Braß responded to the growing tendencies to eliminate Jews from economic life by announcing a change of position; in October, he sent a confidential note to insurance companies that still had contracts with Jewish agents, telling them that

a new situation has developed as a result of the measures generally introduced by the Reich government against Jews in the economy, under which a new situation has also been created for the insurance business. We have to take this into account and now give up our contractual relations to Jewish agents insofar as this has not already happened. This is all the more desired since otherwise the relevant agencies will be inclined to introduce a legal regulation with particular emphasis on the role of the insurance business. But this is not in the interest of the companies as well as the entire sector. With the dissolution of the existing ties to Jews, it will also be possible to prevent the insurance business from being singled out in the press and elsewhere as one of the economic circles which still has to be considered a domain of Jewry.[62]

In fact, the government had on July 6 already issued a change in the commercial code that excluded Jews from a variety of business activities, including real estate and the right to be traveling salesmen. The new regulation was to go into effect on September 30, 1938, and it also deprived the affected Jews of any right to compensation for the economic damage thus done to them. Lencer, the DAF leader charged with banking and insurance, petitioned the RWM for similar legislation in the insurance field, arguing:

The insurance agent should from a purely temperamental point of view be a cheerfully affirmative supporter of Adolf Hitler in the carrying out of his duties. One must therefore consider the consequences of the spoken word and consider how much damage can be visited by the thousand Jews still in the insurance field in the hundred thousand conversations carried on yearly.[63]

The case of one of Allianz's general agents in Magdeburg, Moritz Goldmann – who had served at the front as an officer from 1914 to 1918, had been wounded three times, and had received a host of medals – demonstrates what this growing movement to drive out the remaining Jewish insurance agents (for the grotesque reasons given by Lencer) meant in concrete and human terms.[64] Goldmann had

---

[62] See the form letter of Braß of Oct. 7. 1938, GDV, RS/15; for his earlier attitude, see the Sitzungsbericht über die ordentliche Hauptversammlung des Reichsverbandes der Privatversicherung am 12. März 1937, pp. 21–3, GDV, RS/25.

[63] Lencer an Pg. Alf Krüger, RWM, undated, SM, 1458/1/113, Bl. 84–5. RS of the WG Privatversicherung, 25. Juli 1938, GDV, RS/20.

[64] The correspondence is to be found in FHA, O 1.4.2/8. Especially important for the general history of the case is Goldmann to Heß, Sept. 10, 1937, and Allianz to Rechtsanwalt Beutner, Nov. 25, 1954.

taken over the agency for the Magdeburg branch in 1931 and had proven quite successful, receiving an annual income of 8,000–9,000 RM that was based on commissions for new policies and for collecting premiums on those already in his charge. Thanks to his war record, he experienced few problems in the first years of the regime. In November 1935, however, Allianz imposed a contract that restricted him to the acquisition and servicing of Jewish clients. It is difficult to say whether this reflected a general policy of forcing Jewish agents to give up their Aryan clients or a specific response to the kinds of conditions in Magdeburg that led to Eichbaum's departure that same year. Increasingly, however, the legitimation of retaining Jewish insurance agents was that they were needed to tend Jewish customers; this implied, as did the Nuremburg Laws, having Jews deal as little with Aryans as possible. Whatever the case, the only positive aspect of the contract was that it was formally guaranteed until the end of 1937, with continuance verbally promised until the end of 1938. Goldmann's dilemma was that only 1,200 remained of the Jewish community in Magdeburg, and most of these persons were already his clients. He thus found himself in the humiliating position of not having enough business to cover even the commission guaranteed by his contract.

In September 1937, Goldmann turned to General Director Heß about his plight, since "it is said that *every* employee of Allianz is met by you with understanding and an open heart in his distress and anxiety."[65] Goldmann pointed out that he was being ruined not only materially but also spiritually by the inactivity imposed upon him by the 1935 contract, and noted that other insurance companies were not concluding such contracts with their Jewish agents in other large cities. He pleaded with Heß to be allowed to serve as a general agent in Berlin, where he had good familial and business contacts, and expressed the hope "of finding with you the help that would make it possible for me to secure a future which, even if modest, secures me an honorable existence." Heß agreed to see Goldmann, although the latter ended up meeting with Director Alfred Haase instead, and Haase told Goldmann he would be transferred to Berlin. A grateful Goldmann responded by assuring Haase that he would work with all his strength to fulfill the expectations placed in him and, as if to prove the point, announced that he had just secured three life insurance policies at a publishing house in Berlin.[66] Despite the good intentions all around, however, the plans to transfer Goldmann took a turn for the worse in January 1938 because, as Director Haase learned from his colleague Director König, it was not at all certain that Jewish agents could be further employed in Berlin. By February, it was clear that a move to Berlin was out of the question, and Goldmann decided to seek a settlement and then emigrate. Allianz proposed to give him a settlement of 5,000 RM in return for his portfolio that brought in yearly premiums of 20,000 RM. The advantage

[65] Goldmann to Heß, Sept. 10, 1937, ibid.
[66] Haase to Goldmann, Sept. 22, 1937; Goldmann to Haase, Oct. 23, 1937; Goldmann to Haase, Oct. 29, 1937, ibid.

for Allianz, as Director Haase noted, was that "the entire portfolio will go over to us free of commissions."[67] Goldmann, however, found the proposal "indiscussable," and asked that he continue to work under his old contract. Thereupon he was warned not to have any "illusions," since he could not be promised a renewal of the contract. In July, Goldmann – who now intended to emigrate very shortly – tried to improve the terms of the settlement but was told that he could only receive what had already been offered. This was especially the case since it was by no means certain that the portfolio would have the same value in the future, presumably because of the number of Jewish policies involved.[68] On these icy exchanges, therefore, the good intentions of the previous year and the relationship between Goldmann and Allianz experienced their inevitable dissolution.

Good intentions aside, real assets were involved in the termination of contracts with Jewish insurance agents. This was evident not only in the case just discussed but also in that of another significant insurance agency working for Allianz: Pototzky & Co. (Aktiengesellschaft für Versicherungswesen) in Berlin and Breslau. Allianz's connection with this agency dated back to 1926 and had been renewed in the spring of 1933. Once again, however, the pressure on Allianz to end the relationship increased by 1937 to the point where the Pototzky Breslau branch agreed to give up its Aryan business to the local branch of Allianz in return for a fixed pension totaling 6,000 RM a year – to be divided between the two brothers in Breslau, Hans and Fritz Pototzky. In 1938, the pressure was on to terminate the contract with Ludwig Pototzky, who headed the Berlin branch; in contrast to the Breslau settlement, no direct mention was made of Allianz taking over the portfolio because Director König expressed fears that the Party would get wind of such an arrangement and object to the purchase of such business from a Jew. Ludwig Pototzky therefore agreed to a pension of 4,950 RM a year, but it was fairly obvious (as Pototzky's lawyer argued after the war) that a 49-year-old businessman earning between 18,000 and 20,000 RM a year would not consider this "pension" to be genuine compensation. To make matters worse, when Pototzky decided to emigrate to England in August 1939, he could not collect his "pension" there and thus agreed to a settlement of 25,000 RM; of this, however, only 2,500 RM could be taken out the country – the rest was eaten up by special taxes or put into a blocked account. Pototzky thus ended up losing both his portfolio and his "pension," and here the gainer was clearly Allianz, even if never so planned.[69]

No less deplorable was the case of Martin Lachmann, a subdirector of Allianz in Berlin. As he wrote to his daughter on October 20, 1938:

[67] Haase to Bischoff, Jan. 12, 1938; Aktennote Haase, 12. Feb. 1938; Aktennote Haase, 17. Feb. 1938, ibid.

[68] Aktennote Boetius, 18. Feb. 1938; Allianz, Organisations-Abteilung an Zweigniederlassung Magdeburg, 21. Feb. 1938; Zweigniederlassung Magdeburg an Goldmann, 12. Juli 1938, ibid.

[69] See the extensive documentation of the Ludwig Pototzky case in WGB, Ia 6059, Bayerisches Hauptstaatsarchiv, MW 25275.

My future is now completely unclear. I do not to be sure think that Allianz will leave me in the lurch; that would certainly be the absolute worst. After 31 years of strenuous work in building up a portfolio, the likes of which almost no one else has, being dropped would be a catastrophe for me. I have regarded my portfolio as a security for my old age and to be sure with full justification, for the contract with guaranteed portfolio was made with me for life, so that a breach of faith to me in this respect will be almost like suicide. But I cannot and will not believe it since only a short time ago I have received assurances on their word of honor from my highest superiors.

A few days later, Heß and König informed him that he would have to be let go at the end of the year, but that they fully recognized his achievements and hoped to get him a position in Switzerland. This would mean leaving behind a portfolio which brought him an annual income of 36,000 RM; if things did not work out in Switzerland, Lachmann would become a pensioner at the beginning of the new year. Yet the big problem, as Heß and Goudefroy informed him, was that his long-standing contract could not be carried out because he was a non-Aryan:

I could not get my pension from this portfolio because, from a portfolio whose largest portion has to be termed Aryan, a non-Aryan cannot derive income. This is completely mysterious to me since this business was made at a time when such laws did not exist and, as my contract expressly states, constitutes a specific portion of my honorably earned commission.

Apparently, his prospects in Switzerland did not work out, and his efforts to get out of Germany were not successful, either. In return for his portfolio, Allianz gave him a pension of 12,000 RM a year as well as 4,800 RM a year for his wife. He remained in Germany, was later deported, and died in a Minsk concentration camp on November 16, 1941; his wife was murdered in front of her house in Munich on January 13, 1942.[70]

We have seen that the handwriting was very much on the wall even before the November 1938 Pogrom and the subsequent elimination of Jews from German economic life. One of the numerous difficulties of Hilgard's position was that, as leader of the Reich Group, he found himself mandating policies that contradicted those that he and his fellow directors pursued at Allianz. All he could do was pander to official sentiment, try to play down the issue, and seek to uphold the sanctity of contracts as best he could. In a speech in late 1938, Hilgard insisted that accusations of the external service in the insurance business being filled with Jews were unfounded. There were 20,000 full-time insurance agents in Germany and 250,000–300,000 part-time insurance agents. Of these, only 680 were non-Aryan, according to a survey taken in August. Three quarters of

---

[70] Martin Lachmann to his daughter Ruth Haas and her husband, Leopold, Oct. 10, 1938; Martin Lachmann to Leopold Haas, Oct. 26, 1938. These letters and further information were generously provided by Lachmann's grandson, Peter Haas. See also Charlotte Johann an den Treuhänder der Militärregierung für zwangsübertragene Vermögen, 22. Sept. 1950, WGÄ, 1 WGA 3745/50 (Ruth Ernestine Haas), and *Allianz-Zeitung* 14 (1932), p. 287.

Martin Lachmann (1884–1941), subdirector of Allianz.

these could be expected to leave by the end of the year, while the few that re-mained had long-term contracts but could also be expected to depart soon.[71] It was thus clear that the policies pursued by the government in 1937–1938 were leading to the complete elimination of Jews from the insurance business in Ger-many, and that the efforts of Allianz (such as they were) and other companies to retain Jewish employees were coming to naught.[72]

It is difficult to draw a precise balance about Allianz's treatment of its Jewish employees, and it is important to bear in mind that there were differences among

[71] Undated speech of Hilgard to insurance salesmen and agents, probably late 1938, p. 10, FHA, S 17.6/8.
[72] Thus, at a meeting of the Fachgruppe Versicherungsverteter und Versicherungsmakler on Jan. 31, 1939, the departure of large numbers of Jewish salespersons and agents was reported; see SM, 1458/1/112, Bl. 46.

the various branches of the concern that reflected local conditions and attitudes of the personnel running those branches. It is also hard to make comparisons between Allianz and similar companies in insurance and banking because of asymmetries in the available information. However, the study by Dieter Ziegler of Aryanization in the Dresdner Bank enables comparison in some important respects: Allianz appears to have had fewer Jewish employees to start with and to have made great efforts to treat them well; Dresdner Bank suffered from a considerable willingness on the part of some of its employees to take advantage of the disappearance of Jewish competitors to rise through the ranks. We have no evidence that such motives played a significant role at Allianz, but this does not mean that such motives were not present. Dresdner Bank certainly was much more Nazified at the top than Allianz.[73]

In general, the company's leadership was solicitous of tried-and-true Jewish colleagues in high positions. It also sought to hold on to Jewish agents and salespersons insofar as they had served the concern well and could be useful in dealing with Jewish portfolios, although it was not above taking advantage of the ability to acquire the non-Jewish portfolios of such agents at minimal cost. Insofar as lower-level employees were concerned, Allianz seems to have responded to government pressures without much resistance but not to have taken initiatives itself. As in the case of James Freudenburg, the leaders of the concern showed a strong distaste for suggestions emanating from a Reich court decision according to which "it had to be deemed as improper for an enterprise to pay a pension to a Jew who left his position because of his race and in the context of political developments."[74] They also resisted demands by rabid anti-Semites from the Party (like Anton Roßmann, plant steward at Bayerische Versicherungsbank) who wanted to take away the pensions of three Jewish members of the pension fund in 1939. A survey showed that there were only about twelve Jewish pensioners involved in the fund; though some consideration was given to a one-time financial settlement, the matter was put off in the expectation that the issue would be legally settled after the war.[75]

Thus, dealing with the regime as it consolidated and then became more radical required increasing levels of engagement and involvement in National Socialist goals and practices – whether one liked them or not. A good illustration was Allianz's place in a project dear to Hitler's heart: redesigning the capital city of the Reich under direction of architect Albert Speer. Speer was appointed general inspector of buildings for Berlin on January 30, 1937, after Hitler became fed up

---

[73] See the illuminating study by Dieter Ziegler, "Die Verdrängung der Juden aus der Dresdner Bank 1933–1938," *Vierteljahrshefte für Zeitgeschichte* 47 (1999), pp. 187–216, which benefits from a great deal more data than is available for Allianz and has some general things to say about the banking sector. It would be interesting to compare the use of Jewish representatives abroad.

[74] Reichsgerichtsbriefe 35 (1939), Nr. 39, 25. Sept. 1939, in FHA, O 1.4.2/31.

[75] Lux to Arendts, Nov. 22, 1939. There is a list of Jewish members of the pension fund as well as correspondence about them between 1939 and 1951 in FHA, O 1.4.2/31. See especially the Aktennote of Nov. 17, 1944.

with foot-dragging by Berlin city authorities. The major concern of Hitler and Speer was the construction of the great new north–south axis intended to run through the city and the gigantic civic structures in which they were to terminate and serve as monuments to the (megalomania of) the regime. These plans required a major restructuring of the entire center of the city and involved important new real estate acquisitions and construction for Allianz.[76]

The physical expansion of Allianz, as it was finally conceptualized, was to occur in two areas of the center of the city shown. Allianz was to increase its holdings on the Tauben-, Mohren-, Mauer-, and Kanonierstraße – an area right near the Reich Chancellory, filled with major banks and businesses – into one large complex intended primarily to serve Allianz Leben. An entirely new administrative building was to be created on what was to become the Runder Platz, a new large square for business; this involved tearing down existing structures on the Potsdamer-, Eichhorn-, and Linkstraße. The new building was intended to house the Berlin branch of Allianz, then located on the Bellevuestraße. Allianz was to share this square with another imposing structure that would include the House of German Tourism and the Reich Association for Private Insurance.[77]

After 1945, Allianz claimed that the projected new administrative office building on the Runder Platz was "forced" upon them and that they had "no actual interest" in a new building after having spent a great deal of money before 1930 modernizing their existing properties in the city center.[78] The surviving records show that this claim simplified a complicated story in a rather tendentious manner. In reality, Allianz had plans to expand its Berlin facilities since at least 1933, when Hitler took a personal interest in Allianz's plans by expressing the wish that Allianz hold back the intended expansion of its main headquarters on the Mohren- and Taubenstraße through the purchase of additional properties there. Instead, he proposed that Allianz and Allianz Leben construct one large building at the point where the Potsdamer Straße would cross the projected north-south axis – that is, on what was to be later named Runder Platz in the formal plans for redesigning the city. An alternative idea then developed of putting the Berlin branch of Allianz at the Runder Platz location while also creating a single (and quite imposing) structure on the Mohren- and Taubenstraße complex. In all probability, Kurt Schmitt himself had made the proposal to put up a new building for Allianz on the Runder Platz when he was Reich Economics Minister in 1934.[79]

[76] On the general program, see Albert Speer, *Inside the Third Reich. Memoirs* (New York, 1970), Chs. 6 and 10; Gitta Sereny, *Albert Speer: His Battle with Truth* (New York, 1995), pp. 140–8, 219–20, 265–67. See also Joachim Fest, *Albert Speer. Eine Biographie* (Berlin, 1999).

[77] See the description and pictures in "Die Allianz baut," *Allianz-Zeitung* 20 (1938), pp. 165–8, and the documents in BAB, R 4606/2786.

[78] Allianz an den Senat von Berlin, Wiedergutmachungsämter, 6. Juni 1951, WGÄ, 13 WGA 444/51 (Rose Hirschberg).

[79] Allianz an das Kammergericht Berlin, 15. Zivilsenat, 30. Dez. 1953, WGÄ, 6 WGA 264/51 (Berta Feige), and "Vom Bauvorhaben der Allianz und Stuttgarter Lebensversicherungsbank Aktiengesellschaft an der Mohrenstraße in Berlin," *Der Allianz-Adler,* Dez. 1938, p. 2, FHA, B 3.6/2.

Map of Berlin, 1941; 1: Allianz headquarters; 2: central administration of Allianz Leben; 3: greater Berlin Allianz branch; 4: new building planned for Allianz at Runder Platz.

All these plans hung in the air until early February 1937, when it is highly likely that the appointment of Speer as general inspector inspired or forced decisions to be taken. Allianz had already submitted plans for new construction and reconstruction of its existing buildings on the Mohren- and Taubenstraße to the city authorities, but it had not worked them out in detail because of the possibility that all its offices would be moved to a new location at the Runder Platz. Allianz's director in charge of real estate and construction questions, Clemens Maiholzer, had discussed their plans with Speer on February 9, and a further meeting was planned with Maiholzer, Speer, and Schmitt to examine a model submitted by the Düsseldorf architectural firm that worked for Allianz, Wach und Roskotten. Delays continued, however, quite probably because Allianz was reluctant to construct a new building at the Runder Platz. This is suggested by a meeting in early June, where Maiholzer proposed that the Allianz branch headquarters building on Bellevuestraße be reconstructed. Speer vetoed this proposal, urging that Allianz solve its space problems by expanding on the Kanonierstraße (i.e., purchasing new properties adjacent to the buildings on the Mohren- and Taubenstraße) and also creating a new building on the projected Runder Platz. At this point, Maiholzer himself seems to have personally determined the site where the new building was to be constructed and also asked Wach und Roskotten to work on the plans with Speer. The latter envisioned the Runder Platz very much as a commercial area, with shops on the ground floor of the buildings, eight-meter-high arcades, and substantial electric advertising signs. It was to be graced with a sculpture area in front of the square with works by one of the leading Nazi artists, Arno Breker. Speer's object also was to create a "subordination" of commercial area to the political structures on the north-south axis. This, he argued, would "allow the few large buildings on the NS-axis to appear still greater and more monumental, that is, to be made more prominent by the contrast."[80]

By the fall of 1937, the plans had advanced considerably, including the question of who was to inhabit the other structures on the Runder Platz. Allianz agreed to pay the 4.25–5.52 million RM for the property, demolition work, and new construction required at its site on the Runder Platz – provided the Bellevuestraße building not be torn down until the new building was finished. Speer agreed to recommend these plans to Hitler and urge approval for the expansion of Allianz holdings in the Mohren- and Taubenstraße complex. In addition, Allianz was planning to spend another 4 million RM on new construction costs at the Mohrenstraße. At this point Allianz had holdings on the Mohren-, Tauben-, and Friedrichstraße worth 27.5 million RM, of which 19 million RM's worth were to be used exclusively for Allianz purposes with the remainder to be rented out to friendly and allied companies. This was to be thought of as reserve office

---

[80] Protokoll der Besprechung am 23. Juli 1937, BAB, R 4606/2786. See also Allianz an Speer, 18. Feb. 1937, Wach & Roskotten an Speer, 25. Feb. 1937, Besprechung, 9. Juni 1937, Vermerk, 25. Juni 1937, ibid.

Model of the planned building of Allianz on the Runder Platz not realized owing to World War II. The structure was meant to be used as head office of the greater Berlin branch of Allianz.

space for the future. Thus, by the end of 1937, the basic decisions about the expansion of Allianz's office space in Berlin had been taken, and the process of acquiring the necessary properties and designing the new quarters could begin. In the case of the Runder Platz, the city of Berlin itself undertook to act as agent and trustee of Allianz in the acquisition of the properties on Potsdamer Straße 19–23, Eichhornstraße 3–10, and Linkstraße 34–39 – to have them vacated by October 1, 1938, and cleared for new construction by January 1, 1939. The basic plans became public in the spring of 1938, and work on the details of the design continued on into 1940 and even beyond. It is hard to tell how enthused Maiholzer and his colleagues at Allianz became about the project on the Runder Platz, but some of the megalomania connected with the reconstruction of Berlin must have been infectious: in June 1940, Speer had to ask that a new sculptor be hired to design the Allianz eagle, since he did not want it to appear as an "emblem of Sovereignty" but rather as simply a company logo.[81]

It was stretching things quite a bit, then, for Allianz executives to have claimed (after the war) that they had been "compelled" to plan the construction of a

---

[81] Aktennote, 19. Juni 1940, Protokoll der Besprechung, 21. Okt. 1937, Allianz an Speer, 16. Nov. 1937 (3 Briefe), Oberbürgermeister Berlin an Allianz, 20. Dez. 1937, ibid.

new building on the Runder Platz and to have been sated, so to speak, with respect to their office space needs. Although the concern's preferences may have been pre-empted, it did have plans to expand. The real problem was that the arguments that they had no interest in the project – to which were added claims that everyone in the affected area had to sell off their properties or be subject to eminent domain – were made in connection with restitution claims of Jewish houseowners who had been forced to sell their properties to make way for the Allianz buildings. The conditions under which these properties were acquired suggest that Allianz's postwar leaders were disingenuous about their involvement in the Runder Platz. As noted before, the City of Berlin had the task of acting as Allianz's agent and trustee in the purchase of the properties connected with the Runder Platz and, on the basis of the legislation governing the reconstruction of German cities of October 5, 1937,[82] could use the power of eminent domain to take over and decide on the compensation for properties in cases where an agreement on price could not be reached. It had the responsibility to keep its costs as low as possible and to inform Allianz of the prices it was offering and of any intention to use its powers of eminent domain.

Of the nine properties taken over for the project on the Runder Platz, four were owned by Jews and three by "Aryans"; one had already been Aryanized, and one was in the hands of the Reich Treasury. While it was certainly true, as Allianz argued after the war, that all the properties in question were subject to eminent domain and had to be sold, three of the non-Jewish properties were sold for 25%–30% above their assessed worth and another, that of a high SS officer in the Leibstandarte Adolf Hitler, was sold for 250% above its assessed worth; yet another, held by the Treasury, was sold for 320% above assessed worth. By comparison, three of the four Jewish properties were sold for between 3% and 18% below their assessed worth.[83]

It is important to realize that the assessed value was usually kept artificially low for tax reasons, so that a higher price – especially in cases where property was being sold unwillingly and under threat of eminent domain – was fully appropriate. Thus, despite the ban on price increases in force at this time, the government permitted payments over assessed value. This was always allowed when Aryans were involved, but sometimes it was even permitted with Jews in order to make matters simpler. This may well have been the case with respect to a well-known Jewish gynecologist who was able to sell his valuable property above assessed value in 1938, used a good portion of the return to get his daughter out of Germany, and then committed suicide in 1943 at the age of 82 rather than be deported. In the postwar restitution case brought by his heirs, which lasted a decade, the former director of the chief real estate office of Berlin (Willi Müller-Wieland, who had handled the property sales in question in the Nazi

---

[82] RGBl, 1937, I, p. 1054.
[83] Allianz an Kammergericht Berlin, 15. Zivilsenat, 7. Dez. 1953, WGÄ, 6 WGA 264/51 (Berta Feige), Bl. 137–40.

period) testified that there was no discrimination against Jews in the settlements presided over by his office prior to the economic legislation taken against Jews after November 1938.[84] It is difficult to imagine, however, that the individual in question would not have bargained more rigorously were he a non-Jew. In any case, the evidence shows that the Jewish property owners received amounts below the assessed worth. Most telling, however, was the method by which such low prices could be extracted by persons working in Müller-Wieland's office. Thus, one of the victims, who sold in December 1940, was told by the city official handling the matter that "you know that you are Jews. If you do not accept our offer, we will take other measures against you."[85]

These words were spoken by a government rather than an Allianz official, but it would be absurd to think that those involved at Allianz were not aware of the difference between what was being offered to Jews and non-Jews and of the pressures on Jewish property owners at so advanced a stage of the expropriation of Jewish assets. Indeed, a good example of how aware Allianz officials were of such facts can be found in the case of the property at the corner of Friedrichstraße 184-Mohrenstraße 52 in October 1938 – whose purchase was, however, a far cry from the kind of thuggery exercised by government officials at the Runder Platz. In this instance, the property was purchased for 590,000 RM, which was only 60,200 RM above the assessed value of 1935. The property was needed to round off the holdings at the site of Allianz's other big construction program and was considered especially valuable. Maiholzer justified the price to Speer by pointing out that the Jewish owners were anxious to sell because of their tax debts and so that the sale would benefit the Treasury, but also that it was important to have them sell it to Allianz and thereby avoid the problems connected with turning the disposition of the property into an eminent domain issue.[86]

It is impossible to tell whether a sense of fairness played any role in this transaction along with the opportunistic reasons mentioned, and such sentiments toward Jews certainly would not be stated in a letter to the authorities in 1938. The businessmen at Allianz and in other companies were no longer functioning in a political and social environment that put much stock in civilized behavior toward Jews. In 1935, for example, a Jewish real estate agent offered to sell Allianz a property in Berlin-Charlottenburg for a Jewish businessman who had built it in 1927 with the intention of using it for his family and for renting apartments. He had devoted considerable attention to detail in the construction of the house, and it was a very attractive property that he obviously never would have sold under normal conditions. Allianz claimed after the war that the sale was made at a time when the seller still had considerable freedom to accept or decline conditions, but that was not how the seller (who had fled to Brazil) remembered it.

---

[84] Verhandlungsprotokoll, 27. Feb. 1954, WGÄ, 3 WGA 2642/50, Bd. 1 (Walther Czempin).
[85] Beschluß des 15. Zivilsenats des Kammergerichts Berlin, 18. Dez. 1953, WGÄ, 6 WGA 264/51 (Berta Feige).
[86] Allianz an den Generalbauinspektor, 17. Okt. 1938, BAB, R 4606/2785.

He recalled Director Maiholzer saying: "You Jews should save what you can and get out of here."[87] After the war, Maiholzer could not remember saying such a thing and Allianz argued that this was not his "style."[88] What is depressing is that it was actually good advice – whatever the "style" in which it was given.

This is amply demonstrated by another Allianz real estate acquisition to which Maiholzer was a party, that of Kaufingerstraße 22 in Munich, which housed a number of businesses in the heart of the city's shopping center. The property belonged to Julius and Else Basch and was purchased by Allianz in January 1940. Maiholzer did not deal with Basch himself but rather with SA Obersturmführer Hans Wegner, whom Gauleiter Wagner had appointed head of the "Munich Property Utilization Agency Ltd." that had been set up after the November 1938 Pogrom. Its basic function was the Aryanization of Jewish property and enterprises. Wegner and his organization were later to take on the function of "trustee" for Jewish assets when the Jews were deported. In this instance, Basch was "represented" by an engineer and businessman, Hanns Stumfall, who worked closely with Wegner in such cases to his own considerable profit and to the detriment of the Jewish sellers of properties and enterprises. Stumfall had been appointed to "negotiate" for Basch in 1939, and he received 72,000 RM for his services as a commission on the sale price of 1,674,000 RM. In 1937, the City of Munich had offered Basch 2,225,000 RM for the property, but the Baschs turned them down. This unfortunate attachment to Germany cost them dearly. Following the Pogrom of November 9, 1938, Basch (along with many other wealthy Jews) was dragged off to Dachau and was "persuaded" to sell his assets and leave Germany. The Baschs decided to join their son in the United States, but their decision came too late. Julius Basch took ill and died soon after the property was sold, and his wife was subsequently deported and died in Theresienstadt.[89]

In 1949–1950, when the surviving son (Ernest B. Ashton) launched a restitution case against Allianz, the concern initially claimed, rather astonishingly, that Basch had not negotiated under duress and that the intention to emigrate and the "retaining" of Stumfall antedated the November Pogrom. They also claimed that

[87] Willi Meyer an das Magistrat von Groß-Berlin, 21. Nov. 1950, WGÄ, 5 WGA 4664/50 (Ludwig Jansen).

[88] Allianz an der Senator für Justiz, Berlin, 2. März 1950, ibid.

[89] The documentation on this complicated case, which shall be discussed again in the final chapter of this book, is to be found in the files of the WGB, Ia 919, Bd. 1–3. See especially Allianz an die Wiedergutmachungsbehörde Oberbayern, 12. April 1949, Bd. 1, Bl. 15–16; Samuel Ackermann & Co. an die Wiedergutmachungsbehörde Oberbayern, 26. Mai 1949, ibid., Bl. 24–5; Kaufvertrag 20. Jan. 1940, ibid., Bl. 45–9; Allianz an die Wiedergutmachungskammer beim Landgericht München I, 19. Juni 1950, ibid., Bl. 120–1; Treuhänder an Maiholzer, 28. Dez. 1939, and related correspondence in Bd. 3. For a first-rate discussion of the Aryanization process in Munich, see Marian Rappl, " 'Arisierungen' in München. Die Verdrängung der jüdischen Gewerbetreibenden aus dem Wirtschaftsleben der Stadt 1933–1939," *Zeitschrift für bayerische Landesgeschichte* 63 (2000), pp. 123–84.

the price Allianz paid was 20% above the assessed value of 1,399,200 RM in 1935, that purchasing so substantial a property was a risky business for an insurance company, and that the RAA would not have allowed them to pay more under the conditions of 1940. It is significant to note that Allianz had lost important documentation on the case during the war and that it changed its position once new information was placed at its disposal, although it continued to claim that the price it paid was fair and even asserted that its supervisory board finance committee members recalled twice turning down the price for being too high before finally accepting it. In reality, however, as Allianz told the RAA in requesting permission to make the purchase, the finance committee "particularly welcomes the purchase of the property," whose real worth it considered to be 2.2 million RM in normal times. Indeed, Allianz's valuation was precisely that stated in the files of the Munich Property Utilization Agency, Ltd. in January 1939 and in a list generated by the City of Munich itself in April. Allianz described Kaufingerstraße 22 as "a commercial building … with a unique commercial location …. For this reason we did not hesitate to consider the proposition when the property was offered us for sale so that later our corporation can set up business offices there. The property is also extraordinarily suitable for effective advertising." Allianz thus viewed it as a very good and by no means risky investment. Most significant for the discussion here, however, is that Allianz knew full well that it could strengthen its case by employing the immense tax problems faced by the Basch family after the various impositions on Jews following the November Pogrom:

The present sale of the property is also of significance to the public interest. We submit a letter of the Trustee in conformity to the decision of the Government President of Upper Bavaria of September 28, 1939 in which it is pointed out that the sale is absolutely necessary for the covering of the Jewish Property Levy, etc. Thus, after deduction of the assumed mortgages, at least 90% of the remaining approximately 600,000 RM purchase price will be left for the Reich Financial Administration for the trusteeship fee, for the still unpaid five installments of the Jewish Property Levy owed by the former Jewish owner,[90] for the regular and extraordinary levy owing the Jewish Religious Community under Reich regulations, for the Reich Flight Tax since the emigration of the Jew Israel Basch is immediately impending, as well as the unredeemable levy to the Gold Discount Bank for emigrant merchandise. The remaining amount of at the most 10% will initially stay in a blocked account and then be transfered to an emigrant account after emigration. In view of this public interest in the sale of the property, all of the relevant official agencies, especially the Special Plenipotentiary for Economic Matters for the Capital City of the Movement, President Christian Weber, have supported a sale to us and have opened up the prospect of a speeding up of the necessary approvals.[91]

---

[90] The so-called atonement tax imposed on the Jews after the Pogrom of November 9, 1938, to be discussed in Chapter 5, was payable initially in four installments, but the tax was then increased and a fifth installment added.

[91] Allianz an das RAA, 22. Jan. 1940, SM, 1458/1/143, Bl. 63–4. For the valuation by the Vermögens-verwertung München GmbH, see Staatsarchiv München, NSDAP/38; for the valuation by the City of Munich, see Stadtarchiv München, Film 22 (originals in Yad Vashem, Signatur M-1/DN 17). I am grateful to Marian Rappl for these references.

Allianz thus presented itself as performing a public service in purchasing Kaufingerstraße 22, and one cannot help wondering whether those involved gave a moment's thought – let alone serious contemplation – to the fact that they were thus serving as accomplices in the systematic despoliation of the Baschs and violating the most elementary principles of business ethics, equity, and good faith.

The entire episode reflected the degree to which the Aryanization of Jewish assets – whether the price was fair or unfair and whether the money went to the property owner or the State – had become a part of "normal business." How much this was the case is demonstrated by a consideration of the number of Jewish properties purchased during these years. According to available business reports, the Allianz concern purchased 433 properties between 1933 and 1948–1949. Purchases for the period 1941–1949 are dealt with collectively in the available report, but one can assume that there were few purchases in the years immediately after the war. The vast majority (336) were purchased by Allianz Leben, four of these in common with Allianz, which itself purchased 91 properties. The other ten properties were purchased by daughter companies of Allianz (Badische Pferde, Hammonia, and Neue Frankfurter). Of the 433 purchased properties, 348 were on the territory of what became the West German Federal Republic and, of these, 61 (or 17.5%) became the subject of restitution cases after 1945. The bulk of the remaining 85 properties were in the former German Democratic Republic, Poland, and the Soviet Union, where there was no restitution. In Breslau, 27 properties were acquired by Allianz, 16 of them in 1938–1939, while 14 properties were acquired in Leipzig. Both cities had significant Jewish populations. How many of these 85 properties – many of which are multiple addresses on the same street, counted here for convenience as one – belonged to Jews? Satisfactory information is not available, but there is at least one case to be found where a Jew sought restitution for losses in the East. Hugo Benjamin, who lived in Tel-Aviv in 1950, sought recompense for underpayment in the amount of 85,555 RM for properties at Schmiedebrücke 46/47 in Breslau that had been auctioned off and purchased by Allianz in 1939.[92]

Mortgages, like real estate, were among the assets used by Allianz and other insurance companies to cover their obligations; here, too, one could follow in the wake of an Aryanization to transfer the mortgage once given to a Jew to his successor. An interesting example is the textile firm Landshuter Leinen- und Gebildeweberei F.V. Grünfeld, which had its main offices in Berlin and its factory in Landshut, Upper Silesia. It was Aryanized and taken over by the Max Kühl Kommanditgesellschaft in 1938. Allianz Leben decided to offer the latter a mortgage loan of 1 million gold marks in September 1938 and to transfer the 3 million

---

[92] The statistics on property acquisitions and restitution cases were developed for me by the research team at the Center for Corporate History of Allianz AG. For the Benjamin case, see WGÄ, 5 WGA 484/50 (Hugo Benjamin). Allianz, of course, was not the only insurance company taking advantage of the real estate opportunities created by the persecution of Jews. The Aryanizations by the Alte Leipziger and the Gothaer Lebensversicherung are recorded in the approvals granted by the RAA, BAB, R 3104/20544 and 21966.

marks in mortgages it had previously given to Grünfeld under the same conditions. In asking for the supervisory board's approval, Allianz directors pointed out that – although they had not yet assessed the full value of the properties for which the mortgages served as a guarantee – the property at the Kurfürstendamm, corner of Joachimsthaler Straße in Berlin-Charlottenburg, was alone worth the 1 million of the new loan, to which had to be added the security that the Max Kühl firm offered in the form of its building on Leipziger Straße in Berlin and the factory and villa in Landshut, Upper Silesia.[93] Clearly Allianz was not responsible for the Aryanization of the Grünfeld company, but it was a profiting participant.

The same holds true in the acquisition of shares that came on the market as a result of Aryanization. Thus, on November 1, 1938, Allianz wrote to the RWM that

there is the intention of transferring into Aryan possession a block of Bayerische Vereinsbank in Munich shares in the amount of about 4,000,000 RM (of a total capital of 31,000,000 RM) which are still in Jewish hands at the present time. In view of the purpose involved, we have declared ourselves prepared, presupposing the permission of the Reich Economics Ministry, to take over 1,300,000 RM in shares. In the case of the Bayerische Vereinsbank, one is dealing with what is known to be one of the best Bavarian bank institutes. It has paid a 5% dividend in the last three years. The transfer will be made at 105% of par.[94]

In making this request, which was granted in March 1939, Allianz made specific reference to conversations between Ministerial Director Lange and August von Finck, which is an important clue as to the source of the shares. Von Finck, acting for his own banking house of Merck, Finck & Co., was very much involved in efforts to keep Bayerische Vereinsbank in private hands despite Party interest in gaining control of it. He had purchased 4,200,000 RM in shares of the bank from the banking house of Mendelssohn & Co., itself undergoing Aryanization at this time, and there can be little doubt that the shares Allianz was seeking to gain came from this block.[95]

Needless to say, Allianz kept a watchful eye out for insurance business opportunities when there were Aryanizations. Thus, in April 1939, Hilgard wrote to Director Eduard Mosler of Deutsche Bank about the Schocken AG in Zwickau, a department store chain that had been renamed Merkur AG and whose capital had just been taken over by a bank consortium headed by Deutsche Bank. Neue Frankfurter had provided the old company with insurance against interruption of operations and was apparently now planning to change its fire insurance. Hilgard hoped that Mosler would contact the new management and secure the fire

[93] Allianz Leben an Hans Rummel (Deutsche Bank), 27. Sept. 1938, BAB, 80 Ba 2/P 5774.
[94] Allianz an RWM, 1. Nov. 1939, BAB, R 3104/20524, Bl. 24–5.
[95] See the very informative Vermerk des Parteistabsleiters Saupert of 13. Feb. 1939, BAB, ehem. BDC, PK, August von Finck (*18.7. 1898), and the interrogation of August von Finck, Sept. 23, 1947, NA, RG 260, OMGUS, FINAD, 2/57/4.

insurance contract for Neue Frankfurter as well, a request that Mosler granted.[96] A few months later, Hilgard paid a visit to Director Karl Kimmich of Deutsche Bank to introduce his son, Hanns Hilgard, who was being sent to build up the insurance business for Allianz in the Sudeten area. Eduard Hilgard wanted his son introduced to the branch directors of banks associated with Allianz. As Kimmich reported to Director Paul Vernickel of the Reichenberg branch of the Deutsche Bank, Hilgard "has in mind, among other things, also of the many Aryanizations and the insurance questions relating to them as well as industry in general."[97]

Thus, as the 1930s drew to a close, it had become a part of normal business to transfer old mortgages and insurance relationships to the new owners of Aryanized assets when it seemed profitable to do so. Efforts to be decent and fair sometimes coexisted with but more often simply gave way to the seizure of advantage and opportunity to gain from the plight of Jewish insurance agents forced to give up their professions and portfolios and of houseowners compelled to sell their properties. Even Schmitt could not rise above the temptation to sacrifice principle and honor to advantage in his role as chairman of the AEG supervisory board, and in 1936–1937 he joined with Hermann Bücher (general director of AEG) in taking over the Gesfürel/Ludwig Loewe AG in a manner that violated their previous agreements with Erich Loewe, who was considered a Jew by Nazi definition. Both Schmitt and Bücher had opposed anti-Semitic measures in the economy, but the tide had turned and giving way to Nazi pressures was a price worth paying for recapitalization of AEG via the takeover.[98] Thus, it is difficult to escape the impression that, by the time the more extreme radicalization began in 1938–1939, resistance to Aryanization – of one's own concern or of the careers, properties, and enterprises of others – had not only evaporated but had given way to a goodly measure of cynical opportunism.

---

[96] Hilgard an Mosler, 14. April 1939, and Mosler an Hilgard, 15. April 1939, BAB, 80 Ba 2/P 5786. On the Schocken Aryanization, see Helmut Genschel, *Die Verdrängung der Juden aus der Wirtschaft im Dritten Reich* [Göttinger Bausteine zur Geschichtswissenschaft, Bd. 38] (Göttingen, 1966), pp. 239–40.

[97] Kimmich an Vernickel, 10. Juli 1939, BAB, 80 Ba 2/P 779, Bl. 18.

[98] See Peter Hayes, "State Policy and Corporate Involvement in the Holocaust," in Michael Berenbaum & Abraham J. Pecks (eds.), *The Holocaust and History: The Known, the Unknown, the Disputed, and the Reexamined* (Bloomington, Ind., 1998), pp. 197–218, esp. p. 201.

4

Allianz and the Reich Group:
Politics of the Insurance Business in the
Period of Regime Radicalization, 1936–1939

WHILE it is impossible not to deplore the role of Allianz executives and other businessmen in Aryanizations, it is necessary to understand that they were not operating in a context where either traditional business ethics or capitalist economic rationality counted for much anymore. Having once persuaded themselves that they could "prevent the worst" by joining the Party and working within the context of the regime, they increasingly found themselves in a situation where "preventing the worst" became a daily activity and where increasing engagement with the regime and its goals was the necessary result. This had profound consequences for the investment policies of banks and insurance companies. These were, it must be remembered, regulated institutions that had remained under the cloud of recent scandals and financial collapses and whose social worth was constantly being challenged by powerful elements in the regime.

The cloud was indeed made much heavier in March 1936 by the collapse of the Austrian Phönix Life,[1] the causes of which were painfully similar to those of the Favag's demise. Like the latter, Phönix Life was a very large company – in fact, the third largest on the European continent – and one that did business in no fewer than 22 countries.[2] Just as Favag owed its rise and fall to Paul Dumcke, so was Phönix Life's fate intimately bound up with its leading director, Wilhelm Berliner – by all accounts a remarkable personality with extraordinary talents as a linguist, mathematician, financial expert, and lawyer, and a man who had close connections with the Austrian government. Like Favag, Phönix Life overexpanded after the war and for similar reasons. In order to handle existing obligations, it took on new ones that were often of a highly speculative nature, which was obviously an expensive and dangerous way of doing business. These methods could hardly escape notice. Munich Re, for example, retreated from its engagements with Phönix Life at the beginning

---

[1] Although they cooperated closely, it is important not to confuse Phönix Life with Elementar-Phönix, which handled property insurance.

[2] For good discussions of the Phönix collapse, see Isabella Ackerl, "Der Phönix-Skandal," in Ludwig Jedlicka & Rudolf Neck (eds.), *Das Juliabkommen von 1936. Vorgeschichte, Hintergründe und Folgen. Protokoll des Symposiums in Wien am 10. und 11. Juni 1976* (Vienna, 1977), pp. 241–79, and Marita Roloff & Alois Mosser, *Wiener Allianz. Gegründet 1860* (Vienna, 1991), pp. 135–55.

of the 1930s, as Kisskalt came to the conclusion that its management and financing were unsound, that its costs were too high, and that its premiums were too low.

As noted earlier, he had hoped Allianz would purchase part of the still financially sound Phönix Elementar and put Eichbaum in charge.[3] When General Director Michele Sulfina of the great Italian concern Generali showed an interest in buying up Elementar-Phönix in September 1935, Kisskalt again recommended Eichbaum. It would be impossible to make a non-Austrian Jew the general director at this point, but one could appoint someone suitable – like Eberhard von Reininghaus, who had a distinguished career first with Anglo-Danubian Lloyd and then as deputy general director of Wechselseitige Brandschaden- und Janus Allgemeine Versicherungs-Anstalt a. G. in Vienna – and then "give him an energetic man like Herr Eichbaum at his side for the actual work."[4] But Elementar-Phönix, as will be shown, would be taken over in a different way.

That Phönix Life survived in the 1930s was due to three factors: Austrian distrust – after the collapse of the Creditanstalt in May 1931 – of banks in comparison to insurance companies; Berliner's close contacts with the government; and the laxity and corruption of high officials in the Austrian supervisory authority. As was the case with Dumcke, Berliner's malfeasance, which was almost baroque in its breadth and complexity, came to light only after his unexpected death in February 1936. This was followed by the discovery of lists of all those he had bribed and the turning over of the true accounts of the concern to Berliner's successor, Eberhard von Reininghaus. The result of the exposures, needless to say, was a major international scandal and produced economic difficulties of very serious proportions. This was actually a much larger collapse than that of Favag, involving many more countries and policyholders.

In contrast to Favag, whose insurance portfolios had been taken over by Allianz, it was the Austrian State that regulated the affairs of Phönix Life by separating the insurance from the financial side of the company, liquidating the latter, and requiring the Austrian business community more generally to guarantee a successor insurance company for the Phönix Life insurance, Österreichische Versicherungs-AG (ÖVAG). Participation in ÖVAG was made attractive by the aforementioned collective guarantee of the Austrian insurance business and various restrictions on repurchase of insurance policies by their holders. Thus, both risk and the obligation to policyholders were reduced. Among its most important shareholders were Wiener Städtische, the Italian Generali, and Munich Re. Indeed, Kisskalt and his colleagues considered it a matter of prestige to participate and petitioned Schacht for special dispensation from the foreign exchange regulations in order to do so.

---

[3] See Chapter 3, pp. 126–7.
[4] Aktennote Kisskalt, 17. Sept. 1935, MR, A 2.13/46. In general, this file contains important material on the Phönix Life affair and on Munich Re and Allianz's involvement with Elementar-Phönix. On von Reininghaus, see his Lebenslauf in MR, D/8.

Phönix Life was regarded as a Jewish company. Berliner was a Jew, and the company had a large Jewish clientele. Indeed, the German government was specially hostile to Phönix Life because Berliner had a reputation for helping German Jews rescue their assets. Von Reininghaus turned out to have a Jewish grandmother and to have expressed pride in having Jewish ancestry.[5] In Germany, where Phönix Life had been extremely active, there had been considerable anxiety about the concern's solidity; the supervisory agency had tried to obtain an increased bond from Phönix Life and was worried about it having sufficient coverage. This was a real issue despite all the protective regulations, and while the public was told that there was nothing to worry about, there was a genuine danger that the German branch of Phönix Life could go bankrupt if negotiations for its liquidation and the assumption of its policies failed. Thus, in May 1936, the Economics Ministry summoned the insurance industry organization leaders to discuss the situation. One could argue that the German insurers had no obligation to save the branch of a foreign company from a bankruptcy that it had brought upon itself, but insurance organization leaders dismissed such notions because "they overlook the heart of the matter, which is that the existence of many German families is at stake and on the other side that the bankruptcy of the German branch of the Phönix Life would be a heavy blow to the entire German life insurance business." The conclusion was that a common action by the insurers to prevent such a bankruptcy was necessary in the form of a guarantee for such losses as had been incurred. This was warmly supported by Kisskalt of Munich Re, who pointed out that his company had bowed out of the Phönix Life long before but that he felt an obligation nonetheless. The Hungarian insurance companies had put up a 3-million-pengö guarantee for their Phönix Life branch, and "what the Hungarian insurance business can do is easily possible for the German enterprises which are much stronger in capital.... One has to avoid everything that is likely to promote the view that the German insurance business is not healthy."[6] There was only one negative voice, General Director Tiedke of Alte Leipziger, who argued that Phönix Life had done nothing but ruin their business and that policyholders had gone to Phönix Life primarily for speculative reasons and thus deserved no protection. The prevailing mood, however, was that the reputation of the German private insurance business depended upon them acting collectively. In the end, the guarantee was given and a new company, the Isar Lebensversicherungs-AG, was established to take over the German Phönix Life policies. As we shall see, Isar was to present some special problems on the German insurance scene because it inherited a large Jewish portfolio from Phönix Life.

In contrast to the Favag case, where Allianz had saved the day and left shareholders and financial creditors to pay the bill, the Phönix Life liquidation involved

---

[5] Gestapo an RWM, 23. Okt. 1933, BAB, R 3101/17325, Bl. 39–48. The reports of the German Embassy in Vienna, headed by Franz von Papen, are very useful on the Phönix Life affair; see ibid., especially Bl. 88–96 (1. April 1936), 258–9 (9. Mai 1936).

[6] Meeting of May 12, 1936, BAB, R 3101/17325, Bl. 120–7.

a great deal more direct government action as well as collective action to cover the losses and protect policyholders. It is significant that the Phönix Life issue in Germany was solved under the auspices of the RAA, whose powers had been greatly increased. There were some who even argued that the RAA should, in effect, run the peak association of the private insurance business, and the voluntary collective action of the private insurers undoubtedly reflected their desire to show that they knew how to keep their own house in order. Also, there were important forces in the National Socialist regime arguing for socialization of the insurance business. It was thus important to be able to argue that "the events in Vienna give no cause for a strengthening of the tendencies which run in the direction of a nationalization of the private insurance industry, and certainly not among us, where the National Socialist economic policy by aiming at a spirit of community and securing the necessary state influence has made the means of socialization superfluous."[7]

Between 1933 and 1936, much of business cooperation with government economic policies had been relatively voluntary. Schacht (Schmitt's successor as economics minister) was viewed as friendly to business, and the bureaucracy of the RWM and some of the other ministries was often a haven when having to deal with the new leaders. As noted earlier, there was considerable continuity between the regulatory financial regime established by Hitler's predecessors and that of the National Socialists. The effort to reduce interest rates, always a matter of great importance in the insurance field, had first begun with the Emergency Decree of December 1931, and the National Socialist interest in further interest reductions was hardly a novelty. The value of Allianz Leben's 670 million marks in investments in 1934 was inevitably affected by even the smallest change in rates. Also, Allianz Leben was the fourth largest holder of mortgages in Germany, and the value of these holdings and its coverage – and what it could offer its policyholders in dividends – obviously were tied to interest rates. Still, Director Schloeßmann viewed the reduction of average interest rates from 6.2% to 5.56% in 1933 as a welcome development in the effort to promote investment and economic recovery. At the beginning of 1934, the mortgage rate was dropped voluntarily another half percent, but Allianz Leben responded to the situation by lowering its dividends on life insurance policies. This was not an action that one wanted to take very often, however, and the Allianz directors showed considerable concern in 1935 as they faced yet another reduction at the beginning of 1936 which would mean that the rate had been reduced from 8.5% in 1931 to 5% on both existing and new mortgages.[8]

On the surface, this reduction of 1936 was "voluntary." Both the RWM and the RAA had strongly recommended it, and Hilgard had negotiated various technical aspects with the RWM about the matter before formally urging the

[7] Joseph Winschuh, "Phönix-Gedanken," *Deutsche Allgemeine Zeitung,* April 6, 1936, BAB, R 3101/17324, Bl. 164.

[8] 23. erweiterte Vorstandssitzung am 4. Mai 1934, pp. 6–7, 24. erweiterte Vorstandssitzung am 6. Nov. 1934, pp. 3–4, 26. erweiterte Vorstandssitzung am 29. Okt. 1935, p. 8, FHA, S 17.2/4.

interest-rate reduction to all members of the Reich Group on May 21, 1935. A member of the Reich Group objected to the procedure on the grounds that it was a "market regulating measure," claimed that the measure was damaging to the profitability of his company and, in effect, challenged Hilgard's right to use his position in the Reich Group to exert such pressure. For Hilgard this was a very serious matter, because he saw his role as precisely that of an intermediary between the government and the industry – negotiating the best possible arrangement and maintaining as much voluntarism as possible while at the same time getting his "troops" into line once a decision had been made and thus preventing the "worst." Indeed, Hilgard was anxious to control the manner in which the interest-rate reduction was presented to the public and insisted that it be treated confidentially until he decided on how to describe it to the press.[9]

Hilgard therefore orchestrated a response from the RWM to the rebel in his ranks in the form of a letter addressed directly to himself from State Secretary Hans Posse, wherein the latter at once defended Hilgard's procedure and provided a revealing illustration of how businessmen were supposed to think under the new order. Posse insisted that just because an interest-rate reduction could indirectly reduce profits did not mean that Hilgard's "urgent recommendation" for such reduction was a market regulating measure in any legal sense. He went on:

There is no doubt in my mind as to your authority to call upon the leaders of the enterprises belonging to your group with great vigor and seriousness to reduce the interest rate for long-term loans in the interest of the German economy and thereby to preserve unity. The necessity of climbing down from the excessively high interest rates on the capital market ought also not be contested by the head of the insurance enterprise in question. If he nevertheless turns against such a regulation because high-interest contracts make possible the distribution of high dividends to the insured and, as a result, relatively low insurance premiums in life insurance, then he fails to recognize that the insurance companies have also to consider first and foremost the interests of the entire nation and to subordinate the special interest of their policyholders to these interests.[10]

The insurance executive at whom these lines were aimed was probably General Director Johannes Tiedke of Alte Leipziger, who was unusually outspoken in his attachment to market economy principles and hostile about compromising what he considered to be sound business practice. Like Heß, he had a deep distaste for National Socialism and did not join the Party, although this did not prevent him from praising what he considered to be Hitler's achievements in foreign and domestic affairs: restoring Germany's international position and ending

---

[9] Hilgard an den Leiter der Wirtschaftsgruppen Privatversicherung und den Leiter der Wirtschaftsgruppe öffentlich-rechtliche Versicherung, 21. Mai 1935 und 28. Mai 1935; Oertel an die dem Reichsverband angeschlossenen Fachverbände und Verbandsgesellschaften, 27. Mai 1935, GDV, RS/18. The interest-rate reduction measures were the subject of a host of guidelines and other circular letters from the Reich Group; see BAK, B 280/12237, Bl. 237–47.

[10] Posse an den Leiter der Reichsgruppe Versicherungen, 26. Juni 1935, GDV, RS/18.

class conflict.[11] Unlike Heß, however, Tiedke was impolitic and given to missteps, and he felt that Schmitt and Hilgard – with their ostentatious entry into the Party and their concessions on questions like the interest-rate reduction – were selling out the interests of the industry. Even if Tiedke was the executive in question, he remained quite dissatisfied and, at a meeting of the executive committee of the Reich Association in June 1936, complained that his company had lost 300,000 RM because of the interest-rate reduction, that Victoria had probably lost two or three times as much, and that the savings banks managed to get more concessions from the RWM (with respect, e.g., to revalued mortgages, which retained their 6% interest rate if held by savings banks) than did the insurance business. He called upon the association to secure equal treatment. Schloeßmann opposed arguing for equality, since the savings banks had reduced their average rate to 4.8% while the insurance business remained at 5%. Hilgard was especially irritated at Tiedke for suggesting that the savings banks had a "life of their own" while the insurance business had lost all autonomy, and he responded by saying that he believed,

on the basis of … numerous negotiations,… that there is hardly a group in the entire economy which enjoys a life of its own to such an extent as insurance. The fact that the insurance business has a life of its own is due exclusively to the fact that the Reich Economics Minister has great confidence in the leaders of the insurance business. The savings banks do not in the least have a life of their own; they do not even have the freedom to give even a single mark for donations; everything depends on the agreement of the RWM.[12]

The record shows that there was considerable discussion following these remarks, and though the end result was an expression of confidence in Hilgard, it would be interesting to know if Tiedke stood alone in his criticisms and how concerned the other insurance leaders were about the consequences of further interest-rate reduction.

In any case, there was no reason for optimism about the future, and by 1940 Schmitt told Funk (Schacht's successor as economics minister) that the average interest rate at Allianz was 4.6%, that he anticipated it going down to 4% and dropping further, and at that point "then either the premiums for millions of policies in force will have to be raised or the amounts of insurance reduced," while new insurance policies would be calculated on the basis of a 3% interest rate. Funk responded by claiming that he intended no further reductions during the war but that he hoped to bring down interest rates afterward and that

---

[11] See for example his speech "Zum 50. Geburtstag unseres Führers, 20. April 1939," and also his "Meine Stellung zum Nationalsozialismus überhaupt und die Gründe dafür, daß ich nicht in die Partei eingetreten bin," of July 5, 1945, NL Tiedke. I am grateful to Roland Knebusch for placing these materials of his grandfather at my disposal. There is a very useful discussion of Tiedke and his role as general director of Alte Leipziger in the unpublished manuscript, also kindly placed at my disposal by the author, Volker Weiß, "Ist das, was wir machen, auch gerecht? Zum Gedächtnis an Generaldirektor Johannes Tiedke 1881–1947 (Oberursel, 1995).

[12] Niederschrift über die Sitzung des Allgemeinen Präsidialausschusses des Reichsverbandes der Privatversicherung am 16. Juli 1936, pp. 12–14, GDV, RS/14.

Table B. *Securities Held by Allianz and*
Allianz Leben, 1931–1945 (Reichsmark)

Year	Allianz	Allianz Leben
1931	12,933,833.96	118,900,341.56
1932	18,634,017.46	150,342,718.05
1933	25,972,466.69	164,806,657.99
1934	33,691,063.52	220,781,252.05
1935	48,060,166.34	267,387,318.73
1936	59,024,101.21	311,229,397.36
1937	69,335,711.09	360,416,775.67
1938	61,522,393.32	419,931,346.29
1939	72,498,254.72	477,804,778.32
1940	84,284,428.13	639,265,299.98
1941	108,341,366.60	757,923,440.01
1942	128,072,238.69	875,357,933.16
1943	138,411,664.29	995,696,285.98
1944	158,949,452.25	N/A
1945	155,498,589.92	N/A

Source: Business reports of Allianz and Allianz Leben,
1931–1945.

starting to operate on a 3% basis early was a good idea.[13] It was manifest that the autonomy of the insurance business had become very limited indeed; Funk had every reason to have confidence in the insurance industry organization, and the Allianz executives who led it, since they could be counted upon not only to adapt to the government's policies but even to anticipate them.

Nowhere was this more in evidence than in the massive investment by the insurance industry during these years in securities almost entirely attributable to the holding of government paper. Table B demonstrates the size of this increase in the holding of securities, largely governmental. Whereas the relative percentages of government securities and private stock issues of the total amounts of securities held by Allianz did not change much during the period in question, the change for Allianz Leben was dramatic. In 1931, 11.6% of the total securities held were in government bonds and guaranteed loans; 39% were shares in banks, railroads, and industrial enterprises. In 1939, 54.6% of the total securities were held in government bonds and guaranteed loans, and the 11% held in shares were all invested in Reichsbahn preferential stock. In 1931, 15% of Allianz Leben's securities holdings were in bonds of banks, railroads, and industrial enterprises; in 1939, the amount so invested was only 5%.[14]

[13] Aktennote Schmitt. Besuch bei Minister Funk, 24. Sept. 1940, MR, A 1/7.
[14] Geschäftsberichte, Allianz Leben 1931 (p. 25), 1939 (p. 33), FHA.

As in the case of interest-rate reductions, the process of acquiring increasing amounts of securities to help finance the regime's programs began "voluntarily." Thus, in September 1934, the Reich Finance Ministry approached Director Schloeßmann and asked if Allianz Leben was willing to take over a large portfolio of securities owned by the Reich to assist the work creation program. Not only did Schloeßmann agree, he also informed members of the Association of German Life Insurance Companies of the proposal with the result that 37 companies bought a total of 50 million of the fixed-interest securities. Allianz Leben took 20 million and Allianz took 5 million of these securities, thus together accounting for half the purchase.[15]

This, however, was only the beginning. What could be more convenient and useful than deriving money from the investment of private enterprises in bond issues? – especially where (as with the insurance industry) funds had to be invested "securely" in order to cover obligations. Soon there was a renewed summons to purchase bonds for the Reich railroads, the Reichsautobahn, and the general struggle against unemployment. A more or less standardized procedure developed. Thus, Hilgard would negotiate with the Finance Ministry, the amount and conditions would be determined, the Reich Group and its members would then be informed, and the level of subscription would be based on premiums received by the companies in question. The companies would be asked to pledge their subscriptions, and careful record would be kept of performance. In 1935, for example, the insurance industry was asked to subscribe 200 million marks worth of the Reich bond issue of May 1935, with Allianz alone taking 25% of the subscription. The insurance industry had in fact raised 204,768,500 RM, with 168,644,500 RM being contributed by the private companies. No sooner had these results been announced, in the Presidium of the Reich Group in November 1935, then Hilgard indicated that the industry would be called upon to contribute to a 1936 bond issue – though he knew neither the amount nor the terms. He could only urge that they be prepared and not invest their available money in long-term assets but rather in short-term interest-bearing assets like treasury bills. In fact, the insurance companies ended up with substantial quotas for not one but two government bond issues in 1936. The first was for 195,047,800 RM in Reich bonds; 158,302,600 RM came from the private insurance sector. Allianz bought 5 million RM in these bonds, while Allianz Leben bought 25 million RM. The second bond issue quota for the insurance industry resulted in the purchase of 239,804,200 RM's worth of Reich-guaranteed bonds of Reichsautobahn-Gesellschaft, 198,562,700 RM of which came from the private sector. Allianz purchased 6.5 million RM of this issue, while Allianz Leben purchased 30 million RM. Although these officially were "voluntary" investments – since Hilgard and the Reich Group had no more right to impose investment quotas than they had to impose interest-rate reductions – the Reich Group made a regular practice of "reminding" companies to pledge or asking them why they had refused to do so. Indeed, even foreign insurance companies

[15] Schloeßmann an Ministerialrat Bernard (RWM), 2. Okt. 1934, BAB, R 3101/17009, Bl. 199–200.

doing business in Germany were expected to do something for their "host land," and they did purchase 1,225,000 RM of the 1935 issue and a combined total of 2,527,250 RM of the two 1936 issues.[16]

While the government needed to publicize these bond issues for the purpose of generating public support, it had an obvious interest in suppressing information about the extent to which its success depended on the compulsion being exerted on the business community. The RWM and Hilgard thus regularly warned against unauthorized divulging of information to the press. For anyone employed at a major insurance company, however, it was difficult not to notice what was happening. Thus, in 1937, Socialist informants at an insurance company reported:

The financial situation is viewed much more critically than the international position of the Reich. The employees are at least to some extent aware of the extent to which insurance monies are drawn upon for the compulsory loans of the Reich and ask themselves how the financial difficulties will be solved in the long run. They had expected Germany to join in when the Gold Bloc countries devalued and were astonished that this did not occur. There are already discussions as to whether or not the price increases in Germany are to be viewed as the beginning of an inflation.[17]

Certainly there must have been many vivid memories of the role played by government bonds in the Great Inflation and by their depreciation, although these could neither be discussed in public nor even put on paper. Nevertheless, there were grounds for concern because a fundamental change of economic policy was announced at the Nuremberg Party Congress on September 9, 1936.

The Four-Year Plan – officially the second such plan, since the name was intended to remind Germans of the first and its alleged success in fighting unemployment – was intended to achieve rapid rearmament through mobilization of the economy. However, it ran counter to the conservative economic ideas of Schacht and others who felt that it was necessary to return to more normal economic and financial practices; instead, the Plan was intended to push forward preparedness by promoting high levels of self-sufficiency and vastly increasing the management of the economy. Toward this end, immense powers were vested in the person of Hermann Göring, who was made Reich Plenipotentiary for the Four-Year Plan and given an organization to implement the plan on October 16, 1936. Göring proceeded to coordinate the Economics Ministry with his

[16] See Reichsgruppe Versicherungen an RWM, 16. Aug. 1937, 5. Okt. 1937, Hilgard an den Leiter der Wirtschaftsgruppe Privatversicherung, 2. April 1936, Vermerke Köhler, Nov. und Dez. 1937, and other related documents in SM, 1458/1/65, Bl. 4–5, 10–14, 34–5, 40–1; Niederschrift über die Sitzung des allgemeinen Präsidialausschusses des Reichsverbands der Privatversicherung am 22. Nov. 1935, pp. 17–18, GDV, RS/13. For the lists of companies and the premiums and assessments for the bond drives in 1935–1937 as well as correspondence and "reminders," see GDV, unverzeichnete Akte (Az 20, XI); see also Bericht an die Aufsichtsratsmitglieder, 1. Okt. 1935, FHA, S 17.1/23.

[17] Deutschland-Berichte der Sozialdemokratischen Partei Deutschlands (1937), p. 352. On the efforts to control press reports, see the Rundschreiben of May 22, 1935, Jan. 7, 1936, and April 2, 1936, GDV, RS/18.

own organization to the point where he had the RWM apparatus at his disposal. Schacht resigned in December 1937 and was replaced by Funk in February 1938. Exactly what these personnel developments meant for Allianz was unclear. On the one hand, Schmitt had excellent relations with Göring and Funk, while he and Hilgard continued to have good connections in the ministries. On the other hand, Schmitt's fears about the regime's trajectory toward war could only be increased by the Four-Year Plan, and neither he nor Hilgard and their colleagues in the insurance business could be particularly happy about the expanding role of the government in economic affairs. One of the most serious potential threats came from the appointment of a Reich Commissar for Price Formation on October 29, 1936, in the person of the hard-nosed Gauleiter of Silesia, Josef Wagner. The charge of the new office was to fight inflation, which could otherwise be expected to increase enormously under the Four-Year Plan. Wagner had extraordinary powers and, on November 26, 1936, issued a price-stop decree that subjected all price and wage increases to his approval. Needless to say, the effect of this price stop on insurance premiums was a source of great concern to the industry leadership, since Wagner considered insurance premiums to be prices subject to his authority.[18]

The Four-Year Plan was a test of Hilgard's already well-honed talents for speaking the language of the regime at a time when he was confronting a new wave of conflict – involving such issues as automobile insurance rates – between the private insurers, on the one hand, and the DAF and publicly chartered companies (as well as the Party radicals) on the other hand. The subject of auto rates had assumed special importance because of the Nazi craze for motorization, bad German driving habits, and pressures to tighten the restrictions on insurance salespersons and agents. The more the regime challenged liberal economic principles, the more Hilgard had to encase his defense of private insurer profitability in an ever more elaborate shell of what passed for economic thinking in the National Socialist context.

A splendid example of Hilgard's skill on the National Socialist political tightrope under these circumstances is provided by his speech, "The Task of German Insurance in the New Economy," to the DAF's Reich Working Congress of the Reich Plant Community for Banking and Insurance on October 15, 1936 – that is, virtually coincident with the announcement of the Four-Year Plan. DAF events were always difficult occasions, especially since this one was presided over by DAF leader Paul Lencer. Hilgard shared the platform with Professor Paul Riebesell, who represented the publicly chartered insurance companies but was a man of moderate disposition with whom one could do business. Hilgard's right-hand

---

[18] The significance of the Four-Year Plan is often underestimated, but Richard Overy has rightly called attention to its immense importance for the development of the economy. See his working paper for the Arbeitskreis zur Rolle der Unternehmen im Nationalsozialismus of the Gesellschaft für Unternehmensgeschichte, Frankfurt, "The Four-Year Plan" (Frankfurt, 2000), as well as *War and Economy in the Third Reich* (Oxford, 1994), Pt. 3. It is worth noting that Wagner, although an old Nazi, retained his church ties and was thrown out of all his offices in 1943; he later became involved in the July 1944 plot against Hitler and was probably murdered because of it.

man at Allianz, Director Paul Lux, went over Riebesell's speech carefully and also made a point of giving Riebesell a draft of Hilgard's speech together with assurances that there would be no critical remarks about the publicly chartered insurance companies. Hilgard decided to exercise similar restraint with respect to any mention of rate increases or deductibles for automobile insurance due to the increasing problems with reckless driving. Instead, mention would be made of the faith the insurance companies were placing in the government's "traffic education program." One wanted to avoid public criticism of the private insurance companies at all costs and to tread lightly in dealing with nasty Nazi criticism emanating, for example, from the SS journal *Das Schwarze Korps*. Most recently – and to the great annoyance of Allianz's public relations director, Baron Edgar von Uexküll, and the director of Allianz's life insurance operations, Rudolf Schloeßmann – Karl Samwer (former general director of Gothaer Lebensversicherungsbank AG and chairman of the German Association of Insurance Science) had responded to *Das Schwarze Korps* attacks in the newspapers, greatly irritating young editors in the Party press and potentially encouraging them to engage in further criticisms. Uexküll and Schloeßmann turned to Allianz's general director, Hans Heß, to intervene personally and restrain Samwer, an effort that met with success and nicely illustrates the kind of backroom politics in which businessmen now had to engage.[19]

It thus remained for Hilgard to further still these troubled waters by placing the interests of the private insurers in the context of a pandering National Socialist discourse. The Führer's Four-Year Plan, Hilgard announced, had placed new tasks before the insurance companies and had thereby given "the work of the insurance industry a political meaning." What Hilgard conceded with a short sentence, however, he then relativized in a longer and more convoluted one: "That should not mean that we see the political obligations of our work in politicizing and organizing, but rather that it exists in a clean, objective, forward-striving labor which takes its meaning from service to the State and the people." Hilgard went on to explicate this conception of the role of private enterprise in the new economic order:

Whether we now seek to win over the individual comrade to enter into the community of risks of the insured, whether we have to regulate damage costs or whether we have to take into account certain social or demographic policy considerations in the setting of rates, whether we follow the leadership of the state in the investment of the capital trusted to us or whether we promote large constructive plans and works through the taking over of risks – we *always* have the obligation of testing each of our acts for their effect upon the entire national community.[20]

Six weeks later, on December 2, 1936, in the more agreeable environment of the general meeting of the Reich Association for Private Insurance in Dresden, Hilgard addressed the problems of "The Tasks of Private Insurance in the Four-Year

[19] Lux an Hilgard, 8. Okt. 1936, FHA, S 17.6/8.
[20] The speech is to be found in ibid.

Plan" more directly.[21] To be sure, the concrete issues were once again embellished with dramatic language and embedded in the ideological discourse of the Third Reich, as Hilgard strove once again to save the basic principles of the capitalist economy by bringing them in through the back door. Thus, the immensity of the tasks presented by the Plan were "perhaps frightening," above all for those "who perhaps want to operate on the basis of an economic viewpoint which belongs to a time that has been overcome." Notions of "the greatest profitability" were antiquated and incompatible with the new way of thinking demanded by National Socialism – which was not to say, however, that economic considerations could be dismissed:

Our task must continue to be to work for the profitability and the maintenance of the economic strength of our enterprises. For he, who perhaps out of a fanatical desire to serve the people throws economic efficiency or the striving for profitability overboard and sacrifices his enterprises in a falsely understood sense of sacrifice, will go to ruin just as well as he who does not take any heed of the demands of the general welfare. The one goes to ruin because he believes he can neglect the laws of the National Socialist world view, and the other suffers shipwreck because he believes that he can set aside the eternally valid laws of economics.

Hilgard then moved from these spiritual and intellectual "heights" to the bread-and-butter issues presented by the Four-Year Plan. All areas of insurance would be affected in one way or another, but certain branches would be particularly involved – for example, fire insurance, machine insurance, liability insurance, and flight insurance. In every case, Hilgard was (not surprisingly) worried about the implications of the Four-Year Plan for his industry. Fires, machine breakdowns, accidents and mishaps, and plane crashes were, after all, to be anticipated in an economy about to be so massively overheated. The dilemma was that it would be difficult to increase premiums precisely because the greater risks were being incurred in the national cause. There had been, for example, enormous pressures on the fire insurers to reduce their premiums, and Hilgard claimed there had been substantial reductions during the past few years whose general invisibility reflected the fact that most reductions were handled individually. The high profits came from older policies, and Hilgard urged that they be put into reserves so as to have a basis for dealing with the anticipated increases in damages due to the Four-Year Plan. At the same time, he appealed to the branch to reduce premiums and improve the quality of protection for raw materials producers working for the Four-Year Plan. He expected the machine insurance branch to experience particular stress because of production demands and warned that only "internally very powerful and strong corporations" would be able to handle the insurance in this branch. The obvious implication was again that the big insurance companies would be best suited to meet the requirements

---

[21] The discussion and quotes that follow are based on the copy of the speech in the Sitzungsbericht über die ordentliche Hauptversammlung des Reichsverbandes der Privatversicherung am 2. Dez. 1936, GDV, RS/9.

of the Plan and that their financial soundness was of central importance. For such reasons, Hilgard had some particularly nasty things to say about the price competition and lack of discipline exercised by the liability insurance companies, warning that "at no time and in no area has lack of regulation and discipline led to anything other than downfall."

Hilgard's summons to self-discipline and to providing more service at less cost under the anticipated trying conditions was particularly pronounced with respect to flight insurance and to reinsurance questions. On the one hand, this branch was important as a source of foreign exchange, which the Reich desperately needed. On the other hand, the insurance industry was being criticized for having too passive a foreign-exchange balance, and Hilgard urged that the German companies undertake more of their own reinsurance and reevaluate their foreign reinsurance connections – without, of course, undermining Germany's international trading connections. Here again, the message was that stronger and richer companies were needed to meet the autarchy demands of the new program and still keep Germany active internationally. From this perspective, Hilgard worried greatly about the pressures emanating from critics of the industry in the DAF and Party, anxieties that came through even as he expressed their alleged commonality of interests. He warned against pressures to overregulate insurance agents and agencies, as demanded by the DAF, and was particularly opposed to the expansion of group insurance for each occupational group and profession, which he castigated as "collective selfishness." If each occupational group joined together for insurance purposes, then nothing would be left but high-risk customers, an obviously undesirable situation for insurance companies. In short, the private insurance industry had to be on its guard as it faced the new demands of the Four-Year Plan, for as Hilgard noted in a rare moment of straightforwardness, "[w]e face the mighty block of the German Labor Front which, as you all know, is possessed with an extraordinary urge to activity." Hilgard did insist that the task was not to fight the DAF but to work together with it. Nevertheless, the message was clear to those who understood the language being used. Somehow the industry had to demonstrate its worth in the Four-Year Plan or succumb to its enemies in the party and regime.

The Four-Year Plan meant a substantial increase in the insurance industry's holdings of government paper, as well as a further reduction of the alleged "voluntarism" in their purchase through the systematization of subscription levels and restriction of other investment options. This development became particularly evident in 1938. Whereas the insurance industry was supposed to contribute 125 million RM to the bond drive in the first half of 1938, the contribution was raised to 200 million RM for the second half of the year. Furthermore, life insurance companies were expected to invest a minimum of 15% of their yearly premium receipts in the bond issue, while other branches were required to invest at least 3% of their premium receipts. The RWM assigned the Reich Group the task of monitoring these contribution levels. The Finance and Economics Ministries also expected the insurance companies to continue their existing level of subscription to longer-term Reich loans issued by the government, the 200 million RM bond purchase being considered a supplementary investment. Also, the regime had obviously learned from the experience of the First World War, when companies used previously purchased war bonds to pay for new ones; insurance companies were warned that the investments in question were to be made from current income and not from the sale of previously purchased state securities. Indeed, a secret Reich Economics Ministry decree ordered that the companies were to invest all available monies in Reich bonds, while the provision of money or granting of mortgages for new housing construction was banned. Similarly, the purchase of real estate was allowable only with special permission, and this explains the elaborate arguments in Allianz's purchase of Kaufingerstraße 22 in Munich discussed earlier. The insurance companies hoped that both the size of subscriptions and the restrictions on investments would be reduced in 1939, but they were rapidly disabused of such fantasies. Indeed, Hilgard informed his colleagues in January 1939 that the life insurance companies were expected to provide a minimum of 30% of their premium income to the bond drive, while the Reichsbank reported in April that the insurance industry had purchased 620,231,600 RM in Reich securities issued by the Reich in 1938. It anticipated that the industry would provide 800,000,000 RM in 1939. In that year, Allianz bought 6.7 million RM and Allianz Leben subscribed to 57 million RM of the government loans. By 1940, insurance industry subscriptions reached 1.4 billion marks for the year. Hence, a fundamental consequence of the Four-Year Plan was that the assets of insurance companies were increasingly dominated by state securities. The engagement was made all the more problematic by the 1939 reduction of interest rates on the bonds from 4.5% to 4%. In 1933, Reich loans amounted to 10% of the capital assets of the Allianz or 12% if one added in municipal and other public loans. The respective percentages for 1939 were 21% and 24%.[22]

There were, of course, other important areas of investment aside from real estate, mortgages, and government bonds, but in some cases these had become problematic. Although Allianz held shares in a number of important banks and enterprises – Commerzbank, AEG, IG Farben, and Vereinigte Stahlwerke – share holdings averaged about 13% of securities and participations between 1933 and 1939.[23] The stock market, however, was not an institution that prospered in the Third Reich. The government had legislated a Dividend and Bond Law on December 4, 1934, which set a ceiling on dividends with the object of promoting

---

[22] See the extensive documentation in SM, 1458/1/66, especially Schreiben der Reichsgruppe, July 2, 1938, August 8, 1938, January 1, 1939, and April 1, 1939. For the Allianz subscriptions, see Bl. 218 and 232. See also Bericht an die Aufsichtsratsmitglieder, 19. Sept. 1938, FHA, S 17.1/2, and the Geschäftsberichte for 1933 and 1939.

[23] The holdings are listed in the Geschäftsberichte for 1933–1938, FHA. After that time, they were not individually listed. In addition, of course, Allianz held majority control shares of the corporations in the concern. Its shares in Munich Re and Hermes, however, were listed as normal shareholdings.

its bonds and converting the public debt. Hence there was little incentive to issue new shares or to buy them. This was true of even so promising an enterprise as the ever-expanding Hermann-Göring-Werke, because such shares were not accepted as primary reserve coverage by the RAA.[24] More promising were loans to enterprises connected with the Four-Year Plan, and these were encouraged by the government although they were not without problems of their own. In 1937, for example, the Reich Economics Ministry encouraged Allianz to lend IG Farben the money needed to build worker housing at the new Buna factory in Schkopau near Merseburg, but the entire effort was aborted when the DAF intervened and offered to do the financing itself.[25] Allianz had better luck with an 8-million-RM loan to Harpener Bergbau AG in 1936, which the latter company intended to use to buy shares of Essener Steinkohlenbergwerke AG from Vereinigte Stahlwerke. The latter intended to use the money it received to repurchase the shares of Vereinigte Stahlwerke that Friedrich Flick had sold to the Reich back in 1932. As part of the deal, Allianz also purchased 1.5 million RM in the shares of the Essener Steinkohlenbergwerke from Deutsche Bank. The money was thus being used to promote a reprivatization desired by industry and the government, and Allianz also received as security a mortgage on Harpener buildings worth some 22 million RM. In this case, the RAA accepted the mortgage as primary reserve coverage.[26]

Such promising high capitalist transactions were not a daily occurrence, of course, but Allianz made major loans to utility companies – particularly those connected with Dessauer Gas, whose supervisory board chairman was Kurt Schmitt – and also participated in loan consortia with banks and/or other insurance companies to provide substantial loans to big industrial firms such as Vereinigte Stahlwerke, Wintershall, Henschel & Sohn, and Braunkohle Benzin AG.[27] The concern was indeed hungry for good loan investments, most of which were actually to be made by Allianz Leben, where Schloeßmann handled industrial loan negotiations. Hilgard complained to Director Kimmich of Deutsche Bank that the latter was not as forthcoming in serving as an intermediary for friendly companies, and pointed out that one needed to encourage industrial firms involved in building worker housing or productive facilities under the Four-Year Plan to seek such loans. The way to do this, Hilgard pointed out, was to have the company or its bank approach Reich Commissar Walter Köhler (who handled Four-Year Plan matters in the RWM) and claim a need for a loan. Köhler apparently was easy to deal with under the right conditions: "No

---

[24] See James, "Deutsche Bank," pp. 285–91. On the Hermann-Göring-Werke shares, see RWM an den Braunschweigischen Minister des Innern, SM, 1458/1/59, Bl. 19.
[25] See the correspondence between Warncke and Mansfeld, Feb. 9–25, 1937, SM, 1458/1/59, Bl. 3–5.
[26] See Steinbrinck an Staatssekretär Posse, 1. April 1930, and RAA an RWM, 4. April 1936, Vermerk, 7. April 1936, and other relevant correspondence, BAB, R 3101/17078.
[27] For a utility loan to Stassfurter Licht- und Kraftwerke AG (1935), see BAB, R 3104/20500, Bl. 60–4; for the industrial loans, which were given in 1938–1940, see BAB, R 3104/20492, Bl. 39–40, 46, 57, 62, 121, 132.

Eduard Hilgard, head of the Reich Group for Insurance, giving a speech at the celebration of the 125th anniversary of the Berlinische Feuer-Versicherungs-Anstalt in the conference hall of Berlin City Hall, December 11, 1937.

hard boundaries are drawn, but rather, if someone has special contacts, permissions beyond this narrow program are granted."[28] Thus, Allianz had been able to give out 30 million in loans to such companies, and Hilgard added that Allianz was prepared to act as an intermediary with other insurance companies if the amounts involved were too large for it to handle alone. Kimmich was careful to take note of the information, although his own inclination was to approach other friendly insurance companies directly rather than have Allianz act as the go-between. Also, as Kimmich told Hilgard on another occasion, it was not easy to offer Allianz good prospects because Allianz was very selective and "sets the strictest conditions with respect to the quality of the loans. For example, loans to armaments plants are made only with the greatest reluctance by Allianz – most

[28] Aktenvermerk Kimmich, 13. Dez. 1939, BAB, 80 Ba 2/P 5779, Bl. 35–6.

favored are utilities, or consumer industries, for example breweries, but even here there must be accessory guarantees such as securities, etc."[29]

One senses from such statements that Allianz, Hilgard, and the industry were seeking to reduce the risks of the Four-Year Plan as much as possible even as they became more and more involved in its financing and in making sacrifices to ensure its realization. Allianz certainly sought to demonstrate such a spirit of sacrifice, with Hilgard leading the way. Thus he personally intervened to have the concern renounce all profits on its fire insurance contracts for new factories that were providing raw and other materials for the Four-Year Plan. Allianz also led a consortium of ten insurance companies to insure the Hermann Göring Werke in Germany and Austria.[30] Such "virtuous" acts, however, were part of an elaborate political effort to meet the challenges to the insurance industry on a very broad front, and Hilgard's strategic position as head of the Reich Group for Insurance (with its direct subordination to the economics minister) was an important instrument in his defense of Allianz and the private insurance industry as well as a useful means of exercising a certain restraint on the publicly chartered companies.

It was not a comfortable position to be "leader" of both types of enterprises. As Director Bebler of Swiss Re reported after a June 1935 conversation with Hilgard in Berlin:

Herr Hilgard complains a great deal about the burden and unpleasantnesses which his office as leader of the German insurance business places on him. His position is especially painful because of the publicly chartered companies, who go their own crooked way. While his heart now as before beats for the private insurers, he must powerlessly look on and see how the publicly chartered companies under the leadership of Goebbels, the brother of the Reich Minister, fights the private insurance business by every means, fair and foul. He, Hilgard, stands there as a kind of buffer between the private and the publicly chartered insurance groups.[31]

Hilgard was on edge, and his tolerance for criticism was minimal. While he seemed to have no choice but put up with problems coming from the Party, he was infuriated when Artur Lauinger (of the *Frankfurter Zeitung*), who had played such an important role in exposing the Favag scandal, continued to probe the insurance business:

Herr Hilgard expressed himself very angrily about the *Frankfurter Zeitung*, where the previous economics editor Lauinger had as a Jew to resign but who unofficially is the director and allows himself to criticize and interfere in a way that has become really unbearable. He demands information about all kinds of details from the companies that

---

[29] Kimmich an Rummel, 17. Dez. 1940, ibid., Bl. 66.
[30] Aktenvermerk Moesler, 14. Dez. 1936, BA, 80 Ba 2/P 5787; Allianz an das RAA, 27. Juli 1938, and other relevant correspondence, BAK, B 280/12237, Bl. 312–14.
[31] Bericht über Besprechung am 13. Juni 1935 in Berlin, SR, Feuer 11.

are none of his business. Herr Hilgard intends to move against Lauinger in an energetic manner and put him on ice definitively.[32]

There is no record as to what action, if any, Hilgard took. Lauinger remained in Germany until 1938, was briefly in Buchenwald, and ended up in England. This episode demonstrates how easily the otherwise diplomatic Hilgard could be provoked into an anti-Semitic outburst.

It is clear, however, that this in no way solved his problems with the publicly chartered companies and the Nazi critics who could not be put on ice. While Hilgard was a convinced believer in working with the Nazis to temper them, it must be said that one of his tactics at this time was most peculiar indeed – namely, his support for the appointment of Andreas Braß to replace General Director Oertel (who wanted to leave his post for health reasons,[33]) as head of the Private Insurance Economic Group at the beginning of 1937. Hilgard had first encountered Braß at the Bayerische Versicherungsbank, where he had been employed. Subsequently, Braß was appointed general director of one of the DAF's insurance companies, Deutsche Lebensversicherung AG. Braß was, as he never tired of repeating, an Old Fighter (indeed, Party member no. 10657) who had battled for the movement "at the most forward line" since 1923.[34] Braß continued to struggle for less dramatic causes after 1933, and his fevered commitment brought to the most mundane of issues that proper measure of drama and ideological ballyhoo needed to perpetuate his National Socialist credentials.

Braß had achieved a measure of notoriety in insurance circles because of two campaigns he had launched in 1935–1936. The first of these was for the elimination of the Association of German Life Insurance Companies, which (he argued) had become superfluous with the establishment of the branch group within the Reich Group and the installation of the "leadership principle." In creating the Reich Group and the economic groups, Schmitt's strategy had been to retain the old associations for the various branches of the insurance business alongside them, of which one of the most important was the Life Insurance Association. Braß wished to undermine this strategy, which lay at the heart of the old order of business self-administration. Indeed, Braß wanted to get rid of all the old associations, including the Association of Private Insurers, on the grounds that it was a National Socialist principle to promote simplification and

[32] Ibid.

[33] On Oertel's motive for resigning, see the manuscript of Director Karl Haus of the Kölnische Hagel-Versicherungs-Gesellschaft, "Die Deutsche Versicherungswirtschaft und der Nationalsozialismus," (1946), p. 10, AXA, Bestand Kölnische-Hagel-Versicherungs-AG.

[34] Braß an Feder, 13. Jan. 1934, requesting a position on the insurance committee of the newly founded Akademie für Deutsches Recht, BAB, R 3101/16959, Bl. 7–8. Hilgard, in his postwar interrogation, claims to have first met Braß in 1935 and that Braß was appointed to the DAF position in 1936. Braß, however, already held the latter position in 1934, so Hilgard must have met him at the Bayerische Versicherungsbank earlier. See his interrogation of July 14, 1947, NA, RG 260, OMGUS, FINAD, 2/57/6–8.

avoid double organization. In a series of letters to Schloeßmann, Oertel, and other leaders of the Association in the spring and summer of 1935, Braß promoted his cause but with little success. While other industry leaders conceded that there was some duplication and that the establishment of a single organization might be a future goal, they argued that the two types of organizations were necessary because the legislation creating the Reich Group and economic groups for the various branches had specifically barred them from engaging in market regulating functions, so that price issues continued to be the province of the old associations. Furthermore, the new branch groups depended on the old associations for funding. Coordination, Braß's interlocutors insisted, was guaranteed through the personal identity of the leaders of the associations and the Reich Group and its branch organizations. It is hard not to conclude that underlying these arguments was a strong desire on the part of the industry leadership to maintain its tried and true organizations precisely against the sort of synchronization that Braß held forth as an ideal. They were certainly not as enthused about the leadership principle in business life as Braß, whose commitment to the idea was as total as could be. Schloeßmann, for example, bluntly warned against "a strict carrying through of the leadership principle," since many association members would simply resign (as was their right) if the chairman forced decisions upon them. This would be unfortunate, in Schloeßmann's view, since the Association worked in common to promote the insurance idea to the public.[35]

The second area where Braß distinguished himself, in this case with considerably more success, was with respect to automobile insurance. This was one of the industry's great headaches in the early 1930s because of pressure from the Party to reduce rates and the large number of accidents that helped make automobile insurance a losing business. The insurers had formed a rate cartel, and in mid-1936 they tried to solve their problems by increasing rates and devising a complicated scheme of deductibles for automobile and liability insurance. At this point the DAF insurers – under the leadership of Braß – refused to go along, charged that some automobile dealers were getting as much as a 30% commission on the insurance, and called upon the insurance companies to reduce their costs and, if necessary, subsidize automobile insurance from profits made in other branches. In order to deal with the crisis, Hilgard set up a special commission to find a solution, where Braß roundly declared that the DAF companies

will not go along if the solution is only arrived at on the basis of the view of the insurers. He does not see himself as a representative of his companies but as the bearer of the will of the Movement. As such, he cannot recognize that the only possible alternative for

---

[35] See especially Braß to Schloeßmann, June 26, 1935, and Schloeßmann to Braß, Aug. 22, 1935, BAB, R 3101/9270, Bl. 105–12. See also Braß to RWM, Dec. 11, 1935, ibid., Bl. 103–4, and his correspondence with other industry leaders, Bl. 113–26.

reconstructing the automobile insurance business is by means of premium increases that benefit the insurers or reduction of benefits at the expense of the general public. Rather, as is according to the will of the Führer, sacrifices must be made if necessary ....[36]

Braß denied that any rate increase was necessary, but he did indicate that the Party was not opposed to a deductible and that this would reduce costs. Hilgard seized upon this concession, expressing his agreement with Braß on the need to keep the general public in mind and pointing out that "we are after all not some pile of interested persons but a committee conscious of its responsibility." Hilgard then developed this perspective further by pointing out they could not operate on the basis of voluntarism and that their decisions needed external reinforcement:

There must therefore be the necessary authority behind our decisions, and it is therefore important to assure the agreement of the Party and government. He [Hilgard] has found in dealing with Party agencies that they in part really have much understanding for the difficult situation of the insurers. Nevertheless, one can hardly speak of a united Party will in this connection. One has to work in an enlightening way within the party, especially along the lines of making clear that insurance premiums are no dominating portion of the upkeep costs of a car.[37]

The episode is important, not only as a revealing general illustration of the politics of the insurance business at this time, but also because it helps explain Hilgard's decision to support the appointment of Braß as head of the Private Insurance Economic Group in early 1937. Braß had attained a good deal of popularity because of his role in the automobile insurance question, and he was blessed by good luck since the costs of the insurers began to drop after the second half of 1936 owing to a decrease in new drivers, better traffic education, and stricter traffic regulations. Ultimately, the prices and regulations governing automobile insurance were settled after lengthy negotiations by a decree of the Price Commissar of February 14, 1938, and Braß could take some credit for having led the way and for eliminating abuses such as the automobile dealer provisions. Back in 1936, however, Hilgard seems to have come away with the impression that one could do business with Braß, that his Party connections were indeed useful, and that he might be used for precisely those purposes of "enlightenment" within the Party about which he had spoken. Furthermore, Hilgard was aware through his contacts in the RWM that Party circles were anxious to have Braß appointed, and Hilgard managed to convince himself that Braß would be

---

[36] Bericht über die Sitzung der Kommission für die Kraftfahrzeug-Versicherung am 1. Sept. 1936, GDV, RS/34, p. 5. There is a good discussion of the automobile insurance problem in Arps, *Durch unruhige Zeiten*, Bd. 2, pp. 138–45.

[37] Sitzung, 1. Sept. 1936, GDV, RS/34, pp. 6–7. Hilgard went on to suggest that one also had to work on public opinion in general and divert some of the attention to the profits of the automobile makers so that all the burdens would not be passed on to the insurers!

useful in his struggles with the publicly chartered companies and his battles with Schwede-Coburg and Hans Goebbels.[38]

It was neither the first nor the last instance in which Hilgard was to outsmart himself, as Braß was to prove a Trojan Horse. One of the first things he did was to relegate Privy Councilor Lippert, the tried and true business manager of the Reich Association and the Association of Private Insurers, to the ever-decreasing activities of the Reich Association. Indirectly, Braß was thus achieving his goal of getting rid of the latter organization, while the major work was now turned over to his private secretary Krauss. The 54-year-old Lippert found the situation impossible and resigned in September 1937. Hilgard, who had worked closely with Lippert, found this extremely unpleasant.[39]

Nevertheless, Braß did initially seem helpful with respect to the issue of price controls under the Four-Year Plan. The position taken by private insurers after the price-stop decree of November 26, 1936, was that insurance premiums differed from normal prices in that they depended on the level and extent of claims being made and were often individualized because of different risks. The effort to set fixed premiums or to reduce them would have the effect of harming the "community of risk" served by insurance companies; it would also, argued the insurers, endanger the coverage requirements set by the RAA. Thus, Hilgard and his colleagues sought to protect the insurance industry from the Price Commissar by appealing to the RWM and the RAA for exemption from ceilings on insurance premiums.[40] These agencies, which were responsible for the supervision of insurance, did indeed argue this cause on behalf of the insurance companies, stressing in particular that the liquidity of the insurance companies was very important for the financing of the Four-Year Plan. Nevertheless, Price Commissar Wagner's office insisted that its powers extended to insurance premiums, although it agreed to work with the RAA and RWM in dealing with the industry. Braß, while compelled to recognize the authority of the commissar, nevertheless shared the view of Hilgard and the insurers that insurance premiums could not simply be treated as prices.[41] In May, the conflict was joined at the highest level of government, with Economics Minister Schacht himself intervening to argue that he had ultimate responsibility for the welfare of the insurance industry; Wagner stood his ground with the claim that premium increases on a broad front would inevitably damage price stability. After months of tedious negotiation, an agreement was finally reached on February 1, 1938, setting down complicated guidelines for what did and did not constitute a "price increase" in the insurance field. Final decision-making power was left in the hands of the Reich Commissar, and the agreement provided for use of the RAA

---

[38] See Hilgard interrogation of July 14, 1947, NA, RG 260, FINAD, OMGUS, 2/57/6–8.
[39] See Hilgard to RWM, Jan. 12, 1942, SM, 1458/1/109, Bl. 231–2.
[40] See Reichsverband der Privatversicherung an das RAA, 7. Dez. 1936, SM, 1458/1/2062, Bl. 5–8.
[41] See the correspondence for early 1937 in ibid., and especially Braß's speech of Feb. 11, 1937, "Versicherungswirtschaft im Sinne der Gemeinschaft," ibid., Bl. 402–19.

as an intermediary and accepted the principle that changing levels of risk justified changes of premium.[42]

Far more worrisome than this bureaucratic wrangling were the challenges that came from outside the bureaucracy, which Hilgard and Schmitt had sought to prevent by donations to the SS and the appointment of the Old Fighter Braß. On April 5, 1937, the RAA complained to the Economics Minister about attacks on the private insurance industry, and specifically on Neue Frankfurter, by *Das Schwarze Korps*. Between February and April 1936, the journal ran hostile articles, one of them making charges about the Neue Frankfurter's handling of claims – charges that the RAA had already investigated and that had turned out to be totally false. The customer in question had praised Neue Frankfurter for its handling of his claim; Hilgard had sought a retraction from the *Schwarze Korps,* but the journal had refused. A new series of attacks had been launched in February 1937: one was accurate but most were false and all were designed to put the private insurers in bad repute. The RWM was concerned enough to mediate a meeting between Kurt Schmitt and the 27-year-old fanatic who edited the journal, Gunter d'Alquen, at which the latter promised to give his insurance company victims a chance to respond to false charges.[43]

It was not long, however, before d'Alquen was up to his old tricks, as demonstrated by an article of October 14, 1937, entitled "Unholy Allianz," in which a speech of General Director Heß was cited where Heß noted that the volume of premiums still had not recovered to its 1930 levels because of the decrease in claims. Heß pointed out that, while this was welcome, one also had to recognize that a certain volume of claims was necessary in order to bring costs into a reasonable relationship to premiums and that therefore one also needed claims. The obvious point was that the existence of a certain level of damages and claims was the legitimation for insurance and premiums. The *Schwarze Korps* urged its readers to go out and do penance (for failing to produce enough accidents and damage) by dropping lighted matches in their barns and throwing banana peels onto the street, since there had been too few accidents. If one wished to understand why – as had been the case with automobile insurance – insurers needed to raise rates and introduce deductibles, then they need only turn to the general director of Allianz. Insurance was not there for the insured; rather, the insured was there for the insurance companies and damages were needed so that the concern might survive instead of finding other ways to reduce its costs. For d'Alquen, the view that "business is not there for the people, but rather the people for

---

[42] See the Aktennote Posse, 24. Mai 1937, the inter-agency exchanges that follow, and the agreement between Posse and Flottmann of the Four-Year Plan authority of Feb. 1, 1938, in SM, 1458/1/100.

[43] See Widmann (RAA) an RWM, 5. April 1937 (with extensive supporting material) and Vermerk Fritzsche on the meeting between Schmitt and d'Alquen, April 14, 1937, SM, 1458/1/99, Bl. 43–66. On d'Alquen, see Werner Augustinovic & Martin Moll, "Gunter d'Alquen – Protagonist des SS-Staates," in Ronald Smelser & Enrico Syring (eds.), *Die SS: Elite unter dem Totenkopf. 30 Lebensläufe* (Paderborn, 2000), pp. 100–18.

business," was pervasive in the private economy, and he was appreciative that Heß was so open about such views.[44]

Braß, by contrast, was not given to being sardonic and was filled with earnestness when it came to both bringing the private insurance industry into the National Socialist fold and resolving the conflict between the private and the publicly chartered companies. The greatest incentive to do so was the cost problem plaguing the entire industry and the issue of "Ausspannung" – that is, illicit efforts by insurance agents to win both agents and customers from one insurance company to another. The difficulty with this issue was defining exactly when fair competition became unfair and protecting the right of persons to switch companies and policies. Braß, however, believed that all problems could be solved with the proper National Socialist attitude. Toward this end, he joined forces with Hans Goebbels at the end of 1936 and concocted what became known as the "Goebbels–Braß German Insurance Comradeship." In an agreement signed on December 16, when Braß was still working for the DAF, the two men agreed to engage in "healthy and fair competition." The agreement also provided for joint participation in large insurance risks. The G-B Insurance Comradeship agreement, as it became known, was then expanded on January 12 for the purpose of joining together the private and publicly chartered companies in an effort to collaborate in carrying out the Four-Year Plan by ending their old quarrels and collaborating in the avoidance of unfair competition, the charging of "just premiums," and obligating their representatives and agents to act accordingly. It also provided for an arbitration court to settle disputes. The idea met with enthusiasm in the RWM, and Hilgard apparently also viewed it as promising, provided certain issues could be settled. One of them was the question of non-Aryan insurance agents, where Goebbels and Braß were prepared to concede the continuation of existing contracts provided that no more Jews were hired and that Jewish agents were increasingly limited to the servicing of Jewish customers. The other was the arbitration court, where Hilgard considered it essential that persons not be allowed to be arbitrators in their own cause and that the RWM have a voice in the decision making. Within this context, Hilgard appeared strongly supportive of the endeavor.[45]

Nevertheless, the G-B Comradeship soured fairly rapidly, despite Braß's appointment as head of the Private Insurance Economic Group. Thus, at a meeting of the advisory council on May 20, he complained bitterly that only 45 companies had signed up, 20 of them private, but that not one of the large private concerns had joined. His predecessor General Director Oertel of Colonia tried to explain

---

[44] "Unheilige Allianz," *Das Schwarze Korps,* 14. Okt. 1937, and Heß's speech before the 2. Betriebs-
leitertagung der Allianz, Abteilung für Maschinen-Versicherung, 8. Dez. 1937, BAK, B 280/12237,
Bl. 289–92.
[45] See the agreements of Dec. 16, 1936, and Jan. 12, 1937, as well as Hilgard to RWM, Feb. 4, 1937,
and other relevant documentation in BAB, R 3101/17050, Bl. 210–37.

this by the fact that the terms of the agreement had not been fully hammered out in the RWM, but the reality was that no one could quite figure out what kinds of issues were to be adjudicated by the arbitration body projected in the agreement. The Ministry had lost its enthusiasm and now favored some kind of agreement between the private and publicly chartered companies, while Hilgard noted that more sign-ups were unlikely in view of the agreement's deficiencies. Discussions continued until November 1937, but the entire project came to naught because no one could define what actually constituted "Ausspannung." When Braß suggested that the matter could be decided by practice and experience, Hilgard insisted that this simply would not do if one were going to have an agreement of the kind envisioned by Goebbels and Braß.[46]

Underlying all of these discussions was a great deal more suspicion and sense of impending crisis than comradeship. The Four-Year Plan had created an environment of mobilization in which radical measures attained a higher degree of plausibility and thus legitimacy. This manifested itself at the end of 1937 in the Reich Group for the publicly chartered companies, whose head (Paul Riebesell) was ruthlessly driven from office by Schwede-Coburg for protecting a young Jewish insurance mathematician. He was given a vote of no confidence after an attack on his person by the *Schwarze Korps* and went on to become head of the newly founded Isar Company.[47] The growing radicalization came to the fore in the private insurance industry organization in late February 1938. The advisory council of the Private Insurance Economic Group met on February 24 in Munich, one day prior to its plenary meeting on the following day, where Braß was scheduled to deliver a major speech. Braß was celebrating his first year in office and received a unanimous vote of confidence from his colleagues on the advisory council. Both he and Hilgard then proceeded to inform the council that they were very concerned about reports and rumors of an impending nationalization of the insurance industry. Indeed, there were reports that the matter had been decided already, although he did not think things had gone that far. He also did not think that Göring would act without consultation. Braß claimed that the initiative was coming from State Secretary Johannes Krohn of the Labor Ministry and that circles in the SS leadership were also behind it. Another concern was that Economics Minister Funk had close relations to the SS leadership. Braß felt one had to take the matter very seriously, and he was planning to create a "political committee" of ten Party comrades who had been in the movement before 1933 to serve as a counterweight to the developing tendencies among leaders of the publicly chartered companies. He needed

---

[46] Sitzung des Beirats der Wirtschaftsgruppe am 20. Mai 1937, GDV, RS/25, pp. 3–5; Vermerk, 14. Mai 1937, and Besprechung über Ausspannung, 30. Nov. 1937, BAB, R 3101/17050, Bl. 253, 272–3.

[47] Karl Hauss, "Die Deutsche Versicherungswirtschaft und der Nationalsozialismus," pp. 12–13, AXA, Bestand Kölnische Hagel Versicherungs-AG.

a political apparatus with which he [Braß] can operate. It does not matter whether the individual member is a big cannon in the field, whether he has already appeared before the public. The most decisive thing is that old Party comrades are at hand to challenge the view of the people in the publicly chartered companies that they are authorized representatives from a Party standpoint.[48]

Thus, Braß felt that the Labor Ministry, the SS, and the publicly chartered companies were all working against the private insurers, although he thought Schwede-Coburg was less of a problem here than the people surrounding him. Braß made a point of emphasizing his loyalty to the private insurance business: "As an old National Socialist he [Braß] stands fundamentally and completely in support of private insurance. He rejects every type of collectivization because it contradicts the program and the National Socialist view." Nevertheless, if contrary views were making themselves felt then it was important to deal with their causes, and he hoped to use his speech on the following day to define the tasks of the private insurance business in the National Socialist state and to restore confidence in the industry. It was essential that their commitment to National Socialism be made as clear as possible.

Hilgard underscored Braß's point that they were facing "questions of vital significance" and that Braß was pointing to the correct way of dealing with them. According to reports Hilgard had received, however, the support for nationalization came less from the agencies mentioned by Braß than from what he termed the "Reich Youth Leadership of the SS." No such organization actually existed, and he undoubtedly meant the young fanatics associated with the *Schwarze Korps*. He could report that Schmitt had discussed the question with Göring and had found that Göring did not support nationalization, but Hilgard warned that the strong forces supporting nationalization were constantly trying to win over the highest authorities. In fighting them, two points had to be kept in mind. First, all claims to the contrary, the popularity of the private insurance business between 1933 and 1936 exceeded that of the publicly chartered companies – as demonstrated by the increase in customers, which ranged only from 6.3% to 13.8% for the latter but from 12.4% to 38.2% for the former. That so many people insured themselves with the private companies needed much more emphasis, in Hilgard's view. Second, there was the problem of foreign exchange in the international business of private insurance companies; its balance had been negative to the tune of 15.4 million RM between January and November. The primary reason was the amount of business they were doing with English and Swiss reinsurers. The figures could, of course, change if fires and other disasters increased

---

[48] There are two versions of the minutes of this meeting: one edited, the other unedited. The latter is used here since, despite grammatical problems, it contains a great deal more information and better conveys what really happened. For the quotations and discussion of this meeting, see Niederschrift über die Sitzung des Beirats der Wirtschaftsgruppe Privatversicherung am 24. Feb. 1938, GDV, RS/26, pp. 4–30, quote on p. 5.

or decreased, but the dangerous thing would be for Göring to discover that private insurers were costing him 15.4 million in foreign exchange at a time when his hunger for foreign exchange was boundless. Hilgard feared that their fate would be sealed if this came to Göring's attention. It was necessary, therefore, to reduce dependence on foreign reinsurers at least to some extent.

In a remarkable response, Braß thanked Hilgard for bringing these matters to the fore but then went on to discuss Göring and how to deal with him in a manner that speaks volumes about political leadership principles in the Third Reich:

> It should not be thought that perhaps things are seen too darkly. Whoever knows Göring, knows that for him there is only one perspective: Germany! If Göring determines that something is working to the detriment of Germany, there is no pardon. When Göring is convinced that the steering wheel is turned the other way, then he will also give consideration to our perspectives. If two proposals would be presented, both of which are not adverse to Germany, then it could be that it will be decided in favor of one person. Göring leaves it to the forces themselves to fight it out, just as the Führer lets the currents struggle with one another about great questions. If we fulfill the external preconditions, then he [Braß] is optimistic enough to say that we will succeed with Göring with the means at our disposal and the intentions that he has. The gentlemen present will understand why he is committed to authoritarian leadership. There should be no other opinion than that of the leader of the Reich Group or, in the case of the private insurance, his own. Also in the future this should be the alpha and omega of each individual leader of an enterprise. He asks all the gentlemen present to make this standpoint and perspective be the gospel; then we will form a pool, a closed formation that holds constantly to its goal. Until a decision is made, we will fight against nationalization. Why should not one attain victory here as in other cases in which a battle is fought? Those are the perspectives which he will in part present tomorrow so that the ground is prepared so that the insurance industry is in line with the authoritarian system.[49]

Braß certainly was not a great analytical mind, but he had an intuitive understanding of the role of Darwinian conflict between competing forces in the functioning of the Nazi dicatatorship and what the function of "working toward the Führer," to use the language of another Nazi official, really meant to a practicing National Socialist of this type.[50]

As became clear from the ensuing discussion, the dangers were indeed taken quite seriously by those present. The Labor Ministry, once so supportive of the insurance industry against the DAF, apparently had plans to expand the social insurance system. It sought to take advantage of the failure of private insurance companies to do enough in providing insurance for craftsmen and offering pensions. Thus, there was a strong sense that the private insurance industry was threatened from powerful forces in the government and the SS, and Hilgard and his colleagues apparently hoped that Braß, with his Party credentials, would

---

[49] Ibid., quotes on pp. 6, 13–14.
[50] See Ian Kershaw, *Hitler. 1889–1936. Hubris* (New York & London, 1998), pp. 527–9, who uses the term to explain the dynamics of National Socialist behavior.

contribute to warding off the dangers and reassuring the public about the industry in his forthcoming speech.

If this was the intention, then Braß's speech on February 25, "The Community of Labor in the Insurance Industry,"[51] was a catastrophic failure that caused outrage within the industry while providing welcome fodder for *Das Schwarze Korps*. Braß spent an hour and a half telling his audience that the private insurance industry must mend its ways and overcome the "sins" of the capitalist age, which had given it such a bad reputation. He sharply attacked the investment policy of the industry, arguing that it needed to be more focused and centrally directed and that one would have to do more than have a few great concerns invest in the public good. He called for less competition and more collaboration, and he sharply attacked the stealing away of customers. Insofar as the cost question was concerned, he urged controlling commissions and purging "undesirable elements" from the external service and also called for more pooling of risks, thus creating the impression that the entire industry was very wasteful and inefficient. At the same time, he urged far greater attention to public needs, such as pensions, even if they were deemed unprofitable. He also sharply criticized the companies for charging different premiums for different persons and claimed that there *was* such a thing as a "just premium." As usual, he praised himself for his role in the automobile insurance debate and praised the Price Commissar for settling the matter. Above all, he placed extraordinary emphasis on the primacy of political considerations and expected that the concerns and firms in the industry would place more National Socialists in responsible positions.

Needless to say, the speech did nothing to improve the image of the industry. The *Schwarze Korps,* in an article headlined "Pretty Words Do Not Help" and "Belated Conscience Probing," expressed satisfaction at the acceptance of its criticisms from within the industry but argued that the real question was the right of private insurance to exist.[52] The reaction to Braß's speech within the industry was a high degree of outrage, expressed above all by Johannes Tiedke in a lengthy letter to Hilgard of April 9, 1938. As Tiedke (who, along with other colleagues, had taken careful notes) pointed out, the printed speech in *Neumanns Zeitschrift* left out portions of the speech and thus made it sound less insulting than it actually was. In his remarks about the stealing away of customers, for example, Braß had said: "I repeatedly receive reports that not only insignificant companies but also those with name and reputation sally forth into competition like thieves."[53] Tiedke answered Braß's charges point by point and insisted that, whatever Braß claimed his intentions to be, his speech promoted the cause of nationalization and had done great damage to the industry. He also charged Braß

---

[51] Generaldirektor Braß, "Gemeinschaftsarbeit in der Versicherungswirtschaft. Vortrag auf der Jahreshauptversammlung der Wirtschaftsgruppe Privatversicherung am 25. Feb. 1938," *Neumanns Zeitschrift für Versicherungswesen,* Beilage zu Nr. 10 vom 2. März 1938. There is (perhaps happily for the Anglo-American political culture) no real way to translate the full meaning of *Gemeinschaft* – let alone *Gemeinschaftsarbeit* – into English.

[52] *Das Schwarze Korps,* March 10, 1938.

[53] Tiedke an Hilgard, 9. April 1938, NL Tiedke.

with gross incompetence in handling the affairs of the group, with neglecting pressing issues, and with failing to pay attention to the suggestions and work of his colleagues.

The entire affair was to be very much a test of Hilgard's diplomatic skills. He most certainly was not going to permit a battle royal between Braß and Tiedke. The latter was too given to expressing his outrage at the outrageous, an honorable but not very useful or safe way to deal with such problems in the existing political context. At the same time, there was no way to hide the fact that Braß had put on an absurd performance and had very much disappointed and irritated his colleagues. Braß's capacity to deal with the criticism was weakened by two other developments. First, Braß had been one of those summoned to prepare and carry out the "elections" in Austria following the March 1938 annexation and was thus preoccupied in the months following his speech. Second, the DAF had decided at the end of 1937 to dissolve Deutsche Lebensversicherung (which Braß had headed) by consolidating with its organizations in Hamburg. Braß had thus effectively lost his position as an insurance executive, and his critics claimed that he possibly had lost favor with the DAF as well. Certainly the bad economic situation of the company did not speak well for his management.[54]

Thus, when Braß's speech finally was discussed at the advisory council meeting of June 17, 1938,[55] Hilgard seized the initiative and set the tone. He agreed to the appointment of two new members to the council, the insurance man Staatsrat Christian Bartholatus from Hamburg and Standartenführer Haertel from Himmler's staff, so as to answer criticisms that there were not enough Nazis on the Council. This was not the committee of ten Old Fighters that Braß had contemplated, but it certainly gave the Party a great deal more presence. Hilgard began by pointing out that they all had a duty to express their opinions on matters pertaining to the economic group and that they all were persons who had long served the industry. He recognized that Braß's speech had been the source of some "tensions." This was not, in Hilgard's opinion, because Braß had made programmatic suggestions, which was his right and duty, "especially in view of the fact that Herr Braß was summoned in order to implement the demands of the Party in private insurance."[56] The problem, as Hilgard presented it, was Braß's tone, especially the suggestion that everything was ill with the industry until he took office. It was one thing to say that reforms were needed, yet

---

[54] Braß an Ministerialdirektor Kurt Lange, 11. April 1939, SM, 1458/1/109, Bl. 179–80. See the excellent unpublished Magisterarbeit by Ingo Böhle, "Die Volksfürsorge Lebensversicherungs-AG im 'Dritten Reich'" (Universität Hamburg, 1996), pp. 71–2. See also his "Die Volksfürsorge Lebensversicherungs AG – ein Unternehmen der Deutschen Arbeitsfront (DAF) im 'Dritten Reich'," *Zeitschrift für Unternehmensgeschichte* 45 (2000), pp. 49–78, esp. p. 60.

[55] Sitzung des Beirats der Wirtschaftsgruppe Privatversicherung am 17. Juni 1938. There are two versions of the minutes: an edited one in GDV, RS/15, and an unedited one in GDV, RS/26.

[56] Interestingly, this was inserted in the official minutes that went out to members in GDV, RS/15, p. 2, and was probably intended to remind those who received it that Braß had been put into his office as a representative of the Party.

another to suggest that private insurance was not the blooming industry it was but rather in terrible shape. Turning the table a bit on Braß, Hilgard urged a more comradely spirit and that he consult more with his colleagues before acting so as to create a true community of labor. Borrowing from Tiedke's letter, Hilgard made reference to comments by Schmitt (at the Munich meeting) to the effect that the leadership principle in business meant that the leader should have as his goal inducing the vast majority to support him. The limits of criticism had thus been defined. The problem with Braß's speech was declared to be a matter of form rather than content. This point was emphasized by Bartholatus, who stressed that Braß was above all concerned to serve the National Socialist cause. Another member suggested that Braß had made the mistake of painting too dark a picture. Braß himself seemed much chastened and certainly was aware that his performance in Munich had been a flop. While he absolutely refused to engage the criticisms of Tiedke, which he had read, he did seem anxious to reconcile himself with his colleagues.[57] He expressed gratitude to Hilgard, whom he described as a "master of the art of negotiation," and tediously explained his performance by the fact that he was an Old Fighter, accustomed to political battles and a rough tone, and that he had used the same style and techniques that had been used to win the people over to the Party. The Munich speech, Braß claimed, was intended to be honest and to place the problems in the context of the National Socialist world view. He had worked half the night after the previous advisory council meeting to write a speech appropriate to the occasion and had not intended to wound individuals. His goal, he insisted, was to support and not to harm the private insurance industry.

On the same day that Braß was praising Hilgard and speaking these reconciling words, he sent Ministerial Director Kurt Lange of the RWM a detailed memorandum whose aims included eliminating Hilgard from Reich Group leadership, restructuring the insurance industry's organizations, and compelling the private insurance industry (insofar as it would be allowed to survive) to mend its ways. This memo was no solo flight on Braß's part, which made the matter far more serious and dangerous. Lange was an Old Fighter from Hamburg who had been appointed to deal with financial aspects of the Four-Year Plan within the RWM money and credit division; he was thus an important member of the Göring apparatus. It was Lange who had solicited Braß's recommendations concerning reorganization of the insurance industry.[58]

Braß operated from the premise that the insurance industry and its organizations in all their forms were in need of a "comprehensive reform" so as to make them "instruments of National Socialist economic policy *in every respect.*" This included the Reich Supervisory Office, which (in his view) needed to be politically reformed and much more anchored in the Party, perhaps through the appointment of Schwede-Coburg as its head, and needed to have comprehensive

[57] See the internal note to Gabriel, June 24, 1938, GDV, RS/26.
[58] On Lange, see Boelcke, *Deutsche Wirtschaft,* p. 183. For the origins of the Braß report, see Braß's covering letter of June 9, 1938, in SM, 1458/1/92, Bl. 3. The report is on Bl. 4–13.

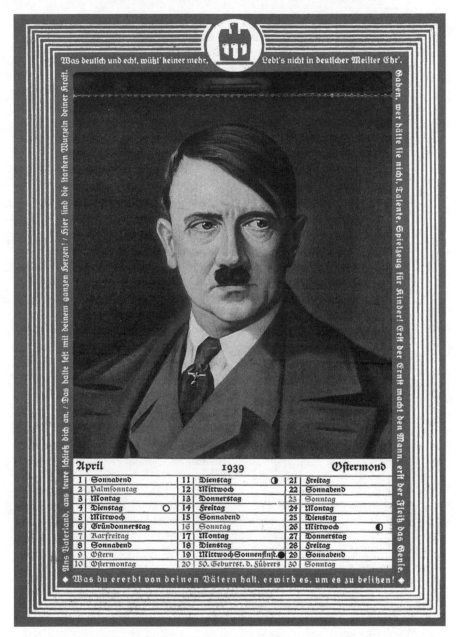

Advertising calendar of Allianz: "Famous Germans. An almanac for the year 1939".

powers over the entire industry in all its forms. The RAA was too overburdened by auditing activities; Braß urged that the auditing duties be left to accountants with specific instructions and that the RAA personnel thereby be liberated for the policy-making and supervisory job it needed to do with respect to substantive issues – for example, premiums, external service, commissions, dividend policy, simplifying of insurance conditions, and reducing costs.

Insofar as the Reich Group was concerned, the goal had to be to turn it into *"the instrument of self-administration* for the policy of the State." Braß thought the separation between an economic group for private insurance and an economic group for the publicly chartered companies "tragic" because it encouraged a "business-hungry attitude" instead of collaboration for the common good. He therefore proposed a Reich Group that would encompass both types of insurance company and a division into seven economic groups for the different types of insurance (e.g., life, fire, automobile, accident and liability, health, transport and reinsurance, and agriculture). As in the Reich Group, so in each of these economic groups: the private and the publicly chartered companies would work together. It was essential in Braß's view that these groups be led not by the "old experts" but instead by "political personalities" who would approach the reorganization of the industry from a political (rather than business or technical) perspective. Indeed, the entire benefit of bringing the two types of insurance companies together would come from the fact that the more politically oriented publicly chartered companies would no longer be criticizing the private companies from the outside; instead they would be working within the same structure and could thereby directly influence the private companies to pursue a National Socialist economic policy.

Braß claimed that he did not wish to make any personnel recommendations (aside from suggesting Schwede-Coburg for the RAA) because he stood in the middle of personnel disputes himself, but he could hardly be accused of subtlety in suggesting from whence the leadership of the Reich Group should *not* come. The challenge to the position of Allianz and Hilgard was scarcely disguised:

I believe ... that everything should be done to avoid what would amount to a continuation of the earlier traditions of the old associations of the German insurance industry. At that time – to some extent such considerations continue still today – the leading positions of the organization were filled in such a way that at the head and in the other positions and offices there were persons who represented a certain economic power complex. As a result, the biggest concern always received the top office and certain other concerns occupied the next positions. The Third Reich has already broken with this tradition .... Very many hopes on the part of willing and faithful persons in the insurance industry will be lost if once again there will be the impression that in a reorganizing the attitudes and wishes of this or that great concern will be taken into account.[59]

Braß had passed these proposals on to Schwede-Coburg and Hans Goebbels, who were invited by RWM Ministerial Director Lange to join in a discussion with other RWM and Party officials on June 28. Among the latter was Georg Amend, who handled insurance for the NSDAP and worked closely with Party treasurer Franz Xaver Schwarz. Schwede-Coburg questioned whether insurance should be a profit-making business at all and complained that the competition had gotten

⁵⁹ Ibid., Bl. 11.

out of control at a time when manpower was needed for more important things. Hans Goebbels insisted that the large risks handled by the private insurers could just as easily be undertaken by publicly chartered companies. Most importantly, however, a new actor had come on the scene in the person of Amend, who had written a memorandum advocating the consolidation of the entire industry into a single publicly chartered company.[60]

Amend's proposal, which was one of a number solicited by Lange after the meeting, was extremely radical in nature. It insisted that insurance was not an appropriate field for private enterprise since, by its very nature, it embraced a risk community. Competition simply raised the costs, and he charged that the private industry had done nothing to prevent damages and accidents. He made much of the scandals involving private insurance, especially at Favag and Phönix. Thus, he urged immediate measures to determine the number and ownership of insurance company shares, a ban on their sale, limitations on executive salaries, and limitation of existing insurance policies to three years. Fundamentally, he was urging nationalization of the industry.[61]

There can be no question that Party radicals were most serious about this plan. On July 12, 1938, Schwarz wrote directly to Göring and claimed that

the true reason for these abuses lies almost exclusively in the self profit seeking of the private insurance companies .... A cleansing of the personal insurance system in Germany and its alignment to National Socialism is not and will never be possible through partial solutions of individual problems but only through an uncompromising radical solution of the basic problem which, in the first instance, my dear Party Comrade Göring, you will have to undertake.[62]

Franz Xaver Schwarz claimed to be speaking for the Party and was very insistent that the necessary reforms could never be carried out by the "liberalists" heading the private companies.

Göring, however, apparently wanted to know what Lange had to say, and Lange reported at the end of September that all the representatives of the private insurance business with whom he had spoken opposed the consolidation of the insurance industry into one privately chartered company. While they had not been given access to the Amend memorandum, they had all insisted that the proposal would "necessarily lead to an ossification of the insurance business and an exclusion of German insurance from world trade. The private insurers consider free competition among a plurality of enterprises necessary for their mutual fructification, for the deepening and promotion of the insurance idea, and lastly, for the opening of new kinds of insurance and new paths toward insurance protection."[63]

---

[60] See the record of the meeting in ibid., Bl. 16.
[61] The Denkschrift zur Reform der deutschen Individualversicherung was forwarded by Schwarz to Lange, 27. Juni 1938, ibid., Bl. 17–33.
[62] Schwarz an Göring, 12. Juli 1938, ibid., Bl. 128–9, quote on Bl. 128.
[63] Entwurf eines Briefes von Lange an Göring, 30. Sept. 1938, ibid., Bl. 130.

A good illustration of these arguments was provided by General Director Walter Forstreuter of the Gerling concern, who had also been invited to the meeting of June 28. He sought to remind the government of the great achievement of the private insurers in rescuing the entire insurance business after the inflation, stressed their creativeness in the fields of machine insurance and other areas, and noted that it was the private insurance business – not the publicly chartered companies – that had banded together in the service of the film industry and flight insurance and that had demonstrated its capacities in the recent Hindenburg disaster. The international role of the German insurance industry was predominantly the work of the private insurers as well. Forstreuter also rejected the idea that private insurers were doing nothing to prevent accidents, arguing that they were at the forefront of research in certain areas and also that they paid high taxes and thus contributed importantly to the government's safety programs.[64]

In the end, Lange came down on the side of the "liberalists." On the one hand, thanks to the situation in Austria and other pressing political and economic problems, he was simply too busy to deal with the problem in all its complexities. On the other hand, he was most inclined to see the continued existence of a variety of types of insurance companies (and of individual companies as well) to be beneficial. He therefore decided to limit reform to improving the supervisory situation and creating a Reich Group organized according to insurance branches. This position was strongly confirmed by Economics Minister Funk in a letter to Göring of November 22, 1938.[65] What this RWM decision reflected was a more general tendency on the part of Four-Year Plan authorities to employ existing structures and the private economy for their purposes rather than ride the radical wave in the Party. Nevertheless, as shown in the next chapter in connection with the November 1938 Pogrom, Party radicals were able to create circumstances that forced Göring to deal more rapidly and radically with certain problems than he might otherwise have. Thus, although the government was not prepared to give way to Schwede-Coburg and Amend, it was now inclined at least to follow Braß's program to reorganize the RAA and the Reich Group and, if Braß were to have his way in these matters, to Nazify these organizations.

Braß, however, had a unique talent for shooting himself in the foot. On November 9, 1938, the insurance agency of Jauch, Hübner & Co. complained to Ministerial Director Lange that Braß had denounced them to the Chamber of Industry and Commerce for being "true examples of what we understand to be Jewish businessmakers," suggested that they might have some Jewish ancestry, and claimed that they were suspect for their international dealings and business with the Soviet Union. The company certainly did do a great deal of

---

[64] Forstreuter an Lange, 3. Aug. 1938, "Einige Betrachtungen zur Frage einer Neugestaltung des deutschen Versicherungswesens," ibid., Bl. 114–25.
[65] Entwurf Lange, 30. Sept. 1938, ibid., Bl. 130; Funk an Göring, 22. Nov. 1938, BAB, R 3101/9275, Bl. 129–33.

international business, but it had brought a lot of foreign exchange into the country. Three of the owners were Party members, and one was a Captain of the Reserve in the Wehrmacht. Apparently Braß had a business grudge against the firm, but whatever his motives, the unfounded charges ruined his position even with the Party people in the economic group. Initially, on November 15, Braß was asked simply to step down from his office while matters were settled. His secretary Kraus seems also to have been involved in the affair and ended up being fired. In the coming months Braß continuously protested his innocence, writing to all and sundry that he was a victim of the capitalists and of his efforts to create a truly National Socialist insurance system. In the process he also informed the Gestapo that there were reports that Hilgard and General Director Heß were homosexuals, which led to a series of interrogations before the charge was dismissed. Braß, in an effort to excuse himself, later told Hilgard that Schwede-Coburg had put him up to the denunciation. Before leaving office, Braß persistently violated his agreements with his colleagues and tried to resume his role, which led to demands for his dismissal from members of the advisory council. His actual term ran out at the end of January 1939, and Economics Minister Funk thanked him for his services and relieved him of his duties on March 3, 1939.[66]

The entire affair, which the RWM tried to keep out of the papers by imposing silence on Braß and the others involved, was of course extraordinarily embarrassing to the Reich Group – whatever the personal pleasure some private insurance executives must have felt about Braß's plight. Given the impending reorganization and the personnel problems, Hilgard had placed his own office at the disposition of the Ministry and apparently was quite serious about resigning if that was requested. There was a strong feeling that someone new with genuine authority had to take over the Reich Group, and General Director Forstreuter (as well as important persons in the RWM) thought that Kurt Schmitt would be the right man in the right place under the existing conditions. When Schmitt was asked, however, he showed no enthusiasm, suggesting that it might be best if someone totally outside the insurance field – like the Baden Minister-President, Walter Köhler, with whom he had spoken and whom he regarded as a moderate – would take the job. The problem was that Köhler would have to take a position with some insurance company and probably did not want the job. As the RWM official with whom he spoke reported:

He, Schmitt, can at the utmost declare himself ready to take over the office if it is really shown that the leadership question cannot be solved in a better way, and if he by taking the position could prevent an otherwise unavoidable severe damage to the insurance

---

[66] For the Jauch, Hübner & Co. complaint of Nov. 9, 1938, see SM, 1458/1/109, Bl. 2–7; for the subsequent correspondence, see the same volume, Bl. 29ff. For the dismissal by Funk, see Bl. 168. See also the materials in BAB, R 3101/9275, Bl. 62–129. On the homosexuality charges, see Hilgard interrogation of July 14, 1947, NA, RG 260, OMGUS, FINAD, 2/57/6–8.

business and finally if the taking over and carrying out of the office would be made possible, by which he understands that he would not be dragged into doing the "dirty work."[67]

That is, Schmitt wanted the old arrangement whereby someone else was dealing with the nasty business and persons in the regime, which had of course been the specialty of Hilgard and in which Hilgard was up to his ears at this time owing to the November 1938 Pogrom and the insurance problems it presented (see Chapter 5).

Concurrently with those problems, Hilgard was facing an attack on the private insurance business and the uncertainty about his own job in the Reich Group. Hilgard had never seen the memorandum of Amend recommending the creation of a single insurance organization, and he was not a participant in the meeting of June 28 to discuss the idea. He was not even privy to the reform proposals of the RWM, which he did not learn about until November. It was only on December 12 that he and Schmitt were finally in a position to discuss the proposals at a meeting called by Göring, a record of which Hilgard made and sent to Schmitt on December 19 because of its potential future importance.[68] Also attending (among others) were Economics Minister Funk, Lange and other high officials of the RWM and the Four-Year Plan office, Schwede-Coburg and Goebbels, Rudolf Lencer, and Braß. Göring informed those present that the issue of nationalization of the insurance business was of such importance that he did not feel he could decide it himself and had taken the matter directly to Hitler on December 4. Hitler came to the conclusion that nationalization was not something that could be taken up in the foreseeable future and was no longer to be discussed. Göring made clear that this did not mean that it could not be taken up again someday, just not within the coming decade. Hence, insofar as there were going to be reforms, they would have to be of another nature. Funk then came forth with his proposals for the reorganization of the Reich Group and also argued for the shutting down of unprofitable small insurance companies.

Schwede-Coburg was obviously disappointed, and he made no secret of his bitter rage. He claimed to be there not as a representative of the publicly chartered companies but rather as a plenipotentiary of the Führer, to whom alone he felt responsible, and that it was his task to bring the ideas of National Socialism to realization. The publicly chartered companies were much closer to these ideas than the private ones, who wanted to leave things just as they were. He sarcastically remarked that the opposition of the private insurers to nationalization would cease if every general director were guaranteed a lifetime income of

---

[67] Vermerk Krause, 17. Nov. 1938, BAB, R 3101/9275, Bl. 61. On the support for Schmitt and Hilgard's willingness to resign, see Vermerk Schmeer, 12. Nov. 1938, ibid., 56–8, and Forstreuter an Lange, 18. Nov. 1938, SM, 1458/1/109, Bl. 56–7. On Schmitt's view of Köhler as one of the moderate Gauleiter, see Friedrich Freiherr Hiller von Gaertringen (ed.), *Die Hassell-Tagebücher 1938–1944. Ulrich von Hassell. Aufzeichnungen vom andern Deutschland* (Berlin, 1988), p. 74.

[68] Hilgard to Schmitt, Dec. 19, 1938, and Aktennote of Dec. 15, 1938, which forms the basis of this discussion, FHA, S 17.5/7.

200,000 RM a year. Schmitt and Hilgard responded to this insulting accusation of venality with outrage, and Göring – who obviously did not like Schwede-Coburg's tone – made it clear that such arguments would go nowhere and that it was time to stop such attacks and establish peace. In the ensuing debate about cost questions and the like, Hilgard and Schmitt strongly defended the private insurance business against charges that its costs were higher than those of the publicly chartered companies; they also emphasized the importance of the industry in German foreign trade. Schmitt made a particularly strong case against Braß's attack on the profit-making and dividend policy of the industry. In the end, there could be no question that Göring had come down on the side of the private insurers:

The General Field Marshal made it clear repeatedly in a very drastic way that a person who bought a share wanted to get something for it. In general it was not a special problem of the insurance business. The question of the joint stock company and its dividend policy was a general economic question and could only be regulated for the entire economy in the same way.

Even Lencer proved cooperative by arguing that if an insurance company fulfilled its obligations to the insured and its employees, then one could not reproach it for giving higher dividends to its shareholders.

Thus, events transpired as Braß had outlined in the Reich Association meeting on February 24, 1938. Hitler and Göring had let the combatants wage their war and – all considerations not being as equal as he had pretended – drawn the balance in favor of the existing structure of the industry and against nationalization. While this did not introduce either an era of good feelings or quite the obedience to Hitler's order demanded by National Socialist ideology, it did provide an important prop for the private insurers (especially Allianz) in the coming years. Nonetheless, a price had to be paid: every successful battle against Party ideologues required personnel concessions and opened new opportunities for their infiltration of the industry and its organizations. On December 15, 1938, Martin Bormann (chief of staff to Party secretary Rudolf Heß) called upon Funk to appoint Amend head of the RAA; on January 7, he told Funk that Schmitt was fully in agreement with this choice. He then urged that Amend be given an advisory council headed by Schwede-Coburg and composed of Schmitt, Hans Goebbels, Braß, and Hilgard – along with Bärmann (who worked with Bormann) to represent the Party, Lencer to represent the DAF, and one of Schwarz's co-workers to represent the insured. Bormann thoroughly approved the unification of private and publicly chartered companies in the Reich Group and the reorganization of economic groups according to branches. Here, too, he had personnel wishes, urging that General Director Rudolf Kratochwill of Deutscher Ring be placed in charge of the life and health insurance group. Bormann thought it critical that the Reich Group be headed by someone from a medium-sized insurance company and proposed Director Max Odenbreit of the Agrippina in Cologne, although he also supported the appointment of Hans Schmidt-Polex of Allianz to head the group for liability insurance and Alois Alzheimer of Munich Re to head the group for reinsurance and credit insurance. Bormann remarked that these appointments were being proposed in full agreement with Schwede-Coburg and Goebbels, and Schmitt (who had also been consulted) agreed.[69]

The obvious goal was to put as many committed National Socialists into the commanding heights as possible, and many of Bormann's proposals were implemented. The personnel question did produce further discussion, however, since Funk initially wanted Kratochwill to head the entire Reich Group, a proposition certainly very agreeable to Bormann. When it came to the top leadership of the Reich Group, however, Schmitt was not quite as agreeable as Bormann had claimed and sought to persuade Schwede-Coburg that Hilgard was still the best person for the job. Schmitt therefore decided to turn to the one person who could decide the issue: Göring. In early February, Schmitt wrote personally to Göring as a follow-up to correspondence Hilgard had been having with Göring and in a manner that suggests Schmitt's long-term cultivation of the Field Marshal was not without advantage. He began by pointing out that "the decision of the Führer and yourself in the question of insurance created a welcome clarity, and the way must now be free so that with the help of an economic leadership guided by National Socialist principles the highest conceivable position in the world can be attained in this field." He had conveyed this view to Schwede-Coburg, but

from a purely practical view the old game continues insofar as in the nominations for the most important positions one is trying very strongly and with understandable success to push the private insurers into the background. The centerpiece of this battle is the elimination of Hilgard, who without doubt must be the natural leader of the insurance business, if the private–public conflict is not quietly to remain the dominating idea beneath everything.

Schmitt insisted that "friendly collaboration" was impossible if the struggle was going to continue in this manner. As a former minister, Schmitt claimed that he was trying to take a neutral position and then asked Göring to arrange a meeting with Schwede-Coburg (in the presence of Göring) in mid-February to settle the matter.[70]

No record has been found of such a meeting. Göring did decide that Hilgard would keep his post, and Schwede-Coburg was compelled to accept the decision. The reason is discoverable from the marginal comment in red by Göring on a copy of the aforementioned letter from Schmitt to Göring. The latter's office sent the document to Lange on February 20 and asked in a covering letter that Göring's marginal comment be brought to the attention of Funk. Lange's own marginal notations show that on February 21 he spoke to Schwede-Coburg, who

---

[69] Bormann an Funk, 7. Jan. 1939, BAB, R 3101/9275, Bl. 158–9; for the subsequent exchange on personnel questions, see ibid., Bl. 160–81.

[70] An undated copy of the letter from Schmitt to Göring was sent to Lange from Göring's office on Feb. 20, 1939, ibid., Bl. 183–4.

agreed to the retention of Hilgard, and that on February 22 he reported to Funk. The decisive handwritten notation by Göring read: "If the private [insurers] are 80%, then Hilgard must remain."[71] In sum, Göring's decision in favor of Hilgard was largely pragmatic and involved an acceptance of the private insurers' argument that they dominated the business and so should provide the organization leadership. As was so often the case, Göring came down on the side of private enterprise when it was the practical thing to do.

After the war, Hilgard was to attribute his retention to more personal factors, and these may have well played some role. Schmitt's letter to Göring began by making explicit reference to recent correspondence between Hilgard and Göring: "My friend Hilgard informed me yesterday about an exchange of letters with you. I feel a need to say a few words about it."[72] The subject of this correspondence may have been a matter that Hilgard brought up in his postwar interrogation and that he considered decisive for his retention as head of the Reich Group. Göring had asked Hilgard to assist in the insurance case of Göring's wife's close friend, the actress Agnes Straub. She was involved in an automobile accident and was insured with the Gerling concern, but she told Frau Göring that she feared difficulties if she filed a claim. Göring personally wrote to Hilgard to ask for help; Hilgard contacted General Director Forstreuter, who assured Hilgard that Frau Straub would have no difficulties with her claim. Hilgard then wrote Göring that he had the pleasure of telling him the problem had been solved. Subsequently, when Hilgard visited the RWM in connection with his reappointment as head of the Reich Group, Lange purportedly showed him the letter Hilgard had written concerning Straub, at the bottom of which Göring had allegedly written in red: "Hilgard stays."[73] Eight years had passed between the events described and the interrogation, and it is possible that Hilgard was conflating events and establishing a cause-and-effect relationship where none actually existed. Hilgard's interpretation of his retention fit in nicely with his own emphasis on the trials, tribulations, and vulnerability of the private insurance industry and on the unpredictable behavior with which he constantly had to contend. The conflation could have been conscious or unconscious, and it is not impossible that Göring may also have been influenced by Hilgard's services even if the decisive reason was the power of large private insurers in the industry.

One thing for certain is that pandering to Göring's material needs and wishes was common practice by those who courted his favor. This was not the first time Hilgard had played Göring's insurance man, although Göring seems to have shown a preference for Allianz as an insurer quite independently of Hilgard. Thus, he had taken out a 30-year policy for 50,000 RM in 1932 with a premium

---

[71] Ibid. I am grateful to Inge Böhle for providing me with a copy of the document in which the Göring marginal comment is decipherable and thus making it possible to refute the Hilgard interpretation discussed shortly.

[72] Ibid.

[73] See Hilgard interrogation of July 14, 1947, NA, RG 260, OMGUS, FINAD, 2/57/6–8.

of 1,620 RM a year, for which he had paid a total of 13,200 RM by 1945. In June 1938, the Luftwaffe gave Göring a present of a 50,000-RM dowry insurance for his daughter Edda, payable on her marriage or in 1963 at the latest.[74] In his unpublished memoirs, Hilgard claims that Göring had summoned Hilgard to his office in 1935 and stated that he wished to take out a life policy but that Allianz's rates were too high. Hilgard explained them to Göring and apparently appeased him, although there is no record that he took out a policy for himself at this time. In 1936, an annuity insurance was taken out for his sister-in-law, Else Sonnemann, but this was not necessarily the problem Göring had in mind in his discussion with Hilgard.[75] In 1937, Göring once again called Hilgard in, this time concerning a policy on his recently awarded Field Marshal's baton (which was studded with jewels and diamonds); he probably took out a policy with Allianz for this as well. Still, it would be excessive to argue that Göring's decision to keep Hilgard was simply a product of the latter's assistance with insurance matters, or because Allianz was a regular participant in the gift giving at Göring's lavish birthday parties, where he would purchase costly works of art and charge them to the account of guest corporations.[76] Göring needed competent people to do his bidding – not types like Braß, who could describe but not master the politics of someone like Göring. Hilgard was a known quantity who had proven himself amidst all the irritating squabbling connected with the insurance business. Why not keep him? In any case, Hilgard stayed at his post and thus presided over the reorganization of the Reich Group during the coming months.

Göring was not the only major figure in the regime to insure with Allianz, which was after all viewed by a substantial number of Germans as the biggest and best insurance company in Germany. Deputy Führer Rudolf Heß had a variety of accident and liability policies with Allianz (on which he paid premiums in 1939 totaling 4,699 RM) as well as what must have been a substantial life insurance policy (on which he paid a yearly premium of 2,076 RM).[77] Adolf Hitler was also insured by Allianz for his palatial home in Obersalzberg, the Berghof, between 1936 (when construction was completed) and 1943 (when the insurance was cancelled for reasons that are not entirely clear). The policies had been mediated through a real estate specialist in Munich by the name of Gotthard Färbers, who officially received a commission of 272.50 RM from Bayerische Versicherungsbank for his services. The commission, however, was actually delivered to Martin Bormann. The five policies covered liability, household contents, glass, water, and storm damage, the last-named four policies each in the

---

[74] AZLB, A 142 696.
[75] Ibid.
[76] Ibid. and Hilgard, "Leben," FHA, NL 2/7, pp. 99–100. Hilgard tells the amusing story of how the Reichs-Kredit-Gesellschaft director (and leader of the Reich Group for Banking) Otto Christian Fischer attended one of the parties and noticed a Cranach as one of the gifts. When he inquired who had bought it for Göring, he was informed that it was his bank!
[77] Aktennotiz, Haftpflicht- & Unfall-Abteilung, 29. Juni 1939, FHA, S 17.10/21.

amount of 500,000 RM. The premiums added up to 1,090 RM a year. After some irritation on the part of Hitler's adjutant SS Gruppenführer Julius Schaub over the way they were being billed (through normal procedures), billing was handled personally by one of Bayerische Versicherungsbank's Munich directors. Obviously, "Our Führer and Reich Chancellor" was not an everyday customer.[78]

On balance, Allianz had done extraordinarily well in maintaining its position as Germany's pre-eminent concern, and its leaders continued to dominate the industry despite the travails of the years before the war. To be sure, Hilgard and his colleagues felt embattled – and would, indeed, continue to feel embattled – in their efforts to defend the private insurance industry from its enemies. However, it would be a mistake to think that they had merely survived. Germany was on the march, and so was Allianz. As the concern approached its fiftieth anniversary in 1940, it was expanding as Germany itself expanded into Austria, into the former Czechoslovakia, and soon into most of the lands dominated by the Third Reich. By the time Germany went to war in September 1939, Allianz and its leaders were well practiced in the grotesque politics of the regime and the ethical compromises required; they had become – sometimes willingly, sometimes reluctantly – mired in its evil purposes. Allianz was in no way unique in these respects, and it ultimately shared the collective responsibility of the German business community. However, certain areas – where the insurance industry was particularly involved in the seizure of Jewish assets – are extremely complicated and controversial. We deal with them in the next two chapters before moving on to the examination of Allianz at war.

---

[78] For this correspondence on Hitler's policies between 1936 and 1939, see ibid.

5

The "Night of Broken Glass" and the Insurance Industry

THE POGROM AS AN INSURANCE PROBLEM AND THE CONFERENCE OF NOVEMBER 12, 1938

ON JUNE 17, 1938, Andreas Braß informed a meeting of the advisory council of the Private Insurance Economic Group that the Jewish question was "picking up strongly again," as his colleagues may have noticed. He had recently been at a small gathering with Hitler, and there was a good deal of anger that so many Viennese Jews were coming to Berlin and that it would not be surprising if something were done about it. Braß indicated that the Hitler Youth were likely to take action and that, in any case, the insurance companies should be prepared. He personally would not insure any more Jews. However, as pointed out by General Director Anton Dietrich Kessel (one of the Berlin glass insurance company executives), there were policies still in force that one could not simply eliminate overnight. He had already received reports of Jewish store windows being defaced during the day and then broken at night. The damage had been considerable. He asked for help, since the damage was not being done to the Jews in the end, a point echoed by General Director Johannes Tiedke of Alte Leipziger, who observed that "the Jew can only be harmed if he himself is the owner and is not insured." Non-Jewish Germans would have to pay in the end – and, worse yet, most of the glass came from abroad. Braß's only response was that they would just have to take the losses. When Kessel urged that they publish newspaper articles pointing out these facts, Braß replied that "if the present action has a political origin, then the press will not take such an article at the present time." Kessel then suggested that they simply turn down such claims, but this was more a counsel of despair than a real answer.[1]

This was revealed three days later, on June 20, when the Association of German Glass Insurance Companies sent a circular to its members dealing with a series of recent reports concerning the shattering of Jewish shop windows in Berlin. Initially, such incidents had been confined to the area around Alexanderplatz, but similar occurrences were now taking place in other parts of the city and

---

[1] See the edited version of this meeting of the Sitzung des Beirats der Wirtschaftsgruppe Privatversicherung am 17. Juni 1938, GDV, RS/15, and the unedited version in GDV, RS/26. The quotation is from the latter, pp. 56–7.

in the provinces. It was standard practice for glass insurers to replace the broken glass of their customers rather than make cash payment, but the Association feared that the immediate installation of new windows would be futile under existing conditions. Because the volume of reports was increasing and "the danger of repetition was great," the association recommended that "the regulation be delayed and the insured be urged to use emergency glass or wood boarding for the time being until a measure of calm has taken hold."[2] It also asked its members to provide, on a regular basis, full details of all such incidents and the costs involved.

There was good cause for concern. The events reported by the glass insurers were the products of a "Judenaktion" that had begun on May 1–2 and did not end until June 21. It had largely been confined to Berlin and was primarily the work of SA men, sometimes in and sometimes out of uniform. In the initial phase, it consisted of the defacement of Jewish shops and businesses with painted identifications, signs, and warnings with the obvious purpose of driving away customers. The first reports of the actual breaking of windows came on May 27, and this was followed at the end of the month with raids on the Kurfürstendamm – in which the police, Gestapo, foreign exchange authorities, and SD (security service of the SS) all participated – whose purpose was to pick up Jews suspected of violating regulations and foreign Jews subject to deportation. A second and far more serious wave of anti-Jewish activity began on June 17, attributed by the police to the Berlin Gau leadership and the direct inspiration of Joseph Goebbels. The propaganda minister had given an inflammatory speech before the Berlin Order Police in which he emphasized that the Jewish question was to be handled with a minimum of laws and decrees and with "a maximum degree of personal readiness to act." In somewhat contradictory fashion, Goebbels then chose as his model the former Weimar Berlin Police Vice-President Bernhard Weiß, whom Goebbels defamed with the first name of "Isidor," who could be presumed to have contemplated what chicaneries he might commit against the Nazis while going to work. Thus, "it is for this reason today nothing more than right and proper when police officials consider on their way to work how they can best employ chicaneries against the Jews that day."[3]

Apparently, the police did not have to strain their minds very much, and about 2,000 Jews were arrested between June 17 and 21, some of them for such offenses as jaywalking. These arrests were accompanied by renewed breaking of Jewish shop windows, along with the plundering of shops, while the police failed to provide adequate protection. The entire "action" was brought to an abrupt halt at 5 P.M. on June 22 by the personal intervention of Hitler himself from Berchtesgaden. Matters were apparently getting out of control, and this order followed

[2] Rundschreiben Deutscher Glasversicherungs-Verband, 20. Juni 1938, GDV, RS/45.
[3] Bericht des Sicherheitsdienstes an das Sicherheits-Hauptamt, 24. Juni 1938, SM, 500/1/645, Bl. 16f., 21f.

meetings the previous day among the Berlin Police President Count Helldorf, Deputy Gauleiter Görlitzer, SA Obergruppenführer von Jagow, and other district leaders and party officials, as well as complaints by Reich Economics Minister Funk to Göring, who apparently intervened with Goebbels. While Funk, Göring, and Goebbels expressed their gratitude to the police and the SA leaders for the action, "which had gone fabulously and had been a complete success," they also announced confidentially that the government 'ntended to buy up all the Jewish businesses. Clearly, the government had an interest in taking them over in good shape.[4]

The actions against the Jews in Berlin and elsewhere had attracted considerable negative attention abroad, which was reinforced by the observations of the many tourists who came to Germany at the beginning of the tourist season. The arrest of some foreign Jews had also led to official protests from their governments. The anti-Jewish actions caused some domestic political embarrassments as well, since they seemed to run counter to the recently issued Third Decree of the Reich Citizenship Law. This law provided that, at some time to be determined, the Reich Economics Minister, in consultation with the interior minister and the deputy Führer, would take responsibility for the "designation" of Jewish businesses. The methods used to "designate" Jewish businesses by the SA obviously were different than those that would be employed by the ministries. Also, SA vandalism inevitably complicated ongoing Aryanization negotiations. Finally, the public was reported to have mixed feelings:

The mood of the population with respect to these actions is divided. While the larger portion of the old Party comrades and the general population have greeted these measures, there have also been a great many negative judgments. It has often been pointed out in this connection that the burdens incurred through the shattering of display windows are carried by the German insurers, but not by the Jewish owners themselves.[5]

Actually, one could argue that these costs should have been carried by the State. In December 1933, the Reich Economic Court had ruled that such damages taking place during the anti-Jewish boycott of April 1, 1933, constituted a domestic disturbance and fell under the compensation provisions of the Tumult Damage Law.[6] But 1938 was not 1933, and the willingness of either Jews or insurers to take the Third Reich to court because of officially sanctioned vandalism by the SA was much weakened. Indeed, the insurers' meeting of June 17 demonstrated that they could not even mention the damage being done to themselves in the

---

[4] Ibid., Bl. 17.
[5] Bericht betr. Judenaktion in Berlin vom 17. Juni bis 21. Juni 1938, ibid., Bl. 32–7. More generally, see Friedlander, *Nazi Germany and the Jews*, pp. 261–3. See also Christian Dirks, "Die 'Juni-Aktion' 1938 in Berlin," in Beate Meyer & Hermann Simon, *Juden in Berlin 1938–1945. Begleitband zu der gleichnamigen Ausstellung in der Stiftung 'Neue Synagoge Berlin – Centrum Judaicum'. Mai bis August 2000* (Berlin, 2000), pp. 33–41.
[6] Longerich, *Politik der Vernichtung*, pp. 36, 595.

newspapers. Worse still, as events later in the year would show, what had still been considered a civil disturbance in 1933 was by 1938 being characterized as the exercise of righteous civic virtue. Saul Friedlander has properly described the "action" in Berlin – although by no means restricted to that city – in the spring of 1938 as a "small-scale rehearsal"[7] for what was to come in the fall after the Sudetenland crisis was over. Similarly, the events of the spring signaled the far more complicated insurance issues that were to be raised by the Great Pogrom of November 9–10, 1938, and also demonstrated that these issues had already attained a measure of consciousness among those who would be called upon to deal with the questions of insurance following the "Night of Broken Glass" ("Reichskristallnacht").

There is by now a substantial literature on the origins and course of the November Pogrom, so that the general aspects need not be recounted here. The Pogrom was launched in the wake of the shooting on November 7 of the Councilor of Legation at the German Embassy in Paris, Ernst vom Rath, by the distraught Herschel Grynszpan, whose family had been among the 16,000 Polish Jews expelled to Poland under the most miserable circumstances in late October. Vom Rath died on the late afternoon of November 9, and Hitler received the news while participating in the "Old Fighters" dinner in Munich following a memorial celebration of the November 9, 1923, putsch. Hitler had been in an intransigent mood on the "Jewish question" for some time, Goebbels was anxious to restore his status (tarnished of late by his propaganda failures and extramarital affairs), and the idea of a pogrom and of a more radical policy toward the Jews had been in the air for months in Party and SD circles. In any case, Hitler decided to take Goebbels off the leash and informed the assembled Party leaders that "spontaneous" actions in response to the vom Rath assassination were not to encounter interference. Thus was unleashed the "Night of Broken Glass," a Party and SA orgy of vandalism, burning, looting, and sadistic mistreatment of Jews throughout the Reich that led to the destruction of several hundred synagogues and 7,500 businesses, the murder of at least 91 Jews, and a wave of arrests in which 30,000 Jews were dragged away for usually brief but always terrifying incarcerations in concentration camps, thereby producing further deaths and suicides. Although Goebbels personally ordered an end to the "demonstrations" on the front page of the *Völkischer Beobachter* on November 10, vandalism and violent actions continued in some places as late as November 13.[8]

Goebbels coordinated his actions, including termination of the Pogrom, very closely with Hitler, and cheerfully noted in his diary that he found Hitler "totally radical and aggressive." Much damage had been done, but Hitler was unconcerned since, as Goebbels noted in reporting their conversation in Munich of

[7] Friedlander, *Nazi Germany and the Jews*, p. 263.

[8] Ibid., pp. 257–79, and Wolfgang Benz, "Der Rückfall in die Barbarei. Bericht über den Pogrom," in Walter H. Pehle (ed.), *Der Judenpogrom 1938. Von der 'Reichskristallnacht' zum Völkermord* (Frankfurt a.M., 1988), pp. 13–51.

The Uhlfelder department store in Munich, Rosental 12, destroyed in the so-called Reichs-kristallnacht, November 10, 1938.

November 10: "The Führer wants to take very sharp measures against the Jews. They must themselves put their businesses in order again. The insurance companies will not pay them a thing. Then the Führer wants a gradual expropriation of Jewish businesses and to give the owners paper payment for them that we can void any time."[9] This diary entry is of immense importance for two reasons. First, in the general sense, it demonstrates that some of the most significant imminent actions reflected the express wishes and intentions of Hitler. Second, with specific reference to insurance, it shows that Hitler was well aware that insurance claims might be made in connection with the Pogrom but had pre-empted any serious discussion of payment by ordering that the Jews were not to receive insurance compensation.

Needless to say, the leadership of the insurance business was also well aware that the fire, glass, and especially burglary and theft branches had a problem on their hands. In contrast to the situation in June, however, it was obvious from the outset that the character and extent of the damage gave the actions of November a very different quality from those of June and that the government was likely to take an active interest in the insurance aspects of the Pogrom. Thus, on November 11, the leadership of the Reich Group sent a most revealing confidential letter to the organization of private insurers pointing out that the damage – the

[9] *Die Tagebücher von Joseph Goebbels,* hrsg. von Elke Fröhlich, Teil 1: Aufzeichnungen 1923–1941, Bd. 6: August 1938–Juni 1939, bearb. von Jana Richter (Munich, 1998), p. 182.

extent of which still could not be determined – had been very great and that one could also not determine "whether the damages are subject to compensation under the terms of the policies." This being the case, "it seems absolutely necessary that the insurance companies proceed in the handling of this matter according to totally uniform principles which have to be adopted in agreement with the relevant authorities and Party agencies." Hilgard, in his capacity as head of the Reich Group for Insurance, therefore asked that they take measures as quickly as possible to ensure that no company do anything to prejudice this unified stance. On the one hand, it was necessary to acknowledge all incoming reports of damages. On the other, it was important that "no payments for damages occur before further instructions are received concerning the handling of these reports." Finally, Hilgard asked that he be supplied with ongoing information about the extent of the damages, which he needed for his reports to the Reich Economics Minister.[10]

This letter clearly demonstrates that Hilgard was very much aware of two factors potentially complicating the handling of claims of Pogrom victims; these factors are of great importance in evaluating his somewhat puzzling performance (to be discussed shortly) at the meeting of November 12, 1938, under Göring's chairmanship in the Reich Air Ministry called to deal with the problems raised by the Pogrom. The first was the general issue of liability – specifically, whether the Pogrom could be viewed as a public disturbance and thus not be subject to compensation under the insurance conditions of most policies. The circular proves that André Botur (who has produced the most important study of the insurance issue and the Pogrom) is absolutely correct in surmising that Hilgard, as an experienced insurance man, was well aware of this legal issue, since the circular specifically raises the question of liability.[11]

Indeed, it is inconceivable that Hilgard could not have been conscious that even the terminology with which liability could be called into question was a touchy issue. On April 20, 1938, the Reich Supervisory Board for Insurance had sent the insurance group a letter pointing out "that in the National Socialist State the marketing of riot insurance and the mention of riot, domestic or civil unrest, disturbance of the peace, mob action, plundering, strikes, lockouts, and sabotage in the general insurance conditions of the other insurance branches is insupportable."[12] At its meeting on June 17, the group advisory council was quite ready to abandon riot insurance, which scarcely existed anymore anyway, but was reluctant to abandon the reference to riots and public disturbance in the general

---

[10] Wirtschaftsgruppe Privatversicherung der Reichsgruppe Versicherungen an die Fachgruppen, 11. Nov. 1938, GDV, RS/46.

[11] Botur apparently did not have access to this important circular, which very much strengthens his general argument but which also shows that Hilgard's policy of nonpayment antedated rather than followed the meeting of November 12 discussed in what follows. Botur, *Privatversicherung*, pp. 179–80, 186.

[12] RAA an die Wirtschaftsgruppe Privatversicherung, 20. April 1938, MR, G 1/1.

Die Wirtschaftsgruppe Privatversicherung
der Reichsgruppe „Versicherungen"
der Gesamtorganisation der gewerblichen Wirtschaft

Fernsprecher: 51 00 26

BERLIN C 2,   den 11.November 38
Kaiser-Wilhelm-Straße 1-3

Tgb.Nr. 12771/38
- - - - - - - - - -
Schw/Bl.

Eilt sehr!

An die

Fachgruppe 1: Feuerversicherung und
Nebenzweige,

V e r t r a u l i c h !
====================

Fachuntergruppe: Glasversicherung,

Fachgruppe 2: Transport-,Luftfahrt-,
Maschinen-,Einheitsversicherung,

Fachuntergruppe: Maschinenversicherung,

Fachgruppe 8: Kraftfahrzeugversicherung.

- - - - -

Betr.: Antijüdische Demonstrationen.

Vom Leiter der Reichsgruppe "Versicherungen" haben wir das
nachstehend wiedergegebene Schreiben erhalten, das wir Ihnen hiermit zur weiteren Veranlassung bekanntgeben:

"Durch die antijüdischen Demonstrationen des heutigen
Tages sind Glas-, Feuer- und E/D.-Schäden grössten Umfanges
herbeigeführt worden. Es lässt sich zurzeit weder der wirkli-
che Umfang dieser Schäden auch nur einigermassen übersehen,
noch lässt sich feststellen, ob die Schäden nach den Versicherungsbedingungen entschädigungspflichtig sind. Unbedingt er-
forderlich erscheint es, dass die Versicherungsunternehmungen
bei der Behandlung dieser Angelegenheit nach völlig einheit-
lichen Gesichtspunkten vorgehen, die mit den in Frage kommen-
den Behörden und Parteistellen abgestimmt werden müssen. Ich
bitte infolgedessen schnellstens Vorkehrungen dahin zu treffen,
dass von keiner Versicherungsunternehmung irgendwelche Mass-
nahmen getroffen werden, die das einheitliche Vorgehen zu
präjudizieren in der Lage wären. Vor allem ist es erforder-
lich, dass die eingehenden Schadenanmeldungen lediglich zur
Kenntnis genommen werden, dass aber irgendwelche Schaden-
zahlungen nicht erfolgen, bevor wegen der Behandlung dieser
Anmeldungen weitere Weisungen ergangen sind.
Ich bitte ferner, über die zuständigen Fachgruppen bei den
einzelnen Unternehmungen umgehend Feststellungen treffen zu
lassen über das Mass der Schäden. Ich bitte um umgehende Erle-
digung, da ich diese Feststellungen zu meiner Berichterstat-
tung an den Herrn Reichswirtschaftsminister benötige."

Die im 2.Absatz gewünschten Feststellungen bitten wir umgehend zu treffen und hierher zu berichten.

H e i l   H i t l e r !
Die Wirtschaftsgruppe Privatversicherung
I.A.

Circular of the Economic Group for Private Insurance of November 11, 1938.

conditions because of its foreign business. It was impossible to have two sets of
conditions in German insurance policies. Furthermore, in the event of war, it
was conceivable that domestic Communists could attempt public disturbances
or that difficulties might arise in areas evacuated in a strategic retreat. Thus,

the insurers argued that it was "in the interest of the National Socialist State" to maintain the clause. Apparently, the insurers and the RAA easily agreed on this compromise – the latter having already indicated that it understood the need to take foreign business into account – but the matter nevertheless continued to hang in the air in late October because the Propaganda Ministry persisted in demanding that the terminology be removed from the general insurance conditions. It would not be easy to openly claim that the events of November 9–10 were a civic disturbance when Goebbels, the very man who had incited them, insisted that civic disturbances no longer existed in National Socialist Germany.[13]

The second factor complicating Hilgard's efforts to find a policy for dealing with insurance claims arising from the Pogrom was that government officials were in a position to exercise dictatorial authority with respect to the payment or nonpayment of insurance claims. This was not only because it was a government-inspired Pogrom that had created the complicated situation in the first place and that one of the unique characteristics of totalitarian states is that they are in a position to arbitrarily "solve" the problems they arbitrarily create; it was also because section 81a of the Reich Insurance Decree gave the government the power to set aside existing clauses in the general insurance conditions if it deemed such action "in the public interest."[14] The insurance industry was in no position to make autonomous decisions on its liability with the confidence that it could fight for its position in court. It would inevitably have to come to terms with the authorities and party agencies. Finally, it is useful to bear in mind that the sense of insecurity in the Reich Group must have been very high at this time because, as discussed previously, it was undergoing reorganization and it was by no means certain that Hilgard would retain his leadership position.

Leader he was, however, and it was only a matter of a couple of days before he was summoned to represent the entire industry with respect to the insurance aspects of the Pogrom. On the morning of November 12, Hilgard received a summons from Göring's "Chancellory" to go immediately to a meeting at the Reich Air Ministry. In the antechamber to the meeting room, as Hilgard reported in his private memoirs, he encountered a number of Göring's adjutants, some of whom immediately approached him with the information that the meeting he was about to enter was a very stormy one, "that Goebbels's position was shaky and that I could contribute to finishing him off entirely."[15] Hilgard was

---

[13] Sitzung des Beirats der Wirtschaftsgruppe Privatversicherung, 24. Feb. 1938, GDV, RS/26; Niederschrift über die 10. Beiratssitzung der Fachgruppe 1 Feuerversicherung, 28. Juni 1938, SM, 1458/1/178, Bl. 105f.; Niederschrift über die Sitzung des Beirats der Fachgruppe Glasversicherung, 9. Dez. 1938, SM, 1458/1/255, Bl. 71.

[14] See the discussion in Botur, *Privatversicherung*, pp. 71–3.

[15] Hilgard, "Leben," FHA, NL 2/7, p. 107. The account by Hilgard given here deviates somewhat from that written at the time of Hilgard's denazification, when he was writing more from memory. His "Aktennote betr. Die Aktion gegen die Synagogen und jüdischen Geschäfte vom 8./9. November 1938," written for the Nuremberg trials, misdates the meeting to November 11 and sets the participation at 40–50 persons. According to his memoirs, it was more in the neighborhood of 100. See FHA, NL 2/5.

understandably surprised by such expectations and, upon entering the room, was confronted by a large assemblage of nearly a hundred Reich ministerial and police leaders assembled about a horseshoe-shaped table with Göring at its head. Göring instructed that Hilgard be provided with a seat next to him, and Hilgard thus found himself squeezed between Göring and Goebbels, who sat at his left. At the same time, he sat directly across from Reinhard Heydrich, chief of the Reich Security Office and SS Reichsführer Himmler's right-hand man, and across from Kurt Daluege, chief of the Order Police. This was no dinner party, and there is every reason to believe that Hilgard found the situation intimidating.

One of the great difficulties in interpreting the 160-minute meeting is that the log is incomplete. The portions taken by one of the two stenographers have not been found. For this reason, we do not have a record of Hilgard's involvement in one of the three parts of the recorded meeting at which he was present. The other presently available sources on the meeting do not add significantly to our knowledge of the insurance discussion. Nevertheless, the total body of available source material is extensive enough to piece together the role of Hilgard in this important event.[16]

Insurance was only one part of the broad agenda of the meeting that Hilgard now joined and that Göring had earlier announced to be of "decisive nature" in taking a unified approach to the Jewish question. He had received a letter from Martin Bormann (chief of staff of the deputy Führer's office) calling for such centralization, and Hitler himself had repeated this demand over the phone with him the day before. Göring viewed the question primarily as a "large-scale economic problem," and this was to be the point of departure for their decisions. The demonstrations of the previous days had made it clear that – despite earlier discussions and decisions – they could not go on dragging their feet on Aryanizing the economy but rather had to act decisively. At the same time, and with scarcely concealed hostility toward Goebbels and his irrepressible egomania, Göring made it clear that he was "fed up with demonstrations" because "they do not hurt the Jews, but in the last analysis myself since I am the final authority for organizing the economy." He argued that not only did destruction of a Jewish store not hurt the Jew (since insurance covered the damages), it also

---

[16] Stenographische Niederschrift von einem Teil der Besprechung über die Judenfrage unter Vorsitz von Feldmarschall Göring im RLA [Reichsluftamt] am 12. Nov. 1933, 11 Uhr, in Der Prozeß gegen die Hauptkriegsverbrecher vor dem Internationalen Militärtribunal. Nürnberg 14. November–1. Oktober 1946, Bd. 28, Nürnberg 1948, Dokument 1816-PS, pp. 499–540 (hereinafter cited as Dokument 1816-PS). One of the two stenographers retained the copy of his portion of the minutes in violation of the regulations, which is why it found its way into the International Military Tribunal. The other two presently available primary sources on the meeting are those of Bernhard Lösener of the Jewish desk in the Interior Ministry and the Undersecretary in the Foreign Office, Ernst Woermann. For the former's account, see "Das Reichsministerium des Innern und die Judengesetzgebung," *Vierteljahrshefte für Zeitgeschichte* 9 (1961), pp. 263–311. Woermann's account can be found in *Akten zur Deutschen Auswärtigen Politik 1918–1945*, Serie D (1937–1941), Bd. V: Polen, Südosteuropa, Lateinamerika, Klein- und Mittelstaaten. Juni 1937–März 1939 (Baden-Baden, 1953), Dokument 649, pp. 761–2.

destroyed goods meant for consumption by the people. Any future demonstrations, he urged, should be directed in such a way "that one does not cut into one's own flesh." Göring repeated again that it was insurance companies who would bear the costs of property destruction, while the shortage of desperately needed clothing and other goods would only increase. In another thrust at Goebbels, Göring stated that he would be appreciative if it were made clear to the people through propaganda that the insurance companies, not the Jews, were the victims of destructive demonstrations. This said, Göring made it no less clear that, "I do not have any desire ... to let the insurance companies pay for these damages. I will therefore issue a decree on the basis of my plenary power – and ask naturally for the collaboration of the relevant ministries – that matters be put on the right track and the insurance companies not have to bear the damages."[17]

This was, of course, in full conformity with Hitler's decision that the Jews receive no insurance payments, of which Göring undoubtedly was aware either through Goebbels or through his own telephone conversation with Hitler of the previous day. Nevertheless, Göring's insatiable thirst for foreign exchange and any assets he could lay his hands on made it impossible for him simply to discharge the insurance companies of any responsibilities they might have had. Thus, he believed there was a second issue to be considered on the insurance front:

these insurance companies could be reinsured abroad. In the case such reinsurance comes into question, then I would not want to renounce it because it will bring in foreign exchange. This must be examined. For this reason I have asked Herr Hilgard of the insurance business to be brought here, who is in the best position to give us information as to the extent to which the insurance companies are covered for such damages for I would not want in any case to renounce it.

The question of how the German insurance companies could be spared payment of Pogrom damages while foreign reinsurance companies continued to pay their share was a mystery concerning which Göring was apparently oblivious. While Hilgard had been on his way to the meeting, those already assembled had engaged in a brutal, ill-tempered, and often simply disgusting discussion of the next steps in the despoliation of the Jews through Aryanization: the replacement of burnt-down synagogues (after the Jews had torn down what remained of them) with parking lots, the segregation of Jews on trains, and their exclusion from cinemas, swimming pools, beaches, public parks, the "German forest," and German schools. Whereas Göring was most interested in details of the Aryanization question, Goebbels paid enthusiastic attention to the "cultural" questions. Göring was anxious to concentrate on the matters most on his mind and made a point of mentioning a plan, long under discussion, to impose a special tax on the Jews. The idea for such an "atonement" tax had first arisen in connection with the assassination of Wilhelm Gustloff (leader of the NSDAP organization in Switzerland) on February 5, 1936. The regime had deliberately restrained "public wrath" in the Gustloff case because of the Olympics. Now that it had been

---

[17] Dokument 1816-PS, pp. 499–500.

unleashed and larger bills were due for both damages and military expenditures, Göring wanted a contribution from the Jews in the form of a high one-time levy rather than a tax surcharge, hungrily remarking that "thereby I am better served."[18]

Turning to Hilgard on his left, Göring now raised the question of how he might be "served" by such insurance proceeds as might be owing to the Jews. Pointing out to Hilgard that the recent events arising from the "justifiable rage of the people toward the Jews" had led to a great deal of damage to property and persons, Göring went on to state that "I assume that a portion of the Jews – probably the majority – are also insured against tumult damages, etc." In the minutes of the meeting, Hilgard is reported as saying "yes" to this remark – "Hilgard: Yes" – although, given what was to follow, this was probably more a "listening noise" than an actual confirmation of Göring's assumption.[19] Göring then went on to assure Hilgard that Jewish insurance entitlements arising from the "justified defense" of the people against the Jews would present no problem: "Here the matter would be relatively simple in that I would issue a decree that these damages that arise from this outburst are not to be covered by insurance." However, the question that was of "burning interest" to Göring (and which was why he had summoned Hilgard) was whether there was any foreign reinsurance for tumult damage insurance. He wanted to discuss "to what extent this reinsurance, which might possibly yet bring foreign exchange, does not come to the Jews but to the German national economy."[20]

Göring was now ready to let Hilgard have his say, first as to the matter of whether the Jews were insured against the damages. There can be no doubt about the fact that Göring's line of questioning put Hilgard in a very difficult position because it was quite the product of utter ignorance. All he could do was attempt to enlighten Göring as to what really was at issue:

The matter is such that we are dealing with three types of insurance, and to be sure not with insurance against disturbances and tumult damage insurance, but with regular fire insurance, with regular glass insurance, and with regular simple theft insurance. The insured, that is, those who have a claim on the basis of these policies, are in part Jews, in part Aryans. With respect to the fire insurance, which is the largest amount here, those involved are probably by and large Jews. In the case of the warehouses, those damaged are identical with the Jews, with the owners, as is naturally certainly the case with the synagogues, aside from the damage to neighbors that came about through the spread of the fires. According to my information, which came in last night, such damage was relatively small. The matter is completely different with respect to glass insurance, which plays a very large role. Here the largest proportion of those damaged by far are Aryan.

---

[18] Ibid., p. 511. On the Gustloff affair, see Friedlander, *Nazi Germany and the Jews*, pp. 181f., 236.

[19] Dokument 1816-PS, p. 511. In contrast to Botur, *Privatversicherung*, p. 177, I am disinclined to interpret Hilgard's "Ja" as an actual affirmation that most of the Jews were insured against unrest, especially since he was soon to dismiss the significance of such insurance.

[20] Dokument 1816-PS, p. 512.

This is namely the house ownership, which is primarily in Aryan hands, while the Jew is in the rule only the renter of the shop – a situation which you can establish all along the line, e.g., on the Kurfürstendamm.[21]

For Göring, all this bad news simply confirmed what he had been saying all along about the economic harmfulness of such demonstrations, and he was not in the least pacified when Goebbels chimed in with "there the Jew must pay the damage." Indeed, Göring flew into a rage: "It doesn't make any sense. We do not have any raw materials. It is all foreign glass; that costs foreign exchange! One could crawl up the walls!" At this point, Hilgard certainly understood very well what Göring's aides had meant with respect to "finishing off" Goebbels. He proceeded to expatiate on the glass problem, pointing out that the shop window glass came from Belgium, not Bohemia, and estimating "that we must expend approximately 6 million under the insurance conditions as replacement mainly to Aryans who have suffered damages." While emphasizing that this could only be an estimate because of time constraints, and modifying his remarks to point out that Jewish merchants did suffer glass damage insofar as they were the owners of the buildings (as was the case with Jewish department stores), he went on to calculate that some 3 million marks' worth of glass was available in Germany, which meant that another 3 million marks' worth of glass would have to be imported. This amounted to half a year of Belgium's production, so that it probably would take another half year for the required glass to be produced. This triggered yet another altercation between Göring and Goebbels over the need to inform the people about Pogrom costs, which the latter did not feel possible at the moment.

Of course, the Pogrom had been an exercise not only in destructive vandalism but also in thievery, and this was the next subject to which Göring turned in what so far had been a very frustrating discussion with Hilgard. Göring wanted to know if theft insurance covered goods that were taken out of shops and then burned, to which Hilgard replied negatively. Was it then a case of civic disturbance (*Aufruhr*)? Here, Hilgard was uncertain, since it was an open question as to whether use of goods after an entrance (or containers) had been forcibly destroyed constituted thievery or simply an extension of the civic disturbance. Göring, apparently still under the illusion that there was insurance against civic disturbances and against damages arising from tumult, first declared the event to be one of civil disturbance, whereupon Hilgard informed him that such insurance scarcely existed anymore. Hilgard took as his example their biggest thievery case, the jewelry store Markgraf on Unter den Linden, which had reported 1.7 million RM in damages and held a so-called combined policy that seemed to insure it against every possible damage. After Göring had gone into another rage – calling on Heydrich and Daluege to round up those responsible and use the Party to go after anyone who seemed to have been involved in

[21] Ibid.

looting – Hilgard went on to say that the damages in question probably did not fall under the policy. Nevertheless, he made this statement with reservation, and asked Göring if he could not make a small request in the name of the insurance industry with respect to their liability, namely, "that we not be blocked in the fulfillment of our contractual obligations." This was necessary, Hilgard declared, because of their international business, which was very important and brought in foreign exchange. It was necessary to maintain confidence in the German insurance business, and failure to meet their contractual obligations would constitute a "black spot on the coat of honor of the German insurance industry."

Göring's initial reaction to this suggestion that the insurance companies meet such liabilities was to reiterate that he would issue a decree that would provide relief, but when Hilgard indicated a desire to discuss this, Heydrich chimed in with the idea that the insurance companies should pay out their obligations and that the money would then be confiscated. In this way the companies could formally save face. Hilgard's response to this and Göring's interruption (along with Hilgard's interjection in the midst of Göring's remarks) are most revealing:

HILGARD: That which Obergruppenführer Heydrich just said is what I actually also consider the right way, first to use the apparatus of the insurance industry to determine, to regulate, and also to pay out, but then to give the insurance industry the possibility, in some kind of fund –

GÖRING: One moment! You have to pay out in any case because Germans are damaged. But you receive a legal ban against making the payments directly to the Jews. You must also pay the damages that you would have had to pay to the Jews, but not to the Jews but to the Finance Minister. (Hilgard: Aha!) What he does with it is his business."[22]

The only sensible way to interpret Hilgard's "Aha!" is that Göring had hoisted Hilgard on his own petard. The latter apparently hoped that the insurance companies could make what was tantamount to fictional payments where they had liability and then get their money back from the State. While there is no direct evidence that Hilgard anticipated that this money would come from the Jews, his agreement with the scenario sketched out by Heydrich and the subsequent remarks made by State Councilor Schmeer (of the Economics Ministry), who was very much involved in the reconstruction of the Reich Group at this time and also was aware of the plan to levy a billion-mark fine on the Jews, could be interpreted as indicative of Hilgard's thinking: "Field Marshal, I was going to make the proposal that one settles on a specific percent of the reported assets – a billion mark is to be collected – in my view 15% and then raises this percent somewhat so that all the Jews pay the same amount and then give the insurance companies the money back from this amount."[23] Göring, however, had obviously changed his mind with respect to the liability of the insurance companies. At the beginning of the meeting he indicated a desire to relieve them of all

[22] Ibid., p. 516.
[23] Ibid.

obligation, but Hilgard's request that the companies be allowed to fulfill their obligations caused Göring to change his mind and to interrupt Hilgard before the latter had a chance to clarify his point: "No. I am not thinking at all of giving the money back to the insurance companies. The insurance companies are liable. No, the money belongs to the State. That is absolutely clear. That would be a gift to the insurance companies. They have made a generous request. They will fulfill it. You can count on it!"

The question of interpretation is important because, after the war, Hilgard claimed his "Aha!" as a "plus point" in his denazification, and he also gave himself credit for saying, presumably in connection with his request that the insurance companies be permitted to fulfill their obligations, that the insurance companies would even pay the Jews if they determined they were liable. He suggested that this required no small amount of courage in the threatening presence of Goebbels and Heydrich. The former was purported by Hilgard to have turned red and to have interrupted him "with the classic words: 'Gentlemen, did you hear that? I think the monkey is picking lice off me. This man wants to pay the Jews.' "[24] Quite aside from the fact that the words attributed by Hilgard to himself and to Goebbels are not found in the extant portions of the minutes, it is difficult to see how or why Hilgard would have made a special point of saying that the insurance companies would pay the Jews when it had been quite obvious (from the remarks made by Göring almost immediately after Hilgard entered the room) that the Jews were not going to collect insurance under any circumstances. Goebbels certainly may have been overwrought, given the way Göring was trying to use Hilgard to make his position difficult, and he could conceivably have misinterpreted Hilgard's remarks or intentions, but it is hard to imagine the stenographer omitting such a sharp remark from so important a personage yet still recording Hilgard's "Aha!" Furthermore, however threatening a personage, Heydrich was positively helpful to Hilgard in suggesting precisely what the latter wanted – namely, a fictional payment by the insurance companies (to help them save face) that would then be compensated. It was the rapacious Göring who elicited Hilgard's "Aha!" by rejecting such a solution and declaring that he was going to confiscate the insurance, so that the companies would receive no compensation at all. Whatever the deficiencies of the minutes, about which Hilgard complained bitterly when they were finally published in 1948, there seems to be no evidence or reason for Hilgard's making a special point about paying insurance to the Jews themselves; most important, the interpretation given here is perfectly consistent with Hilgard's behavior during the negotiations over the coming weeks while the insurance issues of the Pogrom were being settled.

In any case, matters were then made worse for Hilgard – following Göring's announcement that he intended to confiscate insurance payments to Jews without compensation to the insurance companies – by Hans Kehrl, a high official

[24] Hilgard, "Leben," p. 109, FHA, NL 2/7.

in the Reich Economics Ministry whose presence at the meeting Hilgard could not even remember at his interrogation in Nuremberg.[25] Kehrl chimed in that the vast majority of the glass insurance companies were too small to bear the costs and that they had to find out if there was reinsurance. Hilgard responded by pointing out that reinsurance played a very small role here and was primarily of some importance with respect to fire insurance for large department stores. Reinsurance did not exist in the glass branch for the simple reason that the glass insurance business was normally extremely profitable. But it was now suddenly confronted with double the normal damage for a year, so that all calculations had to be thrown out. Whereas glass insurers normally collected 14 million marks in annual premiums and paid out damages to the tune of 4–5 million, their profitability now was truly endangered. Göring was unmoved, however, pointing out that there still would be a 4-million-mark profit; he remained unmoved even though Hilgard insisted that by adding up all the damage one arrived at a loss of 25 million and that this was a "great catastrophe" for the insurance business.

Göring, however, was in a ruthless mood. He only wished 200 Jews had been killed in place of the goods that had been destroyed, and he had no patience either with Kehrl, a convinced Nazi whose apparent concern about the fate of small glass insurance companies ran athwart of Göring's quest for economic rationalization, or Funk, who tried to argue that the insurance companies would not have to pay if the Jews footed the bill. Göring was out to collect from everyone, and the matter was "as clear as day" for him:

At this moment – except for Herr Hilgard, who is here – no insurance company thinks anything other than that it must pay for the damages. They also want to do so, and I have complete understanding for that. They must do so so that they cannot be reproached for not having been strong enough to bear the damages. Glass insurance – this has also been emphasized – was until now the best business. It also has sufficient extra profits, if it did good business, and it has not distributed them as dividends, then it has reserves in order to be able to cover the larger damages. Such a company must be able to cover damages of 10, 12, 15 million, three times that of a normal year's premiums. If it cannot do that, then one must consider whether one should allow such small mutual insurance companies to stay alive. It would simply be insanity to have insurance companies that are not in a position to cover such damages. Such an insurance company would absolutely be a fraud against the people. I now take the following view. The damages are to be determined. The insurance companies have to accept their full legal liability for them and to pay.[26]

At this point, there was a change of stenographers and the discussion that ensued is lost. It would appear to have been concerned with details of the various damages to be covered as well as of a decree, subsequently issued, requiring Jews to repair the damages caused by the Pogrom. This, in any case, was the note on which the minutes resumed, since Göring declared that, if the jewels stolen from

[25] Ibid., pp. 116–18.
[26] Dokument 1816-PS, pp. 518–19.

Markgraf were to be found, they were to be turned over to the State along with any other stolen property from Jews that was recovered. A more serious problem was presented by goods on commission from England or the United States, which may have been insured by British or American companies. For Göring, however, this constituted no problem since the Jews, not Aryans, would report the loss and then be compelled to compensate the non-Jews. Thus, not all the damages would be paid by the German insurers and, as Göring cynically remarked, Hilgard had something "to smile about." Hilgard was not amused and, manifestly unable to control his irritation at the big bill looming before his industry, bluntly stated that not having to pay some damages could not be called a profit. Göring, however, was indifferent to Hilgard's discomfiture (since he seemed to have him where he wanted him) and thought moreover that Hilgard should be grateful for the good deal he was providing:

Excuse me! If you are legally liable to pay 5 million, and suddenly an angel in my somewhat corpulent form comes and tells you: you can keep 1 million, then damn it, is that not a profit? I am to take a direct cut with you, or whatever one calls it. – I only have to look at you; your whole body exudes satisfaction. You are getting a big rake-off.

Hilgard, who had expected that his industry could pass off the bulk of the Pogrom costs, could not share this view. As was his custom by now, he couched his argument in the language of the regime to make a last desperate point, even at the risk of irritating Göring:

It is a self-evident matter for me that the honorable German merchant ought not to bear the burden. I have also spoken to the firms, and I have argued that the damages ought not to remain hanging on the Aryans, and it remains hopelessly on the backs of the Aryans because the insurance community – not the insurance companies! – are thereby affected in that they must pay higher premiums and receive lower dividends. As a result, they are the ones who are damaged in the end. That is so and remains so. No one will deny that to me.

By this time, Hilgard was as irritating to Göring as Goebbels, and Göring dismissed him with the message he had been trying to convey to the Propaganda Minister: "Then please be good enough to take care that not so many window panes are broken. You belong to the people also. Send your agents out. They should explain things immediately!"[27]

HILGARD, THE REICH GROUP, AND THE AFTERMATH OF THE AIR MINISTRY CONFERENCE

Beginning on November 12 – that is, within hours of the meeting in the Air Ministry – there began a new flood of anti-Jewish legislation that distinguished itself

[27] Ibid., p. 520.

from past measures by vastly accelerating their despoliation, exclusion from German economic life, and social and personal isolation. Most important from the perspective of the insurance issue were the three decrees issued on November 12 itself. The first of these, the "Decree for the Restoration of the Appearance of the Streets around Jewish Enterprises," placed the burden of cleaning up and repairing damage from the Pogrom on the Jews and mandated confiscation by the State of any insurance to which Jews of German citizenship could make claim. The second decree imposed an atonement tax of 1 billion marks on Jews of German citizenship. Of great significance in connection with this decree was the implementation decree of November 21. It ordered that all Jews with assets of 5,000 RM or more be obligated to pay 20% of their assets in four payments between December 15, 1938, and August 15, 1939. Especially significant for the insurance question was section 7 of the implementation decree, which provided that insurance payments in connection with the Pogrom to Jews with German citizenship and stateless Jews were to be made directly to the State revenue offices and to be credited against their levy on assets. Insofar as such payments exceeded the latter, however, they were to be confiscated by the Reich anyway. Finally, there was the "Decree for the Exclusion of Jews from German Economic Life," which barred Jews from owning or running any enterprises after January 1, 1939.

As we shall show, the last-mentioned decree promoted a massive repurchase of Jewish life insurance assets and ultimately raised the question of whether Jews were insurable at all. For purposes of clarity, however, it is most efficient to concentrate first on the thorny problem of insurance obligations in connection with the Pogrom itself. As should be obvious, the meeting in the Air Ministry had left Hilgard with an extremely unpleasant and unanticipated problem on his hands: Göring and the government now appeared to be expecting substantial payment of the damages from the insurance companies as well as from the Jews. When Hilgard returned to his office, he immediately arranged for a meeting with his colleagues in the Reich Group. But even before it was held, he received a call from the official in the Reich Finance Ministry (probably Ministerial Director Johannes Schwandt) whom Göring had put in charge of the matter, telling him that Göring "expects a payment of 20 million marks, with which he will then be satisfied." Hilgard and his colleagues had no intention of paying any such sum if they could help it, but they were fully aware that they would have little chance of winning a legal battle "since our real opponent in court would not be the damaged Jews but rather the almighty Göring, who had pronounced the seizure of all Jewish claims by means of a decree."[28] It is unlikely that Hilgard ever believed the insurance industry could take the government of the Third Reich to court over this issue or that the government would engage in a formal legal suit.

[28] Hilgard, "Leben," p. 110, FHA, NL 2/7.

Eduard Hilgard (1884–1982), member of the board of Allianz 1923–1944 and head of the Reich Group for Insurance 1934–1945, about 1934.

Avoiding suits at home and abroad was an important determinant of both industry and bureaucratic behavior in the coming negotiations.[29]

If Hilgard were going to prevent Göring from having his way, he would have to mobilize his contacts in the ministries – especially in the Reich Economics Ministry, which was charged with implementing the decree on repairing damages arising from the Pogrom. Hilgard would also have to keep his "troops" in line. Thus, on November 18, the various insurance organizations were informed about his collaboration with the RWM, and their members were instructed to provide detailed information on the damages and on who had suffered them – German

[29] See Hilgard's interrogation of July 14, 1947, NA, RG 260, OMGUS, FINAD, 2/57/6–8.

Jews, non-German Jews, Aryans, foreigners. The injunction against paying any damages was reiterated and the Reich Group announced its intention of working closely with the various business managers of the insurance branch organizations in assuring a uniform approach to the problem.[30] During the next few days, however, confusion arose due to the RWM's implementation decree of November 21. Three days later, the Reich Group informed its members that nothing was to be paid despite the issuance of the implementation decree and, on November 29, pointed out that the implementation decree said nothing about "whether" the insurance companies were obligated to pay the damages but only stated that, "in so far" as Jews were successful in claiming such obligations, the sums were to be paid to the Finance Ministry. In the meantime, the economics minister had reserved his decision about the actual obligations in question and would probably make a determination only after the extent of the damages had been established.[31]

Hilgard now viewed it as his chief task to persuade the RWM that insurance companies were neither legally liable nor financially capable of covering the damages and, further, that holding them liable made no sense in terms of the goals and purposes of the decrees of November 12. He stated the views of himself and his colleagues in a memorandum to Ministerial Director Lange of the RWM on December 6, 1938.[32] In his covering letter, Hilgard called for a uniform settlement of the issues and urged that the RWM hold a discussion with the relevant insurance industry leaders as well as Justice Ministry officials. He left open the question as to whether the Finance Ministry needed to be asked to join as well, which was quite understandable given the interest of the Finance Ministry in supporting Göring's idea of making the insurance companies liable and collecting their money.

The memorandum itself was signed by Director Hans Goudefroy of Allianz, who served as the legal expert for the Reich Group, and by Hilgard himself. They began by narrowly defining the relevant damages under the two decrees relevant to the issue – the decree for the restoration of the appearance of the streets and the atonement tax implementation decree of November 21. They took the position that the only relevant damages were those that directly affected the appearance of the streets and involved businesses and homes. Thus, damages to the interior of businesses and houses (as well as damages to synagogues, Jewish schools, and other institutions) did not fall under the decrees. They applied a similarly narrow construction to section 7 of the implementation decree, reiterating that it

---

[30] Rundschreiben Wirtschaftsgruppe Privatversicherung, 18. Nov. 1938, GDV, RS/15. The call for speedy transmittal of such information was reiterated in a Rundschreiben of 21. Nov. 1938, ibid.

[31] Rundschreiben Wirtschaftsgruppe Privatversicherung, 24. Nov. 1938 and 29. Nov. 1938, GDV, RS/20.

[32] Hilgard to Lange, Dec. 6, 1938, and his memorandum of Dec. 5, 1938, "Bestehen Versicherungsansprüche deutscher oder staatenloser Juden auf Grund der Vorgänge vom 8.–10. November 1938?" in SM, 1458/1/98, Bl. 147–53.

did not establish liability but only stated that, if liability existed, then insurance payment was to go to the revenue office and be counted in the atonement tax payment. They then turned to the central question: Did liability exist? Unsurprisingly, the answer was negative and was based on the Reich Court decision of June 8, 1923, in the Porto Allegre case, in which an angry mob responded to the German sinking of a Brazilian ship in April 1917 by storming and destroying various German businesses. Those claiming damages from the insurance companies tried to argue that they were entitled to compensation because the disturbances were not directed against the Brazilian government or officials and thus did not qualify as civil disturbances. The court, however, ruled that a civil disturbance existed when "portions of the populace, which do not have to be considered numerically insignificant, are set in motion in a way that disturbs the public peace and order and exercise violence, be it against persons, be it against things." In the view of the authors, this fit the situation of November 8–10 perfectly, as was amply demonstrated (in their view) by Goebbels's call for a cessation to the demonstrations of November 10 in which he urged an end to the "demonstrations and reprisals" taken against Jewry and Jewish property "in justifiable and understandable anger" over the murder of vom Rath. From this, Goudefroy and Hilgard triumphantly concluded that "therefore the damages of November 8–10 were the result of civic or internal disturbances and are consequently not liable to compensation."

However, the two insurance executives left no stone unturned and went on to argue that, even if the conditions defining a civic disturbance were not fully satisfied by the events in question, nevertheless the sense of the general insurance conditions (in excluding compensation for civil disturbances, acts of war, earthquakes, and the like) was to protect the insurers from liability for "elementary events," and this was the sort of event Goebbels described when he wrote – in an article of November 12 on "The Grünspan Case"[33] – that the events in question were "an eruptive outburst of the anger of the population." Thus, if the Pogrom was not a civil disturbance then it was something like an earthquake.

Goudefroy and Hilgard showed themselves to be quite masterful in carrying the logic of the Pogrom, and the decrees arising from it, to their brutal conclusions. Thus, Aryan owners of destroyed Jewish properties could not suffer damages or lay claim to insurance payment because Jews were responsible for making the repairs. They were most emphatic, however, about the lack of Jewish entitlement to compensation:

Through the decrees of November 12, 1938, the entire Jewry, therefore also the German and the stateless Jewry has been pronounced guilty of the Paris murder and thereby of a provocation against the German people. When the provocateur brings about the event provoked, then he must accept being treated like the perpetrator himself. It will not do to

---

[33] *Völkischer Beobachter*, 12. Nov. 1933.

treat the politically condemned Jews as being legally guiltless with respect to insurance. As a consequence, it is justifiable to raise the objection that the German and stateless Jews were responsible for being intentionally, or at the very least being grossly negligent in bringing about the insurance case. Thereby, however, all insurance claims are rendered inapplicable.

It was not enough to argue that the collective guilt of the Jews for the murder of vom Rath deprived them of all rights to insurance, however. Goudefroy and Hilgard found it necessary to go further by insisting that paying the Jews insurance would be "a violation of good morals" since it would involve payment of those who had been found guilty of a crime: "The act of reprisal against the Jews has the character of a punishment approved by the State. It would contradict the general sense of justice in the highest degree if the German insurance companies would have to remove this atonement placed upon the Jews." Yet, this is precisely what would happen. For example, if one compared two Jews, each with 100,000 RM in assets and damages of 20,000 RM but with only the second having insurance, then the former would pay 20,000 RM in damages out of his own pocket plus 16,000 RM in atonement tax on his remaining assets, whereas the latter would pay 20,000 RM in atonement tax but nothing for damages if compensated by insurance. Thus, the 16,000 RM difference would be covered by the insurance companies. And this already unsatisfactory result would be made even more "unbearable" if the money in question came from a mutual insurance enterprise that would then have to raise the money from its members, "for in this case the Aryan members of the enterprise must pay the punishment imposed on the Jews."

This memorandum is a monument to the sophistry and perversion of business and personal ethics that were coming to characterize businessmen like Hilgard and Goudefroy in the pursuit of their interests under the conditions created by National Socialism. That said, it is important to recognize that the issue was not one of paying damages to Jews, since direct insurance payments for Pogrom damages to Jews were manifestly out of the question. Nevertheless, as the example employed at the end of the memorandum demonstrates, the authors were prepared to argue that the liability of the insurers was especially undesirable because it might have the effect of relieving the Jews somewhat of the burdens imposed on them by the decrees. If the chief goal was the avoidance of insurance payment to the government, Goudefroy and Hilgard nevertheless did not shy away from reinforcing their position by arguing that insurance company liability would detract from the punishment being visited upon the Jews. Promoting the efficacy of anti-Semitic measures was thus an integral part of their argumentation against insurance company liability; as we shall see, this was not their last use of such arguments.

The primary goal, of course, was to block insurance company liability, and Hilgard provided the RWM with detailed information as to what the costs would be. If liability were to be assumed, then the amount of money the government would collect from private insurers alone would amount to 25.75 million RM: 21.18 million in fire insurance, 4.42 million in glass insurance, and 150,000 in transport insurance. Payments to foreign Jews, which it was assumed would have to be made for political reasons, amounted to 1.84 million RM, while payment to Aryans would amount to 1.37 million RM, bringing the total to 28.96 million RM for the private companies alone. The publicly chartered companies would owe another 8.4 million RM to Jews, but the total amount of known (but not yet reported) damages to Jews would add 6.5 million RM to the total and, when one added damages to Aryans and non-German Jews, the total for the publicly chartered companies would amount to 15.2 million RM. Hilgard was careful to note that all the information still was not in and that many Jews were not available to assist in the determination of damages – although no mention was made of the fact that their "unavailability" was probably due to their having been carted away to concentration camps. There were other problems as well. Foreign reinsurance companies were refusing payment for the damages. Hilgard did not say why, but they obviously had no difficulty calling a civil disturbance by its name, and that the fire department and police did nothing to mitigate the damages was well known. Also, there was the problem of compensating those who had suffered accidents or shock and illness due to the events. Accident and health insurance had not been regulated under the decree of November 12. Whatever the case, time was of the essence in dealing with these questions because non-Jews were beginning to bring lawsuits against the companies, demanding payment for damages. Finally, to bring home the implications of liability, Hilgard provided a detailed list from German and foreign companies demonstrating that often reported damages significantly and even vastly exceeded the premiums they had collected. This was especially the case with smaller companies, for whom the obligation to pay would have proven "catastrophic."[34]

Nearly every major ministry was by this time engaged in trying to control the damage and complications created by the Pogrom. On December 8, a meeting was held in the Interior Ministry at which representatives of the ministries of justice, economics, finance, and propaganda appeared – along with officials from the Foreign Office and SS – to determine the extent to which the Reich might be liable for Pogrom damages. The RWM was able to present Hilgard's estimates of the damage, thus providing an overview of the enormity of the problem. By this time it was very clear that, for political reasons, certain groups (Jewish and non-Jewish foreigners and non-Jewish German citizens) would have to be compensated for the damages and that public funds would have to be used for at least the immediate handling of some cases. Furthermore, some property belonging to Aryans had been damaged because perpetrators erroneously believed it did belong to Jews, had belonged to Jews, or belonged to persons of "mixed blood"

---

[34] Hilgard an Minsterialdirigent Gottschick, 6. Dez. 1938; Aktennote für Hilgard, 7. Dez. 1938, SM, 1458/1/98, Bl. 154–8, 159–61.

or who were politically suspect for other reasons. There was an entire category of persons who were indirectly damaged because they had just invested all their assets in purchasing Jewish property or had sold goods to Jews who were now completely bankrupt and in no position to pay for the goods. The big question was how to settle claims quickly, avoiding court trials and publicity. Here the government already had a mechanism at its disposal in the form of a law decreed on December 13, 1934, on the "Settlement of Claims in Civil Law," which permitted the Minister of the Interior to terminate claims made to the courts in connection with compensation for damages arising from "the National Socialist uprising and renewal of the State" and to adjudicate such cases himself in accordance with the "healthy feeling of the people." [35] Needless to say, it was a law aimed primarily at preventing Jews from taking the National Socialist regime and its minions to court for acts of vandalism and injustice. Its potential usefulness with respect to stifling court proceedings in cases brought by Jews and non-Jews alike in connection with the Pogrom is easily apparent. Thus, at the December 8 meeting, a decision was made to centralize such decisions in the Justice Ministry so as to ensure uniformity of practice and maintain budgetary control. In the National Socialist state, however, "uniformity of decision making" was really a formula for discriminatory practice (so that only Aryan hardship cases would receive compensation) and it would be possible to distinguish between foreign Jews who had been foreign citizens for a long time and those who had recently emigrated. The Gauleiter would be asked for advice, as provided under the 1934 law, and non-Jews interrelated with Jews would be denied compensation. Indeed, as made clear by the 14th Decree for the Implementation of the Law on the Settlement of Claims in Civil Law of March 18, 1939, which was specifically issued to deal with compensation for damages arising from the events of November 8 and the following days, such compensation would be given only on the basis of need and after political criteria were met. These emergency measures, however, still left open the question of insurance company liability – that is, whether payments by the Reich were purely subsidiary or whether they were to be the primary source of compensation. The insurance companies were able to report their position to those assembled on December 8, but the actual responsibility for dealing with the issue lay with the Reich Economics Ministry. [36]

---

[35] RGBl 1934, I, pp. 1235–6, and Joseph Walk (ed.), *Das Sonderrecht für die Juden im NS-Staat. Eine Sammlung der gesetzlichen Maßnahmen und Richtlinien-Inhalt und Bedeutung* (Heidelberg, 1996, 2d ed.), Nr. I 487, p. 99.

[36] Vermerk über das Ergebnis der Besprechung im RMJ am 8. Dezember 1938 zur Frage der Gewährung von Schadenersatz für Verluste, die im Zuge der Aktion gegen die Juden am 8., 9. und 10. November 1938 entstanden sind, BAB, R 3001/10788, Bl. 356–60. For the 14. Verordnung zur Durchführung und Ergänzung des Gesetzes über den Ausgleich bürgerlich-rechtlicher Ansprüche vom 18. März 1939, see RGBl 1939, I, p. 614, and "Wiedergutmachung von Schäden aus den Aktionen vom 8. November 1938 und den folgenden Tagen," Reichsminister des Innern an die Landesregierungen, 28. März 1939, BAB, R 18/3746b.

Ministerial Councilor Daniel of the RWM, while basically friendly to the position of the insurance companies, was above all anxious to keep the discussion of the issue confined to a small circle and was likewise anxious to avoid any public discussion of whether the damages were the result of tumult and thus free of insurance obligation. He worried that it might indeed prove difficult to avoid court cases. Small and medium-sized firms, whose existence was threatened by the potentially high costs, would certainly do everything in their power to save themselves if held liable, and it would be impossible to prevent foreign insurers and reinsurers from questioning any government decision refusing to recognize the Pogrom as a tumult.[37]

Daniel sought to clarify the matter at a December 16 meeting with insurers and other governmental officials under the chairmanship of Ministerial Director Gottschick of the RWM.[38] By this time, the reported damages (which later turned out to be exaggerated) had risen to 60 million RM: 45 million RM for fire damage, 8–10 million RM for glass, and the rest for burglary. The attendees expected that court cases would be brought by foreign insurers claiming nonliability because of tumult, and Hilgard came well prepared to argue the case for nonliability for German insurers, as well. In the case of burglary insurance, there was no liability because the goods had been stolen after the windows had been broken, rather than by those who had done the initial damage. As for the fire and glass damage, it was the result of civic unrest. Also, the Jews had already replaced almost all the glass that had been broken, as required by decree, so that the obligation of insurers to replace the glass no longer existed. More generally (and quite plausibly), Hilgard argued that he had never told Göring at the meeting of November 12 that the insurance companies would pay in every case, but only "that the companies would remain faithful to their contracts and would pay in those cases in which they were legally bound to compensate."[39] Göring's interruption and the subsequent discussion had created the false impression that Hilgard had accepted full liability. Once again, he and his colleagues reiterated that the costs were unaffordable. The small mutual glass insurers would have to ask their members for additional payments that would exceed by many times their normal premiums, and even the larger fire insurance companies would be hard pressed. As in the memorandum of December 6, so now: industry representatives argued that payment should not be made for reasons of economic policy – namely, that "the Aryan insured would not understand the Aryan community of the insured being the bearer of the burden in the last analysis."[40] They warned

---

[37] Vermerk Ministerialrat Daniel, 9. Dez. 1938, SM, 1458/1/98, Bl. 164–5.

[38] The meeting was originally scheduled for the 14th. There are two reports on the meeting, the first by Ministerialrat Hans Thees of the Justice Ministry, the second by Regierungsrat Segelcke of the RWM. The former is to be found in BAB, R 3001/10788, Bl. 353–4, the latter in SM, 1458/1/98, Bl. 169–72.

[39] Ibid., Bl. 169.

[40] Ibid., Bl. 170.

that foreign reinsurers would refuse to pay, so that the German insurance companies would have to sue them in foreign courts. When asked if the insurance companies also refused to pay for damages to Aryans and foreigners, Hilgard remained consistent. From the standpoint of the law and liability, there was no difference between the Jews and the foreigners. Returning to the proposal (first made by Heydrich and then by Schmeer at the November 12 meeting) at which he had so eagerly grasped, Hilgard suggested that, if the authorities thought it important to regulate the damages done to Aryans and foreigners, then one had to invent a scenario that would camouflage any impropriety yet also be economically palatable to the insurers: "The insurers regulate all the demonstration damages including the Jewish damages without prejudice to their favorable legal situation. But the Reich obligates itself internally to replace 100% of the expenditures of the companies. Approximately 30 to 50 million RM will be necessary that the Reich could pay out of the [Jewish] contribution."[41]

The position of the insurance companies was now quite clear. In the discussion among the ministerial officials following the departure of Hilgard and his colleagues, one of the RWM officials argued that it was "unbearable" to place the damage costs on the insurance companies and that, as intended by the implementation decree of November 21, the costs were to be covered by the Jewish indemnity. The problem, as all admitted, was that the decrees issued in the wake of the Pogrom were contradictory and confusing. It was unclear whether or not the Decree for the Restoration of the Appearance of the Streets was intended to mandate payment by the insurers and thereby exclude application of the civil unrest clause in policies; although the Justice Ministry (RJM) felt that the civil unrest clause was applicable, it was very unhappy with the decree's formulation. Potentially, this left the determination to the courts, which was precisely what all were trying to avoid. The RJM was especially distressed by the implementation decree of November 21 (issued by the Finance Ministry) because they had not been consulted – despite claims to the contrary written into the preamble of the decree, under which the insurance payments could be counted in partial payment of the atonement tax. In the view of councilor Hans Thees of the RJM, "the goal must be to free the insurance companies and extract the contribution without exception from the Jews."[42]

When it came to the modus operandi, however, the RJM wished to issue a decree making the insurance companies liable (thus obviating the need for discussions in the courts) but then actually to spare insurance companies the need to pay by taking the money from the Jewish contribution. The only thing the insurance companies would have to pay under such an arrangement was the money

---

[41] Ibid.

[42] Vermerk Thees, BAB, R 3101/10788, Bl. 373, and complaints of the RJM about nonparticipation in the implementation decree of Nov. 25, 1938, BAB, R 3101/10787, Bl. 118. See also Botur, *Privatversicherung*, pp. 185–6.

owed to Aryan Germans and to foreigners, a sum the officials thought manageable for the insurance firms. This in no way satisfied either the Finance Ministry or the Four-Year Plan representatives at the meeting. The former questioned whether the insurance companies (aside perhaps from some of the smaller glass companies) really were so bad off, feeling that additional evidence was necessary; the latter went further and argued that the assumption of insurance company liability inherent in the various decrees could not be set aside. Section 7 of the implementation decree was interpreted as creating a measure of equity among the Jews so "that the small Jewish businessman, whose windows have been shattered, should not come away worse off than the rich Jew, whose villa remained untouched. For this reason one decided that the payments from the insurance claim should be counted toward the contribution."[43] Neither the RWM nor the RJM could accept this position, which in their view created legal insecurity. The by now infamous section 7 made sense only if insurance companies were liable – but this was not the case, as the companies were in a position to demonstrate. Another way had to be found, and since there was no agreement, the RWM took it upon itself to draft a new decree that would be submitted to the other ministries in an effort to solve the problem.

It had been a nasty meeting. Nine years later, Thees (in a letter to Hilgard) remembered back on their conflict with Schwandt and the Party:

... in that we refused not to recognize the riots of November 1938 as riots. In the end we pushed through with this position, which is that held today, because we saw the entire action as a big *Schweinerei*. I still think back on the first meeting in the Reich Economics Ministry in which among the large circle present you and I were the only ones who had the courage to declare that this event was nothing other than a tumult, although this was sharply contested from the side of the Party with the argument that there could be no tumult in the Third Reich by definition. I also remarked that one would have to issue a decree which would establish the liability of the insurers, but which would have to begin in such a way that under §1 of this decree a tumult is not a tumult.[44]

Hilgard, indeed, remembered Thees as "an ally, as undaunted as he was clever." Writing in 1947, Hilgard quite unabashedly recaptured both his arguments and his sentiments of 1938. The Finance Ministry "dealt with me then as if it were acting on behalf of the Jews." Hilgard, however, argued that the insurers had no responsibility in a civic commotion and that, since the Reich claimed it was punishing the Jews, "it was quite impossible and in contradiction of all sense of justice, to palm this punishment off on the insurance institutions." Thus, "what I aimed at during all of these negotiations was to prevent that the Reich derived from these anti-Jewish demonstrations a benefit of several millions, to the detriment of the insured."[45] By the "insured," of course, he meant the "Aryan" insured who paid premiums to the companies he represented. Apparently Hilgard

[43] Vermerk Segelcke, SM, 1458/1/98, Bl. 171.
[44] Thees an Hilgard, 1. Dez. 1947, FHA, NL 2/5.

had no problem with asking that the Jewish atonement tax be used to compensate the insurance companies for what was tantamount to fictional insurance payments to cover a liability the insurance companies themselves contested. It was, of course, a good thing to keep the Reich from getting still more money from the "night of broken glass." Yet one is struck by the singularity of purpose exhibited by Thees and Hilgard, not only in 1938 but also in 1947, by the absence of any reflection on the fate of the Jews at either time, and by their persistent willingness to instrumentalize the "atonement" imposed upon the Jews – which Hilgard did at least put in quotation marks – in order to argue against liability on grounds of "justice" toward the "community of the insured."

The insurance industry leaders were well aware, even in the benighted Germany of 1938, that they were complicit in a very shady endeavor, if not in the sense that they were directly cheating Jews of insurance entitlements then in the sense that they were aiding and abetting the cover-up of government activities generally viewed as criminal in the civilized countries with which Germany still consorted. This collaboration can be seen most clearly from an extraordinarily frank letter Hilgard sent to Reich Economics Minister Funk on December 17, 1938, as a follow-up to the meeting of the previous day, which was intended as a last-hour appeal to avoid insurance company liability.[46] Hilgard spoke for both the private and public sector insurers in rejecting the idea that the insurance companies should pay for the punishment meted out to the Jews. He made a special point of representing the concerns of the small insurers, like Glasverein Eberswalde, which collected 30,000 RM in premiums a year and was now confronted with an equal amount of damages. The psychological effect of Aryan small businessmen having to pay these costs had to be taken into consideration. He appended a letter from the head of another small glass insurer in Ahaus, a "simple man of the people," to demonstrate his point. In this letter, one Wilhelm Hansen lamented how unbearable it would be for the glass insurer he represented to pay 560 RM for the five windows in the two Jewish businesses insured by his company. As he had argued to his colleagues,

World Jewry is our enemy, with whom we are in a regular state of war. Naturally the Jews of Ahaus also belong to world Jewry. One has to do damage to one's enemy (opponent in war) wherever that might be. And most certainly after the Paris murder. In this case the damages done are to be viewed as a just punishment for this mean deed. This punishment ought not to be compensated with the help of some paragraphs that have been dug up. Every employment of sentimentality and of that famous German objectivity is an evil.

---

[45] "Aktennote betr.: Die Aktion gegen die Synagogen und jüdischen Geschäfte vom 8./9. November 1938" and "Memorandum. Subject: The action against the Synagogues and Jewish shops of November 8./9. 1938," in ibid. Undated but written in 1947 – that is, before Hilgard had access to the minutes of November 12, 1938.

[46] For the discussion and quotations that follow, see Hilgard an Funk, 17. Dez. 1938, SM, 1458/1/98, Bl. 177–82.

Indeed, in Hansen's view, it would be a "mockery of justice," and the people would not understand any law court or lawyer who would defend these Jews.

As Hilgard thus instrumentalized the "voice of the people" for his cause, his own argumentation stuck to familiar arguments designed to strike home to ministry interests as well. Once again Hilgard cited the Porto Allegre case, which demonstrated that disturbances did not have to be directed against the government to count as disturbances, but he warned especially against the idea (suggested in the previous day's discussion) that the government could simply pass a law setting aside the court's decision. It would call forth, Hilgard warned, "a storm of outrage abroad." As evidence he cited an article in the British *News Chronicle,* which reported that many German insurance companies were facing bankruptcy because the damages to Jewish synagogues and businesses amounted to over 50 million pounds. Most German insurers, according to the article, carried reinsurance in England, but the English insurers were well aware that the Germans themselves had eliminated insurance for domestic disturbances from their policies, that the damage was done with the "quiet approval" of the government, and that "the [British] insurers can demonstrate that the police and the fire department did not do their duty, so that the insurers did not receive the measure of official protection that is the precondition for reinsurance." He pointed out that Swiss insurers were also involved, and that it was not in the interest of the State to have such questions brought to trial. Also, the reinsurers would expect the German insurers to demand that the terms of their own policies with regard to civic unrest be effectuated. Thus, the entire industry and also the State would be embarrassed if liability were made an issue.

While Hilgard emphasized the alleged plight of small insurers, he warned very emphatically in the name of the entire industry against letting the question hang on whether or not the existence of individual firms were endangered by liability,

for it is self-evident that, if, for example, Allianz has to pay damages in the amount of perhaps 6 million as a result of the anti-Jewish demonstrations, it will not be toppled over. But one must be clear about the fact that every mark, that is to be paid for this by the German insurance firms, must somehow work out to the disadvantage of the other Aryan insured ....

Hence there was but one solution – namely, the one he had advocated in the meeting on the previous day: that the amount of insurance involved be taken from the Jewish contribution. About 50 million marks in damages had been reported, and by assuming that the synagogues and other Jewish religious buildings were "not worthy of reconstruction," one was left with about 40 million in damages. This was a sacrifice worth making to avoid the "very heavy psychological damages" that he had discussed. Hilgard further proposed that the insurance companies undertake the regulation of the damages and then be paid back in full measure. He did not fail to mention that the use of the insurance apparatus in this way involved considerable administrative costs to the companies in any case, and he pleaded with Funk "not to deny the German insurance business these fully justified demands and to do everything to keep catastrophic harm away from the German insurance industry."

Kurt Schmitt had assigned Hilgard the task of doing the dirty work of the industry, and Hilgard was serving very well. In this instance, however, Schmitt felt he had to intervene himself, as shown by a strictly confidential letter he sent to Justice Minister Franz Gürtner on December 20. It was clearly intended to move the discussion of the November 9 damages up in the hierarchy of both the industry and the government, a privilege Schmitt could allow himself as a former minister. Schmitt claimed that he had assumed that the decree transferring Jewish damage claims to the Reich had been issued so "as to prevent any discussion of the actual and legal issues related to this question." Now apparently "certain circles" in the government were actually planning to call on the insurance companies to pay. Schmitt insisted that, "under the *existing* laws," the companies had no liability because of the civil disturbance involved. Schmitt made it clear that he did not think it very wise to raise questions about this:

Now the very determination as to whether there has been such a violation of the public order or not is unpleasant. But even if this were to be denied, the obligation to compensate would still not be a practical issue because of the possibilities for suits. I can certainly spare myself going into details about this and need only to point out that it would be unbearable if, for example, foreign insurance companies or reinsurers made the question of perpetration or the behavior of the police and the fire department a subject of court proceedings. It is an especially unpleasant complication of the present case that in many instances foreign insurance companies are involved as direct insurers and reinsurers, and according to foreign press reports one can expect that they would refuse to pay voluntarily. In this situation, there is only one practical way of forcing the insurance companies to pay, namely the issuance of a special law. I consider this idea, after the Jews have in general already been obligated to bear the costs of the damages, to be so impossible that I do not have to say a word about it. I believe that a more unusual and unjust special tax and intervention in existing legal relationships could hardly be thinkable.

Apparently, what was being done to the Jews was more "thinkable," and the peculiar juxtaposition of the normal and the bizarre in the relationship between the insurance business and the government at this point was heightened by the Christmas and New Year wishes with which Schmitt ended his letter. In any case, Schmitt noted that he was anxious to bring this "delicate complex of questions" to Gürtner's attention, planned to call him about them, and offered the services of Director Alois Alzheimer to the ministry for further counsel and discussion.[47]

The insurance industry was now mobilizing itself, and while Gürtner invited Alzheimer to take up discussions with Thees, Hilgard had a circular sent on December 27 informing the industry of the line he was taking in dealing with the government, thereby making the position that he and Goudefroy had taken the official position of the industry. On January 4, 1939, Alzheimer met with Thees

---

[47] Schmitt an Gürtner, 20. Dez. 1938, BAB, R 3001/10788, Bl. 361–2.

and other officials and reiterated the usual arguments but indicated also that the insurers would be prepared to accept liability de facto for Aryans and foreigners. The domestic reinsurers would also take on the obligation; although one could try to induce foreign reinsurers to take a similar stance, court cases had to be avoided. The bad news was that a number of insurance companies were already being taken to court, and when Thees asked that the RJM be regularly informed of all such cases, Alzheimer suggested that they contact Director Goudefroy of Allianz, who had apparently been given the job of serving as watchdog in this area.[48] Finally, on January 10, Hilgard sent a new memorandum to the Reich Economics Minister setting forth his position in detail and making concrete proposals for a solution.[49]

What is interesting about this latest memorandum was the extent to which it gave priority to anti-Semitic considerations in making the case against insurance company liability. Thus, because it would be counted toward the atonement tax, payment by the insurers would involve a shifting of the punishment to "purely German insurance communities." It would "weaken the profitability of German insurers in favor of the Jews and contradict the healthy feeling of justice among all national comrades to the highest degree." At the same time, the Reich would receive no additional money because the payment would be credited to the contribution. To be sure, the Jews were also not entitled to compensation because of the civil disturbance involved, and Hilgard quite openly stated that there could be no legitimate charge against the companies for making "unjustified savings" by not paying the damages. Indeed, they were making a "significant sacrifice, if they voluntarily compensate the Aryan insured and thereby would take away the Reich's obligation to compensate." Also, the foreign reinsurers would "leave them in the lurch" and would claim the right to go to court if they felt themselves victims of special legislation that undermined the basic standards written into insurance contracts. The long-term effect would be to undermine the international relations of the industry and its value for the procurement of foreign exchange. Hilgard saw no contradiction between his proposals and the decrees sequestering such insurance claims as may have existed; picking up on an argument used by Schmitt, he viewed the sequestration of insurance claims as necessary "in order to take away from the Jews the legitimacy to launch complaints and to bring the events of November 8–10 before the courts." It was also necessary to prevent "sensational trials before foreign courts" and to prevent foreign Jews from using the issue "in a tendentious manner against the German Reich." He therefore proposed the following way of dealing with the problem: "The leader of the Reich Group for Insurance announces in agreement with the relevant ministries that the insurance enterprises are not obligated to pay the direct or indirect damages to domestic or stateless Jews in connection with the events of November 8–10,

---

[48] Gürtner an Schmitt, 21. Dez. 1938, ibid., Bl. 363, and Rundschreiben Wirtschaftsgruppe Privatversicherung vom 27. Dez. 1938, ibid., Bl. 377, Vermerke Thees, 4. Jan. 1939, ibid., Bl. 381–4.
[49] Hilgard an den Reichswirtschaftsminister, 10. Jan. 1939, ibid., Bl. 388–90.

1938. However, the German insurance enterprises are obligated to compensate insured Jews of foreign citizenship and Aryans."

In the meantime, the pressure for a solution was increasing. On the one hand, foreign insurers and reinsurers were making inquiries with their German colleagues about the situation, and the bad press Germany was getting for the Pogrom in general also contained reports that German insurance companies were threatened with bankruptcy because of the Pogrom's costs. While dangers of insolvency were hotly denied, responses to more general inquiries were vague, usually stating that matters had not yet been decided and sometimes indicating that civil commotion clauses made liability unlikely.[50] On the other hand, the courts were already hearing some cases. A Berlin Jewish optician of Polish citizenship, for example, took a glass insurance company to court in early December demanding 400 marks for the replacement of a window. While the court initially ruled in his favor, the glass company successfully appealed the case. The court ruling on the appeal found that it was legitimate for the company to follow the instructions of the Reich Group and not pay out any monies until the relevant authorities had ruled on the compensation question. Significantly, the court also held that this judgment was in no way affected by the fact that the Nordstern company had been paying damages to foreign Jews. The case was worrisome since it demonstrated that foreigners were not waiting upon decisions in Berlin to go to court. The instructions of the Reich Group to refrain from payment were becoming problematic, and some firms were breaking ranks. Also, the American consulate was showing an irritating interest in the case, claiming the problem was of relevance to its citizens as well.[51]

A similar court complaint was launched against the Allianz branch in Cologne, where the representatives of another Polish Jew, this time one who had been expelled to Poland two weeks before the Pogrom, demanded 467.30 RM for the replacement of windows. The Allianz branch refused to consider the application, claiming that the windows had been destroyed in a civil disturbance; the plaintiffs argued that the events of November 9–10 did not qualify as a civil disturbance. This, of course, was precisely the kind of argument and discussion that insurance industry and government leaders wished to avoid. Once informed of the case, the head office of Allianz decided to pay the bill; in addition, Hilgard sent out a circular letter to members of the Reich Group on February 1, 1939, pointing out that "a bearable result" in the negotiations between the insurers and the government would only be possible if the claims of Aryans and foreigners were resolved without any concern for the reservations stated in previous

---

[50] See, for example, the correspondence between Munich Re and its London correspondent, C. E. Golding, Nov. 24 and Nov. 30, 1938; between B. B. Fischer of the Royal Exchange Assurance and A. Martini of Dec. 1 and 14, 1938; and the correspondence with the Union des Propriétaires Belges between March and May 1939 in MR, G 1/8.

[51] For the correspondence on the American request and a copy of the judgment in the case in December 1938–January 1939, see BAB, R 3001/10788, Bl. 419–24.

circulars about liability. Indeed, Hilgard urged that such payments be made "immediately" and that the companies "proceed in a generous manner." He warned against refusing such payments on legal grounds without first consulting with the Reich Group. At the same time, however, he enjoined the companies to assert their legal nonliability:

In the case of all payments, the insured is to be told in a not-to-be-misunderstood manner that the companies are not legally obligated to pay and that, insofar as compensation is being made, these constitute voluntary payments. This reservation is indispensable so that the payments could not be viewed as prejudicial with respect to claims made by domestic Jews. Insofar as the claims made by domestic Jews are concerned, matters remain the same in this respect as already indicated by my previous circulars.[52]

How much were the insurance companies paying, and how large were the potential claims of German and stateless Jews? At the turn of 1938–1939, the insurance companies had some sense of the actual and potential sums involved. Total damages in all insurance categories (except health and accident) were estimated at the end of January 1939 to be 49.5 million RM, 46.1 million of which was suffered by Jews and the remaining 3.4 million suffered in almost equal measure by German "Aryans" and Jewish and non-Jewish foreigners.[53] Glass was by far the most important category, amounting to 2.1 million marks. The hardest-hit companies with respect to "Aryans" and foreigners were Allianz, Schlesische Feuerversicherungs-Gesellschaft, Albingia, and Neue Frankfurter. Given the international complications involved, one may reasonably assume that the amounts were paid out promptly, although it is worth noting that Hilgard (undoubtedly acting under directives connected with the impending war) issued secret instructions on July 25, 1939, that no payments were to be made to "foreigners of Polish citizenship."[54]

The balance of the potential claims could be made by German Jews. According to the breakdown of damages provided by the insurance companies, they suffered 38.2 million RM in fire damage, 4.4 million RM in glass damage, and 3.1 million RM in theft and break-in. The companies with the greatest liability

[52] Schreiben Hilgard an die Wirtschaftsgruppe Privatversicherung, 1. Feb. 1939, ibid., Bl. 479, and Oberlandsgerichtspräsident Bergmann an RJM, 31. Jan. 1939 und Vermerk, 4. Feb. 1939, BAB, R 3001/10788, Bl. 415–16. See also Rundschreiben der Wirtschaftsgruppe Privatversicherung, 2. Feb. 1939, GDV, RS/19.

[53] Aufstellung, 26. Jan. 1939, SM, 1458/1/98, Bl. 236. This is a more accurate estimate of potential insurance company liability than that employed at the November 12 meeting in the Air Ministry of 225 million RM, taken over by Avraham Barkai in his important "Schicksalsjahr 1938. Kontinuität und Verschärfung der wirtschaftlichen Ausplünderung der Juden," in Walter H. Pehle (ed.), *Der Judenpogrom 1938. Von der 'Reichskristallnacht' zum Völkermord* (Frankfurt a.M., 1988), pp. 94–117, here p. 115. Hermann Graml also speaks of 225 million in his *Reichskristallnacht. Antisemitismus und Judenverfolgung im Dritten Reich* (Munich, 1988), p. 178.

[54] For figures on individual company obligations, see Fachgruppe 1 an das RWM, Ministerialrat Daniel, 21. Dez. 1938, SM, 1458/1/98, Bl. 217–21. For the ban on payment to Poles, see Rundschreiben Wirtschaftsgruppe Privatversicherung, 25. Juli 1939, GDV, RS/16.

in fire were Allianz, Neue Frankfurter, Aachen und Münchener, Nordstern, Albingia, and Victoria. Hilgard, however, reported quite different figures to Ministerial Councilor Daniel of the RWM on January 30, 1939. In his calculations, the final liabilities of the companies for fire damages to German Jewish property were halved, amounting to 19,622,329 RM, while break-in and theft damages were corrected to 3,566,763 RM. There was no calculation for glass damages. The purpose of Hilgard's report was to provide the RWM with the statistical material needed to inform Göring and the Finance Ministry (RFM) of the sums involved and to plead the case for the insurance companies not being held liable. Hilgard well understood that it was to his interest to keep the final figures presented to the government as low as possible, since the more Göring and the RFM thought they might lose, the more they would push for imposition of liability. At the same time, Hilgard and his allies in the RWM were very aware that his figures on German Jewish claims were potentially much higher than those being reported. Thus, in the covering letter to the breakdown of insurance company liabilities – sent in late December to the RWM by Director Karl Autenrieth of Berlinische Feuer and the head of the fire insurance branch of the Reich Group – which formed the initial basis for Hilgard's global figures, Autenrieth warned not only that the numbers were estimates that had to be made without the usual help of the authorities but also that

if the companies are basically condemned to pay, then the sum of the damages would swell extraordinarily. Many Jews are not in a position to make claims [presumably because they were still in concentration camps], while others are holding back with their claims because they do not believe themselves entitled to make them. But if the companies are basically to step forward with regard to these claims, then substantial retroactive claims will be made, namely in the break-in and theft insurance, where the level of claims is least controllable.[55]

The Autenrieth report, of course, made it more imperative for Hilgard to lower the potential liability of the insurance companies. The circumstances of Germany's Jews were of help to Hilgard, since he spoke only of claims made by the Jews up to the time of his letter rather than of potential claims. Furthermore, the ministerial officials had asked Hilgard to report only such claims as might be legally uncontestable. There were some Jews who did have insurance against public disturbance, the total sum involved coming to 38,000 RM, and they could possibly have made claims. Excluding them from the reported claims was tantamount to denying them payment, a rather ironic (indeed, hypocritical) position in view of the fact that insurers considered the Pogrom a public disturbance. In any case, the figures Hilgard now reported were millions short of the amount estimated for fire, theft, and break-in because they included only actual claims and those viewed as uncontestable in court. This did not end the

---

[55] Autenrieth an das RWM, Ministerialrat Daniel, 21. Dez. 1938, SM, 1458/1/98, Bl. 217–18. For Hilgard's use of these figures, see Hilgard an Daniel, 30. Jan. 1939, ibid., Bl. 238–9.

whittling down of the final sum, however, aside from the fact that glass damages were left out. Hilgard then proceeded to argue that 16,055,566 RM of the fire insurance and 79,000 RM of the break-in and theft insurance pertained to synagogues and other Jewish institutional buildings. If one subtracted these amounts, then the amount of insurance that could be claimed was 3,566,763 RM in fire insurance and 2,995,239 RM for break-in and theft, making a total of 6,522,002 RM. This was the amount, Hilgard argued, that the Reich would lose if it accepted his proposal. Although his global figures did not include the publicly chartered insurance companies, which had greater liability in their contracts and were most responsible for insuring synagogues and Jewish institutional buildings, Hilgard urged that those companies be freed of any such liability as well, "since here one is dealing with the destruction of public property not worthy of protection."[56]

One should pause to reflect on these words, since they exhibit a rather novel approach to insurance. Insurance policies had been issued for these synagogues by publicly chartered and private insurance companies both, and no one had ever raised the question of whether they were "worthy" of protection. When Colonia and Iduna-Germania joined together and concluded on June 21, 1938, to insure the structure and contents of the synagogue in Saarbrücken for 320,000 RM and then charged the synagogue congregation a premium for this insurance, no one raised a question concerning the "worth" assigned to the building and its contents. When the Jewish community reported 120,000 RM in damages as the result of the Pogrom, Colonia refused payment on the grounds that the damage was the result of a civil disturbance (citing the Porto Allegre decision) but also indicated that, while it believed its position correct, the decision could be challenged in court within six months. Indeed, Colonia had also insured at least nine other synagogues in various parts of the country (e.g., Bielefeld, Koblenz, Liegnitz, Leipzig) whose total claims added up to 524,000 RM, while claims for damage to contents within four synagogues amounted to 73,000 RM. Manifestly, it had agreed to attach a value to these buildings and their contents, just as it had agreed that the four Torah scrolls, the two mantles covering them, and the prayer books and prayer shawls belonging to the synagogue in Ochsenfurt – items that had been thrown into the street and burned – had a total value of 2,950 RM.[57] In fact, the insurance companies had precise knowledge of what they had and had not insured. Thus, when the mayor of the City of Bühl (which was the owner of the publicly chartered electrical company) wanted to know if Allianz covered

---

[56] Ibid.

[57] These various cases are based on the Akte "Schäden des Judenpogroms vom 9./10. November 1938 ('Reichskristallnacht'), Teil B: Brandschadenberichte," AXA, Bestand Colonia Versicherung AG. See especially the undated report on various claims made in connection with the Pogrom, the copy of the insurance policy concluded with the Synagogengemeinde des Kreises Saarbrücken of June 21, 1938, the correspondence connected with it, and especially the response to the claim of the Synagogengemeinde's claim of Jan. 11, 1939. I am grateful to the AXA Colonia Konzern AG and its archive for making this material available to me.

the technical equipment in the town's destroyed synagogue, worth 204.16 RM, Allianz informed them that the fire insurance policy of the Jewish community covered only such equipment or objects that belonged directly to the synagogue itself. Therefore Allianz "unfortunately" could not pay these damages.[58] Whatever one's moral qualms, one could defend the decision of an insurance company to refuse payment for the synagogues and their contents because the mode of their destruction was excluded under the insurance provisions. But there were no contractual or legal grounds for such refusal by claiming they did not have material value – which had been assigned to them and accepted by an insurance company in return for a scheduled premium. This, however, is precisely what Hilgard was doing in his totally opportunistic and morally reprehensible efforts to reduce the liability of the insurance industry.

Hilgard's sleight-of-hand was thus neatly aided by his employment of anti-Semitic rhetoric. Furthermore, it is necessary to recognize that one important branch of insurance was simply left out of his calculations and arguments – namely, the glass insurance branch, where German Jews had suffered 4,430,000 RM in damages. The companies involved were already liable for 2.1 million RM in damages to Aryans and foreigners. Apparently, Hilgard and the RWM were by this time confident of their case that liability for glass damages would ruin many of the small mutual companies and severely damage others. These costs would simply be left to the Jewish obligation to clean up and restore the appearance of the streets. Potential benefits from insurance company liability (in the form of a reduction of the atonement tax by the amount of insurance paid on a Jew's behalf to the revenue office) would not be allowed with respect to glass damages.[59] Indeed, the Economics Ministry was strongly supportive of Hilgard's position, happy that the amount had been reduced to "only" 6.5 million RM, pleased that the companies were going to pay off Aryans and foreigners, satisfied that the glass companies were not included (since they were supposed to replace damages in kind anyway and were not included in the implementation decree), and relieved to have the question of civic unrest relegated to the sidelines.[60]

Despite the friendly posture of the RJM and the RWM, Hilgard was nervous. There were reports of further court cases, including one by a Jewish community in connection with its buildings, and he was understandably anxious about

[58] Bürgermeister der Stadt Bühl an Allianz, 9. Juni 1939; Antwort Allianz, 16. Juni 1939, Stadt-geschichtliches Institut der Stadt Bühl, BH-Akten (alt) 363.

[59] An estimate of the glass insurance costs can be found attached to an Aktennote for Hilgard of Dec. 7, 1938, SM, 1458/1/98, Bl. 214–15. The company worst hit was Kölnische Glas-Versicherungs-AG, which reported 1.2 million RM in damages, while the list of small mutuals shows that in some cases the damages did indeed exceed their yearly premium. Round numbers on all the damages and a breakdown of the distribution of the glass damage can be found in a RWM list for a meeting on January 26, 1939, ibid., Bl. 235–6.

[60] Schreiben Lange an RJM und RFM, 3. Feb. 1939, BAB, R 3001/10788, Bl. 425–6.

the liability question even though he had managed to whittle down the potential liability to 6.5 million out of a total of 49.5 million RM in reported damages. Thus, on February 7, he called the RJM to find out if there was anything new; he was told that the RWM was composing a memorandum to be sent (in the name of the RWM, RJM, and RFM) to Göring, presumably along the lines desired by Hilgard.[61]

Nevertheless, it would be months before the matter was settled, and there was a good deal of hard bargaining along the way. The projected memorandum for Göring was held up by the Finance Ministry, which apparently first wanted the full 6.5 million. This was opposed by Hilgard and by the two other ministries. Finally, in early May, Schwandt informed Daniel of the RWM that the matter had been discussed with Finance Minister Schwerin von Krosigk. The latter was ready to eschew payment for the fire damage, but he was holding back on the matter of break-in and theft insurance, claiming that the legal situation of the insurance companies was less strong in this area. By this time, however, Hilgard had been emboldened by the support of the RWM and RJM and was prepared to resist the RFM, pointing particularly to the possibilities opened up by the recently promulgated (on March 13, 1939) 14th Decree to the Law on the Settlement of Civil Law Claims, which was directly concerned with the Pogrom damages and enabled the Interior Ministry to close down court cases and settle claims according to its own guidelines. Under section 3 of this decree, German and stateless Jews were not entitled to receive any compensation through such mediation by the Interior Ministry, so that the Justice Ministry or the Interior Ministry could literally throw their cases out of court without a hearing. Hilgard believed that the insurance companies would do well in remaining cases brought before the Interior Ministry, a not unreasonable conclusion since his colleague Goudefroy was constantly reporting all court cases connected with the Pogrom to the Justice Ministry in the hope that they would be suspended and handled under the March 13 decree. Daniel of the RWM was less sanguine, pointing out that the Finance Ministry proposal would cost the insurers some 2–3 million RM but would then end the matter, whereas mediation by the Interior Ministry could prove much more expensive. Nevertheless, Hilgard was adamant, insisting that he had to take the matter before the advisory council of the private insurer group before he could make any concessions.[62]

On May 15, Hilgard wearily informed his colleagues that he still did not have a final agreement; he described his tedious struggle with the Finance Ministry as well as the RWM inclination to go along with the suggested compromise of

---

[61] Vermerk, 7. Feb. 1939, BAB, R 3001/10788, Bl. 418.
[62] Vermerk Daniel, 16. Mai 1939, SM, 1458/1/98, Bl. 273–4. Botur, *Privatversicherung*, pp. 197–202, did not have this information on the RFM demands at his disposal, which explains his puzzlement over the sums at which Hilgard and the RFM finally arrived. See, however, his excellent discussion of the 14th Decree, pp. 202–10.

a reduced lump-sum payment. Hilgard reasserted the position that payment of Jewish insurance claims was tantamount to a "special tax" on the industry. There certainly was no legal obligation, so that "the only thing that can still be involved is a moral and a technical insurance question." General Director Johannes Tiedke of Alte Leipziger was outspoken in his opposition to any compromise with the government, warning that it was important to maintain their legal position and not let other considerations – as, for example, the "moral" and technical ones mentioned by Hilgard – get in the way: "If one surrenders the legal standpoint and lets oneself be directed by other considerations, then one can count on similar difficulties arising in the future in similar cases." Tiedke, however, was always something of a maverick in his uncompromising opposition to National Socialist interference in business matters and efforts to tap insurance industry assets. Apparently, his subordinate directors held similar attitudes; one of whom, Waldemar Adler, had the temerity to discuss his views on the insurance aspects of the Pogrom in a chance meeting with Hans Goebbels on a train ride to Düsseldorf. Goebbels totally rejected the legal position taken by Alte Leipziger and insisted that the matter had to be viewed from a "party-political" point of view.[63] However, Tiedke's colleagues in the Reich Group were not made of such stuff and those present were prepared to be flexible and were doubtless well aware that the days of standing on legal principles – however they might be defined under these circumstances – were a thing of the past. In the end, they authorized Hilgard to struggle as long as possible against any payment but to compromise if necessary. They were certainly most anxious to bring the issue to an end and were quite prepared to discuss payment by means of an assessment on all the insurers, as they did in the case of the Adolf Hitler Donation, rather than only on the firms with liability. While expecting German reinsurers to have some participation, they ruled out any recourse to foreign reinsurers.[64]

The wily and tenacious Hilgard now demonstrated once again his skills as a behind-the-scenes operator in the politics of the Third Reich. By the end of June, Alzheimer was reporting to the reinsurers that the latest payment figure he was hearing was 1.5 million RM, and he knew whereof he spoke. At a meeting at the RWM on July 6, Hilgard refused Schwandt the 3 million the RFM was now demanding and argued that the statute of limitations on claims for break-in and theft had passed, so that the legal situation of the insurers was better than before. Schwandt threatened passage of a new law, and Regierungsrat Segelcke of the RWM pointed out that, while such a law was not likely at this point and

[63] Johannes Tiedke, "Meine Stellung zum Nationalsozialismus überhaupt und die Gründe dafür, daß ich nicht in die Partei eingetreten bin," Leipzig, 5. Juli 1945, NL Tiedke. See also Volker Weiß, "Ist das, was wir machen, auch gerecht?", pp. 57–67.

[64] Niederschrift über die Sitzung des Beirats der Wirtschaftsgruppe Privatversicherung am 22. Mai 1939, SM, 1458/1/109, Bl. 193–6. On Tiedke, see Roland Kneebusch, "Als Versicherungs-Generaldirektor im Dritten Reich," (Leserbrief), *Frankfurter Allgemeine Zeitung*, 17. Nov. 1998.

though the legal situation was favorable to the insurers, Hilgard should really voluntarily offer a "certain compensatory payment" which he "would very much welcome in the interest of the reputation of the insurance industry." After further discussion, Hilgard offered "at the most" 1.5 million RM to the Finance Ministry, a sum that Schwandt declared "only of interest to the RFM if at least one quarter of the damages reported by the Jews are thereby covered."[65] Hilgard was asked to supply the necessary information as well as an accounting of the amounts paid out to foreigners and German Aryans.

There does not appear to be a record of the exact figures and information supplied by Hilgard, but the 1.5 million RM amount seems to have been the accepted point of departure. Synagogues, Jewish buildings, and glass damages had been eliminated from that calculation from the very outset. Indeed, the total amount of such claims as were covered seems to have been less than anticipated because, as Hilgard reported, of "the correction of some damage reports." Whatever the case, Hilgard managed to pay even less than he had promised: in the final accounting with the government on October 14, 1939, he reported a total payment from the Reich Group to the treasury of 1,297,988 RM, with 1,074,828 of it coming from the private insurers of the "Old Reich," 190,010 coming from the publicly chartered companies, and 17,988 from the Ostmark (Austria). Thus, it seems Hilgard managed to save yet another 200,000 RM. The 1.3 million RM paid to the treasury did not, of course, include the sums paid directly to Aryans and foreigners, although money undoubtedly was saved on the Poles.[66] Thus, of the 46.1 million RM in losses by German Jews,[67] the insurers ended up with responsibility for a mere 3% – thanks to the negotiating skills of Hilgard.

This extra benefit to the insurers was the outcome of the charade concocted by insurers and ministerial officials in order to deal with the insured Jews. The projected lump-sum payment to the Treasury was not without its complications, since it was intended to be in lieu of paying the insurance claims of German Jews and Germans in the categories of fire and theft. The Reich Group therefore instructed its members on August 3 to make fictional payments to claim-seeking Jews in the amount of 50% of their claim for fire and theft. They were also to make believe that they were compensating for glass damage if the customer happened to have a comprehensive policy for fire and/or theft insurance. No letter would be sent to Jews who had only glass insurance. The basis of the calculation would not be explained to the customer, and all claims had to be presented by August 15. The model for such a letter to Jewish insurers was as follows.

---

[65] Niederschrift über die Sitzung des Beirats der Fachgruppe 7 (Rückversicherung) am 28. Juni 1939, SM, 1458/1/147, Bl. 71, and Vermerk, 6. Juli 1939, SM, 1458/1/98, Bl. 277.

[66] Reichsgruppe Versicherungen an den Reichswirtschaftsminister, 14. Okt. 1939, ibid., Bl. 290, and Wirtschaftsgruppe Privatversicherung an alle Feuer- und Glas-Versicherungsgesellschaften, 13. Nov. 1939, GDV, RS/16.

[67] See Chapter 5, p. 221.

To the Jewish policyholder.
Re: Fire insurance policy No. ... ...
    Break-in and Theft insurance policy No. ... ...
    Glass-Insurance policy No. ... ...
    (non-applicable categories to be crossed out)

    On the basis of the above insurance policy(ies) a sum in the amount of
RM ....

is granted to you due to the events of November 1938 on the basis of an understanding
with the Reich Finance Ministry and the Reich Economics Ministry, the Reich Justice
Ministry and the Reich Interior Ministry without recognizing a legal obligation in view
of the doubtfulness of the case. The payment of the sum is made on the basis of §2, para. 2
of the Decree on the Restoration of the Appearance of the Streets at Jewish businesses of
12. November 1938, Reich Legislative Journal I, p. 1581, and the Implementation Decree
for the Atonement Tax of the Jews of 21. November 1938, Reich Legislative Journal I,
p. 1638, directly to the Reich.

    You are entitled to deduct the above mentioned sum from the last partial payment due
on 15. August 1939 on the basis of the Decree on the Atonement Payment of Jews of German Citizenship of 12. November 1938, Reich Legislative Journal I, p. 1579.

    No further claims against us exist on the basis of the existing insurance policies as a
result of the events of 8–10 November 1938.[68]

THE "NIGHT OF BROKEN GLASS" AND
BUSINESS ETHICS IN THE THIRD REICH

It is worth taking the effort to appreciate how utterly grotesque this arrangement
was and the extent to which it reflected a state-sanctioned exercise in collective
moral turpitude on the part of everyone engaged in this enterprise of trying to
cope with the results of the Pogrom and cover up responsibility and liability
for the damages. This – and not the legal issue of liability – is the important
point from a historical perspective in any effort to assess the behavior of those
involved. Indeed, it is ironic to note that, if the insurers had maintained their
principles in the manner proposed by General Director Tiedke of Alte Leipziger,
then no Jew would even have received reimbursement in the form of a rebate on
their atonement tax. Those legal principles could only be asserted in another
political environment, however. Thus perceived, it would be hard to fault the
decision of the 2nd Civil Senate of the Federal Court of April 23, 1952, which
rejected the claim of a Jewish émigré for compensation from his insurance company for jewelry stolen in the course of a break-in on the night of November
10–11, 1938. The court, using much the same arguments as were employed in

---

[68] Reichsgruppe Versicherungen an die Wirtschaftsgruppe Privatversicherung und die Wirtschaftsgruppe Öffentlich-Rechtliche Versicherung, 3. Aug. 1939, SM, 1458/1/98, Bl. 283–5 and BAB, R
3001/10789, Bl. 91–3.

the Porto Allegre case and by the insurers in their private meetings with government officials in 1938–1939, declared the Pogrom a public disturbance. It declared the government, not the insurers, liable for making compensation. The 1952 court also rejected the claim of the plaintiff that "the Pogroms of the year 1938 were not considered as disturbances under the official 'legal conception' of that time." The court held that "the legal conceptions in official circles at that time with regard to precisely these questions were so confused that contemporary views on the matter can no longer be taken into account."[69] Nevertheless, the court also noted that Göring (as well as Hilgard and the insurers) had spoken of public disturbance in meetings and court cases at the time. So far, so good – but this hardly exonerates Hilgard or his colleagues from quite consciously and deliberately covering up for deeds and arrangements which they obviously knew were indefensible, which they would have viewed as indefensible before 1933, and which they knew their colleagues in other countries considered indefensible.

The negotiations between the insurers and the authorities over the Pogrom lasted more than a year, not because legal conceptions were "confused" but because the legal conceptions under which Hilgard, his colleagues, and ministry officials had operated simply were incompatible with a government-ordered Pogrom. The mounting radicalization of the regime was rendering standard norms of behavior increasingly incompatible with political requirements. The insurance leaders colluded with the authorities in trying to cover up the true nature of the disturbances and, in the process, persistently used anti-Semitic arguments that the insurers and the "community of the insured" should not pay the punishment visited on the Jews. Ultimately, however, Hilgard and his colleagues found themselves trapped by the hasty conclusions Göring drew from Hilgard's remarks (at the November 12 meeting) about permitting insurers to pay where they did have liability and by the confusing conjunction created between the insurance issue in the Decree on the Restoration of the Appearance of the Streets and the right of Jews to deduct insurance payments to the state from their atonement tax. Although not originally so intended, the efforts of Göring and especially the Finance Ministry to extract as much money as possible from the insurance companies – by making them liable for the damages – created a link between the amount paid by insurers and the amount that could be deducted by Jews from the atonement tax for insurance proceeds confiscated by the revenue offices. Consequently, every reduction in the amount paid by the insurance industry to the Finance Ministry was also a reduction in the amount Jews could deduct from their tax. In the last analysis, Hilgard's success in resisting the demands of the government came at the expense of the Jewish insured. Hilgard, of course, was not concerned about the Jews. He was concerned about reducing the "special tax" he felt the government was trying to impose on his industry, and doing so was something he recounted proudly to Allied interrogators after the war and

---

[69] *Entscheidungen des Bundesgerichtshofes in Zivilsachen*, Bd. VI (1952), pp. 28–35.

in his unpublished memoirs.[70] What he did not say to his interrogators was that he had not the slightest qualm about letting his industry profit from the regime's despoliation of the Jews and that, as we have seen, he was busy seeking out opportunities for Allianz to conclude insurance contracts with newly Aryanized enterprises at about the very time he was negotiating this arrangement.[71]

The goal with respect to the Pogrom, of course, was not to make a profit but rather to control or reduce losses by reducing payments to the government that had become oddly linked to a measure of reduction of Jewish tax liability. In practical terms there was something to Hilgard's claim that the Finance Ministry was cynically playing the "advocate" of the Jews owing to the interaction of legal measures taken in connection with the Pogrom. Needless to say, the Finance Ministry was no advocate of the Jews! Though it instructed revenue offices to deduct reported insurance company payments in connection with credits to be given for the atonement tax, the real payments were actually covered by the lump-sum payment to the Ministry. Jews who had emigrated were not to receive anything. Also, if the insurance payments were in excess of the required atonement tax payment, then the Jew could receive the surplus only if he or she had already made other payments meeting current obligations to the authorities in the form of money, securities, or property.[72] As Thees succinctly put the matter, from the standpoint of the Reich the payment was nothing more than a "political payment" to cover its claims under the insurance confiscation clause.[73]

The fictional character of the entire arrangement was also manifested by the way in which the Reich Group extracted the lump sum from its members. The actual sum in question was paid by the Reich Group and was not paid by the individual companies to the revenue offices of the insured. As demonstrated here, notifications received by the latter were purely for accounting purposes regarding the atonement tax. The actual insurance company payments to the Reich Group were assessed on November 13, 1939. The assessment was divided into two parts. The first was based on the total premium income of the companies in 1937, and each of the involved companies paid 2.29 RM for each 1,000 RM in premiums it had received for that year. The remainder was collected by a charge of 325.74 RM for each 1,000 RM worth of the total damages claimed by the

---

[70] See his interrogation of July 14, 1947, NA, RG 260, OMGUS, FINAD, 2/57/6–8, pp. 8–9; Hilgard, "Leben," FHA, NL 2/7, p. 110. There is not a shred of evidence to support the statement: "After the war Mr. Hilgard told Allied interrogators that he had helped the companies settle Kristallnacht claims at 3 cents to the dollar." See Christopher S. Wren, "Insurers Swindled Jews, Nazi Files Show," *New York Times* (May 16, 1998). Hilgard said no such thing and emphasized that he had reduced the payment to the Finance Ministry; he was and remained angry that the industry had been forced to pay anything to the government at all.

[71] See Chapter 3, pp. 148–9.

[72] Der Reichsminister der Finanzen an die Oberfinanzpräsidenten, 12. Aug. 1939, SM, 1458/1/98, Bl. 283.

[73] Vermerk Thees, 4. Aug. 1939, BAB, R 3001/10789, Bl. 94.

insurers. There was an additional interest charge of 4% for the period between August 14, 1939, when the Finance Ministry declared the money due, and November 19, 1939, when the Reich Group actually paid. German reinsurers were to participate in covering the second half of the costs to the extent of their reinsurance through companies with which they were associated, but foreign reinsurers were not to be involved "in view of the confidentiality of the matter."[74]

It was hardly imaginable that reinsurers in other countries would have been party to such an arrangement in any case – a long road had been travelled since the time when Göring believed he might pick up some foreign exchange from foreign reinsurers – and the reputation of the German insurance business would most certainly have suffered if the settlement had become public knowledge. Indeed, the insurers and government were only partially successful in their effort to keep cases connected with the Pogrom out of the courts. For one thing, many courts and plaintiffs were unaware of the 14th Implementation Decree to the Law on the Settlement of Civil Law Claims; thus Goudefroy was constantly reporting cases to the Interior Ministry so that they could be stopped in their tracks. Furthermore, there were Jews who did not realize that they were barred from taking claims refused by the government to court under section 3 of the implementation decree. Thus, on June 28, the Interior Ministry felt compelled to point out that the entire purpose of the measures was to deny Jews access to the courts and to prevent public discussion of the legal and other issues connected with the events in question. Also, there were complications with interpreting when the Pogrom stopped, so that losses incurred on the night of November 11–12 were considered by one court to be products of violations of the discipline expected in a National Socialist state and hence actionable with respect to insurance. Finally, there were problems with Aryan mortgage holders and others who incurred indirect damages because of the Pogrom. The insurers assumed that these would be somehow covered in the lump-sum payment, but the Finance Ministry refused to consider such inclusion. This led to a conflict with the RJM and the Reich Interior Ministry as to whether Reich money could be used to provide relief in such cases.[75]

Goudefroy's work at having the Ministry terminate court cases (for Allianz and companies connected with it) illustrates insurance company complicity in the legal chicanery of the Third Reich; it also demonstrates the absurd contradictions into which insurers were driven as a consequence of becoming implicated

---

[74] Wirtschaftsgruppe Privatversicherung an alle Feuer- und Glas-Versicherungsgesellschaften, 13. Nov. 1939, and Reichsgruppe Versicherungen an die Unternehmungen, die an der Umlage wegen der Schäden aus den Vorgängen 1938 beteiligt sind, 12. Dez. 1939, GDV, RS/16. An interesting collection of correspondence with the Munich Re on such payment arrangements is to be found in MR, G 1/8.

[75] See the excellent discussion in Botur, *Privatversicherung*, pp. 211–18. See also Rundschreiben des Reichsminister des Innern, 28. Juni 1939, BAB, R 18/3746b.

in the government's treatment of the Pogrom. For example, on August 4, 1939, Goudefroy asked Thees to set aside the case of a Jewish woman from Holzminden who was suing Neue Frankfurter for 737.15 RM in payment for destruction of the glass window of her business on November 25, 1938 – that is, well after the "November action" was declared over.[76] A few days later, he sent another case to Thees asking for termination of the case brought against Allianz by an "Aryan" woman who had divorced her Jewish husband and resumed using her maiden name. Her ex-husband committed suicide in late December 1938, leaving all his property to her; she now asked for compensation from Allianz for a number of policies totalling 8,000 RM. Her lawyer had argued that the Pogrom was a "measure of retaliation against Jewry" and not a criminal act or domestic unrest.[77] Goudefroy was successful in both cases.

Then there was the interesting and indicative case in November 1939 of a Berlin Jewish storeowner with glass damage who could not understand why his revenue office was telling him it could not give him a credit against his atonement tax because it had received no notice from Allianz about an insurance payment. When he contacted Allianz, he was informed that these matters had been relegated to the various ministries and that he had to turn to the revenue office. Undaunted, the policyholder requested his revenue office to ask Allianz to send the necessary information, whereupon Allianz informed the revenue office that the matter was confidential. In the meantime, the policyholder decided to sue, not for his money but rather for information, and this presented an intriguing problem because the court was inclined to hear the case on the grounds that the 14th Decree might not enable termination of cases involving a demand for information. Goudefroy, as can be imagined, was very concerned. He pointed out in a letter to the Justice Ministry that the companies were obligated to maintain silence about the way in which the payments were calculated, and now they were faced with a potential court order to violate this condition – that is, to tell the policyholder that no glass insurance payments were being reported for Jews. Allianz's lawyers were arguing that the 14th Decree was valid in this case because it pertained indirectly to the events in question. It should come as no surprise that Thees lent a helping hand, and the case was stopped on the grounds of the 14th Decree.[78]

An even more egregious case, which also involved a run-around between the revenue office and Allianz, was that of a Jewish merchant in Wesel, who was heavily indebted to creditors and customers because of the damage done to his store and who also owed a substantial sum to the revenue office for unpaid portions of his atonement tax. In correspondence that dragged on between January and August 1940, the legal adviser sought to gain some credit for glass breakage as well as to secure payment for fire and theft damages from Württembergische

[76] Sally Kugelmann gegen die Neue Frankfurter, BAB, R 3001/10789, Bl. 106ff.
[77] Johanna Oberländer gegen Allianz, ibid., Bl. 99–105.
[78] Moses gegen Allianz, ibid., Bl. 162–8, 193.

Feuerversicherung AG in Stuttgart. He received nothing, in the case of the broken glass for the usual reasons and in the case of theft and fire because he had missed the deadline for making such claims under the 14th Decree. Of course, any such claims would have been rejected anyway because he was Jewish.[79]

The reality was that leading officers of Allianz (and undoubtedly their colleagues in other companies) had descended into pure legal opportunism in dealing with the Pogrom, as was evident in the last case considered here, that of the Breslau firm of Wigo Wollwaren GmbH in Breslau. The firm had been 60% in the hands of an Aryan but 40% owned by a Jew, whose husband had been the "soul of the business." For this reason, their establishment had been attacked and suffered severe window and interior damage during the Pogrom. However, this was one of those rare instances in which the party in question had insurance against tumult (*Aufruhr*), and the Aryan owner of the firm took the case to court at the beginning of 1940. Allianz refused to recognize the claim even though the plaintiff was nothing less than a "pure Aryan" and the insurance covered civil disturbance. Goudefroy argued that there had been no civil disturbance because the events in question were not punishable by law and did not constitute tumults or a breach of the peace. As they explained, "the retaliatory actions of November 1938 rather have the explicit character of an elementary event or, to use the words of Reich Minister Dr. Goebbels, the character of an eruptive outbreak of anger by the population."[80] Furthermore, insurance for civil disturbances and glass were not covered under terms of the agreement made between insurers and ministries the previous year – an agreement, one should be reminded, into which the companies entered without giving up their legal standpoint that the Pogrom was a civil disturbance! On this occasion, the position of Allianz did not convince even the Reich Economics Ministry officials, who argued in a meeting with the RAA that Allianz was obligated to replace the glass and to pay on the civil disturbance insurance since an Aryan was involved. Goudefroy hotly contested this position, insisting that companies had to pay such claims only in the event that the criminal code had been violated. His position was strongly supported by Thees, who took the view "that the Reich Supervisory Board for Private Insurance could not hold the companies to payments of civil disorder insurance if they do not want to recognize in their supervisory capacity that one was dealing with a punishable action."[81] This was the same Thees who seven years later was to claim in a letter to Hilgard that only he and Hilgard had shown the "courage" to say that a public disturbance was a public disturbance!

The reality was that both were hopelessly entangled in the mesh created by a criminal regime that was nevertheless committed to certain legal niceties and appearances – primarily because its leaders found them opportune or did not

---

[79] Fall Hugo Brandenstein, BAK, B 280/12238, Bl. 88–113.

[80] Allianz an Rechstsantwalt Hans-Wolfgang Schimmelpfennig, 20. Jan. 1940, ibid., Bl. 121–2, and Allianz an das RAA, 30. März 1940, ibid., Bl. 117–18.

[81] Sitzung, 24. März 1940, ibid., Bl. 123–4.

know how to escape them entirely without creating chaos. Businessmen and bureaucrats found it in their interest and advantage to exploit these windows of opportunity, but they also became increasingly aware that the windows could come banging down at any time. Such efforts did indeed require what, under the circumstances, might be called "courage"; they certainly required constant calculation. It is obvious that Hilgard and Goudefroy wanted to avoid paying Jews, but they also wanted to avoid paying Nazis. The latter were obviously more dangerous than the former, and it is thus not surprising that their memories after the war concentrated on their struggle with Nazi leaders and radicals.

Goudefroy conveniently forgot his role as a watchdog in the effort to shut Jewish claimants off from legal recourse, but it is not surprising that he remembered the struggle over the insurance issue in terms of the rather more threatening and anxiety-producing role he had to play in dealing with the Party. Goudefroy was no enthusiastic Party member, and in 1945 he recalled the issue of glass damages as the "high point" of his conflicts with the Party:

When after the murder of vom Rath, Jewish businesses were destroyed through a "spontaneous expression of the anger of the people," the Party wanted to secure substantial compensation from the glass insurance policies of the Jewish business people for their successors. In negotiations that I had to conduct with high Party agencies, I refused such demands with the argument that, according to the terms of insurance, no compensation could be given in cases of plundering or public disturbance. This argumentation led to a breakdown of negotiations with the Party functionaries and led again to undisguised threats against my person. Attention was diverted away from me only because the Reich Supervisory Board took up the matter and that this led to negotiations with the Reich Economics Ministry, the Reich Finance Ministry, and the Bureau of the Prussian Minister President. But from this time on my phone conversations were controlled and I was observed and reported upon.[82]

Thus it did take some kind of courage to refuse to provide the Nazi expropriators of Jewish businesses undeserved benefits from the original glass insurance of the expropriated, although certainly not the same kind of courage that it would have taken for Goudefroy and his colleagues to have refrained from using anti-Semitic arguments and to have stuck to their legal principles in trying to cope with the demands of Göring and the Finance Ministry. One can reasonably assume that this latter form of courage would have cost the insurance industry a great deal more money and might have led to serious consequences for those involved. Once again, one must remember how heavily engaged Hilgard and his allies were in fighting off the National Socialist opponents of the private insurance industry at this time. One could expect no advantage from stubbornly

---

[82] Goudefroy, "Lebenslauf," Staatsarchiv Hamburg, 221-11/F 17350. I have found no record of Goudefroy's negotiations with Party personages about such demands, but there is no reason to question his account since it is precisely what one would expect of those enriching themselves at the expense of the Jews.

maintaining one's honor, although the essence of honor, of course, is that it is not maintained for advantage but for its own sake. In any case, the performance of Goudefroy, Hilgard, and Thees in the months following the November Pogrom demonstrated how successfully and easily the regime had undermined the most elementary principles of legal and business ethics and how readily the leadership of the insurance industry had succumbed to an often unprincipled opportunism. The adaptations made since 1933 had paved the way for their self-serving performance in 1938, as well as for what was to follow in the wake of that fateful year.

6

Allianz, the Insurance Business, and the Fate of Jewish Life Insurance Policies, 1933–1945

INDIRECT CONFISCATION OF JEWISH LIFE INSURANCE ASSETS

ON NOVEMBER 17, 1938, the directors of Isar Life Insurance Company sent an urgent request to the RWM and the RAA for permission to refuse payment to Jews seeking to cash in their life insurance policies at their current repurchase value. As company directors Paul Riebesell (who, ironically enough, had been driven out of his position as head of the Reich Group for Publicly Chartered Insurance for helping a Jewish student) and Eckert reminded the government authorities, Isar had taken over the German portion of the Austrian Phönix life insurance stock when that company collapsed in 1936 and – with the financial support of the Party, the government, and its corporate backers – had managed to guarantee the acquisition of this portfolio and to acquire a considerable amount of new business since then. As discussed in Chapter 4, Isar Life Insurance Company's portfolio was guaranteed by the entire German insurance industry, which of course included Allianz.[1] Isar company directors warned that its successes were now threatened by Jewish cancellations because 20%–25% of Isar policyholders were non-Aryan. Although policy cancellations had increased significantly prior to November 9–10, the demands of the previous few days had been such, Riebesell and Eckert alleged, as to threaten the very existence of the company. For this reason, they asked for the speedy issuance of a regulation in the final version of the new "Jewish law" being drafted – presumably the already issued decree of November 12, 1938, excluding Jews from German economic life – that would permit insurance companies to refuse payment of the repurchase value of Jewish-owned policies and instead transform such policies into paid-up policies, free of premium obligations. Furthermore, with the approval of the RAA, "special conditions" were to be set for the calculation of the value of these paid-up policies.[2]

This was an unabashed effort by the Isar Life Insurance Company to cheat its Jewish policyholders – and, indeed, to cheat them under conditions where

---

[1] See Chapter 4, p. 152. The Isar Lebensversicherungs-AG was acquired by the present-day Allianz in the mid-1990s as part of Vereinte Lebensversicherung AG.

[2] See Isar Lebensversicherung an den Reichs- und Preußischen Wirtschaftsminister, 17. Nov. 1938, BAK, B 280/3867, Bl. 75; Walk, *Sonderrecht*, Nr. III 8 (p. 254).

they were desperate for cash because of the levies imposed on them and the costs of emigration. Not only did Isar propose to deprive such persons of the cash value of the policy to which they were entitled, the company also claimed an arbitrary right to transform it into a paid-up policy pegged at its present worth – and hinted at creating a special mode of calculation for such policies that would entail a further reduction of their value to the policyholders. Isar Life Insurance Company's request was rejected; the RWM took the position that there were no existing legal regulations limiting the repurchase of life insurance policies held by Jews.[3] As a result, Isar Life Insurance Company had to pay out. Its repurchase expenses in 1938 were 6.41 million RM as opposed to 2.43 RM in 1937, while the "cancellation profit" (to be explained shortly) rose only to 284,000 RM from 1937's value of 177,000. When queried by the RAA as to why profits were so low, Isar Life Insurance Company explained that 2 million RM's worth of the repurchases in 1938 went to policies paid for by means of a single lump premium, which had a particularly low cancellation profit. These policies had been purchased primarily by Jews. Moreover, there was the repurchase of a large portion of the policies held by the Jewish Family Protection Society, which also carried a much lower repurchase profit than large individual policies.[4] Clearly, then, the government's insistence that Isar Life Insurance Company fulfill its obligations to its Jewish customers imposed a substantial – albeit temporary and ultimately sustainable – drain on the company's resources. The episode is instructive, however, because it points to the complexities of one of the central issues of concern in this study: the fate of Jewish insurance assets under National Socialism.

Isar Life Insurance Company's situation was typical in certain respects and not typical in others. Because the company had been created to take over the Phönix assets in Germany, it had an inordinate number of Jewish policies, and no other company asking to be relieved of the obligation to pay its Jewish customers can be identified by name.[5] From this perspective, its exceptional request "proved the rule" that neither the leading insurance companies nor the RAA considered it legitimate to refuse payment of Jewish policies. Isar Life Insurance Company was typical, however, in experiencing a run on its Jewish-owned insurance stock in the wake of the Pogrom of November 1938. As the Isar story suggests, the Pogrom was a central event in sealing the fate of these and (it is important to note) other Jewish assets. The Pogrom was the bridge linking an earlier period of accelerating despoliation of the Jews and promotion of their emigration and a subsequent period of rigorous exclusion of Jews from German economic life, comprehensive extraction and confiscation of Jewish assets by the National Socialist regime, and a large-scale wave of emigration that was followed in 1941 by forced deportation to the East and extermination. The causeway leading to

---

[3] RWM an RAA, 14. Dez. 1938, ibid., Bl. 76, and RAA an RWM, 6. Dez. 1938, SM, 1458/1/98, Bl. 27–9.

[4] Isar Lebensversicherung an RAA, 1. Feb. 1940, SR, Leben 14, Isar.

[5] BAB, R 3104/261, Bl. 71–3.

this bridge was built on the Four-Year Plan and its voracious financial demands, which gave the expropriation of Jewish assets a significant place in Göring's efforts to manage the financial situation and helps to explain why the period from early 1937 to November 1938 marked a qualitative increase in the pressure on German Jewry. This pressure was greatly intensified by the brutalities following the Anschluß in March 1938 and the occupation of the Sudetenland in October. The causeway leading from the November Pogrom to what followed was shorter and more sharply descending, allowing for a final burst of emigration and attendant despoliation before murder replaced emigration as the pendant to thievery. As shall be shown in this chapter – which concentrates on the fate of the life insurance assets of Jewish policyholders in Germany, Austria after the Anschluß, and the Sudetenland and Protectorate of Bohemia-Moravia – the confiscation of Jewish insurance assets mirrors these trajectories.

Nevertheless, the manner in which these insurance assets were confiscated has been the source of much confusion, and there have been charges that Allianz and other German insurance companies were engaged in holding on to Jewish policies, refusing to pay their customers, and profiting as a consequence.[6] Analogies have been made, for example, between unpaid life insurance policies and numbered Swiss accounts. The analogy is false. All life insurance policies have names as well as numbers. By law, every policy had to be covered by assets equivalent to its current worth. As will be demonstrated in Chapter 9, there was no incentive for German insurance companies to hide or refuse to pay out on insurance policies of Jewish or non-Jewish policyholders. Be that as it may, the real tragedy of the life insurance assets of German Jews – namely, that a large proportion of them were forced to give up their coverage and cash in their policies in order to pay extortionist taxes and costs connected with emigration and persecution by the National Socialist regime – can only be obfuscated by a narrow concentration on the possible existence of unpaid policies.

To understand what really happened, it is essential to place the postwar situation in the context of the way in which Jewish insurance policyholders were compelled to deal with their insurance assets between 1933 and 1945 and the roles played by the insurance companies and the National Socialist authorities with respect to Jewish life insurance assets. The policies under consideration here are primarily the so-called large life insurance policies (Großleben). Such policies could run from 2,000 to 100,000 RM, although most of the policies examined by this author had a face value of between 10,000 RM and 30,000 RM. Larger policies were quite rare. Normally, these were policies taken out in the mid-1920s that were to come to term after 20 years. They were a form of capital investment, and the owner was entitled to dividends as well as normal accrual

---

[6] For a useful account of the cases – albeit one that persistently accepts the arguments of the plaintiffs and their lawyers – see Michael J. Bazyler, "Nuremberg in America: Litigating the Holocaust in United States Courts," *University of Richmond Law Review* 34 (2000), pp. 1–283, esp. pp. 93–148.

value. These policies differed from small life insurance policies (Kleinleben) of less than 2,000 RM, which were based on fixed monthly premiums, or group policies in which there was no direct relationship between the insured individual and the contracted insurance company.

In dealing with the fate of these larger life insurance policies, it is essential to recognize that the concrete material interests of the companies and the National Socialist authorities with respect to Jewish insurance policies ran counter to one another owing to the very nature of the insurance business. An insurance company has an obvious interest in holding on to its customers for as long as possible, having them continue to pay premiums, and having the policies it has issued come to their full term. Under normal circumstances, this interest runs parallel to those of the policyholder, who is making a long-term capital investment from which he or she would wish a full return. If an Allianz Leben policyholder held on to the policy then, beginning in the fourth year, he or she could anticipate interest in the form of a dividend based on the profit made on the company's capital investment. Such dividends could be expected to increase in the course of the policy's lifetime and were credited against premiums. This meant that the policyholder could anticipate a time when he or she would have to pay no premiums at all – and might even have a leftover accumulation if the dividends exceeded the premiums. Allianz also offered supplementary dividends resulting from profits made because of lower death rates and administrative costs. Lastly, it offered a guaranteed closure dividend payable for the last five years of the policy, starting at three years before maturity. These were the expectations when the policies were taken out and issued. In the pre-1933 period, the chief threat to such expectations came from the economic difficulties experienced because of the Great Depression. The insurance companies had an obvious interest in trying to persuade their customers to hold on to their policies. Customers could borrow against the repurchase value of their policies, and customers were urged not to repurchase their policies but instead to turn them into paid-up policies. Provision was made for reconversion of paid-up policies back into policies requiring premiums. That is, the companies worked hard at keeping cancellation business to a minimum.

The immediate consequence of a policyholder cancelling a policy was that he or she lost life insurance protection but also no longer had to pay premiums. The long-term implication was that the policyholder and the insurer had to forego the aforementioned expectations in connection with dividends and profits. At the same time, the policyholder received the repurchase value of the policy, and this raises the question of how that repurchase value was calculated and what kind of loss and gain, if any, the policyholder and the company made. The answer is that the repurchase value was calculated in such a way as to cover acquisition and administrative costs already incurred by the insurer, and a cancellation charge (which constituted such profit) was allowable from the cancellation. The repurchase value was based on calculations that were in no way arbitrary but rather were based on the business plans all private life insurance companies had to submit to the RAA for examination and approval. The premiums were designed to cover acquisition and administrative costs, that is, insurance agent fees and commissions, medical examinations, and administrative costs. By a method known as Zillmerung – named after the insurance mathematician August Zillmer (1831–1893), who first devised the mode of calculation involved – the repurchase value was calculated in such a way as to ensure that certain acquisition costs were fully covered at the very beginning of the policy's life while other costs were equally distributed over the years.[7] The costs were immediately added to the reserves that the company was required to have for the policy. In the case of Allianz, using a standard premium and the 1927 business plan (which remained valid through the 1930s and 1940s), this meant that the policy had no value during the first two years – that is, until the acquisition costs were paid off. If the policyholder cancelled in the first two years then he or she received nothing, and the company had a cancellation loss rather than a cancellation profit. Beginning in the third year, the policy had a repurchase value from the primary reserve that was subject to a 4.0% Zillmerung and, in each subsequent year, to 3.5% of the face value of the policy. In the event of a repurchase, the policyholder received the worth of the policy as determined in the manner just described. This, however, included a cancellation deduction that amounted to 10% of the reserve in the third year, sinking down to a minimum of 2% of the reserve beginning in the eighteenth year of the policy. It was this deduction from the reserve that constituted the cancellation charge. It should be noted that the percentage of the reserve subject to the deduction declined as the reserve itself grew, so that the absolute amount of the reserve taken as a cancellation profit by no means declined but rather increased.

Insurance policies that were allowed to come to term, however, produced considerably higher profits than those cancelled prematurely. The repurchase value of a policy was thus always somewhat lower than the actual reserve set aside for the policy. Furthermore, the cancellation charge was required to meet that part of the costs which had been equally distributed over the whole life of the policy. Otherwise these costs would have remained uncovered owing to the early cancellation. Finally, additional administrative costs arose from the great number of cancellations. The actual profit made by the company, insofar as there was one, was thus considerably lower than the cancellation deduction. Table C, based on the cancellation figures for Allianz Leben between 1935 and 1941, shows the relationship between repurchases made during these years and cancellation deductions.

This way of calculating the costs of cancellation business antedated the National Socialists and continued after they came to power. No one anticipated what would happen to Jewish insurance assets, and the level of cancellation would have been viewed as an increasing problem if it had continued, which it did not. The table shows that there was a cancellation charge of about 1.5 million RM in 1938 and 1.6 million RM in 1939. The actual profit, as explained

---

[7] See Arps, *Auf Sicheren Pfeilen*, pp. 383–4, 662–3, and *Durch unruhige Zeiten*, Bd. 1, pp. 306–14.

Table C. *Repurchases and Cancellation Deduction of Allianz Leben,*
1935–1941 (million RM)

	1935	1936	1937	1938	1939	1940	1941
Repurchases	14,382	15,209	13,800	28,922	30,301	6,717	5,042
Cancellation deduction	757	800	726	1,522	1,595	354	265

Note: Since exact figures for cancellation deductions are no longer available, these figures are based on the general assumption that 5% of the available capital coverage is accumulated for cancellation reduction; this is an upper boundary estimate.

earlier, was much lower than these amounts and clearly could not weigh heavily in the balance. This does not mean that no attention was paid to the cancellation profit.[8] Manifestly, more money would have been made in the longer run if the cancellations had not taken place.

As will be shown, insurance companies worked hard to keep cancellation business to a minimum, whether or not the customers were Jewish. The longer the National Socialists were in power, however, the more they wanted to gain control of Jewish assets and to do so as quickly as possible. Theoretically, there were two ways in which the confiscation of Jewish insurance assets might have been of no cost or even of slight profit to the insurance companies. The first method would have been to postpone confiscation until the insured had paid off most of the acquisition costs equally distributed over the life of the policy. Then the cancellation charge would meet both the cancellation costs and those acquisition costs not paid off at this point. It is obvious that the regime wanted the money quickly and was not going to pace its confiscations to suit insurance company calculations. The second method would have been for the government actually to assume the title to policies and wait until they came to term. I have found no evidence in the period prior to 1942 that insurance company officials ever suggested such a thing or that those in the National Socialist regime ever contemplated or indicated any interest in confiscating insurance policies per se, paying premiums, and patiently awaiting the day when it could collect the full sum to which its Jewish victims would have been entitled. Such an arrangement would undoubtedly have served the interests of the insurance companies. Furthermore, neither before nor after 1942 was the welfare of the insurance companies with respect to Jewish life insurance assets a National Socialist priority. Hence, from the regime's perspective, the central problem was to create circumstances in which the Jews or the companies were compelled to monetize these insurance assets and to then find ways and means of gaining access to this money.

[8] Kisskalt an Meuschel, 23. Feb. 1940, MR, B 12/19.

Insurance policy of a Jewish customer of Allianz Leben, started in 1930 and running for sixteen years. The sum insured amounted to 5,000 RM.

This could be done indirectly, by placing Jews in the position where they had to monetize their insurance assets in order to cover the costs of government impositions and emigration, or directly, by forcing the insurance companies to disgorge the cash value of the policies they held. Either way, it involved policy cancellations. If one wishes to understand what happened to Jewish insurance assets then it is a mistake to concentrate attention on the problem of unclaimed insurance policies, since the ultimate goal of the National Socialists was to make sure that there were no unclaimed policies.

The record before 1940 suggests that, in Germany and the areas annexed to the Reich, the National Socialists were highly successful in achieving their purpose of relentlessly collecting the cash value of most Jewish life insurance policies in one form or another. What should be obvious from the foregoing description is that the National Socialist government, not the insurance company, benefitted from the confiscation of such insurance assets, and that it was the government, not the insurance company, that cheated the customer of the fruits of his policy. The reality is that confiscation of Jewish insurance assets was a realm in which the insurance business had nothing to gain and, indeed, something to lose from the despoliation of the Jews by the National Socialist regime. Insurance companies trying to hold on to their Jewish customers were thus doing so at the very least because it was in their interest. Even though the industry and its leaders increasingly adapted to the demands of the regime out of self-interest and thereby became increasingly implicated in its misdeeds, there were nevertheless points at which the interests of the regime were simply incompatible with those of the insurance industry. One of these was the transformation of life insurance policies – from policies on which premiums were regularly paid to premium-free policies – or the premature monetization of insurance assets through the repurchase of policies by their owners before they achieved their full potential value. What is involved here is not a question of "resistance" on the part of the insurance companies to measures of the regime but rather of an ultimately futile self-interested effort (though not without some evidence of humane concern in significant instances) to hold on to a group of valued customers.

The importance of Jews as customers was recognized even where insurers were anything but friendly toward Jews, as was the case with the German Lawyers and Notary Insurance Company of Halle. Hostility toward Jews within the over-populated German legal profession was notorious, and Jewish lawyers were a favorite target of anti-Semites in the public at large. Unsurprisingly, then, they were already the target of special measures aimed at undermining their economic existence – especially in connection with the purging of the civil service soon after the Nazis took power – and were singled out in the anti-Jewish boycott at the turn of March–April 1933. As one of the company's officials noted, this presented some unpleasant problems:

The consequences of the present political movements in Germany for the lawyers insured by us, especially the Jewish lawyers, cannot be predicted with any certainty. I do not know how many Jewish lawyers are insured by us and also do not know for how much they are insured. Since in general the Jew is not exactly lax when it comes to the care of his family, I must assume that the number of Jewish lawyers insured by us and also the amount of the insurance corresponds approximately to the number of Jewish lawyers in the bar. I must therefore assume that a substantial portion of the 900,000 RM in premium payments due on April 1 will not come in because the gentlemen will probably hold back their cash for the time being due to the intransparency of their own situation. I must also calculate that, despite the most urgent advice against doing so on our part in each individual case, a large number of the gentlemen, in order to have cash on hand, will not only prematurely transform their insurance into premium-free policies but will also even buy back their life insurance or at a minimum ask for a prepayment. The sum of such demands made upon us cannot for the moment be in any way calculated. Where before I could view an average liquidity in the amount of 500,000 RM as completely sufficient, I must for the forseeable future count on the necessity of raising this to a million RM.[9]

However, when calculations were made by another official of the company later in April, the situation appeared less gloomy, with an anticipated loss of only 10%. Indeed, as the official in question cynically noted, loss might be turned into opportunity:

On the other hand, we cannot tell today whether or not the income of other lawyers would not rise through the loss of a large number of Jewish lawyers in such a way, that once a certain equilibrium is attained, the former will be able to make larger payments for their insurance than before. We must assume that this momentary loss will be thereby balanced out over time.[10]

One of the ways this organization sought to protect itself in the meantime was to take a tough position whenever it could manage *not* to accommodate its Jewish customers. Thus, it pursued a policy of refusing to allow buy-backs by persons affected by the Law on the Cleansing of the Civil Service, insofar as the policies were held for too short a time or did not qualify for some other reason. When it came to pensions, however, the organization abandoned such legal niceties. For instance, when a Jewish lawyer who had purchased a pension (but could no longer be a member of the Lawyer's Association) asked for the return of his eight years' worth of premiums, he was rudely invited to take the association to court: "payment is refused, and we leave it up to you to take legal action. We would like to see the German court that would find against us in favor of a Jewish lawyer."[11] A refusal to pay back premiums, however, did not constitute the right to deny Jewish lawyers with life insurance the fruits of their investment. Thus, until the "striven after goal of cleansing the bar of Jewry" was achieved

---

[9] Schreiben an Oberjustizrat Barth, 1. April 1933, FHA, H 18 II/21, Bl. 51. On the treatment of Jewish lawyers in 1933, see Simone Ladwig-Winters, *Anwalt ohne Recht. Das Schicksal jüdischer Rechtsanwälte in Berlin nach 1933* (Berlin, 1998), pp. 33–9.

[10] Auswirkungen des etwaigen Ausscheidens jüdischer Rechtsanwälte auf die Ruhegehaltskasse, 21. April 1933, HM, A0308-00013.

[11] AZLB, F 227781. See Erste Aufsichtratssitzung der Ruhegehalts-, Witwen- und Waisenkasse für deutsche Rechtsanwälte und Notare zu Halle a. d. S., 25. Juni 1933, FHA, H 18 II/16, Bl. 1.

by the 5th Decree to the Reich Citizenship Law of September 27, 1938, a great many Jewish lawyers seemed to have held on to their policies. Only then did practically all the Jews buy back their policies. Although the costs were high, the company reported that it had weathered the drain quite well and was managing to pay the costs out of current accounts, thereby demonstrating the solidity it had achieved since 1933.[12]

This ugly little example was paradigmatic for the manner in which Jewish insurance assets eroded in the first five years of the Third Reich and of the mixed feelings with which even an anti-Semitic insurance company confronted the process. Whatever the views on the "Jewish question" held by officials and employees of the Allianz concern, Jews were good customers with a favorable attitude toward insurance as a means of investment and toward providing security for themselves and their families, and a company like Allianz wanted to hold on to them. A measure of the value placed on their business – albeit a somewhat bizarre one, in hindsight – can be seen in the response of Allianz to the first wave of Jewish emigration during the early years of the National Socialist regime. Thus, in February 1935, one of Allianz's daughter companies, the Wilhelma in Magdeburg, sent a circular to its branches that read:

As is known, the Swiss National Insurance Company in Basel is connected to our company. It is therefore to our interest that our policyholders who move to Switzerland become customers of the Swiss National. If you hear about the emigration of a policyholder to Switzerland, we should be informed about this as quickly as possible so that we can recommend that the customer take out a policy with Swiss National. We reiterate that this information should be provided as quickly as possible. If it transpires a few months after the move has taken place, then it will not seldom be the case that the policyholder will already have concluded a new policy with another company. Allianz however also has its own representatives in other countries or has close business connections with indigenous companies. Where other German customers emigrate to such areas, Palestine for example, we also would like to bind them to us in their new homeland. It is therefore necessary that we receive report of such cases as speedily as possible so that we can report the moves to the international section of the company in Berlin.[13]

While it is interesting to note that one of the signers of this circular was the Jewish director Eichbaum, who ended up working for Allianz in the safety of Johannesburg, South Africa, it should be clear that this was general Allianz policy in the period before radicalization of the regime set in. Such a circular would have been inconceivable two years later. While it is difficult to tell how well Allianz and its subsidiaries abroad managed to hold on to Jewish customers who emigrated, the will to do so certainly was there, and it corresponded to the company's efforts to maintain the policies of its Jewish customers at home in the face

[12] Erster Bericht des Vorstandes über das Geschäftsjahr 1938, FHA, H 18 II/16, Bl. 53.
[13] Rundschreiben vom 25. Feb. 1935, Versicherungen der aus Deutschland auswandernden Versicherungsnehmer, FHA, S 17.7/62; see also Rundschreiben Allianz vom 15. Feb. 1935, FHA, AZ 5.1/4.

of mounting economic pressures that were forcing them either to cease paying premiums or to monetize their policies by repurchase.

Before turning to further discussion of the relationship between Allianz and its Jewish customers, it is important to describe the evidence available for the ensuing discussion and to provide some quantitative sense of the process by which Jews surrendered their insurance entitlements as well as some procedural models for the liquidation of Jewish insurance policies and the fate of the monies received for them. Fortunately, a substantial number of life insurance policies and records thereof survived the war and have been stored by Allianz Leben – specifically, 1.3 million policies held in Berlin. In addition, there are another 600,000 policies for the Vereinte Versicherung (successor of the Isar Life Insurance Company and Magdeburger companies taken over by Allianz in recent years) that are stored in Munich. This second collection is composed primarily of very small policies that provide only the sparsest information about the policyholder and the fate of the policies. Taken together, the Allianz collection is the largest such collection of policies available in Germany; the policies of other companies appear to have been destroyed in the war or in the aftermath of the restitution process. Nevertheless, it is by no means a complete collection, and the majority of the older small life insurance policies may well have been destroyed over the last decades when the required preservation period expired. It is extremely important to recognize that policies held by Jews were not subject to special identification, and while some policyholders had names that were clearly Jewish, many did not. "Rosenberg," for example, as the personage of Nazi ideologue Alfred Rosenberg demonstrates, need not be a Jewish name. The regime tried to solve this problem of identification by decreeing on August 17, 1938, that every Jew had to have a clearly recognizable Jewish given name or to take on the middle name of "Israel" or "Sarah" by January 1, 1939, but this was not evidenced in insurance policy documents unless there was correspondence after that date in which the policyholder specifically used the names. Also, Jews who had already emigrated were not covered by this decree. Thus, the identification of Jewish policyholders is possible only if the policies contain some other evidence – for example, correspondence indicating an intention to emigrate, termination of the policy at the time of the November Pogrom, or Gestapo demands for the repurchase value. The best evidence, in fact, is provided by policies involved with postwar restitution claims and compensation calculations, which apparently led Allianz employees to write the word "Jude" on some policies to make reference easier. In short, Jewish insurance policies are difficult to single out and identify from the mass of policies available.

To deal with the problem of possibly unpaid policies in connection with recent lawsuits, Allianz employed the auditing firm of Arthur Andersen to go through its policy holdings and develop a representative sample of policies for analysis.[14]

---

[14] For all the information pertaining to the Arthur Andersen investigation, see "Investigation of Life Insurance Files (Presentation for NAIC Task Force, June 23, 1998, Boston)" and the relevant preliminary reports. These documents were placed at the disposal of the author.

Allianz Leben also undertook efforts to examine and refine the data available from this sample. A repetition of this extraordinarily complex undertaking was beyond the capacity or skills of this writer and would have been pointless besides. However, I did examine about 300 policies that belonged to Jews, some from the group closely examined by Andersen and some from a group of policies clearly identified as belonging to Jews because of restitution information not included in the Arthur Andersen sample. My impressionistic survey, which was above all aimed at finding qualitative evidence in the form of correspondence between the company and its Jewish customers, gave me every reason to have confidence in the conclusions drawn by the Arthur Andersen investigators with respect to the character and fate of the policies. These conclusions will be discussed next. Finally, it is important to note that most insurance policies are rather matter-of-fact documents containing little or no correspondence; as noted before, the only way one can identify many of those belonging to Jews is because they contain forms and calculations required by postwar restitution authorities. A few insurance policies, however, include revealing and at times moving correspondence that gives us some sense of the trials and sufferings of these Jewish policyholders.

First, however, let us consider the statistical record provided by Arthur Andersen, which selected and systematically examined some 35,538 policies and then randomly chose another 31,798 out of a total of 1,188,000 files. Thus, a total of 67,336 files were examined. Of these, 6,338 were believed to be policies owned by Jews. Most of the persons in question were businessmen, lawyers and notaries, medical doctors, or other professionals. Jews constituted 1% of the German population under the racial laws of 1935 – and only 0.77% insofar as they self-identified as Jews – and it is difficult to say whether as a group they were more or less inclined to take out life insurance than others.

The Austrian evidence suggests not.[15] However, the amounts for which Jews insured themselves would appear to have been higher than average. Thus, where the average large life insurance policy at Allianz Leben, which had only been founded in 1922, was 5,902 RM in 1933 and the average small life policy was for 1,025 RM, the corresponding sums for the Jews identified in the Andersen sample were 15,235 RM and 1,812 RM, respectively. Needless to say, the lion's share (90%) of these policies, many of which were written by Favag and inherited by Allianz when it acquired that firm, were taken out between 1923 and 1932; the 10% taken out after 1933 came from the acquisition of other companies and their old stock. This explains why the number of Jewish-owned policies grew slightly during the early years of the National Socialist regime and did not diminish as dramatically as might otherwise have been the case in 1935–1936. Thus, the number of Jewish policies in force in 1934 was 4,904 and had only diminished to about 4,500 in early 1937 before a dramatic reduction to 801 by

[15] Helen B. Junz, "Report on the Pre-War Wealth Position of the Jewish Population in Nazi-Occupied Countries, Germany, and Austria," in Independent Committee of Eminent Persons, *The Volcker Commission: The Report on Dormant Accounts of Victims of Nazi Persecution in Swiss Banks* (Bern, 1999), Appendix S; ⟨http://www.icep-iaep.org⟩.

1939. In that year, the value of Jewish policies was 10% of what it had been in 1928, while that of the remainder of the Allianz portfolio was 240% of its worth in 1928. The cash value of Jewish policies in force, which was about 650% of what it had been in 1928 at the beginning of 1937, was reduced to 20% of its 1928 value in 1939–1940, while the actual RM value of the policies in force had decreased from 14.4 million to 0.4 million.

What had happened to these policies? Some, of course, came to term and were paid off, while the exact fate of some others is unknown. Nevertheless, clear conclusions may be drawn about the majority of the policies. Turning first to the 1,708 Allianz Leben policies identified as belonging to Jews whose insurance assets were lost because of Nazi persecution, 80% were cancelled and 30% were converted into paid-up status. The percentages add up to more than 100% because some policies were first converted and then cancelled. Of the policies whose repurchase date is known, 91% were repurchased before 1940 and 9% were repurchased after 1940. The initiator of the surrender can be determined in 1,273 cases: in 92% it was the policyholder, 6% the government, and 2% the company. Prior to 1940, 96% of the policies were terminated by the policyholder and 2% each by the government and the company. After 1940, 47% of terminations were initiated by the policyholder, 50% by the government, and 3% by the company.[16] This pattern demonstrates the powerful effects of intensified persecution of the Jews in the late 1930s and also the increasing role of the government – above all, the 11th Decree to the Reich Citizenship Law (to be discussed shortly) – in the 1940s.

The Allianz Leben sample of 1,708 policies is obviously a small one, so there is something to be gained from adding the Vereinte policies in order to see if analysis of the two together confirms the aforementioned pattern. It clearly does.[17] Of the 5,715 Jewish policies surveyed between 1928 and 1945, 3,683 (64%) were cancelled and 967 (17%) were converted into paid-up policies. As these statistics and Table D[18] demonstrate, the number of cancellations far outweighed the number of conversions, with the latter most preponderant in the early years of the regime and in 1938. Conversion, of course, involved a significant diminution of cash value, but it was a way of holding on to the policy without the burden of premiums. In many cases, however, conversion was a prelude to cancellation. Manifestly, cancellation reduced the life of the policies – in the case of the large life policies, by an average of half (i.e., from 20 to 10 years) – and this meant that the cash value on average was reduced to almost 38% of the sum insured.

Finally, it is useful once again to consider who initiated the cancellations. In a survey of 2,603 policies prior to 1939, 95% of the policies had been cancelled

---

[16] Darstellung der Zahlenermittlung, Kündigungen und Beitragsfreistellungen im jüdischen Portfolio der Allianz Lebensversicherungs AG (Ausarbeitung Allianz Leben, 16. Juli 2000), FHA, S 17.22/181.

[17] Life Insurance in Germany 1928–1940 (Ausarbeitung Allianz Leben, 1998), FHA, S 17.22/181.

[18] Ibid.

Table D. *Allianz-Vereinte Jewish Portfolio:*
Policy Cancellations and Conversion to
Paid-up Policies, 1928–1946ff.

Year	Cancellation	Conversion
1928	0	0
1929	0	4
1930	0	21
1931	1	32
1932	7	69
1933	90	170
1934	99	145
1935	93	122
1936	357	93
1937	406	69
1938	1,213	140
1939	1,100	60
1940	91	14
1941	50	7
1942	66	8
1943	58	2
1944	21	1
1945	14	2
1946ff.	17	8

by the policyholders, who collected the repurchase value of the policies, while 3% involved direct appropriation of the repurchase value by government agencies and 2% were cancelled by the company itself. These proportions changed after 1940. Of the 249 cancellations that took place after 1940, 44% were at the request of the policyholder, 50% by order of the government, and 6% by the company. Hence, what emerges from these figures is that most policies were cancelled by policyholders themselves and that, insofar as proceeds from the repurchase of insurance policies were then confiscated (as most of them indeed were, in one way or another), the confiscation was indirect in that it took place after the cancellation. Only after 1940 did direct confiscation of insurance policy proceeds by government agencies predominate.

Even if the record shows that Allianz and its allied companies paid off their Jewish customers and followed their instructions about disposition of their insurance assets, this does not mean that the policyholders could freely dispose of the money they received or, indeed, that they had not acted under constraint when they transformed or cancelled their policies. To be sure, there were rare cases like that of a Frankfurt lawyer who read the handwriting on the wall early in the game. As he later reported in claiming compensation after 1945:

In March 1933 I was arrested by the Nazis twice. I saw the disaster coming and made plans to flee. Naturally, I wanted to have as much cash as possible when fleeing. Between the first and the second arrest, that is in March 1933, I therefore went to the Favag and declared that I wanted to buy back my insurance. The Favag official told me that I should think long and hard about the matter since I would lose "a crazy" amount of money. I explained my situation and bought the insurance back.[19]

He managed to get the money out and changed his marks into francs in Saarbrücken.

This, however, was early in the regime. Later on, when Jews cancelled their policies and received their money, there was little mystery as to why they were doing so. Sometimes, as in the case of a merchant from Würzburg in November 1939, the simple facts were made explicit: "Now that I do not have any further means of existence for myself and for my family and need cash for living, I herewith cancel my life insurance policy with you and ask for its repurchase value."[20] In many cases, however, the disposition of monies derived from life insurance assets was far more complicated and was to increase in complexity. Insofar as Jews intended to emigrate, their assets were subject to the Reich Flight Tax of 1931, a measure instituted at the high point of the Depression and which therefore antedated the National Socialist regime; it was intended to discourage Germans from leaving the country and taking their capital with them. The National Socialists, who wished the Jews to emigrate but also wished to seize their assets, transformed the tax into a mechanism for despoiling the Jews. Thus, where the original law provided that all persons having a yearly income of 20,000 RM or taxable assets of 200,000 RM had to pay 25% of their assets upon emigration, the changed law of May 1934 provided that those earning over 20,000 RM a year or having assets worth 50,000 RM were required to pay 25% of their net worth as a tax if they wished to emigrate. This substantial reduction in the threshold amount of assets liable to taxation, and the inclusion of assets like Reich Railroad bonds (which had previously been exempt from consideration), were clearly aimed at the Jews: the new law was designed to force them, in the language of the rapacious Finance Ministry, to make "a last large contribution" as compensation for the taxes thereby lost in the future.[21] The repurchase values of insurance policies were assets subject to taxation under the Reich Flight Tax, and Jews intending to emigrate found themselves cashing in their policies in order

[19] AZLB, F 227781.

[20] AZLB, F 244902.

[21] Dorothee Mußgnug, *Die Reichsfluchtsteuer 1931–1953* [Schriften zur Rechtsgeschichte, Heft 60] (Berlin, 1993), pp. 30ff. See also Stefan Mehl, *Das Reichsfinanzministerium und die Verfolgung der Deutschen Juden 1933–1943* [Berliner Arbeitshefte und Berichte zur Sozialwissenschaftlichen Forschung, Bd. 38] (Berlin, 1990), pp. 41–50. This was a lucrative tax, with the Reich collecting 941.7 million RM between April 1, 1933, and March 31, 1944. During this time, 270,000 Jews emigrated; 135,000 were deported between 1940 and 1944. The peak year, as might be expected, was the fiscal year 1938–39, when 342.6 million RM was collected; ibid., pp. 44–5.

to raise the money they needed to pay this tax and other impositions, especially the infamous atonement tax, after the November 1938 Pogrom. In order to ensure that payment was made, insurance proceeds were deposited into a so-called emigrant blocked account – usually the normal bank account of a Jew who had stated his intention to emigrate, or the normal bank account of a Jew that had been blocked by order of the local revenue office. Take, for example, the case of a Breslau lawyer and notary who held a 15,000-RM policy, which he had taken out in 1925 and which was to reach full term in 1940. Although he had planned to wait until February 28, 1939, to cash in his policy and thus benefit from the interest he would receive, the events at the end of 1938 made him think again; on January 5, 1939, he wrote to Allianz as follows.

I herewith exercise my cancellation and repurchase right and sincerely request that you do not wait until February 28 to make payment but rather undertake payment immediately, if necessary by calculating back interest since the payment is urgently needed for purposes of paying the Reich Flight Tax. In view of my many years as one of your policyholders and your known fairness, I can certainly assume that you will fulfill my request.

In the case of Allianz and its associated companies, there was no need for such anxiety; the customer's request was fulfilled when 13,794.66 RM were placed, as requested, in the blocked account under the control of the president of the revenue office in Silesia.[22] At this point, of course, Allianz had paid off the policy. The real problem was that the right of the "owner" of such accounts to dispose of the assets contained in them was subject to the permission of the revenue authority, and release of the funds (of which the insurance payment was usually only a part) depended upon satisfaction of the Reich Flight Tax requirement as well as other tax obligations. Thus, what was confiscated was not the insurance asset but the money derived from it.

The anxiety that was somewhat muted in the last-discussed case was often made very explicit in others. For instance, a Berlin lawyer held two 20-year policies taken out in 1924 with a face value of 10,000 RM; the repurchase value of one of the policies had already been seized by the authorities to cover liabilities, and he wrote to Allianz on November 12, 1938, about his second policy:

I sincerely request the *immediate* reporting of the repurchase value as of November 12, 1938. The matter *is very pressing*, since I must already report the repurchase value on early Tuesday morning. I would be very grateful if the matter could be taken care of with the greatest possible speed and as an urgent matter and if you could give me the information by telephone. The costs can be charged to me.[23]

For whatever reason, Allianz was not able to provide the information until the late afternoon of November 28, but by this time the revenue office had placed a

---

[22] AZLB, F 235109.
[23] AZLB, F 220947.

lien against the policy, which was finally lifted in February 1939 after the policy-holder had used other resources as security for payment of the atonement levy. In the process, he had turned the policy into a paid-up one and was able to buy it back for 3,356.78 RM in February 1939.

One of the more depressing aspects of the correspondence between Allianz and its policyholders was the witting or unwitting race against time and circumstance to which it bore witness. A good illustration was a 55-year-old Berlin lawyer with a 50,000-RM policy that he had taken out in 1924. On October 28, 1938, he wrote to Allianz pointing out that his biannual premium was due on November 1. However, all Jewish lawyers were losing their licenses effective November 30, and whether he would be allowed to practice as a consultant (i.e., a specialist in handling the legal problems of Jews) was doubtful. If he could not be licensed then he would probably have to buy back his policy, since he needed the interest it had accrued, and he wanted to know what the difference in the repurchase value of his policy would be if he paid the November premium or if he waited until January 1, 1939, and then bought back the policy. That is, would he lose money by paying the premium and then cancelling at the beginning of the year, when he would know for sure about his appointment as a consultant? Allianz responded to him almost immediately, first misunderstanding his question but then answering it once he had clarified matters. By the beginning of December, however, the question had become irrelevant, and the policyholder asked for the repurchase value of his policy to be paid to a blocked account at the Commerz-und Privatbank "since I need the money for the levy on Jewish assets."[24]

Here, obviously, the insurer was in no position to help the customer beyond paying out promptly, but it is worth noting that the company did seem to strive to explain its regulations to Jewish customers and to bend the regulations when it seemed possible to show a modicum of decency. This is well illustrated by the case of a Jewish merchant from Lehrensteinsfeld, who turned his policy into a paid-up policy in 1936 when he could no longer afford the premiums. When he discovered that the value of the policy was now reduced below the total sum of the premiums paid, however, he was quite shocked and complained to his agent. The latter pointed out that the premiums were calculated in such a way that risk of early death had to be taken into account as well as other costs connected with acquiring customers, and that these weighed more heavily the earlier the customer decided to stop paying premiums. The policyholder in question remained upset, however, and Allianz made a point of sending him a lengthy letter explaining its policies. Whether this satisfied him or not is unknown, but he maintained the policy until the end of December 1938, when he informed the company that he was planning to emigrate and wanted to cancel the policy. Although paid-up policies could normally be cashed in only at the end of the "insurance year" – in this case, August 1939 – Allianz informed him that, in view of his intention to emigrate, they were prepared to accommodate him and pay immediately if

[24] AZLB, F 234892.

he supplied the necessary documents within two weeks. At the same time, they urged him to bear the currency exchange regulations in mind and make the necessary arrangements should he be planning to emigrate before the money was paid. Whether this was "company policy" is impossible to say, but it is by no means the only instance of such efforts to inform and assist Jewish customers.[25]

It was indeed quite important to inform emigrating Jews to take the currency exchange regulations into account, for they were a crucial barrier to many Jews acquiring full disposition over their paid-out insurance assets. There were two aspects of this question, which should not be confused with one another. The first pertains to life insurance policies denominated in gold marks, fine gold, or foreign currencies such as the dollar or the Swiss franc. The second and, for Jews, far more important aspect pertains to the money emigrants could take out of Germany.

A substantial number of life insurance policies (particularly larger ones) held by Germans, whether Jewish or not, were held in "real values." This was an understandable response to the hyperinflation of 1922–1923, when the value of the paper mark simply evaporated. Although life insurance policyholders were entitled to some revaluation of their insurance assets, the experience of hyperinflation made Germans wary, despite the stability of the Reichsmark. It is understandable that, after 1923, many Germans did not want to take out insurance policies denominated in Reichsmark but rather wanted policies denominated in what they considered secure values: gold mark values. They continued to do so even after passage of the Reich Currency Law of August 30, 1924, establishing the Reichsmark. These efforts took various forms. Some policies were denominated in fine gold, this being measured as 1/2790 kilograms fine gold equaling one gold mark or, at a minimum, 1 RM, thereby ensuring the customer receipt of at least the Reichsmark equivalent in fine gold. Policies denominated in gold marks were presumed to be on a dollar basis (i.e., 4.2 gold marks to the dollar), thereby allegedly ensuring the customer whatever the real value might be in Reichsmark. Other policies were denominated in dollars or Swiss francs. For good measure, some people took out their policies with Swiss or other foreign companies operating in Germany, and there were even some cases where policyholders reserved the right to cash in their policies either in Germany or in Switzerland. In early 1925, the RAA sought to strengthen support for German currency by urging that insurers issue policies denominated in foreign currencies only in exceptional cases.[26]

What those seeking security by gold mark and foreign currency policies did not anticipate was the currency instability of the Great Depression – especially after September 1931, when England went off the gold standard. The Germans did not go off the gold standard in theory but they effectively did so in practice by

[25] AZLB, S 268967.
[26] RAA, Rundschreiben vom 23. Jan. 1925, Basler Lebens-Versicherungs-Gesellschaft, Altarchiv, Registraturnummer 000 034.

introducing exchange controls during the banking crisis of July 1931. With the end of currency convertibility and the controls on foreign exchange, the RAA began to take a tougher line, since it was very much to the German advantage to have insurance assets denominated in Reichsmark and to reduce the amount of foreign exchange held by insurance companies to guarantee their policies. Thus, on September 10, 1931, the RAA insisted that premiums for policies denominated in foreign currencies had to be paid in such currencies and strongly urged that the insurance companies cease promoting insurance in gold marks or foreign exchange. In June 1932 there were warnings that the insurers were not going to find the coverage they needed for such policies because of the exchange control regulations.[27]

In April 1933, however, the benefits of gold mark–denominated insurance on a dollar basis were dealt a severe blow when the United States went off the gold standard and then devalued the dollar by 40% in January 1934. Two years later, the Swiss devalued their franc by 35%. Thus, beginning in 1933 (when the news of the dollar devaluation came out), one could make a good case for the transformation of such policies into Reichsmark-denominated policies. To encourage such transformations, Allianz directors decided in May 1933 to offer to change gold mark–denominated policies at a rate of 4.20 RM, which was generous indeed since the rate was to become 2.50 RM to the dollar. The company decided to conduct this operation by sending all its policyholders a letter informing them of this offer and an addendum to be returned if they agreed, charging the flat rate of a mark for the operation. Those who did not reply were visited by insurance agents who explained the situation and benefits to them.[28] Not surprisingly, most customers took advantage of this offer, among them Kurt Schmitt himself, who converted his own policy to RM on June 28, 1933, "whereby a gold mark is replaced by a Reichsmark and a dollar by 4.20 Reichsmark."[29] These efforts by Allianz and other insurers were promoted by actions of the RAA. In October 1933 it announced that no foreign exchange would be provided to customers who had concluded policies in foreign currency after December 20, 1931; at the end of May 1934, it banned outright the conclusion of policies in gold mark on the basis of a foreign currency. Soon after, the RAA turned its attention to policies denominated in foreign currencies themselves, ordering in September that future premium payments on such policies – as well as their future denomination – were to be in Reichsmark and announcing that no foreign exchange would be released to pay premiums on such policies. Hence, such policies now had a "foreign currency portion" and an RM portion. Once again, Allianz sent out a notification to its customers and a form for them to fill out agreeing to the transformation of their policies. However, this time they pointed out that they were, in effect, acting out of constraint because they were no longer in a position to obtain the foreign exchange necessary to cover such policies in full and could

---

[27] RAA, Rundschreiben vom 29. Juni 1932, ibid.; Rundschreiben vom 10. Sept. 1931, BAK, B 280/583.

[28] 21. erweiterte Vorstandssitzung am 10. Mai 1933, FHA, S 17.2/4.

[29] Nachtrag zum Versicherungsschein Nr. A 2 250 885, FHA, NL 1/7.

thus only guarantee full coverage for policies whose remaining portions were denominated in RM. Since the courts ruled in 1935 and again in 1936 that the insurer rather than the policyholder had to bear losses attendant upon devaluation of the dollar in January 1934, policyholders had every interest in agreeing to the offer made to transform their policies.[30]

Nonetheless, those portions of life insurance policies denominated in foreign currency and backed by foreign currency assets still remained an object of irritation to the government, especially as the regime's thirst for foreign exchange became desperate in 1937–1938. Early in 1937, the RWM came to the conclusion that its earlier plan to promote the voluntary conversion of policies with a foreign currency component would not achieve its purpose and that compulsion would be necessary. The form that this would take, however, was a complicated matter. Clearly this would constitute a breach of contract between the insurers and their customers – 81.6 million RM in such coverage was involved – and the companies were anxious to have it appear as a government-imposed measure rather than have it reflect badly on the German insurance industry itself. Also, they saw the change as an opportunity to shift the risk of any depreciation in the Reichsmark, which they would now receive in return for their surrender of hard currency to the Reichsbank upon cessation of hard currency coverage.

The government faced particular difficulties with the Swiss. Four companies – the Schweizerische Lebensversicherungs- und Rentenanstalt in Zürich, Basler Lebens-Versicherungs-Gesellschaft, the Vita Lebensversicherungs-AG in Zürich, and Winterthur Lebensversicherungs-Gesellschaft – had policies denominated in foreign currencies and were much concerned about their future credibility if they did not receive some guarantee from the Reich respecting their long-term obligations under the life insurance policies they had issued. Lengthy negotiations were thus conducted with the wily Hans Koenig (general director of Schweizerische Lebensversicherungs- und Rentenanstalt and chief negotiator for the Association of Swiss Insurance Companies) and his colleagues. In the end, the government decided to issue a law whose ultimate justification was that the Reichsbank needed the foreign exchange used as coverage for these policies in order to pay for the Four-Year Plan. The law of August 26, 1938, mandated the conversion into RM of all forms of policy protection denominated in foreign exchange or in the form of exchange-rate guarantees.[31] It was a lucrative piece of legislation for the German government and was made all the more so by its requirement that insurance companies invest the RM they received (in return for the surrendered foreign exchange) in Reich bonds. The Swiss companies, for

---

[30] On the court decision, see Rundschreiben 144/135 des Verbandes Deutscher Lebensversicherungsgesellschaften vom 2. August 1935, GDV, 2-094/1. For the forms sent out by Allianz in 1934 in dealing with this question, see BAK, B 280/1453, Bl. 79–92.

[31] Vermerk, 2. Feb. 1937, SM, 1458/1/154, Bl. 26f.; RAA an die Reichsstelle für Devisenbewirtschaftung, 13. April 1937; Vermerk RWM, 3. Juli 1937, ibid., Bl. 45f. For the negotiations with the Swiss in early 1938, see the Koenig memorandum of March 10, 1938, Bl. 143–52 and the other relevant documents in this volume. The final version of the law is in ibid., Bl. 168–74.

example, had to surrender 19.4 million Swiss francs, 378,000 U.S. dollars, and 66,000 Dutch florins in return for Reichsmark.[32] The amounts at Allianz were considerably smaller, adding up to only 100,000 RM in coverage. When one examines the list of 36 persons who still held such policies in March 1939, nearly all were living abroad and at least 15 can today be plausibly identified as Jews by their names and places of residence.[33] It is important to bear in mind, however, that this was not a policy aimed specifically against Jews. All German insurance policy holders were subject to these conversions.

There were apparently some cases of Jews (as well as non-Jews) who did not change the denomination of their policies into Reichsmark, although Allianz continued to offer the favorable exchange rate as late as September 1936 and to urge conversion on its customers. In one such case – that of a Jewish merchant in Stuttgart whose policy had been denominated in dollars – this stubbornness worked in favor of the insured, since his lawyer was able to arrange a deal in 1935 whereby the policy dividends were paid in RM while the dollar portion of the policy was paid in dollars via an account in New York. It would appear that the policy may have been transferred to the Allianz assets in the United States. Whatever the case, the policy was repurchased in 1938, and $900 was paid to the customer's account at the Chase Manhattan Bank after his lawyer presented a confirmation by Allianz that the foreign exchange was paid from its own sources and did not involve using the Reichsbank.[34] This, however, was most certainly a rare instance in which nonconversion worked to the customer's benefit. In contrast, the agent of a Regensburg merchant (who still had not converted to RM while this was still voluntary) was asked by Allianz to persuade the merchant to change his mind; but as the agent reported in November 1936:

Herr V. is for the moment not to be moved to transform his insurance denominated in Goldmark into Reichsmark. Rather he prefers to ask that the repurchase value of the aforementioned insurance should be paid if at all possible. According to what he says, he has to anticipate that his commercial license will soon be revoked because he is a non-Aryan and that he is compelled to consider the necessity of emigrating from Germany.

A month later, the customer himself wrote personally (as was required) to buy back his policy, pointing out that he was doing so "since I am in financial difficulty at the moment and am dependent on every penny." In receiving the Reichsmark equivalent of his policy, however, he actually lost money because of his previous failure to transform the policy into RM at a favorable rate.[35]

The case of a Nuremberg lawyer is an even more revealing illustration of how the expectations entertained at the time when a life insurance policy was taken out could be brutally disappointed by the conversion policy. In this case, the

[32] Besprechung, 2. Dez. 1938, SM, 1458/1/156, Bl. 20–6.
[33] Allianz an das RAA, 18. März 1938, BAK, B 280/1480, Bl. 22–7.
[34] AZLB, F 271147.
[35] AZLB, F 220318.

lawyer had a 50,000–gold mark policy taken out in 1925 that was to reach term in 1947. However, the policyholder chose to convert it to a paid-up policy in 1930. In early 1939, he asked for a payment in advance on the repurchase value of his policy, assuming that it would be 6,764 RM, but he received only 3,571 RM. He complained to Allianz in a letter dated April 27 and received the following reply:

If you read the addendum precisely, then you will find that the premium-free insurance sum is given, not as RM 11,364, but rather as GM 11,364 (1 GM = 10/42 USA$). The insurance sum originally was namely GM 50,000 with the provision that 1 GM = 10/42 USA$. The measure of value of the insurance, therefore, was the USA$. When this was devalued in 1933, you along with all other insured were offered the insurance at a rate of RM 4.20 for a USA$. You did not pay attention to our offer and we therefore informed you on June 7, 1934 that we will continue your insurance on a dollar basis and will measure our obligation according to the dollar rate at the time. You have accordingly also paid the supplementary premiums for the prepayment granted to you at the going dollar rate for Reichsmark. On the basis of the law of 26. August 1938 and the orders of the RAA connected with this law, the policy had to be changed into a policy denominated in Reichsmark. In accordance with the rate agreed upon with the RAA of RM 2.50 for one USA$, there was an insurance sum of RM 6,764. Naturally the advance payment granted on the 6,000 GM was transformed according to the dollar value of the Reichsmark. The prepayment is therefore now 3,571 and supplementary premiums will also be charged only for this amount.

The policyholder, however, still found the situation insupportable, since he had been making supplementary premium payments – presumably in order to qualify for prepayments in 1935 and 1937 on the basis of the original gold mark value. Now, when he desperately needed the money to pay the levy on the Jews, he was getting far less than that which the company had led him to believe was his due a short time earlier. He therefore did "not consider it permissable that the insurance be continued on another basis without my express agreement." As Allianz explained, however, their position was based on the change required by the law of August 26, 1938. At this point, the customer, who was planning to emigrate, decided to cash in not only this policy but his two others and received 10,660 RM from Allianz, which was placed in his blocked account at his bank.[36] Clearly, he felt cheated, and the new law certainly gave him good reason for such feelings. Allianz obviously was following the law and, as the correspondence shows, was prepared to give the old dollar rate until the new law was passed. However, the salient point with respect to this man's insurance would have held whether he received the money at 4.20 RM to the dollar or 2.50 RM to the dollar: any received money that was not immediately eaten up by taxes and impositions would not be at his disposal anyway, owing to the exchange regulations governing the rights of emigrants.

This leads to the second and more important aspect of the foreign exchange regulations imposed on the Jews – namely, their role as an effective barrier to

[36] AZLB, F 235862.

emigrating Jews who wished to gain access to proceeds of their insurance policy cancellations. From its inception, the National Socialist regime had been
watchful of how Jews might use insurance as a means of evading the Reich Flight
Tax and foreign exchange controls. Thus, on April 6, 1933, an informer in Hamburg notified NSDAP leadership in Munich of Jews who were transferring capital
abroad by taking out policies with the branches of foreign companies in Germany, paying for them with a single premium in RM, and then borrowing as
much as 90% of their worth abroad in foreign currency. This led to immediate
inquiries by the RAA as well as to measures aimed at plugging this gap in the
regulations. Allianz flatly insisted that it never transferred money from its holdings at home to its holdings abroad, but the Italian firm Generali admitted that
the conditions stated in its existing contracts permitted loans on policies taken
out in Germany and suggested that a new regulation might provide for payment
only in blocked marks in the case of its German customers.[37]

The exchange regulations proved increasingly complicated from the perspective of transferring insurance assets to customers living abroad when the amounts
exceeded the allowance. In early 1934, an emigrant could still take as much as
10,000 RM in cash and another 5,000 RM in securities and other forms of paper
assets out of the country. On June 23, however, the allowance was reduced to
2,000 RM. Special provision could be made for the transfer of monies for repurchase of insurance or loans against policies in cases of hardship. Special
provisions were also made for Jews emigrating to Palestine. In certain instances,
as we have remarked, one could even transfer a policy into the company's foreign
holdings. It is important to remember that the insurance business was subject to
favored treatment with respect to the foreign exchange regulations, and correspondence with customers in the earlier years of the regime suggests a measure
of confidence and flexibility with respect to the management of their assets that
soon became less relevant as the regulations tightened.[38]

An interesting illustration of this process – and of relations between the company and a Jewish customer – is provided by case of a theatrical agent who fled
Germany for Paris in 1933.[39] He ceased to pay the premiums on a 10,000-RM
policy taken out in 1928 and, after warning letters from Allianz went unan-
swered, was informed that the policy had been transformed into paid-up life
insurance but could be reinstated in its previous form if he decided to pay premiums again. In January 1934, the policyholder finally replied:

I took out a policy with you some years ago and paid the premiums for many years. In
the meantime, I have been summarily fired from my semi-public position on April 1, 1933

---

[37] See Auskunftei Kramer an die Reichsleitung der NSDAP, 6. April 1933, and the ensuing correspondence in BAK, R 3104/3.
[38] Rundschreiben 63/34 of 10. Feb. 1934 of the Reichsverband der Privatversicherung, GDV, RS/5,
and Rundschreiben 278/34 of 2. Aug. 1934, ibid., RS/6. See also Walk, *Sonderrecht*, Nr. I 409
(p. 84) and Nr. II 147 (p. 160).
[39] AZLB, S 1886079.

because of the National Movement and have been robbed of every possibility of carrying on my career in Germany. I therefore saw myself forced to leave Germany without a job and without means and to try to find the possibility of an existence in France. I present these facts initially to justify my previous silence.

He wanted to know if the policy still had any value, and was told by Allianz that it was worth 950 RM but could not be cashed in for another year. The policyholder, whose wife had remained in Germany, seems actually to have corresponded with Allianz about paying the necessary premiums and renewing the policy, finally deciding against it in July 1934 "because I have learned that according to the new legislation that, in the case of the demise of the insured, payments to Germans who have lost their profession in their homeland under the pressure of the National Socialist Revolution are not allowed to be compensated."

The legal department of Allianz responded almost immediately, assuring him that he was misinformed:

The view that under the newest German legislation the payment of an insurance obligation that has fallen due is not permitted upon the decease of a domestic person who has emigrated in connection with the German Revolution is in no way correct. On the contrary, the German currency regulation has shown wide-reaching consideration for the insurance industry and has allowed it to maintain its considerable foreign business as before. What is involved is by and large certain limitations and control measures which are chiefly intended to prevent emigrating domestic persons from being in a position to bring a substantial portion of their domestic wealth abroad without any control. What is to be prevented therefore is the flight of capital. Any reservation that one is dealing with capital flight basically and naturally does not at all exist if one is dealing with the death or the insurance payments becoming due on a policy taken out by a foreigner. In such cases there are only certain limitations with respect to the taking of the replacement value, prepayments (loans on the policy), and by clearing questions, while insurance payment obligations arising through death or the coming to term of the policy are easily permitted payment on the basis of an empowerment to make payment repeatedly given us at regular intervals.

For such payment, death was always viewed as a qualifying hardship that excluded all suspicion of capital flight; his wife would certainly get the money. Apparently, this reassured the policyholder enough to maintain the policy because, in June 1936, Allianz was again insisting that his wife would be paid in the event of his death and that the foreign exchange agency regularly gave the permission required. By this time, however, foreign exchange regulations had become tougher. Allianz informed him that payment of the policy to him abroad would depend on the "foreign exchange situation." In the following year, both the policyholder and his wife went abroad, which made them both "currency foreigners." Needless to say, they could no longer gain access to their asset unless they returned to Germany, which they happily did not do. The policy was reported to the revenue authorities in 1942 under the decree of November 25, 1941 (discussed later in this chapter), and in 1960 Allianz sent a letter to the policyholder in Paris offering him a special policy arrangement for persons over 85.

No response was received; although the compensation due was calculated, there is no evidence of what happened subsequently.

What makes this case interesting is the peculiar combination of normality and abnormality in the relationship between the company and its customer. On the one hand, the Allianz legal department clearly was genuinely interested in maintaining the policy and helping its customer to understand and deal with the government regulations. No attention whatever was paid to the political comments of the customer except to suggest to him that he underestimated the goodwill and fairness of the regulations, a belief reinforced at Allianz by the special treatment of the insurance industry with respect to currency matters. On the other hand, the policyholder himself was genuinely uncertain about what to do. He was justifiably angry at the regime that had put him into this situation and was uncertain about whether his wife should join him in exile and whether or not to continue his policy. Fortunately, he and his wife seem finally to have made the right existential decision and so were spared the terrible events of 1938 and what was to follow.

The role played by the currency and exchange regulations was thus of central importance because they effectively denied Jews the possibility of taking their insurance proceeds with them when they emigrated. Insofar as they had any money left after paying the Reich Flight Tax, the later Jewish asset tax, and other impositions, they had the choice of either leaving their money in a blocked account that could only be used in Germany – sometimes for relatives who stayed behind – or cashing in what money they had for a pittance of its worth at the gold discount bank.

The significance of foreign exchange and currency controls for the confiscation of Jewish insurance and other assets is not, however, exhausted by the regulations themselves. The organizational structures connected with these controls also played a crucial role, especially because of changes that took place in 1936–1937. In August 1936, Göring created a Foreign Exchange Investigation Bureau in Berlin, which he placed under Himmler's right-hand man in the SS, Security Police Chief Reinhard Heydrich. As a result, not only the customs investigation bureaus but also the foreign exchange and currency bureaus became subject to instructions from the more ruthless and fanatically anti-Semitic elements in the regime. One of the concrete consequences of this change was a decision taken at the end of 1936 that allowed the foreign exchange agencies to take control of the disposition of all assets of anyone suspected of capital flight, and this came to mean all Jews planning to emigrate. Despite the frictions this created between the Finance Ministry and the SS, these changes proved to be an important administrative bridge between the indirect and direct confiscation of insurance and other assets from blocked accounts. What was missing, however, was an informational bridge, and this was created by the decree of April 26, 1938, on the reporting of Jewish assets, which required all Jews with over 5,000 RM in assets to give a full and complete statement of their holdings, by category and worth, as of the date of the decree and to update it yearly. The head of the Four-Year Plan was empowered "to take measures that are necessary to secure the mobilization of the assets subject to reporting for the benefit of the German economy."[40] This meant that the Nazi authorities would now have a list of a large proportion of the policies and policy numbers owned by Jews that was provided by the Jews themselves. Thus, a substantial amount of administrative and informational machinery was in place prior to the Pogrom of November 1938, and naturally this facilitated the confiscation of Jewish assets. In the case of insurance, most confiscation remained indirect – that is, it was subsequent to monetization of the policies. By early 1939, the processes of indirect confiscation were becoming barely distinguishable from those of direct confiscation.

Whether direct or indirect, however, one must emphasize the importance of monetization in the confiscation of insurance assets, since their value was based on the payment of premiums and since both the face value and the dividends depended on collection by the insured or on his or her "behalf." This made insurance policies different from securities, which the Reich Finance Ministry permitted to be used as payment where cash was not available to pay the Reich Flight Tax, installments on the atonement tax, or fees necessary for emigration.[41] In such instances, securities were deposited to the account of the Prussian State Bank, known as the Seehandlung. Dividends could then be paid into these accounts, and the shares could also be marketed if the government chose to do so. An examination of 30,000 (or 15%) of the 200,000 Allianz shares issued before and during 1928, for example, reveals that some 761 were forcibly sold to the Seehandlung between 1939 and 1944, 686 in 1939, 54 in 1940, 12 in 1941, 7 in 1942, and 2 in 1944. The evidence from this source indicates that about 2.5% of Allianz's shares were held by Jews.[42] These shares were deposited to the account of the Seehandlung at the shareholder's bank, and Allianz paid dividends to the account and apparently continued to correspond with the original shareholders insofar as they could be located. In 1941, for example, Allianz sought to contact Heinrich Jacobi in Mannheim, who held 60 shares worth 11,880 RM (each share was worth 198 RM on the market). When the letter was returned as undeliverable, Allianz wrote to the Deutsche Bank branch in Mannheim, which had deposited his 1940 dividend, and was informed that Jacobi had been deported to an unknown address.[43] This, then, was a procedure very different from the confiscation of life insurance assets, yet in both cases the regime was profiting

---

[40] Walk, *Sonderrecht*, Nr. II 457 (p. 223), and Verordnung über die Anmeldung des Vermögens von Juden vom 26. April 1938, §5, Abs. 1, in RGBl 1938, Teil I, pp. 414–15. On the organizational measures see Frank Bajohr, *"Arisierung" in Hamburg. Die Verdrängung der jüdischen Unternehmer 1933–1945* [Hamburger Beiträge zur Sozial- und Zeitgeschichte, Bd. 35] (Hamburg, 1997), pp. 190–5; Mehl, *Reichsfinanzministerium*, pp. 24–31.

[41] Ibid., pp. 81–4.

[42] These calculations have been made from eight available books of shareholder listings by the research team at the Center for Corporate History of Allianz AG.

[43] Allianz an Deutsche Bank Mannheim, 24. Dez. 1941 and reply of 29. Dez. 1941, HADB, Filiale Mannheim, Polizeipräsident/Finanzamt, HC-I.

from assets related to Allianz and other insurance companies even though Allianz could in no way be considered to have gained from the asset's transfer. Only where Allianz (or one of its chief shareholders) was in a position to purchase Jewish-held shares directly, as we have shown in the case of real estate, could there be a private profit. Such an instance was the sale of a large block of the Allianz-controlled Berlinische Lebensversicherungs-Gesellschaft AG to the house bank of Allianz, Merck, Finck & Co. in the summer of 1939 by the private Jewish banking house of Samuel Neumann. The shares of Berlinische Leben were not traded on the open market, and Neumann had purchased the shares at the request of one of the Berlinische Leben directors. They viewed the price they received as well below the worth of the shares, which it was subsequently adjudged to be in the postwar restitution proceedings.[44]

DIRECT EXPROPRIATION OF
JEWISH LIFE INSURANCE ASSETS

The expropriation of Jewish assets was a theme with a number of variations, and it is now necessary to turn our attention to the direct confiscation of Jewish insurance assets. This had different foundations from the indirect confiscation in connection with tax and other currency and financial obligations discussed previously. The basis for direct confiscation already existed in the Law for the Repeal of Nationalization and Recognition of German Citizenship of July 14, 1933, and the accompanying Law for the Seizure of Assets of Enemies of the People and the State of the same date, which allowed the government to confiscate the assets of Communists and other designated enemies of the regime who had gone abroad.[45] The confiscation of the assets of Jews and others deprived of citizenship was centralized in the revenue office of Moabit-West, which was under the command of the chief regional revenue officer of Berlin – after February 1942, Berlin-Brandenburg. Some use of this legislation was made to confiscate Jewish assets throughout the 1930s, particularly of Jews who had emigrated and those who had aroused the ire of the regime through their activities abroad. The names of those deprived of citizenship were normally published in the official government journal (*Reichsanzeiger*), and the Gestapo then proceeded to inform the relevant banks and insurance companies that the assets in question were confiscated and were to be turned over to the financial authorities. The lists of names were also published regularly in the form of circulars sent out by the Reich Group for Insurance to its members. This meant that repurchase values were to be calculated by the insurance company and the sum transferred to the designated revenue office. In April 1939, for example, the Gestapo informed Allianz of the revocation of the citizenship of a Munich lawyer, his wife, and his four children – all of whom had emigrated to Australia – and announced that

---

[44] For this case, see WGÄ, 62 WGA 3397/51 (Peter Newman, früher Neumann).
[45] Walk, *Sonderrecht*, Nr. I 172 (p. 36) and Nr. I 177 (p. 38); Mehl, *Reichsfinanzministerium*, p. 33.

their property was confiscated. Allianz was asked to pay the repurchase value of the 10,000-RM policy, which came to 3,611.85 RM, to the revenue office in Moabit-West, from whom the company subsequently received a receipt. It is interesting to note that this policyholder had been paying premiums up until this time from his emigrant blocked account, an arrangement he had made with the company in return for the company's assurance that it would ultimately pay the proceeds of the insurance into the blocked account when the policy fell due in 1952.[46] It is indeed true that where there is life there is hope, and this was by no means the only Jewish emigrant who maintained a life insurance policy through premiums from a blocked account and apparently entertained the illusion that something might come of such an investment in the end. In October 1941, for example, the regional revenue office in Moabit-West demanded and received the repurchase value – in this case, over 60,000 RM – of an unusually high 100,000-RM life insurance policy of a denaturalized German Jew living in the United States that he had taken out with the Cologne branch office of a Swiss insurance company. He, too, had paid his premiums through his agent in Germany. In other cases, of course, the policyholder had already cancelled the policy, received the money, and placed it in his or her blocked account. In such cases, Allianz duly reported to the Gestapo that the policy had been paid and to whom.[47]

The initiative to terminate insurance policies in these cases clearly came from the Gestapo and other relevant authorities, and it is difficult to tell how much energy the companies themselves demonstrated in dealing with the lists provided by the insurance industry's peak associations. By 1938–1939, those lists were growing in size and were being augmented constantly owing to the stepped-up measures against the Jews. On September 15, 1939, the Economic Group for Private Insurance announced that it would no longer circulate the names published by the government – in order to save paper but also because the publications were losing value since they came out so late owing to the load of work at the Reich Printing Office. Member companies were now referred to the official announcements themselves.[48]

The piecemeal approach to revocation of Jewish citizenship and confiscation of Jewish property came to an end in November 1941 with the issuance of the 11th Decree of the Reich Citizenship Law of November 25, 1941. This decree had been long in preparation, the first discussions taking place in the Ministry of the Interior on January 15, 1941. Sometime in March, Hitler was engaged directly in the matter and was reported to have issued an order; but when members of the Foreign Office asked to see it, they did not receive an order bearing Hitler's signature but rather a letter from the head of the Party chancellory and the Minister of the Interior stating that "the Führer wishes purely and simply the

[46] AZLB, F 239003.
[47] AZLB, F 234839, and a policy placed at the author's disposal by the policyholder's heirs.
[48] Rundschreiben B197/39 der Wirtschaftsgruppe Privatversicherung, 15. Sept. 1939, GDV, RS/19.

withdrawal of citizenship from Jews living abroad and the confiscation of their property."[49] Apparently, there had been a disagreement as to which Jews were to fall under the decree, and Hitler had resolved the conflict in this manner. At the same time, however, the projected decree became linked with plans to deport Jews from Germany, which may help to explain the delay in its issuance. Even in early November there were objections to the draft of the decree from the Foreign Office and military authorities, who were fearful that the measure would lead other nations to seize German assets abroad in retaliation.[50]

Undoubtedly, had banks and insurance companies been consulted about the 11th Decree, they also would have expressed reservations and objections – especially with regard to section 7, which read:

All persons who are in possession of some portion of the forfeited assets or who have liabilities to it are to report the thing in their possession or the debt to the superior revenue office president in Berlin after the forfeiture goes into effect. Whoever violates this reporting obligation deliberately or through negligence, will be punished by jail for up to three months or a fine.[51]

This was nothing less than an effort to shift the responsibility for locating, identifying, and surrendering Jewish assets to the nongovernmental sector, above all to banks and insurance companies. Thus, the reporting and confiscation of Jewish assets was turned into a requirement by the 11th Decree of the Reich Citizenship Law of November 25, 1941, whose basic provisions mandated the revocation of citizenship and the confiscation of assets of all German Jews who were regularly residing abroad. By this time, of course, most of those who had not emigrated were being deported to ghettos or concentration camps in the East. Jews deported to such places were viewed as having "regular residence abroad" and were now systematically deprived of their citizenship. Indeed, the decree was directly connected with the effort to deport all Jews remaining in the Reich who had not already been deported under an order issued on November 4, 1941, mandating the transfer of all Jews not employed in plants important to the war effort. On June 1, 1943, a 13th Decree to the Reich Citizenship Law

---

[49] Vermerk über eine Besprechung im Auswärtigen Amt am 7. Nov. 1941, Bundesarchiv-Militärarchiv, RW 19/1584, Bl. 170–3. There is an excellent discussion of the decree in Hans Günther Adler, *Der verwaltete Mensch. Studien zur Deportation der Juden aus Deutschland* (Tübingen, 1974), pp. 491–545.

[50] See the Vermerk of 7. Nov. 1941, Bundesarchiv-Militärarchiv, RW 19/1584, Bl. 170–3. Most remarkable is a letter from Hans Oster, later an important member of the Resistance, of the intelligence (Abwehr) branch to the military representative in the Foreign Office, Gen. Lt. Reinecke, of Nov. 11, 1941, warning not only of setting a dangerous precedent that might lead to retaliatory actions but also, on the one hand, that there were Jews abroad working for German intelligence whose role would be endangered by the measure and, on the other, that it would complicate the punishment of Jewish former citizens for crimes if they were no longer Germans; see ibid., Bl. 168–9.

[51] RGBl, 1941, I, pp. 722–4; Adler, *Der verwaltete Mensch*, pp. 500–3.

was issued which declared that the property of all deceased Jews – whose numbers were, of course, increasing dramatically as they were being murdered – were the property of the Reich. Finally, because of the massiveness and complexity of the confiscations mandated under the 11th Decree, an effort was made to decentralize the administration of the confiscations. The regional revenue offices now became the recipients of the property and assets of the Jews in question, which meant that the collection point no longer was Moabit-West. Nevertheless, a measure of centralization continued to exist in the person of the chief regional revenue officer in Berlin-Brandenburg, who was given responsibility for the maintenance of a central registry of those affected by this decree.[52]

The November 25, 1941, decree raised serious legal and administrative problems for banks and insurance companies by shifting so much of the responsibility and initiative for searching out accounts and policies of persons living abroad. The banks complained that they could not be certain which of their account holders living abroad were Jews, especially if the names were not clearly Jewish names. Even if the bank knew that a person was a Jew, it did not necessarily know if the individual in question had not taken up some other citizenship before the official date set under the decree for losing German citizenship. Under existing laws, persons who requested a foreign citizenship automatically lost their German citizenship, and this would hold especially true for Jews who had emigrated early. There was also the question of whether an account holder living abroad was doing so temporarily or permanently. The banks were reluctant to take it upon themselves to treat the accounts in question as subject to government seizure without the express confirmation of the Reich Security Head Office (Reichssicherheitshauptamt), as required under section 8 of the decree. Otherwise, there was a danger that the reputation of German banks abroad would be damaged and also that they would be liable to lawsuits by the countries that had granted Jews citizenship. Furthermore, since the Gestapo was insistent that the persons involved not be informed of the surrender of their assets to the revenue office, the banks were barred from making the necessary investigations.[53] It is important to recognize that the persons in question were not Jews being deported or Jews whose loss of citizenship had been officially declared prior to 1941, because such actions were considered sufficient in and of themselves to assure the legality of the property confiscation; rather, they were emigrants who had sought and gained foreign citizenship. Finally, a further concern of the banks, and especially the closely regulated savings banks, was that they were required by law not to surrender monies in savings accounts without presentation of the savings account book; here, too, they wanted protection against future claims and suits. Of course, what the banks were seeking by means of the

---

[52] Walk, *Sonderrecht*, Nr. IV 261 (p. 354), Nr. IV 272 (p. 357), and Nr. IV 480 (p. 397); Mehl, *Reichsfinanzministerium*, pp. 89–98.
[53] Wirtschaftsgruppe Privates Bankgewerbe an den Reichsminister der Finanzen, 10. Jan. 1942, BAB, R 2/9172b, Bl. 62–3.

grotesque correspondence on this matter was a shifting of responsibility, both legal and financial, to the State. The government sought to provide such relief in the form of procedures under which the Reich Security Office would act expeditiously to confirm that the persons in question were held to have been German citizens on November 27 and were thus liable to property confiscation. Similarly, the government relieved savings banks of their legal obligation to require savings account books in these cases and assumed responsibility in the event of legitimate financial claims against the banks.[54] Whether the traditional business principles of equity and good faith had now been preserved, and whether those involved believed this, were of course two entirely different questions.

The considerations raised by the banks were not irrelevant to the insurance business, since there was no way of telling whether or not an insurance asset whose repurchase value was ordered to be deposited at the regional revenue office belonged to a Jew who had acquired foreign citizenship prior to November 27, 1941. As far as the material at my disposal is concerned, there is no evidence that the insurance companies raised this particular issue with the same intensity as the banks; the evidence does show that they requested such information from the Gestapo, however. Legal cases did arise with respect to insurance confiscations, but these were against Swiss companies operating in Germany and against Swiss reinsurers of German companies. Jewish emigrants took Swiss companies to U.S. court, before and during the war, charging that the Swiss companies had no right to turn their assets over to the German government. Ironically, American courts rejected such arguments; they pointed out that, under international law, branches of a foreign company were subject to the laws and regulations of the country in which they operated. In the words of the Supreme Court of the State of New York, "as for the very obnoxious and offensive character of the German decrees, the court is obliged to hold that governing law is no less controlling because it is bad law."[55]

Even more ironically, Swiss courts took a more critical stance toward these insurance companies. There was a considerable body of opinion that held that it was also true under international law that the central headquarters of a company was ultimately responsible for the obligations of its branches and, more generally, that the anti-Jewish legislation of the Third Reich violated the Swiss *ordre public*. Swiss courts decided in favor of Jewish plaintiffs in instances where the policies were payable either in Switzerland or Germany and where a Swiss reinsurance company was the guarantor of a policy taken with a German customer. Naturally, the German authorities sought to assert their position in

[54] Rundschreiben Nr. 73 vom 21. Mai 1942 und Rundschreiben Nr. 81 vom 5. Juni 1942 der Wirtschaftsgruppe Privates Bankgewerbe, ibid., Bl. 105–10; RWM an RFM, 12. Feb. 1942, ibid., Bl. 84.

[55] Decisions of the Supreme Court of the State of New York, New York County, Kleve et al. v. Baseler Lebens-Versicherungs-Gesellschaft in Basel, Dec. 24, 1943, 182 Misc. 776, 45 N.Y.S. 2d 882. See also Bloch et al. v. Basler Lebens-Versicherungs-Gesellschaft in Basel, June 24, 1947, 73 N.Y.S. 2d 523.

negotiations with the Swiss, and the ever-compromising Hans Koenig of Schweizerische Lebensversicherungs- und Rentenanstalt promised to present the German position to his colleagues for use in future court cases. It is revealing, however, that the Reich Justice Ministry in November 1943 argued against appealing recent unwelcome decisions before higher courts, considering it too risky given the attitude in certain Swiss legal circles.[56]

At home, of course, the German government did not have to worry about such formalities. Even so, the authors of the 11th Decree had – as in the case of the November 9, 1938, Pogrom and the decrees issued in connection with it – given little heed to the implications for banks and insurance companies. Under section 7 of the 11th Decree, banks and insurance companies had six months to report accounts or policies liable to confiscation, after which time penalties were to come into force and the companies would also be liable for interest payments. In 1941, there were 85 German-owned life insurance companies in Germany with premium income of over 1 million RM. They had portfolios that included 4.875 million large life policies with a value of 18.9 billion RM and 24.5 million small life policies with a value of 8.9 billion RM. They had also issued group risk insurance policies involving 1.3 million persons with a value of 18.9 billion RM and other group insurance policies involving 6.2 million persons with a value of 3 billion RM. Additionally, there were four Swiss-owned companies operating in Germany with 80,600 large life policies worth 648 million RM and 108,000 small life policies with a value of 84.5 million RM. They had also issued group policies involving 4,600 persons which were worth 14.7 million RM. Finally, the insurance industry also serviced burial funds for 1.3 million members and pension funds for 152,000 persons.[57] Combing through these policies was a massive operation, especially at a time when the number of those working in the insurance industry was being reduced to serve the war effort. With the first deadline approaching, the Economic Group for Life Insurance informed its members in late February 1942 that it had asked the RAA to do something about the impossible situation, and the RAA stepped in more than once in an effort to deal with the problem. Thus, at a meeting on May 20, 1942, a representative of the RAA informed his colleagues in the Finance Ministry – above all Regierungsrat Böttcher, president of the revenue office in Berlin-Brandenburg – that the effort to comply was "difficult and time consuming" and that the companies were having problems in defining the legal status of the Reich in replacing the original

---

[56] See RJM an RAA, 12. Nov. 1943, SM, 1458/11/229, Bl. 29–30. This volume contains extensive correspondence on the case made against Swiss Re, which had guaranteed a Jewish policy issued by Der Anker Allgemeine Versicherungs-AG in Vienna. For the discussion among Swiss authorities, German authorities, and insurers concerning cases involving insurance policies issued by Vita Lebensversicherungs-AG giving double places of payment and the claims of emigrants in general and the role of Koenig, see BAR, E 2001 (E) 2/582.

[57] *Zusammengefaßter Geschäftsbericht über die Tätigkeit des Reichsaufsichtsamtes für Privatversicherung 1939 bis 1945* [Veröffentlichungen des Bundesaufsichtsamtes für das Versicherungs- und Bausparwesen, Sonderheft 3] (Berlin, 1955), pp. 64, 80.

owners of the life insurance policies. Insofar as the delay of the deadline was concerned, the RFM had already taken action on behalf of the banking sector in this respect and now chose a similar solution for the insurance industry – namely, periodically suspending the legal penalties for not meeting the deadline without changing the deadline itself. At the same time, the RAA, using its virtually dictatorial powers under section 81 of the Reich Insurance Law as revised in 1934, agreed to regulate the legal status of the policies in ways favorable to the Reich. The insurance companies also intended to be as accommodating as possible to the Reich. Thus, while having the right to deduct insurance premiums due from the repurchase price, they automatically set December 31, 1941, as the date on which all policies falling under the 11th Decree were officially terminated. In other words, discovery of policies after that date would not lead to further deductions of premiums. Furthermore, the insurance companies agreed to pay a repurchase price on annuities and pensions even though they did not carry repurchase provisions.[58]

At a meeting between representatives of the RAA, the Finance Ministry, and the insurance industry on May 29, 1942, the RAA was able to report a half-year suspension of the penalties for noncompliance. They also informed insurers that the Reich would continue the property liability and other forms of insurance on property taken from Jews under the 11th Decree until disposition of the properties was determined. No one, of course, objected to continued collection of premiums, but the companies did complain that half a year was not enough time to comb through the policies, especially those that were paid up and contained little tell-tale correspondence. Böttcher suggested that the companies report to him on their progress shortly before the next deadline came up, and he would then show consideration for justified petitions for exemption from penalties: "the most important thing is that individual companies can demonstrate at any time that they have not violated their obligation to do their duty." A particularly grotesque aspect of the situation was that the Reich, after all, had in a certain sense replaced the Jewish policyholder as a customer itself. This became clear when it was pointed out that the Reich did not have to take advantage of the general cancellation date of December 31, 1941, but could opt instead to continue paying premiums on the policy if this seemed advantageous – as might indeed be the case with a policy nearing its term. The companies agreed to pay interest on the repurchase values they held until surrendered effective January 1, 1942 (in the case of policies still in force), and as of July 1, 1942 (in the case of paid-up policies). They would also pay to the Reich 75% of the maintained coverage for confiscated pensions.[59] These provisions did in fact receive codification by President Amend of the RAA in an order to the insurance companies

---

[58] Rundschreiben vom 23. Feb. 1942, GDV, RS/30, and Niederschrift, Sitzung am 15. Mai 1942 im Reichsfinanzministerium, BAB, R 2/9172b, Bl. 91–4.

[59] Niederschrift, Sitzung am 29. Mai 1942 im RAA; RAA Rundschreiben vom 29. Juli 1942, ibid., Bl. 123–4, 127.

of June 29, under which insurance policies on Jewish assets forfeited to the Reich were to remain in force until the Reich decided to terminate them. Concerning life insurance policies, Amend provided that "the Reich can continue individual policies by further payment of the scheduled premiums, if it asks for the continuation of already reported insurance policies within three months after the appearance of this writing and by renewal requests up to the reporting date of the end of the quarter following on the proximate quarter."[60]

Despite such opportunities, the government found itself having to continue to grant de facto (if not de jure) extensions to the insurance companies on into 1943 and 1944, and the situation was made more complicated by still other factors. The Gestapo was too stretched in its duties and obligations to provide confirmations under section 8 in a timely manner, and insurance companies were authorized to send the superior revenue office in Berlin-Brandenburg a copy of its inquiry with the Gestapo in order to demonstrate that the inquiry had been made and that a response would be forthcoming. Probably the most serious complication, however, resulted from the Allied air forces, whose bombing missions were destroying insurance policies in ways that were making it difficult for the companies to service their regular customers, let alone Böttcher's office in Berlin-Brandenburg.[61] Under such circumstances, the insurance companies could hardly have been expected to show an excess of enthusiasm and diligence with respect to the 11th Decree. There is no visible evidence that this had anything to do with resistance or sympathy for those being dispossessed so much as the sheer absurdity of being asked to comb through millions of policies under such conditions and for such purposes. Where the task was easy, however, it was carried out. Thus, on May 19, 1942, Allianz reminded its branches of the responsibility to report the pensions and other claims of former Jewish employees as required under the 11th Decree by the next deadline – and also of the penalties involved in failure to do so.[62]

What kind of evidence does Allianz's collection of insurance policies provide with respect to implementation of the 11th Decree? The first point to be made is that most of the policies paid out directly to authorities of the Third Reich were paid out before the decree – in the form of cancellations that went directly to the revenue offices at the request of the customer or into blocked accounts that had to be dealt with by the banks, not the insurers. A second point is that the task of discovering Jewish assets often remained in the hands of the authorities. A good illustration is provided by a Frankfurt policyholder who had taken out a 20-year policy in 1926 for 60,000 RM. This was turned into a premium-free policy at the request of the policyholder at the end of 1938. Subsequently, the

---

[60] Schreiben Amend, 29. Juli 1942, BAK, B 280/1880, Bl. 4.
[61] On the problems of the Gestapo, see Rundschreiben Wirtschaftsgruppe Lebens- und Krankenversicherung, 14. April 1943, GDV, RS/30, which also contains numerous Rundschreiben concerning loss of insurance policies.
[62] Rundschreiben of 19. Mai 1942 signed by Lux and Seyffert, FHA, O 1.4.2/31.

Cover of the life-insurance file of the customer whose policy was shown on p. 242. After the insured had emigrated to Beirut in 1935, the policy was transformed into a paid-up policy free of premiums at a value of 1,880 RM. This amount was to be paid out when the contract expired on January 1, 1946. On March 30, 1943, Allianz Leben reported about this policy to the president of the revenue office of Berlin-Brandenburg in accordance with the 11th Decree of the Reich Citizenship Law. The sum insured was not requested by the office probably because the citizenship of the customer had remained unclear. In 1952, Allianz Leben paid out the policy to the insured.

policyholder emigrated to England, but it was only on July 6, 1943, that the revenue office informed Allianz that the policy fell under the 11th Decree and asked for the repurchase value; Allianz then paid 29,218 RM to the revenue office on July 27. The significant point is that this was an obviously Jewish policy (because of its conversion at the end of 1938) but nevertheless was not found or reported by Allianz; rather, it was cashed in at the demand of the revenue office.[63] Matters went much more "smoothly" in the case of deported Jews, since there was a procedure in place involving fairly rapid acquisition of the monies collected from repurchase. For example, Samuel and Nora Hellmann of Würzburg, before their deportation, were forced to sign over their life insurance policy with Berlinische Lebensversicherungs-Gesellschaft and two other life insurance policies to the Bavarian district office of the Reich Association of Jews in Germany. As was so often the case once the war started, Jewish organizations were used to collect the assets of the deported, thus making confiscation easier and more efficient. Within two weeks after their departure for Theresienstadt at the end of July 1942, the money from the repurchase had been collected, a total of 3,388 RM, more than enough to cover the "home purchase contract" of 2,500 RM for their domicile in Theresienstadt. It was a measure of the bureaucratic scrupulousness of Berlinische Lebensversicherungsgesellschaft that the company had insisted on Gestapo permission before turning the money over to the Reich Association.[64]

A third point is that there was often a considerable time gap between the issuance of the decree and the identification and transfer of insurance assets. A good illustration was a Jewish businessman from Baden who wrote to Allianz in April 1940 asking advice about changing his 25-year 10,000-GM policy, taken out in 1925, into a paid-up policy so that "later, when the time of my emigration comes into prospect, to consider possibly repurchasing it." Allianz responded within ten days and urged him to maintain the policy in force if possible. In late January 1941, they sent him another letter urging him to pay his premium, and in February 1941 Allianz tried to locate him through the Residents' Registration Office – only to discover that "he and his family were deported to an unknown destination on October 23, 1940." Nevertheless, Allianz went through all the formalities connected with the policy, writing to his old address in March 1941 asking for payment of his premium plus interest, and then sending the standard form letter on April cancelling the policy and subsequently transforming it into a paid-up policy worth 5,298 RM to be paid either on the death of the insured or on April 1, 1950. Unknown to Allianz, as postwar correspondence with the policyholder's daughter showed, the policyholder and his wife were killed in 1942. Needless to say, this would not have mattered at all given the 11th Decree: the policy was easily identifiable as belonging to a Jew, and it contained correspondence demonstrating that he was "regular resident abroad" well before November 27, 1941. Nevertheless, it was not until February 8, 1943, that Allianz

[63] HessHStA, Wiedergutmachungsakten, Wsb-566.
[64] Adler, *Der verwaltete Mensch*, pp. 832–4.

wrote once again to the Residents' Registration Office about the policyholder's whereabouts. They reported the repurchase value of the policy to the president of the revenue office in Berlin-Brandenburg a month later and finally sent the money to the office for the Administration of Jewish and Enemy-of-the-Reich Property of the Mannheim revenue office on November 12, 1943.[65]

Once again, there is no reason to construe the leisurely pace of these expropriations as "resistance." The available evidence suggests that Allianz employees duly reported Jewish policies qualifying under the 11th Decree as they found them. Moreover, the revenue offices did not always proceed with alacrity, so that months would sometimes pass between reporting to Berlin-Brandenburg and collection by the regional revenue office. What is unsettling is the matter-of-fact quality to the entire business and the sense one has of a brutal depersonalization of the life insurance business – the inclination to treat the Nazi State as some kind of natural successor to the former Jewish policyholder. This is exemplified not only by the discussions in the RAA and RFM about perpetuating certain policies in order to maximize their return to the government – which also meant maximizing their return to the company – but in more concrete ways, too. This can be seen in the case of a 44-year-old Jewish men's clothing manufacturer from Munich. In April 1942, Allianz was still sending him bills for premiums due on the 25-year 10,000-RM policy he had taken out in 1931. The policyholder had paid premiums in 1940. In 1942, however, Allianz received a reply from the policyholder's legal adviser or consultant that read: "I am required to inform you that Herr Israel G. was assigned to emigrant transport from Munich already on November 20, 1941 and that he, as every other evacuated person, was provided with a declaration under which his property will be declared forfeit in favor of the German Reich." The consultant suggested that Allianz write to the regional revenue office in Munich and ask if they wished to pay the premiums. This was promptly done by the relevant office of Allianz, which asked whether the revenue office wished to pay the premiums or dissolve the policy and collect the repurchase value. The correspondence continued with the revenue office asking for more details about the policy. In the meantime, another premium became due and the bill was sent to the address of Herr G. In July 1942, however, Allianz wrote again to the revenue office, pointing out that a decision had to be made because the policy was losing value through the failure to pay premiums. In this instance, as was indeed probably the case most of the time, the revenue office decided it had a greater interest in securing cash than in playing successor to the policyholder. It cancelled the policy and requested the repurchase value of 2,820.10 RM.[66]

Obviously, those responsible for dealing with this case at Allianz were quite ready and prepared to replace one "customer" with another – in this case, a customer who had paid premiums for almost a decade with one who had despoiled and probably murdered him – while the revenue office assumed the role of "trustee" for the deported Jew who had taken out the insurance. It was another

---

[65] AZLB, F 235590.
[66] AZLB, F 274892. Policyholder treated as anonymous by author.

legal charade, not as complicated and opaque as the one put on in connection with insurance "payments" for the November 1938 Pogrom but well in keeping with the deviousness and disingenuousness that characterized the systematic robbery of the Jews. For reasons already explained in connection with the events of 1938, the number of German Jewish life insurance policies subject to the 11th Decree probably was relatively small, and even a company (e.g., Isar) with many such policies probably lost most of its Jewish customers in the course of 1938–1939 through policy cancellations. The difficulty in finding the Jewish policies subject to direct confiscation was indicative of this.

In one exceptional case, however, there was a substantial number of easily identifiable Jewish insurance policies: the Austrian Jewish policies in the portfolio of Deutscher Ring Österreichische Lebensversicherung-AG. The number was large because Phönix Life was much favored by Jews, and the policies were more easily identifiable because of the efficiency and speed with which the Austrians identified Jewish assets after the Anschluß.[67] Furthermore, the policies taken over from Phönix Life in Austria had certain special qualities deriving from the arrangements made when the concern collapsed in 1936. These policies were subject to special restrictions, which made borrowing on them (or their cancellation) either very difficult or impossible.

Even before the 11th Decree, the revenue offices in Vienna and in Moabit-West had a substantial number of Jewish-owned Phönix Life policies on their hands as security for payment of taxes and especially for payment of the Jewish assets tax of 1938. Moabit-West officials were particularly irked by the special conditions attached to the policies and sought some means of monetizing them rapidly; in the summer of 1941 they were negotiating with the Zentralkasse Norddeutscher Volksbanken about selling the Phönix Life portfolio it had been building up in order to obtain cash. No agreement had been reached when the 11th Decree came into force and substantially increased the number and value of the policies subject to confiscation. Deutscher Ring, however, argued that the policies should be held in its own portfolio until they came to term, and it sought to block the sale of the portfolio. Its views were shared by the RAA, which felt that there was no rush since the policies were guaranteed by the entire industry. However, Regierungsrat Böttcher of the Berlin-Brandenburg office was not at all taken with this delaying tactic; as he pointed out in December 1942:

The death rate of the Jews in question has, as experience has shown, increased greatly. Among the many emigrated Jews it will hardly or never be possible to provide evidence for death. As a consequence, the purchaser or cessionary of the policies will have regularly to await the due dates of the policy and must therefore renounce profit from [the policyholder's] early death, which will therefore bring Deutscher Ring a special considerable profit. But a purchaser of the policies has tied up his substantial means for a long period and therefore performs a valuable service as option holder.[68]

---

[67] See the important discussion of the Austrian "model" in Friedlander, *Nazi Germany and the Jews,* Ch. 8.

[68] Denkschrift Böttcher, 1. Dez. 1942, BAB, R 2/13531, Bl. 41–4.

Böttcher, who certainly had a good idea of what was happening to the Jews, wanted the Phönix Life portfolio treated as a type of security; he justified this stance in terms of the guarantee given for them by the insurance firms at the time of the Phönix Life collapse in 1936. Securities can be bought and sold and, from his point of view, it was more important to get cash for the Reich immediately by selling the portfolio than to allow Deutscher Ring to enrich itself by holding on to the assets until they matured. The issue was finally settled when Deutscher Ring agreed to pay 20 million RM to the Finance Ministry in return for being allowed to absorb the bonds that had been guaranteeing the policies. In this way, both the Finance Ministry and the insurance company were able to secure for themselves the benefits of these policies. In August 1944, Deutscher Ring Hamburg paid 1 million RM to the revenue office in Vienna-Niederdonau, while Deutscher Ring Vienna paid 5 million RM. In addition to this down payment of 6 million RM, the other insurance companies in Austria reported paying 1.4–1.5 RM under the 11th Decree to the finance authorities in repurchase value on confiscated Jewish life insurance assets.[69]

As in Austria, so in the "Protectorate of Bohemia and Moravia"; the latecomers in the business of confiscating Jewish assets were able to proceed with greater thoroughness and brutality than had been the case in the Old Reich. As early as April 29, 1939, the Interior Ministry issued instructions that Jewish insurance policyholders were forbidden from changing the terms of their policies and could only receive insurance payments into blocked accounts of a selected group of banks. Although Jews were allowed to receive a certain amount of payment from insurance companies and to withdraw a certain amount of money from their accounts without permission, the regulations were progressively tightened.[70]

The discussion here has concentrated on the confiscation of life insurance assets, but it is important to bear in mind that the Jews were increasingly denied the right to insurance itself. This was most explicit and direct in the case of private health insurance, where the branch group for private health insurance had petitioned the Economics Ministry as early as 1935 to exclude Jewish customers. By this time, numerous health insurance companies had already written the exclusion of Jews into their general insurance conditions or had instructed their agents not to sign up Jews. As the branch group pointed out,

the companies were not only compelled to take these measures for reasons of world view, but also because the Jewish insured turned out to be the subjectively worst risks and

---

[69] A fuller documentation of this case and its postwar aftermath is to be found in ÖStA-AdR, BMF, VA, Karton 329, Akte 80/1. See especially Österreichische Lebensversicherung-AG Deutscher Ring an das Staatsamt für Finanzen, Versicherungsaufsichtsbehörde, 18. Juni 1945, with appended Aktennotiz, and the Verband der Versicherungsanstalten Österreichs an das Bundesministerium für Finanzen, Versicherungsaufsichtsbehörde, 2. März 1946.

[70] See Tomas Jelinek, "Insurance in the Nazi Occupied Czech Lands: Preliminary Findings," in J. D. Bindenagel (ed.), *Washington Conference on Holocaust-Era Assets November 30–December 3, 1998, Proceedings* (Washington, D.C., 1999), pp. 612–15.

grossly exploited the community of insured to the detriment of the insured of German origin. One could not therefore expect the Aryan insured to belong to a community of risk with the Jewish insured.[71]

The RWM had turned down the group's exclusionary request on the grounds that subordinate bodies were not to undertake such measures unless and until legislative measures had been enacted. In November 1938, however, the branch group was emboldened – by the recent decree on the exclusion of Jews from German economic life – to renew their request because the decree had excluded Jews from participation in cooperatives effective January 1, 1939. The similarity between cooperatives and insurance mutuals was so great, it was argued, that one could also exclude Jews from health insurance. Such an interpretation was all the more necessary because many insurance companies did not have the right to terminate the policies of members after three or five years, so that the membership of Jews who had joined before 1933 could often not be terminated.[72]

The "problem" in question exercised the corrupt talents of Franz Schlegelberger of the Justice Ministry, who had distinguished himself by perverting civil law in the service of the regime.[73] He did not think the issue fell under the decree excluding Jews from economic life, but he also did not think that a special law was necessary. The desired goal could be attained instead by measures of the RAA. If one accepted the proposition (as Schlegelberger obviously did) that Jews were the worst possible risk then the distinction between mutuals and corporations was irrelevant, since both were communities of risk and thus were entitled to protect themselves. They could do so by agreeing not to insure Jews and by terminating the policies of Jews, insofar as their statutes allowed this. Where the statutes did not allow termination of Jewish policies, however, the RAA could step in and require that Jews – as especially severe risks – be required to pay exceptionally large premiums.[74] In the end, Amend used his sweeping powers to settle the matter in an RAA decree of April 13, 1940, under which the private health insurance companies were ordered to change their business plans in such a way that "Jews could neither take out insurance nor be insured."[75] All policies held by Jews were to be terminated as of April 30, 1940, and no further premiums were to be collected from them; premiums already paid for the period after that date were to be returned. Non-Jewish relations of Jews could continue their insurance. The decree did not encompass special Jewish health insurance organizations. Thus, the five-year effort by private providers of health insurance to have a legal basis for excluding their Jewish customers had finally met with success.

[71] Fachgruppe Private Krankenversicherung an den Reichswirtschaftsminister, 14. Nov. 1938, SM, 1458/1/98, Bl. 19–20.

[72] Ibid.

[73] See Michael Förster, *Jurist im Dienst des Unrechts: Leben und Werk des ehemaligen Staatssekretärs im Reichsjustizministerium, Franz Schlegelberger, 1876–1970* (Berlin, 1995).

[74] Schlegelberger an den Reichswirtschaftsminister, 31. Jan. 1939, SM, 1458/1/98, Bl. 57–8.

[75] Amend an die privaten Krankenversicherungsunternehmungen, 13. April 1940, BAB, R 22/2017, Bl. 112.

No similar effort seems to have been made with respect to other forms of insurance, but the exclusion of Jews from economic life effectively meant a steady reduction of Jewish customers. Since Jewish lawyers and other professionals could no longer practice, they ceased to take out liability insurance. In the case of doctors, the government took away their right to treat all but Jewish patients effective October 1, 1938, under the 4th Decree of the Reich Citizenship Law.[76] Allianz reacted to this action by instructing that all professional liability insurance for Jewish doctors was to terminate on that date. There was to be no reimbursement for premiums paid for the year, but premiums paid in installments and due after September 30, 1938, were not to be billed. It was made clear that only professional liability insurance policies – not other forms of liability insurance, covered in combined liability policies – were to be terminated and that premiums were to be reduced accordingly.[77] The ultimate worth of the little insurance Jews held may be gathered from the fact that all insurance claim payments to Jews exceeding 500 RM had to be reported to the revenue offices. Here, as elsewhere, the likely beneficiary of Jewish policies would be the Nazi State.[78]

The decision about insuring Jews appears to have rested with the companies themselves, and it is depressing to record that Allianz took action very rapidly after the November Pogrom. At its expanded meeting of directors on November 29 that was held in connection with the recent anti-Jewish demonstrations, the matter of insuring Jews was taken up; on December 8, guidelines were issued (under the signatures of General Director Heß and Director Haase) barring any new insurance contracts with Jews.[79] Although an exception had been planned for automobile insurance, the withdrawal on December 3 of the right of Jews to drive automobiles eliminated the need to offer Jews such insurance. At the same time, the exclusion of the Jews from German economic life meant that insurance policies of Jewish enterprises would immediately terminate if they were closed down; the insurance would continue in cases where the enterprises were operated under Aryan owners. Finally, the various branches of Allianz were allowed to decide for themselves as to what further measures they might take with regard to Jewish insurance policies – for example, negotiating with Jews on early termination of their jewelry insurance or reducing the amounts of their accident insurance. There is, unfortunately, scant evidence as to how this directive was implemented. Curiously, Wiener Allianz waited until December 1941 before instructing that all Jewish requests for insurance be refused in principle. The only exceptions would be for government requests for insurance of Jewish property, and such cases were to be referred to the management.[80]

---

[76] RGBl, 1938, I, p. 969–70.
[77] The giving up of liability insurance by Jewish lawyers was already noted at the Vorstandssitzung of 10. Mai 1935, FHA, S 17.2/4. For the liability insurance for physicians, see the Rundschreiben of 25. Aug. 1938, FHA, AZ 7.1/9.
[78] Direktionsverfügungen der Wiener Allianz vom 24. März und 5. Mai 1939, AZ Wien.
[79] Rundschreiben, Nr. 37/38 betr. Jüdisches Versicherungsgeschäft, 8. Dez. 1938, FHA, AZ 5.1/5.
[80] Direktionsverfügung der Wiener Allianz, 12. Dez. 1941, AZ Wien.

In concluding this sorry tale, it is important to record that the government did indeed insure what had once been Jewish property – namely, the transport of jewels, platinum, gold, silver, pearls, and other valuable items from the municipal pawn shops throughout the Reich to the central bureau for pawn shops in Berlin, where the Jews had been forced to deposit them. In circular notes of early February 1940, the central bureau provided precise instructions regarding the manner in which the expected value of these items should be determined as well as their packaging and modes of transport. Hence, in each case the insurer would know precisely what was being sent and its value. The cost of the insurance would be carried by the central bureau itself, which had concluded a general insurance policy for the transportation of these valuables with a single company: Allianz.[81]

[81] Städtische Pfandleiheanstalt Abt. III/Zentralstelle an alle Pfandleiheanstalten, 3. Feb. 1940; Rundschreiben (eingetroffen in Frankfurt am 19. Feb. 1940) an alle gemeindlichen Pfandanstalten im Reich betr. Verwertung der aus jüdischem Besitz stammenden Edelmetalle, Jewelen und Perlen, Institut für Stadtgeschichte, Frankfurt a.M., Bestand 812/109. I am grateful to Ralf Banken for bringing these documents to my attention.

7

Allianz, Munich Re, and the
Insurance Business in "Greater Germany"

ALLIANZ IN 1940

WHEN the Allianz concern celebrated its fiftieth anniversary on January 13, 1940, Germany was once again at war, and thus a certain sobriety was in order despite the victories of 1939. The concern presented itself to its various constituencies in a two-volume Festschrift: the first, an informative and useful history of the company by Wilhelm Kisch entitled "Fifty Years Allianz. A Contribution to the History of German Private Insurance"; the second, a picture chronicle of the concern that was a balance of photos of major executives in times past and present, leading representatives of the concern's external service, festive events, various headquarters buildings, vacation homes belonging to the concern, and sporting events.[1] Certainly the goal was to present Allianz and the role of private insurance in the most favorable light possible, but Kisch's narrative was not heavy-handed and was reasonably free of hyperbole. Not surprisingly, it contained a number of positive references to the National Socialist regime and its values; the photo volume showed what can only be termed a requisite number of pictures of uniformed employees and Swastika flags, so that one was aware who held power in Germany and of the Allianz concern's "devotion."

The film Allianz produced for the occasion, *Allianz 1890–1940*,[2] which can justly be called a high-quality cinematic self-presentation of the concern, was similarly constructed. Slightly less than half the film is devoted to the business side of Allianz, which is presented as a story of growth and success. The landmarks were Allianz's founding in 1890, the fusions of 1921 and the appointment of Schmitt as general director, the merger with Stuttgarter in 1927 and the onset of the "concern" idea, and 1929 – when Allianz sprang into the breach after the collapse of Favag. The acquisition of Elementar-Phönix in 1938 (discussed later in this chapter) was presented as a new phase of growth in the concern's history. Much attention was also paid to the expanding number of fields of insurance, employees, branches, and new and modern office buildings, with pictures of the ongoing construction in the Mohrenstraße areas as well as a model of the projected Runder Platz. It is only in connection with Allianz's emphasis

---

[1] Kisch, *Fünfzig Jahre Allianz.*
[2] *Allianz 1890–1940*, FHA, Filmarchiv, 80.F.001.

on damage prevention and in the portion of the film showing the Allianz laboratories for materials testing that mention is made of the economic ideas of National Socialism, which are otherwise blessedly absent from the film. Indeed, the Nazi role in Allianz is placed very much in the background: a portrait of Hitler distantly visible on the wall of an office, a flag-raising ceremony on the roof of the Cologne office building that almost seems to be speeded up and lasts barely more than a few seconds, and a glimpse of the work brigade marching in the background (and then briefly in the foreground) of the fall sporting event at Mariendorf in Berlin, along with a great many Swastika flags in a row at the same occasion.

Still, the film could be interpreted as a sustained effort to satisfy DAF values of a model factory. There is a great deal of emphasis on the well-lighted, comfortable offices – especially at the newer Cologne headquarters, but also elsewhere – and on the various social measures taken at the company branches, including canteens, libraries, and recreation areas. Indeed, more than half of the film is devoted to various vacation homes of Allianz and their idyllic qualities, where "Allianzers" and their families are shown enjoying the facilities, and to the sports facilities and sporting events of the concern. The emphasis on gymnastics and other sports – involving female and male employees both – is extraordinary; it is notable that the presentation of Allianz's major executives was quite limited. There was a picture of Allianz's "Big Four" (Schmitt, Heß, Hilgard, and Schloeßmann). The only speech in the entire film is that of the "old sportsman" Hans Heß, an impressive figure and energetic speaker, who was most convincing in his argument for the importance of sport for body and soul and relating the emphasis on sports to the healthy competitive spirit at Allianz – as reflected in the competition for the Spear Thrower and other prizes. This was presented as the essence of the "Allianz spirit." In general, Allianz is certainly shown to be serving the nation and ready to meet every new danger that requires implementation of the "insurance idea," propagated across the length and breadth of the land by a well-trained external service. But it is also presented as a world unto itself, and the Allianz flag and emblem are so omnipresent that they do indeed appear to be more the symbols of sovereignty (that Speer objected to in the design proposed for the Runde Platz building) than a company logo. The film gives the impression of a corporate culture with familial and organic pretensions – displaying itself in ways that certainly satisfied DAF desiderata, primarily because DAF desiderata were quite compatible with Allianz's own corporate self-understanding.

It would be a mistake to think that the opportunism of Allianz's leadership in the Third Reich was "pure," that is, totally cynical and hypocritical, and that the linguistic turn of people like Hilgard was completely artificial and unnatural. Opportunism requires an environment with at least some familiar and even congenial elements if it is to succeed in achieving the goal of being acceptable to those whose favor is being courted. Germany had never been a land of "shareholder values," and even today corporations like Allianz stress their responsibility to their "stakeholders," that is, a broader community encompassing employees,

General Director Heß making a speech to employees assembled at the jubilee meeting to celebrate the 50th anniversary of Allianz, May 29, 1940.

customers, and the public at large as well as those holding shares.[3] Nevertheless, German corporate culture, thanks to the long struggle with both dirigisme and Socialist tendencies, was well practiced in legitimizing the quest for profit in a vocabulary of service to State and community. There was a conceptual affinity between the language used in corporate strategies of self-defense before 1933 and that used when dealing with the National Socialist regime. The "ideals" and "values" of the regime were, after all, themselves products of the "nationalist" and "socialist" movements that had played so powerful a role in German history, and though the National Socialists certainly were more threatening and unpredictable than anything the German insurance business had previously encountered, its leaders were already familiar with talking about their function as "trustees" for "risk communities" and working to serve the "national economy" and "national community." They said little or nothing about their right to demand a profit for their companies and a dividend for their shareholders in

---

[3] See, for example, "Die Allianz trägt auch soziale Verantwortung," an interview with Finance Director Paul Achleitner in the *Allianz Journal,* 2/2000, pp. 21–2. These differences in national corporate cultures and the language they employ are important because they are grounded in different political, legal, and business traditions. German corporations taking over American companies, for example, try to adapt to the notion of being "good corporate citizens."

exchange for the risk of capital.[4] Kisch, for example, did not treat the existence of private insurance as self-legitimating; he fully accepted the principle of State direction of the economy and the right of the State to abolish private insurance. If the State wisely maintained the private insurance sector, it was because the latter had demonstrated that it put community interests before its own and because private enterprise was better able to respond flexibly to new demands and requirements, since its management faced a higher degree of accountability than did the civil servants who would run a state monopoly.[5]

The leadership of Allianz was well aware that one major criticism of such a huge concern was that it was so large that it might lose coherence and suffer the attendant costs, a danger Allianz sought to meet through its policy of combining centralization and decentralization. As noted previously, the 1930 takeover of Favag marked a pause in Allianz's growth. This was to usher in a period of consolidation and rationalization, interrupted in 1938–1939 by new acquisitions in Austria and what had been Czechoslovakia. As part of this period of consolidation, a major restructuring took place in 1939 that was designed to simplify the concern's organization and to complete the absorption of companies created or brought into Allianz in 1930. At the shareholders meeting on June 13, 1940, the old name – Allianz Versicherungs-Aktiengesellschaft – was restored; "und Stuttgarter Verein" was dropped. As Chart II shows, Neue Frankfurter, Vereinigte Berlinische und Preußische Lebensversicherungs-AG, Karlsruher Lebensversicherungsbank, and Hammonia – along with its sister firm Providentia – were severally joined in a community of interest with a single company, now named Frankfurter Versicherungs-AG, that became a concern within Allianz under the Frankfurt regional headquarters. A similar arrangement was made for the recently acquired Elementar-Phönix, which was renamed Wiener Allianz Versicherungs-AG and made identical with the newly established regional headquarters in Vienna. At the same time, the branch in Danzig was downgraded, while Königsberg was made the center of a new regional headquarters for East Prussia and Memel.[6]

Consolidation in the concern was accompanied by an equally important restructuring of the relationship between Allianz and Munich Re. The two concerns still formally operated under a 50-year joint contract of 1921, under which Munich Re agreed to center its German direct insurance interests in Allianz – receiving in return 25% of Allianz's capital stock and 50% of its reinsurance business.[7] Munich Re then participated in the massive development of Allianz,

---

[4] See the refreshing criticism of this obfuscating language by Arps, who felt that it prevented rather than helped the public to understand the nature of capitalist enterprise; Arps, *Durch unruhige Zeiten,* Bd. 1, p. 187, Bd. 2, p. 29.

[5] Kisch, *Fünfzig Jahre Allianz,* pp. 186–8, 223–6.

[6] Ibid., pp. 93f., 108–12, and Allianz Geschäftsbericht 1939, pp. 11f., FHA. See also the Aktennotiz of Schmitt, 11. Aug. 1939, MR, A 1/20. The shares of Neue Frankfurter, Hammonia, and Providentia were divided between Allianz and Munich Re.

[7] See Chapter 1, p. 10.

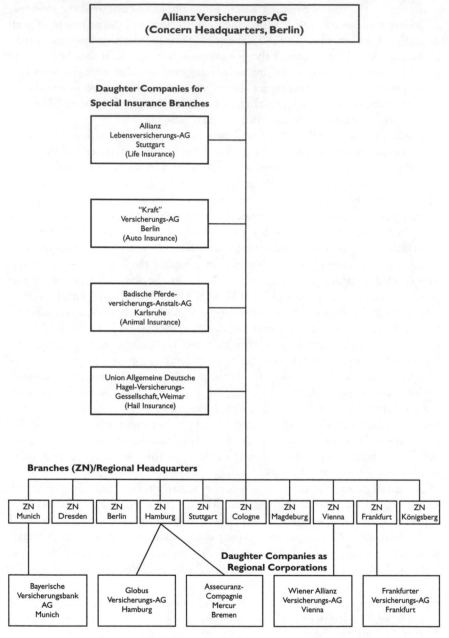

Chart II. Organization of the Allianz Concern in 1940. *Source:* Kisch, *Fünfzig Jahre Allianz.*

with many of the fusions indeed depending on the former's liquid assets. In the process, however, Munich Re's quota of Allianz's reinsurance business dropped from 50% to 37.5%. The reality was that Allianz's growth and premium income had taken on entirely different dimensions, from 50 million marks in 1913 to 500 million, if one included the Karlsruher and Berlinische companies, in 1938. At the same time, Munich Re's profits had also risen dramatically, so that there were grounds to question whether it was justifiable for Allianz, with its huge reserves, to pay so much to Munich Re for reinsurance. Munich Re may have founded and dominated Allianz for a substantial period, but the days of junior partnership were long past and the continued dependence expressed in the 1921 contract provisions on reinsurance was proving bothersome. It was time, Schmitt told the Munich Re supervisory board at a meeting on April 16, 1940, to revise the contract.[8]

Everyone, of course, recognized that Munich Re could stand on its own rights and could morally justify such a course by its past and continuing contributions to Allianz's success. In Schmitt's view, however, such a posture made little practical sense. It would produce an atmosphere of tension that would increase over time and undermine the relationship, which was to be formally up for renewal in 1970 but which obviously could not be thought of in such formal terms. At the same time, it would be difficult (if not impossible) for Munich Re to secure its stance by gaining sufficient control of Allianz's capital shares. Most importantly, however, this seemed to be the time to settle the differences between the two concerns and to found their future relationship not only on holding one another's shares and business arrangements but "above all on mutual friendship and trust." It was essential "that the younger generation feels the carrying on of their *common* endeavor to be a personal obligation."[9]

The situation was probably more difficult than Schmitt was indicating. Important evidence for such tension is that Allianz was much concerned about a potential effort by Munich Re to control its shares. This was revealed when Allianz began to liquidate its real estate companies under RAA pressure that it hold all its real estate in its own name. The one exception was Freia Grundstücksverwertungs-AG, to which Allianz actually planned to transfer a property in 1939 before this met with objections from the RAA. Allianz representatives responded that the concern needed to keep Freia alive since, as they confessed, its real purpose was to administer a large block of Allianz shares. Director Ernst Rausche

justified this by pointing out that Allianz must unconditionally prevent that further Allianz shares are bought up by the Munich Re because it would then get a majority holding. Allianz does not want to place itself completely in the hands of the Munich Re. The sale of the shares on the stock market exchange is impossible because there is no interest in

[8] 251. Sitzung des Aufsichtsrats, 16. April 1940, MR, A 3.4/5.
[9] Ibid.

shares at the present time. Even small-scale sales would therefore lead to a drop in the quotation.[10]

This argument led the RAA to relent in its pressure, although it expected Allianz to dissolve the Freia company eventually. Allianz, however, continued to hold the company throughout the war.[11]

The significance of this silent control of its own shares through Freia may be measured by a brief review of the shareholding in Allianz. At the shareholders meeting in May 1938, the number of shareholders voting totalled 529 – 12 by themselves personally, 517 through an assigned representative. A total of 19 persons (i.e., 12 individual shareholders and 7 proxies acting for corporations and individuals) voted some 27.3 million RM in shares. The importance of Munich Re was made evident by the fact that it held 17.3 million RM shares, which were voted on its behalf by Schmitt, who additionally held and voted 173,400 RM shares on his own account. Kisskalt held 122,700 RM in shares personally. The next largest corporate block of votes cast was that of Merck, Finck & Co. August von Finck, who headed the bank and was also presiding as chairman of the Allianz supervisory board, voted 2,625,000 RM in shares for the bank and a few hundred thousand RM in shares for small shareholding individuals and companies. The banking house of Sal. Oppenheim jun. & Cie. in Cologne held over 600,000 RM in shares, Dresdner Bank 400,000 RM, Bayerische Vereinsbank 150,000 RM, and Henckel & Cie. GmbH 240,000 RM in shares. The Deutsche Bank did not hold its shares as a corporation, but leading directors and persons associated with the bank held substantial amounts of shares, possibly exceeding that of Dresdner Bank. The Stuttgart chemical industrialist August Brüggemann was a significant individual shareholder with 408,600 RM in shares. The various Allianz and Allianz Leben directors held modest but significant amounts in shares, after which came a substantial group of shareholders – many of them women and often wives and widows of prominent businessmen – who held shares ranging from 1,500 RM to 15,000 RM in value.[12]

The total share capital of Allianz was 60 million RM, and it is thus obvious that many shares were not present at the shareholders meeting and were not voted – among them the 7,436,100 RM in shares held by the Freia.[13] What the described distribution of shares demonstrates, however, is that Allianz was vulnerable to a Munich Re takeover unless it continued to control a substantial number of its shares through Freia. However, given the history of the two concerns and their common interests, the goal was now to prevent the development

[10] Niederschrift, 28. Feb. 1939, BAB, R 3104/20513, Bl. 191.
[11] RAA an den Vorstand der Allianz, 25. März 1939, ibid., Bl. 197. The Allianz business reports for 1940–1945 continue to mention that Allianz had 100% of the 300,000 RM in Freia shares.
[12] Verzeichnis der in der 48. ordentlichen Hauptversammlung der Allianz und Stuttgarter Verein Versicherungs-Aktien-Gesellschaft in Berlin am 31. Mai 1938 erschienenen Aktionäre und Aktionäre-Vertreter, BAB, R 3104/20522, Bl. 77–85.
[13] Vermerk, undated but from 1940, ibid., Bl. 60.

of an adversarial relationship. Schmitt – whose personal history was largely bound up with the growth of Allianz and who was a newcomer to the general directorship of Munich Re – favored a revised joint contract over an unfriendly attempt at domination that was probably doomed to failure and would undermine a long-standing and mutually beneficial relationship. Hence Schmitt, Heß, and other members of both concerns negotiated a new contract whose formal terms were intended to continue until 1990 and beyond if neither party objected. Finally signed on November 11, 1940, the contract began with a remarkable preface that traced the history of the relationship and argued that the ultimate proof of its correctness was to be found in the fact that Allianz had emerged as the greatest German direct insurer and that Munich Re was the most important reinsurance enterprise in the world. (Actually, in 1939 Swiss Re was the largest reinsurer in the world.[14]) It was now their purpose to restructure the old collaboration, "which has become a proven partnership," to satisfy changed conditions and "to anchor it in an unchangeable manner for all times."[15] Thus, section 1 of the contract obligated the two corporations "to support one another in every way and mutually promote the interests of one another along with their own." This was to be especially the case in times where one might be in difficulty; the firms were expected to come to each other's aid – without any legal obligation to do so – insofar as it did not involve doing serious damage to their own interests.

From a practical standpoint, the most important revision was probably contained in section 2, which declared that shareholding in one another's enterprises was to be based on the principle of parity. At the moment, Munich Re held 30% of Allianz's shares whereas Allianz held only 7.5% of Munich Re's shares. Munich Re was not to increase its Allianz holdings above 30% without permission, and Allianz was allowed to increase its Munich Re holdings to 30% – provided it did so gradually and without disturbing the stock market quotations. Insofar as there was a disparity between the shareholdings of the two concerns, Munich Re obligated itself not to vote its additional shares at the shareholders meetings if Allianz so requested.

As was the case with the 1921 contract, provisions were made for personal and institutional reinforcement of the relationship, but these were now strengthened in significant ways. Thus, each supervisory board was to include the other firm's chairman of the board of managers; the goal was for each supervisory board to include at least three members from the other firm's board. They were expected to support each other at their respective shareholders meetings and, of great importance, three quarters of the members of the smaller committees that made the major decisions on the supervisory boards were to be persons who were members of both supervisory boards. At the same time, a new institution was created in the form of a "joint managerial council," composed of the chairmen of the boards of management of the two corporations, two members of each

[14] *Assecuranz-Compass, Internationales Jahrbuch für Versicherungswesen* 47 (1939), pp. 364, 1055.
[15] Gemeinschaftsvertrag, 11. Nov. 1940, MR, A 3.4/5.

of the boards, and previous chairmen of the boards who might still be serving on the supervisory boards. The new body was to serve a purely advisory function and was assigned the task of promoting cooperation, especially in business conducted abroad.

The division of labor between the two corporations was to remain as before: Allianz doing direct business in Germany and Munich Re refraining from direct insurance in those areas where Allianz was active, which for all intents and purposes was every branch of insurance of any significance. Munich Re was allowed to have minority holdings in other companies, however, which was essential given that it reinsured a variety of other companies. The two corporations were to promote one another's business as much as possible, and Allianz was to refrain from competing with Munich Re and from signing contracts to which the latter objected or concerning which it had reservations. Furthermore, section 6 of the agreement gave Munich Re a considerable participation in Allianz business: 30% of all business done by Allianz or its daughter companies at home and abroad, 50% of the foreign business that Allianz might take over from its foreign daughter companies, and 50% of the shares of Allianz in domestic and foreign daughter companies. In the first two categories, participation was to take the form of reinsurance contracts on the business in question. In the case of establishing new companies or capital participations, Allianz was to offer Munich Re 30% of the shares, and Munich Re was to offer Allianz 50% of the shares of new companies or participations in which it might engage. However, arrangements that Munich Re might make with friendly companies abroad were not covered by these conditions. Finally, the contract provided for arbitration provisions and for the silent renewal of the contract for fifty years after 1990 unless one of the corporations announced a desire to terminate the contract by 1985. In the event that the contract was to be terminated by one of the parties or to effectively end for some other unforeseen reason, Allianz was obligated to compensate Munich Re the price of its lost reinsurance portfolio – a provision more important than it might appear, since it was intended to compensate Munich Re for surrendering its right to acquire 50% of Allianz's shares – and both corporations could insist on the sale of their respective shares to designated purchasers.

The significance of this contract and relationship, which was maintained until very recently (albeit with changes to meet new circumstances), was neatly stated by Kisskalt at the Munich Re supervisory board meeting in April 1940 where the draft contract was considered. The establishment of parity in shareholding rights meant that Munich Re "would be changed from the mother to the sister, that there would be two independent corporations bound together by the joint contract and common interests."[16] They did not and would not constitute a single concern, which would have required a single supervisory board and board of management at the very top of the organization or of a holding company. While the connection between the two corporations since 1921 had caused some bad

---

[16]   251. Sitzung des Aufsichtsrats der Münchener Rück, 16. April 1940, ibid.

feeling in the industry at the time of Allianz's major acquisitions, the basic relationship was hardly a secret, since everyone knew that they were shareholders in one another's corporations and that they had supervisory board members in common. Nevertheless, in January 1941 it was thought wise to supplement section 2 with a clause that, in the interest of Munich Re's other business relations, the acquisition of more than 10% of its shares by Allianz was to be treated confidentially, with the shares placed in portfolios of daughter companies that were not in the insurance business.[17] The advantages clearly outweighed the disadvantages for both sides, and this was to be all the more the case when Germany was expanding abroad. While wartime obviously reduced business with Germany's enemies, foreign business with Germany's allies and with neutrals would increase in importance, as would acquisitions there and in the occupied areas. Thus, in January 1941, another change was made under which the Munich Re would also have to offer Allianz participation in new acquisitions abroad for daughter companies "which perhaps should have to be disguised for political reasons."[18]

What these arrangements also make clear is that the historian of Allianz must not neglect the history and role of Munich Re, especially for the years 1938–1945 when the two corporations expanded in tandem. They were, taken together, a truly formidable economic power. Also, one should not forget that Allianz Leben had been a party to the relationship between the Allianz and Munich Re since 1928, when a syndicate contract was concluded that gave each of the two last-named corporations more than a quarter of the Allianz Leben shares and also gave Munich Re 25% of Allianz Leben's reinsurance business. At the shareholders meeting in 1942, Allianz held 6,168,200 RM's worth of voted Allianz Leben shares, while Munich Re held 6,151,400 RM. The total value of the shares voted was 13,992,400 RM out of a total capital share value of 20 million RM. The only other shareholders with significant amounts to vote were banks and bankers as well as individuals with substantial holdings – for example, Schloeßmann, who owned 162,000 RM in shares.[19]

All three corporations stood far above their next leading competitors at the outbreak of the war. Thus, among the 81 insurers of property, accidents, and liability in 1939, Allianz took in 217.9 million RM in premiums; coming next were Kraft (a daughter company of Allianz), with 50.4 million RM in premiums, Nordstern, with 48.9 million RM, and Gerling, with 44.9 million RM. Neue Frankfurter followed with 39.2 million RM in premiums, but it, too, was a member of the Allianz concern – as was Bayerische Versicherungsbank, which ranked eighth with 23.9 million RM. The other companies in the top ten were Aachener und Münchener (30.9 million RM), Albingia (25.2 million RM), Agrippina (23.7 million RM), and Magdeburger Feuerversicherung (22.5 million RM). In the case

---

[17] For par. 2, section 2, see Briefwechsel 4./16. Jan. 1941, ibid.

[18] Schreiben der Münchener Rück vom 4. Jan. 1941, ibid.

[19] Syndikatsvertrag, 25. Juni 1928, MR, A 3.4/6; Verzeichnis der in der ordentlichen Hauptversammlung der Allianz Lebensversicherungs-Aktiengesellschaft in Berlin am 24. September 1942 erschienen Aktionäre und Aktionäre-Vertreter, BAB, R 3104/20486, Bl. 136–8.

Wilhelm Kisskalt (1873–1958), general director of Munich Re 1922–1937 and member of the supervisory board of Allianz 1922–1945, about 1940.

of reinsurance, there were 21 companies with premiums above a million Reichsmark; Munich Re ranked first with 210.1 million RM in premiums, followed by Kölnische Rückversicherungs-Gesellschaft with 45.5 million RM, Frankona Rück- und Mitversicherungs-Gesellschaft (39.1 million RM), Bayerische Rückversicherung AG (31.7 million RM), and Gerling-Konzern (22.4 million RM). Among the 74 private life insurance companies with over a million in premiums listed, two were far ahead of the pack: Allianz Leben, with 232 million RM in premiums, and Volksfürsorge, with 99.9 million RM. The latter was listed as a private company because it was organized as a corporation (AG). It was followed by Victoria (66.4 million RM), Gerling (50.4 million RM), Deutscher Herold Volks- und Lebensversicherungs-AG (46.9 million RM), Deutscher Ring (45.7 million

RM), Karlsruher Leben (41.6 million RM), Alte Leipziger (37.9 million RM), Gothaer Leben (37.2 million RM), Vorsorge Lebensversicherugs-AG (33.3 million RM), and Berlinische Leben (32.8 million RM). Since both Karlsruher and Berlinische belonged to Allianz, the receipts of the concern in life insurance policies was even stronger than the place assigned Allianz Leben would suggest.[20]

At the same time, the life insurance rankings – where Volksfürsorge is a strong second and Deutscher Ring is among the top companies – points to the existence of serious competitors from the ranks of the DAF companies, whose successes (above all, those of the Volksfürsorge) produced serious concern at Allianz Leben. Thus, in a report of March 5, 1940, General Director Schloeßmann – who, along with his staff, had been following the growing competition from the publicly chartered companies – came to disturbing conclusions. In the period 1934–1938, the number of policies at Volksfürsorge increased 144% while the number at Allianz Leben increased only 44%. Fixed capital investment increased 110% at Volksfürsorge and 100% at the publicly chartered companies, but only 67% at Allianz Leben. Company costs for new business in 1938 at Volksfürsorge were 30.9% and 33.5% at the publicly chartered companies; they were 51% at Allianz Leben. Once behind Victoria and Gerling, Volksfürsorge was now well ahead of them and, most serious of all, was competing with Allianz Leben in large policies by offering lower premiums. Schloeßmann and his colleagues concluded that the Volksfürsorge advantage could not be attributed to its propaganda and instrumental use of its DAF connections. Rather, it must lie in lower costs, not in internal administration (where it had far more policies to handle than Allianz Leben and thus inevitably had higher costs) but rather in the costs of external service – that is, in the acquisition of new customers. It is not without irony that the general director of Volksfürsorge, Diedrich Pollmann, came from the middle management of Allianz. Along with its nazification, which included the integration of many former Socialist and Christian trade unionists into the Nazi fold, the company developed an extraordinary dynamism and used its every advantage, including access to film facilities for its effective advertising. At the same time, it cut costs, offered lower premiums, and was obviously an increasingly troublesome competitor to Allianz Leben in precisely those areas where the latter had previously been most triumphant.[21]

ALLIANZ AND "GREATER GERMANY": EXPANSION INTO AUSTRIA AND THE SUDETENLAND

This was not the only realm in which DAF insurance companies were to prove a dangerous competitor, as demonstrated by developments following the Anschluß (annexation) of Austria on March 12, 1938. The Anschluß, it should be

---

[20] Anlage b, f, and 6 to Anlage 4 of the draft of a report to be sent for commentary to insurance leaders by Hilgard on April 6, 1941, intended for the RWM and dealing with the problem of competition in the industry, FHA, S 17.4/6.

[21] See Schloeßmann's letter of March 5, 1940, and its appended reports by his staff, FHA, B 1.3.1/20, and Böhle, "Die Volksfürsorge Lebensversicherungs-AG im 'Dritten Reich'," pp. 64–91.

noted, took place shortly after Braß's highly controversial speech of February 25, 1938, to the Reich Association of Private Insurers in which – to the great irritation of Hilgard and leaders of the industry – he seemed to concede that many of the charges against the private insurance industry were correct and called for reforms. It was also coincident with some of the most severe attacks on the private insurance business by the *Schwarze Korps* and the efforts mounted by Schwede-Coburg, Hans Goebbels, and Amend to nationalize the insurance business. It was inevitable that the substantial ambitions of German insurers, both public and private, would be intertwined with their internecine conflicts. Schwede-Coburg swung into action as soon as he could, asking in early May 1938 for an interview with Gauleiter Josef Bürckel, the Reich Commissar for the Reunification of Austria with the German Reich.[22] He was anxious to learn of decisions being taken regarding insurance in Austria and to influence them. It does not appear that Bürckel was able to fit Schwede-Coburg into his schedule, but either he or his chief aide, Oberregierungsrat Kratz, met with Thiele of Rudolf Heß's staff in Munich on May 24 – a meeting at which the Party's interest in the insurance question was made clear. An agreement was reached that Bürckel's office was to conduct an investigation of the state of Austrian insurance, after which the NSDAP in Munich would be informed of the results. Thiele made a point of the fact that Schwede-Coburg, whom he described as the "leader of the Reich Group for Insurance," intended to bring about the nationalization of the insurance industry and was negotiating toward this end with Ministerial Director Lange of the RWM. He urged that Bürckel's office get in touch with Lange, and also warned that "the strictest secrecy is necessary so that the private insurance companies do not get premature information. An especially strong opponent of the plan is the previous Reich Economics Minister Schmied [sic!] who is Chairman of the Board of the Munich Reinsurance Company."[23]

As might be expected, Hilgard – the actual leader of the Reich Group – was anything but inactive. He had already made contact with Lange at the end of March and, in a good illustration of his close connections with the RWM, actually drafted instructions for Lange to send to Hilgard, as leader of the Reich Group, setting up a committee to examine the condition of the Austrian insurance business, both private and publicly chartered. The committee was to be kept as small as possible and to include a representative of the Austrian insurers. Until it reported in, no actions were to be taken with respect to the reorganization of the Austrian insurance business. When Hilgard appointed a committee whose majority consisted of persons from the private insurance field, Hans Goebbels – who was acting as deputy for Schwede-Coburg's Reich Group for

[22] Schwede-Coburg an Bürckel, 3. Mai 1938, ÖStA-AdR, Bürckel/Materie, Karton 94, Akte 2170/o. Bürckel had held a similar position after the population of the Saar area voted to join the Reich in 1935. On Bürckel, see Gerhard Paul, "Josef Bürckel – Der rote Gauleiter," in Ronald Smelser, Enrico Syring, & Rainer Zitelmann (eds.), *Die braune Elite II. 21 weitere biographische Skizzen* (Darmstadt, 1993), pp. 51–65.

[23] Aktennotiz, 25. Mai 1938, ÖStA-AdR, Bürckel/Materie, Karton 94, Akte 2170/o.

the publicly chartered companies – claimed that he had been double-crossed because Hilgard had promised a smaller committee and also parity between the groups. He warned that, if Hilgard failed to act in good faith, then the publicly chartered companies would refuse to do anything more through the Reich Group and would instead deal directly with the RWM. Hilgard responded by sending Funk a copy of Goebbels's letter, pointing out that it was not consonant with the leadership principle on which the organization of the economy was based, and refusing to put up with Goebbels's tone. The management of the insurance industry problem thus served to intensify the war between Hilgard and Schwede-Coburg, who (Hilgard constantly argued) had neither the competence nor, as an active Gauleiter, the time to properly deal with insurance questions.[24]

Nevertheless, the commission as constituted went to work with the approval of the RWM; by summer, it turned up with fifteen reports on the Austrian insurance business. At the same time, insurance companies in the Old Reich were not permitted to set up their offices in Austria until at least October 10, 1938, a regulation not limited to insurance but rather part of a decree of April 14, 1938, aimed at protecting the Austrian economy from being subjected to an "economic invasion" in which the stronger German business enterprises would simply overwhelm their weaker Austrian counterparts. In his dealings with the RWM, Hilgard claimed to be uncertain as to what the implications of this temporary freeze against German companies unlicensed to operate in Austria would be for obligatory or preexisting insurance relationships in the Reich (e.g., hunting insurance, automobile accident insurance, and insurance of vehicles at the Hermann-Göring-Werke in Linz). Hilgard was as cautious as he was shrewd, and he was anxious to play the honest broker and assure the head of the Austrian insurance organization, Hans Sittenberger, that he was concerned to prevent unlicensed German companies from illicitly trying to drum up business in Austria. The Reich Group offered its services, since the Germans obviously wished to avoid having such matters show up in the courts. At the same time, there were practical problems to be solved, and Hilgard was successful in getting Sittenberger to urge Bürckel's office to have existing contracts – certain types of group insurance and the insurance of large companies like the Hermann-Göring-Werke – settled between the Austrian organization and the Reich Group in a way that would give the Austrian companies some portion of the business in question while allowing the Old Reich insurance companies to extend this business into Austria.[25]

Indeed, it did not take long for Sittenberger to find Hilgard possibly more sympathetic to Austrian insurance interests than the NSDAP headquarters in Munich. Having contemplated what the Austrian companies had to offer the Party and its member organizations from the standpoint of both coverage and cost, NSDAP treasurer Schwarz told Bürckel in late June 1938 that he could not

---

[24] Hilgard an Gottschick, 31. März 1938, Entwurf Hilgard an Funk, 18. Mai 1938, Goebbels an Hilgard, 15. Mai 1938, and Vermerk RWM, Juni 1938, SM, 1458/2/200, Bl. 3–5, 48–51.

[25] Hilgard an RWM und Sittenberger, 31. Mai 1938; Sittenberger an Kratz, 21. und 25. Mai 1938, ÖStA-AdR, Bürckel/Materie, Karton 94, Akte 2170/0.

give Austrian companies exclusive insurance rights to Party insurance in Austria. He was willing to give them 10% of some insurance business of the Party and urged that Sittenberger be sent to negotiate with Amend, who was still handling Party insurance matters. However, when these negotiations finally took place on September 15, 1938, Amend was more generous. The chief reason was undoubtedly that the lion's share of the business in question was given to "Austrian" insurance companies that already were under the control of companies and concerns from the Old Reich.[26]

Thus, one of those present was Hans Schmidt-Polex, the former deputy director of Bayerische Versicherungsbank who had become general director of Elementar-Phönix, whose name would soon change to Wiener Allianz. While there were temporary regulations against the licensing of firms in the Old Reich to operate in Austria, there were no barriers to the acquisition of Austrian firms by German ones. Elementar-Phönix had been owned since 1936 by a consortium composed of the Munich Re, the Italian Assicurazioni Generali, and Creditanstalt; the company had been struggling to make a profit under General Director Eberhard von Reininghaus since the debacle of Phönix Life. From the perspective of Munich Re, the Anschluß with Austria provided an opportunity to conduct an "Anschluß" of its own by giving Allianz a dominant role in the company and either subordinating or driving out the Italians. Thus, at a meeting on May 23, 1938, in Venice with the Generali leadership – President Edgardo Morpurgo, General Director Michele Sulfina, and Central Director Camillo Gentilli, who represented Generali in Phönix's administrative council – General Director Schmitt and Director Walther Meuschel of Munich Re announced that the problems of Elementar-Phönix, whose shares had suffered a reduced real value because of the schilling's overvaluation and which was expected to continue to suffer business losses, could best be solved by collaboration with Allianz and the latter's placing "of an industrious man in the leadership who knows the methods commonly employed in Germany and can bring them to fruition and that the Allianz then deliver its name, leadership, and responsibility, so that there will be a relationship similar to that of the Bayerische Versicherungsbank ...."[27] The big difference, however, was that the latter company made a profit, while Phönix was in bad shape. Schmitt pointed out that something could be made of Elementar-Phönix, whose name he claimed a willingness to retain, if it had the support of Allianz and Allianz Leben and if it was spared competition from Allianz in Austria and other areas where Elementar-Phönix was active. If Generali wished to remain a participant then it could do so, provided Allianz assumed the leadership. Alternatively, Generali could be bought out and the company divided between Munich Re and Allianz. Schmitt also suggested a variety of combinations that would keep the Creditanstalt involved, something he knew the Italians wanted. Generali raised no objection to this proposal or to Allianz

[26] Schwarz an Bürckel, 24. Juni 1938, and Aktenvermerk über die am 15. Sept. 1938 in München im Amt für Versicherungswesen der NSDAP-Reichsleitung stattgehabte [sic] Besprechung, ibid.
[27] Aktennotiz, Venedig, 23. Mai 1938, MR, A 2.13/46.

becoming the leading participant in Elementar-Phönix, but insisted that it had made a heavy investment. It did not want to lose money and hence was more interested in participating as a reinsurer of Elementar-Phönix – in its Austrian and Czech business, and also in the Old Reich – than as a shareholder. It was, after all, an insurance company and not a bank. When Morpurgo suggested that the organization that Generali had built up in Austria should be taken into account in calculating the compensation due Generali, the Germans dismissed the idea, pointing out that the organization of Elementar-Phönix in Austria was largely Jewish and had already "cleared out."

The fact was that Morpurgo was himself Jewish, as was a good deal of the leadership of both the leading Italian companies – Generali and the Riunione Adriatica di Sicurtà (RAS) – which were products of the enterprising Jewish community of Trieste that had assumed a very important position as insurers in Central, Eastern, and Southeastern Europe. We will show that the leadership of Allianz and Munich Re was by no means averse to working with their Italian-Jewish counterparts where it did not cause unpleasant difficulties, but it made little sense for the Italians to hang on in the Austrian Elementar-Phönix or in Austrian companies more generally. Morpurgo informed Schmitt on June 9 that Generali had decided to sell its entire holding in Phönix, so that the majority group would have greater freedom of action, and also agreed to the appointment of Hans Schmitt-Polex as general director. Generali also agreed to the alienation of its shares in Polish and Romanian companies held by Phönix but received a percentage of Phönix's reinsurance business in Yugoslavia and Czechoslovakia as well as in Austria. Its desire to procure such business in the Old Reich, however, was denied.[28]

Manifestly, Generali would have preferred to hold on to its position in Phönix but was compelled to yield to the situation created by the new constellation of political and economic forces in Austria. There is no evidence that the affair was damaging to the relations between Munich Re and Generali and or that it in any way prejudiced their substantial future collaboration. Indeed, in 1939–1940 Allianz and Munich Re agreed to let Generali become a third shareholder in their Milan-based Italian firm La Pace.[29] An equally friendly settlement about Austrian shares in Italian hands was reached between Munich Re and the RAS at a meeting in Trieste in March 1939, where the latter agreed to sell shares that had given it an "eternal" right to a portion of Elementar-Phönix's direct and indirect business in return for modest compensation. Among those present on the Italian side were the former President of the RAS, Arnoldo Frigessi di Rattalma; he was Jewish and had been forced to leave his position by the racial laws

---

[28] Morpurgo an Schmitt, 9. Juni 1938; Generali an Münchener Rück, 28. Juni 1938; Vertrag, 6. Juli 1938, ibid. See also the fine account of the Allianz takeover in Roloff & Mosser, *Wiener Allianz*, pp. 240–7.

[29] On La Pace, see the documents in MR, A 2.8/32. The three companies continued to work together into 1944, and Generali looked after the interests of the firm after the German shares were liquidated at the end of the war. See especially: Aktennote Schmitt, 25. Mai 1939; Aktennote, 19./21. Nov. 1940; Aktennote, 20./23. April 1944; Aktennote von Reininghaus, 3./6. Mai 1948.

introduced in Italy in late 1938, but he continued to play a major role in RAS affairs. He also was to maintain an excellent personal and social relationship with
at least two of the Munich Re leaders present, Schmitt and Alois Alzheimer –
the latter a participant in Hitler's Munich putsch of 1923, albeit as a 22-year-old
member of the Free Corps Oberland. Nevertheless, he did not become a Party
member until May 1933, when he and Kisskalt came to the conclusion that this
would be in the interests of Munich Re. His relations with Frigessi and his general attitudes suggest that he was anything but a true believer.[30] Frigessi also
had excellent working relations with his successor as President of the RAS, Ful-
vio de Suvich, and the concern's managing director, Enrico Marchesano, both
of whom were present at the meeting. The "Anschluß" had promoted a measure
of restructuring in a still very much intact axis in the insurance business – above
all, the reinsurance business – between Germany and Italy.[31]

Nonetheless, the takeover of Elementar-Phönix by Allianz and Munich Re
was as complete as it could be, and it cannot be said that the Austrians were
treated with equal friendliness. Thus, the Creditanstalt was actually compelled
by the German government to sell its shares in Elementar-Phönix and other enterprises, and the chief Austrian shareholder was thus eliminated. At the end of
October and beginning of November 1938, Schmitt met with Heß, Hilgard, and
others to discuss policy toward Elementar-Phönix, which was to be ruled jointly
by Allianz and Munich Re with the goal of making it profitable. The new management was to run Elementar-Phönix "like a branch of Allianz" and was to
build up the direct business, while Munich Re was to control the indirect business. In the end it was unified with the Vienna branch of Allianz.[32]

Indeed, it was not long before the very name "Phönix" was eliminated and
replaced by "Wiener Allianz." As Schmidt-Polex pointed out to the special general assembly that met on December 28, 1938, the effort to maintain the name
"Allgemeine Versicherungs-Gesellschaft Phönix" for reasons of tradition and in
the hope that the public would distinguish it from the life insurance branch had
been fairly successful with customers. Nevertheless, the name continued to be a

---

[30] Alzheimer had a so-called *Dauerausweis*, which was a special permit giving him the right to attend reunions of the participants in the Hitler putsch, but he claims to have attended only the first
of these in 1933. See his interrogation of July 17, 1947, NA, RG 260, OMGUS, FINAD, 2/56/1.
Also, see Schmitt an SS-Obergruppenführer Karl Wolff, 5. Juni 1940, BAB, ehem. BDC, SL 62,
Bl. 79f.; on Alzheimer's membership in the Party in May 1933, see Schreiben an Gratama, 6. Nov.
1945, MR, D/2.

[31] On the meeting in Trieste of March 6, 1939, see MR, A 2.13/46. Much can be learned about the
Italian insurance scene and relations with the Germans from the remarkable papers of Arnoldo
Frigessi di Rattalma in the Archives of the Banca Commerciale Italiana in Milan. On the warm
relations between Frigessi and his Munich Re colleagues, see for example the postcard with greet-
ings to Frigessi from a vacation spot in Hungary of Sept. 21, 1942, signed by Schmitt and Director
Mattfeld, BCI, NL Frigessi, cart. 80, fasz. 1. As late as June 9, 1943, Alzheimer, who seems to
have paid visits to Frigessi in Cortina d'Ampezzo with his wife, thanked Frigessi for the friendly
reception he had recently received in Trieste and the opportunity to discuss business matters; see
Alzheimer to Frigessi, June 9, 1943, ibid., cart. 62, fasz. 5.

[32] Aktennote Schmitt, 2. Nov. 1938, MR, A 2.13/46.

liability and had become something of a "slogan" among the Austrians. The last straw, apparently, was a picture of the Elementar-Phönix building in the *Deutsche Volksblatt* with the name of the company in hebraic-style lettering.[33] Politics and "race" also determined the personnel changes. Although von Reininghaus had some Jewish ancestry, political rather than racial motives were responsible for his departure as general director: he (along with a number of others) were removed from office by the authorities right after the Anschluß because of their prior connections with the collapse of Phönix Life. Although released from custody, he was later to be charged with a variety of crimes and misdemeanors in connection with his work at Phönix Life; such harrassment was apparently intended to intimidate prominent members of the Austrian authoritarian corporatist State that ruled Austria prior to the annexation. The Munich Re, however, continued to value his services, providing him with an inconspicuous position in its Munich offices where he became what he himself described as a "travelling uncle," negotiating reinsurance contracts for Munich Re in Western and Southern Europe.[34]

Von Reininghaus was a special case, an internationally respected figure who would be safe if he got out of the brutal atmosphere in Vienna and could be sent travelling from Munich. The dismissal of Jews in Austria, however, was imposed with special vehemence, and the insurance business – where Jews played an especially important role – was severely affected. All Jews lost their positions effective June 30, 1938, and were placed on leave for the requisite month allowed after notice had been given. They were, however, given only 40% of normal severance pay. Nevertheless, as in Germany, there was a certain differentiation in the "processing" – to use the brutal term employed by Schmidt-Polex – of Jewish employee terminations. Thus, Georg Schlesinger, the former general director who had remained on as a consultant to the executive committee after leaving office in 1936, was given a full year's consultancy fee and actually managed to receive it in Hungary by March 1939 through the company offices. He and his wife were able to escape to South America, from whence he was summoned back to his old position after the war, and "as a faithful Austrian, who had suffered from homesickness the entire time in Chile, happily agreed."[35] Employees who had worked for the Elementar-Phönix a long time received a letter of appreciation and sometimes a letter of recommendation rather than the usual summary form letter of dismissal, and the company also gave special financial help to long-serving employees who wished to emigrate or were in particularly dire straits. In one peculiar instance, a Jewish female employee was given her full severance pay

---

[33] See his remarks at the Außerordentliche Generalversammlung vom 28. Nov. 1938 and to the Verwaltungsrat am 19. Jan. 1939, AZ Wien.

[34] On Reininghaus, see Gertrude Enderle-Burcel (ed.), *Christlich-Ständisch-Autoritär. Mandatare im Ständestaat 1934–1938. Biographisches Handbuch der Mitglieder des Staatsrates, Bundeskulturrates, Bundeswirtschaftsrates und Länderrates sowie des Bundestages* (Wien, 1991), pp. 196f. He was a prominent member of the Bundeswirtschaftsrat. There is a substantial compilation of materials on him by Martin Herzog in MR, D/8. On von Reininghaus's arrangements with Munich Re, see Fey to Frigessi, July 7, 1938, BCI, NL Frigessi, cart. 68, fasz. 1.

[35] Aktennote von Reininghaus, 25. März/5. April 1947, FHA, S 17.14/78.

after a leading Austrian Nazi (Josef Mayrhofer, to be discussed shortly) testified that she had not reported illegal Nazi Party meetings even though she had been aware of them. Such "good conduct" in the time of the "system" – the Nazi expression used to describe the preceding regime – deserved special consideration. There does not appear to be an exact record of how many Jewish employees were thrown out of their jobs at Wiener Allianz, but the number was reported to be substantial. This is also suggested by General Director Schmidt-Polex, who remarked especially on the costs of "processing" Jewish employees at the supervisory board meeting of December 16, 1939.[36]

Elementar-Phönix was not the only takeover of a major Austrian insurer by a concern from the Old Reich during the period when Austrian business was allegedly being protected from the entry of Germans into the Austrian market. The counterpart to the taking over of the Phönix and its transformation into Wiener Allianz was the acquisition of control over the ÖVAG by the insurance companies of the DAF in the late spring of 1938, although the renaming to "Deutscher Ring. Österreichische Versicherungs-AG der Deutschen Arbeitsfront" would wait until 1940. The actual takeover of ÖVAG began even before its shares came into DAF hands and was accomplished by the recall of all its representatives on the supervisory board of the majority shareholder – the Municipality of Vienna – including the president, Heinrich Foglar-Deinhardstein. Thus, the shareholders' meeting on June 2, 1938, was chaired by a dedicated Austrian Nazi, Josef Mayrhofer, at that time director of Nordstern Allgemeine Versicherungs-AG and of Nordstern Lebensversicherungs-AG in Vienna. Among his many dubious distinctions, Mayrhofer could boast a father who had been Hitler's guardian and membership in the NSDAP since 1931. He was also the highest Party judge in Austria. Mayrhofer, whose fundamental assignment was to serve as conductor in the orchestrated transfer of control to the DAF, began his brief tenure in this office by announcing that he considered it his special task to turn the ÖVAG into a model National Socialist company and create a "retinue" with a single political orientation. Resignation of the representatives of the Vienna Municipality was accompanied by their proposal for replacements on the administrative board that included Schwede-Coburg and Gustav Mattfeld of Munich Re. The new supervisory board then performed its assigned duties at an special shareholders meeting on July 16, where the DAF was able to claim a majority of the shares. Indeed, between the two meetings, the Austrian companies holding shares in the ÖVAG were persuaded to sell them to the DAF and thus help strengthen its majority holding. Because the statutes barred such a change in majority control during the first two years of the ÖVAG's existence, the statutes were changed; Mayrhofer resigned as chairman along with his colleagues, and a new administrative board was voted in that included Mayrhofer himself, Rudolf

---

[36] Protokoll über die Aufsichtsratssitzung vom 16. Nov. 1939, AZ Wien. The account of Aryanization in Roloff & Mosser, *Wiener Allianz*, pp. 502–5, is a fair and accurate description of what I have found in the archive of Wiener Allianz, where Mayrhofer's testimony of July 29, 1938, on behalf of Dora Schapire is also to be found.

Kratochwill of Deutscher Ring in Hamburg, Andreas Braß, Dietrich Pollmann of Volksfürsorge, and other DAF officials. The dynamic Volksfürsorge did not stop here, however. It also purchased the Vienna-based Allianz und Giselaverein Versicherungs-AG, whose shares were held by an Italian company and by the Prague-based Star Company. At the beginning of October, the new acquisition was renamed the Ostmärkische Volksfürsorge; some Austrian executives were put into the board of directors for tactical reasons, but the company was dominated by persons from Volksfürsorge in Germany. In fact, Alfred Pohlmann, Dietrich's brother, ended up on the board of directors in 1940.[37]

It is thus clear that insurance enterprises from the Old Reich, led by Allianz and Volksfürsorge, were moving aggressively in Austria by simply taking over Austrian companies. In the last analysis, they had the strength and capacity to provide the insurance needed (e.g., by the Party and its organizations in Austria). This was why Schmidt-Polex and Mayrhofer, along with representatives of other German-controlled companies, were invited to the aforementioned discussions at Party headquarters in Munich of September 15 about the distribution of insurance contracts to Austrian and German companies, with results so favorable to Austrian companies owned by German concerns. Of course, this ended neither the competition nor the hostility, which was now even more complicated because DAF companies were competing with Austrian publicly chartered companies in making new acquisitions.[38]

The big battle, however, was over the question of just when the German companies who did not control Austrian enterprises could be licensed to practice in Austria. The law of August 14, 1938, protecting the Austrian economy was set to expire on October 1 of that year. The committee to investigate the Austrian insurance business recommended that the ban on licenses for German companies be extended to the end of 1939. The RWM refused to accept this proposal but did extend the regulation until the end of 1938. But opposition to further prolongation of the licensing ban was already mounting in the summer of 1938 and, as might be expected, it came from one of the excluded companies. Albingia responded to the RWM's August denial of its request by pointing out that it was false to argue that the Austrian insurance business needed protection for the very simple reason that there was scarcely any truly Austrian insurance business to protect. Albingia had made a survey of the various private non–life insurance companies in Austria and found that the most important of them were either under German or foreign control. In the case of fire insurance, the Germans dominated the Austrian firms. Hence, in the last analysis, the protection

---

[37] See Hans Thuer, "Die Österreichische Versicherungs-AG und Deutscher Ring Österreichische Lebensversicherung AG der Deutschen Arbeitsfront (1936–1945)," in Wolfgang Rohrbach (ed.), *Versicherungsgeschichte Österreichs, Bd. 3: Das Zeitalter des modernen Versicherungswesens* (Vienna, 1988), pp. 705–41, esp. pp. 728–32; see also Böhle, "Die Volksfürsorge Lebensversicherungs-AG im 'Dritten Reich'," pp. 114–20. On the pressure to sell the shares to the DAF, see Fieger to Frigessi, July 6, 1938, BCI, NL Frigessi, cart. 68, fasz. 2.

[38] Fieger to Frigessi, July 28, 1938, ibid.

April 1938 edition of the *Allianz-Adler* magazine covering the annexation of Austria.

of "Austrian" life insurance was in reality "the protection of the interests of a few German and foreign large concerns and a disadvantaging of interests of single medium-sized companies, which according to the National Socialist economic view should be closer to the heart of the government than the large concerns."

Albingia already had built up a transport and automobile insurance business in Austria, and its employees there had worked hard to keep it going, despite the bad economic conditions, in the hope that Albingia could expand its activities into fire and other insurance areas. Now this seemed impossible and, because of the departure of Jews from the insurance field, there was a shortage of skilled insurance people and a danger that their employees would be won away from Albingia by competing firms.[39]

The criticism that the existing regulation was unfair was also shared by General Director Ullrich of Gothaer Versicherung, who argued on September 22 in a meeting of the Reich Group Advisory Council that "those companies which have an Austrian company in their possession are able thereby to do business in the Ostmark, while the others are excluded from doing business in the Ostmark." Hilgard agreed with Ullrich, but he also pointed out that the RWM was not only proposing a continuation (until April 1, 1939) of the embargo against Old Reich firms selling property insurance but wanted also to treat each licensing application individually. This led Hilgard to suggest that the embargo be eliminated and that the RWM immediately go over to a system of concessions. He thought it even more unfair that the RWM was asking to extend the embargo against Old Reich life insurance companies for five years while also asking the excluded companies to participate for five years in contributing to the funds guaranteeing the old Phönix policies in the ÖVAG. This was obviously a matter of no small interest to General Director Schloeßmann of Allianz Leben, who did take the "high road" by arguing that the licensing of Old Reich life insurance companies would benefit the Austrian consumers, "who would get cheaper insurance protection from the German than from the Austrian corporations."[40]

Schloeßmann, who was head of the branch organization for life insurance within the Reich Group, followed up these remarks with a series of aggressive moves designed to persuade the RWM to let Old Reich life insurance companies into Austria. He was able to play upon the reports being issued by the committee investigating the Austrian insurance business, which argued both that the Austrians would need time to adjust to the German system and that they would probably still be uncompetitive even if the embargo were lengthened. In a lengthy memorandum to the RWM of October 24, Schloeßmann contended that the life insurance premiums charged by the Austrian companies were about the same as those charged by the Germans but, in contrast to the latter, did not offer any share of profits. Thus, Austrians were actually paying 15%–20% more than their German counterparts:

The systematic development over many years of life insurance with profit sharing by the German companies of all types has enabled the life insurance business in the National Socialist State to fulfill its tasks in the service of the People's Community in the best possible

---

[39] Albingia to RWM, Aug. 26, 1938. Albingia made a renewed plea on Oct. 24, 1938; see ÖStA-AdR, BMF, VA, Karton 315, Akte 55/A, a-4, 1, Bl. 46–50, 85–91.
[40] Beiratssitzung vom 22. Sept. 1938, GDV, RS/26, pp. 8–13.

way. *The advantages of this development cannot any longer be withheld from the national comrades of the Ostmark who have returned to the Reich.*[41]

Schloeßmann claimed to be in no way convinced that such protectionism for
the Austrians was necessary: not for the original publicly chartered companies
of the states and cities who were mobilizing into one association, nor for the
DAF companies, nor for foreign dominated companies like Der Anker (which
was controlled by Swiss Re), nor for Donau Allgemeine Versicherungs-AG, in
which Magdeburger Feuerversicherungs-Gesellschaft had the leading influence.
Furthermore, these foreign-owned Austrian firms did most of their business outside Austria. As far as Schloeßmann was concerned, the companies in question
should either be able to compete or should leave the scene, both in Austria and
in Germany. As was the case with Albingia, the life insurers also sought to mobilize the rapid dismissal of Jewish employees in the insurance business for their
purposes:

The workforce of the Austrian companies should experience a marked diminution through
the departure of the non-"Aryan" employees so that the manpower available will be needed
to deal with the remaining tasks. By permitting the entry of the German companies there
will be a rising demand for insurance personnel. In any case, the totality of the German
life insurance companies can undertake to guarantee that there will be no social hardships for the insurance employees.[42]

As Schloeßmann was well aware, however, the real argument of the investigatory
committee for continued protection of the Austrians from German competition
was the unfavorable cost structure in the Austrian insurance industry. This had
arisen from its underdeveloped provision of customer service, the legacy of the
Phönix Life affair, and the bad economic conditions that had plagued the Austrian economy. In his view, these deficits could not be repaired in one year or
in five but could only be corrected by improved economic conditions – to be expected from the Anschluß – and improved business methods. He viewed it as
totally unfair that German companies should be expected to pay for Austria's
failures and be excluded because of their productivity or that the Austrian population should be deprived of the blessings of the German life insurance system.

The demand – with which he concluded his memorandum – of Schloeßmann
and his group that the German companies be allowed to set up shop in Austria no later than January 1, 1939, met with strong resistance at a meeting of
the RWM on October 26. Mayrhofer bluntly accused the German insurers of
caring only about the extension of their business and, along with Hans Sittenberger and Franz Fieger of RAS, called for an expansion of the deadline until the
end of 1939. They claimed they needed at least that long to adjust to the new

---

[41] Italics in original. Fachgruppe Lebensversicherung an den RWM, 24. Okt. 1938, SM, 1458/2/194,
Bl. 241–50, quote on Bl. 243.
[42] Ibid., Bl. 246.

conditions. Braß took the side of the Austrians, which compelled the other Germans (Schloeßmann and Ullrich) to retreat from their position. The latter had, as Schloeßmann later confessed to Fieger, committed a grave tactical error in not first consulting with the Austrians to come to some understanding instead of thinking the Germans could simply ride roughshod over them. After the industry representatives left the meeting, the RAA also came down on the side of the Austrians, although the RWM held back on its decision. In a subsequent memorandum of November 24, the RAA supported maintaining the barrier against German property insurers until March 31 or June 30, 1939 – the latter date was to be chosen in the end – and that against life insurers until December 31, 1939.[43]

These prospects mobilized the ever-watchful Schwede-Coburg, who was anxious to strengthen an alliance he had forged among the leading publicly chartered companies in Austria – Landesbrandschaden-Versicherungsanstalten, Ostmark-Versicherungs-AG, and Städtische Versicherungsanstalt der Gemeinde Wien – and who was still conspiring to nationalize the industry. In November he thus turned to Bürckel once again and urged the summoning of the Austrian Gauleiters to take special measures designed to protect Austrian companies and counter the German companies once they came in; when he received no response from the busy Bürckel, he wrote again on December 21 and January 18. Bürckel finally replied on February 3 and flatly turned down Schwede-Coburg's proposal, a decision that was determined by events in Berlin. Through his personal representative Kratz and a letter from Lange of the RWM, Bürckel had been informed about Hitler's order suspending all further debate on the insurance nationalization issue for ten years and Göring's demand that the two sides cease their quarreling. As Bürckel informed Schwede-Coburg, Göring wished a cessation of all discussion of insurance matters "in order not to disturb or endanger the efficiency of the German insurance business at the present time."[44] Bürckel took this opportunity to express greater optimism than Schwede-Coburn about the capacity of the Austrian insurers to survive the end of protection, especially since the RAA would have to approve all requests by German companies to do business in Austria.

Like Göring, Bürckel was a pragmatist about the insurance business. A good illustration was his Aryanization policy. Bürckel was a vicious anti-Semite and promoter of Aryanization who was firmly convinced that his supposedly long-suffering Austrian comrades deserved "restitution" for the alleged political and economic discrimination they had suffered at the hands of the Jews. This was shorthand for saying that the Austrian Nazis felt that they had been deprived of power and wealth by the Jews and that, having now attained power, they had a

---

[43] See Fieger to Frigessi, Oct. 29, 1938, BCI, NL Frigessi, cart. 68, fasz. 2; Vermerk, Nov. 1938, SM, 1458/2/194, Bl. 251f., and RAA an RWM, 24. Nov. 1938, ibid., Bl. 256–9.

[44] Bürckel an Schwede-Coburg, 3. Feb. 1939, ÖStA-AdR, Bürckel/Materie, Karton 94, Akte 2170/0. This was a verbatim repetition of the language used by Lange in a letter to Bürckel of Jan. 18, ibid.

right to plunder Jewish assets. Nevertheless, he was insistent that Jewish businesses not fall into incompetent hands and that export interests be taken into account in the transfer or shutting down of Jewish enterprises.[45]

The investigations into Austrian insurance had demonstrated that it was an overpopulated industry with an excessively high cost structure and was victim of a variety of ills stemming from the collapse of the Austro-Hungarian Empire, inflation, depression, and the Phönix Life mess. It was clear that some companies could and should not survive, and that takeovers by Allianz and the DAF had a stabilizing effect and constituted the most acceptable form of reorganization by German companies. The call for a period of adjustment probably was justified, and the lesson taught Schloeßmann seemed to have taken hold. There was considerable cooperation between the German and Austrian insurers in 1939–1940, as old group insurance contracts for party organizations (and also for major industrial companies) spread to Austria, just as compromises were made in adjusting the premium rate structure in Austria to those of the Reich. If the reports and comments of the Austrian insurance leaders after the dismissal of their Jewish employees are to be believed – and there is no reason why they should overstress the importance of the Jews to their business – Austria suffered considerably from a shortage of skilled insurance personnel because of the dismissals, the need to take on young and inexperienced persons to replace them, and the fact that such persons were increasingly being drafted into the army. In this realm, however, economic rationality had severe limits.[46] Nevertheless, it was obvious that Germany was expanding, and an important incentive to stabilizing the insurance business situation in Austria was that Vienna was assuming an especially vital position at this point because it was "to serve as a gateway for the economic expansion of Germany in the south eastern space."[47]

Such promising prospects were brightened further by the "peaceful" acquisition of the Sudetenland in the fall of 1938, the invasion of the rump Czech state in March 1939 and its transformation into the Protectorate of Bohemia and Moravia, as well as the establishment of a nominally independent Slovak state. Needless to say, when the Wehrmacht marched in, German business was never far behind; this, of course, included the insurance business. As Martin

---

[45] See his "Zur Judenfrage in Österreich" in ÖStA-AdR, Bürckel/Materie, Karton 89, Akte 2160/2, Bl. 44–8.

[46] For the various reports on the state of the Austrian insurance business, see SM, 1458/2/187 and 215. See also the report on the Umstellungen im ostmärkischen Versicherungsbetrieb nach dem Anschluß, Bezirksstelle Wien der Reichsgruppe "Versicherungen" to Amend, 17. April 1941, ÖStA-AdR, BMF, VA, Karton 329, Akte 80; the report of a speech by Tanzner on "Die Versicherungswirtschaft in der Ostmark," *Neumanns Zeitschrift für Versicherungswesen* 61 (1938), pp. 1162–4; and Hans Sittenberger an Pg. Regierungsrat Ernst, 29. April 1939, ÖStA-AdR, Bürckel/Materie, Karton 94, Akte 2170/0.

[47] Josef Posselt, Direktor Internationale Unfall, an Frigessi, 17. Okt. 1938, BCI, NL Frigessi, cart. 101, fasz. 1. See also Sittenberger an Ernst, 29. April 1939, ÖStA-AdR, Bürckel/Materie, Karton 94, Akte 2170/0.

Herzog – a bright young assessor appointed by the Reich Group to assist Hilgard around this time and in whom Hilgard was to find a reliable and trusted helper – pointed out in a memorandum of November 10, the situation in the Sudetenland was quite different from the one found in Austria. The only German company with a significant presence was Concordia of Cologne, which had an office in Reichenberg, while the rest of the Sudeten insurance business consisted of the branches of Czech companies based primarily in Prague and some small local Sudenten-German companies. If one wished to transfer Sudeten-German portfolios into German hands, care had to be taken to avoid German or Sudeten companies simply winning away former Czech customers, since this would give the Czech companies disposal over the reserve coverage of the cancelled policies and also saddle the German companies with reserve requirements on unfavorable terms. At the same time, there was a similarity with Austria insofar as the RWM sought to protect Sudeten business from being overwhelmed by companies from the Reich and, with respect to insurance, wished to have existing portfolios transferred to local Sudeten companies as much as possible.[48]

This fit in well with the recent business politics in the Sudetenland. Konrad Henlein and his Sudetendeutsche Party had been striving for some time to unite the business interests of the region, while Concordia had sought to win over the pro-German elements by stressing its strong attachments to National Socialism.[49] In the course of November 1938, the local Sudeten insurance companies united into a publicly chartered Sudetendeutsche Union Versicherungs-AG; then both the new company and Concordia made a bid to more or less monopolize the taking over of Czech portfolios in the region – the former with respect to property insurance, the latter in life insurance. This plan, however, ran afoul of both RWM policy and other interests. On the one hand, the German government was concluding a treaty with Czechoslovakia that gave Czech companies control of the sale of those Sudeten portfolios at their disposal. On the other, German companies could see no justification for a Concordia monopoly and were also being asked by client industrial companies who were moving into the Sudetenland whether it would be possible to continue using their old insurers.[50]

---

[48] Notiz Herzog für Gambke, 10. Nov. 1938, GDV, unsignierte Akten, Sudetenland 10 IV, 2. On Herzog, see the remarks by Hilgard, "Leben," FHA, NL 2/7, p. 122. Braß, of all people, had assigned Herzog to Hilgard, which turned out to be the only positive thing Braß ever did for him. In his later years, Herzog was to demonstrate a remarkable sensitivity and interest in the history of the insurance business that one wishes were more widely shared by his colleagues and that is amply demonstrated in his unpublished history of the Munich Re, "Was Dokumente erzählen können," FHA.

[49] See the revealing reports by Hugo Kornfeld, who headed the RAS office in Prague, to Frigessi of June 30 and July 7, 1938, BCI, NL Frigessi, cart. 79, fasz. 3. This development was not entirely unwelcome to the Prague-based companies, who saw it as an opportunity to take on Jewish customers who would obviously not be very happy insuring with the Sudeten insurance companies or with Concordia.

[50] See the various reports by Herzog, especially Herzog an Braß, 7. Dez. 1938, in GDV, unsignierte Akten, Sudetenland 10 IV, 2.

Whatever the case, the amount of insurance involved was too large and the pressures from companies in the Reich too great for the aforementioned monopolistic efforts to work, and other companies were permitted to assume Sudetenland portfolios. One of these was Allianz Leben, which concluded a contract with the Slavia Insurance Company in Prague at the beginning of May 1939 in which it took over a portfolio worth 8.4 million RM (70 million Czech kronen). At the same time, Allianz, Wiener Allianz, Bayerische Versicherungsbank, and Kraft took over the Sudeten general portfolio of the Slavia. Additionally, Wiener Allianz took part of the general portfolios of the První Česká and Rolnická companies.[51] The Slavia portfolio marked the last significant prewar acquisition by the Allianz concern. Its future gains and international activities, including those in the Protectorate of Bohemia-Moravia created after the German entry into Prague in March 1939, were to be made in the context of war that began at the beginning of September 1939. As before the war, however, so during the conflict; Allianz was also to depend on the insurance industry's success in representing and defending its interests under the National Socialist regime, and the enemies of the private insurance business were anything but stilled by the coming of war.

THE NATIONALIZATION CONFLICT REDIVIVUS AND THE REWARDS AND TRAVAILS OF COLLABORATION

The twentieth century produced a variety of tyrannical and bizarre regimes, of which National Socialism and Stalinist Communism were certainly the most extreme. If the former has nevertheless engendered a unique fascination for historians and the historically-interested public, this stems not only from its extreme aestheticization of politics and unfathomable brutality but also because it held sway over one of the most institutionally advanced, industrialized, and cultured societies of Europe. The German elite had played no small role in helping the National Socialists come to power and, in the case of the business elite, to consolidate their position. A good many had entertained notions of being able to control or dominate the Nazis and bend the purposes of the regime in the direction of their ambitions, but certainly all such illusions had evaporated by 1938–1939; the overheating of the economy by the Four-Year Plan, the Pogrom of November 1938, and Hitler's manifest willingness to risk war and wage war to achieve his goals demonstrated that the regime had entered a radical phase. This was a new kind of regime and a new kind of politics. One of the major problems for the historian is trying to comprehend how the elites – in this case, the

---

[51] For a listing of the companies involved, see Tomas Jelinek, "Insurance in the Nazi Occupied Czech Lands," Table 2: The Transfer of Czechoslovak Insurance Activities in the Sudetenland, to be found at the website ⟨http://www.hrad.cz/kpr/holocaust/pojistky_uk.html⟩. For the contract, see BAK, B 280/1446, Bl. 8–13; for the estimated worth of the portfolio, see Allianz Leben an RAA, 30. Sept. 1939, ibid., Bl. 37f.

leaders of the German private insurance industry – assessed the domestic and international situation. This needs to be coupled with an effort to determine where they felt some freedom to maneuver and capacity to shape events or, at least, to determine from whence they thought containment of the regime might come. The insurance industry has good reason to prefer peace to war, since the latter increases the death rate, is by definition risky in every respect, disrupts international connections, and makes the conduct of business much more complicated. Insurance is not a vital war industry in the same sense as, for example, coal mining, and its claims to manpower are of a lower priority. At the same time, it is an important financial resource for the government to tap in its war efforts, and this makes it particularly vulnerable to the vagaries of war financing. Naturally, victorious war also offers opportunities, just as defeat imposes special penalties, as had been demonstrated after 1918. How the leaders of the insurance business dealt with the new war that began in 1939 was therefore a function of their assessment of the opportunities and risks that war under National Socialist leadership brought. The problem here is to reconstruct the real strategies of offense and defense available within the existing range of possibilities as they were understood by these businessmen – that is, to be as historical as possible. There is little point in abusing the advantages of hindsight and imposing present-day knowledge and sensibilities in judging past actions where there is little historical basis for doing so. Similarly, as has already been shown, it is absurd to take the post facto accounts by insurance leaders at face value, and it is essential to reconstruct what they were really up to at the time. One of their goals, which often conveniently slipped their minds after 1945, was taking as much advantage as possible of the war to expand their enterprises and interests. Finally, it would be utter folly to treat the decision making of the businessmen in question as an exercise in some pure form of business history and economic decision making, assuming there is such a thing.[52] Certainly there was no such thing in the Third Reich. One of the great "achievements" of the National Socialists was to politicize all economic decision making. It is therefore useful to begin this section by considering the available evidence concerning how some insurance leaders viewed the situation on the eve of war.

In a letter to his father of November 18, 1935, Kurt Schmitt's eldest son Günther ruminated about the hostile attitude of Hitler toward the university fraternities, to whose existence and values both father and son were firmly committed. Günther gloomily stated that "we no longer have any complete freedom of existence today – no one contests this – and we will *never* attain it in the National Socialist State! And the National Socialist State exists and will *remain* in existence!" While some of the Corps brethren thought that the way to go was to convert into a National Socialist organization, it all reminded Günther of the Stahlhelm, Weimar's famous veterans's organization, which had allowed itself

---

[52] Here I find myself very much at odds with the arguments of Toni Pierenkemper, "Was kann eine moderne Unternehmensgeschichtsschreibung leisten?", pp. 15–31.

to be coordinated right out of existence. The reality was that "one cannot compare the present time with any earlier one; never yet has a State represented the
totality principle so strongly and – this is the chief thing   *carried it through!"*[53]

Günther Schmitt's desire to preserve the autonomy of the fraternities apparently did not extend to other spheres of life, however, since he joined the SS and
was to become a member of the SS Leibsstandarte Adolf Hitler. Indeed, he and
his father were quite upset when they believed Günther's SS membership and
withdrawal from the church had led to his rejection for a Cecil Rhodes Fellowship in 1938. This demonstrated that Schmitt, Anglophile though he may have
been, had very little understanding of the limits of British toleration for German
peculiarities under National Socialism. Schmitt's neighbor in the Starnberg Lake
area (and frequent visitor at the Schmitt estate Tiefenbrunn), the diplomat Ulrich von Hassell, who would be executed five years later for his participation in
the Resistance, had more understanding for Günther's rejection by the selection
committee. In von Hassell's view, the selection committee had a responsibility
not to send people to England who would give offense, something the Schmitts
were apparently too obtuse to comprehend. Von Hassell was a genuine opponent of the regime, but in 1938 he noted that Kurt Schmitt was anything but
happy about the state of affairs in Germany:

> In general, Schmitt was just as despairing about the domestic and economic situation as
> all of us, especially over the fact that the historical opportunity provided by the Jewish
> Pogrom to put a stop to the development has not been used by Göring despite his bet-
> ter understanding and by the army through its lack of political power. If Hitler, through
> further passivity of the Western Powers attains a new success in the East against Poland
> and Soviet Russia and in making a large economic area in the form of the Ukraine ser-
> viceable to Germany, then the steamroller will continue on, the economic crisis will be
> put off or avoided, and the destruction of all ethical values will progress further. With
> regard to the Jewish matter, he [Schmitt] maintained that Hitler to be sure had given
> his agreement to measures of reprisal at Goebbels's instigation but that he was himself
> surprised and painfully affected by their actual scope and character. Göring had unfor-
> tunately failed to recognize this and believed that he was dealing with the clear will of the
> Führer.[54]

While von Hassell quite rightly did not find this interpretation of the roles
played by leading Nazi actors in the November Pogrom very convincing, what
is remarkable is the extent to which Schmitt understood Hitler's ultimate goals
in the East, the economic dislocation that had been created by the rearmament
program, the potential role of conquest and plunder in its solution, and the absolutely unethical nature of the regime. As was the case with respect to Goebbels,
Schmitt tended to overstate Göring's rationality. Indeed, when von Hassell asked

---

[53] Günther Schmitt an Kurt Schmitt, 18. Nov. 1935, FHA, NL 1/125; for Schmitt's view of the stu-
    dent organizations, see his "Erinnerungen," pp. 25–9, FHA, NL 1/133.
[54] Gaertringen (ed.), *Hassell-Tagebücher,* pp. 73–4 (29. Dez. 1938).

Schmitt whether he could discern any person or persons about whom opposition might rally, Schmitt was very pessimistic. He thought that Göring and the army still had the potential to force their will on Hitler, but not for long. When von Hassell suggested that Göring was not really the right man because of his fear of Himmler and Heydrich, Schmitt responded that he had heard rumors that opposition to Hitler's policies was forming. He considered Heydrich and Goebbels the most dangerous persons in the regime but "did not want to give up on Himmler entirely,"[55] despite the SS leader's fanaticism about religion and certain other subjects. He thought Himmler had a good understanding of some of the dangers, but he took a dim view of most Gauleiters, especially Julius Streicher in Nuremberg, Martin Mutschmann in Saxony, Adolf Wagner in Munich, and Schwede-Coburg.

Manifestly, the disillusioned Schmitt was grasping at straws in thinking that Himmler might somehow moderate the policies being pursued, but such appeared to be the options from his perspective at the end of 1938. Schmitt in any case continued to cultivate Himmler as best he could, not only through his membership in and contributions to the Circle of Friends (discussed in Chapter 2) but also by yearly contributions of 240 RM between 1938 and 1942 to the Lebensborn e.V., an SS organization aimed at promoting the production of "racially pure" children through the protection and care of their married and unmarried mothers. He also made monthly contributions of 100 RM to the "special fund for SA leaders" between 1938 and 1943.[56] Not only did Schmitt make personal contributions to such causes, he also sought to gain the personal interest of Himmler in the Munich Re and perhaps exert influence on him in other matters as well. Thus, in July 1939, Schmitt used the occasion of his intervention with Hilgard about a contribution to some cause of interest to Himmler to ask SS-Gruppenführer Karl Wolff, the chief of Himmler's personal staff, if he, Himmler, and their wives might not come out to Tiefenbrunn for a visit. The estate was particularly beautiful in the summer, and Agriculture Minister Darré was supporting its transformation into an entailed hereditary estate, a goal whose attainment certainly would be promoted by a visit of high-ranking SS leaders. Schmitt suggested that they meet at the headquarters of Munich Re, "the greatest enterprise of its kind in the world and one of the most beautiful buildings in Munich," and then travel out to Tiefenbrunn.[57]

The preparations for war in the summer of 1939 allowed Himmler and Wolff no time for such visits, but the invitation demonstrates that Schmitt had remained persona grata for Himmler and his inner circle. Nevertheless, there was no way that Schmitt could protect Günther from the fatal consequences of membership in the SS Leibstandarte Adolf Hitler. Günther was about to take his university

---

[55] Ibid.
[56] Report on the investigation of Kurt Schmitt, Exhibit 42, NA, RG 260, OMGUS, FINAD, 2/58/2–7.
[57] Schmitt an Wolff, 6. Juli 1939, BAB, ehem. BDC, SL 62, Bl. 72–4, and Wolff's reply, 5. Sept. 1939, ibid., Bl. 70.

examinations, his studies already having been delayed by the call-up of his unit during the Czech crisis, and he was sent to fight at the Polish front in September 1939. Understandably, Kurt Schmitt was extremely anxious about his son's safety as well as his welfare, and when he learned from his academic connections that students who had been called up could be placed on temporary furlough in order to take a special examination, Schmitt sought to arrange through Wolff for Günther to be given such an opportunity once the campaign in the East ended, so that he could take his examination at the University of Munich. Before getting the favorable news on this effort, he learned from Wolff that his son had "fallen for his Führer and his homeland" and found himself requesting that Günther's body be exhumed from a cemetery in Silesia and returned to Tiefenbrunn.[58] Hitler and Himmler sent wreaths for the occasion – certainly no consolation to Frau Schmitt, who had opposed her husband's involvement with the National Socialists from the start, and a hollow tribute to Kurt Schmitt's first but not last great personal sacrifice for a regime he increasingly disliked but which, in contrast to von Hassell, he continued to treat with ambivalence and ambiguity. The news of Kurt Schmitt's loss was a shock to many of his compatriots in the insurance business. As Arnoldo Frigessi, surely not a person one would normally have expected to mourn an SS man, wrote to Alzheimer, "I cannot refrain from giving expression to you also the genuine emotion which has seized all of us by the news that the son of Reich Minister Schmidt [sic] has fallen."[59]

Schmitt was indeed living in two worlds, the civilized, cultivated international world of European insurance business and the one inhabited by the National Socialists. People cope with their personal tragedies and life's exigencies in different ways, however, and Schmitt seemed to be his old self when Ulrich von Hassell encountered him again in Ebenhausen at the end of January 1940. Schmitt reported attending Göring's birthday party in Berlin on the 12th, and von Hassell went on to note

that in general one had succeeded in cloaking and securing the foreign interests of the Munich Re in time, mainly by a kind of dissimulation toward the enemy powers. All lines of contact have not yet been irrevocably cut off, as was the case in 1914. His [Schmitt's] report on Berlin reflected his so easily impressionable nature, fundamentally completely negative but with exploding fireworks of optimism along the way. When Funk tells him that our continuously on-again, off-again offensives against Belgium and the Netherlands are a calculated war of nerves, then he believes this. Göring spoke "moderately and calmly." Yet he was horrified by Himmler who, with his jiggling pince-nez and the dark expression of his proletarian face, told him that the Führer had assigned him the task of making sure that the Poles could never rise up again. Therefore, a policy of extermination.[60]

---

[58] See Kurt Schmitt an Günther Schmitt, 19. Sept. 1939, and Prof. Theodor Süss an Schmitt, 9. Sept. 1938, FHA, NL 1/125, which also contains the last letters between Günther and his parents. See also Schmitt an Wolff, 19. Sept. 1939, Wolff an Schmitt, 9. Okt. 1939, Schmitt an Wolff, 14. Okt. 1939, and other relevant correspondence in BAB, ehem. BDC, SL 62, Bl. 62–9, 77f.

[59] Frigessi to Alzheimer, Oct. 3, 1939, BCI, NL Frigessi, cart. 62, fasz. 3.

[60] Gaertringen (ed.), *Hassell-Tagebücher*, p. 158 (28. Jan. 1940).

Clearly, Schmitt's access to the high and mighty of the regime did little to clarify his never particularly analytical political judgment. Instead, it intensified his oscillations. At one moment he looked to Himmler to bring some reason into the situation; at another, he placed hopes in Göring's "moderation." He could never face up to the reality that he was consorting with monsters, let alone decide to make the kind of existential moral choice of von Hassell and the men and women of the Resistance. Nor, indeed, was he prepared to support the path of open opposition to the regime of Pastor Martin Niemöller, whose family were regular visitors at the Schmitts. In 1936, Schmitt told Niemöller during a conversation in Berlin that "you stand before the choice of clearly and single-mindedly carrying on the battle you have begun – if you do so you will definitely be put out of the way – or continuing to serve your church even beyond the present time by cautious self-restraint." Niemöller's response was that "this policy might be correct for an economic enterprise but it is not applicable in questions of belief. Here there are no compromises. I must go my way."[61] That way led to a concentration camp; to Schmitt's great credit, he not only sought to intercede on Niemöller's behalf but also looked after the care and education of Niemöller's son Hermann at his estate Tiefenbrunn, where he also housed and protected his son's teacher and others who were non-"Aryan" under the Nuremberg laws.[62] Schmitt was no hero, but he was no coward either and, as will be shown, could at times be quite reckless in his speech and actions. At the same time, he sincerely believed – even after the grim experiences since 1933 – that his path was the correct one and that it was his duty to protect the enterprises in his care and fight for them within the system rather than pursue a "catastrophic" policy of futile opposition.

Ever since his time as economics minister, Schmitt had feared that the regime was heading toward war, and certainly by 1938 this anxiety was widely shared among some of his colleagues. Hilgard, who had travelled with his family from his nearby estate in Irnberg to witness the events surrounding the Munich Conference in September–October 1938, later claimed that one could see from the "naked rage" in Hitler's eyes that the entire effort at a peaceful solution to the Czech crisis ran counter to his real intentions. Still, Hilgard seems to have entertained some hope that the English had contained Hitler, but he rapidly gave it up after experiencing the renewed bellicosity of Hitler's post-Munich speeches and especially after the occupation of Prague in March 1939.[63] Gloomy foreboding now dominated the atmosphere and luncheon conversation among the members of what Hilgard described as "our Allianz family." As the political situation became worse, Hilgard met daily with the section heads in the supervisory board room at Allianz, where they could get the latest information from

[61] Schmitt, "Erinnerungen," FHA, NL 1/133.
[62] See Niemöller's testimony on Schmitt's behalf in the denazification tribunal, Oct. 7, 1947, AM, Spruchkammerakten Dr. Kurt Schmitt, Akten der Spruchkammer Starnberg, 2. Teil.
[63] See Hilgard, "Leben," FHA, NL 2/7, p. 121f.

Director Georg König, who had served on the General Staff during the last war and who was slated to take up an important military post in a new war. It was difficult to act on König's information, however, since the government insisted that nothing be done to suggest that the Third Reich wanted war. Ultimately, one was forced to fall back on the flexibility of the Allianz organization itself and its blend of centralization and decentralization – which, as Hilgard proudly noted, did indeed serve the concern well during the war.[64]

In contrast to Schmitt, Hilgard was not one to exhibit any anguish about the regime. If he had any purpose in life then it was to serve the "Allianz family," to hold it together and to preserve the private insurance industry in victory or, finally, in defeat. He accepted the cards dealt to him, never pretended or imagined that they were anything but what they were, and played to win according to the rules defined by those who had determined the nature of the game. His great skill was to stay in the game as long as possible by finessing every dangerous situation, choosing powerful partners, and knowing when to call his opponent's bluff and when to cut his losses. That was how he managed to enter the war as head of the Reich Group for Insurance, despite all the efforts to push him out, and to play the key role in defining its policies.

Hilgard's was most certainly not the way of the Alte Leipziger General Director Johannes Tiedke, who (as has been shown elsewhere[65]) had sought to maintain the integrity of his enterprise and independence from the regime. Tiedke had actually summarily dismissed two NSBO plant foremen in 1934 for engaging in impermissible agitation and interference in company operations. Were it not for the intervention of his friend, the later Reich Economics Minister Schacht, the ruthless Saxon Gauleiter Mutschmann would have had Tiedke arrested. Tiedke's outspoken opposition to Braß and to the handling of the insurance industry's payment to cover damages of the November Pogrom only increased the enmity toward him in Party circles. As he was to discover from documents found after the war, powerful forces had been intriguing to bring him down. On the one hand, the Nazi plant steward at the Alte Leipziger (a man named Schneider) and his Gestapo crony Gothe were conspiring with various directors to remove Tiedke. On the other, the DAF leader for banking and insurance Rudolf Lencer wanted to place Alte Leipziger, which had been doing quite well under Tiedke's leadership, under a commissar and transform it into a publicly chartered company. Tiedke made the mistake of failing to have the entire company assemble to hear Hitler's speech of September 1, 1939, as was expected by the Party, with the claim that suitable facilities were not available in the building and that the speech could be heard again later. This played right into the hands of his enemies. He was denounced, arrested on September 2, placed in the Leipzig prison, and interrogated for five hours about his political affiliations. Released later in the day, he

---

[64] See Eduard Hilgard, Die Allianz im 2. Weltkrieg [ca. 1955] (unpublished ms., FHA, AZ 1.3/2), pp. 3–4.

[65] See Chapter 4, pp. 154–5, 176–7.

was arrested again on September 4 at Lencer's instructions because of Tiedke's refusal to join a DAF committee connected with Lencer's office in which all leading insurance directors were expected to participate. This time, he spent five days in jail before being released. When he asked on what charges he had been arrested, he was told by the Gestapo official that he had committed no formal offense but that it was hoped he had learned his lesson and would be compliant with the Party and DAF in the future. But Lencer wanted him out, so Tiedke was declared "politically unbearable," removed from all his offices, prematurely retired, and refused a position on the Alte Leipziger supervisory board – where his advice and experience would most certainly have been welcomed. Lencer was able to accomplish this by threatening the remaining directors and the supervisory board of Alte Leipziger with a takeover of the company by a commissar if Tiedke were not removed. To add insult to injury, Tiedke later discovered that Hilgard had cooperated with Lencer in the affair and had simply left Tiedke in the lurch. Ironically, however, Tiedke also came to the conclusion that the most important thing was to protect the Alte Leipziger from Lencer and that the supervisory board did the right thing in dropping him as general director and appointing one of the functioning directors, Fritz Hensel, as his successor. It is clear that Tiedke cannot be described as a resister in the sense of Niemöller or von Hassell, and his anti-Nazi posture was rooted in his principled business conservatism. He did not openly challenge the regime ideologically. There were simply limits to the political compromises he was prepared to make and to the types of persons with whom he was prepared to consort. He was bitter about being removed from active life seven years before retirement age. Hilgard and Schmitt undoubtedly would have argued that Tiedke was a good illustration of the futility and impotence to which one condemned oneself by failing to make the necessary public and visible compromises they had made in order to save what could be saved. In any case, the German business community certainly did not suffer from any abundance of persons like Tiedke, let alone from full-blown opponents of the regime.[66]

From this perspective, Hilgard was the right man in the right place for the majority of his colleagues, especially when seconded by the potent support of Schmitt. As has been shown, Hilgard, with the help of Schmitt, emerged to be confirmed by Göring as head of the Insurance Industry Reich Group in February 1939 despite a strong movement to have him removed during the previous months.[67] This by no means terminated the dangers presented by Schwede-Coburg and his followers, and the appointment of Amend as head of the RAA was hardly a promising development from the perspective of the private insurers. Essentially, Hilgard and Schmitt were engaged in a two-front war with the Nazi

---

[66] Johannes Tiedke, "Meine Stellung zum Nationalsozialismus überhaupt und die Gründe dafür, daß ich nicht in die Partei eingetreten bin," of July 5, 1945, NL Tiedke, and Weiß, "Ist das, was wir machen, auch gerecht?", pp. 45–75.

[67] See Chapter 4, pp. 185–7.

leaders. On the one hand, they had to keep a watchful eye on organizational developments and "reform" proposals in Berlin so as to ensure that the dominant position of private industry was maintained. On the other hand, especially under wartime conditions, the contest for power between the private and the publicly chartered companies – as demonstrated in Austria and the Sudetenland – was also carried into the areas in which Germany expanded. The success of private industry in taking the lead in insurance expansion and forging international contacts under the new conditions would be critical to its position at home and abroad. The domestic context is important for understanding the international effort and must be considered first.

Göring's choice of Hilgard in February 1939 came as a great surprise to Schwede-Coburg, the officials of the RWM, and many insurance industry leaders; it had simply been assumed that the DAF insurance general director from Hamburg, Rudolf Kratochwill, would be Hilgard's successor. He was expected to preside over a reorganization of the Reich Group in which the private and publicly chartered companies would be combined and in which there would be anywhere between five and nine economic groups for the key insurance areas, with specialized branch groups under them. Additionally, plans were afoot to create an advisory council for the RAA under the chairmanship of Schwede-Coburg, with Kurt Schmitt and Hans Goebbels as deputy chairmen, that would include heads of the various economic units of the Reich Group as well as other prominent persons. It was not only to advise the RAA but also to propose fundamental reforms of the industry. The Party leadership followed these developments closely. On January 7, 1939, for example, Chief of Staff Martin Bormann approved these plans in the name of Party secretary Rudolf Heß, pointing out that he had discussed them with Schmitt and that they seemed to have general approval; on February 7, Heß informed Ley of his approval of Kratochwill.[68]

Thus, everyone seems to have been caught off-guard by Göring's change of heart on the leadership question, and it was only on April 21 that a meeting was held involving Schwede-Coburg, Hilgard, Schmitt, Goebbels, Amend, and Ministerial Director Lange in an effort to move matters forward. Now, Hilgard was given the task of organizing five economic groups within the Reich Group and to create special branch groups for each of them: (1) property under General Director Heinrich Bothe of the Landschaftliche Brandkasse in Hannover, a publicly chartered company; (2) life and health insurance under General Director Kratochwill; (3) vehicles under Director Max Odenbreit of the Agrippina company in Cologne; (4) accident and liability under Director Bruno Reuter

---

[68] In general, see Karl Adolf Schwartz, "Die Verbände der Versicherungswirtschaft bis 1945," pp. 86–9, GDV, 0-201/1. See BAB, R 3101/9275, Bl. 152ff. for the details of these developments; see especially Bormann an RWM, 7. Jan. 1939, ibid., Bl. 158–9, and Heß an Ley, 7. Feb. 1939, ibid., Bl. 179.

of Öffentliche Versicherungsanstalt des Landes Sachsen in Dresden, a publicly chartered company; and (5) reinsurance, credit insurance, and other types of insurance under Director Alzheimer of the Munich Re. Hilgard had not been happy about this reorganization plan when it was first accepted in December 1938, arguing then that one should set up either economic groups or branch groups but not both, since it would produce nothing but overorganization and duplication of effort. He was overriden by the RWM officialdom on the grounds that every Reich Group had to have economic groups and insurance could be no exception. At the April 21 meeting, however, he did achieve agreement that the branch group question would be put off since leaders of the economic groups had first to be approved by the Deputy Führer's office (Rudolf Heß); once this happened, one could then discuss the personnel for the branch groups. Further, the meeting of April 21 authorized the creation of the advisory council planned earlier, now with Schwede-Coburg as chairman and Schmitt as deputy chairman and a variety of members ranging from Lencer of the DAF and Hans Goebbels to Ullrich of Gotha Versicherung.[69] Matters then dragged on until mid-July with Schwede-Coburg becoming increasingly angry that Göring had not delivered on certain promises from when they first discussed an advisory council – namely, Hans Goebbels as co-deputy chairman and a small committee with fewer representatives of the private industry.[70]

What is obvious from both the passage of time and the developments since February is that Schwede-Coburg was losing the initiative and that his intended instrument for the "reform" of the insurance business, the advisory council, was being turned into an unwieldy body filled with people he did not want. Even the reorganization of the Reich Group was being delayed. A decree had been issued on September 8, 1939, mandating that the reorganization take place on October 1, but Hilgard suddenly took ill in late September and was expected to be bedridden for at least a month. The RWM felt it essential to delay the implementation of the reorganization, since Hilgard had been personally selected by Göring to undertake the reorganization and it simply could not be done without Hilgard if one did not want to run the risk of the old conflicts of interest – which Hilgard had been assigned the task of eradicating – showing up yet again. The RWM went further than originally intended, however, by not simply delaying the reorganization until the new year but actually empowering Hilgard to integrate the old apparatus with the new one, to appoint the committees that were to function immediately, and to appoint commissars for the special branch organizations falling under the economic groups. Hilgard also appointed Alzheimer to act as his deputy until he returned to work. Hilgard's "indispensability" had obviously been powerfully ratified by Göring's imprimatur, and he knew how to use

---

[69] Entwurf, RWM an Braunes Haus, 31. Mai 1939, and Hilgard an Staatssekretär Landfried, 30. Okt. 1939, ibid., Bl. 201–2, 300–6.
[70] Schwede-Coburg an Ministerialrat Krüger, 12. Juli 1939, ibid., Bl. 210–11.

it. Hilgard's illness provided him with an excellent opportunity to preempt future decisions, both with respect to organization and with respect to personnel.[71]

This did not go unnoticed by Bothe and Reuter, who were from the publicly chartered companies and allies of Schwede-Coburg and were slated to head economic groups. They went so far as to refuse to recognize the commissarial and other appointments that had been made by Hilgard on the grounds that these required approval from Heß's office. The RWM responded by characterizing their behavior as "crude insubordination," a violation of the leadership principle and cause for dismissal if not corrected.[72] At the same time, Schwede-Coburg was now taking the position that one did not need branch groups after all and that one could settle on having five economic groups with the persons already appointed.

For Hilgard, however, this was no longer satisfactory, and he apparently felt that both his renewed authority and the outbreak of the war gave him the opportunity to demand that the private insurance sector receive its due. As he pointed out in telephone calls to Schwede-Coburg and in a lengthy letter of October 30 to Landfried of the RWM,[73] the only area where publicly chartered companies had a market share comparable to that of the private insurers was fire insurance, with 40% for the former and 60% for the latter. There was no other area in which the publicly chartered companies could boast more than 15% of market share; in many cases, it was considerably less. Furthermore, the private insurance companies were exclusively involved in the most risky areas of wartime insurance: transport, where special community transport insurers had been organized to share the additional risk, and machine insurance. Ninety percent of flight insurance was provided by the private insurers. Hilgard found it inappropriate that the most important economic groups in which private insurers dominated were nonetheless under leaders of the publicly chartered companies, while those groups led by private insurance industry leaders were almost exclusively the province of the private insurers anyway. The only head with whom Hilgard was reasonably satisfied was Kratochwill, since the policies pursued by the private and the DAF life insurance companies tended to be similar. Hilgard demanded that the weight of the private insurers be increased by dividing property insurance into two groups, one under Bothe for fire insurance and the other under General Director Blase of Aachen-Leipziger Versicherungs-AG for other forms of property insurance. Similarly, while willing to leave accident insurance with Reuter, Hilgard proposed that Schmidt-Polex be placed in charge of a separate liability insurance group. Hilgard was quite blunt in stating that the acceptance of his proposals was essential if he were to lead the Reich Group

---

[71] Vermerk, 28. Sept. 1939, and Vermerk, 7. Okt. 1939, ibid., Bl. 229–30, 251–2.
[72] Vermerk Ministerialrat Homann, 21. Okt. 1939; Schreiben Neumann an Homann, 16. Okt. 1939, ibid., Bl. 280–7.
[73] Hilgard an Landfried, 30. Okt. 1939, ibid., Bl. 300–6.

effectively and maintain the confidence of the private insurers. After further bickering in which Hilgard and Schmitt pressed Ministerial Director Lange to concede the demands of the private insurers, an organizational arrangement was finally agreed upon that was acceptable to all sides. There would be seven economic groups, with transport under General Director Edgar Schnell of Nordstern forming a special group (for the wartime period) with all the rights and powers of an economic group. Property insurance was divided into two groups: the first, under Bothe, had domain over fire, water, interruption of plant operations, storm, hail, and livestock; the second, under Blase, was charged with insurance against theft, civic unrest, rain damage, machinery and machine assemblage, and glass. Apparently, theft and glass insurance had first been given to Bothe's group but were now transferred to Blase's because of pressure from Hilgard and Schmitt. The other groups were life and health insurance, vehicle insurance, accident insurance, liability insurance, and reinsurance and credit insurance. Five of the economic group leaders came from the private sector and three from the publicly chartered sector. If the purpose of the reorganization initiated by Schwede-Coburg and his friends had been to give domination to the publicly chartered insurers, then the combined forces of Hilgard, Schmitt, and Lange (and the crucial indifference of Göring) had defeated those efforts.[74]

One of the reasons that the number and composition of the leadership of the economic groups was so important was that they were to be represented in the insurance advisory council for the RAA and RWM, by this time referred to as the Reich Insurance Committee, which was to be chaired by Schwede-Coburg and upon which he pinned great hopes of carrying through his proposed reforms of the insurance business. Here too, however, Schmitt and Hilgard had claims to make. Thus, on December 7, Schmitt wrote to Lange expressing appreciation for his efforts on their behalf but pointing out that there was yet one more issue that needed to be settled. While insisting that he was glad to work under the chairmanship of Schwede-Coburg, he could not accept being a co-equal deputy chairman with Hans Goebbels – not because he had anything against Hans Goebbels personally but rather because it seemed inappropriate to have both the chairman and the first deputy chairman come from the publicly chartered companies, given that "85% of the German insurance, and to be sure the most difficult areas, are in private insurance."[75] When Lange tried to make light of the problem, pointing out that the danger of an anti–private insurance industry majority had been obviated and that the goal was a distinguished committee to provide advice, Schmitt assured him that the issue was not one of prestige but rather a practical one, and that he would be satisfied if he (Schmitt) would

[74] See the correspondence and draft decrees of December 1939 in ibid., Bl. 353–72. See also Tagesmeldung, 30. Nov. 1939; Hilgard an Lange, 2. Dez. 1939, Lange an Hilgard, 13. Dez. 1939, Schmitt an Lange, 2. Dez. 1939, SM, 1458/1/282, Bl. 26, 32–8.
[75] Schmitt an Lange, 7. Dez. 1939, ibid., Bl. 47.

be named first deputy chair and Goebbels second deputy chair. Otherwise, he really could not serve on the advisory committee. Nevertheless, in the end he gave way since the formal announcement of the creation of the committee listed Schmitt, along with Goebbels, as deputy chairmen. What would become of the committee remained to be seen, but Schmitt and Hilgard had clearly established a strong position for dealing with Schwede-Coburg and his cronies by the beginning of 1940.[76]

The Reich Insurance Committee did in truth turn out to be an extremely unpleasant, even bizarre, experience. The committee held its first meeting on January 26, 1940, where Schwede-Coburg and Amend – with no prior warning – presented members with the draft of an amendment to the Reich Insurance Law under which reinsurance would be placed under RAA supervision and every reinsurance contract would be subject to RAA approval. Schwede-Coburg also announced that he intended to send the legislation on to the RWM and claimed that it had the unanimous agreement of the committee. It cannot be said, however, that he got very far with this tactic. Hilgard and Alzheimer immediately objected that this would destroy Germany's position in the international reinsurance business entirely, since no foreign insurer would or could wait upon the approval of some Berlin office before concluding an agreement with its German counterpart. Schwede-Coburg's response was that such arguments did not impress him since the war would be won "in three months and foreign insurers will be happy if they are allowed to reinsure with German companies."[77] Schwede-Coburg's effort to achieve a fait accompli failed, and the matter was put off for negotiation among the interested parties and commentary from the Reinsurance Economic Group. The latter produced a long letter of protest stating that reinsurance often required speedy action, that the business would be undermined by the proposed requirements, and that a form of state supervision that entailed the granting of permission for each and every piece of business constituted an interference "in the independence and self-responsibility of business." The reinsurance business was too complex to be made hostage to a ruinous "schematization and bureaucratization."

Alzheimer also wrote personally to Amend, warning of the dangers to German international economic interests posed by the Schwede-Coburg proposal. He dismissed the latter's claim that reinsurance was completely free of all supervision, pointing out that it had to open its files just as every other branch of insurance. What it could not produce was a business plan in the style of other insurance branches. He reminded Amend that German reinsurance, especially his concern, had played a leading role in spreading the idea of reinsurance internationally, and he claimed (less accurately) that Munich Re was the leading reinsurance company in the world, ahead even of Swiss Re. He noted that five

---

[76] Lange an Schmitt, 13. Dez. 1939, and Schmitt an Lange, 21. Dez. 1939, ibid., Bl. 48–9.
[77] This account is taken from Alzheimer, "Die deutsche Rückversicherung 1938–1945. Ein Rechenschaftsbericht" (1948), MR, D/2, pp. 3–4.

German companies were in the top ten. Germany's enemies were well aware of the importance of German reinsurance in the neutral countries, and he reminded Amend that Munich Re alone accounted for 16% of the participation in the air insurance pool, a portion that was higher than that of all publicly chartered companies put together. Similarly, German reinsurance played a major role in the fire insurance of big industry under the Four-Year Plan. The RAA simply did not have the resources to go through every reinsurance agreement. More importantly, such surveillance would serve Germany's competitors in the field. Germany, Alzheimer reminded Amend, was competing not only against its rivals in enemy countries but also (and even more) against reinsurers in Italy, who had strong state support, and in neutral countries, especially Switzerland. If Germany won the war, then it could recover its losses against enemy competition but not its losses against allies and the neutrals. He also warned against a policy of limiting concessions to foreign reinsurance companies, since the countries in question would only retaliate and might indeed cooperate in doing so. Finally, Alzheimer emphasized a "psychological consideration":

As you can imagine the German companies have to fight hard for their positions abroad, and to be sure less against English and French than against neutral competition. The sources of our difficulties lie to a large extent in the fear that we will be hindered some day through German government measures – against the previous practice of the Reich Economics Ministry and the Reichsbank – in the fulfillment of our obligations or that our operations will be made more difficult. Why should we here deliver another excuse without thereby gaining any tangible advantages?[78]

This was not the only proposal that Schwede-Coburg presented to the opening meeting of the committee. He also proposed a change in section 81 of the Reich Insurance Law that would give the RAA new powers to dissolve insurance companies or merge them with other insurance companies – and even transfer their portfolios, if this were deemed justifiable for the good of the insurance industry. This would have enabled the RAA to place private insurance companies under public control and, more generally, to dispose of such private assets at will. Needless to say, Hilgard and his colleagues from the private insurance field raised a strong protest, emphasizing the danger to private property rights and the pure arbitrariness of the projected legislation. Schwede-Coburg was not a man who took well to being contradicted, and when Hilgard's arguments began to get on his nerves, he turned on the radio in the room and drowned out Hilgard's remarks with a military march.[79]

Just as Alzheimer had sought to counter Amend's attack on the reinsurance business with rational arguments to Amend, so Schmitt attempted to use persuasion in dealing with Schwede-Coburg – with whom he went so far as to meet for breakfast – on both issues but especially on the question of shutting down

---

[78] Alzheimer an Amend, 22. Jan. 1940, BAB, R 3104/11.
[79] See Hilgard's manuscript, "Die Allianz im 2. Weltkrieg," FHA, AZ 1.3/2, pp. 8–10.

Franz Schwede-Coburg (1888–1966), Gauleiter and president of the province of Pommerania, about 1938.

enterprises. He took (or at least pretended to take) seriously Schwede-Coburg's claim that rationalization was necessary in the industry and that some of the smaller enterprises needed to be shut down or merged with other companies, but he insisted that the companies so designated should be given the opportunity to choose the placement of their portfolios or their new partners. Only if they refused to do so in a timely fashion should the RAA have the right to make these decisions. What he wished to prevent was Schwede-Coburg's use of such shutdowns to transfer the portfolios to publicly chartered companies of his choosing.[80]

All in all, this proved a formidable counteroffensive. Although Schwede-Coburg claimed he had the support of all the representatives of the Party institutions in the Reich Insurance Committee, he was clearly opposed by the most

[80] Schmitt an Schwede-Coburg, 19. März 1940 mit Anlagen, BAB, R 3104/11.

important leaders in the private insurance business.[81] There was no way these proposals were going to be implemented with any alacrity, especially since Hilgard could count on Hans Thees in the Justice Ministry to raise all kinds of objections, and the continuing war made it more and more difficult to interfere in the operations of the active reinsurance business.

Nevertheless, Schwede-Coburg and his allies continued to use the committee for purposes of harassment and as a potential vehicle for a long-term restructuring of the industry. Thus, at the second meeting on May 28, 1940, Bothe began raising questions about whether German reinsurance contracts abroad were being used for purposes of espionage by the enemy as well as costing Germany needed foreign exchange. That Hilgard, Alzheimer, and Edgar Schnell of Nordstern had all consulted with the Army command about these matters and had made special provisions in no way mollified Bothe, who stated that the behavior of the reinsurance economic group "bordered on treason" since they were indirectly helping British bombers to find their targets in Germany.[82]

Needless to say, this was a canard, with an especially vicious and dangerous undertone because of the regime running Germany. It is very important, however, to place the intense conflict between Schwede-Coburg and his associated Nazi ideologues within a context beyond the rather simple politics of self-defense against socialist-minded Nazis that was so strongly emphasized by Hilgard, Alzheimer, and Schmitt after the war. The politics of the German insurance industry leaders was much more complex and had its own offensive thrust, especially at this point when the war was going so well for Germany. Thus, in June 1940 and fresh in the wake of German military victories in the West, Schmitt wrote to SS-Gruppenführer Wolff requesting permission for himself and Alzheimer to travel – as soon as the military situation permitted – to Norway, Denmark, the Netherlands, Belgium, and Sweden in order to renew their business contacts at a time when those countries had been cut off from England and were finding it difficult to make contact with Switzerland – a time when Germany could rush in to fill the gap. The English insurers, with over a century of international experience behind them (especially in the field of transport insurance but also in other branches) and with strong competitive advantages, had profited from the Allied victory in 1918 to establish a powerful position for themselves in West European markets.[83] This aggressive approach was also evinced by Alzheimer at the November 1940 meeting of the Reich Insurance Committee, where he took the initiative and went into a lengthy argument that "the

[81] Schwede-Coburg an den Reichswirtschaftsminister, Mai 1940, ibid.

[82] Alzheimer, "Die deutsche Rückversicherung 1938–1945. Ein Rechenschaftsbericht" (1948), MR, D/2, p. 13, and 2. Sitzung des Reichsversicherungsausschusses am 28. Mai 1940, SM, 1458/1/282, Bl. 79–82.

[83] Schmitt an Wolff, 5. Juni 1940, BAB, ehem. BDC, SL 62. See also the useful discussion of the English insurance business by Martin Herzog, "Beispielsammlung für die Kriegswirtschaftsgeschichte: Behandlung der englischen Versicherungsbestände in den von deutschen Truppen besetzten Gebiete," 18. Sept. 1941, GDV, Personenarchiv/Akte Martin Herzog.

opportunity to now recapture the German position on the foreign market and to build it up must be exploited by every means."[84] At the same time, Schnell pointed out that the German transport insurance had successfully organized itself to replace the English market, although he complained that IG Farben still made a practice of insuring its foreign trade abroad.

Indeed, the view was widely held that the separation of the European insurance market from London provided an important opportunity for the German insurance industry,[85] and Kurt Schmitt saw the situation as one particularly propitious for reorganizing the entire European insurance market. In the late summer of 1940, he and his colleagues at the Munich Re began discussing the idea of creating a reinsurance community to replace the role of Lloyd's of London and other British firms on the continent. It is important to note that this was no easy task, given the previous role played by the British, the vast increase of insurable risks on the continent during the war, and the inability of Germans alone to assume responsibility for them. One would have to mobilize the conquered and the neutrals to serve the needs of Europe's new masters. Furthermore, Schmitt and Alzheimer found independent enthusiasm for such a step among their Italian partners. Thus, when Alzheimer met with the RAS leaders Frigessi and Marchesano in Venice in October 1940, Frigessi remarked that

it should at the present time be the task of the German and Italian insurance companies to create an institution that can as far as possible take over the position of the English Lloyd's. In most areas, the continental reinsurers have understood how to replace the English market, there having been certain difficulties only in transport insurance, excess loss and other exotic business. But even for these companies it is desirable to set up continental coverage possibilities on the basis of a consolidation of a large number of insurance carriers in the form of a consortium in which groups of insurance carriers voluntarily sign up. The initiative for this should come from the Italian and German companies.[86]

Alzheimer informed Frigessi that these ideas were already being discussed in Munich, but that one also wanted to bring in the Swiss along with the Italian and German markets.

Schmitt himself held discussions with leaders of the other major Italian concern, Generali, as well as with the Swiss Re, and he seems to have won them over to his basic and rather novel conception by the end of 1940. This conception was to create a community of all the insurance carriers on the continent for the purpose of covering those risks whose size and character were such that they could not be covered by existing mechanisms. He thought it important that the community be continental and not German–Italian, but he also felt that the management had to be centered in Germany, which was the largest and most

[84] 3. Sitzung des Reichsversicherungsausschusses, 19. Nov. 1940, SM 1458/1/282, Bl. 88–91.
[85] "Loslösung der europäischen Versicherungsmärkte von London. Deutschlands Versicherungswirtschaft vor neuen Aufgaben," *Neumanns Zeitschrift für Versicherungswesen* 63 (1940), pp. 517–18.
[86] Aktennotiz, 2. Okt. 1940, MR, B 15/23.

central power; he suggested that it be placed in Munich under von Reininghaus. The Association for the Coverage of Large Risks was only to deal with those risks that could not be dealt with under existing market conditions and not to take over risks that were uncovered because of the customer's refusal to pay an appropriate premium. Furthermore, the liability was to be shared in proportion to the contribution made by the individual members, and these were not to be fixed but to vary as the companies took stock of the situation and how much liability they were undertaking. Schmitt was anxious to clear the entire matter with the German government and also to use the founding of the association to prevent any formation of state reinsurance bodies or institutions specifically for the purpose of replacing Lloyd's. Rather, he wanted to make sure his projected association would serve as an organization that all insurance companies could join and would function as a kind of clearing agency for specific risks not otherwise coverable in any single market.[87]

After a meeting was held among leading insurance companies in early 1941, Schmitt was able to announce the formation of the association formally in March and invited the various European insurance companies to participate. Schmitt, not surprisingly, was made chairman of the association, and its management was located in the Munich Re, but its presidium was to be representative of the leading continental European insurance companies. The announcement stressed the voluntary nature of the organization and the need to maintain a healthy insurance market and to act only where conditions so required. Von Reininghaus was sent off to France and Belgium to recruit for the new association, finding considerable interest in France but having some difficulties in Belgium, where several companies did not want to do anything that might suggest they accepted the "new order."[88] By mid-May, Schmitt was able to announce a pecking order of companies who were to be favored in instances where insurance was required for great risks. At the top of the twelve German, Italian, and Swiss companies listed stood Munich Re and Swiss Re, each with 25% participation, followed by Kölnische Rück with 10% and Generali and RAS with 5% each; Frankona Rück followed with 10%. Should more help be needed, however, clients of the association could turn to large primary insurers like Allianz and Nordstern. The new organization did insure a storehouse filled with furs in Norway worth 600,000 Norwegian kroner as well as eleven Finnish electrical machines for the making of paper from wood (worth 5–58 million Finnish marks) – which were illustrations of the sort of "large risks" it was set up to handle – but it did not, in the end, do a significant amount of business.[89]

---

[87] Aktennote Schmitt, Zürich and Milan, Nov. 15–21, 1940, ibid. It is interesting to note that Frigessi would have preferred less identification with the Munich Re by locating the Association in Vienna or Hamburg. On the extent of the business done by the organization, see Herzog, "Was Dokumente erzählen können," Bd. 3, pp. 1219–22.

[88] Aktennote von Reininghaus, 26. März–8. April 1941, HMR, B 15/2.

[89] Aktennote Schmitt, 12. Mai 1941, ibid.

This European cartel for the management of great risks was a good illustration of how Munich Re (and, as will be shown later, Allianz) was taking the lead in the expansion of German insurance as Germany's armies advanced in all directions. Those involved, however, continued to think in terms of an international economic order with Germany as the leading but not sole protagonist in the field. It was precisely this liberal perception that Schwede-Coburg and the Party ideologues detested, and it was embodied in the German–Swiss connection, the strong participation of the Swiss in the German market, the German involvement in the Swiss market, and the agreements on the exclusion of reinsurance obligations from clearing requirements under foreign exchange decrees. These connections and arrangements had already been attacked from circles hostile to the German private insurance business before the war, but they had been beaten back with considerable success by arguments that the relationship was vital to German trade and commerce. With the coming of the war, however, there was a renewal of such hostility on both security and economic grounds, and the issue had become something of a centerpiece in the struggle over "insurance reform."

The leadership of the Swiss Re was well aware of these tendencies, especially owing to their large interest in Bayerische Rückversicherung AG; a report of May 1940 expressed concern about "what is being cooked up in Berlin."[90] Rumor had it that Swiss Re was simply to be driven out of Germany but that Schmitt had intervened and urged that a less drastic approach be taken. The particular vulnerability of Swiss Re lay in charges from a subordinate office of the military high command that secret information on German industry had fallen into enemy hands because of the Swiss Re. The military insisted not only that foreign reinsurers no longer be used but also that Hofrat Ernst Drumm, head of Bayerische Rück, be thrown off all German supervisory boards because of his Swiss connection. As a compromise Hilgard, who was extremely concerned about the military pressure and the way it played back into the domestic debate with Schwede-Coburg, suggested that Swiss Re's German business be placed under trusteeship for the duration of the war. The Swiss were infuriated at the proposal, which they termed "catastrophic and unacceptable,"[91] and were resentful as well. They reminded Hilgard of all they had done for Germany during the First World War, the losses they had taken in the inflation, the fact that they had left 12 million RM with German companies to help the foreign exchange situation, and of their participation in the German war transport community and the German air transport pool, which was bound to bring losses but which they nevertheless joined in order to show solidarity with their German business partners. At the same time, Hilgard was warned that the Swiss government was bound to respond to such interference in Swiss operations in Germany with countermeasures against German interests in Switzerland. Finally, the Swiss emphasized

[90] Report from Berlin on "Deutsches Geschäft," 4. Mai 1940, SR, FA A7.3-03.
[91] Report, May 1940, ibid.

their close personal friendships with their German counterparts and the desirability of maintaining these relationships.

It was not Hilgard, of course, who needed persuasion. Although the pressure on the Swiss insurance companies abated after May, a new issue arose in the late summer and early fall – namely, whether the Swiss companies doing business in Alsace and Lorraine, where they had been active before their return to France in 1918 and had remained prior to the German occupation in 1940, would be allowed to continue to do so. Schmitt discussed the danger of excluding the Swiss from their old business with Reich Economics Minister Funk in late September, and the latter agreed with Schmitt that the Swiss should not be excluded; indeed, he could see no legal basis for excluding them.[92] Nevertheless, by early November Schwede-Coburg had used his influence with Amend, Robert Wagner (the fanatical Gauleiter in Alsace), and Minister-President Köhler in Karlsruhe to withdraw not only the permission given to the Swiss but also the licenses accorded to six German insurance companies to do business in Alsace – among them Allianz, Karlsruher, and Victoria. Schwede-Coburg was anxious to gain control of the leading French company in the area, Rhein und Mosel, in order to shape the insurance business in Lorraine and Alsace. As General Director Kurt Hamann of Victoria explained to an alarmed General Director Koenig of Schweizerische Rentenanstalt, spokesman for the Swiss insurance business,

Schwede-Coburg ... is a strong party-political personality, who is unhampered by any traditions and has as his highest goal the nationalization of insurance, namely, the creation of a great central institution divided into Gaue [districts] which takes care of everything. For this reason, he demanded that first a publicly chartered company be granted a dominating position in Alsace and Lorraine and that the "Rhein und Mosel" provide the foundation for this purpose. The goal that is to be attained in Alsace is the speediest possible mobilizing of the territory for National Socialism. For this reason also, no foreign life insurance ought to be in any way active in Alsace, for otherwise "dissidents" will be cultivated and supported and everyone will run to the foreigners.[93]

Hamann also noted that Schwede-Coburg was furious at the anti-German tone of the Swiss press and wanted to make an example, but also that he was working hand-in-hand with his friend Hans Goebbels to undertake similar measures in Eupen-Malmedy. He doubted that all the Swiss firms would be licensed to operate in Lorraine and Alsace and that the Swiss should concentrate particularly on life insurance and on those companies that had been operating in the area before 1914.

Clearly Hamann was trying to help the Swiss as much as possible, and Hilgard was even more explicit about the reasons in his discussions with Koenig. As Koenig reported, Hilgard

---

[92] Aktennote Schmitt, 24. Sept. 1940, MR, A 1/7.
[93] Vertrauliche Notiz Koenig, 5. Nov. 1940, SR, FA A7.3-03.

assured me that the German insurance business has the greatest interest in not having the Swiss companies driven out of Lorraine and Alsace – which is the goal of certain Party agencies – for that is moving in the direction of autarky, which would be damaging to private insurance because it will lead to nationalization. For these reasons we can be sure to count on his support.[94]

Schmitt was no less pointed in his discussion with Koenig, to whom he stressed that Munich Re stood behind the Swiss in Alsace and that Funk – as well as State Secretaries Landfried and Clodius in the RWM – were also opposed to the Party desires. Koenig reported Schmitt saying that "the German private insurance industry has the greatest interest that we Swiss corporations remain in Germany because we are the best bulwark against the nationalization of the insurance business"[95] and also urging the Swiss to take diplomatic steps to assert their rights where they had a historical foundation. At the same time, Allianz and Munich Re were expanding, and Schmitt had important plans for setting up a private insurance corporation in the Generalgouvernement in Poland and working with Swiss Re and other friendly companies on the formation of a reinsurance community on the continent. At a meeting with Directors Emil Bebler and Hürlimann of Swiss Re in Zürich on November 13, 1940, he found them very pessimistic. The Swiss insurance men felt that their friends in Germany were deserting them under government pressure, and they were inclined to sell out their holdings despite Schmitt's warm words for this Swiss rival, his renewed advice to work with the right people in the RWM, and his stress on the need to protect the private insurance business through the Association for the Coverage of Large Risks that he was proposing.[96]

Bebler certainly appreciated Schmitt's good will and friendliness, but his experience with RAA President Amend, with whom he had a "discussion" on January 16, 1941, was every bit as unpleasant as he had been led to anticipate. Amend let loose with complaints about the anti-German tone of the Swiss press. Bebler did not deny that certain portions of the Swiss press were not appropriately neutral in their attitude, but – in one of the few bright moments in this otherwise bleak history – he paid more heed to his role as a citizen than to his function as a businessman; his reported "conversation" with Amend deserves to be honored with extensive citation:

Switzerland is the oldest Republic and a democracy of a special kind which cannot be compared with others. We are not National Socialists and do not want to be, but rather to remain what we are. Although Hitler has more than once declared that National Socialism is no export product and that he does not want to impose it on other countries, we are compelled to defend our democracy. No one can prevent us from doing so. Hitler has declared in his speeches that a people that does not defend itself does not deserve to

[94] Ibid.
[95] Ibid.
[96] Aktennote Schmitt, 13. Nov. 1940, MR, B 6/9.

Hans Goebbels (1895–1947), general director of Provinzial Feuer- und Lebensversicherungsanstalten der Rheinprovinz, brother of Reich Propaganda Minister Joseph Goebbels, about 1933.

survive. – Herr Amend: "We have done nothing to you, although it would have been a trival matter for us to take Switzerland." – I: "We are grateful to fate that you have decided to leave us in peace. I must however say, Herr President, that Switzerland would not be so easy to take as the Netherlands, Belgium, and other nations. They who would attack us will meet up with a well-armed and trained army and a resolved people." "To be sure," he replied, "you have your mountains; but nothing can be done against our soldiers, our Stukas, and our tanks." – I: "You will permit me to have another opinion. In general, may God prevent that Switzerland is also drawn into the vortex." – Herr Amend: "We do not have anything against Switzerland insofar as it accepts the circumstances as they have been created by our victory in Europe. The European economy will be newly ordered under German leadership. There will be a European economic block and a central clearing – Switzerland cannot exclude itself from it." – My answer: The position of Switzerland to the new ordering of the economy and to a European central clearing is a matter for our government to decide. I imagine in any case, that Switzerland cannot remain on the sidelines but must come to an arrangement with the new circumstances. A central clearing seems necessary to me if payments from country to country are to function again.[97]

After this exchange of "pleasantries," Bebler reminded Amend of the many services of Swiss companies to Germany and urged that the old Alsatian companies in which they had an interest be maintained. Amend then complained that Swiss Re did not have any Germans in its administrative council, to which Bebler responded that it was an international concern and needed to maintain its independence of any particular country. When Amend pointed out that there was a Swiss on the Munich Re supervisory council, Bebler diplomatically responded that Swiss Re worked with companies from many nations and could not give each a seat on its board, although what he would have liked to have said was that "a Swiss on a German supervisory board could allow himself to be visible, but the reverse was not the case."

Needless to say, the question of how to deal with the Swiss was a matter of German government policy and not simply a matter of Schmitt's plans for the European insurance business or Amend's xenophobia. At a meeting in the RWM attended by members of the Foreign Office and by Amend, the issue of whether to encourage the Swiss to maintain their interests in the Reich or rather to pressure them to sell their holdings was seriously discussed. Amend, of course, was quite clear on the subject, arguing "that in his view everything has to be done to repress the Swiss influence. One has to consider that liberal influences make themselves felt in German insurance through Swiss insurance interests ...."[98] In the ensuing discussion, however, Amend stood alone; the Foreign Office representatives emphasized the foreign exchange advantages provided by the Swiss and that credit business with the Swiss was of great value to the German war economy. It was thus important not to annoy the Swiss gratuitously. The Foreign Office had nothing against the Swiss selling some of the German holdings, but warned against the employment of any pressure. Similarly, while they thought that the Swiss had accepted a measure of limitation on their engagement in Alsace and Lorraine, "an irritation of the Swiss is undesired at the present time." Thus, in early January, Gauleiter Wagner in Alsace, Gauleiter Bürckel in Lorraine, and Gauleiter Gustav Simon (head of the civil administration in Luxemburg) were instructed to pay due respect to old Swiss interests in their respective territories. There is no evidence that they were in any rush to do so, since State Secretary Landfried reported in early February that the matter still had not been decided. The Swiss knew that the prime reason was the power struggle in Berlin, and they had no expectation that all nineteen Swiss companies would be issued a license – especially since, in the fall of 1940, the RAA had allowed only a limited number

---

[97] Bebler, Besprechung mit dem Präsidenten des RAA, Herrn Amend, in Berlin am 16. Jan. 1941, SR, FA A7.3-03.

[98] Vermerk, Besprechung vom 16. Nov. 1940, SM, 1458/11/53, Bl. 224–5.

of German companies in the area and only two Italian companies. For example, Allianz was granted a license to conduct new business but not Neue Frankfurter, which was told to make no further applications.[99]

However, what really triggered concern and alarm among the private insurance company leaders was the news that authorities in Lorraine had, with RWM authorization, created a publicly chartered property insurance institution to preside over compulsory building insurance and that there were plans to extend such insurance to the Alsace, the Saar, and Luxemburg. In short, Schwede-Coburg and his Gauleiter friends in the West were now extending as a fait accompli the system of compulsory building insurance already existing in various parts of Germany to the reconquered areas. The danger that this would serve as a wedge for expansion of the publicly chartered system into other areas and for the nationalization of insurance was obvious. Schwede-Coburg and his friends were obviously using the occupied areas to preempt future development of the insurance business therein, rather than placing any further faith in meetings of the Reich Insurance Committee that consistently evaded their control.[100]

Where, then, to turn? As in the past, so now: Hilgard and Schmitt capitalized on their cultivation of Göring, which dated back to the days before the Nazis took power. Thus, on March 21, 1941, Hilgard responded to a birthday greeting from Göring by taking the liberty of expressing his cares to the Reichsmarschall, cares that reflected the "unlimited confidence" that Hilgard had placed in him since their first meeting in 1931. Hilgard reminded Göring that the latter had mandated peace in the insurance business in their meeting on December 10, 1938, and he and his colleagues in the private industry had followed the injunction. The same, however, did not hold for the publicly chartered companies, which in the past months had introduced compulsory building insurance and propagated the idea of a socialized building insurance. Neither the Reich Insurance Committee and its deputy chairman Schmitt nor he, as head of the Reich Group, had been consulted. Hilgard had only learned of these actions in Lorraine and Alsace through the newspaper. Furthermore, Schwede-Coburg had claimed that the Führer himself had ordered the nationalization of this type of insurance. Before the war, building fire insurance had been the exclusive province of the private companies in Lorraine and Alsace, "and it would be for every just-thinking person self-evident, that it would receive restitution for the robbery it experienced which had been imposed upon it by the Treaty of Versailles."[101] Instead, this compensation was being taken by the publicly chartered insurance companies through the use of their political influence. Hilgard feared that this would

[99] Schreiben RWM, Jan. 1941, ibid., Bl. 226f.; Tagesbericht, 3. Feb. 1941, SM, 1458/1/693, Bl. 12; SR, Verband Konzessionierter Schweizerischer Versicherungsgesellschaften, Vorstandsprotokoll, 4. März 1941; RAA an Allianz, 14. Okt. 1940, BAK, B 280/12253, Bl. 288f.; RAA an Neue Frankfurter, 22. Nov. 1940, BAK, B 280/13206, Bl. 166–7.
[100] Tagesbericht, 3. Feb. 1941, SM, 1458/1/693, Bl. 12.
[101] Hilgard an Göring, 21. März 1941, FHA, S 17.5/76.

then be extended to the Saar, with its substantial private industrial holdings, and also to the newly created Warthegau in what had once been a part of Poland. He undoubtedly knew whereof he spoke, since the Gauleiter of the Warthegau, Arthur Greiser, had written to Deputy Führer Rudolf Heß on January 3, 1941, asking that Posensche Feuersozietät be given a fire insurance monopoly in the Warthegau, defending this position in a lengthy memorandum. Heß's chief of staff Martin Bormann had backed Greiser in a letter to the Economics Minister on February 5.[102] Hence the danger was real that the private insurers would simply be shut out of the fire insurance business for buildings in the newly annexed areas. Hilgard complained to Göring that the private insurers were never consulted about these measures and that they were now being deprived of the most lucrative insurance, which they needed if they were to play the role of creating German preeminence in the insurance field internationally. Hilgard pointed out that he could easily just ask the Reich Economics Minister to accept his resignation but did not feel entitled to do so, "since the soldier in war cannot resign and since on the other side, even if I have been formally appointed by the Reich Economics Minister, I still feel myself appointed by you." Thus, so long as he had Göring's confidence, he would stay on the job, and the best demonstration of this would be if Göring would put an end to the development he had described.

As was so often the case, this was a coordinated effort between Hilgard and Schmitt, and the former referred to a letter Schmitt had sent Göring on this subject that sought to spell out the dangers presented by the monopoly on compulsory fire insurance that had been granted to the publicly chartered companies in some of the occupied areas. Funk had informed Schmitt that the monopoly was the product of a basic decision of Hitler himself, but Schmitt felt it only proper – given his lifetime devotion to the insurance business – that he express his objections. Schmitt sought to frame his argument in the context of general national economic developments and especially the Anglo-German economic rivalry. He stressed the interaction between British insurance and its position in world trade, as well as the importance of England's capacity to compensate for the broad range of risks in its insurance business through its expanding commercial capacity and ability to spread its system worldwide. Germany had challenged Britain through the development of the reinsurance idea and its commercial power until the setback of the Great War, after which it had to struggle to regain something of its former position despite its political powerlessness. Schmitt emphasized the importance of the role of insurance as an "invisible" factor that enabled England to cover half its foreign trade deficit.

Schmitt went on to stress what Germany's "final victory" would mean from the perspective of replacing England internationally as the leading insurer, as well as the significance of this combination of shipping, commerce, and insurance for Germany's balance of foreign trade and currency. Germany could establish for

---

[102] See Greiser an Heß, 3. Jan. 1941, and Bormann an den Reichswirtschaftsminister, 5. Feb. 1941, APP, Reichsstatthalter/2801, Bl. 18–42.

itself the kind of world trading position that England had previously enjoyed in places like China. Furthermore, this was not only an economic vision but also a political one, since a large trading organization and network of representatives were excellent sources of both political and economic intelligence. These benefits, however, could only be provided by the merchant and private person, not by public agencies, and Schmitt pointed out how ineffective was the Soviet state insurance monopoly, which other countries did not trust and did not use. The victorious war now gave Germany the opportunity to take advantage of its position, and Schmitt mapped out a clear strategy:

We already see today during the war that it is not at all difficult to orientate the insurance market completely toward Germany. German companies are licensed which work in competition with their domestic counterparts. German companies will acquire capital participation and practically turn the foreign enterprises into daughter companies and thereby to branches, and finally the domestic insurance business in the various countries, which wisely should not be destroyed, will become accustomed to placing large portions of their business in Germany. Thus, without the use of force and naturally, the business of the countries under our influence will flow naturally into a unity with a German center of gravity and, to be sure, all the more naturally, the less external pressure and force will be perceived and felt.

In this connection, Schmitt pointed out that the recently created Association for the Coverage of Large Risks that included practically all the nations of Europe "is the first practical expression of the development described."[103]

All these advantages, however, were now threatened by the nationalization plans of Schwede-Coburg and his allies. Building insurance was the keystone of the insurance business because of the large premiums involved and the easy calculation of risk, and the provision and calculation of other forms of insurance provided by the private insurers depended on this building fire insurance market. Therefore, the insurance business would be severely weakened by nationalization and its general credit undermined; it would then be in no position to work effectively abroad. Indeed, it would be totally dependent on foreign insurers when working internationally. It would also encourage other countries to take similar measures and so lead to a policy of mutual exclusion in the international insurance market. Schmitt proposed that the publicly chartered companies in the field of compulsory building insurance all be turned into a Reich corporation that would compete with the other insurance institutions offering building insurance, that special provisions be made for inexpensive insurance for settlement construction projects, and that the entire business be treated like the compulsory hunting insurance, which required no bureaucratic structure and which offered insurance from a variety of sources at a reasonable price. (Schmitt pointed out that, as Reich Hunting Master, Göring seemed to be quite satisfied with the arrangement.) In Schmitt's view, however, the issue was actually a basic decision

---

[103] Schmitt an Göring, 22. März 1941, FHA, S 17.5/76.

as to whether or not Germany wanted to have an effective private insurance system that operated on international markets – that is, whether one wanted an insurance business run by public officials or by businessmen. For Schmitt, at least, the proper National Socialist economic leadership for Germany and the world was one in which the economy was guided but not managed by the State, in which Germany would be prepared to assume a great role in the world with the coming of peace, and in which the German people were serviced by an effective insurance system after the war had been won. He thus appealed to Göring to secure a basic decision from Hitler in this area.

In fact, Göring had already issued an order (on March 3, 1941) banning formal discussion of nationalizing the insurance industry during the coming years and suggesting that the question be suppressed in order to avoid further confusion; this was officially communicated on April 26, 1941.[104] The trouble was that individual actions in the occupied territories had implications for the future, and the polycratic nature of the regime meant that any number of policies could be pursued at the same time. For example, Schmitt in desperation turned to Himmler and sent him a copy of his letter to Göring, but Himmler refused to grant Schmitt an audience on this subject since he did not want to interfere in the insurance controversy.[105] The most extensive response to Schmitt's letter, which was widely disseminated, came from Martin Bormann, who was anything but convinced by Schmitt's arguments. Bormann was clearly on the side of Schwede-Coburg and suggested that, if the private insurance business was so vulnerable that it needed fire insurance premiums on buildings in order to cover its more risky ventures, then it should be totally nationalized. Insofar as the international issue was concerned, Bormann argued that the insurance business gave out more in foreign exchange than it took in, that Germany's economic role in the world would ultimately depend on the political situation and not the status of the insurance business, that the insurance business suffered from an excess of companies and of employees, and that the money it received would be better spent on damage prevention than on dividends.[106]

What all this meant was a constant testing and sparring between the private insurance leaders and Schwede-Coburg and his supporters. The latter continually tried to expand the scope of compulsory building insurance in the occupied areas, while the private insurers hunted about for support from other leading Nazis. Because National Socialist economic doctrine was extremely opportunistic in practice, it was very hard to tell in what direction it was going. Ley, for example, thought his DAF had proven every bit as effective and efficient as Allianz: paying its directors a great deal less and needing only a 3.5% rather than a 4.5% interest rate. At the same time, the Schwede-Coburg position was incompatible

---

[104] Göring an RWM, usw., 3. März 1941, ibid.; Gauleitung Hamburg an Staatssekretär Landfried, 26. April 1941, SM, 1458/1/94, Bl. 41.
[105] Brandt an Kranefuss, 9. Juni 1941, BAB, NS 19/2220, Bl. 56.
[106] Bormann an Schmitt, 25. April 1941, BAB, NS 6/328, Bl. 8–13.

with that of the DAF and Ley's empire building. Funk and the RWM obviously were friendlier to private enterprise, and though Funk thought that some areas of insurance were best managed by the bureaucracy, he was convinced that the most important fields required free competition in order to achieve the highest level of performance. This heartened the advocates of private industry, as did the news that Göring was in favor of reprivatizing the aluminum industry and other enterprises under state control.[107] Another major issue was the nationalization of hail insurance, a measure supported by Schwede-Coburg but strongly opposed by some agricultural interests, who felt they were better served by the private companies and feared that decisions would be made while the major experts were serving in the military.[108]

Officially there was supposed to be a Burgfrieden – a truce of the fortress – between the two sides for the war's duration, but it was constantly violated in deed and word by Schwede-Coburg and his allies. Schwede-Coburg's response to Schmitt's letter to Göring, sent sometime in April 1941, was brutal and blunt. The Gauleiter, after all, also claimed a mandate from Göring – namely, the one given to him in December 1939 to chair the Reich Insurance Committee and reform the insurance system. Originally, he had intended to do so by attacking what he conceived to be the most serious deficiencies and only then turn to reordering the entire system, but Schmitt's memorandum now forced him to take a more basic position. In Schwede-Coburg's view, the purpose of insurance was to protect the German people against the consequences of accident, disaster, and other harms and to serve as the trustee of the premiums paid for this purpose – not to act as a gathering point of large amounts of capital. By collecting capital in the manner in which it had, insurance

has completely alienated itself from its purposes and become a milking cow for large shareholders and a pile of directors and general directors. Well over 2,000 companies bustle about in the insurance field today. The result is that insurance protection has gone into the background and unearned capital profit and big salary earnings have come into the foreground. The cancerous evil of this insurance system, however, is above all that in order to earn these sums an organization has to be built up that no longer stands in any relationship to the economic purpose of insurance.[109]

Schwede-Coburg charged that even huge concerns like Allianz used half their premiums to cover administrative costs, while the liberal competitive system had multiplied the number of insurance agents and salesmen. All one really needed to deal with Germany's domestic insurance needs was about 15 or 20 regional mutual insurance companies that would treat the premiums they received as a trust

---

[107] See the revealing exchange between Ley and Funk, May 24, 1941 and June 3, 1941, FHA, S 17.5/10, as well as Samwer an Hilgard, 26. Juli 1941, FHA, S 17.5/76.

[108] Memorandum on "Verstaatlichungsbestrebungen," Köln, 3. Mai 1941, ibid.

[109] Stellungnahme des Gauleiters Schwede-Coburg zum Schreiben des Generaldirektors Reichsminister a.D. Dr. Schmitt vom 22. März 1941 an den Reichsmarschall, betr. Neugestaltung des Versicherungswesens, SM, 1458/1/94, Bl. 291–5, quote on Bl. 291.

and not a source of profit. At the same time, one could form a single Reich Insurance Corporation to cover risks abroad. Schwede-Coburg was totally opposed to the system of international insurance and reinsurance that Schmitt obviously wished to eternalize. The German economy, in Schwede-Coburg's view, had to be built on German labor and was not to serve as an object of "capitalist exchange." He claimed that the system proposed would truly spare labor and costs and would be less rather than more bureaucratic. Finally, he was very explicit about the next steps to be taken: the introduction of compulsory building insurance in the non-Prussian areas and of compulsory hail and vehicle liability insurance along the lines he proposed.

Schmitt, as might be imagined, was infuriated by Schwede-Coburg's response. In a reply sent to Göring's office, Schmitt pointed out that Göring had assigned Schwede-Coburg the task not of reconstructing the insurance business but rather of heading an advisory body, reducing conflicts between private and publicly chartered insurers, and keeping the peace – since the Führer had ordered a ten-year truce with respect to the question of nationalization. Naturally, Schmitt defended the private industry against Schwede-Coburg's charges that it was making undue profits without really taking any risks; he argued that most of the money made was given back to customers, that the industry had made great sacrifices to ensure that policyholders were paid when a company failed (as in the case of Favag), that the industry was contributing hugely to government loans, and that most of its shareholders came from the middle class. He contested Schwede-Coburg's claim that there were 2,000 insurance companies in the private market, pointing out that of the 3,114 private organizations in 1938–1939, most were small mutuals and local companies or specialized companies that fulfilled a valuable function in the market and that there were actually only some 300 true private insurance companies in the sense normally used. As always, he defended the importance of customers having a choice and the role of competition, insisting that Schwede-Coburg was using false and arbitrary statistics to make the case of excessively high costs. Finally, he defended the significance of the insurance industry abroad and especially emphasized how much the industry had suffered from the last lost war and how much it had to gain from victory in the present one.[110]

The position of the RWM lay somewhere between Schwede-Coburg's ferociously anticapitalist approach and the liberal position of Schmitt and Hilgard, which was (as usual) veiled in politically correct language. Thus, an internal memorandum of April 26, 1941, suggested that there was something to the charges that the industry needed rationalization and that reforms could be made in building, vehicle, and hail insurance – but it rejected nationalization in other areas owing to the dangers of bureaucratization.[111] Whatever the case, the RWM

---

[110] Schmitt an den Persönlichen Referenten Görings, 10. Mai 1941, FHA, S 17.5/76.
[111] Regierungsrat Trepte, "Verstaatlichung des Versicherungswesens," 26. April 1941, SM, 1458/1/94, Bl. 325–32.

was anxious to follow Göring's injunction and remove the entire discussion from the public forum. Thus, Schwede-Coburg was instructed to develop a reform program and carefully prepare any reconstruction of the industry he might wish, but to use the Reich Insurance Committee toward this end. Hilgard was also instructed to avoid all public polemics. Schwede-Coburg complained regularly, even about the appearance of an article by an Old Fighter like Professor Heinrich Hunke, who edited the journal *Die nationalsozialistische Volkswirtschaft* and who was to end up on the managing board of Deutsche Bank as part of that institution's effort to have more Nazis in high places. Hunke was every bit as much a supporter of a directed economy as Schwede-Coburg and, like him, had been graced with the Party's "gold badge of honor"; thus the RWM did not feel it could censor so high and mighty an economic expert, especially since his article did not really deal with polemical issues. The reality was that Schwede-Coburg, backed by Bormann, simply did not want insurance discussed at all until he could come forth with a plan of his own, and then he wanted to make sure that any discussion or actions taken transpired on his own terms.[112]

Apparently, he also decided that he needed to give that plan academic backing and to produce a carefully laid-out scientific argument from his Reich Insurance Committee, as called for by the RWM. In May 1941, Schwede-Coburg asked the Reich Group to provide the committee with 50,000 RM for a study on the development of the insurance business, a request which Hilgard referred to the RWM and which the latter turned down on the grounds that the insurance business was already burdened enough without being additionally burdened for no compelling reason.[113] Undaunted, Schwede-Coburg summoned the committee to its fourth meeting on June 17, 1941, and announced that, with the approval of the RWM, he was appointing Professor Klaus Wilhelm Rath of the insurance seminar at the University of Göttingen to join the Reich Insurance Committee and was charging him with the task of developing a full-scale memorandum dealing with this problem. He was to be aided by a subcommittee of practitioners in the field from the Reich Insurance Committee: Director Bothe from the publicly chartered companies, Director Katochwill from the DAF, and someone (to be named by Hilgard) from the private sector.[114]

The proposal enraged Hilgard, who had procured Rath's vita and found that Rath, who came from Anklam Pommerania, did indeed have a lengthy publication list – but one that featured communal finances (especially of Anklam), the elimination of Jewish influences from economic life, and other general themes dealing with public finance. His only publication on insurance was an article in *Neumanns Zeitschrift* of March 1940 on the reorganization of the study of the science of insurance. Hilgard considered Rath totally unqualified to undertake

[112] For this correspondence, see ibid., Bl. 342–71, 402–4. On Hunke, see James, *Deutsche Bank*, pp. 343–4.

[113] Reichsgruppe Versicherungen an Schwede-Coburg, 18. Juni 1941, GDV, 3-003/1.

[114] Schwede-Coburg an Hilgard, 30 Juni 1941, ibid.

the projected study and refused to send the subcommittee a representative of private industry; he also informed the RWM that he saw no purpose in appointing a "complete novice" to deal with the complexities of the insurance business.[115]

Needless to say, Schwede-Coburg was not going to take such a reply lying down. In an angry response to Hilgard, he pointed out that the RWM had approved Rath's appointment and the latter had been chosen in consultation with a Party agency dealing with academic qualifications and appointments – namely, the Reichsdozentenführer. He saw no excuse whatever for Hilgard to prejudge Rath's work before it had even been completed. Furthermore, personnel choices were not simply a matter of scholarly qualifications: "Decisive for the judgment of a person and his work are not his publications, but rather *his will and capacity as demonstrated by National Socialist deed*." Schwede-Coburg could see no reason why a financial specialist could not do work on insurance, especially someone who was teaching insurance regularly, and he demanded of Hilgard "comradely collaboration" in the Reich Insurance Committee.[116] Unhappily for Hilgard, the RWM supported Schwede-Coburg on this question, and Hilgard found himself not only naming Alzheimer to the subcommittee but also agreeing that the private insurance industry would pay a fifth of the subcommittee's expenses.[117]

At the same time, Hilgard was no less upset by the actions taken by Schwede-Coburg's allies in the occupied areas. Luxemburg was a particular sore point because Gustav Simon, the head of the civil administration, issued a series of decrees that totally changed the insurance situation in the former Grand Duchy. Initially, he had allowed some 40 German companies in the region and charged many of them with trusteeship over enemy companies. Now, all these concessions were suddenly withdrawn. As Hilgard complained to Göring on November 22, 1941, Simon had at the same time established publicly chartered companies in life and property insurance where they had never existed before and given them special monopoly privileges in various spheres. All the work done by the German firms, and especially the preparations they had made to take over Luxemburgian companies, now seemed to have been for naught. Most important, from Hilgard's point of view, was that Simon's actions had implications that stood in direct contradiction to Göring's orders concerning cessation of the socialization debate of December 10, 1938, and its reiteration on March 3, 1941, since the Gauleiter had simply shifted the balance between the two types of insurance companies by creating publicly chartered corporations and giving them

[115] Klaus Wilhelm Rath, "Zur Neuordnung des versicherungswissenschaftlichen Studiums," *Neumanns Zeitschrift für Versicherungswesen* 63 (1940), pp. 151–4; Hilgard an Schwede-Coburg, 6. Juli 1941; Hilgard an Ministerialdirigent Klücki, 6. Juli 1941, GDV, 3-003/1. For Rath's vita, see Notiz für Herrn Amtsgerichtsrat Schwartz, 21. Juli 1941, ibid.

[116] Schwede-Coburg an Hilgard, 31. Juli 1941, ibid.

[117] RWM (Landfried) an Hilgard, 20. Aug. 1941; Hilgard an Schwede-Coburg, 13. Sept. 1941; Schwede-Coburg an Hilgard, 21. Jan. 1942; Hilgard an Mandt, 15. April 1942, ibid.

a special position. Furthermore, the actions in Luxemburg were not isolated, since similar actions were being taken in the Eastern areas. As Hilgard angrily (and accurately) concluded:

What most outrages myself and the entire German private insurance business by all the events described is that, under the rule of the truce which you yourself have ordered repeatedly between public and private insurance no opportunity has been passed up by the publicly chartered companies or their leaders to use the conditions created by the war to harm the interests of private insurance wherever this is possible and by surreptitious means to achieve what is the irreversible goal of the opponents of private insurance, namely the elimination of private insurance itself. And all this is taking place despite the fact that immediately after the end of the war and in general already now the insurance business faces enormous tasks to overcome that can only be solved by private insurance.[118]

In the meantime – unhappily for Schmitt, Hilgard, and their colleagues – Rath was working away at improving his publication record in the field of insurance. In early September 1942, Hilgard heard rumors that Rath was going to publish an article in Hunke's journal and was worried enough to write to Hunke, reminding him that Göring had established a Burgfrieden and that, if Rath broke it with a published article, then the private insurance industry would have to respond. However, Hunke assured Hilgard that he had received no such article and did not intend to be an instrument for breaking the truce.[119] Initially, Alzheimer was somewhat puzzled why there were no meetings of the subcommittee headed by Rath, who had initially consulted him about a few matters of detail but then had remained silent for almost a year. Hilgard was wary and asked Alzheimer to contact Rath, while also writing to Funk that he was constantly being asked what he thought of the Rath report but was in no position to answer, since he had not seen it even though he heard it had been sent to Göring, Ley, and Bormann. In the meantime, Rath replied to Alzheimer that he had been able to gather all the material on his own and did not want to burden the busy committee members.[120]

They were burdened soon enough: not only did the Reich Insurance Committee receive Rath's "The Present Condition and Problems of German Insurance," but its basic ideas also appeared in the press – even though Schwede-Coburg, in the presence of Rath, read an instruction from Bormann that the document was to be treated as an internal one. Schmitt, who was in contact with Göring concerning various proposals on compulsory hunting insurance that had pleased Göring greatly, immediately turned to the Reichsmarschall. After reminding him that Hitler had decided that the insurance nationalization issue was supposed to be put off for at least a decade and that they were in the midst of a

---

[118] Hilgard an Göring, 22. Nov. 1941, FHA, S 17.5/76.
[119] Hilgard an Hunke, 5. Sept. 1942, and Hunke an Hilgard, 7. Sept. 1942, GDV, 3-003/1.
[120] Hilgard an Funk, 3. Nov. 1942, Alzheimer an Rath, 31. Okt. 1942, Rath an Alzheimer, 10. Nov. 1942, Alzheimer an Hilgard, 3. Dez. 1942, FHA, S 17.5/10.

war in which there were more important things to do (hunting insurance questions apparently were among them, despite the military situation on the Eastern front!), Schmitt noted that Schwede-Coburg had nevertheless solicited the Rath report. Schmitt was quite blunt in stating what he thought of it:

This opus is, as we certainly could not otherwise have expected, one-sided, incorrect, inobjective, and tendentious. There has been such criticism at all times. Experience is that it is quickly overturned. But it is much more difficult to really present something better in its place. For good or for ill, now that the report lies before us, we must deal with it despite its superfluousness and our great shortage of labor.[121]

Schmitt found it upsetting enough that the profession to which he had devoted his life was given such treatment, but the publication of the findings and the damage to the reputation of private insurance gave him the sense that he was being led around by the nose. Schmitt felt that the time had come to enforce Hitler's order. He was quite willing to discuss reforms after a victorious war, "but I do not want to be present if an industry of which I am proud to be a member, and whose members are today standing before the enemy or doing their work in silent fulfillment of their duty, is to be destroyed through tactical and tendentious subterfuges."

There is little point here in going over Rath's arguments for the replacement of the allegedly costly existing insurance system with a "völkische System" based on competition in performance rather than salesmanship. His analysis included such mental flights as comparing the cost of a person putting out a fire with the number of people and hours it took to process a claim on fire insurance. His basic goal was the replacement of private companies with publicly chartered monopolies. What really exercised Hilgard was the notice that Rath's work received in such newspapers as the *Hamburger Fremdenblatt* and the *Essener National-Zeitung* as well as the distress it was causing the private insurers.[122] He was convinced that the publication of Rath's ideas was designed as a trap to drag the private insurers into the fray, have the onus of breaking the Burgfrieden placed on private industry, and reopen the nationalization controversy.

Hilgard's first goal, therefore, was to use the influential connections he had in the government to restore the ban on discussion of the issue. At the same time, he felt it important to rally his colleagues and get their support for his approach, which he did at a meeting of the leading private insurance directors on December 17, 1942, held in the Berlin offices of Allianz. Some of the leaders were terribly concerned that they had no political friends in high places and that confidence in the industry was being undermined. General Director Hermann Hitzler of Hamburg-Mannheimer, for example, was outraged by the "pseudo-scientific nonsense" used to put together the statistics but was impressed with the way in which evident problems of the industry were highlighted to create

---

[121] Schmitt an Göring, 16. Dez. 1942, ibid. For the Rath memorandum, see ibid.
[122] Rath's various articles and writings are to be found in ibid. A good illustration is "Eine neue Epoche der Versicherung," *Hamburger Fremdenblatt*, 11. Dez. 1942, ibid.

the impression of a drastic need for reform among those who knew little about the business. Another director observed that most of the Party people had been brought up on the Party program, which was written at a time when Hitler did not have much by way of economic advice, and that the insurance industry had not done enough to influence Party leaders on the regional and local level. Most of the Gauleiter, for example, simply supported socialist ideas intuitively, and this made it difficult to convince them that Rath was spouting rubbish. Hilgard placed particular stock in proposals by General Director Adolf Samwer of Karlsruher Leben, who agreed that they should not engage in polemics at this point but rather should do more to present industry achievements to the press and prepare the way for battles to come. They also had to pay attention to reforms that were needed, especially reducing the number of small companies – a position strongly seconded by Hilgard.[123]

It was no easy matter to silence Schwede-Coburg and renew the gagging order on discussion of the nationalization issue. Schmitt actually wrote to State Secretary of the Reich Chancellory Hans Lammers asking for a personal interview with Hitler on the question. Schmitt emphasized that there was a great danger that the German insurance industry would be discredited and wanted at least for Lammers to urge that Hitler reaffirm that the discussion should be closed until after the war.[124] Schmitt did not get an interview with Hitler but instead a letter from Göring on December 31, 1942, in which Göring promised to talk to Hitler about the matter but also warned Schmitt against misinterpreting Hitler's desire to have the subject not discussed during the war as some basic decision on nationalization. Here, Göring insisted, the issue remained open. The Führer had not decided. As for Göring himself, "I am personally now as before of the opinion that this question should rest during the war in every respect, therefore also with respect to agitation. A new world will arise after the outcome of this mighty struggle about which no one can say today what kind of economic necessities will present themselves."[125] Nevertheless, both Schmitt and Hilgard had done everything possible to stay in Göring's good graces. In January 1941, for example, a statute of the Holy Hieronymus had been bought in Schmitt's name to be given as a birthday present to Göring from various corporations with which he was associated. It came from the private collection of Konsul Otto Bernheimer, a prominent Jewish businessman, and the proceeds of the sale went to pay his Reich Flight Tax and atonement tax.[126] Göring appreciated personal as well as corporate giving, and there was a price to be paid for Hilgard's and Schmitt's

---

[123] For materials from this meeting of Dec. 17, 1942, see ibid.

[124] Schmitt an Lammers, 22. Dez. 1941, ibid.

[125] Göring an Schmitt, 31. Dez. 1941, ibid.

[126] This was not the only item from the collection bought in Schmitt's name, since on March 13, 1941, a Baroque fauteuil (armchair) was purchased for 2,500 RM. The Bernheimer family, which had fled to South America, sought restitution for the items, but Schmitt never really had them in his possession. See Süddeutsche Treuhand-Gesellschaft AG an die Wiedergutmachungsbehörde Oberbayern, 12. Juli 1949, and Schmitt an die Wiedergutmachungsbehörde Oberbayern, 24. Nov. 1949, FHA, NL 1/108.

taking advantage of their invitation to Göring's fiftieth birthday party (on January 12, 1943) to press their cause. Göring's aide Gritzbach had already suggested to Schmitt that, if the latter was uncertain what to give, then Göring would appreciate a valuable statue that had caught his eye. Schmitt thus "properly" made the requisite contribution, as did the other business leaders invited.[127]

It had thus been a good opportunity to appeal to Göring' sensibilities. A few days later, Hilgard reminded Göring of their brief conversation about the insurance problem and sent him the copy of a letter from a colonel and regiment commander on the Eastern front named Wrengler who worked in the insurance field and expressed great distress at the assault on their profession in the middle of the war, when so many insurance people were facing the enemy. This was one of a number of such letters, and Director Kurt Pomplitz of Nordstern Lebensversicherung had written directly to Hilgard to point out that "it is just our soldiers in the East who have been able to form their own view of the socialization of the economy. If they learn that similar plans are being seriously considered in the homeland, then many will ask: why am I actually fighting, when one at home is propagating the introduction of insurance collectives?"[128]

Such evidence that the debate launched by Schwede-Coburg and Rath was demoralizing to troops expecting to return home to their insurance profession was certainly a shrewd form of propaganda for halting the debate, but Hilgard still had a hard time getting a consistent policy from the authorities. Thus, on the same day (January 2, 1943), Bormann sent a note to Hilgard declaring that publications and discussion of the reform of insurance were undesirable and should be avoided as well as a note to Schmitt declaring that one could not deny Rath, in his capacity as a university professor, the right to discuss insurance questions scientifically – provided that such publications did not engage in a debate about Rath's report.[129] Hilgard found the entire situation maddening. When the articles of Rath came out, he was successful in having the RWM issue a ban on further press discussion. Schwede-Coburg, however, used the Reich Propaganda Ministry to lift the ban on the grounds that Rath was a professor. Then there were the contradictory instructions of Bormann. It was hard to know where one stood, but what seemed clear was that "despite the war and despite the order of the Party chancellory the enemies of private insurance think their hour has come and do not want to let go."[130]

The leaders of the private insurance business realized that they had only minimal protection against Schwede-Coburg and Rath and thus, as early as December 18, 1942, decided to hire an expert of their own: Professor Jens Jessen of the University of Berlin, who had joined the Party in 1930 and was a highly regarded

[127] Gaertringer (ed.), *Hassell-Tagebücher*, p. 346 (22. Jan. 1943).
[128] Kurt Pomplitz an Hilgard, 22. Dez. 1942, Hilgard an Göring, 16. Jan. 1943, Wrengler an Hilgard, 8. Jan. 1943, Paul Schmitz (Vorstand Karlsruher Leben) an Hilgard, 27. Jan. 1943, FHA, S 17.5/10.
[129] Bormann an Hilgard und Bormann an Schmitt, 2. Jan. 1943, ibid.
[130] Hilgard an Ernst Wüster, Donau-Concordia Allgemeine Versicherungs-AG, Budapest, 11. Jan. 1943, ibid.

and respected (if somewhat controversial) national economist. Jessen was asked to draw up a reply to Rath, and the leading insurers agreed to provide the necessary information. Jessen, to be sure, demanded a stiff price for his work, but apparently he had the name and reputation they wanted and so they agreed to pay 50,000 RM as a retainer and another 50,000 RM when the work was done. The first payment was made by Victoria (7,500 RM), Munich Re (10,000 RM), Gerling (7,500 RM), Allianz (10,000 RM), Colonia (12,500 RM), and Albingia (2,500 RM).[131]

During the ensuing months, Jessen was to generate an incomplete but important report with a massive amount of material of great interest on the German insurance business, and the battle over publications by Rath – who believed that the private insurance system was more or less an invention of the English Jewish banking house of Rothschild – was to continue well into 1944.[132] All this, however, became increasingly of academic rather than practical interest, as the tide of war turned against Germany and the problems of the insurance industry became more and more a function of the general economic and manpower situation of Nazi Germany in its prolonged demise. Clearly, the battle over the future of the German insurance system was ultimately a struggle between the radical wing of NSDAP – who thought themselves social reformers and wished to realize antiliberal as well as various eugenic and racial programs – and the businessmen who had come to terms with the regime but usually had an entirely different vision of the world and continued to hope that the regime could be bent to their purposes, or at least be made more rational.

Schwede-Coburg understood this very well. In an angry letter to Schmitt of March 5, 1943, he expressed his deep resentment at the way in which the private insurers were seeking to silence Rath and himself and to denigrate the scholarly credentials of Rath. He was struck by the similarity between the techniques used against himself and Rath and those used in England by the "plutocratic insurance corporations" against the plans of Lord Beveridge for a reform of the English insurance system. He really was not interested in Schmitt's judgment of Rath's scholarly qualifications, since Schmitt had collaborated in the insurance dictionary published by emigré Professor Alfred Manes in 1930 and thus had contributed to the propagation of "Jewish-capitalist make-believe science." Old Fighters like himself understood how people could change their views, but they did not intend to be told what was real science and what was not.[133]

---

[131] Ibid., and interrogation of Hilgard, 16. July 1947, NA, RG 260, OMGUS, FINAD, 2/57/6–8.

[132] See the report on Rath's speech in Posen on Jan. 21, 1944, FHA, S 17.5/10.

[133] Schwede-Coburg an Schmitt, 5. März 1943, ibid. The work in question was Alfred Manes (ed.), *Versicherungslexikon. Ein Nachschlagewerk für alle Wissensgebiete der gesamten Individual- und Sozial-Versicherung*, 3. Aufl. (Berlin, 1930). The list of collaborators on the front page, which was conveniently sent by Schwede-Coburg to the SS, was a "who's who" of the German insurance field and, as the underlining showed, contained almost twenty Jews. See Schwede-Coburg an Himmler, 5. März 1943, along with the page in question, BAB, ehem. BDC, SL 62. SS-Führer Beinzger, also an insurance man, was on the title page, and Schwede-Coburg made sure to mention him as well.

Schmitt properly refused to dignify this charge with a response, but some of the leading lights of scholarship in the insurance field – like Manes, who was then teaching at the University of Indiana – were Jews, and Schmitt had once upon a time been proud to have his name appear among the collaborators in a leading publication in his field. Times had changed, but Schmitt had enough character to refuse to abjure his involvement in the publication. Nevertheless, he continued to worry about his standing in the SS and, in the spring of 1942, asked the head of the Circle of Friends, SS-Oberführer Fritz Kranefuss, whether his lack of promotion from SS-Brigadeführer since 1934 reflected some kind of criticism of his behavior by Himmler or a snub. Kranefuss tried to reassure him that he did not believe this to be the case and that the next rank, SS-Gruppenführer, was reserved for persons in active government service involving regular work with the SS. Schmitt seemed relieved, as Kranefuss reported to SS-Obersturmbannführer Rudolf Brandt of Himmler's staff. Brandt did discuss the matter with Himmler, however, and the Reichsführer made it clear that Schmitt had to understand that one could not receive endless promotions and that rank was related to real activities on behalf of the SS.[134]

Schmitt was, in fact, something of a problem for the SS. As chairman of the supervisory board of Deutsche Continental-Gas-Gesellschaft, Schmitt backed the efforts of its general director (Eduard Schalfejew, who had worked with Schmitt as an RWM official before leaving in 1935) to retain Count Rudolf Westarp, who was considered a "non-Aryan," on the managing board of one of the company's larger works. Westarp was kept on until the end of 1942, when the danger became too great and Schalfejew sent him to Hungary to represent the company. All this led to attacks from the Party, and Westarp finally was arrested by the Gestapo in Budapest and sent to the concentration camp at Matthausen, which he managed to survive. Schalfejew was obviously in bad odor with the Party, and when Schmitt included him in efforts to secure a contribution for the Circle of Friends and some charity supported by Himmler, the Reichsführer found the matter embarrassing and "painful." He had sent a letter of thanks to Schalfejew before learning about the latter's position on Westarp. Himmler returned the money, and Schmitt was told never again to use his membership in the Circle for business purposes.[135]

Kranefuss had more problems concerning Schmitt at the beginning of 1943, when Wilhelm Keppler tried to mobilize higher SS leaders – among them the leading economic figure in the SS, Oswald Pohl – to promote Schmitt. Kranefuss was able to ward this off by speaking to Keppler about the problem.[136] At the same time, Schmitt also asked for an interview with Himmler about "acute questions of the insurance business" when the Reichsführer was next in Berlin, to

---

[134] Kranefuss an Brandt, 2. Juni 1942; Brandt an Kranefuss, 14. Juni 1942, ibid.
[135] See the correspondence between Brandt and Kranefuss, Nov.–Dec. 1942, ibid. See also the statement by Schalfejew of Feb. 7, 1946, in connection with Schmitt's denazification, FHA, NL 1/74.
[136] Kranefuss an Brandt, 15. Jan. 1943, BAB, ehem. BDC, SL 62.

which Himmler formally agreed but, as his staff noted, on the assumption that "this will not be the case in the forseeable future."[137] The attack of Schwede-Coburg, therefore, simply compounded an already existing problem with respect to Schmitt's SS position, but it also demonstrated both the advantages that Schmitt's pandering to Himmler brought and his profound miscalculation of where he really stood with the SS. The advantage, quite simply, was that Himmler was not going to feed Schmitt to Schwede-Coburg. On March 15, 1943, Himmler thanked him for the information on Schmitt and then went on: "You know that in your struggle which you lead in the matter of insurance, I stand absolutely on your side. But I will ask you, insofar as is possible, to avoid personal attacks on Party comrade Schmitt, who belongs to the SS and whose son fell for us as an SS-Untersturmführer."[138]

Obersturmbannführer Brandt asked Kranefuss to convey this information to Schmitt and try to get the two combatants to calm the debate down. Kranefuss agreed that Schmitt deserved their respect and consideration as the father of a splendid young man who had died heroically for the SS. At the same time, Kranefuss made it clear that he had no illusions about Schmitt and what he really represented. He pointed out that Schmitt had achieved his prominence through his role in the Favag affair, which Kranefuss in fact thought deserving of criticism, and through his close contacts with Göring, who was responsible for Schmitt becoming economics minister. It was this that led to his being invited into the SS. Kranefuss himself, however, bluntly told Brandt that "I have never considered Dr. Schmitt a National Socialist and I also do not today." Kranefuss classified Schmitt as one of a number of economic leaders who had developed powerful contacts in the regime but who deserved an even less favorable judgment than Schmitt himself. Manifestly, Kranefuss was suggesting that this was built into the compromise the Nazi leadership had made with the business world. These, however, were worlds apart:

When one as a National Socialist and an SS-man discusses economic and political questions, then one has the feeling that one is living on two separate planets. In human terms, such conversations are always very nice and polite but in the last analysis they are completely unsatisfying with respect to world view. He has often demonstrated how he thinks and feels .... Probably he will never understand why we have such a basic difference of opinion than he, and one actually cannot hold it against him that he does not understand us.[139]

Kranefuss thought it pointless to try to reconcile Schmitt and Schwede-Coburg and was quite critical of the latter for the way he dealt with the insurance problem. At the same time, there was no way Schwede-Coburg could understand the mentality of a businessman like Schmitt or even care about Schmitt's personal loss.

---

[137] Vermerk, 30. Dez. 1941, ibid.
[138] Himmler an Schwede-Coburg, 15. März 1943, ibid.
[139] Kranefuss an Brandt, 18. März 1943, ibid.

This indeed was true, and it is well worth noting that Schmitt's and Hilgard's opponents in the insurance battle were truly dangerous people. Schwede-Coburg was a killer who pushed forward a highly effective euthanasia program in Pommerania and who had no qualms about eliminating his political enemies in the most brutal fashion. Similarly, the ever-troublesome DAF man Lencer was to be found in Minsk in 1943 heading a liaison agency between economic authorities and the SS and police, where he was responsible for combing Jews and others out of production plants and for reducing the population's food supply.[140]

It is significant that the man chosen to respond to Rath and provide the weapons to fight Schwede-Coburg was Jens Jessen, a person with National Socialist credentials who was nevertheless already involved in the Resistance. Jessen, who would be executed in connection with the July 20, 1944, attempt to kill Hitler, was in fact a member of the Goerdeler Circle of conservative opponents of the Nazi regime who were drawing up plans for an alternative government. He was also a member of the "Wednesday Society" (Mittwochs-Gesellschaft), a Berlin discussion group of intellectuals, government officials, and military leaders to which many of the leading conspirators – of whom General Ludwig Beck was one of the most noteworthy – belonged.[141] In their conversations on the Jessen project, Hilgard discovered not only that Jessen was an opponent of the system but also, in July 1943, that Jessen was involved in a plot to overthrow Hitler with Minister Johannes Popitz. Jessen asked that Allianz make a contribution of 100,000 RM without explaining exactly how the money would be used. Hilgard did discuss the matter with Alzheimer at Schmitt's estate Tiefenbrunn in the summer of 1943 but not with Schmitt himself, "because he is known to be a man who cannot keep a secret." According to Alzheimer, who was interrogated by Allied authorities in July 1947, Hilgard specifically stated that "Jessen required the RM 100,000 for the preparation of an attempt on Hitler's life." Hilgard and Alzheimer agreed, however, that the danger of making such a contribution was too great and Hilgard told Jessen that Allianz could not take the risk. Apparently, Jessen then suggested that the second installment on the book be paid shortly; Hilgard and Alzheimer (who discussed the matter again

---

[140] On Lencer, see Christian Gerlach, *Kalkulierte Morde. Die deutsche Wirtschafts- und Vernichtungspolitik in Weißrußland 1941 bis 1944* (Hamburg, 1999), p. 149 mit Anm. 135, pp. 315, 318–19, 444, 485. About Schwede-Coburg's role in the context of euthanasia see e.g. Ernst Klee, *"Euthanasie" im NS-Staat. Die "Vernichtung lebensunwerten Lebens"* (Frankfurt a.M., 1985), p. 95, Heike Bernhardt, *Anstaltspsychiatrie und "Euthanasie" in Pommern 1933–1945. Die Krankenmorde an Kindern und Erwachsenen am Beispiel der Landesheilanstalt Ueckermünde* (Frankfurt a.M., 1994), and Heinz Faulstich, *Hungersterben in der Psychiatrie 1914–1949. Mit einer Topographie der NS-Psychiatrie* (Freiburg i.Br., 1998), esp. pp. 455–63.

[141] Jessen worked closely with Johannes Popitz, Ulrich von Hassell, and Carl Goerdele. For this group and Jessen's place in it, see Hans Mommsen, "Gesellschaftsbild und Verfassungspläne des deutschen Widerstandes," in Hans Mommsen, *Alternative zu Hitler. Studien zur Geschichte des deutschen Widerstandes* (Munich, 2000), pp. 53–158. On the Mittwochs-Gesellschaft, see Klaus Scholder (ed.), *Die Mittwochs-Gesellschaft: Protokolle aus dem geistigen Deutschland 1932 bis 1944* (Berlin, 1982).

in Berlin a few weeks later) agreed, and Jessen was given a check in early August 1943 by Allianz, recorded as the second payment for the work Jessen was writing. Alzheimer agreed that Munich Re should pay half the cost, although Alzheimer could not say whether it did so in his 1947 interrogation. Hilgard never consulted with or charged the other companies involved, and Jessen never asked for any further funds. After the war, Jessen's widow, Käthe, claimed not only that Hilgard was a political ally of her husband who was among those believing it necessary to assassinate Hitler but also that "Hilgard promised my husband every needed financial support for the conspirators and was made privy to all the plans by my husband." In his denazification proceedings after the war, Hilgard claimed, on the basis of this letter and a statement of Alzheimer, that he promised and delivered money for the Resistance cause and that his intentions were matched by deeds. Although Alzheimer's statement of February 1947 and Hilgard's own testimony make no reference to giving the Resistance any money it might need, Alzheimer's interrogation in July 1947 does explicitly speak of a plot to kill Hitler. Both Hilgard and Alzheimer made no claim to doing more than giving Jessen half of what he requested – and that in the form of an added advance for his study, with the cost booked to Allianz. Strictly speaking, there was no payment for the Resistance cause and no evidence about why Jessen, who was on the margins of the actual conspiracy, needed the money and to what use it was put. Hilgard never claimed to have detailed knowledge about the conspiracy, although he obviously knew of its existence and may indeed have wished it well without becoming personally involved. And he never actually claimed that Allianz was contributing to the Resistance, even if he implied a connection between his knowledge of Jessen's views and the prepayment of the honorarium.[142]

The struggle between Schmitt and Hilgard, on the one hand, and Schwede-Coburg and his allies, on the other, is not a story of resistance to National Socialism but rather of conflicting elements within the National Socialist system. It was a conflict that had to be suspended because of the war, and even Gauleiter Greiser had to give up – albeit with great reluctance and not until August 1943 – on pursuing compulsory building insurance in the Warthegau because it would have cost manpower. He took the view that the question would have to be regulated for the entire Reich and believed "that in the area of insurance a certain socialization will take place and that the introduction of compulsory insurance will certainly be easier to introduce in this context."[143] Having to fight this battle

---

[142] Interrogation of Hilgard, July 16, 1947, NA, RG 260, OMGUS, FINAD, 2/57/6–8, and Hilgard, "Leben," FHA, NL 2/7, pp. 140–4, which contains statements by Frau Jessen on June 23, 1946, by Alzheimer on Feb. 23, 1947, and by the chief bookkeeper of Allianz, Ernst Rausche, on April 24, 1946. Interrogation of Alois Alzheimer, July 17, 1947, NA, RG 260, OMGUS, FINAD, 2/56/1.

[143] Vermerk Siegmund (Persönlicher Refernt Greiser), 13. Aug. 1943, APP, Reichsstatthalter/2801, Bl. 210. Until this time, he tried to hold out against powerful agencies anxious to see the discussion terminated for the duration of the war. See the complaining letter to the RWM and to Greiser from Finance Minister Schwerin von Krosigk of April 7, 1943, and the rejection of the plan by Körner of Göring's Four-Year Plan office, ibid., Bl. 141–3, 162–4.

was one of the prices Allianz and the insurance industry – represented so effectively by Schmitt and Hilgard – had to pay for their involvement with the regime, and important weapons in this struggle (or at least so they thought) were their connections with Göring, Himmler, Funk, and other major Nazi leaders. They had to present the private insurance business and its leadership as a better alternative to that being proposed and supported by Nazi Party radicals, and this meant becoming increasingly implicated in National Socialist imperialism and the crimes that attended it.

8

Allianz and Munich Re
in the Second World War

THE TERM "community of danger" belonged to the language of the politically correct in German insurance circles, but that National Socialist Germany itself was a "community of danger" in a quite literal sense was not lost upon those leading the industry. The greater the drift toward war, the more obvious this became. Although Hitler's willingness and ability to take great risks and revise the Treaty of Versailles "peacefully" until 1939 – and then move on to yet further triumphs in 1939–1941 – may have been viewed with admiration and satisfaction, those involved in the management of the German insurance industry, as was the very nature of their enterprise, remained anxious to minimize risk but also to maximize opportunity. This meant constant assessment of the situation, and the two goals were inextricably related to one another. Risk reduction was an imperative when Germany faced war before 1939 and when Germany faced defeat after 1942, while opportunity maximization was of greatest importance during the period when it appeared that Germany might be victorious. Nevertheless, it was the very nature of the regime to insist that peace was being maintained while it was driving toward war and to speak of final victory while facing total defeat. Thus for only a brief period was there some correspondence between claims and reality. Especially after 1942, those who managed to maintain their capacity for rational perception inevitably faced an increasing tension between their engagement with the regime and their effort to continue "doing business," on the one hand, and such measures as they could take to deal with the manifest disaster they were confronting, on the other.

EXPANSIONIST EFFORTS AND
BUSINESS OPPORTUNITIES IN WAR

The Lessons of Spain, War Risks, and Wartime Business

Ironically, one of the developments that made German insurers particularly aware of war risks was the Spanish Civil War, where Germany and Italy had stood on the side of Franco's successful insurrection against the Republic but where the war action of 1936–1939 and Franco's victory produced a host of disagreeable and costly problems for all foreign companies who had sold insurance in Spain or acted as reinsurers. Spanish policies covered civil unrest and a few actually went so far as to mention civil war, although this was rare. Foreign companies, including the Germans (who, as shown in connection with the November Pogrom, tended to refuse such coverage) agreed to include civil unrest coverage in Spain in order to compete against or provide reinsurance to the indigenous companies. The problems involved were especially relevant to Allianz, which controlled Plus Ultra (one of Spain's major companies) and Munich Re, which was a partner of Allianz in such ventures and handled a considerable amount of reinsurance. The Germans were thrown out of Madrid in August 1936 and so the managers in question were then handling Plus Ultra affairs from the foreign section of Allianz in Berlin.[1] By 1937 there was already much discussion in the international insurance community of how to define the liability of the companies – that is, how to distinguish between damage caused by tumult or public disturbance and the damage caused by the Civil War. The entire problem was the subject of international conferences, and an international committee of jurists had actually been set up to define (which it did, quite narrowly) what constituted a public disturbance.

The Germans, friendly as they might be to Franco, had nevertheless an obvious interest in not losing more money than necessary in Spain. As Franco increased his sway in 1938, there was good reason to worry that he would play the dictator also in the insurance field and simply decree what the obligations of insurers working in Spain were to be. Directors Meuschel and Alzheimer of the Munich Re were particuarly alarmed that some companies and reinsurers, especially the Swiss, were making premature concessions that Franco could use to increase demands, and the Germans were anxious to work closely with the English and French to create some solidarity in dealing with the problem.[2] The Franco regime, however, was less interested in disputing legal definitions than in having the foreign insurance companies make a solid contribution to reconstruction of the destroyed areas. It referred to the events since 1936 as a "war" when doing so was useful for taxation purposes without worrying in the least about the implications for insurance claims; ultimately, the regime was after as much as it could collect in taxes and in "contributions" from the insurance companies for national reconstruction. Franco was not only in desperate need of reconstruction aid, he was also short of foreign exchange and was thus particularly interested in what he might extract from reinsurers.[3] Schmitt naturally worked closely with the German Foreign Office to try to moderate the potential claims and demands of the new Spanish regime, and in the spring of 1939 he prevailed on Ulrich von Hassell to go to Spain and deal with their insurance organizations

---

[1] See the Rundschreiben der Organisations-Abteilung der Allianz of Aug. 19, 1936, FHA, AZ 5.1/4.

[2] Aktennote Meuschel, 1. April 1938, MR, G 1/14. This file contains a wealth of information on the evolution of the issue and the problems of defining civil unrest and riot.

[3] Aktennote Alzheimer, 24. Okt. 1938, MR, G 1/14; Pablo Philipp y Stadler, General Direktor Plus Ultra an Allianz, 3. Mai 1939, MR, G 1/11.

and public authorities. Von Hassell was also asked to report on the dangers of nationalization, which seems to have been on the agenda of the Spanish Fascist Party, the Falange. Von Hassell, however, did not think this much of a problem and also was able to report that the Spanish were moving toward a settlement that would introduce predictability to the entire insurance compensation scenario.[4] Still, there were plenty of indications in the various negotiations taking place that the Spanish were thinking in terms that could only be plausible if they were expecting to get the money they wanted from abroad. Allianz was anxious for Plus Ultra to use its connections with the Spanish government to moderate its demands. Matters were further complicated when the French and British withdrew from their collaboration with the Germans because of the outbreak of war.[5] Thus, by April 1940, Plus Ultra was reporting to Allianz an estimate of 150 to 180 million pesetas in damages to be asked of the insurers, an amount considered alarmingly high.[6] Finally, after much tedious negotiation, an agreement was reached in the spring of 1941 on a global insurance amount of 100 million pesetas to be paid in installments by the insurance companies involved as a consortium, 40% immediately in June 1941, 30% in October, 20% in December, and 10% by the reinsurers when final obligations had been calculated for them. It was a substantial payment, especially since it had to be paid in pesetas. In the case of Allianz, however, it could call on Plus Ultra to pay 10 million.[7]

It should thus come as no surprise that the Spanish Civil War served as a warning bell for European insurers to think more systematically about their obligations in the event of a European war. An important indication of this effort to deal with the war danger was the decision of the British Fire Officers' Committee in early 1937 that its members would issue no more policies that might even imply coverage of civil war and war risks. The Reich Group, following their lead, instructed that all its members refuse any further coverage of civil war damages because they were scarcely distinguishable from covering an actual war. At the same time, it was deemed in the public interest to continue the insuring of war correspondents, personnel and ships operating in Portuguese harbors and in Spanish harbors under control of Franco's forces, and personnel working for German enterprises in areas controlled by Franco's forces.[8] What worried Hilgard most, however, was that Germany did not seem to be following the British lead in cancelling all war risk obligations, a policy to which the

[4] Schmitt an Philipp, 15. April 1939, ibid.; Aktennote von Hassell, 19. Mai 1939, MR, G 1/14.
[5] Bericht Grieshaber, 23. Feb. 1940; Allianz an Münchener Rück, 22. Aug. 1939, MR, G 1/12.
[6] Allianz an Müncher Rück, 25. April 1940, MR, G 1/11.
[7] Alzheimer an die interessierten Gesellschaften, 8. Aug. 1941, GDV, RS/48; Alzheimer an die Wirtschaftsgruppe Rück- und Kreditversicherung, 18. Jan. 1941 und 12. Mai 1941, GDV, RS/17; Bericht an die Mitglieder des Aufsichtsrats, 12. Dez. 1941, BAB, 80 Ba 2/P 5781.
[8] See the Rundschreiben der Organisationsabteilung der Allianz of April 19 and June 28, 1937, FHA, AZ 5.1/5, the Rundschreiben des Deutschen Aufruhrversicherungs-Verbandes, 24. März 1937, and Anlagen, the Rundschreiben der Wirtschaftsgruppe Privatversicherung, 15. April 1937 und 16. June 1937, GDV, 2–108/1.

German ministries were opposed on the grounds that it would make it appear as if Germany thought war imminent. Hilgard was reproached for his attitude when he pointed out that this left German insurers with an intolerable level of exposure in the event of war.[9]

Nevertheless, the need to do something became increasingly obvious, and the form this took was the creation of a German war clause for transport insurance in 1938 and the subsequent establishment of the German War Insurance Community in July 1939. The former was an addendum to all transport insurance contracts that provided, in return for a special premium, coverage for all goods damaged, destroyed, or seized by acts of war between the time they were loaded aboard ship and unloaded. The clause was extended at the beginning of the war to shipments by Lufthansa and by other forms of transportation. The German War Insurance Community was an association composed initially of some 48 direct transportation insurance companies and a dozen reinsurance companies that functioned as a pool covering such war risks. In addition to the special premiums charged customers, the transportation insurers involved agreed also to increase their coverage capacity by providing a fund of 10 million RM, to which would be added another 10 million from the entire private insurance industry. Finally, should these resources be used up, the German government then agreed to undertake full liability for remaining costs. Hilgard formally headed the new organization, which was managed (very effectively, it seems) by his Director Ludwig Neumüller of the Allianz transport division. The tasks it faced were certainly complicated, involving different premiums for various areas depending on their relative dangers and taking into account Germany's borders and areas of control as they expanded and then contracted.[10]

In contrast to the somewhat conflicted and short prehistory of the War Insurance Community, there seems not to have been any question on the part of the government or the insurers that life insurance would continue at existing levels and that war-related deaths would be covered. At the same time, it was obvious that the life insurers would need some protection against the consequences of the increased death rate, and the RAA therefore mandated a "risk supplement" on premiums of 20% on the first 3,000 RM, 30% on the next 17,000 RM, and at least 30% on amounts exceeding 20,000 RM.[11] With recent memories of the First World War and its enormous death rate, the insurers naturally faced the situation with some trepidation, but they seemed reasonably confident that a combination of the supplements and an assessment among the various companies would cover their needs. The primary thing, as Hilgard and Schloeßmann

[9]   Hilgard, "Die Allianz im 2. Weltkrieg," FHA, AZ 1.3/2, pp. 24–5.

[10] Ibid.; for the Kriegsklausel and the constitution of the Kriegsversicherungsgemeinschaft, see SM, 1458/34/66, Bl. 78–9, 227–35; for the meetings and procedures and policies see this entire volume and the Beiratssitzungen der Wirtschaftsgruppe Rück- und Kreditversicherung, SM, 1458/1/27 and 88. On the complexities of some of this trade see the interesting material on Allianz's insurance business in Iran, SM, 1458/1/87.

[11] Rundschreiben RAA, 1. Sept. 1939, SM, 1458/1/157.

Calendar for students edited by Allianz Leben, 1940/1941.

argued, was "that the German life insurance should have so complete a capacity at the end of the war as if the consequences of the war had remained without any influence."[12] In the heady days of victory, however, the consequence of the war was a considerable reduction in the number of persons taking out life insurance because "there is no inclination among the insured to pay increased war surcharges in view of the soon to be expected peace."[13] The public noted the low death rate and the reduced number of those drafted and also looked forward to Ley's plans for an old-age pension system for the entire German people.

[12] Vermerk, 14. Sept. 1939, ibid.
[13] Lagebericht, 4. Sept. 1940, ibid.

By 1941–1942, however, the situation had changed dramatically. At the beginning of April 1942, Allianz Leben reported to the RAA that 9,629 of its insured had died and 25.1 million RM had been paid out for 1941 and that the weekly death rate was 415 in March 1942. Under the circumstances, the capacity to serve policyholders required an increased war supplement and the levying of an assessment on the insurance firms.[14] The ravages of war made themselves felt even more strongly between January and November 1942, when 17,537 Allianz Leben insured died, resulting in claims amounting to 40.3 million RM.[15] The Battle of Stalingrad was, of course, to prove particularly disastrous, and by April 1943 the number of wartime deaths had increased to 37,000 for a total sum of insurance of 90 million RM. Oddly enough, however, the life insurance companies did well – thanks to increases in premium supplements allowed by the RAA and to the general assessment made on all companies for ensuring that those with old policies were not unjustly deprived of their dividends because of the increased deaths of those who took out insurance later. The number of large life insurance policies increased by 55,410 in 1941, by 63,689 in 1942, and by 34,535 in 1943, so that, after deducting policies that ended or were terminated, the total number of such policyholders rose from 629,009 policies at the end of 1940 to 728,428 at the end of 1943. The number of insured with small life and group policies increased by 435,391 persons in 1941, by 432,073 in 1942, and by 519,144 in 1943, so that the total number of such insured rose from 3,194,606 at the end of 1940 to 4,803,333 at the end of 1943. Between 56% and 58% of the total value of these policies were group policies.[16] The effect of the increased number of insured and the higher premiums meant, on the one hand, that survivors could be paid off rapidly and, on the other, that a considerable reserve was building up for investment. Naturally, the concern would have done better without a war: the gross profits of Allianz at the end of August 1942 were 26.4 million instead of the 60 million they might have been had peacetime and normal interest rates prevailed.[17]

During the early stages of the war, the attitude toward liability for property damage caused by the war was relatively casual. The insurance companies were not liable for property damage caused directly in the course of military operations, but it was difficult to determine liability for indirect war damage and sometimes to distinguish between damage that was normal and damage that was war-related. The RWM and the Reich Group urged companies to be generous and liberal in their attitudes and – so long as things were going well, as they were in 1939–1940 – to cover indirect war damage. The economic groups for property insurance in the Reich Group set up special commissions to adjudicate individual

---

[14] Allianz Leben an RAA, 8. April 1942, BAK, B 280/1490, Bl. 80.
[15] Schreiben Allianz Leben, 25. Nov. 1942, ibid., Bl. 96.
[16] Geschäftsberichte Allianz Leben, 1941/1943, FHA, p. 8.
[17] Schloeßmann an von Finck, 26. Aug. 1941, FHA, B 1.3.1/9; Schloeßmann an von Finck, 21. April 1943, FHA, B1.3.1/4.; Hilgard, "Die Allianz im 2. Weltkrieg," FHA, AZ 1.3/2, p. 26.

cases. There seemed to be a consensus, for example, that damages incurred during blackouts were not to be considered war damages whereas damages incurred in defense against enemy air attacks were war damages. Needless to say, these issues were to become much more complicated as the war progressed.[18]

Nevertheless, Allianz increased its intake of premiums substantially during the war, above all in fire insurance on industrial facilities and transport. Although private vehicle insurance decreased sharply in the first year of the war, there was growth in premiums paid for vehicle transport after December 1941, thanks to the high volume of transport in the occupied areas and in Southeastern Europe. Only thereafter did collection of premiums slow down, because construction of military production facilities had reached its limits and nonessential plants were being shut down. As the fortunes of war began to turn, premium increases reflected the higher amounts for which industrial and other assets were assessed for insurance purposes (because of the increased danger) and also general inflationary tendencies but were ultimately overshadowed by losses incurred through bombing and the shrinking of areas under German control.[19]

Nevertheless, the war effort had offered plenty of business over a wide geographical area. An important type of insurance provided by Allianz during the war was construction insurance. This form of insurance was first introduced in 1934 and announced with considerable fanfare to the RWM as coming "at the beginning of the second working year of the National Socialist Government" and reflecting the renewed interest in construction and the promise of further work creation. Because it had a large organization and trained technical personnel, Allianz was in a position to offer insurance against construction mishaps by sparing the builder from having to calculate them itself and then also providing the customer with cash security against them. Thanks to its engineering bureau and experience in machine insurance, Allianz would do the job and let the builder concentrate on what he was really supposed to do. In providing such insurance, Allianz proudly claimed it was providing "a building block for the reconstruction of the economy."[20]

During the war, of course, there was more than enough "work creation" going on, and the need for construction insurance increased substantially. Premiums from this form of insurance had tripled between 1938 and 1942, and in 1942 Allianz was insuring 750 million marks worth of construction and 30 million marks worth of construction equipment. The Organisation Todt, which was responsible for much of the construction work in the war effort, made almost exclusive use of Allianz and praised it for turning risks into fixed costs. Albert Speer's ministry also supported working with Allianz and taking out this form of insurance,

[18] See the Organisations-Rundschreiben of Allianz of Dec. 28, 1939, Jan. 15 and 23, Feb. 26, March 4, April 6, 16, and 29, 1940, FHA, AZ 5.1/5.
[19] The reports to the Aufsichtsrat in BAB, 80 Ba 2/P 5781, chart the ebb and flow of premiums during the war.
[20] Allianz an RWM, 2. Mai 1934, BAB, R 3101/17078.

as did the Air Ministry. Indeed, Allianz construction insurance had as its field of operations

collaboration in the drawing up of government and industrial construction contracts, evaluation of construction work done, supervision of construction sites, handling of damages, at present only for building sites important and decisive for the war effort in the Reich, the occupied western and eastern areas, in friendly nations abroad, such as coastal protection, U-boat bases and plants, airfields, road and bridge constructions, steel shipbuilding, air defense, armaments and energy development (raw materials production, hydrogenation, Buna, and munitions works, weapons plants, water and steam power works) – utilization of building equipment.[21]

Therefore, in thinking about Allianz's wartime activity, it is important to distinguish between its short-term activities for the war effort throughout Europe, which were very substantial, and its longer-term ambitions. In Norway, for example, Allianz was denied the right to sell various types of insurance (fire, theft, accident, auto, etc.) because the market was viewed as overcrowded, but it was allowed to sell machine and construction insurance. In Denmark, Allianz was permitted to reestablish connections with a Danish agent it had used before to handle its general business and was also permitted to sell machine and construction insurance. The machine and construction insurance business in the occupied areas obviously was closely connected to the war effort, but Allianz was no less anxious to participate "in step with the expansion of German insurance interests in the occupied foreign area" by renewing its ties to the firm of Axel L. Bramsen & Co. in Copenhagen. It is to this second type of wartime activity that we now turn.

The Drive to Expand

How much Allianz, its chief partner Munich Re, and the German insurance business in general participated in Germany's expansion – and the character and quality of their engagement – are complicated questions, and it is important to deal with them in a realistic context. Some insurance leaders were more interested than others in external expansion. One of the differences between Kurt Schmitt and Hans Heß, for example, was that the former was enthusiastic about Allianz's international development whereas the latter was opposed to significant development of the concern abroad.[22] The coming of the war put a limit on such personal predilections, though it helps explain why Schmitt (in contrast to Heß) was often so visibly active on behalf of Allianz interests in the occupied areas. A decision to be totally uninvolved and to "stay home" would be tantamount to going out of business, and it would be unrealistic for the historian to expect such behavior. The service of insurers was a required part of the

---

[21] Bericht an das RAA vom 27. Apr. 1943, Anlage 6 vom 27. April 1943, FHA, S 17.4/6.
[22] E. J. Ruperti an Federico Morway, 31. März 1948, MR, D/7.

war effort, especially in areas where British insurance and reinsurance had been of great importance, and it was by no means unusual to place British and other enemy insurance branches in conquered territories under the trusteeship of German firms.[23] The more serious question concerned the intentions of German insurers toward the insurance businesses themselves in the occupied countries and toward the future shape of the European insurance business. Thus, as Hilgard noted correctly after the war, a good deal more than occupation measures and necessities of the moment were involved, since "it was in the nature of the German political leadership at that time that it was ready to seize this economic booty with ruthless brutality."[24] Hilgard claimed that he (and those of his colleagues with any insight) realized this approach could only damage the future reputation and interests of the German insurance industry, which depended on functioning in an international market, and that it was his goal – especially in the western occupied countries – to minimize the influence of the Nazi-dominated RAA and, with the support of the RWM, to create mechanisms through which German insurers would work with their counterparts in the occupied countries as partners rather than dictating victors.

We will show that these claims should not be dismissed entirely out of hand, yet some well-informed persons viewed the matter less favorably. For example, the well-known writer Ludwig Arps, who taught insurance at the University of Munich and authored the 75th anniversary history of Allianz, spoke bluntly in correspondence with Director Walther Meuschel of Munich Re in 1948 of the "imposed participation of German insurance in foreign corporations." He had apparently intended to make this comment especially with respect to the DAF insurance companies in an article but then decided to drop the issue. However, as he told Meuschel,

[t]hose participations were in fact imposed, in southeastern Europe, in France, in Poland, in what was then the Protectorate, in the Netherlands; and that not only by the DAF group, also not from reinsurers alone, but also from primary insurers in various branches. Who would want to maintain that all the businessmen in German contractual insurance were angels or even politically persecuted? Is it useful to the German insurance business when one suppresses or even maintains that the German insurance business was guiltless or harmless with respect to all the economic sins of the Third Reich? I believe much more that one is better served by candid expression and criticism of such excesses.[25]

Meuschel was not very taken with this criticism and, while expressing a willingness to face real evidence, claimed that he and Hilgard had always behaved

---

[23] Martin Herzog, "Beispielsammlung für die Kriegswirtschaftsgeschichte: Behandlung der englischen Versicherungsbestände in den von deutschen Truppen besetzten Gebieten," 18. Sept. 1941, GDV, Personenarchiv, Akte Martin Herzog.

[24] Hilgard, "Allianz im 2. Weltkrieg," FHA, AZ 1.3/2, p. 30.

[25] See Arps an Meuschel, 5. Jan. 1948, MR, E 4/15. It cannot be said that Arps's account of the Nazi period in *Wechselvolle Zeiten* followed this injunction in any respect or was much more than a standard Festschrift.

correctly and that this had been confirmed by the foreign insurers.[26] However, the real problem was that it was difficult for Meuschel (or Hilgard, or Schmitt) to recapture the sense of opportunity and ambition one felt in 1938–1941 amidst the wreckage and immense task of reconstruction one faced 1945–1948. Thus, at a meeting in Vienna in October 1940, Heß and Schmitt met with Schmidt-Polex to discuss the affairs of Wiener Allianz – a company, it should be recalled, that Allianz and Munich Re had taken over by forcing both the Italian and the Austrian shareholders out. The first item on the agenda was the future activity of Wiener Allianz abroad: "It was made basically clear that Wiener Allianz is the given corporation for the cultivation of the narrower eastern region (Balkans) and that as a consequence Allianz will operate not from Berlin but rather from Vienna in Hungary, Yugoslavia, Slovakia, Romania and Greece, initially also the Protectorate."[27] A few weeks later, on November 11, 1940, Munich Re and Allianz held the first meeting of the joint council of directors, with Schmitt serving as the first rotating chairman. The directors present then reported on "expansion of business carried out and introduced until now in the occupied areas by their corporations."[28] They reported on considerable activity in France, Belgium, and the Netherlands, although they found the possibilities in Norway and Denmark more limited. At the second meeting, on May 9, 1941, there was further discussion of expanded activity in France, and Schmidt-Polex had a chance to report on his search for concessions in southeastern Europe and his other plans.[29] All this made neither devils nor angels of the executives running these concerns, but it did demonstrate that the war seemed to give them opportunity and power and that they intended to use them for the benefit of their enterprises. It also made them participants in the generally accepted proposition that, in the event of a German victory, Berlin would replace London as the center of European commerce. Schmitt's Association for Large Risks had this explicit goal at the time of its founding, and he – as was most of the German business world – was engaging in economic warfare on behalf of the Third Reich. Howsoever they may have interpreted their actions then and later, the Allies understood their behavior to have such a purpose and monitored their activities with as close a watch as was possible under wartime circumstances. This does not mean that Allied observers always got the details straight, and the historian today is obviously more advantaged. As is well known, German rule varied in different parts of Europe and in different countries, being more "civilized" in the West and barbaric in the East, and it was also affected by differing conditions in the various areas and countries to be considered. Finally, the questions of whether one was dealing with a satellite or an enemy

---

[26] Meuschel an Arps, 6. Feb. 1948, MR, E 4/15.

[27] Aktennote Schmitt, 18. Okt. 1940, MR, A 1/30.

[28] Niederschrift über die erste Sitzung des gemeinsamen Vorstandsrats am 11. Nov. 1940, FHA, S 17.2/73.

[29] 2. Sitzung am 9. Mai 1941, ibid.

(these categories became rather fluid in the later part of the war) and of the type of German administration imposed on conquered areas were both relevant in defining the behavior of the insurance business outside Germany. Therefore, in understanding the actions of Allianz, Munich Re, and the insurance business in Europe, it is important to take these geographical and other factors into account.[30]

Frustration in Southeastern Europe

In the case of southeastern Europe, the situation in the region was the source of a considerable and surprising amount of disappointment, despite some lucrative if rather temporary opportunities. The disappointment was particularly evident in the Protectorate of Bohemia and Moravia and in the puppet state of Slovakia. In the former, there was basic agreement among the German authorities in charge, above all the "Reich Protector" Reinhard Heydrich, that the basic economic structure of the area should not be changed insofar as military requirements did not dictate otherwise: "All other decisions, along with all those pertaining to insurance, should be set aside until after the war when the Führer decides what the political future of the Protectorate shall be."[31] What this meant was that, despite Schmidt-Polex's protestations that Wiener Allianz should be allowed to return to those areas in which it had been active in the old Austro-Hungarian Empire (before the rude interruption created by the establishment of the Czech state), Wiener Allianz was denied a license. German, Austrian, and Sudetenland companies like Victoria, Agrippina, Donau-Concordia, Internationale Unfall- und Schadensversicherungs-Gesellschaft, Sudetendeutsche Union Versicherungs-AG, and Sudetendeutsche Volksfürsorge, which were already established in the area (along with the Italian Generali and RAS and with the Swiss Helvetia, Schweizer National, and Basler), were permitted to continue doing business alongside a

---

[30] See the important essay by Richard J. Overy, "The Economy of the German 'New Order'," and Dietrich Eichholtz, "Institutionen und Praxis der deutschen Wirtschaftspolitik im NS-besetzten Europa," in Richard J. Overy, Gerhard Otto, & Johannes Houwink ten Cate (eds.), *Die "Neuordnung" Europas. NS-Wirtschaftspolitik in den besetzten Gebieten* (Berlin, 1997), pp. 11–28, 29–62. More generally, see Dietrich Eichholtz (ed.), *Krieg und Wirtschaft. Studien zur deutschen Wirtschaftsgeschichte 1939–1945* (Berlin, 1999), Wolfgang Benz, Johannes Houwink ten Cate, & Gerhard Otto (eds.), *Die Bürokratie der Okkupation. Strukturen der Herrschaft und Verwaltung im besezten Europa* (Berlin, 1998), and Johannes Houwink ten Cate & Gerhard Otto (eds.), *Das Organisierte Chaos. "Ämterdarwinismus" und "Gesinnungsethik." Determinanten nationalsozialistischer Besatzungsherrschaft* (Berlin, 1999). For an important illustration of American efforts to understand what the German insurance business was up to, see "Axis Penetration of European Insurance," Board of Economic Warfare, Economy Branch, June 15, 1943, NA, RG 60, 230/31/1/6. The U.S. government also tapped the knowledge and experience of Alfred Manes, who produced a memorandum on reinsurance on July 31, 1942, NA, RG 60, 230/32/1/4.
[31] Aktennote, 8. Dez. 1941, MR, A 1/23. On general policy matters, see Alice Teichova, "Instruments of Economic Control and Exploitation: The German Occupation of Bohemia and Moravia," in Overy, *"Neuordnung" Europas*, pp. 83–108.

host of Czech companies.[32] Naturally, these companies were subject to the usual racial measures. Thus, a ban on the further payment and employment of Jews in insurance was instituted immediately, a matter that proved very "painful" for a company like Internationale Unfall, which had a majority participation by RAS and had extremely able Jewish leadership that had to be let go.[33] The companies licensed to operate in the Protectorate were also affected by the particularly rigorous and systematic seizure of Jewish insurance assets, so that by July 1942 the Prague Gestapo was able to report 54.4 million Czech crowns in confiscated repurchase values, the bulk of which came from the portfolios of Generali (20.1 million), Victoria (13.8 million), RAS (5.9 million), and Star-Versicherungsanstalt (4.6 million). The Allianz portfolio was not affected in this case because of its exclusion from the Protectorate, and although 2.1 million Czech crowns in Jewish insurance assets had been taken from Slavia, this was presumably from the non-Sudetenland portfolio and thus did not involve Allianz either.[34] Jewish policies with a value of 2.1 million Czech crowns were confiscated from Slavia, but these were exclusively policies from the Protectorate. The entire portfolio of Slavia in the Sudetenland was transferred to Allianz companies after the annexation. Allianz was not licensed to operate in the Protectorate.

German authorities in the Protectorate had two goals regarding the insurance business there. First, they wished to capture Czech business for German companies and increase German influence. Since Czechs preferred to buy their insurance from Czech companies, they sought to veil the role actually being played by German companies. Second, there was general agreement that the Czechs had too many small mutual insurance companies and that concentration and rationalization were essential. Thus, Schwede-Coburg, in his capacity as chairman of the Reich Insurance Committee and with an eye toward extending the role of the publicly chartered companies, opposed giving the insurance business in the Protectorate any organizational autonomy, telling the RWM in 1940 that "I would consider it far more correct to place the insurance business in the Protectorate under far-reaching German influence and to put the supervisory authority in a position to carry out the concentration of insurance, especially in the question of the consolidation of enterprises and the setting aside of the unjustified number of premium schedules."[35] Fundamentally, Schwede-Coburg wanted to coordinate the business organizations of the Protectorate with those of the Reich, whereas the authorities in the Protectorate chose to maintain existing Czech insurance organizations and ensure German influence through the

[32] Robert Rosenkranz, *Die Versicherungswirtschaft im Protektorat Böhmen und Mähren, im Sudetenland und in der Slowakischen Republik* (Prague, 1941), pp. 33f.

[33] R. Weydenhammer an Marchesano, 8. März 1939, BCI, NL Frigessi, cart. 108, fasc. 4.

[34] See Tomas Jelinek, "Insurance in the Nazi Occupied Czech Lands," Table 2: The Transfer of Czechoslovak Insurance Activities in the Sudetenland, to be found at the website ⟨http://www.hrad.cz/kpr/holocaust/pojistky_uk.html⟩, p. 5.

[35] Schwede-Coburg an RWM, 11. Okt. 1940, SM, 1458/1/282, Bl. 83.

appointment of the German Robert Rosenkranz as chief agent of the Reich Protectorate to oversee developments in the insurance field.[36]

Rosenkranz's basic attitude toward the Czech insurance business was not much different from that of Schwede-Coburg, though it was much friendlier to private enterprise. He thought the industry overpopulated and wished to set aside the multiple system of premiums designed to preserve small companies. Thus, in a meeting in January 1941 with Protectorate insurers, he advised them that their protection against competition from Old Reich companies could not last forever and that there was no room for 40 companies. If the insurance companies did not consolidate on their own then it would be done for them; he bluntly added that

the insurance business is not to be viewed as a productive occupation, that is, the officials in it do not perform productive work. It is the intention of the economy, however, to transfer people from unproductive enterprises to productive enterprises and to retrain them accordingly. No consideration can be given in the concentration of the insurance enterprises if a few hundred or thousand officials are eliminated and retrained, for that is in the interest of the economy.[37]

This did not sit at all well with the Italian insurers, and Riunione sent a report on the meeting to Director Alzheimer of the Munich Re, pointing out that this was a matter of mutual concern (because of agreements they had reached about their roles in the Protectorate) and stressing that certainly Munich Re had a particular interest in the matter since it was the largest reinsurer in the Protectorate and so desired an orderly rationalization of conditions there.[38] Indeed, whereas neither Wiener Allianz nor Allianz itself was active in the Protectorate, Munich Re – which had so many common and overlapping interests with the Allianz concern – played a significant role in the Protectorate's insurance affairs.

These affairs had a rather Byzantine character, as was amply demonstrated by the remarkable involvement of Munich Re with the Prague-based Volks-Versicherungs-Anstalt Čechoslavia AG. This company was founded in 1919 as one intended to service persons of modest means; it was a creation of the Czech consumer cooperatives and, to a lesser extent, the trade unions. The Munich Re had served as their reinsurer and as a significant shareholder since the early 1920s, and a good deal of mutual confidence had developed between the two sides. On the one hand, it was unusual for a Czech firm to develop so intimate a relationship with a German reinsurer, given the difficulties between the two countries. On the other, Munich Re had great confidence in the management of the Čechoslavia. Shortly after the German invasion, Directors Mattfeld and Alzheimer approached their counterparts at the Čechoslavia (Directors Nejedlý and Svoboda) and urged that Munich Re be allowed to secure a 51% majority,

---

[36] Reichsprotektor an RWM, 15. Jan. 1941, ibid., Bl. 85.
[37] Report to Frigessi, 21. Jan. 1941, BCI, NL Frigessi, cart. 108, fasc. 3.
[38] Frigessi an Alzheimer, 3. Jan. 1941, ibid., cart. 62, fasz. 4.

promising to maintain the Czech character of the company and to avoid unwarranted interference in its operations. In late July, Mattfeld pressed the case,
pointing out that there were other interested parties. He had spoken to one of
the directors of Böhmische Eskomptebank, which was under the control of the
Dresdner Bank, who strongly suggested that Čechoslavia was a logical prospect
for takeover by Deutscher Ring. Mattfeld asked that the bank not pursue the
matter (since Munich Re controlled a large share of Čechoslavia's stock) and
warned the chairman of the supervisory board, Frantisek Vesely, that he was not
sure how long he could ward off such attempts from the DAF quarter. Thus the
situation remained between the summer of 1940 and the first months of 1941.[39]

It radically changed when Chairman Vesely and his deputy chairman (Ko-
meda), who were possibly engaged in resistance activities, were arrested in May
and executed as "enemies of the State" in late October 1941. This information
was conveyed to Schmitt by Rosenkranz on November 1, who indicated that
"those responsible for the security of this area are of the view that thereby a new
situation has been created that the enterprise has to take into account ...."[40]
This was certainly the case with respect to shareholding in the Čechoslavia because the victims held shares (belonging to other shareholders) that they had
apparently used to block Munich Re, which held 38% of the shares, from gaining majority control. As Rosenkranz informed Schmitt, those Czechs now holding the shares were prepared to sell them in order to give Munich Re a majority.
Whatever Schmitt and Mattfeld thought of the manner in which these shares
had been made "available," they leapt at the opportunity to gain the majority.
Time was indeed of the essence, because Volksfürsorge was also after the shares
in question and argued that they belonged to the consumer cooperative and thus
should properly go to DAF, which also was the proper agency to run a popular
insurance organization. Apparently, DAF officials thought this argument would
be particularly appealing to the Gestapo for political and social reasons and that
security interests could be combined with an appeal to anticapitalist sentiments
in attempting to promote the DAF cause. Munich Re, however, claimed that it
had a prior option, an argument that Rosenkranz was prepared to accept since
the crucial issue was placing control of Čechoslavia in German hands. Nevertheless, as Mattfeld reported, Rosenkranz – obviously well aware of anti–big
business sentiment among the more radical Nazis – did remark that Munich Re
"as a plutocratic-democratic and liberal corporation is not exactly popular in
many quarters."[41] It was typical of the National Socialists to define Western
capitalist enterprises as "plutocratic" and to conflate plutocracy with democracy and liberalism. It is only fair to note, however, that the relations between

[39] See especially the Aktennote of 17. April 1939, 21./22. Juli 1939, and 17./19. Juni 1940, and the
      exchange between Mattfeld and Pokorný, June 25 and July 6, 1940, as well as other related cor-
      respondence in MR, A 1/5.
[40] Rosenkranz an Kurt Schmitt, 1. Nov. 1941, ibid.
[41] Aktennote, 27. Nov. 1941; Schmitt an Rosenkranz, 4. Nov. 1941; Aktennote, 25. Nov. 1941, ibid.

the two corporations seem to have been quite cordial and that Munich Re apparently struggled to maintain the Czech character of the company. Thus, when the Reich Protector's office sought to force a change of the company's name in late 1942, Munich Re resisted the idea, remarking that they had 55% control by this time and that "it therefore lies in our German interest that the transformation and further work of the company is made easier and to be sure just within its Czech circle of customers in order to bring them along indirectly into the German sphere of Influence."[42] As a compromise, they proposed that "Čechoslavia" be changed to "Cechoslavia." This compromise seemed to win some approval, but in January 1944 "Cechoslavia" was changed to "Bohemoslavia."[43] After the war, Director Meuschel of the Munich Re credited his company with showing "strong resistance" on behalf of its old business partner and "saving the insurance company of the Czech Social Democratic Party."[44] Certainly Munich Re showed prudence and as much decency as the situation allowed, but if it saved Čechoslavia from anything it was from Volksfürsorge, and that was very much in Munich Re's interest.

Munich Re also had close reinsurance relations and shares in other important Czech insurance firms, particularly Slavia and Corona-Slovanska, and the consolidation of these firms extended Munich Re's holdings in 1942. Here again, Munich Re's continuing interest in Slavia holdings seemed much appreciated since – as Director von Reininghaus reported in August 1944 – the general director of the company (Václav Peča) praised Schmitt for rescuing Slavia and remarked that "he and his institution will never forget it, for one learns who one's friends are in one's distress."[45] Munich Re's big problem in the region was the ambition of Volksfürsorge and the proposals of its General Director Pollmann that his company and Munich Re enter into joint control of the leading Czech companies, which would continue to be cloaked as Czech firms but in reality be Germanized.[46] The goal was ultimately to make Volksfürsorge the leading company in a consortium of German firms controlling a concentrated Czech insurance system, and while it was undoubtedly the course of the war that frustrated the pursuit of these efforts, Munich Re's and Schmitt's watchfulness, interventions, and wire pulling certainly played an important role in making it much more difficult for Volksfürsorge to achieve its goals. Needless to say, this is not to be interpreted as an effort to block Germanization of the Czech insurance business but rather to have it take place under private auspices that would be less brutal in dealing with Czech interests.

---

[42] Münchener Rück an den Reichsprotektor, 31. Okt. 1942, ibid.

[43] Aktennote, 14. Jan. 1944, ibid.

[44] Walther Meuschel, "Die deutsche Rückversicherung 1938–1945" (1948), p. 6, MR, D/6.

[45] Aktennote von Reininghaus, 21./26. Aug. 1944, MR, A 1/23, which also contains an Aktennote of 15. Mai 1942 and the relevant agreements with the Slavia.

[46] Aktennote, 3. Feb. 1943, 8.–10. Feb. 1943, MR, A 2.21/130. See the discussion in Böhle, "Die Volksfürsorge Lebensversicherungs-AG im 'Dritten Reich'," pp. 132–5.

None of this, however, changed the exclusion of Wiener Allianz from the Protectorate, and neither a personal letter by Schmitt to the Reich Protector Konstantin von Neurath in 1940 nor attempts by Mattfeld and Schmidt-Polex to gain the ear of other influential persons had any effect. Schmidt-Polex suffered similar frustration in his attempts to influence Slovakian authorities.[47] Thus, on July 30, 1940, Wiener Allianz applied for a concession to engage in transport, machine, and aviation insurance in Slovakia on the grounds that they held a decades-long interest in Danubian river transport and that Bratislava was a key city in that business. Similarly, they had interests in the industrialization of the area (especially since German companies could be expected to move in) as well as an established role in aviation insurance. These concessions had been lost in 1932 when the Czech government forced them to turn their Slovakian portfolio over to a Czech company, and they now asked that their position be restored. Nevertheless, on August 19, the RAA turned down this request on the grounds that an agreement had already been reached between the German and Slovakian authorities as to which German companies could do business in Slovakia, and Wiener Allianz was not one of them.[48] This was indeed the case, and an agreement had been worked out under German pressure to consolidate the overcrowded Slovakian insurance industry. Thus, a consolidated Slovakian group was established, and some of the more important Protectorate companies were also licensed to do business in Slovakia. At the same time, five German companies were granted concessions: Allgemeine Elementar, Der Anker, Donau-Concordia (for both property and life insurance), Sudetendeutsche Union, and Victoria. Only Victoria had its base in Berlin. Finally, Generali and RAS were also allowed to do business in Slovakia.[49]

However, the complexities of organizing the insurance business in what was once Czechoslovakia were as nothing when compared with the situation in Yugoslavia following the coup that brought down the pro-German government in April 1941 and led to the Axis conquest of the country. The country was divided into no fewer than nine parts, with northern Slovenia being annexed by Germany, Italy taking central and south Slovenia as well as portions of the Adriatic coast, and Hungary, Bulgaria, and Albania taking over areas adjacent to their territories. At the same time, Montenegro was made independent, and a state of Croatia was set up under a brutal Ustasha regime. What was left of Serbia was placed under German military administration along with the Banat, whose fate remained undecided.[50] Prior to its conquest, Yugoslavia enjoyed a reasonably

---

[47] Aktennote Schmitt, 18. Okt. 1940, MR, A 1/30.

[48] Wiener Allianz an RAA, 30. Juli 1940; RAA an Wiener Allianz, 19. Aug. 1940, ÖStA-AdR, BMF, VA, Karton 269, Akte 35/A, A2.

[49] The negotiations and agreements of 1940 are to be found in BAB, R 3101/20306. See also Rosenkranz, "Versicherungswirtschaft," p. 295.

[50] For a valuable general account, see Holm Sundhausen, "Improvisierte Ausbeutung – der Balkan unter deutscher Okkupation," in Houwink ten Cate, *Das Organisierte Chaos*, pp. 55–76. There is a good report on the division and resources of the former Yugoslavia by the Volkswirtschaftliche Abteilung of the Dresdner Bank of June 30, 1941, which is to be found in SM, 1458/9/215, Bl. 2–8.

well-developed insurance system constructed along liberal lines. For obvious reasons, the big Italian companies were the most important foreign influence, but the Germans (especially Munich Re) played a respectable role as well, along with the Hungarians. Munich Re had interests in three Yugoslav companies. Most important was Ujedinjeno Osiguravajuce Dionicarsko Drustvo, which was centered in Belgrade and Agram (Zagreb) and in which Munich Re held 31.3% of all shares in May 1931 with an option to purchase another 30%. (The two other interested foreign concerns were Scandia in Stockholm and Erste Ungarische Allgemeine Assecuranz-Gesellschaft in Budapest.) The second company was the Jugoslavija in Belgrade, a family enterprise for which Munich Re had served as reinsurer since the end of the Great War. The third was the Europäische Güter- und Reisegepäck-Versicherungs-AG in Belgrade, where the Munich concern owned 86% of the shares. Naturally, Munich Re sought to watch out for its interests as soon as the situation permitted. Once again it broke a lance for Wiener Allianz, arguing that it was only fair that it receive what had been taken from it when the Austro-Hungarian Empire broke up and the successor states took over its portfolios. Thus, Munich Re argued that portfolios of Ujedinjeno and Jugoslavija in the areas annexed to Germany be turned over to Wiener Allianz. At the same time, it suggested that the three companies continue to function, with Ujedinjeno perhaps centering its activities in Croatia and using Agram (Zagreb) as its base and with Jugoslavija operating in Belgrade.[51] Indeed, Mattfeld had been hard at work laying the groundwork for such arrangements once he had heard from the very pro-German general director of Jugoslavija, D. J. Majalkovitsch, who blamed the entire disaster on Serbian officers, Jews, and especially successful English propaganda. Mattfeld suggested that Majalkovitsch's interests would be best served if he authorized Munich Re to sell the portions of its portfolio in the German and Hungarian parts of Yugoslavia to Wiener Allianz, its portfolio in Laibach to the Pace company in Milan (in which Munich Re had a substantial interest), the Bulgarian portion to the Orel company in Sofia, and the Croatian portion to Ujedinjeno in Agram (Zagreb). Majalkovitsch readily followed this advice.[52]

The Ujedinjeno became a purely Croatian firm headed by Oskar Maurer, an old Nazi who had worked for the company for some 15 years. Although he, along with Munich Re, worked hard to transfer portfolios to Wiener Allianz, this did not meet with much success, and in November 1942 Wiener Allianz itself was denied a license to do business in Croatia.[53] All in all, the insurance business in the region for Germany was a disaster. On the one hand, unrest in the area (the combination of partisan warfare and ethnic violence) made it a difficult place to do business. On the other hand, the Italians remained a potent

[51] Münchener Rück an RWM, 3. Mai 1941, MR, A 2.11/36.

[52] Mattfeld an Majalkovitsch, 5. und 6. Mai 1941; Majalkovitsch an Mattfeld, 9. Mai 1941; Mattfeld an Majalkovitsch, 13. Mai 1941, ibid.

[53] RAA an Wiener Allianz, 9. Nov. 1942, ÖStA-AdR, BMF, VA, Karton 269, Akte 35A, A2. See also the documents in MR, A 2.11/38, especially Deutsche Vereinigte Versicherungs-Aktiengesellschaft an RWM, 30. Juni 1941.

force until they left the war, and by then further Germanization had little point. Hilgard, who visited the region in the fall of 1942, was told by his German colleagues that the Croatians had killed a half million Serbs and that, of 30,000 Serb partisans in a camp, only 1,800 remained because the rest had been allowed to starve. He thought Belgrade a city of "criminals" and Croatia an "unbelievably unconsolidated land" that "justified the greatest anger." This certainly was no paean to Axis policy, and Hilgard did not think things could remain as they were in the Balkans. Manifestly, he was not very sanguine about business opportunities.[54] Insofar as the insurance business itself was concerned, the German authorities thought themselves hampered by the strong Italian influence, and it was only after "Italy's treason" that plans were laid for a consolidation of the insurance business in the region as well as for dealing with war damages without the obstruction of the Italians, who tended to neglect "economic necessities." As the final report of the German economic authorities ruefully noted, however, "because of the political developments the first measures promising success were made illusory"[55] – that is, German rule collapsed and those who worked for the German effort, like General Director Maurer of Ujedinjeno, retreated with the German forces or were left to their fate.

Compared with the former Yugloslavia, Greece appeared to be a land of at least some possibilities because of its important commercial and transportation activities. The Greek government had irritated not only the German and Italian insurance companies but also the English by passing a law creating a state reinsurance company that compelled all primary fire insurers to reinsure at a level of 50% of their policies with the government company, for which the insurance firms received a low commission; the state company then reinsured with Lloyd's of London and an Argentinian company but charged a much higher commission for itself, thus pocketing the difference between the commission it paid to the primary insurers and received from the reinsurers. Fundamentally, the state reinsurance monopoly provided no services at all beyond collecting money for the government while excluding foreign reinsurers, who could do the job more cheaply, and so increasing the costs of insurance in Greece for all concerned. The matter particularly galled the Germans and Italians, who were constantly fighting against critics of the reinsurance business at home and were anxious to eliminate all foreign models. Thus, one of the first things Alzheimer did after surveying the situation in Greece was to prevail upon the RWM to put pressure on the Greek government to eliminate the reinsurance monopoly, an effort that was successful.[56]

At the time of the Axis takeover in April 1941, seven German companies were operating in the country – among them Allianz and Wiener Allianz, so that here

---

[54] Stenographische Notizen über die Beiratssitzung der Reichsgruppe Versicherungen am 6. Nov. 1942, GDV, RS/28. See also the earlier very pessimistic report by Mattfeld of Nov. 26 and 27, 1941, MR, C 2/10.

[55] Abschlußbericht der Gruppe Wi I A 4. Banken und Versicherungen, undated but clearly from late 1944, SM, 1458/9/222, Bl. 10f.

[56] Alzheimer an Daniel (RWM), 16. Juni 1941, MR C 2/9.

at least licensing was not a problem – as well as the leading two Italian insurers, Generali and Riunione. In this respect, Alzheimer urged the RWM to bar any further insurance companies from entering the country, since this would serve to limit the Italian competition as well. The most important question, however, was what to do about the 60% of Greek fire insurance in the hands of English companies. The Germans and Italians had 15%–20% of the business, while the Greek companies had the remainder. An agreement was reached between the Italian and German companies to divide the English portfolios among the Germans, Italians, and Greeks on the basis of a 40:40:20 split. However, this scheme proved difficult to implement, owing to the confused administrative situation in Greece, which was allowed to retain a government with the appearance of sovereignty and which was in the process of changing its occupation regime from a German to an Italian one. As a result, the English companies had not been placed under trusteeship, and there was a danger that the English portfolio would end up in the hands of the Greek companies because there would be no authority to prevent this. Furthermore, the Greeks were constantly founding small new insurance companies, a fairly easy task because the inflationary situation and monetary "overhang" made it possible to meet the minimal cash requirements of starting a new company. Yet another problem was that no survey existed of the actual English portfolios and their value, a task turned over by the German authorities to the Allianz representative in Athens, Director Siegmund. In September 1941, the Germans and Italians came to an agreement in Venice to place the English companies under Italian and German trusteeship and to use the reinsurance of their portfolios as a mechanism for eventually taking them over. Nevertheless, the technical difficulties of assessing the portfolios dragged on to the point where Alzheimer and his German colleagues met with their Italian counterparts in Venice at the end of April 1942 and indicated that the passage of time had made any further effort to implement the agreement useless and had the potential of "causing moral damage for the insurance businesses of both countries" among the Greek insurers, since the Italo-German efforts to deal with the question were obviously having no results.[57]

The biggest problem of doing business in Greece, however, was the inflation, which reminded the Germans of their own experiences in 1923 and which meant that the insured were inevitably underinsured because they were unable to keep up with rising premiums.[58] A report of October 1942 argued that the founding of new companies, some of them of "microscopic size," was reaching "epidemic" proportions, that both domestic and foreign insurers were primarily inspired by the prospect of commissions, and that these companies would disappear under normal circumstances. For the moment, fire insurance business was

---

[57] Report on meeting of April 29, 1942, and Aktennote, 7. Mai 1942, as well as other relevant documentation in ibid.

[58] On the incredibly chaotic economic conditions in Greece, see Gabriella Etmektsoglou, "Changes in the Civilian Economy as a Factor in the Radicalization of Popular Opposition in Greece, 1941–1944," in Overy, *Die "Neuordnung" Europas*, pp. 193–240.

good, but there was concern that sabotage and English commando and undercover units would undermine the business. Although transportation insurance was also doing well, the war damage premiums were no longer really covering the dangers involved; some of the insured were not bothering to take out the war damage premiums on the theory that if the ship and its entire crew were lost then one could not demonstrate war damage anyway. The inflation was ruining life insurance, while the unreliability of the police made it impossible to offer break-in and theft insurance, and the amount of automobile insurance required of drivers was set too low to cover accidents. The most positive news was that the German insurers had gained a good reputation for themselves and were becoming as highly regarded as the English and more highly regarded than the Italians. Nevertheless, the basic problems remained the inflation, the fact that the Greeks could not pay the high occupation costs, and the unwillingness of the Greeks to accept the lira as their new currency because they saw this as complete subjugation to the Italians.[59] By April 1944, of course, the Italians were out of the picture, while Greece was in the throes of a nascent civil war, anarchy, and hyperinflation. The founding of new insurance enterprises had been banned, but normal coverage and business had become impossible, and Munich Re sought to save what it could by transferring its business to the Union Rückversicherungs-Gesellschaft in Zürich.[60]

Obviously, the promise of business in the Balkans was limited, even before the Germans were driven out. Hilgard, in his trip through the area in the fall of 1942, was certainly sober about the prospects. Regarding Bulgaria, for example, he found the opportunities quite limited. Sofia was a pleasant enough place, but the country was too small for 22 insurance companies whose existence mainly depended on wartime insurance business. Hilgard advised Wiener Allianz, which had already applied for permission to operate in Bulgaria in November 1940 but had still not received a reply from the Bulgarian authorities by March 1942, to refrain from trying to join the competition and advised Amend to allow no more German companies into the area. As Wiener Allianz reported to the RAA in March, Allianz and Munich Re had not yet come to a determination about the matter. Given Hilgard's attitude following his Balkan journey later that year, the matter was obviously going nowhere.[61]

Hilgard was much more sanguine about business prospects in Romania and Hungary – especially the former, which he thought had great economic potential, although he did find the insurance business more consolidated and disciplined in the latter. He was well received in both countries, although their hatred of one another over territorial issues was quite intense. Hilgard noted that the Romanian business class was oriented toward the West and felt forced into the

[59] Report by Hütz, Oct. 7, 1942, ibid.
[60] Report by Hütz, April 25–May 2, 1942, and an excerpt from his memoirs "1948," ibid.
[61] Stenographische Notizen über die Beiratssitzung der Reichsgruppe Versicherungen am 6. Nov. 1942, GDV RS/28; Wiener Allianz an RAA, 20. Nov. 1940, Wiener Allianz an RAA, 14. März 1942, ÖStA-AdR, BMF, VA, Karton 269, Akte 35/A, A2.

alliance with Germany. Nevertheless, despite these and other problems, the future promise was such that "here one must first gain a position and try to make things better after the war."[62] Gaining such a position, however, was no easy matter. On the one hand, there was the problem of the Volksdeutsche – that is, the ethnic German minority – and the competition between their insurance organizations and the other German companies licensed to operate in Romania, among them Wiener Allianz. On the other hand, German efforts were threatened by the strong nationalist "romanizing" tendencies of the Romanian governments.

The Romanian Volksdeutsche in Transsylvania and the Banat were among a number of such minorities in Europe (similar problems had been created for the insurance business in Croatia) who were organized through the Ethnic German Liaison Office, which coordinated all activities pertaining to Germans abroad with the object of promoting German racial and settlement policies.[63] In June 1941, for example, the liaison office complained that the Romanian government, which was notoriously and murderously anti-Semitic but made exceptions for Jews of a certain class and service to the State, was not doing enough to promote Aryanization and, in an effort to promote Romanization, was hindering the takeover of Jewish assets by the ethnic Germans.[64] All of this greatly complicated matters for the German insurance companies operating in Romania and elsewhere, since the ethnic Germans had a strong tendency to set up their own insurance organizations and, in Transsylvania, had actually created two companies, Transsylvania Allgemeine Versicherungs-AG and Landwirte Allgemeine Versicherungs-AG ("Agronomul"). RAA President Amend had a number of meetings with the ethnic German and German insurance company representatives in Vienna in an effort to find a way of dealing with the two goals being pursued. On the one hand, one needed to satisfy the special needs and desires of the ethnic Germans. On the other, one wanted to penetrate into the Romanian insurance business itself in competition with the native and other foreign insurance companies. While some of the ethnic Germans proposed creating a single ethnic German insurance company for all of Europe, the regular German insurance companies warned that this would be viewed as a political construction and would defeat efforts to sell insurance to the native populations. Insofar as creation of individual ethnic German companies for the various countries of southeastern Europe was concerned, the only viable ones would be those in Transsylvania. It seemed most logical, therefore, to consolidate some of the business of the regular German insurers and the ethnic German companies while combining Transsylvania and Agronomul and creating committees for the different countries that would likewise combine the ethnic German and regular German insurers. However, it proved difficult to prevent competition between German

---

[62] Stenographische Notizen über die Beiratssitzung der Reichsgruppe Versicherungen am 6. Nov. 1942, GDV, RS/28.

[63] See Valdis O. Lumans, *Himmler's Auxiliaries. The Volksdeutsche Mittelstelle and the German National Minorities of Europe, 1933–1945* (Chapel Hill & London, 1993).

[64] Volksdeutsche Mittelstelle an RWM, 6. Juni 1941, SM, 1458/14/61, Bl. 1–7.

and ethnic German companies, and in September 1942 a decision was taken to leave the ethnic German customers in Romania to their own companies, at least in Romania. The reality was that the liaison office viewed those companies as part of an ideological effort "in the fight for order against Jewry, Bolshevism, and capitalism"[65] who were not at all interested in selling insurance to the Romanians themselves.

Those who were interested in that market, however, were having a difficult time. In the first phase of the war, the native Romanian companies had sought to compete with the British by forming a cartel that underbid British premiums; when the British left, they pursued the same policy toward the Germans. The Germans eventually pressed for a more rational organization of the entire insurance business and formed a fire insurance cartel along with the Romanians – a matter of particular importance to Wiener Allianz, which held a significant portion of the fire insurance market.[66] By 1942, Schmidt-Polex complained bitterly about the inflationary conditions in Romania and Hungary. Although high premiums for war risk were being demanded, especially in the most important field of transportation insurance, there was great difficulty procuring the foreign exchange needed to pay off on damages. Alzheimer was particularly disturbed by the introduction of a high tax on reinsurance, which made the entire operation unprofitable despite the promising fire insurance business.[67]

Yet another important aspect of the peculiarities of doing business in Romania was that there was considerable foreign participation in the Romanian insurance – especially in the most important of the Romanian companies, Dacia-România – yet an increasingly ambivalent attitude toward such foreign investment. In 1939–1941 Generali was a large shareholder, controlling 40%, while Munich Re played a major role as a reinsurer but also began to gain shares with the support of the company, which hoped to prevent Generali from gaining a controlling interest. At the same time, Munich Re, which had a friendly relationship with Generali, did not wish to appear as a competitor and suggested that the Dresdner Bank buy up shares using a Romanian front, a proposal supported by Economics Minister Funk. In the spring of 1942, however, the Romanian Government – which was striving to distance itself from Germany in any case – suddenly decided to treat every company with more than 50% foreign participation as a foreign company. Since Generali would not surrender any of its shares and since Munich Re was anxious to continue having Dacia treated as a Romanian company, it worked closely with the General Director Romalo, who had once served as Romanian Ambassador in Berlin, to transfer shares to the Banka Romaniaska. In the process, contrary to Munich Re's original intention, this

[65] Protokoll über die Abschlußbesprechung über Sachversicherungsfragen am 29. April 1943; see also die Besprechung im RAA Wien, 30. Jan. 1942, and Besprechung des Rumänien-Ausschusses in Wien, 22. Sept. 1941, ÖStA-AdR, BMF, VA, Karton 323, Akte 61.

[66] Aktennote Alzheimer, 23./28. Aug. 1940; Protokoll über die in Wien am 13. und 14. Nov. 1941 abgehaltenen Sitzungen, MR, C 2/16.

[67] Niederschrift über die Beiratssitzung der Reichsgruppe Versicherungen am 6. März 1942, GDV, RS/28, pp. 9–12.

came to involve the consolidation of some of the leading Romanian companies. The creation of a substantial Romanian national insurance enterprise, Alzheimer noted to his chagrin, "would make the psychological position of the foreign companies more difficult,"[68] especially given Romanian xenophobia. As it turned out, the Romanians were not sufficiently organized to realize this possibility.

Their true problem, in any case, was not creating a competitive insurance company but rather the impossible task of escaping the consequences of their alliance with Germany. By the summer of 1944, the country was suffering from severe war damage, and the government came up with the idea of creating a "Federation for the Support of the Bombed-Out" and requiring that the six leading insurance companies contribute 115 million lei to the cause in five installments. The quota for Transsylvania & Agronomul and for Victoria was 30 million lei each, while Wiener Allianz was to be charged 10 million lei. The sums in question amounted to more than their capital holdings in the country, and they asked the German government to protest the Romanian action.[69] As Josef Mayrhofer (now general director of Wiener Elementar and a major figure in the negotiations with the ethnic Germans and in Balkan insurance affairs) reported to the Reich Economics Ministry in May 1944, the German insurance companies in Bucharest, including the Wiener Allianz, had themselves suffered bomb damage. Thanks to the English raids, Bucharest itself was partially paralyzed, while the occupation of various portions of Romania by the enemy had led to a loss of premiums. Damages during the first four months of 1944 were less than in 1943, to be sure, but the loss of premium income could be expected to have "unfavorable consequences." Mayrhofer was quite critical of the disorganization and helplessness of the Romanian authorities in the face of the bombing; in his view, it was important for the insurance companies to maintain discipline, especially since both the Romanian and the German companies had signed on. As he concluded, with studied obliviousness to Romania's impending fate: "The German insurance business will suffer heavily from all of these conditions in Romania. It is therefore essential that the German insurance companies operating in Romania, but also the Romanian institutions, keep to the rate agreements concluded in February 1944 under all circumstances."[70] At the end of August 1944, the Romanian government was overthrown and then joined the Allied side. There is no record as to whether they maintained the insurance rates that Mayrhofer thought so important.

The last country in southeastern Central Europe in which German insurance ambitions went awry – along with German political and military ambitions – was Hungary.[71] The country was a linchpin in Schmidt-Polex's plan, which he considered more or less realized by April 1941, to have an area of operations

---

[68] Aktennote Alzheimer, 12./13. April 1943, and other relevant correspondence on the Dacia in MR, A 1/7.

[69] Eingabe an die Deutsche Gesandtschaft Bukarest, 26. Juli 1944, SM, 1458/14/42, Bl. 107f.

[70] Mayrhofer an Ministerialdirektor Riehle, 11. Mai 1944, MR, C 2/16.

[71] See Péter Sipos, "Hungary in the German Sphere of Interest," in Overy, *Die "Neuordnung" Europas,* pp. 241–56.

for Wiener Allianz stretching from Lake Constance to the Black Sea. Here, as elsewhere, the strategy was for Wiener Allianz to play successor to the defunct Phönix concern. This was no easy task in the Hungary of 1940, for two reasons. First, the old Phönix company continued to exist there, albeit in the form of a company in liquidation. Second, the Hungarians had banned all further foreign concessions. Thus, while Amend and the German authorities supported a concession for Wiener Allianz, the barriers were substantial. The saga of how Schmidt-Polex managed to gain such a concession by the spring of 1941 – too long and complicated to recount here, but which he reported with considerable pride to Kurt Schmitt – speaks well for his tenacity and negotiating skills. Suffice it to say that he began by transforming Phönix in liquidation into Wiener Allianz in liquidation and then used the available legal mechanisms to take it out of liquidation. At the same time, between September 1940 and May 1941 he cultivated every conceivable connection in the Hungarian officialdom, nobility, and insurance world. The culmination was a breakfast of the high and mighty at the Grand Hotel in Budapest on April 3, 1941, whereafter he was assured that Wiener Allianz would receive a concession.[72]

Matters did not move quite that quickly, however, because Schmidt-Polex and the home offices of Allianz apparently had larger ambitions: they wanted to offer not only property and accident insurance in Hungary but also life insurance. The idea was that Wiener Allianz would sell the life insurance directly but be 100% reinsured by Allianz Leben. This was, in fact, a very odd proposal, since the liability would still rest with Wiener Allianz and the proposal violated the RAA principle that life and property insurance might coexist in the same concern but *not* in the same corporate entity. When the RAA inquired of Goudefroy what Allianz had in mind, Goudefroy claimed that there was a good market for foreign companies in Hungary, as demonstrated by Victoria and the Italian insurers operating there, and that German corporations would be particularly welcome because of all that Germany had done to rectify the dictated peace of Trianon. Furthermore, there were potential customers among the many Germans in the regions of Romania and Yugoslavia that had been given to Hungary. Goudefroy concluded that "we believe therefore that Wiener Allianz can build up a larger life insurance portfolio in Hungary than we have until now been able to do in countries that are not as politically close to us as, for example, Greece and Egypt."[73] The RAA, however, was not at all convinced. They did not think that the Hungarians would consider it legitimate for Wiener Allianz to sell life insurance when its business had been property insurance and, more importantly, they did not believe that the market was there since the insurance field was already too overcrowded in the old and new territories both.[74] In the end, Wiener Allianz received its concession in late November 1941, but only

---

[72] For Schmidt-Polex's extraordinary account, see his dramatic report to Kurt Schmitt of 22. April 1941, MR, A 1/30.

[73] Allianz an RAA, 29. Juli 1941, ÖStA-AdR, BMF, VA, Karton 269, Akte 35A, A2, Bl. 59.

[74] Schreiben 4. Aug. 1941 und 3. Sept. 1941, ibid., Bl. 56–8.

for property insurance and not life insurance.[75] As noted earlier, Schmidt-Polex was soon complaining about inflationary conditions in the country, which were indeed already the subject of complaint and worry in late 1941.[76]

As might be expected, conditions in Hungary increasingly reflected the devastating effects of integration into the German war economy and war effort, but one of the country's great peculiarities was that the Jewish community remained more or less intact in 1942–1943 and – despite discriminatory measures against them – continued to play a significant (though diminishing, because of the quotas) role in areas like insurance. One factor that made possible the employment of Jews in Hungary was that the laws defining who was a Jew were much less rigidly racial than in Germany, so that even German companies employed persons who would have been "Jews" in Germany but were not in Hungary. The leaders of Munich Re, especially Meuschel and Alzheimer, seemed to have no difficulty in dealing with Jewish directors and insurance personnel in Hungarian enterprises nor even in breaking a lance for them with respect to their continued employment. This was especially the case with Director Emmerich Balaban, the earlier general director of Erste Ungarische Allgemeine Assecuranz-Gesellschaft, and Josef Szönyi, a director at Europäische Güter- und Reisegepäck Versicherungs-Aktiengesellschaft.[77] However, the German occupation of Budapest in March 1944 and the establishment of a new Hungarian regime under Döme Sztójay led to a sudden and utterly brutal series of measures against the Jews by the new regime, despite the crucial role they continued to play in the economy. The situation was described in a deplorably cynical and inhumane report from Budapest by the itinerant Mayrhofer to the RWM on May 11, 1944, just at the time when he had also reported on the situation in Bucharest:

At the moment the situation is dominated by the dejewification of Hungary's political and economic life. This makes it noticeable in that the largest portion of the capital city's businesses, which as is well known were in Jewish hands, are locked up. Only very few shops, whose owners are national Hungarians, are open. There is lively activity on the streets; the yellow of the sun flowers on the clothing of the Jews is dominant. But one also sees on the streets as a result of the closing of the businesses, the coffee houses, etc. unemployed employees, waiters, etc. In a word, there is dejewification but no work is being done. This strikes one immediately as a businessman, and I think that the leading circles should be reminded that nothing is accomplished by dejewification alone.[78]

As Mayrhofer noted, the new legislation (which included adopting the German racial definitions) was having a profound effect on the insurance business

---

[75] See Wiener Allianz an RAA, 26. März 1942, and other relevant documents, in ibid.

[76] See the report by Hütz of Oct. 16/20, 1941, MR, C 2/23.

[77] Interestingly, both Alzheimer and Karl Kún of the Hungarian Foncière company (in which Munich Re and RAS had an interest) corresponded with Frigessi about protecting Balaban and others. See Kún an Frigessi, 11. März 1939 and Alzheimer an Frigessi, 17. März 1939, MR, C 2/23. The claims made in a 1945 exposé on the Munich Re in MR, B 22/35, Anlage 1, p. 3, would tend to be confirmed by this evidence.

[78] Mayrhofer an Riehle, 11. Mai 1944, MR, C 2/23. There is an excellent account of the Hungarian situation and development in Hilberg, *Vernichtung*, 2, pp. 859–926.

at a variety of levels. Not only were many employees now being let go, but the companies were no longer collecting premiums from Jews – an important part of their business – because the government had seized their assets, ceased to pay pensions, and so forth. In short, a host of issues had been created for the entire Hungarian insurance business that needed to be settled by all members of the industry, and Mayrhofer proposed that Hilgard, Alzheimer, and Herzog (who dealt with foreign questions for the Reich Group) come to Hungary to talk "business to business" and find a solution to these new problems.

Hilgard apparently was unable to make the trip, but Mayrhofer, Alzheimer, and Herzog went to Hungary in mid-July 1944 and reported back to the RWM on the situation. They cynically criticized the Hungarians for thinking, in contrast to the Germans and Austrians, that one "had to solve the Jewish problem in Hungary with one blow."[79] This was apparently a mistake because of the economic consequences, as the Germans were indifferent to the human losses that transpired. Thus, the effect of the driving out of the Jews was to cause an initial phase of serious economic stagnation; this was understandable in a city like Budapest, where 250,000 of the 1.2 million inhabitants were Jews. The personnel consequences were also serious for the insurance industry, especially with respect to the importance of Jewish adjusters, who were specialists in areas like textiles and leather. The loss of premiums from 18,000 Jewish businesses was also regrettable because it was hard to say when non-Jews could replace them, since so many Hungarian men were now being called up by the military. The only relief was that new owners were not allowed to change insurers, thus sparing administrative costs. Nevertheless, "constructive plans" were devised for the future. One was reducing the size of the insurance business and concentrating the industry in a manner more suitable for the population of 13 million non-Jews who were potential customers. Insurance business was satisfactory in fire (but becoming more problematic owing to sabotage), stagnating in life insurance, and increasingly costly overall because of the calling up of men to the front. Costs were also increased because the Hungarians were legally required to continue to pay commissions to their Jewish agents, and it was to be hoped that they would soon be freed from this obligation with the support of German agencies. Finally, the three German insurance leaders noted that the Hungarian insurance organization had leadership problems and that the companies themselves were suffering from severe staffing difficulties because the Hungarian government's military draft did not leave even a minimum of personnel. The situation was thus too much in "flux for intervention with general decrees from the German side." As is well known, the only "success" the Germans could boast in their final spurt of activity in Hungary was the murder of the vast majority of Hungary's Jews. They were, of course, despoiled to the extent that conditions allowed, but the evidence suggests that time was not available to confiscate their insurance assets

<hr>

[79] The discussion that follows is based on "Bericht über die gegenwärtige Lage der Versicherungs-wirtschaft in Ungarn," 12. Juli 1944, SM, 1458/18/104, Bl. 3–7.

(as had been done, for example, in Czechoslovakia). Yet Wiener Allianz was never allowed to sell life insurance in the country and so would not have been subject to such regulations – not that Jews would likely have purchased their life insurance from the company in any case.[80]

Taken as a whole, the German insurance industry (and the Allianz concern in particular) had rather limited success in Southeastern Europe, even in the early period of the war, because of the less developed nature of the countries involved and the rather chaotic political and military conditions. There was, to be sure, some big business for German insurers – the Rumanian oil fields, for example, and the military production facilities outside the Reich – but immediate and long-term prospects were much greater in the occupied countries of Western Europe that already had well-developed insurance industries serving more advanced economies.

Expansion in the West between Force and Conciliation

Both Allianz and Munich Re had long-standing interests and relationships in France, Belgium, and the Netherlands. Allianz's license to do business in France – the most important of these countries from the perspective of insurance and the one that will receive most attention in the ensuing discussion – was periodically renewed since 1926 (it had first been licensed to do business there in 1905) and had close contact with one of the leading insurers connected with the Minerve company, Béraud-Villars. As for Munich Re, it was not only an active reinsurer in France but also had significant shareholdings in La Cité-Vie, La Cité-Accidents, and Les Réassurances in Paris. Also, as Hilgard frankly noted, the fact that he was in charge of the most important negotiations meant that Allianz was "interested to a special degree" in these developments; since Alzheimer worked so closely with Hilgard, this meant that Allianz and Munich Re as a whole were in the forefront of the German insurance industry involvement in occupied Western Europe.[81]

Once France succumbed to German arms in June 1940, Hilgard was immediately active in trying to influence the RWM to create the most advantageous situation possible. On the one hand, it was necessary to eliminate French measures of economic warfare against Germany: the French ban on trade with Germany, of course, but especially the blacklisting – that is, the refusal to deal with companies that did business with German-owned or -controlled firms in Switzerland like Union Rückversicherungs-Gesellschaft in Zurich and Schweizerische National-Versicherungs-Gesellschaft in Basel. These companies were closely connected

[80] See Tamás Földi, "Insurance Claims in a Historical Context with Special Regard to the Holocaust in Hungary," in J. D. Bindenagel (ed.), *Washington Conference on Holocaust-Era Assets. November 30–December 3, 1998. Proceedings* (Washington, D.C., 1999), pp. 629–48.

[81] Hilgard, "Die Allianz im 2. Weltkrieg," FHA, AZ 1.3/2, pp. 31–2. On the licensing of Allianz in France, see BAK, B 280/12253, Bl. 51–3, 111–13; on Munich Re's participations, see Aufsichtsratssitzung, 3. Nov. 1936, MR, A 3.15/29.

to Allianz and Munich Re and had suffered policy cancellations because of the blacklist. On the other hand, the role of English reinsurers had been extremely important in France, as they had been in the Netherlands, and the German victory created something of a reinsurance emergency for the direct French insurance companies. As Hilgard pointed out, "there is in and of itself a great chance for the German companies if it is exploited quickly." But time was of the essence, since otherwise the Swiss companies, which had close relations with the French anyway, would be "the lone exploiters of this chance." Insurance was a special field in that both the insured and the insurers were loath to allow the slightest vacuum in their coverage.[82]

Naturally, the German military authorities decreed an end to the French measures about which Hilgard complained. Hilgard was, of course, most anxious to take advantage of the situation thus created and requested permission on July 19, 1940, to go with Alzheimer to France and Belgium in order to reestablish connections with the insurance businesses in those countries and to replace English with German reinsurance before the Swiss and American reinsurers got there first. The RWM agreed that the idea was a good one and that the matter was urgent, but nothing happened for over a month and Hilgard felt compelled to write again on August 21, forwarding a letter from a German insurance colleague serving as a staff officer in France that emphasized the importance of the French insurance business, the powerful influence of the English, and the failure of the military authorities – who were engaging other areas of French economic life – to have staff knowledgeable about insurance matters. Hilgard also reported that Alzheimer had seen signs for the Deutsche and Dresdner banks all over Strasbourg but no signs for German insurance companies. As Hilgard gloomily noted, "my company constantly receives piles of inquiries, requests, and cries for help from the occupied areas, to which we cannot respond other than in a consoling manner, with the probable result that the companies and representatives, etc. in question turn to Switzerland or Italy where, as I know, they are rubbing their hands over German inactivity."[83]

When Hilgard finally began his trip to Paris on September 16, there had already been significant contact with some of his colleagues who were in uniform and had been assigned tasks in the occupied areas by the Wehrmacht. One of these was Gerd Müller, a member of the Allianz board of management, who was serving as a military administrative councilor in Paris and who actually drove Hilgard to Paris from Saarbrücken in his military auto. Although assigned other duties, Müller had looked after insurance matters on the side and had been advising Hilgard about the situation, as had Director Meuschel of Munich Re and

---

[82] Hilgard an Ministerialrat Daniel, 26. Juni 1940, SM, 1458/5/271, Bl. 217–18; for the French decrees, see ibid., Bl. 229–35.

[83] Hilgard an Riehle, 21. Aug. 1940, ibid., Bl. 244. See also Aktennote, 19. Juli 1940, ibid., Bl. 236–7, and Wolfgang Bauerreiss (Vorstandsmitglied der Wechselseitigen Versicherungsanstalt Südmark) an Hilgard, 4. Aug. 1940, ibid., Bl. 245–7.

Rudolf Audebert, also a manager at Munich Re. The latter was a German citizen (and now an officer on Göring's staff) who had been born in Metz and had played a role in the development of the Cité automobile insurance firm in Toulouse until the war. Rumor had it that Audebert had saved Toulouse from bombing, a happy fate not shared by Marseilles, and this added to his popularity at the company.[84]

Both men were concerned about the confusion in Paris and France. Meuschel reported that the French insurers were upset by being cut off from their British reinsurers but were not certain they could take out reinsurance with the Germans. He was trying to get his staff, above all the director at Les Réassurances, to offer reinsurance in place of the British. At the same time, the French were seeking to maintain as much independence as possible, with the French supervisory office, for example, asking that the Réassurances continue to maintain its French majority, something Meuschel would not guarantee. Actually, Les Réassurances had not had a real French majority for some time. Munich Re owned 70.4% of the shares in 1929 (when it participated in the company's reorganization) and 71.9% in 1939. In April 1940, as part of a cloaking operation designed to veil the German control of Les Réassurances prior to the German military victory, the French firm of Demachy & Cie. acquired 30,045 shares of Les Réassurances from Munich Re through the Schweizerische Bankgesellschaft and then sold back 24,395 shares to Munich Re in December 1940–January 1941.[85]

Nevertheless, since the French were not being deprived of their sovereignty, Meuschel was concerned about possible nationalization efforts and felt it important to be as reassuring as possible that one could do business with the Germans:

In this connection, there is anxiety in Paris about the forthcoming visit of Hilgard, because one fears that he will dictate something that will inhibit the freedom in the management of business. I was able to have a strong calming effect here and used the opportunity to say that it is a matter for the companies to convince us through their own measures that there is a will to loyal collaboration.[86]

Meuschel thought it extremely important that Director Müller work behind the scenes to look after German insurance interests and that Hilgard make contact with the French insurance authorities as soon as possible. Meuschel was somewhat ambivalent about what he expected from the French. On the one hand, he praised the French businessman in charge of the Réassurances, Eugéne Poidebard, for maintaining a dignified posture and refusing to accept an invitation to

---

[84] Meuschel an Münchener Rück, 10. Aug. 1940, MR, B 12/19.
[85] Interestingly enough, Demachy & Cie claimed after the war that the sale to Munich Re had been made under duress and French courts nullified the sale. What was involved, however, was not duress but rather a cloaking operation in which Demachy violated French law in April 1940. See Melvin Fagen of the Inter-Allied Reparation Agency, Brussels to Debergh, Office des Sequestres, Brussels, Sept. 12, 1949, MdF, EN.17.136.
[86] Meuschel an Münchener Rück, 10. Aug. 1940, MR, B 12/19.

dine with the German military until a peace had been signed. On the other, he noted very positively that Poidebard was anxious to do business and, as head of what had been an Anglo-French maritime shipping company in Le Havre that he had allowed to be destroyed before the German arrival, he was now ready to consider a partnership with the Germans once the facilities had been reconstructed. What was important to both the German and the French businessmen was that these things be done privately and not dictated, and Meuschel was very anxious to have a civilian suit brought to him in Paris so that he did not have to appear in uniform when conducting such business. The Germans, to be sure, did not want to be too genteel about protecting their interests, and in August Meuschel urged that the French government be persuaded to simply ban further French contact with English reinsurers and that everything be done to prevent the French authorities from setting up pools or official (or semiofficial) reinsurance funds instead of turning to the Germans.[87]

A similar ambivalence was to be found in the report of Audebert, who met with Béraud in early September and found "that he apparently suffers very severely under the development of the existing circumstances and avoids every general conversation."[88] Like Poidebard, however, Béraud was willing and anxious to do business, especially to take over English portfolios for Minerve. When Hilgard finally met with his friend Béraud at the beginning of his September trip to Paris, the two men found the experience quite shattering. As Hilgard remembered: "In Béraud-Villars there seemed to me to be the embodiment of beaten France that stood uncomprehending before the ruins of his national self-consciousness."[89] Apparently, however, friendship and the necessities of the moment made it possible for them to work together and, thanks to Béraud, Hilgard was able to come into rapid contact with the head of the French Insurance Supervisory Board, Gabriel Chéneaux de Leyritz, and with his own counterpart, the president of the French insurers organization, Jacques Guérard.[90] Hilgard was evidently able to develop considerable rapport with the two men, which "demonstrated itself also to be very promotive for the building up of Allianz interests in France." Béraud also introduced Hilgard to Emile Jouvet, who had represented a variety of English insurers in Paris and who now decided to place his experience at Allianz's disposal and who (along with his secretary, Mme. Martin) remained faithful through all the "storms and dangers" of the coming years.

Hilgard's by no means atypical exercise in postwar nostalgia for the harmony of the early German occupation tended, of course, to bypass some of the hard politics of his journey to Paris. Just as he planned to build up Allianz in France,

---

[87] Schreiben Meuschel, 21. Aug. 1940, ibid.
[88] Aktennote Audebert, 3. und 14. Sept. 1940, MR, A 2.6/16.
[89] Hilgard, "Allianz im 2. Weltkrieg," FHA, AZ 1.3/2, p. 34.
[90] On these two men and the French insurance industry under the occupation in general, see Philippe Burrin, *France under the Germans. Collaboration and Compromise* (New York, 1996), pp. 238–43.

so his colleague Kurt Schmitt was working hard in the same cause back in Berlin, where he met with Amend on September 25. Amend had just returned from France and Alsace and informed Schmitt that, in agreement with the French supervisory authority, he planned to license some fifteen German insurance companies to operate in France. Among these would most certainly be Allianz and Victoria, which "would be given assigned trusteeship in the administration of the English portfolios with the intention of turning them over to them definitively as soon possible."[91] Amend was uncertain regarding the status of the German companies in the unoccupied areas of France, and he pointed out that the German companies would have to charge French rates but that the standard bond (i.e., the amount of money deposited as security for insurance companies operating in France) could be made by bank guarantee rather than in cash. He worried that the French would set up some kind of pool rather than allow free commerce in insurance and feared that the French supervisory board was behind the idea. Insurance companies operating in Lorraine and Alsace – which still formally belonged to France but would be reintegrated into the Reich – would be subject to special restrictions due to the special wishes and plans of the Gauleiter. Amend promised in any case that Karlsruher Leben and Badische Pferdeversicherungs-Anstalt AG, both part of the Allianz concern, would be licensed in Lorraine and Alsace, and that Karlsruher Leben would be given trusteeship over the firm of Rhein und Mosel – that is, placed in control of its operations and assets on behalf of the German government. Indeed, he promised that Allianz would have the most significant English and French portfolios in the area, while the publicly chartered companies would gain trusteeship of the Elsaß-Lothringen Versicherungs-Gesellschaft. Schmitt protested on the grounds that Allianz had such large shares of the latter firm; Amend held fast on the question of property insurance, but he was prepared to concede Allianz trusteeship of the company's life insurance portfolio. Finally, Schmitt pointed out that the interest of German insurers in the occupied countries stemmed from the fact that one could anticipate growing German industrial and commercial activity in these areas that needed insurance, but he thought it important that indigenous insurance companies be maintained to deal with normal business and that the German role be that of reinsurers rather than direct insurers. Here, too, there seemed to be basic harmony of views between Amend and Schmitt.

This was extraordinary enough, but what is particularly striking is the complete identification of Allianz and Munich Re interests reflected by the conversation and the extent to which Allianz was being given a most favored position with regard to the English portfolios. This was no trivial matter, since the British held half of France's insurance portfolios in 1939, which amounted to 90 billion francs.[92] Indeed, in Alsace and Lorraine alone, Allianz received a dozen English

---

[91] Aktennote Schmitt, Berlin, 25. Sept. 1940, MR, C 2/8.
[92] "Axis Penetration of European Insurance," Board of Economic Warfare, Economy Branch, June 15, 1943, NA, RG 60, 230/31/1/6, pp. 33–4.

and French portfolios – and this does not include the portfolios turned over to Kraft and Karlsruher Leben.[93] Thus, when Hilgard held a number of meetings with Chéneaux de Leyritz, he was defending Allianz interests in representing German interests. Chéneaux's plans to set up a reinsurance pool had been justified by his obligation to provide coverage for French industry, and he was prepared to drop the idea if the Germans would guarantee their capacity to cover French needs – an assurance that Hilgard gave, thereby burying the plan. He was less accommodating when it came to recent French legislation setting up a state reinsurance fund for transport insurance, which he claimed was insisted on by the French naval authorities in order to cover war risk. Hilgard pointed out that the German authorities had the right to review all such laws in the occupied zone, although rejecting the legislation would solve only part of the problem, and Chéneaux seemed to suggest that the implementation of the law (which was limited to eight months) might be such as to obviate this question as well. There was also some discussion concerning the appointment of trustees for the English firms operating in France, with Chéneaux arguing that there was no need for German trustees and that many of the English firms had moved their offices and documentation into the unoccupied area of France. Hilgard recognized that the German companies could hardly provide the personnel to administer the hundred English firms in France (doing so would require each German corporation licensed for business in France to administer seven English companies), but he was insistent that Germans have trustees of their own appointed for general oversight while the French did most of the actual administrative work.[94]

Actually, the Germans were already doing a bit more than that, and Hilgard intended to act upon the points of difference between himself and Chéneaux in ways that would determine the outcomes in Germany's favor. Thus, on October 3, 1940, he expressed outrage to the RWM about the French law setting up a transport reinsurance fund; he viewed it as a backhanded way of excluding the Germans and undermining already existing contracts with the French for the transport of valuables and items worth more than 500,000 RM. Hilgard suggested that using various mechanisms to monopolize all shipments of goods in the occupied areas would give the French something to think about, but he also urged that the matter be handled officially in the Armistice Commission.[95] Nor was Hilgard prepared to accept French domination in the trusteeship question. The RAA not only licensed Allianz to do business in France on October 4, it acceded moreover to Hilgard's request that Director Müller be made trustee for the portfolio of the Commercial Union Assurance Company Ltd. He was to work under Oberregierungsrat Hebel, who had been initially assigned as

---

[93] Anordnung über die treuhänderische Verwaltung der im Elsass frei gewordenen Versicherungsbestände vom 7. Nov. 1940, MR, A 2.6/12. See also Rundschreiben der Organisationsabteilung of Allianz of Feb. 15, 1941, FHA, AZ 5.1/5.

[94] Aktennote Hilgard, 9. Okt. 1940, MR, C 2/8.

[95] Hilgard an Daniel, 3. Okt. 1940, GDV, 3-234/1.

general administrator by the RWM. Sometime in the fall, Hebel was replaced by Director Karl Autenrieth, who was general agent of Berlinischen Feuerversicherungsanstalt in Stuttgart and head of the branch group of insurance agents within the Reich Group. His experience as an insurance agent was especially useful because of the important role played by local agents for the English companies.[96] There were other pre-emptive actions as well. Deutscher Luftpool, which was headquartered and managed at Allianz, was anxious to take over the English role in aviation insurance. When the Armistice was signed, the Luftpool was approached by French aviation insurers asking for German reinsurance, which had taken over 90% of the risk of Air France in the occupied areas and was assuming reinsurance risk for the major airplane companies in the occupied areas. Although French airplane production was now under German supervision, it was a French risk for which the Luftpool received permission from the RWM. Not only did the RWM and Luftpool consider the replacement of the British in this field to be in the German national economic and security interest, but the Luftpool also asked the German government to bar Italian competition from Consorzio Italiano di Assicurazioni Aeronautiche in Rome.[97]

Allianz had considerable ambitions in France, and it went to work almost immediately building up both its business and presence there. Director Ernst-Justus Ruperti – who had extensive experience abroad and knowledge of languages and had headed the foreign division of Allianz until 1935 before becoming deputy director of the Dresden branch – was summoned to oversee the work of Emile Jouvet, the French insurance man who (as previously mentioned) had left his English clients to work for Allianz. Ruperti had considerable rapport with the French agents who dominated the Parisian business, and Allianz soon outgrew its initial relatively modest but well-located quarters in the Place de Trinité; within two years it had to find larger and more elegant offices at 2 Rue Blanche. Ruperti was summoned for military duty in 1943, but he had already been replaced by Director Karl-Friedrich von Schlayer, who apparently had artistic tastes and hired one of the best architects in Paris to renovate the new quarters. It was a measure of how well established and respected Allianz had become that the grand opening of the new offices was attended by all the leading French insurers.[98]

Furthermore, Allianz intended not only to establish its own presence but also to play the role of a "French" insurer. Here the old interests of Munich Re in Minerve and the Cité firms came into play; in a discussion with Béraud in December 1940, Schmitt suggested that, after the conclusion of peace, "we offer Allianz the Cité as a French corporation alongside its direct representation."[99] Allianz had not yet been consulted about this idea, but by May 1941, Hilgard

---

[96] RAA an Allianz und RAA an Hilgard, 4. Okt. 1940, BAK, B 280/12253, Bl. 276–7. For Autenrieth's career and qualifications, see BAB, R 3101/92781, Bl. 164–6.

[97] Deutscher Luftpool an RWM, 5. Nov. 1940, SM, 1458/5/271, Bl. 164–6.

[98] Hilgard, "Allianz im 2. Weltkrieg," FHA, AZ 1.3/2, pp. 34f.

[99] Aktennote Schmitt, Paris, 5. Dez. 1940, MR, A 2.6/16.

Joint meeting of Allianz and Munich Re directors, including Kurt Schmitt (standing) and, facing him (starting left), Gerd Müller, Alois Alzheimer, and Hans Goudefroy, about 1940.

and Alzheimer presented a full-blown plan to the joint directors meeting of Allianz and Munich Re under which the English fire insurance portfolios given to Allianz would be turned over to Minerve, which would then fuse with Cité-Accidents; another French firm (Préservatrice) with long-standing reinsurance connections to Munich Re would have a minority share in the new company.[100] It was viewed as important to give the company the appearance of being French, so Munich Re and Allianz would control only 38% of the 15 million francs in shares, which might be increased to 45% if they acquired the portfolios of the British Victory Insurance Co. Although this would be the upper limit, the German concerns were granted veto power over the acquisition of the French shares by any single company, and Munich Re was to assume 60% of the Minerve-Cité fire business.[101] The RAA approved the arrangement – the merger taking place in September 1941 – although it thought it "unusual that the portfolio of English companies, that is, enemy property, should be transferred to an enemy corporation without the German corporation being given a majority and thereby a dominating influence."[102] Allianz argued, apparently persuasively, that this was the most that could be attained and that they could undoubtedly dominate in any case because the actual German control was cloaked: 10,000 shares of the

[100] Niederschrift über die zweite Sitzung des gemeinsamen Vorstandsrats am 9. Mai 1941, FHA, S 17.2/73.
[101] Aktennote Alzheimer, 7. Mai 1941, MR, A 2.6/16.
[102] Allianz an Münchener Rück, 4. Nov. 1941, ibid.; for the fusion agreement, see MR, A 1/16.

new company were owned in the name of Préservatrice, but three fifths of these were really the property of Allianz and merely held in trust by Préservatrice. This caused something of a problem in the fall of 1942, when Béraud feared the actual situation would have to be revealed at the Préservatrice shareholders meeting. They were doing such good business that the competition would then be in a position to take advantage of the revelation and claim that Minerve was nothing but a "disguised German institution." Béraud suggested this could be avoided if the Allianz shares were placed under the trusteeship of a French bank, so that Préservatrice would not have to reveal the true nature of the shares and the bank could be presented as yet another French shareholder. Eberhard von Reininghaus of Munich Re, who was involved in these discussions, strongly supported Béraud, as apparently did von Schlayer.[103]

Indeed, Béraud had long overcome the shock of France's defeat, and his appetite for the portfolios of Germany's enemy had grown with the eating. After the United States entered the war, Béraud, who administered the Hartford Insurance Company portfolio, was anxious to take it over as quietly and quickly as possible by offering the customers in question three months of free insurance. Ruperti was quite willing to help out in this 6-million-franc operation, and both Guérard of the French association and Chéneaux de Leyritz were willing to look the other way while Béraud and Ruperti skipped an official transfer of the portfolio to Minerve and engaged in "self-help." Ruperti and his German colleagues appreciated the cooperation of what he referred to as "our French friends," and when Guérard and Chéneaux visited Berlin in December 1941, Ruperti took the time to show them the impressive sights of Potsdam. The Frenchmen seemed very pleased by their reception, but they also wanted reciprocity in their business relations and were anxious to see one or two French insurance companies allowed to do business in Germany. Ruperti wished that he could send them home with something to show their colleagues but could only console them with the prospect that this would come later. As he told Alzheimer, "I would consider this – which is nothing much more than a gesture on our part – indispensable for the entire German–French work in our field."[104]

These French businessmen, of course, had a good deal in common with their German counterparts. They were collaborators, and just as Hilgard defended his role as one of saving his industry by taking a responsible position and working with the government, so he appreciated the efforts of his French colleagues to save the interests of their industry as best they could and to seek reciprocity. Indeed, Chéneaux de Leyritz explained his role using language very similar to that of Hilgard; the former claimed that he was out to save his industry while at the same time "maintaining courteous relations with German insurance"[105] and

[103] Von Reininghaus an Schneider, 14. Sept. 1942, MR, A 2.6/16.
[104] Ruperti an Alzheimer, 19. Dez. 1941, ibid.
[105] Quoted in Annie Lecroix-Riz, *Industriels et Banquiers sous L'Occupation. La Collaboration économique avec le Reich et Vichy* (Paris, 1999), p. 33.

that he wished to continue doing so regardless of how the war ended. Hilgard thus thought it deplorable after the war that, "instead of receiving the thanks of their country, they were burdened with the blot of 'collaboration.' "[106] Assuming they did not wish to join de Gaulle, which was the case with most Frenchmen in prominent positions, they did have short-term interests to defend. Their German colleagues certainly intended to take advantage of the situation to make a profit. Schmitt stated the position very clearly in discussions at the RWM in August 1940:

... in my view it is very important that, on the German side, everything be done in the countries that must work with us to employ our influence so that the insurance business is not built up under conditions that bring a loss either to the German direct insurer or to the reinsurer, even if, as for example in the French accident and also fire insurance the working conditions there were previously unfavorable or that through the appearance of German companies in the new countries the market is ruined for competitive reasons on the German side.[107]

In short, Schmitt (like Hilgard) wanted to use the authority of the RAA and the RWM – and especially the self-administration of the industry in the Reich Group – to create favorable conditions for German insurers to work profitably.

One of the most pressing matters in this respect was raising premiums, especially in fire insurance, which was in a chaotic and insufficiently profitable state. The British insurers had apparently undermined the high premiums existing in the industrial regions of France before the First World War by coming in after postwar reconstruction of devastated regions and offering lower premiums appropriate to the modernized facilities. Furthermore, the lower premiums were not, as originally intended, limited to northern France but rather spread to the rest of the country, so that the French companies were as anxious as the German to raise the level of premiums. Nevertheless, the German insurers suffered from rather contradictory feelings about this program of reconstructing the premium system to make it appropriately profitable. In the Franco-German commission that met in Paris between March 6 and March 12, 1941, there was general agreement on the need for "disciplining" the system; the Germans wanted to go as high as a 50% increase but the French did not think their supervisory authority would accept such a level, though Chéneaux de Leyritz himself was willing to go up to 30%. On the other hand, the Germans also demanded special consideration for themselves because they were well aware that they were uninvited newcomers on the French insurance scene and were at a competitive disadvantage in France owing to the reluctance in some quarters to do business with them and to the fact that high-risk customers disproportionately turned to the Germans. Thus, while the French accepted a 25% price increase for themselves in the end, they also gave the Germans a three-year period in which they could charge only 15% more than the old rates and only 10% more in the case of the English

---

[106] Hilgard, "Allianz im 2. Weltkrieg," FHA, AZ 1.3/2, p. 31.
[107] Aktennote Schmitt, 28. Aug. 1940, MR, C 2/8.

portfolios. The Germans were caught in a contradictory situation. On the one hand, they believed premiums needed to be raised substantially and wanted to force the French in this direction. On the other hand, they were anxious to secure French business by offering lower premiums themselves and thus had to accept lower premium increases than were economically desirable.[108]

When they met on March 14, however, the German insurers wondered if this was enough, since the agents who actually sold the insurance were rather uncertain as to whether they could win over French customers even with so low a premium. Hilgard admitted this was true, but he defended the commission's work on "higher" grounds:

The commission in its negotiations in Paris did not only carry on its negotiations with present business in view, but rather had especially the future of the greater European space in mind. The commission takes the position that where a chance is offered to reconstruct industrial business, it should do so, and to be sure even if in French circles it is said of the German companies that it was they who demanded the increase of premiums.

It was up to the German insurers, in Hilgard's view, to prove that they really had something to offer, especially in the generous and speedy regulation of damage claims. In general, "[t]he German companies must demonstrate that they are better than the English. One has to keep in mind and understand that one is dealing with an industrious predecessor and that things can only move forward with the most extreme effort." The chief task was to build up solid portfolios, and

it is impossible for the task of the German companies to employ German money in an exaggerated way in favor of French large insurers. It is much more correct at first to observe how things develop and impose measures of holding back. There will certainly be a general improvement of the French market when the reconstructive measures once have taken effect.[109]

Allianz was a strong supporter of binding premium arrangements in France, Belgium, and the Netherlands, whether in industrial fire insurance or in machine insurance, which fields they subsequently sought to enter in France as well.[110] Nevertheless, making the increased premiums effective was something of a problem, and by the end of 1942 most of the discipline was on the French rather than the German side. The unexpectedly high claims in 1942, which were to increase in subsequent years, made the French insurance companies anxious to raise their premiums. Insofar as the German companies were co-insurers with their French counterparts, they went along with the increases, while the German

---

[108] Hilgard an alle in Frankreich zugelassenen deutschen Versicherungsunternehmungen, 14. März 1941, GDV, RS/17.
[109] Niederschrift über die Sitzung der in Frankreich zugelassenen deutschen Versicherungsgesellschaften am 27. März 1941, GDV, ibid.
[110] Bericht über die Reise nach Frankreich von Direktor Gerboth (Alte Leipziger), Sept. 1942, FHA, H-4-II/44, Bl. 74.

companies kept their low premiums in order to increase business. Alzheimer promised that the Reich Group would support the French insurers' position, but nothing was actually done.[111] Even more telling was the paralysis with respect to the English portfolios. These had been guaranteed by the German companies who held them in trust through reinsurance, but the initial plan and hope was to consolidate the entire collection of English insurance holdings, so that one could not differentiate among them, and thus basically wipe out the English presence as insurers in France. The French were supposed to pass a law making this possible, according to an agreement with the Germans concluded in the spring of 1941. Two years later, however, the law still had not been issued, and it was quite clear that it would not be issued. The reason, as Director Heinz Gerboth (of Leipziger Feuer-Versicherungs-Anstalt) stated in May 1943, was "the change in the military situation."[112] Director Gustav Hartig of Gladbacher Feuerversicherungs-AG was even more explicit about French motives following remarks by the French negotiator Joseph Ripert, who admitted that the projected transfer law was dead. He made a new proposal that the German companies formally remain the trustees for the British and American portfolios but turn their administration of Anglo-American portfolios over to the French companies with which the Anglo-American companies were associated. These French companies would then have the responsibility of negotiating a settlement with the British and American companies for the portfolios. The true motives for this French proposal were quite transparent to Hartig. The Germans had wanted title to these portfolios; Ripert was willing to give it to them, but at the same time he wanted to leave the final settlement of the status of the portfolios until after the conclusion of peace. Hartig believed that the French were "calculating that Germany will lose the war, so that the portfolios will have to be given up or at least negotiated about with the English or Americans," thereby showing "that the French government had protected the interests of the English or American insurance companies in the best possible way."[113]

What is interesting, however, is that the Germans themselves were prepared to accept this French proposal. As Gerboth reported concerning a meeting on the subject: "The representative of the military administration as well as the gentlemen from the Reich Supervisory Office as well as the German insurance directors had the view, as came out clearly enough, that one would one day have to give an account to the English insurance companies ...."[114] There were numerous practical and technical reasons for not pressing the issue at this point, especially given the attitude of the French, but the German tone had clearly changed from

[111]   Bericht des Herrn Direktor Gerboth über die Reise nach Frankreich in der Zeit vom 19.–24. Mai 1943, ibid., Bl. 32–4.

[112]   Ibid., Bl. 38.

[113]   Harting, "Betrachtungen zum Transfergesetz in Frankreich," 15. März–2. April 1943, AN, AJ 40/836, Bl. 111–21, Zitat Bl. 114.

[114]   Bericht Gerboth, 19.–24. Mai 1943, FHA, H-4-II/44, Bl. 38.

one of confidence and insistence with respect to the English portfolios to one that was considerably more hesitant.

Indeed, the German insurers dealing with their French counterparts reflected not only the extent but also the increasing limits of French collaboration and their own uncertainty regarding how to respond. In December 1941, for example, Gerboth noted

that the idea of collaboration has gradually lost out, that is, the unconditional going together with Germany even in the circles which are dependent on economic cooperation with us and who carry this through now as before in a correct and loyal manner, and also in their personal attitude show the same friendliness. One has the impression that the idea of *attentisme* increasingly gains ground.[115]

The unexpected prolongation of the war, the food difficulties, and the growing discomfort over subordination to Germany and the uncertainty of German intentions were all taking their toll. While the French were willing to accept the loss of Alsace, they chafed at the loss of Lorraine. At the same time, Gerboth, who appears to have been a true believer, did note a positive attitude toward the war against the Soviet Union in bourgeois circles and the extent to which "the movement against the Jews appears to have gained ground very strongly in the course of the year."[116]

Set over against such grim "progress," however, was the increasing tendency of French insurers to hold back in their cooperation with the Germans, about which Gerboth had already complained. At a March 1942 meeting of the advisory council of the Reich Group, for example, General Director Heinrich Bothe complained that the French had reinsured the American portfolios in their control exclusively with the Basler firm in Switzerland. He considered this an "unfriendly act" and did not find the behavior of the French to be "nice." Yet similar behavior had been observed in the Netherlands and Belgium, and Hilgard decided to remind his colleagues that it was only "natural" for people whose country was occupied to respond in this way:

He reminded them of the occupation of the Palatinate after the World War. At that time one also did everything possible to prevent a French company from getting a German insurance policy. Why should it now be different there? If we at that time had the possibility, we would have also given everything to the Swiss. We will be having illusions if we thought that it would be done otherwise on the other side. That is why the work in the occupied territories is so difficult. We live from hand to mouth in these areas. The development of the general political situation is of great significance here. The attitude in the occupied territories is to a certain extent a barometer from which one can read how things are on the Eastern front. It will remain thus until the conclusion of peace. One must simply have to see how to do as good business as possible there.[117]

[115] Bericht Gerboth, 8. Dez. 1941, ibid., Bl. 179.
[116] Ibid., Bl. 284. In general, see Burrin, *France under the Germans*, Pt. II.
[117] Stenografische Notizen über die Beiratssitzung der Reichsgruppe Versicherungen am 6. März 1942, GDV, RS/28.

Telling words indeed – which provide evidence that even under the Nazi regime one did not have to lose all sense of reality and that businessmen could (and did) speak more frankly about the military and political situation than might be supposed. At the same time, Hilgard's words were wisely subjected to heavy editing in the official minutes to omit all references to his comparison of German and French behavior and to the Eastern front.[118]

As we have shown, the situation a year later (i.e., after further deterioration of the German position on the Eastern front due to the defeat at Stalingrad) made the French even more skeptical of German military chances, to which must be added that the occupation of the entire country – and the growing hardships and German impositions – increased French hostility and the tendency of French insurers to drag their feet in meeting German demands. If the French no longer believed in German victory, the "reasonable portion of the French bourgeoisie" (according to Gerboth, echoing the Nazi line) worried about German defeat and viewed the German Reich as defending not only Germany but also "European culture against Bolshevism." As Gerboth noted, however, neither these Frenchmen nor the Belgians with whom he had contact were convinced that Russian victory over the Germans would mean the victory of Bolshevism in Europe, because "England and America would prevent such a development."[119] Given such expectations, the gingerly handling of Anglo-American portfolios discussed earlier was indeed the better part of wisdom!

Thus, as Hilgard repeatedly stressed, doing business in France was no easy matter. At the same time, there was considerable pressure to maintain high performance. This was emphasized strongly by Autenrieth, who (on September 1, 1941) was made military administrative councilor to the military commander in France charged with insurance questions. Autenrieth had excellent Nazi credentials, having joined the Party as member no. 384,626 on December 1, 1930. He held a variety of Party positions and was also connected with the DAF, but he nevertheless appeared to be a friend of the private insurance industry, seemed to have worked well with Hilgard, and was made chief business manager of the Reich Group in May 1943.[120] Therefore, Autenrieth strongly urged the German companies to provide, as required, precise information on their premiums to the military commander's office in Paris and to do so on time. Since the military commander sent in periodic reports that were passed on to Hitler himself, Autenrieth was anxious to have the insurance sector appear in the reports since "it is absolutely necessary that the Führer also hears something about the insurance companies in the working report from France." In Autenrieth's view, this was important to the insurance industry for long-term reasons: "At a later

---

[118] See Niederschrift über die Beiratssitzung der Reichsgruppe Versicherungen am 6. März 1942, ibid., p. 6.

[119] Bericht Gerboth, 19.–21. Mai 1943, AN, AJ 40/836, Bl. 30.

[120] For Autenrieth's vita and appointment to the Reich Group, see Hilgard an RWM, 17. Mai 1943, BAB, R 3101/9728, Bl. 123–4.

time, when the nationalization idea will come up again from some source, the Führer will recollect these reports on the work of the private insurance in France and the work of the private insurance industry that was performed and captured in reports will without doubt be taken into account by the Führer in later decisions."[121]

Whether the Führer paid any attention or not, the reports demonstrated a nominal increase in premiums between 1941 and 1942: from 456.7 million francs to 701.9 million francs. This included reinsurance, which amounted to 50.7% of the total in 1942. As was its wont, Allianz led the pack of 25 German companies with 64.5 million francs in premiums, followed by Nordstern with 51.6 million and Victoria with 18.5 million in premiums. Allianz did 6.5 million francs in fire insurance, as compared to 10.3 million for Berlinische Feuer and 8.8 million for Gladbacher; its chief sources of income came from transport insurance (16 million francs for the fourth quarter of 1942 alone) and reinsurance, with a premium income of 5 million for the same period. The German companies scarcely did any business in life insurance, although Allianz Leben was one of a number of companies petitioning for the right to sell such insurance in March 1942.[122] They did, however, do an increasing amount of business in the unoccupied area of France, because the English companies were no longer operating there independently and because French companies did not have the resources to cover some of the large risks – such as the docks and port facilities of Marseilles and the Galeries Lafayettes.[123]

One did not, to be sure, want the Führer or his potential advisers in the insurance question to see everything, as became evident when German insurance companies licensed to operate in France were confronted with the French requirements that they publicize their balances yearly by July 15 and supplement their reserves to meet the required percentage of claims. The latter requirement did not have to be met until the following June 30, but there was great pressure to have the reserves in place at the time the balances were published because the deficit would clearly be noticed and might adversely affect the status of the firms in question. Because of the rising number of claims, however, this imposed a drain on foreign exchange and even required special permission from the German authorities. When the Württembergische Feuerversicherung AG proposed at the end of 1942 that the Reich Group seek an exemption from the requirement owing to the abnormal fluctuations in the number of claims under wartime conditions, Hilgard turned the request down on the grounds that such special favoring of the German insurers and lack of openness would damage the image and competitive capacity of the German companies. Autenrieth agreed with

---

[121] Bericht über die Reise des General-Inspektor Müller nach Frankreich und Belgien vom 9. April bis 26. April 1942, FHA, H-4-II/44, Bl. 127–8.

[122] Militärbefehlshaber in Frankreich an die Reichsgruppe, 15. April 1943, GDV, 3-234/1; Le Directeur des Assurances an Allianz, 13. März 1942, AN, AJ 40/835, Bl. 243.

[123] Reichsgruppe Versicherungen an den Militärbefehlshaber, 20. April 1942, ibid., Bl. 33–6.

Hilgard, although he was sufficiently worried to at least suggest negotiations with the French authorities – for the same internal German domestic political reasons that had made him so anxious to bring the German industry's accomplishments to Hitler's attention. In this case, he feared that "perhaps the often raised criticism that the German private insurance is not a source of foreign exchange but rather requires substantial supplements of foreign exchange could be repeated."[124]

These were good illustrations of how the shadow of Schwede-Coburg and Rath hung over the private insurers as they tried to establish a permanent foothold in France, but there were increasingly more immediate and practical concerns plaguing these efforts in 1942–1944. These were exhibited in considerable plentitude by La Minerve, when Munich Re had one of its officials take a close look at the sum-up lists – that is, the lists of reported claims and damages that direct insurers provide to their reinsurers – at the end of 1943. While the official in question thought that Minerve's exposure was excessive in comparison to the other insurance companies involved in some of the cases in question, the real problem was that 90% of the company's portfolio was industrial business, where the damages were extremely high and where the cause was in general "unknown" – primarily because it was difficult to demonstrate sabotage except in specific cases. Nevertheless, sabotage was regularly suspected. In the first nine months of 1943, Minerve had collected 10.6 million francs and was reporting 12.8 million francs in claims. Needless to say, this put a considerable strain on Minerve's reinsurers, and in March 1944 Munich Re was asking for a revision of the terms of its agreement with Minerve so as to reduce its loss.[125] In the final phase of the occupation, the question of insuring and covering sabotage costs became a much-discussed subject among the German and French insurers as well as with the German military authorities in France. Insofar as the insurance companies were concerned, neither the Germans nor the French were keen on introducing sabotage risk into their policies, since the question of defining sabotage and demonstrating that it had taken place was not always easy. To make matters still more complicated, the big French companies were not averse to covering sabotage damages because they thought the costs would destroy some of the small mutuals. What ultimately seemed to force some action, however, was the growing number of cases and the possibility that companies would contest the demands of the insured in court on the grounds that sabotage risk was the equivalent of war risk. Since the French government was in no position to pay the costs, the burden had to fall on the French insurers, and a law was planned to go into effect in April 1944 under which sabotage damages would be covered by a special fund derived from a tax on French insurance companies. Given that discussion of this question dated back to 1942, it is rather remarkable that it took until early 1944 for a solution to be found. One insurance industry leader explained this by the difficulties of negotiating

---

[124] Autenrieth an Hilgard, 11. Dez. 1942, and related correspondence, in ibid., Bl. 7–11.
[125] Bericht, 15. Dez. 1943, and Münchener Rück an Minerve, 24. März 1944, MR, A 1/16.

with the French authorities and by the fact that German insurers tended to concentrate on the affairs of their own companies when they came to Paris.[126]

Whatever the case, there was obviously a great deal of give and take between the German insurers and their French counterparts as well as a clear unwillingness on the part of the former to press their advantages to the point where they behaved like conquerers. This was far less true in Lorraine and Alsace, which were intended for incorporation into the Reich. Somewhere between two thirds and three quarters of the area's insurance business was in French or English hands, and from the very outset of German control of the area Alzheimer considered the goal to be "to bring these portfolios into the hands of Reich-German enterprises." At the same time, he thought it important to protect the venerable two purely Alsatian companies – Rhein und Mosel and Elsaß-Lothringen Versicherungs-Gesellschaft – both of which had always been oriented toward Germany and had close reinsurance relations with the Munich Re. Indeed, with the exception of Rhein und Mosel General Director André Mouchard, who was French, the personnel of the companies was purely Alsatian. Thus, for both business and political reasons, Alzheimer thought it important to transfer the French shares in these companies to German companies and to reorient their reinsurance from the Swiss to the Germans but to maintain their integrity.[127] This, however, was not to be, since Amend and the Gauleiter in the region were intent on transferring the property insurance part of Elsaß-Lothringen to the publicly chartered companies, while Gauleiter Robert Wagner and Minister-President Walter Köhler in Baden were intent on having Baden profit from the situation by transferring Rhein und Mosel to Karlsruher Leben, which was of course in the Allianz group.

Nevertheless, the Alsatian firms caused considerable tension between the German and French members of the standing Armistice Commission, since the French had moved the reserves and part of the administration to France itself. The basic goal of the French appears to have been to hold out for a final settlement until peace came, while the Germans were anxious to have everything centered in Strasbourg.[128] It would appear, however, that General Director Samwer of Karlsruher Leben was most impatient of all. A protégé of General Director Heß and widely respected for his skills and abilities, Samwer was also ferociously ambitious and had cultivated Wagner and Köhler, who had not only recommended Karlsruher as a "model plant" but had also made Samwer the commissarial administrator over Rhein und Mosel. Samwer's colleagues at Allianz and Munich Re were extremely unhappy about Samwer's obvious interest in the job and in

---

[126] For a revealing discussion of the sabotage question, see Bericht über Reise nach Frankfurt, Dir. Gerboth, Sept. 1942, FHA, H-4-II/44, Bl. 76–9. On the law, see the discussions and memorandum of early 1944 in SM, 1458/5/274, Bl. 4–10.

[127] Aktennote Alzheimer, 20. Aug. 1940, MR, A 2.6/12.

[128] For these alterations see the reports of May 29, 1942, June 5, 1942, and Aug. 5, 1942, SM, 1458/5/319, Bl. 34–44.

absorbing Rhein und Mosel, since Swiss Re had a substantial holding in the company and also did most of its reinsurance business; the German insurance leaders had apparently promised the Swiss not to use the military situation to their own advantage in this case. Impatient to pocket Rhein und Mosel, Samwer (as Chéneaux de Leyritz informed Hilgard) denounced Mouchard and had him imprisoned by the Gestapo. When criticized for this action, Samwer defended himself by claiming that the German government, as Amend and the Foreign Office had informed him, intended to put an "iron curtain" between Alsace and France and that it was necessary to denounce Mouchard because the latter had falsified papers and was trying to reassert his old position and remove Rhein und Mosel assets to Vichy France. Schmitt felt Samwer's performance "to be the only black spot on the wartime record of the Münchener-Allianz Konzern." While regarding Samwer as an "exceedingly able but extremely self-centered man," Schmitt and his colleagues sharply criticized Samwer to his face about his methods and did not think much of his self-defense. As Schmitt admitted, however, no effort was made to do more than call Samwer to account verbally for his actions.[129]

As demonstrated in this volume, there were some other "black spots" on the Allianz-Munich Re escutcheons, albeit of a different nature. Yet concerning their behavior toward their colleagues in Belgium, the Netherlands, and France, the situation in its basic characteristics was not much different than it had been in France. Allianz had already been operating in Belgium since 1936 through its agency Maurice Deckers in Antwerp, while Frankfurter Versicherungs-AG worked through the Antwerp firm of Martroye & Luth & Varlez & Marx. Neither company sold life insurance, and the Frankfurter was limited to fire and transport.[130] Similarly, Munich Re was also active in Belgium, where it had acquired 32.5% of the shares of La Minerve de Belgique; 65.3% of the shares were held by Les Réassurances in Paris, which (as we have seen) was controlled by Munich Re.[131] Despite these examples of foreign direct and indirect insurers in Belgium, the German role was quite small in comparison to the English, French, and Swiss. From the German perspective, the Belgian market was overpopulated (with no fewer than 250 companies, loosely organized in voluntary organizations), undisciplined in its premium policies, and poorly supervised.[132]

---

[129] Interrogation of Kurt Schmitt, July 15, 1947, NA, RG 260, OMGUS, FINAD, 2/58/5; interrogation of Baron Edgar Uexküll, June 7, 1947, ibid., 2/57/4; interrogation of Hilgard, July 15, 1947, ibid., 2/57/6–8; interrogation of Samwer, July 17, 1947, ibid., 2/56/1. See also Samwer's postwar explanation, "Meine Tätigkeit für die Rhein & Mosel Versicherungs-Gesellschaft-Straßburg," sent to Director Hermann Hitzler on Aug. 30, 1945, HM, A0001-00056, Bd. 2. Samwer claimed that Cheneaux suspected him of wanting to take over the Paris operations of the company, which Samwer claimed he did not want to do. For a more critical stance on the role of Cheneaux in this matter, see Lecroix-Riz, *Industrielles et Banquiers*, p. 237.

[130] Rundschreiben von 15. Feb. 1941, FHA, S 17.7/72.

[131] Munich Re to OMGUS, Property Division, June 28, 1949, MdF, EN.17.136.

[132] See the Lagebericht der Oberfeldkommandantur, 11. Nov. 1940, pp. 90–4, CREH, LL 1/1.

As in France, the German insurers at once sought to win over the Belgians and to make sure that they derived maximum advantage from their position. In a letter of September 1940 to Military Administrative Councilor Sperl in Brussels, who handled insurance matters, Alzheimer thought it psychologically important to keep measures of administrative intervention to the minimum required for re-organization and to assume that replacing British and French insurers would lead the Belgians to turn to the Germans. It was important, however, to prevent any kind of organization of Belgian reinsurers, and Alzheimer also urged that the number of German companies licensed to work in Belgium be limited so as to keep the market as stable as possible. Like Schmitt, Alzheimer favored a liberal approach to the transfer of English portfolios, undoubtedly sharing Schmitt's expectation that the better portfolios would fall to them or to friendly Belgian companies.[133]

This calculation, however, soon proved rather problematic for the sixteen German companies licensed to work in Belgium. On the one hand, the Belgian companies took advantage of their relative lack of organizational and supervisory constraints to compete with the German companies. On the other, they were quite aggressive in trying to gain control of English portfolios. This was especially evident at a meeting of the Belgian committee of the Reich Group with representatives of the Belgian insurers in September 1941. In response to Hilgard's question of how the German insurers could be assured participation in the former English business, the Belgian director Francis Diercxens responded that the English had gained so large a share of the Belgian market after the Great War by underpricing their Belgian competitors and taking away the better risks while leaving the Belgians with the poorer ones. For this reason, "the Belgian insurance companies now have the wish to get back again this business which originally belonged to their portfolio. They therefore have been striving not to share this business with any foreigner, and to be sure also with no Englishman." Hilgard apparently found this a bit much and responded that

the dropping out of the English is a consequence of the war won by Germany, and it will not do that the fruits of this war now be exclusively claimed by the Belgian companies. If the desire of the German insurance companies for a reasonable participation in Belgium is not satisfied, then he [Hilgard] does not know what will happen. He also considers it better in the interest of the Belgian corporations to come to an understanding and considers it in their own interest if they themselves do something about it.[134]

These remarks left little to the imagination, and the Belgians came up with a self-denying proposal that limited their participation in English policies to no more than 50%.

---

[133] Alzheimer an Sperl, 18. Sept. 1940, MR, C 2/4, and Aktennote Schmitt, 28. Aug. 1940, MR, C 2/8.

[134] Niederschrift über die gemeinsame Sitzung in Brüssel am 23. Sept. 1941, SM, 1458/16/86, Bl. 161–5, zit. Bl. 162–3.

As in France, so in Belgium. There was an increase of premium income for both the German and the Belgian companies after 1941, in part because of new business but increasingly because of the higher risks. Similarly, the issue of sabotage was of growing concern and importance, especially in agriculture, since the farmers were refusing to grow endangered products like flax and rapeseed. The Belgian insurers refused to cover clear cases of sabotage, but the burdens of paying out on unclear cases were causing increasing difficulty. Ultimately, the Reich Group asked the authorities to impose a premium on all insurance policies with the object of covering these added damages. By the summer of 1944, of course, business was collapsing. German insurers had already reserved the right to cancel transport contracts in the event of an Allied invasion – and this after charging an extremely high premium on the movement of goods to and from Germany. Once the invasion took place, the entire transportation insurance business simply came to a halt.[135]

The Netherlands were the remaining western European country where the German insurers pursued their policy of firm but negotiated infiltration and creation of greater homogeneity between the insurance organization in Germany and the occupied territory. The Allianz concern was represented in the Netherlands by no less than three member companies: the "mother" company Allianz itself, Frankfurter, and Globus, with the latter concentrating on fire and transportation insurance. These companies operated through Dutch agency firms, since the role of agents was extremely important in the Netherlands. In order to avoid undesirable competition and duplication of effort within the concern, the business of all three companies was coordinated by the foreign business section of Allianz in Berlin. Munich Re also maintained contact with agencies in the Netherlands and had close connections with the Dordrecht fire insurance firm of "Holland van 1859" as far back as 1896. However, the role of English insurers and reinsurers was of particular importance in the Netherlands, and the Nazi invasion created substantial reinsurance difficulties.[136]

Needless to say, there was strong hostility toward the Germans, especially given the many friendly and indeed vital economic services performed by the Dutch for the Germans during the post-1918 period, which included credits and a venue for German companies to operate under Dutch names and do international business from which they might otherwise have been excluded. The first response of the Dutch insurers, whose industry was better organized and disciplined than that of the Belgians, was an attempt to fill the vacuum created by the disappearance of the English by forming a special corporation with 5 million

---

[135] See the Lageberichte der Oberfeldkommandantur, Oct.–Nov. 1943, p. C-21, and June 1944, B-4/5, CREH, LL1/1.

[136] Rundschreiben vom 15. Feb. 1941, FHA, S 17.7/72; Gratama an das Hauptquartier der III. Amerikanischen Armee, Bad Tölz, 7. Jan. 1946, MR, D/2. See also the article by Martin Herzog, "Versicherung in den Niederlanden," *Der Deutsche Volkswirt,* 8. Nov. 1940, GDV, Personenarchiv, Akte Martin Herzog.

florins in capital to cover large risks in the event that they could not be covered by the individual firms. Whatever individual Dutch feelings may have been, this action was not taken in an atmosphere of rejection of the Germans; at a June 1940 meeting in the Hague, Hilgard and Alzheimer expressed strong approval of the efforts of the Dutch to deal with their problem through their own resources. In short, there was no rejection of the Germans establishing their own agencies in the Netherlands and trying to fill the vacuum but only a request that the Germans play by Dutch rules, keep to premium rate agreements, limit the number of agencies they might found, and not compete with Dutch companies in the provinces, since the latter had a surfeit of coverage. Hilgard was perfectly agreeable to the idea of not overstraining market capacity and was pleased to find what he felt to be a concordance of views and a good basis for future collaboration.[137] Hilgard also assured the Dutch representatives that the Germans had no intention of demanding that the Dutch create an organization comparable to the Reich Group, but he did hope there would be a counterpart organization available so that one could settle matters efficiently. This existed in the form of an insurers committee – to whose head, Director Heering of De Niederlanden van 1845, he could turn. An agreement was reached that the insurance agents would refer half of the English portfolios to German companies.[138]

Thanks to this situation, the German companies could boast some economic success in the Netherlands during the occupation, and the insurance industry had a positive balance of payments in 1940 for the first time in years.[139] However, in the Netherlands (probably more than in Belgium or France) German insurers had to deal with a highly nazified occupation regime of particular ruthlessness. In contrast to the central role of the military authorities in France and Belgium, the Netherlands was placed under the Reich Commissar for the Occupied Netherlands Arthur Seyß-Inquart, whose right-hand man for economic affairs was Hans Fischböck – one of the more brutal and imaginative despoilers of the Jews during his tenure as economics minister in Austria. Hence the occupation regime in the Netherlands was far more ruthless and ideological than in either Belgium or France, and the Holocaust was much more thoroughgoing in the Netherlands than in the other two countries. Not surprisingly, Schwede-Coburg and Hans Goebbels took a particular interest in the area and hatched plans to set up an organization of the fire insurance mutuals in the provinces with a central headquarters in the Hague. J. W. Gratama, a leading Dutch insurance man who headed the Dordrecht fire insurance company of Holland van 1859 (which as noted had close connections with Munich Re), was asked to join the supervisory board and was deeply troubled about getting involved. Indeed, he even declined to join Schmitt's Association against Large Risks because it was

[137] Besprechung im Finanzministerium, 19. Juni 1940, MR, C 2/14.
[138] See Martin Herzog, Beispielsammlung für die Kriegswirtschaftsgeschichte, 18. Sept. 1942, GDV, Personenarchiv, Akte Martin Herzog.
[139] Monatsberichte des Kommissars bei der Niederländischen Bank, 1940–1941, RIOD, FiWi 47, 7b.

under German leadership. In his dealings with his colleagues at Munich Re, he was very frank about these matters and apparently had their sympathy.[140] This was amply demonstrated in the spring of 1943, when Gratama and three colleagues and relations were picked up as hostages by the Gestapo. Not only did Alzheimer send an agent to procure their release, but Schmitt sent an urgent telegram to Seyß-Inquart emphasizing Munich Re's close relationship to Gratama's company and the importance of having those involved released for the continuation of operations. This probably saved their lives and certainly earned the gratitude of Gratama, who was actually a member of the Dutch underground.[141]

It was one thing to help and save business colleagues who were endangered by the regime, but quite another to refrain from exploiting the business opportunities created by the systematic expropriation pursued by German authorities in the Netherlands. The occupation regime demanded that insurance companies report the extent to which they were owned by Jews as well as the names (and extent of participation) of Jewish shareholders, and the Jews were forced not only to surrender their shares but also to pay what usually amounted to 1% of the share capital.[142] The German rulers in the Netherlands were successful in forcing Jews to account for their assets; they even set up a former Jewish bank, Lippmann, Rosenthal & Co., to collect Jewish assets – including shares in insurance companies owned by Jews and life insurance policies. For German insurers connected with such companies or wishing to buy shares in Dutch insurance firms, Lippmann, Rosenthal became a useful source for such shares. Thus, on March 16, 1942, the Handelstrust West N.V. wrote to the office in charge of Jewish assets asking that it instruct Lippmann, Rosenthal to "offer the shares of the Assur. Mij. De Nederlanden van 1845, Den Haag for the account of the German interested party, the Allianz Lebensversicherung AG, Berlin."[143]

However, the most important source of this Dutch company's shares was the Dresdner Bank. On March 17, 1942, its securities section wrote to Allianz that it was pleased by the interest expressed by Hilgard in the Dutch company and that, as agreed, it had consulted with the Reich Commissar for the Occupied Dutch Territories to arrange that Allianz have first call on all shares of the company – above all, those that had been in Jewish possession. Thus,

---

[140] See Aktennote, 2. März 1942 und 8. März 1943, MR, C 2/14.

[141] For Schmitt's undated telegram, see RIOD, T 63.3; for the postwar correspondence on Alzheimer's role, see the correspondence with the Allied authorities of 1946 in FHA, NL 1/157, and Gratama an das Hauptquartier der III. Amerikanischen Armee, Bad Tölz, 7. Jan. 1946, MR, D/2.

[142] Vermerk zu den Besprechungen der Versicherungsreferenten der besetzten Westgebiete im Haag am 31. Okt. und 1. Nov. 1941, AN, AJ 40/835, Bl. 11–15.

[143] Handelstrust West N.V. an Generalkommissar für Finanzen und Wirtschaft, Der Sonderbeauftragte, z. H. von Herrn Pfeffer, CABR, Dossier LIRO. On Lippmann Rosenthal, see Gerard Aalders, "Three Ways of German Economic Penetration in the Netherlands: Cloaking, Capital Interlocking and 'Aryanization'," in Overy, *"Neuordnung" Europas*, pp. 273–98. See also Gerard Aalders, *Geraubt! Die Enteignung jüdischen Besitzes im Zweiten Weltkrieg* (Cologne, 2000), esp. Chs. 6–8.

it can be expected that very shortly the Jewish securities, under which shares of the afore-mentioned company can be found, will be up for sale. In view of the desired amalgamation between the German and Dutch economies, the relevant German agencies naturally have an interest in seeing that the delivery of the blocks of shares gathered among the Jewish goods, wherever possible as complete blocks, be directed over to the German hands most appropriate for such amalgamation. It should therefore be possible, to gain in the relevant cases as complete blocks not only the shares originating in Jewish goods but eventually also the blocks of shares stemming from the confiscated enemy property. Beyond this, the interested German party will as a rule have the sole permission to buy up all the wares offered on the Dutch exchange.[144]

Jewish as well as enemy assets were therefore to be used to promote German economic imperialism, and Hilgard and Alzheimer (who was kept informed) were very interested parties indeed. Thus, in late April Allianz bought 300,000 guilders' worth of shares in the Dutch company previously in Jewish and enemy hands; Dresdner Bank offered another 61,000 guilders of former Jewish holdings a month later, another 45,000 guilders in June, and 10,000 guilders in August. Only in March 1943 did Allianz hold back when offered another 142,750 guilders in shares from enemy assets.[145] Finally, it is worth noting that Allianz not only bought Jewish securities of Dutch insurance companies from the Dresdner Bank and Lippmann, Rosenthal, it also provided transportation insurance in 1943–1944 for the shipment of securities and other valuables from Lippmann, Rosenthal to Germany.[146]

The driving out of Jews from the insurance business and the confiscation of insurance assets were not limited to the Netherlands and were pursued vigorously in France and Belgium. The evidence suggests that Allianz was not alone among German companies in showing interest in insurance company shares made available by Aryanization. Thus, at a meeting of the Reich Group Advisory Council on March 6, 1942, Director Bothe complained that the French were resisting participation of the newly licensed German companies in French companies and mentioned that the Jewish shares were to be sold off.[147] It should be clear, however, that the measures themselves were initiated by the German authorities – namely, by the military in the occupied areas of France and Belgium[148] and, in France, by the Vichy regime. Furthermore, insofar as life insurance policies were concerned, we have seen that the German companies played only a small role in the occupied areas in the West, so the confiscation of Jewish insurance assets primarily involved indigenous companies. Insurance policies were not, after all,

---

[144] Copy of Dresdner Bank an Allianz, 17. März 1942, sent by Hilgard to Alzheimer on March 19, 1942, FHA, AZ 8.1/1.
[145] The detailed documentation of both offers and shares is in ibid.
[146] CABR, Lippmann/Rosenthal, 81379, I Asd. This file also contains a policy of the Gerling Concern.
[147] Stenographische Notizen über die Beiratssitzung am 6. März 1942, GDV, RS/28, p. 7.
[148] There is a good collection of these orders in CREH, LL 3/12.

negotiable, and they do not appear to have been deposited initially with other negotiated assets and valuables. In the Netherlands, for example, both the Jews and the companies in question were required to report Jewish-owned policies, but there was some question as to whether Jews might not be allowed to continue to pay premiums and thus defray some of the administrative costs of the companies. It was only in 1943 that Jews and insurance companies were actually required to surrender their policies to Lippmann, Rosenthal, presumably for the purpose of procuring their cash value.[149] The process was also fairly slow in Belgium, where Jews in late 1941 were actually buying rather large policies based on large single-premium payments, presumably as a means of reducing their seizable assets, whereafter the German authorities began to consider banning such sales.[150] Nevertheless, a decree of May 31, 1942, required that all Belgian insurance companies making payments to Jews be obliged to deposit them in a blocked account at the Société Française de Banque et de Dépôts.[151]

As demonstrated by the report of the Mattéoli Commission on the despoliation of Jewish assets in France, the French authorities and business community, including their insurance companies, were by no means innocent in their application of the Aryanization process in their own economy. In the case of insurance, payouts to Jews were blocked beyond certain specified limits – 18,000 francs before the summer of 1941 and then 10,000 francs in cash or 6,000 francs as a pension – and Jews were thus deprived of the full value of their insurance assets by the French government and the insurance companies. Such monies as were paid could often go only into blocked accounts. It is believed, however, that insurance assets in France were of less value than other types of assets and that less interest was shown in confiscating them.[152] At the same time, there was a bizarre competition between the occupied and unoccupied areas in the appropriation of Jewish assets, as demonstrated by the grotesque reports of Ferdinand Niedermeyer, the German "Administrator of Assets Forfeited to the Reich in the Territory of the Military Commander in France," who had been installed to ensure the confiscation of assets belonging to non-French Jews, especially German, Czech, and Polish emigrés. Niedermeyer – who deserves a special place in the history of organized governmental thievery and an even more special place in the history of

---

[149] See the statement by the Dutch Government on "Restitution of legal rights with regard to Jewish life insurance policies in the Netherlands after the war," United States Holocaust Museum, ⟨http://www.ushmm.org⟩, Holocaust assets by country.

[150] Niederschrift über die Besprechungen der Versicherungsreferenten der besetzten Westgebiete im Haag, 21. Okt. 1941–1. Nov. 1941, AN, AJ 40/835, Bl. 3–10. See also "Second World War: Final Report of the Second World War Assets Contact Group: Theft and Restoration of Rights" (Amsterdam, Jan. 12, 2000), esp. pp. 82–91.

[151] See the Lageberichte der Oberfeldkommandantur, 1. Juni bis 1. Sept. 1942, CREH, LL 1/1, Nr. 21, p. C-17.

[152] Contribution sur les Préjudices Subis en Matière d'Assurance au Cours et au Lendemain de la Seconde Guerre Mondiale par les Personnes visée par les Lois de Discrimination Raciale" (Nov. 1999), which is part of the general report of the Jean Mattéoli Commission's Les Rapports de la Mission d'étude sur la spoliation des Juifs de France, in ⟨www.ladocfrancaise.gouv.fr⟩.

art theft – was deeply upset that, prior to his arrival, many of the proceeds of such expropriations had found their way into the French treasury, a situation he corrected with fanatical dedication. His booty included insurance assets, although it was clearly but a small part of an immense catalogue. In any case, what is now known about the performance of the French insurance companies – as well as the French State – with respect to treatment of the Jewish insured in no way suggests a moral (or any other kind of) superiority over their German counterparts.[153]

Conquest and Expropriation in the East

It has been shown that German insurance companies exhibited considerable self-restraint in the West European occupied countries. The same was not true in the East. It was in Poland after the German conquest of 1939 that German insurers, more than anywhere else, were tainted by the regime in the wake of whose conquests they sought to do business. It is not surprising that Hilgard, in his apologetic account of Allianz after World War II, writes extensively about Allianz's role in the West European countries but does not even mention Poland; he claims that Allianz's purpose in the East was primarily to provide insurance protection and peremptorily states that "the territories north of old Austria were handled by Allianz and in part by its daughter companies, especially the Bayerische Versicherungsbank."[154] The latter did indeed have a presence in Poland since the 1920s, although the operating conditions there, particularly in automobile and fire insurance, were such that by April 1939 it was seriously contemplating cutting its losses and, along with the other German company operating there (Aachener und Münchener), simply pulling out.[155] The position of Munich Re in Poland was much more active and powerful; often cloaking its role and working with Generali, the two companies controlled the majority of the largest Polish insurance companies: Generali-Port-Polonia Insurance Company, Patria Insurance Company, and Warsaw Insurance Co. (all domiciled in Warsaw) as well as Florianka in Cracow. Taken together, they accounted for half of Poland's insurance business.[156]

The German invasion of Poland created a complicated situation for the insurance business because Poland was divided into three parts.[157] The first of these were the areas annexed to Germany: the Wartheland, Danzig–West Prussia, and

---

[153] See Niedermeyer's report to the Militärbefehlshaber in Frankreich of July 4, 1942, and his report of Nov. 20, 1944, on his "achievements" in France, Bundesarchiv-Militärarchiv, RW 35/1188.

[154] Hilgard, "Allianz im 2. Weltkrieg," FHA, AZ 1.3/2, p. 38.

[155] Aufsichtratssitzung der Bayerischen Versicherungsbank, 27. April 1939, FHA, B 3.3.1/2.

[156] Münchener Rück an RWM, 28. Sept. 1939, MR, A 2.14/55. As the documents in this file (and in MR, A 2.14/54) show, Munich Re often used straw men to cloak its role and it also used Generali as a cover.

[157] For a good view of the German economic policies in Poland, see Werner Röhr, "Zur Wirtschaftspolitik der deutschen Okkupanten im Polen 1939–1945," in Eicholtz, *Krieg und Wirtschaft*, pp. 221–51.

the Upper Silesian territories previously annexed to Poland. The second part was the Generalgouvernement, and the third was the territories taken over by the Soviet Union as a consequence of the Hitler–Stalin Pact. The Generalgouvernement initially encompassed the area of Poland between the areas annexed to Germany and the areas occupied by the Soviet Union. It constituted an occupied area under the governorship of Hans Frank, whose rule was notorious for its exploitative and brutal character. The policy in the annexed area, as Assessor Herzog of the Reich Group put it, was "the elimination of everything Polish," and this meant the transfer of Polish and British assets to German companies. A different policy was pursued in the Generalgouvernement, where most insurance companies had their headquarters and where, for political reasons, the assets of British companies were not confiscated and the formal existence of the Polish companies was continued throughout the remainder of the German occupation. Matters remained to be clarified for the third area, portions of which were to become part of the Generalgouvernement (Galizia) while others were to become parts of the Reich Commissariates for the Ostland and Ukraine after the Germans launched their attack on the Soviet Union in June 1941. Prior to this time, Munich Re took the position that the assets of the Polish companies under its control be considered German and/or Italian property and be compensated by the Soviet regime.[158]

Despite these complexities, Allianz and Munich Re were very well positioned to do business in a repartitioned Poland, and the arrangements made were another illustration of the way in which Munich Re and Allianz worked hand in hand. Thus, on November 9, 1939, Allianz sent a circular to the entire concern defining its role in the former Polish territories.[159] The point of departure of this circular was explaining the control of Generali-Port-Polonia, Warschauer, and Patria by Munich Re and Generali. The circular then described the subsequent history of Allianz's involvement. Thus, following Poland's collapse, the German government had initially appointed trustees for the various Polish companies in the annexed areas while banning German companies from doing business there. These trustees were assigned the tasks of running the companies in question, both financially and administratively, and either liquidating them or presiding over their transfer into German hands. While formally an uncompensated public responsibility, trustee status obviously gave the company so designated an "inside track" in benefitting from the disposal of the assets assigned to it. In the instance of Munich Re's assigned trusteeships, for example, the concern intervened to ask that Allianz (along with Allgemeine Elementar, which belonged to Generali) be made trustee for the aforementioned Polish companies under its control in the to-be-annexed areas – in return for a guarantee of a portion of the portfolios. This was not exactly a chance development. The person charged with assigning the

---

[158] See Martin Herzog, Beispielsammlung für die Kriegswirtschaftsgeschichte, 18. Sept. 1942, GDV, Personenarchiv, Akte Martin Herzog. On the properties in the Soviet area, see Schmitt an RWM, 9. Okt. 1939, MR, C 2/16.

[159] Orga-Rundschreiben an die Direktionen, 9. Nov. 1939, FHA, S 17.7/70.

trusteeships in the insurance field (the so-called General Trustee for Individual Insurance for the Civil Administration of the Occupied Former Polish Territories of the Eastern High Command) was none other than Wilhelm Arendts, general director of Bayerische Versicherungsbank, who had been drafted into military service and, as an insurance expert, was charged with handling the non-German insurance companies in the region. Though obviously given responsibility to serve the occupation authority and not private interests, Arendts was nonetheless in a position to act according to his lights and certainly must have found it easy to reconcile the public and the private interest. He knew, of course, that Munich Re was a major shareholder in the Polish companies, and asked it to name trustees for the companies. These were trustees who could be counted on: Rudolf Schneider (for Patria), who had worked for a decade in the service of Munich Re; Renato Sambri (for Generali-Port-Polonia), who had long experience working for Generali in Poland along with a retired Regierungsrat Cuntz from Vienna; and Edwin Magnus (for Warschauer), a lawyer and highly trusted Latvian ethnic German who had worked for Munich Re in the region for some time and who was to play a key role for Munich Re and Allianz during the occupation.[160]

With this authorization from the trustees for Munich Re, Allianz first negotiated with the original government-appointed trustees in Kattowitz, and then in Posen for the so-called Warthegau, and finally in Danzig for Danzig–West Prussia. Allianz took over trusteeship of the portfolios of the Kattowitz branches of Warschauer and Patria as well as the fire, break-in and theft, and glass insurance of the Bielitz branch of Generali-Port-Polonia. Erste Allgemeine became trustee for the Kattowitz branch of Generali-Port-Polonia and for the accident and liability insurance of the branch in Bielitz. At the same time, Allianz Leben negotiated to act as trustee in the annexed territories for the relatively small life insurance portfolio of the English company Prudential. By the beginning of January, these petitions were approved and Allianz and Allianz Leben had established themselves in the annexed areas, with branches in Kattowitz under Director Hansgeorg von der Osten and in Posen for Warthegau under Branch Director Günther Klein. By early February 1940, negotiations over the Prudential portfolio were completed, and Allianz Leben along with Allianz were licensed to work in the annexed areas. Furthermore, Bayerische Versicherungsbank transferred its interests in the area over to Allianz and to Kraft and also closed down its operations in Upper Silesia in favor of Allianz. Further changes in organization were undertaken at the beginning of 1941, when the Allianz administrative control of Wartheland was transferred to Breslau (along with responsibility for Kattowitz) and von der Osten was put in charge in Breslau, while Branch Director Rudolf Bartholome was placed in charge of the Kattowitz agency. Allianz remained officially excluded from the Generalgouvernement, where Bayerische Versicherungsbank continued to operate from its branch in Cracow, but it did

[160] Arendts an Münchener Rück, 21. Okt. 1939, and Antwort, 24. Okt. 1939, MR, A 2.14/54; Arendts an Münchener Rück, 21. Okt. 1939, and Antwort, 24. Okt. 1939, ibid.; Münchener Rück an Arendts, 24. Okt. 1939, MR, D/6.

its business for the account of Allianz. However, Allianz did receive permission to handle the policies of ethnic Germans in its own name.[161]

To a significant extent, the Allianz concern was able to capitalize on the special claims made by Bayerische Versicherungsbank, which as early as September 1939 joined with Aachener und Münchener in complaining that the RAA was allowing other German companies to conclude insurance contracts in Upper Silesia instead of giving special consideration to the two companies that had stuck it out against the discriminatory behavior of the Polish government. It was on this basis that Bayerische Versicherungsbank also made appeals to be licensed in the Generalgouvernement. The Poles, however, were gone, and in October 1940 Allianz made clear to its daughter company that "we intend to pursue business in the Generalgouvernement more intensely than before."[162] If Allianz held back in simply replacing Bayerische Versicherungsbank, it was because Generalgouvernement authorities feared their efforts to control the number of German companies wanting concessions would be undermined. At the same time, Allianz was able to to make use of the Bayerische Versicherungsbank's claims of mistreatment by the Poles to support and collaborate in the 1941 attempted takeover of the non–life insurance portfolios of the only major Polish insurance company actually controlled by Poles: the Vesta. Bayerische Versicherungsbank asserted that it had lost 1.2 million zloty because the Polish government had required a huge bond and other guarantees for allowing Bayerische Versicherungsbank to do business in Upper Silesia in 1929, after which its business was undermined by the government's Polandization program. Nevertheless, Bayerische Versicherungsbank had stayed on "under the greatest difficulties and sacrifices in the interests of Germandom in Eastern Upper Silesia" and was now requesting the entire business of the Vesta (excluding life insurance) be given as compensation.[163] As in the previous year, when Allianz hoped to replace its daughter company, so now it wished to get the Vesta portfolios directly; but once again the authorities in the Generalgouvernement were quite insistent that the concession not be exchanged at the expense of the daughter company – in order to keep the number of insurance companies in the area under control and reduce paperwork. Everyone knew, after all, that Bayerische Versicherungsbank belonged to Allianz, and that it was the latter whose resources were now driving the concern's activity in the area.[164]

---

[161] Orga-Rundschreiben an die Direktionen, 9. Nov. 1939, 16. Jan. 1940, und 7. Feb. 1940, FHA, S 17.7/70; Rundschreiben vom 15. Feb. 1941, FHA, S 17.7/72. On the booking of Bayerische Versicherungsbank's work in Poland, see the Sitzungsprotokoll des Aufsichtsrats, 24. Juni 1942, FHA, B 3.3.1/2. See also Clemens Maiholzer, "Die Berliner Allianz-Betriebe vom Beginn des 2. Weltkrieges (3. Sept. 1939) bzw. vom Beginn des 51. Geschäftsjahres der Allianz Versicherungs-AG (1. Jan. 1940) bis zu den ersten Jahren des Wiederaufbaues 1945/1946 nach dem Zusammenbruch im Mai 1945" (Munich, 1960) (unpublished ms.), FHA, pp. 5–7.

[162] Allianz (Lux und Haase) an die Bayerische Versicherungsbank, 3. Okt. 1940, and correspondence between Walter Schmidt, General Director of Aachener und Münchener, and Arendts, Sept.–Okt. 1939, FHA, B 3.6/6

[163] Allianz an das RAA, 7. Juli 1941, ibid.

[164] Aktennote, 9. und 25. Aug. 1941, ibid.

There was more business for Allianz to do in the Polish areas annexed to the Reich, and a great deal of it was quite ugly. For one thing, it was impossible not to be involved in the activities of the dominant economic institution of these areas: the Head Trusteeship Office East (HTO), whose central headquarters were in Berlin. This institution was created by Göring on October 10, 1939, for the purpose of taking over the assets of the Polish State and undertaking the measures necessary to Germanize the Polish economy by acting as a trustee for Polish and Polish-Jewish enterprises and assets through confiscation, administration, and (insofar as worth doing) sale to German enterprises and ethnic German settlers in former Polish territories. The director of the HTO, Max Winkler, directed a substantial staff in Posen, Zichenau, and Kattowitz. The office was, to put it quite simply, assigned the task of despoiling Poles and Jews for the benefit of Göring's Four-Year Plan and the Nazi racial resettlement programs. It was the HTO, for example, that oversaw the liquidation of the Vesta, most of it done through the publicly chartered Posensche Feuersozietät. In June 1943, the HTO branches could boast a balance of 1.5 billion RM as a result of almost three years of organized and systematic government-sanctioned thievery.[165]

At the beginning of its operations, all Polish insurance companies – including those owned by Munich Re and Generali – fell under the purview of the HTO, so that the German insurers acting as trustees for Polish insurance enterprises were formally acting as "commissarial administrators" of these companies and guaranteed the insurance obligations undertaken by Polish firms. In the case of life insurance, this extended only to ethnic Germans, thus eliminating all claims by Poles and Jews to payment for their life insurance policies. Property insurance, however, was fully guaranteed with the understanding that the insurance companies would receive compensation as part of settlements in the liquidation of Polish assets. Recognizing that most of the real ownership of the major Polish companies had been cloaked and desiring to cut down on time-consuming work and administrative expenses, the HTO terminated the commissarial status of these companies in January 1942. This was also in recognition of the fact "that here under difficult circumstances pioneering work in the German interest entailing heavy losses had been performed and therefore now the Polish daughter companies had to be recognized as German enterprises."[166]

Allianz, Munich Re, Aachener und Münchener, and other German companies were not relieved of their obligations to pay out on prewar Polish policies and on policies of Polish Jews, but they were instructed to make payment of these obligations to the German State. As the HTO made clear in a circular of August 1941, claims by Polish citizens against German companies were to be reported

[165] Jeanne Dingell, "Die Haupttreuhandstelle Ost, Treuhandstelle Posen: Staatliche Raubzüge, 'deutsche' Kolonisierungsbestrebungen und deren Auswirkung auf das warthelländische Geschäftsleben im Zweiten Weltkrieg," unpublished paper presented at the "Arbeitskreis zur Rolle der Unternehmen im Nationalsozialismus" of the Gesellschaft für Unternehmensgeschichte, Frankfurt a.M., January 2000. Ms. Dingell is finishing a full-length study of the HTO.
[166] Report by Krier, HTO, 26. Nov. 1942, BAB, R 144/194.

to the local HTO. Such claims were then subject to sequestration by the branch of HTO nearest to where the claimant lived and were confiscated when they fell due. Indeed, since the assets of Poles in the annexed areas were subject to confiscation, most such claims could simply be ignored since they would be confiscated anyway. The value of their insurance policies were to be surrendered to the financial authorities.[167] It is a measure of the cynicism and criminal rapacity to which German banks and insurance companies were party that the HTO in August 1942 concluded it would be good to further encourage the Polish propensity to save. As the HTO noted matter-of-factly, this had been significantly diminished by the confiscation of all Polish savings, but from the outset the idea of encouraging new capital formation among Poles had been contemplated for "reasons of credit policy." This was why assets acquired after December 31, 1939, were exempt from confiscation – along with a thousand RM of old assets. As argued in an HTO circular of November 13, 1940, "so long as Poles and Polish Jews remain in the areas that have become German and participate in economic life, it has to remain possible for them to form new wealth and especially to keep funds from newly saved or earned money free of confiscation in the German credit institutes."[168] The question in 1942 was whether to bring this further to the attention of the Polish public – the Polish Jews obviously did not come into consideration by this time – and encourage saving. In the Economics Ministry there was some skepticism as to whether the Poles had anything to save under existing conditions and also whether it would be a good idea to spell out what the confiscation policy had been.[169] Nevertheless, Krier, the HTO official charged with insurance, thought that not only savings but also insurance should be encouraged among ethnic Poles. As he brutally concluded, "this should in no way be viewed as a danger to the German interests, since a newly forming upper strata would undoubtedly, as soon as it becomes expedient and necessary, be deported to the Generalgouvernement."[170] The fate of their "new" savings and policies can well be imagined.

While it is doubtful that many Poles insured themselves with German companies during these years, the HTO itself and its activities were a source of business for the German insurers and particularly for Allianz. Beginning in 1940, Allianz provided the HTO with liability insurance, automobile insurance (through Kraft), and break-in and theft (!) insurance, as well as a group accident policy for 125 persons that was issued in May 1944.[171] It also provided fire and liability insurance for the Catholic Church properties placed under HTO trusteeship.[172] As was the case with Lippmann Rosenthal, the Dutch bank used

---

[167] Rundverfügung Nr. 126, 10. Aug. 1941, APP, HTO/2129.
[168] Quoted in Krier an den Reichswirtschaftsminister, 4. Sept. 1941, BAB, R 144/199.
[169] See RWM an HTO, 22. Aug. 1942, BAB, R 144/193.
[170] Krier an RWM, 4. Sept. 1942, BAB, 144/199.
[171] For these policies, see APP, HTO/2128.
[172] See the correspondence with Bleckmann, who was in charge of church assets for the HTO, and other relevant documentation from November–December 1941 in APP, HTO/13241.

to collect Jewish assets, Allianz also provided insurance for the transport of confiscated assets, in this case securities from the HTO to the Reichsbank.[173]

The conquests in the East indeed seemed to offer all sorts of opportunities, and oddly this sense of pioneering effort seemed to linger on in an unpublished 1960 account by Director Clemens Maiholzer of the Berlin branch of Allianz during the war. Thus, in describing the building up of the Posen branch, he reminisced: "Here something completely new had to be created out of nothing, whereby the taking over of the portfolios of free Polish insurance companies provided the first basis."[174] This comes out even more strongly when he turned to the further expansion of Allianz:

Soon the business operations of the Wartheland branch expanded to Lodz (Litzmann-stadt), where the Wartheland direction set up a district office under the leadership of the previous organization head of the branch direction in Pommerania, Dr. Hübner .... The first visit in 30° cold, the most difficult lodging conditions and the initially completely disordered circumstances. It was a ray of light that the German insurance companies and especially the Allianz were welcomed in the most friendly way by the old German firms in Lodz, mainly large textile mills.[175]

There were, of course, other old textile and other firms in Lodz, one of the major industrial cities of eastern Europe, and it was a standard piece of HTO self-legitimation to claim that a combination of "Polish methods of oppression and Jewish greed for profit" had made it possible for Jews to dominate the industry, drive back German entrepreneurship, and inhibit modernization. The HTO reversed this alleged situation, taking over all the Jewish firms, closing down 1,600 of the 2,600 textile firms, and managing the rest until they could be sold to ethnic Germans and other suitable purchasers.[176] As for the Jews, the Wartheland's Governor Arthur Greiser ordered that they be sealed off in a ghetto in December 1939 in the anticipation that they would soon be transported into the Generalgouvernement. The plan, in the meantime, was to extract what remained of their assets in return for food, which was tantamount to a policy of slow starvation. This policy became problematic, however, when the plan to evacuate Jews to the Generalgouvernement was put off indefinitely. The policy of attrition then appeared counterproductive since, given the death rates, it was becoming clear that the limits of extracting were being reached and that feeding the Jews, however miserably, was still going to cost money. This paved the way for a reversal of policy in which the "productionists" – that is, those who felt the Jews should work for their survival and that the Reich should benefit from their labors – won out. There developed a grotesque community of interest – between the head administrator of the Ghetto, Hans Biebow (who took the "productionist line") and the head of the Jewish council, Chaim Rumkowski – to make

[173] See, for example, HTO an Allianz, 7. April 1942, BAB, R 144/191.
[174] Maiholzer, "Die Berliner Allianz-Betriebe," FHA, pp. 253f.
[175] Ibid., p. 254.
[176] See "Die Industrie in Litzmannstadt," 27. Aug. 1940, APP, HTO/79, Bl. 139–47, and Rechenschaftsbericht HTO Posen, 1939–1942, APP, HTO/1, Bl. 98–103.

the Ghetto self-sustaining and so permit the Jews to survive in return for work. Biebow not only procured the necessary machinery toward this end but also went about Germany and persuaded various companies (above all, the military) to give the Ghetto contracts for clothing and other items.[177] He was always on the lookout for sewing machines, and what better place to find them than at the revenue offices that had confiscated them from deported Jews all over Germany. They created enough plant and production to require insurance, and Hübner and Allianz were in the forefront of those trying to satisfy these insurance needs. Indeed, they insured the transport of those sewing machines to Litzmannstadt from places like Eschwege, Heppenheim, and Gemünd.[178]

The first policy taken out with Allianz seems to have been on July 19, 1940, to cover stored Wehrmacht-supplied textiles intended for clothing manufacture in the Ghetto against theft. The value was 100,000 RM and the premium 250 RM. It was to run for three months unless renewed. A similar policy for fur goods valued at 1.2 million RM (with a premium of 864 RM) was issued on November 22, 1940. A fire policy on the same items was issued jointly on the same date with Posensche Feuersozietät in which each company received a 450 RM premium.[179] A year later, however, Biebow and his chief deputy Friedrich Wilhelm Ribbe were asking Hübner to arrange for much larger policies to be issued out of the Posen office that required sharing of the risk among a number of companies. Typical was a three-month January 1942 fire policy for 40 million RM on military-supplied materials stored all over the Ghetto, for which Allianz issued the policy on behalf of itself (with 20% participation) and a consortium composed of Iduna-Germania (20%), Posensche Feuersozietät (15%), Schlesische Feuerversicherungs-Gesellschaft (12%), and seven other companies whose participation ranged from 2% to 8%.[180] It would seem that Allianz and Iduna-Germania had reached an agreement in handling such large policies, since there were occasions when Iduna-Germania took the lead for an equal percentage with Allianz. The leading company in such a consortium received a special commission for negotiating the contract on behalf of the others and took responsibility for the basic arrangements. The forms used for the contract itself were provided by the leading company of the consortium. Finally, there was the transport of the finished products to the military and various companies that

---

[177] On these policy shifts, see the Niederschrift der Beauftragten des Rechnungshofs des Deutschen Reichs über die örtliche Prüfung der Ernährungs- und Wirtschaftsstelle Ghetto des Oberbürgermeisters der Stadt Litzmannstadt of April 1940 and the other relevant documents in BAB, R 2/56159. See also the helpful discussion in Christopher Browning, *Nazi Policy, Jewish Workers, German Killers* (Cambridge & New York, 2000), pp. 65–70, 83–8, and Hanno Loewy & Gerhard Schoenberner (eds.), *"Unser einziger Weg ist Arbeit." Das Ghetto Lodz 1940–1944* (Vienna, 1990).

[178] Biebow an Finanzämter Dieburg, Eschwege, Heppenheim, Gemünd, 24. April 1942, und Schreiben Allianz, 24. April 1942, APL, Ghettoverwaltung/31179, Bl. 69–73.

[179] The policies are to be found in APL, Ghettoverwaltung/31182.

[180] Allianz an den Oberbürgermeister von Litzmannstadt, 18. Dez. 1941, APL, Ghettoverwaltung/31179, Bl. 25–6.

had ordered them, and the insurance companies had to be provided with specific lists of both insured raw materials being stored in the Ghetto and finished
products to be transported.[181]

Needless to say, these lists are a remarkable record of what was being produced
by the Jews who labored in this terrible place, but this account must concentrate
on the issues raised in assessing the role of those who insured Biebow's enterprise. One of these is the extent to which those present at the negotiations with
Biebow and Ribbe ever actually entered the Ghetto and had direct contact with
the conditions and persons involved. It is, after all, normal for insurers to in-
spect the properties they are insuring and make certain they are not undertaking
improper risks. This issue came up in the spring of 1941 when the Ghetto administration was raising its combined policy (which provided comprehensive
insurance against fire, theft, etc.) from 6 to 11 million RM because of its great
expansion; Allianz introduced a clause in the new policy calling for a yearly inspection by the Association of Private Fire Insurance Companies to determine if
the safety measures were up to standard. Allianz was informed, however, that
permission to enter the Ghetto for such purposes could not be given. Also, there
was little point since no materials were available to bring the electric facilities
beyond prewar Polish standards. At the same time, Allianz was assured that the
Ghetto fire department and the Litzmannstadt urban fire department could deal
with any emergency. Another effort was made at the end of 1941, when Allianz –
acting on behalf of the consortium for a total policy that had risen to 40 million
RM – suggested that a lower premium might be offered if at least the areas of
greatest risk could be directly inspected. Alternatively, it provided a questionnaire that might be filled out to help insurers calculate their risks. It was the
questionnaire that won out, and no on-site inspections were allowed.[182]

These rejections of inspections could only heighten the sense that conditions
in the Ghetto were very different from those on the outside. However, there is
no reason to think that the insurers engaging in the negotiations actually cared,
since they were asking to enter the Ghetto not out of curiosity but rather out
of concern for running risks by not engaging in on-site inspection. And even
though insurance company representatives never had any direct negotiations
with Rumkowski, it was clearly stated by Biebow and Ribbe that the insurers
were ultimately dealing with the Jewish council and its leader because it was the
responsibility of the Jews to account for the material being insured, make sure
it was kept safely, and in effect to cover the costs of the insurance. As Ribbe informed Hübner, "I continue now as before to judge the risk favorable, since the
Jewish elder places a permanent guard in the work room day and night and besides this has an interest in being able to work since this is the only possibility

---

[181] See, for example, the lists for May–September 1942, which often include information as to the
destination of the produced goods; ibid., Bl. 526–610.
[182] Degner an Biebow, 26. Juni 1941, APL, Ghettoverwaltung/31180, Bl. 22; Degner an Allianz, 30.
Juli 1941, ibid., Bl. 52; Allianz an Ribbe, 15. Dez. 1941, APL, Ghettoverwaltung/31179, Bl. 23–
4; Allianz an Biebow, 14. April 1942 und Antwort, 24. April 1942, ibid., Bl. 67–8.

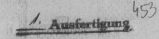

Geschäftsstelle:
Filialdirektion Wartheland
Posen, Berliner Straße Nr. 10

1. Ausfertigung 453

ALLIANZ UND STUTTGARTER VEREIN
VERSICHERUNGS-AKTIEN-GESELLSCHAFT
Abteilung für TRANSPORT-Versicherung

UMSATZ-POLICE NR. T - 8 9 4 -
für Gütertransporte zu Lande

Die ALLIANZ UND STUTTGARTER VEREIN Versicherungs-
Aktien-Gesellschaft versichert hiermit dem Firma Herrn Oberbürgermeister zu Litzmannstadt, Ernährungs- u. Wirtschaftsstelle
Getto, L i t z m a n n s t a d t , Moltke-Straße Nr.211
gegen einen Prämiensatz von --0,6 °/°° nachstehend bezeichnete Güter:

alle Uniform-Herstellungen für die Luftwaffe, die
Wehrmacht, die Marine, den Arbeitsdienst, SA., SS.,
NSKK sowie ähnliche Formationen, ferner Ausrüstungs-
gegenstände aller Art, wie: Militärstiefel und andere
Lederwaren, Bekleidungssäcke, Kleidersäcke für Marine,
Rucksäcke, Sturmgepäck, Brotbeutel, Zelte, Wäsche etc.,
und zwar Rohstoffe, Halb- und Fertigfabrikate, ferner
Zutaten und alle regelmäßig wieder ergänzten Material-
ien sowie auch Verpackungsmaterialien aller Art

für alle Transporte per Eisenbahn, Post, Fuhre, Boten und Kraftfahrzeug
innerhalb Deutschlands nach Maßgabe der beigefügten Allgemeinen Versicherungsbedingungen für den Gütertransport zu Lande mittels Eisenbahn,
Post oder Fuhre und der Allgemeinen Versicherungsbedingungen für den
Gütertransport mit Kraftfahrzeugen sowie der umstehenden Besonderen
Bedingungen. Die Besonderen Bedingungen gehen den Allgemeinen, die
geschriebenen den gedruckten überall, wo sie voneinander abweichen, vor.
Diese Police ist von den Parteien geschlossen, genehmigt, vierfach aus-
gefertigt und ausgewechselt worden.

L'stadt , den 22. Jan.1942.   Posen , den 6. Jan.1942.

ALLIANZ
VERSICHERUNGS-AKTIENGESELLSCHAFT
FILIALDIREKTION WARTHELAND

a. § 10 der
Besonderen
Bedingungen.

Ausfertigungs-
gebühr   RM 3.00

Versicherungs-
steuer   RM 0,10

Zusammen   RM 3,10

Dieser Police sind als ergänzende Bestand-
teile beigefügt: T.33, 3.40./ T.42,
7.40./ T.32, 3.39./ T.231
4.39./ T.47, 11.39./ T.118,
10.37./ T.214, 7.40./ T.206,
5.41./ T.214, 5.41./ - - -

Allianz transport insurance policy for clothes manufactured in the Lodz Ghetto, issued
January 6, 1942.

for the Jewish community to eke out their subsistence."[183] Rumkowski was indeed required to inform Biebow what was to be insured (and its value) on the 10th of every month, and the insurance companies were thus well aware of the procedure involved.[184]

Insuring the Ghetto, however, was viewed as a lucrative and desirable business – once the companies involved engaged in it. Initially it seemed rather risky, and Allianz was virtually alone in pursuing it; as soon as the amounts involved required a consortium, Iduna-Germania became an equal of Allianz in the business. Since there were risk limits, Allianz did not seem to object, but it was furious when the Mayor of Litzmannstadt began to push for the publicly chartered Posensche Feuersozietät to take the lead in the Ghetto's fire insurance. The old battle between the private companies and the publicly chartered ones thus flared up once again, and in September 1942 the Posensche reminded the Ghetto administration that the Allianz policy would soon come to an end and required a three-month notice. Ribbe opposed such a change, telling Biebow: "Allianz is the company which laid the basis for our insurance contracts and was the first that was at all ready to conclude an agreement with us." He thought it disloyal to change, but the pressure on Biebow seemed to be too great; he annoyedly told Ribbe to "dissolve the present contract so that the tiresome matter is finished once and for all."[185] Allianz did not take this rejection lightly. It had been told by the Mayor of Litzmannstadt that, all things being equal, he had to favor the publicly chartered company. Allianz did not think that things were equal and pointed out that the Posensche did not even do its own transportation insurance but rather acted as an agent for the Zentropa firm in Berlin. Given that Allianz was pursuing such transportation insurance when other companies were not taking the risk, it felt it should receive more consideration.[186] There is no record, however, of Allianz having recovered its leading position in Lodz during the period prior to the dissolution of August 1944, a period of increasing deportations of its inhabitants and their murder at the death camps in the vicinity.

Lodz was by no means the only site of Jewish forced labor insured by the Allianz concern, as is demonstrated by the case of the forced labor camp Krakau-Plaszow, which lay behind Cracow's Jewish cemetery.[187] The camp, which was controlled by the SS and police leader of the Cracow district, grew from 2,000 prisoners when opened in October 1942 to 12,000 in the fall of 1943; following liquidation of the Cracow Ghetto, it swelled to 22,000–24,000

[183] Ribbe an Allianz Litzmannstadt, 7. Juli 1941, APL, Ghettoverwaltung/31180, Bl. 34.

[184] See Biebow an den Ältesten der Juden, APL, Ghettoverwaltung/31179, Bl. 37.

[185] Posensche Feuersozietät an der Oberbürgermeister, Ghettoverwaltung, 11. Sept. 1942, and Notiz für Biebow mit handgeschriebener Antwort, 15. Sept. 1942, ibid., Bl. 283–4.

[186] Allianz an den Herrn Oberbürgermeister, 27. Okt. 1942, ibid., Bl. 482.

[187] I am grateful to Marian Rappl for a very useful analysis of the materials on Krakau-Plaszow in BAB, NS 3/688, upon which in part I rely here. On the forced labor camps, see Dieter Pohl, "Die großen Zwangsarbeitslager der SS- und Polizeiführer für Juden im Generalgouvernement 1942–1945," in Ulrich Herbert, Karin Orth, & Christoph Dieckmann (eds.), *Die nationalsozialistischen Konzentrationslager. Entwicklung und Struktur* (Göttingen, 1998), Bd. I, pp. 415–38.

44

BAYERISCHE VERSICHERUNGSBANK AKTIEN-GESELLSCHAFT
VORMALS VERSICHERUNGSANSTALTEN DER BAYERISCHEN HYPOTHEKEN- UND WECHSELBANK MÜNCHEN
BEZIRKSDIREKTION KRAKAU

BAYERISCHE VERS.-BK., KRAKAU, POSTFACH 196	FERNSPRECHER NR. 168-80, 168-81, 132-74, 200-57

An den

SS und Polizeiführer
im Distrikt Krakau

z . Hd. des Herren SS Obersturmführers

W e h d e

K r a k a u , Oleanderstr. 4.

Ihre Zeichen	Ihre Nachricht vom	Unsere Nachricht vom	Unsere Zeichen K≠L	Krakau, 2. 12. 1943. Hauptstrasse 1 (Slawkowska) Postfach 196

Betreff Feuerversicherung des Zwangsarbeitslagers in Krakau-Plaszow
hinter dem jüdischen Friedhofe.

Auf Ihren uns mündlich am 25. Oktober 1943 übermittelten Antrag ge-
währen wir Ihnen hiermit, gleichzeitig im Namen der mitbeteiligten
Gesellschaften , vorläufige Deckung in Höhe von

Zl. 35.000.000.-- Zloty Fünfunddreissig-Millionen
für die beantragte Feuerversicherung auf:

    1.) Gebäude und Baulichkeiten   Zl. 15.000.000.--
    2.) Technische und kaufmännische
        Betriebseinrichtung, einschl.
      - der Wohnbaracken, für eigene
        und/oder fremde Rechnung   Zl. 8.000.000.--
    3.) Betriebs-und Rohmaterialien,
        Halb-und Ganzfabrikate für eige-
        ne und/oder fremde Rechnung, mit
        Stichtagsmeldung, gemäss der Stich-
        tagsklausel, Grundversicherungs-
        summe Zl. 6.000.000.-- Höchstver-
        sicherungssumme   Zl. 12.000.000.--
                   insgesamt Zl. 35.000.000.--
                   =====================

befindlich: in Krakau-Plaszow, hinter dem jüdischen Friedhofe,
Zwangsarbeitslager.

Gleichzeitig bestätigen wir Ihnen das heute zwischen Ihrem SS-Obersturmführer W e h d e und unserem Bezirksdirektor Bormann ge-
führte Ferngespräch , im Verlauf dessen Ihnen Deckungszusage in
obiger Höhe bereits zugesagt wurde.

Die vorläufige Deckung wird gewährt unter den Ihnen bekannten
Allgemeinen Versicherungsbedingungen für die Feuer- Versicherung
und den Ihnen noch mitzuteilenden Sonderbedingungen gegen Zahlung
der tarifmässigen Prämie und Nebenkosten.

b. w.

Die Deckungszusage gilt für die Zeit vom 1. Dezember 1943
12 Uhr mittags bis zur Einlösung der Versicherungsurkunde,
längstens aber bis 1. Februar 1944 12. Uhr mittags.

Wie Ihnen in unserer Deckungszusage vom 24. Nov.ds. J.,
die gegen diese Deckungszusage erlischt, mitgeteilt, be-
ginnt die Haftung der Gesellschaften nur dann, wenn innerhalb 14 Tagen, also spätestens am 10. Dezember ein Prämienvorschuss von Zl. 140.000.-- entrichtet wird, anderenfalls
die Gesellschaften von der Entschädigungspflicht frei sein
würden, wenn ein Schadensfall vor der nicht rechtzeitigen
Zahlung eintreten sollte. Bei Einlösung der Versicherungsurkunde wird dieser Prämienvorschuss in Anrechnung gebracht.

Der vorgenannte Betrag von Zl. 35.000.000.-- wird von
folgenden Gesellschaften mit den dabei vermerkten Quoten
gedeckt.

Bayerische Versicherungs-Bank, Krakau	mit	12 1/2 %
Florianka Vers. Ges. Krakau	"	12 1/2 %
Generali Port-Polonia "	"	12 1/2 %
Riunione Vers. Ges. "	"	12 1/2 %
Allgemeine Versicherungsanstalt Krakau	"	12 1/2 %
Warschauer Vers. Ges. Krakau	"	12 1/2 %
Aachener und Münchener, Kattowitz	"	10 %
Silesia, Vers. Ges. Krakau	"	10 %
Vesta, Vers. Ges. Krakau	"	5 %
	zus.	100 %

Wir bitten Sie, uns baldmöglichst mitzuteilen, wann die
bei Ihnen in Arbeit befindliche Wertaufstellung beendet
ist, damit wir die notwendige Besichtigung des Lagers
vornehmen lassen können.

H e i l H i t l e r !

BAYERISCHE VERSICHERUNGS-BANK AKT.-GES. (...)
(vorm. Versicherungs-Abteilung der Bayerischen Hypotheken- u. Wechselbank)
Bezirksdirektion Krakau
Feuer. Abteilung

Letter of Bayerische Versicherungsbank in the name of eight further insurance companies (December 2, 1943) about the conclusion of a fire insurance policy for the forced labor camp Krakau-Plaszow for a temporary coverage of 35 million zloty.

prisoners by June 1944, when it was formally turned into a concentration camp under the chief economic department of the SS in Berlin. The camp initially serviced private firms in the area, the most famous of which was the Deutsche Emailwarenfabrik Krakau Oskar Schindler, which actually developed a sub-camp of its own. The disorderly conditions and lines of authority in the camp may have served Schindler well in his heroic rescue work, but the camp itself was notorious for the inadequate provisioning of its inmates and the arbitrariness and brutality with which they were treated. Be that as it may, a consortium headed by Bayerische Versicherungsbank (which, as noted earlier, was allowed to operate in the Generalgouvernement) offered to insure the entire camp for 3 million zloty (1.5 million RM) for a 5% premium which was then further reduced by 10%.[188] This offer was made after the officials of the Cracow branch of Bayerische Versicherungsbank had visited the site, which was in marked contrast to what had been allowed in Lodz – and which means that they had direct experience with conditions in the camp. Bayerische Versicherungsbank led the consortium with a 20% share, while Florianka, Generali-Port-Polonia, Orzel, Silesia, and Vesta joined with 16% apiece. In February 1943, the value of the insurance was raised to 6 million zloty (3 million RM), with Orzel leaving and Aachener und München-chener, Adler Versicherung, Allgemeine Versicherungsanstalt Krakau, RAS, and Warschauer joining. Bayerische Versicherungsbank took a 12.5% quota while the others took 10%, except for Warschauer, which took 7.5%.[189] In December 1943, a contract for temporary coverage in the amount of 35 million zloty (17.5 million RM) was concluded, and this was followed in January by another temporary policy for 29.8 million zloty.[190] At this point, it is unclear whether insurance on the barracks continued; it is highly unlikely since this would be unusual for a concentration camp, into which Plaszow had been transformed. This change of status meant that Bayerische Versicherungsbank was now doing business with Deutsche Ausrüstungswerke, because the latter managed the concentration camp factories. This supports the assumption that the policies at this point covered only production and not prisoner barracks. Thus, the final policies in April and October 1944 were for 6 and 1.3 million zloty, respectively. This, especially the last-named sum, was much more in line with the insurance provided in connection with other concentration camps (to be discussed shortly) and shows by comparison how large were the policies arranged for Krakau-Plaszow – at least before it became a "normal" concentration camp. One thing is for certain: Bayerische Versicherungsbank paid very close attention to safety provisions in the woodworking plants, complaining in a letter of June 1944 that its inspection "did not lead to very happy results." The furnaces of the types employed were not

---

[188] Bayerische Versicherungsbank an die Wohn- und Siedlungsgesellschaft Krakau, 9. Okt. 1942, BAB, NS 3/688, Bl. 59–62.

[189] Bayerische Versicherungsbank Krakau an den SS- und Polizeiführer im Distrikt Krakau, 26. Feb. 1943, ibid., Bl. 63–4.

[190] Bayerische Versicherungsbank an den SS und Polizeiführer Krakau, 2. Dez. 1943, and SS und Polizei-Führer an die Bauleitung des ZAL, 30. Nov. 1943, ibid., Bl. 44–5.

normally used in such plants; Allianz insisted that the furnaces be replaced and that proper equipment be installed.[191]

Doing Business with the SS

This was hardly the only concentration camp to be graced by visits of Allianz concern inspectors, since it had an insurance engagement with SS enterprises in most of the principal concentration camps: Auschwitz, Lublin, Neuengamme, Stutthof, Buchenwald, Ravensbrück, Sachsenhausen, and Dachau. Although highly suspicious of Biebow's operations at Lodz and preferring concentration camps to forced labor camps, Himmler had long encouraged the development of an SS economic empire in connection with the concentration camps under Oswald Pohl. The latter, already involved in the economic activities of the SS, was formally appointed chief of the head economic office of the SS in 1942. Here, then, was another set of productivist ambitions, which were already evident in 1938–1939 with the creation of Deutsche Erd- und Steinwerke GmbH and Deutsche Ausrüstungswerke GmbH. The latter developed into a holding company for more than 39 companies and 100 plants, many of them in concentration camps and their sub-camps, where they produced, using forced labor, a variety of products (primarily wooden furniture, clothing, and metal objects) for use by the SS and in the camps themselves. Himmler's pretensions to the contrary, they were never the major producers of weapons and munitions he had intended.[192] Allianz's opportunity to insure these plants came in the early fall of 1940, when they ceased to work for the account of the NSDAP and hence the Party treasurer would no longer insure them. Since they now formally became private enterprises run by the SS, they required insurance; the first fire insurance policies for the plants in Dachau were concluded through Bayerische Versicherungsbank.[193]

The head start in this engagement, however, had apparently come a few months earlier in connection with insuring the production of the SS Dachau factories, and it seems by and large to have been the product of the connections of an Old Fighter on its staff. The person in question was subdirector Max Beier, a committed Nazi activist and an energetic insurance man who had

[191] Bayerische Versicherungsbank Krakau an die Deutschen Ausrüstungswerke, 27. Juni 1944, ibid. Bl. 16–18.

[192] Walter Naasner, *Neue Machtzentren in der deutschen Kriegswirtschaft 1942–1945. Die Wirtschaftsorganisation der SS, das Amt des Generalbevollmächtigten für den Arbeitseinsatz und das Reichsministerium für Bewaffnung und Munition/Reichsministerium für Rüstung und Kriegsproduktion im nationalsozialistischen Herrschaftssystem* [Schriften des Bundesarchivs, Bd. 45] (Boppard am Rhein, 1994), pp. 234–40, and the useful critical article by Jan Erik Schulte, "Das SS-Unternehmen 'Deutsche Ausrüstungswerke GmbH'," in Ulrich Herbert, Karin Orth, & Christoph Dieckmann (eds.), *Die nationalsozialistischen Konzentrationslager. Entwicklung und Struktur* (Göttingen, 1998), Bd. II, pp. 558–83.

[193] Chef des SS-Hauptamtes an Chef des V.u.W. Hauptamtes, Amt IIIc, 19. Sept. 1940, and Bayerische Versicherungsbank an Allianz, 28. Sept. 1940, BAB, NS 3/279, Bl. 154–7, 168.

Max Beier (1889–1945), subdirector of the Berlin branch of Allianz, about 1934.

qualified for the Large Life Insurance Club in 1937 (i.e., he had sold insurance worth a million marks or more in premiums). Beier had made his earlier career in Magdeburg but spent most of his time during the war at the Berlin branch, from which he did a considerable amount of business for Allianz with the DAW. He seems to have courted the high and mighty, and there is a record of his giving a Christmas present to Göring in 1937. He died in a prison in Naumburg in 1945; when his wife claimed a pension, the factory council of the Berlin branch raised no objection but recorded that: "We consider it important to note that Herr Beier is to be considered completely as a Nazi activist and profiteer whose business deals could only be attained through his strong political connections to the SS and the NSDAP."[194] He was regarded more highly by the executives in Berlin. Heß had granted him entitlement to a higher pension in 1944 because he was earning so much beyond his normal salary through commissions and premiums,[195] and when Frau Beier requested that she receive some payment from

---

[194] Zweigniederlassung Berlin an die Allianz-Versorgungskasse, 13. Jan. 1949, FHA, AVK/909872B. He gave Göring a framed picture of the Karl-Göring-Straße, IfZ, Sammlung Irving, Ed 100/267.
[195] Internal Note of Jan. 21, 1944, ibid.

his life insurance in 1965, Allianz General Director Alfred Haase responded very warmly – saying that he "gladly remembered Max Beier with whom we experienced so many pleasant hours."[196] Haase, in recommending that Frau Beier be helped out, made a point of mentioning how successful her husband had been and that he was well known to Heß.[197] This was probably a reference to the prewar period, however, since Haase spent the entire war in the Army. Whatever the case, Beier's activities clearly were well known to the leading directors in Berlin; he was considered an asset when he lived, and his timely demise kept him from becoming a visible liability when that might have mattered.

Beier provided a variety of insurance products to his SS clients, including automobile insurance and accident insurance for German personnel supervising and working in the plants in the various camps.[198] Most important, however, was the fire, theft, and damage insurance for the factories themselves. Beier usually worked through the local Allianz or Bayerische Versicherungsbank offices near the relevant camps, but on at least one occasion, in June 1940, he went himself to Dachau to estimate the value of the stored wood and plant facilities.[199] Needless to say, all the concentration camp plants Beier and Allianz insured in Germany were grim establishments, but those at Auschwitz and in Eastern Poland had a special quality because of their proximity to the Holocaust. In the case of Auschwitz, Beier was first contacted by the SS office in Berlin overseeing Deutsche Ausrüstungswerke and informed that a new factory complex had been set up in Auschwitz – similar to those in Dachau and Sachsenhausen – containing plants for cabinet making and carpentry, a machinist plant, and similar plants that needed insurance; he asked Beier to contact the Kattowitz branch and arrange for the necessary on-site inspection with SS Obersturmführer Wagner, who was in charge of plants located on the concentration camp grounds. As was the case throughout, the Kattowitz branch handled the actual drawing up of the insurance policies; a Herr Plints undertook the inspection on May 2, 1941, and described the facilities in the four-story building and its fire safety and firefighting arrangements. Premiums were set at 1.75% for the building, 2.50% for the equipment, and 3% for the stored materials needed for the carpentry work – which together were estimated to have a worth of 570,000 RM. Allianz asked, however, that a further inspection be made once the plant went into actual production. The policy was backdated to April 10, 1941; the premium was 1,360.95 RM.[200] Another inspection was made at the end of January prior to the renewal of the policy by Alfred Sack of the Kattowitz branch. By this time 250 prisoners were working in the plant, which was expected to employ 700, and the report was more

---

[196] Haase an Gertrud Beier, 8. Sept. 1965, ibid.
[197] Haase an Meister, 8. Sept. 1965, ibid.
[198] There is material on the collective policies for both types of insurance in BAB, NS 3/1479.
[199] Notiz, 21. Juni 1940, BAB, NS 3/279, Bl. 193.
[200] Chef des Amtes III C an Beier, 15. April 1941, Bericht Plints, 8. Mai 1941, Allianz an die Deutschen Aufrüstungswerke Auschwitz, 16. Mai 1941, Chef des Amtes III C an das Werk Auschwitz, 2. Juli 1941, BAB, NS 3/280, Bl. 43, 45–7, 60, and related documents and policies in this volume.

detailed. It noted that "as a result of the constant military supervision, there is perfect order and cleanliness. The work is located within the concentration camp Auschwitz, so that the entire area will always be under military guard."[201]

By October 1942, the plants were valued at 1,535,100 RM, and Allianz now gathered a consortium to insure them; it took 25% of the risk, with consortium members Aachener und Münchener (20%), Magdeburger (20%), Schlesische Feuer (15%), Victoria (10%), and Silesia/Bielitz (10%) taking the rest.[202] A year later, the value was estimated at 3,217,000 RM and the premium was set at 14,758.15 RM, of which Allianz received 3,704 RM. Although some supplementary policies were drawn up to deal with short-term needs, the basic policy continued at these levels in July 1944. Sack undertook further inspections, although there is no record of them, but the policies themselves were treated as a "State Secret." In September 1944, a new building was put up and there were also new woodworking machines that required a supplementary policy; the final policy made by the consortium for Auschwitz, which was to cover the period 1944–1945, beginning October 15, provided Allianz with a premium of 4,220.75 RM. There were, however, some costs: there was a fire in one of the barracks storing textile materials in the women's camp on December 22, 1944; the combination of material loss and other costs, including the wages calculated for prisoner labor, was estimated at 30,000 RM.[203] But the Russians were about to arrive, so the matter would have to be settled back in Germany.

The correspondence between Allianz and Bayerische Versicherungsbank, on the one hand, and the SS authorities and plant managers in the concentration camps, on the other, have a remarkably bland quality and an extraordinary consistency. It was, indeed, "business as usual," with some changes in the makeup of consortia, some quibbling over prices, and some demands that safety standards be met. With only a few exceptions, one would never know that the Russians were coming or that there was no future in the business as one reached the end. It is almost a shock when one reads a note of August 15, 1944, from Bayerische Versicherungsbank to the sawmill in the Lublin-Pulawy camp, to which it provided liability insurance, that the policy might as well be terminated since insurance policies "have become illusory" because "of the military conditions that have developed in the area."[204]

In the last analysis, however, the surreal seems to dominate in the insurance history of the concentration camp plants. Thus, in the fall of 1944, SS officials in charge of the factories were trying to work through the problem of whether they should offer their employees a pension plan or group insurance with Allianz, as proposed by the ever-active Beier. The discussion had begun in September 1943 and had dragged on over a year while the SS mulled over Beier's proposals and

---

[201] Besichtigungsbericht, 29. Jan. 1942, ibid., Bl. 13–17.
[202] Allianz an Reichsführer-SS, Amt W IV, 27. Okt. 1942, BAB, NS 3/217, Bl. 103–5. This volume contains a record of the subsequent history and development of the policies discussed here.
[203] Schadensregulierung, Dez. 1944–Jan. 1945, ibid., Bl. 2–8.
[204] Schreiben, Bayerische Versicherungsbank, 15. Aug. 1944, BAB, NS 3/686, Bl. 13.

compared them to the much less competitive proposals of the Deutscher Ring insurance. Whereas Allianz offered a policy that promised care for the policy-holder or his family in old age, the latter had a much more rigid policy that did not do so. Though the decision still was not reached at the end of 1944, it appeared in 1945 that Allianz would get the contract![205]

Although Allianz seemed to be winning on this front, it was losing on another. In February 1945, SS-Obersturmführer Reinartz of Pohl's office informed Beier that his contracts at Auschwitz, Buchenwald, Dachau, Ravensbrück, Sachsenhausen, Stutthof, and Neugamme were terminated. This was because the agent used by the SS, Hans Bergler, had apparently been able to put together a new consortium to take over the policies on better terms; it was headed by Agrippina-Gruppe and composed of Iduna-Germania, Erste Allgemeine Unfall- und Schadens-Versicherung AG, Helvetia, Gerling, and Nordstern. Nevertheless, Beier seems to have fought back, and Reinartz agreed to review the two premium schedules on March 6. Beier was thus able to inform Deutsche Ausrüstungswerke on March 25, 1945, asking for an appointment to discuss the question so that the policies could continue. Whether these discussions took place between then and the unconditional surrender of May 8, 1945, and what the outcome might have been, is not recorded.[206]

One can imagine why an old Nazi like Beier would cling to his SS business to the very last, but it is difficult to fathom what would move the new consortium to seek this business in 1945. One answer may lie in the fact that the business world and the insurance companies had become so habituated to working and expanding with the regime that it became difficult not to continue – even as the camps and their factories were being captured by Allied forces and the insured plants were shut down, leaving nothing to insure. This is well demonstrated by another episode of the Eastern ambitions of Allianz and the Munich Re, which by no means stopped at the Warthegau and Generalgouvernement. In September 1941, they had petitioned the RWM for permission to found a Versicherungs-Aktiengesellschaft für das Ostland – that is, a new company to cover Lithuania, Latvia, Estonia, and White Russia. They already had daughter companies in the area and warmly recommended Edwin Magnus, who headed up their operations in the Generalgouvernement. Schmitt wrote personally to Hinrich Lohse (Reich Commissar for the Ostland) as well as to the RWM in support of this effort. Nevertheless, the influence of Schwede-Coburg seemed to dominate here, and in February 1942, Allianz and Munich Re teamed up with Deutscher-Lloyd, Magdeburger Feuerversicherungs-Gesellschaft, and Nordstern in a new effort to create the proposed company. However, this effort failed, too.[207]

It was probably just as well, since within a year the insurers were complaining bitterly about damages for which they were forced to pay, which they considered to be war damages but which were not treated as such. As they lamented: "The

---

[205] For the discussions and proposals, in which Beier was very active, see BAB, NS 3/1058.
[206] For this correspondence between Feb. 2 and March 25, 1945, see BAB, NS 3/216, Bl. 4–9.
[207] For this correspondence, see MR, A 2.14/61.

political leadership does not want to hear about partisans, and those organs responsible for the security of the State from now on only know about robber bands."[208] But this was not a luxury that the insurance companies could afford, and they began a lengthy battle to have such damages recognized as war damages and to increase premiums to cover such events. These, however, were as nothing compared to the problems of 1944. In September, following the Warsaw uprising, Magnus reported that 80% of Warsaw had been destroyed, including most of the insurance offices with which he and the Munich Re had been associated. The time had come to cut losses. Magnus ordered that new business was to be cut off as much as possible and the known existing damages paid off as quickly as possible – so as to cut down on potential claims against their Polish companies. As this and other reports demonstrated, the German insurance business in Poland had come to a miserable end.[209] It was time to save what could be saved back at home.

There was no way, however, that Allianz could be saved from the taint of its engagement in the barbarities of the German war effort and of the proximity of the concern and its personnel to the crimes of the regime and the Holocaust. Lodz surely was the worst of its engagements in this connection, and it was certainly a product of the concern's continual and oft-stated ambitions to be more "active" in the East. It was hard to be "active" without being aware of some of the unfolding events – certainly not for those who dealt with the ghettos and the camps nor for those who insured the assets of the persecuted back to the Reich for agencies whose purposes and activities were well known. There were certainly some instances where Allianz officials could quite plausibly not be aware of the horrors underlying their business activity. In 1943, for example, Allianz insured substantial shipments of gold for the Dresdner Bank to Istanbul, with some of the gold in coins and some in bars. All the gold, of course, was stolen, since the Reich by this time did not have any gold of its own, but the fact that some of the gold was victim gold (i.e., gold smelted at Degussa, the point of origin for some of the shipments) was something the insurers were unlikely to know.[210] However, it was impossible not to know that the Würzburg construction firm of Ernst Grün, which was working in the East for Organisation Todt, employed 200 men of whom three quarters were Russian POWs or other forced laborers – especially since Allianz's insurance agent in Schweinfurt informed Bayerische Versicherungsbank of this fact in order to show that the prospect of providing liability insurance for the firm entailed a very low risk because these workers were not paid by the firm and had no entitlement against it.[211] Similarly, as noted earlier, Allianz eagerly sought contracts for construction insurance and

[208] Niehuus an das Aufsichtsamt für das Versicherungswesen im Generalgouvernement, 4. Jan. 1943, MR, C 2/16.
[209] Magnus an Münchner Rück, 19. Sept. 1944, and other reports, MR, A 2.14/55.
[210] Altbankarchiv der Dresdner Bank, Konsortial-Abteilung Nr. 430, 4. Etage, Regal 20, Akte "Allianz Versicherungs-AG"; Industriebüro, 4. Etage, Regal 35, Akte Nr. 94049. One of the shipments was actually stolen and Allianz had to pay 32,038 Swiss francs for the loss. On the gold shipments of the Dresdner Bank, see Bähr, *Goldhandel*.
[211] Abschrift Schreiben von Meukel an Generaldirektion München, 13. Okt. 1942, FHA, B 3.6/6.

took considerable pride in all the areas in which it worked, including the construction of works for the production of Buna. The most important construction site connected with Buna, after all, was at Auschwitz-Monowitz, but one did not have to go there to find examples of terrifying exploitation of forced labor taking place practically wherever construction was going on in Germany and the areas it occupied. Unfortunately, the remaining records are too thin to specify exactly where the Allianz construction insurance men were at work and who they were, but clearly they were everywhere they could be at home and abroad, and they must have seen and experienced a great deal. This does not make them or the concern they served criminal, any more than it was criminal for Allianz, which provided group accident insurance to IG Farben, to request and receive permission to extend such insurance – 10,000 RM in case of death and 30,000 RM in case of disablement – to Austrian engineers working for the company at Auschwitz in 1943.[212] It was just one more piece of business in the Third Reich, but it demonstrated that such pieces on any large scale made contact at some point with all that is represented by the name "Auschwitz" – from slave labor to extermination – virtually inescapable.

TOTAL WAR AND DOING BUSINESS IN THE FACE OF DEFEAT

Needless to say, Allianz – like every other German firm and concern – suffered significant losses of workforce as a result of the war and had to undertake a variety of measures to deal with the problem. Some 5,000 Allianz employees were called up in 1939 and an equal number in 1940; the numbers were to increase substantially in 1942–1944, when 6,996, 8,340, and 8,700 were called up, respectively. Nevertheless, the number of Allianz employees increased from 13,511 in 1939 to 15,190 in 1940, and then climbed in 1941 to 15,967 and to 16,325 in 1942 before descending to 16,030 in 1943 and 15,598 in 1944. The increases of personnel, however, were primarily young trainees, female workers unrequisitioned for other duties, disabled, and retired persons – in short, less qualified personnel. By 1943, however, Allianz was employing no more than 40% of its prewar personnel, and quantity could never really replace quality.[213] At the same time, these persons were laboring under conditions of increasing physical destruction from the air and, in the end, on the ground.

The burdens of leading the Reich Group became both physically and psychologically heavier for Hilgard in the last two and a half years of the war. In the late fall of 1942 he came to the conclusion that Germany was facing a severe catastrophe and actually said so to his colleagues at the fourth joint meeting of the directors of Allianz and Munich Re on October 28, 1942, at which time he urged measures designed to save some of Allianz's most important assets by getting them out of Berlin. Needless to say, such defeatist attitudes did not find their

---

[212] See Neue Frankfurter und Allianz an RAA, 16. und 23. Sept. 1943, BAK, B 280/13214, Bl. 37–40.
[213] Hilgard, "Allianz im 2. Weltkrieg," FHA, AZ 1.2/2, pp. 14–15.

Der Allianz=Adler

FELDPOST-NACHRICHTENDIENST
DER ALLIANZ-BETRIEBSGEMEINSCHAFTEN

Nummer 2	Berlin, September / Dezember 1943	1. Jahrgang

Kämpfer

Ölgemälde von Rudolf
Lipus, Leipzig, auf der
Großen Deutschen Kunst-
ausstellung München 1943

Aufnahme: Delke M.

IN DAS NEUE KAMPFJAHR 1944

Liebe Arbeitskameradinnen und -kameraden! Wieder geht ein Kriegsjahr zu Ende.
Eine gewaltige Kraftentfaltung hat das deutsche Volk gezeigt. Unsere herrliche Wehrmacht hat unerhörte Ruhmestaten vollbracht, die in die Geschichte als einmalige
Leistungen eingehen werden, und die Heimat kann dem Heldentum deutscher Soldaten
zu Lande, zu Wasser und in der Luft ihren Dank vorläufig nur durch treueste Pflicht-
erfüllung und unermüdliche Arbeit abstatten. Darum bedenke ein jeder, wie klein

1

Der Allianz-Adler Feldpost-Nachrichtendienst (Allianz Eagle Military Postal Information Service) was sent to drafted employees of Allianz on a regular basis.

way into the minutes of the meeting, but there is no reason to disbelieve Hilgard's postwar assertions in this regard since, as will be shown later, Allianz pursued precisely the policy he advocated.[214] At the same time, he was in constant struggle with the challenges created by the fanatical Nazis. He was especially plagued by General Director Heinrich Bothe, who headed one of the two property insurance groups in the Reich Group and whom Hilgard believed had been assigned the task of shadowing him in his various trips abroad. Hilgard certainly liked his trips to Western Europe, where he felt he could deal with cultivated fellow insurance men with whom he had a great deal more in common than Nazis like Bothe and other Party people who were in his company from time to time. Bothe was relatively bearable on such occasions because he spoke not a word of any foreign language, so Hilgard could say what he wished without fear that Bothe would understand a thing. At the meetings of the advisory council to the Reich Group, however, there were a series of nasty altercations. On one occasion, when Bothe aggressively complained that his group was insufficiently represented on a committee, Hilgard "asks Director Bothe to adopt a more polite tone in this circle. He [Hilgard] is used always to deal politely with those around him .... He has had enough of being subjected to Herr Bothe's loutish behavior before the entire group."[215] Hilgard was particularly irritated by Bothe's tendency to work around him and the advisory council and try to settle questions with Amend.[216]

Hilgard's own tone had undoubtedly become harsher as he faced the antics of Schwede-Coburg and the proposals of Rath for the nationalization of the insurance business. In his capacity as head of the German insurance industry, Hilgard had to do everything possible to meet the demands for total mobilization of the economy as part of total war, at the same time trying to save what he could of the German insurance business in the face of total war enthusiasts like Schwede-Coburg and Bothe. The military and economic situation did seem to put an end to the "reform" efforts of Schwede-Coburg and Rath. Hilgard placed considerable hope in a decree of Economics Minister Funk of February 6, 1943; referring to a confidential Hitler order that all activities not supportive of the war effort were to be terminated, Funk counted among these the debate over reform of the insurance business and ordered a termination of all such discussion. He banned further theoretical discussion as well as the carrying out of plans not relevant to the immediate war effort. While the renewed ban on the reform discussion seemed to provide the private insurance sector with some breathing room, the total war program was another vital threat to the industry.[217]

---

[214] Ibid., pp. 27–9. The only such meeting in the late fall was on Oct. 28, 1942; the minutes are to be found in FHA, S 17.2/73.

[215] Stenographische Notizen über die Beiratssitzung der Reichsgruppe am 25. April 1941, GDV, RS/28, p. 1; Hilgard, "Allianz im 2. Weltkrieg," FHA, AZ 1.3/2, p. 130.

[216] Stenographische Notizen über die Beiratssitzung der Reichsgruppe am 1. Feb. 1943, GDV, RS/28, p. 19.

[217] This decree of Feb. 2, 1943, was communicated to all members of the Reichsgruppe on Feb. 6, 1943, GDV, 3-001; see also Niederschrift über die Beiratssitzung der Reichsgruppe am 5. Feb. 1943, GDV, RS/28, pp. 7–8.

Indeed, in early 1943 Hilgard faced the grim prospect of presiding over the virtual dismantling of important portions of the insurance business in carrying out
total war measures demanded by the regime. Thus, he felt compelled to sum-
mon an emergency meeting of the Reich Group Advisory Council on February 5,
1943, after the RWM asked for proposals to significantly reduce the number of
those employed in the insurance field. In Hilgard's view, three groups of activity
had to be distinguished from one another. First, there was the gathering of new
business, which encompassed the entire process that began with advertising and
ended with issuing a new policy. Second, there was the administration of existing portfolios. Finally, there was the handling of claims. In Hilgard's view, the
latter two activities were of importance to the war effort and could not be shut
down. Thus, the only areas in which Hilgard thought personnel savings were
possible were advertising and sales. Even here, however, Hilgard wished to avoid
a total shutdown, pointing out that those over 65 years of age were not mobilized
and that many such persons needed the money and were available – as were those
permanently disabled by the war. He thought that one could also continue to use
persons for whom insurance selling was a side activity, although this would have
to be in the context of the labor-mobilizing efforts of the government. He was
also prepared to release officials and inspectors insofar as they were primarily
concerned with gaining new business, and in general thought that the industry
could release 10% of its employees by such work reduction measures as cutting
back or eliminating auditing and accounting requirements for the rest of the war.
In order to maintain effectiveness, however, task reduction would be necessary,
and Hilgard urged that – for the duration of the war – policyholders not be permitted to terminate policies in order to take out new ones. This would at once
reduce the quest for new business and protect insurance salesmen who had been
complaining about losing business while at the front. Hilgard was quite doubtful about efforts to consolidate the industry at this point. The experience at
Allianz had demonstrated that concentration and consolidation were measures
whose benefits became visible only with the passage of time and could not be
expected to bring immediate savings of labor.[218]

In the discussion that followed, Hilgard met with little opposition from the
heads of the various economic groups, although there was a good deal of skepticism as to whether one would really reduce the number of employed by 10%.
As had frequently been the case at these meetings, Hilgard openly clashed with
Bothe. The latter, making reference to developments on the Eastern front, felt
that Germany had to conduct total war in the manner of the Russians and argued that all advertising and sales efforts should cease. Hilgard, however, could
see no reason "why I should destroy a large number of existences, people 65–70
years old. There are also among them war-disabled. Why should I drive them into
the arms of public welfare?"[219] In any case, the ultimate responsibility rested

---

[218] Stenographische Notizen über die außerordentliche Beiratssitzung der Reichsgruppe am 1. Feb.
    1943, GDV, RS/28.
[219] Ibid., p. 12.

with him, and Hilgard pointedly told Bothe: "I can as leader of the Reich Group listen to my advisory council, but then I can always still decide as I will. For the proposals come from me."[220]

Those proposals were sent to Funk on the following day and demonstrated Hilgard's willingness to more or less shut down the external service of the insurance business while keeping at least some portion of it alive by employing the old and the disabled. He claimed there were approximately 82,000 persons (38,000 men and 44,000 women) working in the insurance business in May 1942 and that manpower measures had reduced the total number of employees to between 70,000 and 75,000 since then. He estimated the number of insurance agents and their employees at 13,500. It was this group that he was prepared to see placed at the disposal of the war economy, while keeping their activities as alive as possible with the types of workers mentioned earlier. Hilgard also supported a ban on advertising, the carrying through of measures to simplify the insurance tax, and a ban on change of insurer for the duration of the war. He stressed that the last measure would save a great deal of administrative labor. Finally, he urged the RWM to consider eliminating auditing and financial reporting requirements for a year. Hilgard rejected proposals for consolidating firms or shutting them down, just as he warned against trying to concentrate operations like the handling of all damage claims in one firm, on the grounds that the effort to deal with different types of forms and procedures would create nothing but more work and confusion to boot. A very difficult problem that Hilgard felt needed more consideration was of policyholders seeking added insurance, because underinsurance had become a major problem owing to inflation and increased damages. Although companies were prepared to provide a margin of increased insurance of about 30% without increasing premiums, actual underinsurance amounted to a great deal more. Announcing the policy would lead to a wave of policyholders asking to increase their insurance, and this would cost much labor. If one said nothing, however, then the policyholders would be ignorant both of what the companies were prepared to do and of the potential problems they would have.[221]

On February 16, 1943, the RWM issued a decree based on Hilgard's suggestions, and Schwede-Coburg immediately raised objections. It is one of the more grotesque ironies of the politics of the insurance business under National Socialism that the last hope of Schwede-Coburg and others seeking to nationalize the insurance business now lay in those measures of total mobilization, taken especially at the beginning of 1943, which signalled that Germany was firmly on the road to defeat. Schwede-Coburg complained to Funk that he had not been consulted either about the decree on labor force mobilization or the decree stopping work on reorganization of the insurance business. He hastened to remind Funk that many of the preparations for reorganization were designed to simplify the business and reduce labor needs. Schwede-Coburg's chief proposal was to

---

[220] Ibid., p. 19.
[221] Hilgard an RWM, 2. Feb. 1943, FHA, S 17.4/6 and SM, 1458/1/95, Bl. 278–8.

give his ally Amend and the RAA the right to order measures for simplification of procedures in the insurance business.[222] This effort to switch the responsibility for the labor-saving measures from Hilgard to Amend succeeded and, as Alzheimer gloomily reported:

Amend can today decide which employees are dispensible and which have to go to military service; he can have the operations of insurance branches shut down; he has the right to set up joint operations between the operations of individual companies or to undertake a fusion, etc. .... [O]ne must fear that he will use the plenary powers granted to him to achieve his plans.[223]

Amend did indeed live up to the expectation that he would use his powers to reduce staffs of insurance companies still further, and this took the form of a decree of March 12, 1943, that threw Hilgard and most of his colleagues into something of a panic. Emphasizing the need for the insurance industry to recognize the demands of the hour, Amend called upon leaders of the larger firms, private and publicly chartered, to undertake an examination of all aspects of their operations with respect to significance for the war effort. He warned that this would lead to the termination of many activities important to the business but not necessary for the war effort.[224] Toward this end, Amend ordered a cessation of advertising and sales. At the same time – and this was the portion of the decree that was most disturbing to the industry leaders – he set up percentual guidelines for the release of labor, proposing that life insurance companies strive to retain a maximum of one third of their staffing levels of July 1, 1939, with a target level of 40% for most other staff; health insurance was to limit itself to 40%–50% of its prewar staff size. Even in cases where companies had already cut back to these levels at the beginning of 1943, Amend expected further personnel reduction of 10%–20% due to the elimination of sales operations. Amend specifically noted that these requirements already took into account the fact that portfolios had increased in size and value since the beginning of the war and that the quality of the personnel employed had decreased. Among the further measures Amend proposed was a severe reduction in accounting and bookkeeping. Finally, he warned that the sooner the firms undertook to meet these standards, the less likely they were to have interference from his side. To check on performance, he provided a rather detailed questionnaire for the purposes of verifying the measures taken.

At the Reich Group advisory council meeting on March 26, 1943, a very upset Hilgard pointed out that Amend had promised to keep him informed before taking measures but had not done so. In the case of Allianz, this would mean giving up 35% of its property insurance staff and 46% of the staff at Allianz Leben. In Hilgard's opinion, neither Allianz nor the other companies could continue to operate in an orderly manner under such conditions. The problem, as Hilgard

[222] Schwede-Coburg an Funk, 23. Feb. 1943; Stellungnahme, ibid., Bl. 217–21.
[223] Mitteilung Alzheimer, 8. März 1943, SR, FA A7.3-03.
[224] RAA an die größeren Versicherungsunternehmungen, 12. März 1943, GDV, 0-101, Bd. 1.

saw it, was that Amend's guidelines reflected the basically false assumption that most of the labor-saving measures he was proposing needed to be undertaken. In reality, they had already been put in place so that further savings of manpower could not be expected from them. Hilgard's concerns were widely shared by his colleagues (with the exception of Bothe, who apparently felt that any order from on high was more or less feasible by definition), and they added other considerations not present in the Amend decree – namely, the effects of bombing on productivity and the complication of operations arising from these and other war-induced conditions (e.g., increased death rates). The dilemma was to either carry out the orders and answer the questions by the unrealistic deadlines or face the charge of engaging in economic sabotage.[225]

As was so often the case, Hilgard turned to the RWM for help, and on March 31 he sent a long letter of criticism and protest aimed at Amend's decree. Hilgard spoke for himself and his colleagues – a point to which Bothe objected, claiming to be misrepresented by Hilgard – in arguing that the demands were not feasible and would only bring disorder into the insurance business without benefitting the war economy. He went on to detail the false assumptions under which the RAA was operating and to reiterate his claim that sales by the elderly and war wounded were in no way costly in manpower.[226] Indeed, some ten days later, Hilgard was able to describe the futility of the RAA's demands with the example of Bayerische Versicherungsbank, which had placed 70 of its employees at the disposal of the labor exchange in Munich on April 1 as required in the RAA decree – only to find that the labor exchange refused to take them and asked that no such further actions be taken since it was not in a position to process them. Hilgard noted various cases where employees thrown on the market by insurance companies were unable to find the suitable war-essential jobs for which they were let go.[227]

Although certainly not so intended, the decree is useful to the historian seeking to gain some sense of Allianz's situation in the final phase of the war, since Allianz (along with all the other companies) had to fill out the RAA questionnaire.[228] Hilgard provided the answers, which reflected the current situation of Allianz and how involved the company had become in the war effort. He pointed out that rationalization – once undertaken to cut costs and increase profits – had since, because of military requirements, increasingly taken on the exclusive purpose of wringing as much productivity out of as little labor as possible. The concern had lost half its trained male and female personnel to the war effort, and these had been replaced by wounded and disabled persons and pensioners over 65. It had become highly dependent on untrained employees, and sick leave, which had doubled since 1938, had increased 20% between 1941 and 1942. Air raids increasingly taxed the physical and mental endurance of the work force.

---

[225] Stenographische Notizen über die Beiratssitzung am 26. März 1943, GDV, RS/28.

[226] Hilgard an RWM, 31. März 1943, SM, 1458/1/95, Bl. 82–91; Bothe an die Reichsgruppe, 10. April 1943, ibid., Bl. 131; Hilgard an Bothe, 13. April 1943, ibid., Bl. 132.

[227] Hilgard an RWM, 12. April 1943, ibid., Bl. 134–5.

[228] For this discussion, see "Bericht an das R.A.A. vom 27. April 1943," FHA, S 17.4/6.

At the same time, wartime conditions had multiplied paperwork. Many policy-holders were changing their residence or were difficult to locate because of the war, while others had lost their policies. Despite all this, Hilgard was prepared to offer another 1,122 persons to the labor exchanges, but he warned that this was the outer limit of sacrifice.

He went on to remind the RAA that Allianz performed a variety of services vital to the war effort: heading the Luftpool, running a testing laboratory for materials in Berlin-Mariendorf, and providing machine insurance (whose premiums had doubled between 1938 and 1942). The same held true for transport insurance. Though the automobile insurance business had decreased, the paper-work connected with it had become more complicated and time-consuming. In fire insurance, the war had certainly brought more business, with premiums for Allianz climbing from 31.9% of their business in 1938 to 41.5% in 1942. The problem was that damages and claims, especially those due to air raids, had climbed even more, from 54.5% in 1938 to 72% in 1942. While the traditional foreign business of Allianz had been reduced or eliminated in areas under Allied control, Allianz was highly active in the conquered areas and had been com-pelled to set up a host of new offices that faced not only their normal tasks but also the special tasks associated with working in non–German-speaking areas. In short, Allianz was overextended, and the efforts to master the tasks involved with unskilled employees and 60-hour work weeks necessarily had their limits.

Yet in making his case, Hilgard also demonstrated how inextricably involved Allianz had become in the German expansion and German war effort. This was particularly evident with respect to the East, where Hilgard stressed that Allianz had been granted the right to provide insurance protection to German interests in the Generalgouvernement, and this involved building up a complicated new portfolio and the setting up of a major business office in Cracow as well as offices in various Polish cities. Even more important in adding to the labors of Allianz, however, was the expansion in the Eastern territories annexed to Germany. Hil-gard's summary demonstrated the scale and scope of Allianz's activity:

Here there was an uncommonly complicated reviewing and liquidation of what had re-mained of former business offices of three Polish corporations in Gotenhafen, Posen, Kat-towitz and Bielitz and, alongside their administration in the capacity of a trustee (which included also a number of properties) and the taking over of ethnic German and Polish personnel, there was the building up of a large, new, German portfolio. Our branch in Königsberg, which now had to care for the Memel territory, and the districts of Sulwalki, Bialystok and Zichenau, had to be built up along with the Danzig branch responsible for the Gau Danzig–West Prussia and the new District Office in Bromberg. Also, the branch office in Breslau had to be built up into an independent regional headquarters, to whose area of competence belongs Lower and Upper Silesia, the East Sudetengau, and the Warthegau with the newly established branch offices of Posen and Kattowitz and the district office in Litzmannstadt.[229]

[229] Ibid., pp. 8f.

In arguing for the retention of as much of the Allianz labor force as possible, Hilgard understandably placed great emphasis on the role of construction insurance, whose importance to the German war effort has already been discussed. Hilgard stressed that no competition among insurance agents was involved because the premiums were defined by the price commissar, who also determined what the construction companies could charge. Nevertheless, it was necessary to have staff on the spot to determine costs and risks under wartime conditions. He employed testimony from Organisation Todt, which warned that reducing the company's effectiveness would have negative consequences for the drawing up of proper contracts and the control of prices. Speer's Armaments Ministry and the Air Ministry also testified to the importance of Allianz's services in this area. Here at least Hilgard had a good case – but from a historical perspective, his argument constitutes strong evidence of the concern's direct and heavy involvement in the war effort.

Such contributions to the war effort did not end all efforts to comb out nonessential industries like insurance, but both the RAA and the RWM seemed to become quite concerned by late 1943 and during 1944 that call-ups were reaching the point where the entire financial sector (i.e., banks and insurance companies) would become nonfunctional. The situation was worsened by the tendency of Gauleiter and Party officials to take matters into their own hands and take actions that ran contrary to the ministry instructions. Yet another problem was the military call-up of key persons in the companies and the threat this carried of decapitating the company operations for which they were responsible.

It is interesting to note that the Allianz offices in Berlin were permitted by the labor office to use some 40 foreign employees, who were either prisoners of war or foreigners obligated to work in Germany (12 of them French officers and 20 Czechs, all of whom had worked in the insurance or banking sectors back at home) as well as such employees from Belgium, the Netherlands, and Latvia. Director Maiholzer described them as "forced laborers," but he hastened to add that relations with these persons were especially good, that they pitched in with their German compatriots in air raids, and that they were well treated. Given that these individuals were familiar with the kind of work being done at Allianz, which was certainly less onerous than that done by forced labor in industry, Maiholzer's claim seems plausible. Apparently, the Berlin offices also employed some Jews and part-Jews supplied by the labor office, and Maiholzer claimed they were never subjected to abuse by supervisory personnel. In any case, the concern cannot be considered a significant employer of forced labor because the priorities for assigning such labor lay elsewhere.[230]

Therefore, in the last years of the war, Allianz clearly had more business than it could handle – both because of the volume and increasingly high premiums in

---

[230] See the Niederschrift über die Beiratssitzungen von 1. Okt. 1943 und 14. April 1944, GDV, RS/28, and Maiholzer, "Berliner Allianz Betriebe," pp. 22–3. See, in general, Ulrich Herbert, *Fremdarbeiter. Politik und Praxis des "Ausländer-Einsatzes" in der Kriegswirtschaft des Dritten Reiches* (Berlin & Bonn, 1985).

certain cases due to war risk and damage and also because it did not have the personnel it needed to deal with the situation. It would be utterly senseless to try to account for the concern's status during this period in terms of profit and loss, since one would not be dealing with anything remotely resembling a normal economic or financial situation. To begin with, Allianz – especially Allianz Leben, which was the repository for the concern's major investments – was investing more than ever in a losing war. The headline of one newspaper article in late 1942, "Life Insurance in the Service of War Finance," accurately stated the inescapable reality.[231] As of September 1, 1942, insurance firms were required to invest three quarters (rather than two thirds) of their available means in Reich bonds, and these bore 3.5% instead of the previous 4.5% interest.[232] Such investment was made all the more necessary by the severe restrictions imposed by the RWM on loans to industry and municipalities in the final war years. Such loans had to be demonstrated as absolutely essential to the war effort in order to justify not using the available funds to invest in Reich bonds. Also, insurance companies were forced to charge a higher interest rate for industrial loans (so as to make them less attractive), and the rate could only be lowered in the case of wholly or partially government-owned companies.[233] It was a sign of the times, however, that the insurance firms were urged not to request that the Reich bonds in which they were investing be sent to them, since they were in danger of burning up in air raids, but rather have their investment noted in the Reich Debt Ledger, which was allegedly safe. Indeed, while the companies were compelled to invest their paper Reichsmark in paper assets, their real assets were burning up. In its report to the supervisory board of December 8, 1944, Allianz Leben noted that, at the end of 1943, 10.5% of its property holdings had been totally destroyed. The net book worth of this property amounted to 21.2 million RM – that is, 27% of the total net book worth of its properties. Another 56% of its properties were partially damaged, the repair of which was roughly estimated at 4.2 million RM. At the same time, 12% of the properties on which Allianz Leben held mortgages were totally or very severely damaged – 40.8 million RM in value, or 9.5% of its entire mortgage investment.[234] Naturally, more was to come in 1944 and the first months of 1945.

Needless to say, the business headquarters of insurance companies were in no way immune from bombing, and one of the decisions made at the meeting of the Allianz and Munich Re directors on October 28, 1942, where Hilgard stated that the war was lost, was to deal with the implications of Allianz's exposed situation in the center of Berlin. A decision was taken to begin removing all the securities held by Allianz to areas that were less endangered. Thus, starting in early

[231] *Münchener Neueste Nachrichten,* 28./29. Nov. 1942, GDV, 2-066/1.
[232] Rundschreiben vom 23. Jan. 1941, 13. Jan. 1943, 6. Jan. 1944, GDV, RS/22.
[233] RWM an Reichsgruppe, 14. Aug. 1943, and correspondence within Allianz Leben concerning the problem of industrial credits of Feb.–March 1944, B 1.3.1/23.
[234] Bericht vom 8. Dez. 1944, BAB, 80 Ba 2/P 5776.

The Allianz headquarters on Mohrenstraße 63/64 after being severely damaged during Allied air raids of Berlin in 1944 and 1945.

1943, especially reliable members of the finance department were given the task of undertaking numerous trips to transport these securities to friendly banks in various towns – such as Straubing and Deggendorf in Bavaria, but also to Weimar and Sonnenberg in Thuringia – for safekeeping. Given the war situation in Germany, these actions were undertaken at no small risk to those involved. Some of those responsible continued to demonstrate their company loyalty and initiative at the end of the war: Director Ernst Manteufel took the securities stored in Thuringia to Coburg before the Russians came, and Walter Bredow of the financial section (along with his wife) violated American orders to stay in Straubing and managed to carry all the heavy sacks filled with securities registers some 25 kilometers for safekeeping in a peasant's barn. This enabled Allianz to have demonstrable title to these assets later on.[235]

Unhappily, Allianz was less solicitous of its historical and managerial records, most of which – especially the papers of the central management in Berlin – suffered destruction or became widely dispersed as a consequence of the bombings of its Berlin buildings. The first of these bombing raids took place on the night of November 23–24, 1943, when the recently built Allianz Leben building on the Mohrenstraße was virtually destroyed. Some days later, the spacious quarters of Frankfurter Versicherungs-AG on the same street was totally demolished. A hiatus followed until April 29, 1944, when further devastation was visited on the buildings in central Berlin, this time on the Taubenstraße, which housed the headquarters for the Air Insurance Pool and Kraft. The latter shortly afterward moved its central offices to Höflitz in the Sudetenland, one of over a hundred safety areas used by the various divisions and branches of Allianz and other companies seeking to escape the Berlin bombing and to continue operations as best they could. In contrast to the first two big raids, the third raid affecting the Berlin headquarters took place on February 3, 1945, during working hours and cost the lives of seventeen employees as well as other persons from the vicinity who used Allianz facilities and shelters. The area around the Allianz headquarters was severely damaged by the bombing, as were the buildings of Allianz. By this time, however, air-raid shelters had come to serve as workplaces as well as places of refuge against Allied raids. Indeed, even after the war, on November 28, 1946, an Allianz building on Taubenstraße, in which Allianz Leben archives were stored and which was also used to continue such operations as were possible, was destroyed in a fire that could not be put out owing to inadequate water supply. The days of Allianz's presence in this part of Berlin were numbered anyway, and the dreams of a great administrative building on the Runder Platz had certainly dissolved in the ongoing catastrophe that was destroying much of the record of the past and leaving a very uncertain future in its wake.[236]

Nevertheless, there were still immediate problems to be solved by the end of 1943, and matters were not made easier by the fact that Allianz had to share some of its quarters with government agencies and personnel whose own quarters had been bombed out. In November, Allianz sought permission to purchase a property in Berlin-Schöneberg as a temporary solution to the problem of housing its Berlin branch until such time as the buildings on the Runder Platz could be built. They estimated it would take at least two years or more for the building to be completed, quite aside from the fact that the plans for the façade, which would require Hitler's personal approval, had not yet been drawn up.

---

[235] Hilgard, "Allianz im 2. Weltkrieg," FHA, AZ 1.3/2, pp. 47–51.
[236] On the bombing raids, destruction of documents, and fire, see Maiholzer, "Berliner Allianz-Betriebe," FHA, pp. 81–9.

Originally, Speer had granted permission for the branch to stay at its headquarters in the Bellevuestraße 14 but had then gone back on his promise because the Bellevuestraße building would have to be torn down to make room for a new Reichsmarschallamt. Apparently Allianz intended to take out a credit to purchase the building. The RAA refused the request in February 1944 on the grounds that such purchases could only be allowed in special cases; they could not view the proposal as either necessary for the war effort or particularly pressing. A renewed petition in August 1944 was also turned down at the end of the year by both the RAA and the RWM despite the backing of Speer's office, which claimed that construction on the Reichsmarschallamt would continue despite the use of construction workers to repair bombed buildings. But the RAA was not impressed by the arguments of Allianz that the purchase was important for the war effort and that the Reichsmarschallamt, even if not built during the war, would most certainly be built right after its end. While these surrealistic exchanges were going on, portions of the Berlin staff seem to have been transferred to safer quarters on the outskirts of Berlin – along with documents needed for their everyday activity – and had to be compensated for their travel costs. It was a measure of the desperateness of the situation that Allianz Leben showed interest in the offer of a Hamburg broker of Dutch houseboats and other vessels that might be used as offices, some of these having already been sold to agencies in Berlin. The Allianz Leben officials involved thought the houseboats too small, but asked to be informed should larger ships come on the market.[237]

Despite all these difficulties encountered at home in Germany, Allianz and Munich Re sought as much as possible to protect their old interests in neutral nations: Spain, where they controlled Plus Ultra; Sweden, where the Bore stood under their domination; and Switzerland, where Allianz held the majority of Schweizerische National-Versicherungs-Gesellschaft and Munich Re controlled the Zürich-based Union Rückversicherungs-Gesellschaft. In contrast to the occupied areas (where the Germans could anticipate being thrown out) and the enemy states (where assets had already been confiscated and, if at all returned, then only with the greatest difficulty), Allianz and Munich Re could at least entertain the hope of having a continued presence in neutral states after the war. Also, even before and then increasingly during the war, Munich Re had pursued a policy of acquiring assets abroad with which its business partners in neutral countries could fulfill Munich Re's obligations to those it reinsured, even in the occupied areas, in the event that Germany lost the war and was barred from fulfilling its business obligations.[238] All this made efforts to cloak and protect their interests in these countries – especially Spain, Sweden, and

---

[237] For the correspondence on the building purchase in Berlin, see BAB, R 3104/20512, Bl. 3–15. On the transfer of work to Berlin safe areas, see Maiholzer, "Die Berliner Allianz-Betriebe," FHA, pp. 48–51. On the ship offer, see the Notizen of the Vermögensverwaltung, Berlin, 26.–28. Feb. 1944, FHA, B 1.3.1/23.

[238] Von Reininghaus an Prölss, 3. Sept. 1946, SR, FA A 7.3-03.

Switzerland – appear worthwhile, despite the fact that they were all on the Allied blacklists and were coming under increasing pressure as the outcome of the war became more obvious.

Notwithstanding the costs and difficulties of the Spanish Civil War, Plus Ultra, which Allianz had built up from a small Catalan insurance company to one of the major companies in Spain, continued to enjoy the solicitude of Allianz and Munich Re. The latter had sold its interests in the company to Allianz in 1933, but then repurchased 50% in 1940 under the new common interest agreement of that year. In 1943 there were strong tendencies toward economic nationalism in Spain, and the fear arose that the Spanish government would demand that the majority control of the company be placed in Spanish hands. Allianz had long pursued a policy of instructing its employees to always refer to Plus Ultra as a "friendly company" rather than the "daughter company" that it really was, but this no longer fooled anyone, if it ever had.[239] That Plus Ultra was on the Allied blacklist compounded the problem, since it hurt the company's business and provided yet another reason for reducing German control. The problem was thus to find reliable Spanish shareholders who could be counted upon to administer the company properly and at the same time look after German interests until they could be recovered under more auspicious circumstances. Needless to say, no guarantee that they would so act could be demanded or given, and so the entire cloaking effort was both risky and adventuresome. The key figures in carrying out this plan were Hilgard and Karl-Friedrich von Schlayer, who headed the Paris office of Allianz and regularly travelled to and from Madrid – the formalities of his journey made easier by the assistance of a young border guard who had been in Allianz's service. In the spring of 1944, Hilgard and von Schlayer met together in Madrid with Spaniards whom they believed reliable enough and concluded an arrangement for the transfer of the largest portion of their holdings into Spanish hands. All this was accomplished with a great deal of friendliness and hospitality; at a dinner party in March 1944 hosted by the supervisory board of Plus Ultra, there were expressions of confidence in Germany and a German victory. Hilgard found it all quite painful, but he was confident that he had done the right thing. The same cannot be said for Hans Heß, who, as Hilgard reported, "viewed my trips to Madrid with disapproving eyes and condemned my position in Madrid in every respect." Heß, who apparently felt that Hilgard's arrangement was too risky, actually travelled himself to Madrid a number of times in the unfulfilled hope of changing the arrangement. Hilgard proved right in the end with respect to the probity of his Spanish shareholders, although their management of the business was less than satisfactory.[240]

Allianz was to have much less luck with the Bore company, which was headed by a very pro-German Swede, G. Juhlin-Dannfelt. Hilgard made numerous trips

---

[239] See the Rundschreiben der Organisations-Abteilung der Allianz, 4. Dez. 1935, FHA, AZ 5.1/4.
[240] Hilgard, "Leben," pp. 131–3, FHA, NL 2/7. See also the documents in MR, A 2.20/127, especially the Aktennote of 1. Okt. 1943 and MR, A 2.20/128.

to attend to its affairs but became increasingly skeptical about chances for keeping the company in view of the growing hostility toward Germany and Juhlin-Dannfelt's excessive public support of Germany. Toward the end of the war, German assets were frozen at Allied request, and the Germans apparently had great difficulties getting back anything. As Hilgard bitterly noted in his postwar memoirs: "I cannot get over the fact even today that Sweden, upon whose loyalty we had all counted as being as firm as a rock, was after the war among the countries that showed the most enmity with respect to the return of German property, at least insofar as we were concerned."[241]

However, Switzerland was the most important country from the standpoints of Allianz and Munich Re foreign holdings and international insurance business. Quite aside from the significant business conducted by the Swiss daughter companies of these German concerns, Schweizer National and Union Rück took on additional significance in wartime as a means of continuing to conduct business in enemy states and as instruments to cloak some of the German interests in the occupied areas. Nevertheless, by May 1940 Schweizer National was already complaining about the burdens of the Allied blacklist. In a meeting between Schmitt and General Director Hans Theler, the latter pointed out that Schweizer National had suffered a loss of half a million Swiss francs and was suffering attacks from the competition; something had to be done to meet Allied conditions, since there was no point trying to negotiate with the Allies. Theler proposed that Paul Jaberg, president of Schweizerische Bankgesellschaft and vice-president of Schweizer National, resign from the supervisory board of Munich Re and that business dealings with the German companies be suspended. Schmitt found this too much and, while respecting Theler's managerial capacities, believed that his sympathies lay with the Allies. Nevertheless, these actions were approved since even Heß, to Schmitt's irritation, believed them necessary.[242]

In late May 1940, of course, the Germans were in control of Paris and the French were no longer blacklisting German-owned firms, but by May 1943, Theler was once again complaining to Heß that the blacklist was ruining his transportation insurance business and was hurting in other areas. Through Schweizer National's agent in Bern, they had come into contact with the British embassy and believed that they could get off the blacklist if only the Germans refrained from appearing at administrative board meetings and limited their reinsurance involvement to 20%. Heß understood the relationship between Schweizer National and Allianz/Munich Re to be one of partnership, however, and would only agree if there was a clear commitment to prolong the relationship and to keep funds in reserve for subsequent reinstallation of the German quota. Heß's opinion was shared by Rudolf Ernst (president of the administrative board) and Vice-President Jaberg, both of whom agreed to reaffirm the commitment to the relationship without putting this into the minutes of the

[241] Hilgard, "Leben," pp. 133f., FHA, NL 2/7.
[242] Aktennote Schmitt, 10. Mai 1940, MR, A 2.19/109.

official administrative board meeting. Yet another point of discussion was that Theler asked the two German companies to reduce their shareholdings from 43% to 20%, which meant surrendering 1,180 shares. In the negotiations over this issue at the end of 1943 with Ernst and Jaberg, Alois Alzheimer insisted that such a reduction in no way prejudice the existing reinsurance quotas. In Alzheimer's negotiations with Theler, he sought to pin the latter down by conceding a reduction of the reinsurance quota from 50% to 33-1/3% if Schweizer National would agree to continue to view the relationship between Schweizer National and themselves as one similar to the relationship existing bctwccn Allianz and Munich Re. Once again, the leaders of Schweizer National appeared to agree to the German proposal. It rapidly turned out, however, that Theler also wanted the reinsurance quota permanently reduced to 20% so as to avoid being put on the blacklist again decades down the road, and that there had been a misunderstanding in the negotiations.[243]

This issue was a matter for the Swiss bankers on the administrative board, and it soon became apparent that they were trying to get as much of the best of both worlds as they could under difficult circumstances. On the one hand, Ernst and Jaberg were anxious not to offend the Americans, since their Schweizerische Bankgesellschaft had substantial interests in the United States.[244] On the other, Jaberg seemed prepared to give a verbal promise that Schweizer National had the right to give the shares back to the Germans within five years. Schmitt found this too vague and unsatisfactory a commitment, however, and emphasized the historical relationship between the two German concerns and Schweizer National. Munich Re had played a great role in getting Schweizer National back on its feet and supporting it financially in 1921, and this transaction between Allianz and Schweizer National had established a special relationship. Allianz had given up its majority to help Schweizer National out at the beginning of the war, and now it was reducing its holdings still further, but it could not tolerate a total alienation of its holdings without jeopardizing its own future prospects. Schmitt was prepared to have the shares placed in a deposit but was not prepared to sell the 1,180 shares in question. After a considerable amount of complicated negotiation, much of it created by the fact that Ernst and Jaberg had already promised to let two private bank houses sell the shares to their customers, an agreement was reached under which the bank houses in question received 250 shares; the 930 remaining shares were to be deposited with Schweizerische Bankgesellschaft. The repurchase of these shares by the German companies was to be guaranteed by the creation of a special deposit of securities of equivalent value. That this was intended to be a cloaking operation was made manifest by the second point of the agreement as outlined by Schmitt, "that the Münchener and Allianz have not agreed to this transaction and do not know anything about it. In their view they remain shareholders and consequently will not place this transaction on their

---

[243] Aktennote 18. Mai 1943, and Aktennote Alzheimer, 18. Dez. 1943, ibid.
[244] The bank was the forerunner of the United Bank of Switzerland (UBS).

books."[245] Finally, after the war and "the calming of the political situation," the conditions as understood by the two German concerns would be restored in that the 930 shares would be returned at the going market quotation and paid for from the aforementioned deposit. At the same time, it was hoped and expected that the private banks of Roguin and Lombard and Odier & Cie. would hold the shares for resale to the two German concerns. Jaberg assured Schmitt that his arrangement had the agreement of his colleagues, and Director Hans Grieshaber of Union Rück was subsequently asked to serve as trusteee. Hence, for all intents and purposes, the 1,180 shares (1,000 of which belonged to Allianz and the remainder to Munich Re) were secure, as was the relationship between the two German concerns and Schweizer National. Indeed, this impression was strongly confirmed when Alzheimer met with Theler in March 1945 in Zürich and the latter emphasized his desire to continue the relationship as soon as conditions allowed. As became evident after the war, however, the agreement turned out to be the stuff of which lawsuits are made.[246]

The other important direct holding in Switzerland that was in increasing jeopardy as the war came to a close was Union Rück, founded in 1923 by Munich Re, which held 80% of its shares despite its Swiss management under Director Hans Grieshaber and the administrative board headed (as in the case of Schweizer National) by Ernst and Jaberg. Schmitt, Alzheimer, and other Allianz and Munich Re leaders were constantly travelling to and from Switzerland, dealing with the affairs of Union Rück as well as of Schweizer National. In July 1943, for example, Schmitt and Alzheimer visited Grieshaber for the purpose of transferring Munich Re Italian business to Union Rück because of the political situation in Italy, and Union Rück was granted all kinds of powers to act for Munich Re as the political situation for Germany steadily deteriorated.[247] In November 1944, Munich Re petitioned the RWM to permit Alzheimer to travel to Switzerland and look after its affairs, pointing out that Union brought in 40 million in premiums and handled many kinds of business in other countries where Munich Re had difficulties working because of Allied pressure. This included portions of Munich Re's earlier Argentine, Portuguese, Turkish, Finnish, Bulgarian, and Romanian business, as well as Spanish and Swedish business of more recent vintage. The question of how to declare such business in the balances of Union Rück in a manner that was acceptable to the Swiss supervisory authorities was a special problem under the existing circumstances, but the Union Rück also needed regular advice on technical issues in the management of the portfolios being sent its way if Anglo-American competitors were not to gain control of them. Union Rück's problems became worse in December 1944, when the French government

---

[245] Streng vertrauliche Aktennote von Schmitt, 20. Jan. 1944, ibid.
[246] Aktennote Alzheimer, 15. März 1945; see also the contract between Union Rück and Schweizerische Bankgesellschaft and the Zusammenfassung der Verhandlungen, 26. Mai 1944, ibid.
[247] The remaining files of the Union Rück are to be found in the archive of Swiss Re. See especially the Aktennote and correspondence of July 1943, SR, R-Union Rück: Kriegsfall 1935–1944.

under Charles de Gaulle basically took over the American blacklist and thus banned Union Rück from business in France, although Grieshaber hoped to keep up at least his life insurance business in France (if the ban did not last too long); he and Alzheimer agreed to hold back on transferring the French portfolio of Union Rück to another company.[248] In contrast to the case of Schweizer National, however, no arrangement was made for the transfer of shares prior to the end of the war, which meant that Grieshaber and the Union Rück would have not only to find a way off the blacklist on their own when the war ended but also to deal with a Swiss commitment to the Allies to liquidate German assets.

It is very important to recognize that the Swiss-German connection in the insurance field was highly prized by both sides, and this was because it brought a multitude of advantages. One of these, hard to pin down precisely but certainly of great moment, was that Switzerland and the Swiss insurance leaders provided something of a respite for the German insurance executives. It provided a venue to visit valued and more fortunate colleagues, to speak about their worries back home more freely, and to get away (however briefly) from the Third Reich. This was especially evident in the case of Kurt Schmitt and his close relationship with Heinrich Fehlmann of Winterthur, but Hilgard, Alzheimer, and Heß also made regular trips to Switzerland in which business was mixed with social relations.[249]

At the same time, the business relationship in insurance between the two countries was extremely important. In 1943, German business provided two thirds of Switzerland's foreign premiums in life insurance, or 27% of its entire premium income. Swiss Re, which handled the lion's share of Swiss reinsurance, received 20% of its premium income in reinsurance from Germany, which translated into 25% of total profits on reinsurance.[250] An important aspect of this business was the five-year German-Swiss Reinsurance Agreement of March 1940 and its counterpart for the Protectorate of Bohemia-Moravia. The central problem dealt with in these negotiations was how to allow the Swiss to receive profits they made from their German operations (which they obviously did not want to hold in Reichsmark) in Swiss francs, despite German exchange controls. Thanks to this agreement, between 1940 and 1945 the Swiss insurers were able to draw on Reichsbank accounts at the Swiss National Bank and take their German

---

[248] See Münchener Rück an RWM und Gauwirtschaftskammer München, 14. Nov. 1944, RAA an RWM, 25. Nov. 1944, Gauwirtschaftskammer Oberbayern an RAA, 17. Nov. 1944, SM, 1458/11/174, Bl. 119–22, 157–9. See also Aktennotiz über Union Rück, 21. Mai 1946, MR, B 22/35, and Aktennote Alzheimer, 14.–19. Dez. 1944, MR, B 12/19.

[249] The importance of these relationships will become more apparent in the next chapter, but see the correspondence between Schmitt and Fehlmann (e.g., Fehlmann an Schmitt, 2. Mai 1947, NL 1/14), where the former notes their frequent conversations on Schmitt's grim forebodings concerning the war.

[250] See Unhabhängige Expertenkommission Schweiz – Zweiter Weltkrieg, *Die Schweiz und die Goldtransaktionen im Zweiten Weltkrieg. Zwischenbericht* (Bern, 1998) (hereinafter: *Bergier Kommission, Zwischenbericht*), Ch. V, esp. pp. 188–90.

profits in Swiss francs. These accounts, established under the general German-Swiss Economic Agreement, contained a certain percentage of Swiss payments for German imports that could be used to pay German debts to Swiss creditors. Appendix D of the agreement enabled the Swiss insurers to make immediate use of the accounts to cover their German business in Swiss francs. This arrangement was doubly advantageous to the Swiss, enabling them to receive their own hard currency as payment and also to keep their Reichsmark balances low, ensuring that – in any depreciation or devaluation of the Reichsmark (and a loss in the value of the RM could certainly be anticipated) – they would have made an exchange profit from the ability to pay such German obligations as they had in RM while having collected their German earnings in Swiss francs.[251]

By late 1944, however, it was becoming clear that this "happy" state of affairs – for the Swiss because it was so profitable, and for the German insurance business because it permitted them to pay their obligations and maintain their most important international connection – was coming to an end. General Director Hans Koenig of the Rentenanstalt, who was also chief negotiator for the Swiss Insurer's Association and the Swiss government in negotiations on insurance questions with the Germans and who had largely been responsible for negotiating the insurance side of the German-Swiss economic agreement, was a remarkably tenacious and effective representative of Swiss insurance interests. He noted in October that the transfer had been beneficial but that the account available for Swiss creditors was now running out of money because the Germans were selling so little to the Swiss. The Germans, who at the beginning of the arrangement of 1940 anticipated annual payments of 12 million Swiss francs for insurance (divided roughly as 45% for direct insurance and 55% for reinsurance) found themselves facing increasing cost overruns, so that 13 million Swiss francs were paid for 1943, 17.2 million for 1944 (of which 9 million was still owing at the end of the year), and a 20 million debt was anticipated for 1945.[252] Both sides were anxious to continue the agreement, but how was this to be done given the German situation? In January 1945 new negotiations were held, with Hans Koenig and Paul Guggenbühl of Swiss Re negotiating for the Swiss and Ministerial Director Hans Storck of the RWM heading the German delegation. The two sides reached a compromise under which the Germans would immediately pay the 9 million Swiss francs owing for 1944, while the Swiss would agree to a ceiling of 13 million Swiss francs for 1945 that would not be payable until the end of the year. An important aspect of this arrangement was the anticipation that the Reichsbank would be able to sell gold to the Swiss National Bank to cover its obligations, although by this time – thanks both to Allied warnings

---

[251] Ibid., pp. 190–2; for Anlage D, see SM, 1458/11/142, Bl. 95–102. See the revealing report by P. Guggenbühl, Verwaltungsratssitzung vom 28. März 1945, SR, Protokolle der Verwaltungsrats-Sitzungen, Bd. X, pp. 175ff.

[252] Koenig an Hotz, Kohli, usw., 4. Okt. 1944, Besprechung mit den Herren der deutschen Delegation, 18. Dez. 1944, BAR, E 2001 (E) 2/582.

and other information – it was quite clear that such gold was almost certainly stolen and, indeed, possibly gold taken from Jewish victims.[253]

Manifestly, everyone involved knew that Germany was on the verge of collapse, and the Swiss were unabashedly trying to get as much from the Germans as they could before the end came. This effort was complicated further on February 16, when the Swiss Federal Council finally succumbed to Allied pressure and issued a freeze on all German assets as well as a ban on business with Germany. Needless to say, this put the entire arrangement with the insurers in danger, along with the plans to assist other Swiss creditors in a similar manner. Nevertheless, the arrangement between the Germans and Swiss with respect to insurance was confirmed on February 28 as if it had no bearing whatever on the agreement with the Allies and especially on the negotiations with President Roosevelt's representative Lauchlin Currie. Much would depend, therefore, on the impending Swiss negotiations with the vice-president of the Reichsbank, Emil Puhl.

Puhl did indeed offer gold. Some of the Swiss officials – such as Robert Kohli, head of the legal and private assets abroad section of the political section of the Federal government – thought that it might be accepted to cover the insurance obligations. He admitted that

it is certainly difficult to take gold, since one does not know from where it comes and one cannot tell by the smell from whence it was stolen or robbed. But he, Kohli, hopes that the Allies would see that it is better if Germany pays us this gold to fulfill its obligations than when the gold otherwise goes floating about.[254]

But Walter Stucki, the much-harrassed head of the political department of the Swiss Foreign Office, had no more taste for gold purchases and further Allied protests on this score, and he told Koenig that the Swiss government could not accept the gold. Nevertheless, Koenig did manage to get the insurance business excluded from any payment ban with respect to the Reichsbank accounts, so that something could still be saved of the agreement.

What could be saved was still an open question, but it is striking how anxious the German insurance leaders were to maintain the relationship in these last months of the war and to continue doing business in Switzerland. The blocking of German accounts and freeze on German business very much alarmed the Germans, and they were even more upset to learn that the agreements (between Storck and the insurers) of December 1944 and January 1945 might be unfulfillable because there might not be enough in the Reichsbank accounts to cover them. Thus, in mid-March, Alzheimer and Schmitt requested permission to visit Switzerland to negotiate with their Swiss contacts and friends about gaining an exception for the German insurance business – just as the Swiss insurers had

---

[253] Koenig an Hotz, Kohli und Homburger, 24. Jan. 1945, BAR, E 2001 (E) 2/575; for the general account see *Bergier Kommission, Zwischenbericht,* pp. 190–2.

[254] Quoted in ibid., p. 194.

managed so successfully to put themselves outside the general regulation of February 16. Alzheimer reported on his mission in a detailed account to Storck of March 26.[255] His first goal apparently was to induce the Swiss to agree to excluding German insurance firms and interests from provisions of the February 16 order. Although Alzheimer held an official position as head of the reinsurance economic group, he emphasized that he was coming as a private person rather than as someone empowered to negotiate and sought "to employ the business connections of the Munich Re to Swiss enterprises over many years and my personal friendly relations with the leading persons of the Swiss insurance business, in order to make possible the continued operation of the German insurers and especially here the strongly interested German reinsurance business." As Alzheimer reported, his Swiss colleagues demonstrated "great understanding" for his proposals and he found "completely loyal support." He thus believed he had accomplished his goals of excluding the German insurers from the freezing of their assets and permitting those under German influence to continue operations, although this involved very complicated arrangements with the Swiss authorities with respect to the kinds of accounts that could be used by the Germans for their business. Emil Boss, the head of the Swiss Insurance Office, also indicated full support for Alzheimer's effort to keep the German-influenced reinsurance companies operating. Alzheimer in turn promised to do everything in his power to make Swiss operations in Germany as functional as possible.

Despite all good will, it was now a race against time to see if anything could be saved of the arrangement to pay the Swiss insurers from Reichsbank funds. As Guggenbühl reported on March 28, one could no longer expect the 9 million due in 1944 to be paid, since the money was not there and there were pressing claims for some 27 million RM by Swiss creditors. Of these, if the transfer was still technically possible before Germany collapsed, 4.5 million would be available for the insurance payments. Obviously they had hoped for more but, as Guggenbühl noted, the transfer agreement had enabled 40 million Swiss francs to be transferred and had thus been a great success.[256] Finally, a new agreement was reached with Puhl in early April on the Reichsbank accounts to be used to pay off the Swiss creditors, and a "Girokonto I" was set up on April 11, 1945, upon which the Swiss insurers could supposedly draw.

Indeed, the capacity of the Allianz and Munich Re leaders to look after these interests and move back and forth across the border was quite remarkable, given the problems they were having at home. On January 5, 1943, Paul Lux – a member of the board of management who was also Hilgard's right-hand man and the

[255] "Bericht über meine Reise nach der Schweiz," Zürich, 24. März 1945, SM, 1458/11/140, Bl. 227–36. The Union Rück Akten in the archive of Swiss Re report that Schmitt and Alzheimer travelled back to Munich by auto on March 27, which demonstrates that Schmitt came along despite some problems in his getting permission reported in the documents of Feb.–April 1945 in SM, 1458/11/193.

[256] Verwaltungsratssitzung vom 28. März 1945, SR, Protokolle der Verwaltungsrats-Sitzungen, Bd. X, pp. 175ff.

plant manager in Berlin – died following an operation at the age of 41. Lux was greatly admired for his competence and personal qualities; his death was a hard blow and meant the loss of a rising star in the concern. Richard Krause, a member of the board of management of Allianz Leben and its chief mathematician, also died of natural causes in 1943. The war years were taking their toll of the concern's leadership. Director Georg König, Herbert Mathy (head of the assets division of Allianz Leben), and Steffen Boetius (head of the Magdeburg branch) were victims of combat.[257]

At the same time, the top management of Allianz was aging. Heß turned 60 in 1941, and he and Schmitt – who was deputy chairman of the Allianz supervisory board as well as general director of Munich Re, and who continued to discuss all important questions bearing on Allianz with Heß – hoped to continue the Allianz policy of having the general director step down within a year of turning 60 so as to open the way for younger leadership. Heß believed in this policy and did not want to make an exception for himself, to which was added the problem of his heart condition and his inability to control his natural urge to be overly active. A further consideration was that Heß was having increasing difficulties with his housing situation. He had homes in Berlin and an estate in Saxony at Agnesdorf, and maintaining them was a problem under wartime conditions. While both men knew the war was lost, they were also aware that the end could take a few years and feared that Heß would not be up to facing the potentially revolutionary social situation that might develop and the attendant loss of income. Schmitt hoped that Heß would move to the supervisory board and serve as a semi-delegate to the board of management. In thinking about a successor, first Lux and then (after Lux's death) Goudefroy and Schmidt-Polex came to mind, since Hilgard was only a few years younger than Heß. Schmitt and Heß were uncertain about which of the two would be better, and thus discussed with Hilgard the possibility of his taking over as general director for a two-year term with Goudefroy and Schmidt-Polex as deputy general directors. This would provide an opportunity to determine which of them would be best.[258]

A major barrier to this solution was the head of the Allianz supervisory board, August von Finck, who disliked the idea of having anyone with a special position that might diminish his own on the supervisory board and also seemed averse to changes so long as the war lasted. Von Finck and the supervisory board had agreed in 1941 that Heß could effectively work half-time if he wished, but Heß had never taken advantage of this offer and asked to resign at the end of 1942. With unusual passion, however, von Finck urged Heß to stay on and made him promise to do so until the war ended.[259]

---

[257] On Lux, see the moving tribute by Hilgard in "Allianz im Zweiten Weltkrieg," pp. 14–21, FHA, AZ 1.3/2. For the deaths in Allianz management, see Maiholzer, "Berliner Allianz-Betriebe," pp. 93–4.

[258] Schmitt, "Meine Beziehungen zu Dr. Heß," 17. Aug. 1949, FHA, NL 1/20.

[259] Heß an August von Finck, 4. Dez. 1944, FHA, NL 3/4.

Nevertheless, in September 1943, Heß used his housing situation to make a new effort to resign, informing von Finck that his country home had been sequestered for bombing victims and this was forcing him to make a decision between his Berlin and his country homes, since he could not expect to retain both under existing circumstances. He decided to return to Agnesdorf, which meant that his Berlin quarters would be sequestered for bombing victims. Under these circumstances, he needed to resign since he thought it improper to serve as general director from the safety of his estate while the other employees confronted air raids, but he was prepared to serve the concern in any other way the supervisory board might deem appropriate.[260] Once again, however, von Finck dissuaded Heß from this purpose and frustrated Schmitt's efforts to create a new succession.

Schmitt was probably correct in later surmising that Heß really found it hard to leave his position and stop being active, but what was truly remarkable was that Heß remained an asset to the concern during these years despite his fairly obvious hostility to the Nazi regime. He apparently refrained from using the Nazi salute, demonstrably did not sign his business correspondence with "Heil Hitler," and did not let his three children join the Hitler Youth. His youngest son was jailed while doing labor service in Belgium for making anti-Nazi remarks. As has also been shown in the case of Maximilian Eichbaum, he was known to protect Jews. Most serious, however, was that Heß had some close contacts to the Resistance and was apparently aware of the existence of a circle of officers planning to kill Hitler, although it is unclear if he knew the specifics of the July 20 plot. As he explained somewhat misleadingly after the war, "I drew the ultimate consequence when I joined with the men who over the years had continuously forged plans to bring down the entire Nazi structure with an act of force."[261] This suggests a participation in the movement for which there is no evidence. His chief contact with the Resistance was Count von Helldorf, the Police President of Berlin, certainly a dubious character but nevertheless someone who had decided to abandon the regime and support the plotters. Both were members of the Club of Berlin, and Heß claimed to have seen him almost daily before the events of July 20; Heß went on to point out that "[i]f Count Helldorf, who was an old National Socialist and committed all sorts of stupidities in connection with the Jewish question in the early years, totally changed during the war, if he turned from a Saul into a Paul, then that is something specially to be credited to myself."[262] This may have been taking too much credit, indeed. Helldorf was

---

[260] Heß an von Finck, 21. Sept. 1943, FHA, NL 1/20.

[261] "My attitude toward National Socialism" ("Meine Stellungnahme, die ich zum Nationalsozialismus eingenommen habe"), FHA, NL 3/6.

[262] Heß, "Meine politische Einstellung, in Sonderheit [sic] zum Nationalsozialismus," an die Kreisboden-Kommission Sangerhausen, Agnesdorf, 16. Dez. 1945, FHA, S 17.2/165. This was written in an effort to save his property from sequestration. It is curious that a slightly different version, composed for similar purposes in Berlin and dated Jan. 23, 1946, is less clear about Helldorf's conversion, stating simply that if Helldorf joined the conspiracy then it was to Heß's credit. See FHA, NL 3/6.

an old putschist, having participated in the Kapp putsch of 1920, the Munich putsch of 1923, and possibly the SA putschist plans in 1932, but by 1944 he felt unappreciated and neglected by the regime's leaders and dissatisfied with the war and its progress.[263] Hence, the extent of Helldorf's conversion and his motives remain unclear. There can be no question, however, that Heß knew him well, knew there was a conspiracy, and was thus guilty of a capital offense. He was in fact arrested shortly after Helldorf and questioned for hours by the Gestapo before being "temporarily" released, and it is probably true that, as Heß claimed to have learned later from a Gestapo official, that he was saved by Helldorf's refusal to implicate him in any way. Helldorf himself suffered a particularly cruel fate, being forced as a renegade Nazi to watch his compatriots slowly strangle after being hung on meat hooks before suffering the same fate himself.[264]

Heß's narrow escape initially was without consequence for his position at Allianz, but his engagement in the events of July 20 – which seems to have been limited to knowledge about the plot, the encouragement of Helldorf, and contact with some of the others involved – was soon to produce problems. Heß managed to procure a visa to travel to Switzerland for eight days on business in early September, but then had a heart attack a few days after his arrival and ended up in a Basle hospital. He sent a telegram to August von Finck that he was ill and that he hoped to return in about three weeks. This meant, however, that he had to miss an important meeting of the executive committee of the supervisory board in Munich on September 8. Von Finck, who had been informed of Heß's Gestapo interrogations by Heß himself, apparently thought that Heß was trying to flee the country; he took Schmitt aside before the meeting and told him that he was going to propose that the committee send Heß a telegram asking him to return to Germany immediately. Schmitt was alarmed at the suggested procedure, pointing out that such a telegram would be noted by the German border authorities and would produce misunderstandings. At that meeting, von Finck nevertheless proposed to those present – Kisskalt, Carl Goetz of Dresdner Bank, Schmitt, Hilgard, Goudefroy, and Schloeßmann – that the telegram be sent. Kisskalt made a compromise proposal that Heß submit a medical statement confirming his illness, whereupon Schmitt pointed out that he was going to Switzerland in a few days and could convey the message personally. As a result, the committee sent a simple message to Heß wishing him a speedy recovery and hoping that he would return soon.[265] Schmitt then saw Heß in Basel, and the latter confirmed his illness by sending a medical report back to von Finck and declared that he would return as soon as possible.

[263] This is the argument of Ted Harrison, " 'Alter Kämpfer' im Widerstand. Graf Helldorf, die NS-Bewegung und die Opposition gegen Hitler," *Vierteljahrshefte für Zeitgeschichte* 45 (1997), pp. 385–423.

[264] *Die Tagebücher von Joseph Goebbels, hrsg. von Elke Fröhlich, Teil II: Diktate 1941–1945*, Bd. 13: Juli–Sept. 1944, bearb. von Jana Richter (Munich, 1995), p. 245 (Eintrag vom 16.8.1944).

[265] Protokoll, 8. Sept. 1944, FHA, NL 1/14, and Schmitt, "Meine Beziehungen zu Dr. Heß," 17. Aug. 1949, FHA, NL 1/19.

This was the beginning of a great deal of nastiness and bad feeling between Heß and von Finck and eventually between Heß and his old friend Schmitt. Von Finck was annoyed at the manner in which Heß had communicated with him and worried about what might happen. Apparently, von Finck felt it important for the executive committee to cover itself in the event that Heß decided to stay in Switzerland and thus for those on the committee to demonstrate that they had taken action in case an investigation took place – since it clearly was odd for the general director of so large a concern as Allianz to be absent from so important a meeting.[266] However, when Heß heard from Schmitt about the discussion of his absence at the meeting, he was infuriated, pointing out in an angry letter to von Finck that, at the age of 64 and after 26 years of service to the company, he knew what his obligations were and did not need to be informed of them by a supervisory board. He was especially annoyed because it was von Finck, after all, who had persuaded him to stay on the job in the first place. On October 3, Heß then sent von Finck his electrocardiogram and a medical report attesting to the seriousness of his illness. Heß, who wished to impress on von Finck how much he was sacrificing for the concern by staying on under the existing circumstances, remarked that the worsening of his condition had much to do with his experiences during the last bombing attack on Allianz in Berlin. He then reported further on his condition on October 13. Although his doctor in Basel had urged him to rest and continue treatment, and although he had also contracted bronchitis, Heß decided to return home to their safety areas in Weimar and Erfurt and then go to a clinic in Bad Nauheim. By this time, the relationship with von Finck had become very troubled indeed. Von Finck was angry that Heß had been so critical in a letter – especially since it had been opened by the censors – and believed that such questions should be dealt with verbally rather than in writing. As for Heß, he felt deeply hurt that he had received an undeserved vote of no confidence. In fact, von Finck had come to the conclusion that Heß was a liability and, in a letter of November 21, used Heß's health as an excuse to declare that the supervisory board would not ask him to stay on for 1945. Heß, however, had no intention of letting himself be fired in this manner. In a response of December 4, he announced to von Finck that he would be happy to hear that he was now fully fit to return to work. He reminded von Finck that he had never taken advantage of his extraordinary offer to work half-time for the concern back in 1941 and also that, at their meeting in late 1942, they had solemnly shaken hands in agreement that Heß would stay on until the war ended.[267]

The exchanges between Heß and von Finck put Schmitt in a very difficult position. On the one hand, he felt that Heß had neither a legal nor a moral claim on his position for 1945, since his contract ran from year to year and his health made

---

[266] Von Finck an Dümmler, 10. Okt. 1947, FHA, NL 1/14.
[267] Heß an von Finck, 23. Sept. 1944, 3. und 13. Okt. 1944, von Finck an Heß, 14. Okt. 1944, Heß an von Finck, 27. Okt. 1944, von Finck an Heß, 21. Nov. 1944, Heß an von Finck, 4. Dec. 1944, FHA, NL 1/20.

it quite natural for von Finck (and other members of the personnel committee) to feel that a change was necessary. On the other hand, Schmitt was anxious to restore harmony and felt that this could best be done through personal meetings rather than through exchanges of letters and the misunderstandings they generated. Apparently, von Finck and Heß did meet in December, and the latter asked that he be allowed to make the announcement of his resignation at a meeting of the supervisory board. Such things were difficult to arrange in the first months of 1945, however. Von Finck hoped to hold a meeting of the executive committee of the supervisory board in February or March, but one could not be certain as to its feasibility. Heß, however, was as testy as ever, claiming that he above all wanted to continue to settle matters in person but also insisting that he had been unfairly treated and that von Finck had no right to make sudden use of his illness to let him go, especially since he was well aware that the illness was anything but new. This bickering by mail and Heß's increasing resentment – not only against von Finck but also against Schmitt – over the feeling that he was being undeservedly pushed out was bound to intensify in the absence of a genuine possibility to hold a meeting in which all the difficulties and problems could be aired. Schmitt not only thought Heß increasingly unreasonable but also seemed to be nursing bad feeling toward Heß for not consulting with him as much about Allianz matters as he would have liked. But there was no possibility of airing such issues, or of holding a supervisory board meeting, given the general problems of travel and also Schmitt's journey to Switzerland in March to assist Alzheimer with negotiations on the future relations between the two insurance industries and on the transfer problem. This was to be the situation until war's end.[268]

Although it is difficult to fathom all of Heß's emotions and motives, there is strong evidence that he did feel a high degree of moral and personal obligation to stay at the helm so long as no one else was there to do the job. As he told von Finck,

in one point we are in agreement, namely that just in these times a man in his best years should stand at the head of Allianz who would be possessed of robust health, the strongest nerves, and the greatest initiative. If the supervisory board has such a man, then I will cheerfully step down tomorrow. The entire question is less that of my person than of Allianz, for whose welfare and fate I feel morally obligated to care because of my entire course of life, and this also in the sense of our 50,000 co-workers, who have given me their unlimited confidence at all times.[269]

One of the persons who – while certainly not young – might have helped fill the breach was Hilgard, who had the good fortune to be laid up in bed owing to a nerve inflammation resulting from a fall on a icy staircase shortly before Christmas 1944 during a visit to Schmitt at Tiefenbrunn. He was thus compelled

[268] Von Finck an Heß, 22. Jan. 1945, Heß an von Finck, 30. Jan. 1945, ibid.; Heß an Schmitt, 30. Jan. 1945, Schmitt an Heß, 21. Feb. 1945, Goudefroy an Schmitt, 27. März 1945, Schmitt an von Finck, 21. März 1945, Schmitt an von Finck, 4. April 1945, FHA, NL 1/19.
[269] Heß an von Finck, 30. Jan. 1945, FHA, NL 1/20.

to be away from Berlin for the last months of the war and, as he later noted, was possibly thus spared the fate of the head of the Reich Group for Banking, Otto Christian Fischer, who was seized by the Russians and disappeared without a trace. Herzog sought to fill in for Hilgard during these months, but the Reich Group's effectiveness appears to have suffered rather badly at this time.[270] Whatever the case, business in Berlin was shutting down, and Heß's description of conditions at Allianz in a letter sent to Hilgard for the latter's 61st birthday at once describes the horrendous conditions under which it was functioning and attests further to Heß's motives for staying on:

Things are frightful at our Allianz. The last attack, during which I once again distinguished myself by my absence, once again caused all kinds of damage. The old damages to windows and doors could only be partially repaired before then, and now everything has gone to the devil again. There can be no thought of doing any real work. Everyone is going about in their winter coats, their collars turned upward, their hats on their heads, walking about in the bureaus without sitting down. Whatever one grasps is filled with dust and dirt. No heating, no water, no telephone, and added to it the most unbelievable transportation circumstances. Your proposal to leave Berlin with a staff was therefore certainly worthy of notice, but it is unfortunately not implementable because none of the men of whom you specially thought can leave Berlin anymore today. And where would one still be safe from destruction today in Germany? I travel back and forth between Berlin, Agnesdorf and Erfurt with my car. I cannot perform any really positive work today either. But it is also not necessary. It suffices that one is seen over and over again, so that the retinue does not appear without leadership since the board of management shrinks increasingly. At the moment only Goudefroy, Maiholzer, Müller and Eggerss are present.[271]

Employees continued to show up for work at Allianz in Berlin – albeit in decreasing numbers and under increasingly intolerable conditions – until April 21, 1945, when transportation for such purposes shut down and Berlin was declared a fortress.[272]

Although certainly not free of air raids, the situation of those working for Allianz and the Munich Re was less dramatic and frightening than in Berlin. Hilgard and Schmitt had homes in the countryside, and Schmitt's estate Tiefenbrunn became particularly important for meetings of the top echelon of the concerns. The last joint meeting of the directors of the two concerns, for example, took place at Tiefenbrunn on December 8, 1944.[273] Here also Schmitt conferred with his colleagues on planning for the future, and he drew in some of the more important branch directors who might have to assume responsibility in the event something happened to the top leadership. One of these was Director Walther Boehm, who succeeded Eggerss as liaison man between Schmitt and

---

[270] Hilgard, "Leben," FHA, NL 2/7, p. 135; Goudefroy an Schmitt, 27. März 1945, Schmitt an von Finck, 21. März 1945, FHA, NL 1/20.

[271] Heß an Hilgard, 1. März 1945, ibid.

[272] Maiholzer, "Die Berliner Allianz-Betriebe," pp. 96–7.

[273] FHA, S 17.2/73.

Göring before 1933; currently he was head of the Allianz branch for Saxony and Silesia and was headquartered in Dresden. The two men apparently discussed the military situation because, after returning home, Boehm wrote that – despite the seriousness of the situation – he continued to maintain his "confidence in a turn for the good" and cited a letter he had just read from Field Marshal Model that the Allies would be stopped at the German border. He also sent along portions of a letter from a general with whom he was acquainted who insisted that the Allies would be stopped once their armored vehicles began to experience the problems of being refueled as they advanced. Most important, however, was that "a people of 80 million with a fanatical will and belief cannot be driven off the face of the earth." As for the plotters of July 20, this general thought them too clever for their own good, arguing that their cleverness had destroyed their understanding of the need to subordinate themselves and put their confidence in the leadership. At their trial, he found their mental state and attitudes "not only frightening but nauseating." Boehm had obviously not learned much over the previous twelve years, and he undoubtedly was responding to Schmitt's open or veiled pessimism. Schmitt chose to thank Boehm for his letter and to remark that "your confidence and reports pleased me. After all the heavy sacrifices and fantastic accomplishments of our people, a victory of our arms would be no gift but rather something well earned."[274] It is hard to believe that Schmitt really believed this. The issue, after all, was not the sacrifices and accomplishments but rather the cause in which they had been made. Schmitt was definitely in no position to speak his mind about that cause in a letter, and certainly not to the likes of Boehm.

Furthermore, there is good evidence that Schmitt was sympathetic to the Resistance and had an unusually good understanding of the political problems involved, if not a very practical solution to them. Thus, sometime in 1943, he entertained Fritz Walter (an insurance executive) and Colonel Hans Otfried von Linstow. Schmitt knew they were both opponents of the regime and began to talk about the war and military situation. He feared that eliminating Hitler would feed another stab-in-the-back legend, turn Hitler into a hero, and place all the blame for the failures of the regime on his close associates. He tried to persuade von Linstow that the best solution would be to simply throw all the German forces against the East and then let the Allies conquer Germany from the West, impose unconditional surrender, and occupy the country. He hoped Linstow would persuade his fellow conspirators to pursue this course. Linstow, who was in the Paris headquarters, was arrested for his involvement and was executed on August 30, 1944, while Walter was placed in Moabit prison but then released.[275]

In fact, Schmitt was suspect to the Gestapo, and with good reason. It was not simply a matter of his efforts to release Pastor Martin Niemöller and his care for

[274] Boehm an Schmitt, 18. Sept. 1944, Schmitt an Boehm, 26. Sept. 1944, FHA, NL 1/12.
[275] Eidesstaatliche Erklärung Fritz Walter, 9. Nov. 1948, FHA, NL 1/104.

Niemöller's son. Schmitt and Alzheimer had turned the Munich Re into something of a haven for persons connected with the Resistance, specifically Ulrich von Hassell, Eduard Hamm (a former economics minister and head of the German chamber of commerce), and Franz Sperr (a diplomat who had been Bavarian envoy in Berlin until 1934). All three were arrested after July 20. Von Hassell and Sperr were executed at Plötzensee prison; Hamm committed suicide in his Gestapo cell. The Schmitts were on particularly intimate terms with Franz Sperr and his wife Traudl, and Schmitt later told her that he had turned to the chief miltary judge of the Luftwaffe, Eugen Schmidt, whom Schmitt knew to be sympathetic and who had important Jewish clients in civilian life, after their arrest – only to be told that nothing could be done and warned that he would be well advised to keep as much out of the picture as possible. Indeed, before their arrests, all three had cautioned Schmitt and Alzheimer against trying to do anything for those arrested in connection with July 20, Sperr having the sense that the regime was not only trying to eliminate those who were implicated but also persons who might become popular as politicians. In any case, Schmitt was very suspect to the regime. As he later learned, another close friend (Theodor Süss, a professor of insurance science at the University of Berlin) had been regularly interrogated by the Gestapo about Schmitt and appeared more suspect to the Gestapo than Heß or Kisskalt, especially because of his friendship with von Hassell.[276]

Thus, when Schmitt alluded to heavy sacrifices, he knew whereof he spoke. For Schmitt and his family, the war ended in the same kind of personal tragedy with which it had begun. The Schmitts' 20-year-old son Klaus was missing in action. Klaus had first served as an air intelligence officer, and Schmitt tried to use his connections with Göring's adjutant to keep him in that service and to have him stationed in Italy or on the Western front, rather than on the Eastern front. This, however, was not to be, and the last news the Schmitts received from him was a letter that arrived on February 23 from Koblenz. Schmitt and his wife hoped Klaus had been taken prisoner by the Americans, and it was only in late November 1945 that they learned Klaus had been killed. Initially they thought he had fallen in the Harz in April, but they then found out that he had taken a bullet in the chest and died instantly during the fighting in the Eifel on February 19, 1945, thus giving his young life – as Schmitt bitterly told his daughter and son-in-law – "for a cause that was so distant from him."[277]

---

[276] See the sworn testimony of Alzheimer, 16. Juli 1945; see also Schmitt an Traudl Sperr, 23. Juli 1946, FHA, NL 1/94, and Süss an Schmitt, 29. Nov. 1945, FHA, NL 1/13. For the connections among von Hassell, Sperr, and Hamm, see Gaertringen (ed.), *Hassell-Tagebücher,* pp. 98–9, 148. See also the report of the interrogation of Schmitt by Dr. Harry Philippi, 5. Juli 1946, AM, Spruchkammerakten Dr. Kurt Schmitt, Akten der Spruchkammer Starnberg, 1. Teil, Bl. 25, and Eugen Schmidt's testimony before the Spruchkammer Starnberg, Sept. 1947, ibid., 2. Teil, Bl. 278.

[277] Schmitt an Otto und Hildegard Pape, 20. und 28. Nov. 1945, FHA, NL 1/15; Schmitt an Gritzbach, 23. Jan. 1945, Herbert Becker an Schmitt, 26. Dez. 1945, as well as other relevant correspondence in FHA, NL 1/120.

9

Confronting the Past:
Denazification and Restitution

IT IS a mistake to claim, as had often been the case until recently, that Germans in general and German businessmen in particular did not "confront the National Socialist past" after World War II. The real problem is the manner in which they did so. Recent research on West German industry has shown that its leaders were preoccupied and – in cases where they were subjected to lengthy denazification proceedings or threats of socialization – even obsessed with the Nazi past and their role in it. They developed both personal and organized ways of trying to deal with that past that were personally bearable but that also permitted them to present a case to the outside world that at once legitimized the personal rehabilitation of those who were accused of working with the National Socialists and made the case for reconstruction of German industry along traditional lines.[1] As shall be demonstrated here, this was also true of the leaders of the insurance business and of the insurance industry itself.

Indeed, this confrontation with the Nazi period was an inescapable necessity for three reasons. First, business leaders were subject to denazification. If, in retrospect, the denazification appears to have been poorly conceived and inconsistently and inadequately implemented, it nevertheless required the filling out of lengthy and detailed questionnaires, liability to internment in some instances (as well as dismissal and blockage of accounts in many others), and subjection to legal proceedings that could lead to significant penalties if those appearing before the tribunals did not succeed in exonerating themselves. In the last analysis, the entire enterprise proved something of a monument to two American manias, questionnaires and letters of reference. The latter become known as the "Persilscheine" – attestations (named after a popular German laundry soap) that someone was not really a Nazi or had done good deeds during the Nazi period despite Party membership. Nevertheless, denazification generated a great deal of concern and a remarkable amount of information that deserves more attention

---

[1] See Jonathan Wiesen, *West German Industry and the Challenge of the Nazi Past* (Chapel Hill, 2001), and his "Overcoming Nazism: Big Business and the Politics of Memory," *Central European History* 29 (1996), pp. 201–26. More generally, see Robert G. Moeller, "War Stories: The Search for a Usable Past in the Federal Republic of Germany," *American Historical Review* 101 (1996), pp. 1008–48.

than it has received.[2] Second, the resurrection of the old economic order was anything but guaranteed. This became rapidly apparent in the Soviet zone of occupation, but the Western powers (especially the Americans) were also highly critical of German big business. There were powerful political currents in the Social Democratic Party – and also in what was to become the Christian Democratic Union – that were anxious to make major changes in the economic order. Thus, decartelization, deconcentration, and even socialization were very much on the table after Nazi Germany's military and political collapse.[3] Finally, there were the issues of *Wiedergutmachung* (restitution and compensation) to those who had been robbed, persecuted, physically exploited, and murdered under the National Socialist regime. The efforts to settle these issues inevitably involved the German business community, either directly or indirectly. This was the case because business leaders had been involved and often complicitous in the dismissal of its Jewish employees, the disposal or acquisition of Jewish assets, the expropriation of Jewish and non-Jewish assets in the occupied territories, and doing business connected with the use of forced and slave labor and sites of extermination. While these questions of *Wiedergutmachung* returned to haunt not only the German but also significant segments of the European and even American business world in the 1990s, the initial confrontation of Germany and its business community with these issues occurred during the occupation and first decade of the German Federal Republic.[4]

The resurrection of these questions at the end of the twentieth century is intelligible only against the background of the inadequacies, failures, and peculiarities of the postwar efforts, however substantial these efforts may have been in many respects. Undoubtedly, more time was needed to grasp the full magnitude of National Socialist criminality and the extent to which German society as a totality became implicated in it, and it is doubtful that fuller knowledge could have been either intellectually digestible or psychologically bearable at the time for the victors or the vanquished. What the practical consequences of such knowledge

---

[2] There is a substantial literature dealing with the American role in the denazification. See John Gimbel, *The American Occupation of Germany. Politics and the Military, 1945–1949* (Stanford, 1968), pp. 101–10, 158–74; Harold Zink, *The United States in Germany 1944–1945* (Princeton, 1957), pp. 150–65; Lutz Niethammer, *Die Mitläuferfabrik. Die Entnazifizierung am Beispiel Bayerns*, 2. Aufl. (Berlin & Bonn, 1982); Carolyn Eisenberg, *Drawing the Line. The American Decision to Divide Germany 1944–1949* (New York, 1996), pp. 36f., 118f., 122–38, 262f. For a good survey of the newer literature, see Cornelia Rauh-Kühne, "Die Entnazifizierung und die deutsche Gesellschaft," *Archiv für Sozialgeschichte* 35 (1995), pp. 35–70.

[3] Eisenberg, *Drawing the Line*, pp. 139–51; Volker Berghahn, *The Americanisation of West German Industry 1945–1973* (Cambridge, 1985), Ch. 1; Anthony J. Nicholls, *Freedom with Responsibility. The Social Market Economy in Germany 1918–1963* (Oxford, 1994), Chs. 5–8.

[4] Constantin Goschler, *Wiedergutmachung. Westdeutschland und die Verfolgten des Nationalsozialismus (1945–1954)* [Quellen und Darstellungen zur Zeitgeschichte, Bd. 34] (Munich, 1992), and Ludolf Herbst & Constantin Goschler (eds.), *Wiedergutmachung in der Bundesrepublik Deutschland* (Munich, 1989).

could or should have been is also unclear. As is well known, the management of *Wiedergutmachung* questions in the first decades after the war was very much affected by the problems of German and European reconstruction and the Cold War. From this perspective, the solutions found and the issues left unresolved at that time were virtually inevitable results of the historical conditions existing in the years immediately following the war. Nevertheless, the attitudes of German businessmen toward their obligations with respect to *Wiedergutmachung* were very much conditioned by their understanding of their role in the Third Reich as it found articulation during denazification. If there was a change in business consciousness in the 1990s when these issues came up again – and there is good evidence for such a change – then it is important to understand what the old consciousness was and how and why it might have been transformed. Allianz had left behind a substantial record of its efforts to cope with restitution issues in the years after the war, a matter of no small importance because Allianz was and is Germany's largest insurance concern. More recently, it has been at the forefront of the restitution discussion insofar as this has pertained to the insurance industry. Allianz, therefore, is significant as a case study of this protracted but interrupted history of a great German concern coming to terms with its National Socialist past.

SELF-EXCULPATION AND IMAGE RECONSTRUCTION

In trying to fathom the complex story of reconstruction and denazification at Allianz and in the German insurance business in general, it is important to recognize that the division of both Berlin and Germany into four zones of occupation created considerable opportunity for inconsistency and confusion. The discussion that follows makes no attempt to deal in any detail with denazification in the Soviet occupied areas and also does not pretend to present a comprehensive discussion of denazification in the West. Insofar as the Soviet area is concerned, the insurance business was socialized fairly rapidly; its leading personnel appear to have fled to the West, and the Soviets were not terribly interested in denazification in any case since they perceived the problem as one of changing the economic system itself. Indeed, they were quite casual about keeping on former Nazis in the economic sphere.[5] At the same time, no attempt is made here to provide a full account of the denazification of Allianz's employees, since the available records make such an effort pointless. What is provided here is a discussion of denazification of the leadership of the concern and of some available cases of denazification at the middle management level – insofar as existing records permit.

The problems of reconstruction and denazification were not only complicated by the division of Germany into four zones but were also compounded by other peculiarities of the occupation regime – for example, the initial division of the

---

[5] See Norman Naimark, *The Russians in Germany. A History of the Soviet Zone of Occupation, 1945–1949* (Cambridge, Mass., & London, 1995), esp. pp. 172, 191–2.

American zone into four military commands. Efforts to begin reconstructing a national business organization like Allianz, assuming it would even be possible, were something akin to flying blind, and the terrible transportation and travel conditions and the difficulties of communication in any form made matters much worse. The situation in Berlin was particularly messy because of the massive destruction of major Allianz buildings and their location in the Soviet zone. Also, the leading directors were absent from Berlin when the war ended. Heß was in South Germany, as was Hilgard, who had retired early in 1945 but whose formal retirement date was backdated to December 31, 1944. The ailing Schloeßmann, who had also retired at the beginning of 1945, was in the South as well and died on December 10, 1945. The postwar management in Berlin was thus initially in the hands of Directors Hans Goudefroy, Clemens Maiholzer, and Gerd Müller of Allianz Leben; Müller would eventually become Schloeßmann's successor. In addition to trying to get the Berlin offices functioning again, they also sought to maintain contact with Heß and with the various Allianz branches in the West, where some branches were able to open even earlier than in Berlin. Thus, the branch in Hamburg, which had closed May 3, opened again on May 7; the Frankfurt branch was allowed to reopen on May 11, albeit only in the open air since the building on the Taunusanlage was being used by the occupation authorities.[6]

Director Gerd Müller had already demonstrated considerable initiative at the Berlin offices following the defeat. He posted a sign on what was left of the Taubenstraße doorway advising the Allianz staff that they should meet on May 18 and see what to do next. Some 250 persons showed up on that date and set to work cleaning up, rescuing material and machines, and removing the dead bodies of seventeen soldiers who had died in the struggle for Berlin. Temporary permission to start up business in Berlin again was granted by the local authorities on May 22. The cleanup continued until July, and formal permission to conduct business was granted on October 20 by the financial section of the Berlin Magistracy. The first two months after the collapse had been particularly difficult because of the absence of the leading directors and the difficulty of making binding commitments. Also, Allianz employees were forced to do general clearing of rubble in the city itself by the authorities. Maiholzer complained that some of the other private insurance companies took advantage of Allianz's situation to compete with particular ferocity for customers in the much-reduced postwar Berlin insurance market. The situation in the Soviet sector led to an early decision to seek new headquarters in the West. By the end of August, a suitable building had been found in Charlottenburg, and the general headquarters moved to Jebenstraße 1–2 in October 1945, although the move of the entire Berlin operation was not completed until February 1946.

---

[6] This account is based on Maiholzer's valuable study of 1960, which is often based on accounts he had gathered from those involved in the reconstruction of Allianz in Berlin; see Maiholzer, "Die Berliner Allianz-Betriebe," Parts II and III, FHA.

The permission given by the mayor of Berlin-Friedrichstadt to reopen business in May 1945 was tied to the appointment of a committee of four shop stewards, three recommended by Allianz and one appointed for political reasons by the mayor. However, at least one of those appointed at the behest of Allianz also had a distinctly political flavor – namely, Max Scholber, the Social Democrat who had headed the factory council that was forcibly removed by the Nazis in 1933. In late July 1945, Scholber began attending the regular Tuesday meetings of the leading managers of the Allianz offices in Berlin as one of the representatives of the employees, and Goudefroy made a special point of welcoming him to this body. Scholber and his colleagues appear to have enjoyed the confidence of the employees as well, since they won the factory council elections held in March 1946. The three members originally recommended by Allianz received the greatest number of votes, with Scholber topping the list.[7]

This was, of course, hardly proof that the Allianz leadership or its personnel had been transformed into democrats overnight. Writing of these events as late as 1960, Maiholzer could not refrain from describing his first post-capitulation visit to Potsdam in February 1946 in a manner that suggested that he remained susceptible to the spell that certain events of 1933 must still have held for him. Thus, he was shocked by the condition of the Garrison Church and noted particularly the unprotected and miserable condition of the grave of the "Old Fritz across from which had been placed the seats of honor for Reich President von Hindenburg and the Reich Chancellor named by him in the midst of a forest of old venerable flags at the celebration of the seizure of power on March 21, 1933."[8] Apparently, Maiholzer found it impossible to let reflection about the connection between the unnamed Reich Chancellor, the Day of Potsdam, and the condition of the Garrison Church in 1946 interfere with such sentimental reminiscence. But a quick tour of Potsdam and his observations of the Russian generals and troops who ruled there rapidly brought him back to reality and "taught me anew to be satisfied with our conditions in the British zone of occupation in Berlin."

In any case, the more immediate goal after German capitulation was denazification, and here Maiholzer, who had never joined the Party,[9] was actively engaged in the process as it affected the Berlin branches of Allianz. The first steps taken toward this end were based on a general order by Marshal Georgij K. Zhukov of June 15, 1945, calling for the dismissal of all Nazis in Greater Berlin and for verbal agreements with the Russian authorities and the city agencies they had appointed as well as with the two relevant unions, the Association of Commercial and Bureau Employees and the Federation of Free German Trade Unions. The initial denazification measures of possibly tainted employees at Allianz were

---

[7] Ibid., pp. 126, 140–2, 151.
[8] Ibid., p. 148.
[9] See the letter of Maiholzer to the Bezirksbürgermeister des Verwaltungsbezirks Zehlendorf of July 6, 1945, Staatsarchiv Hamburg, 221-11, F 17350.

undertaken on July 15 together with a program of staff reduction of male and female employees hired during the war. Such reductions were necessary in order to make room for Allianz employees returning from the front, but they were used to eliminate former Nazi Party members in the process. Thus, of the 239 Allianz employees, 82 were put on leave without pay, and 31 were dismissed for purposes of denazification. At Allianz Leben, where there were 313 employees, 127 were put on leave without pay and 25 were dismissed as part of the denazification. Nevertheless, the ranks of both companies were rapidly refilled by returning soldiers, and denazification continued to be used as a mechanism to reduce staff in connection with the more systematic denazification program that developed in 1945–1946.[10]

The nature of that program was initially discussed on July 23, 1945, at one of the regular Tuesday meetings by Goudefroy, who had been travelling in West Germany. He reported on a U.S. military forces directive of July 7, 1945, that required persons in responsible positions to fill out a 131-item questionnaire designed to elicit as much information as possible about their political affiliations and attitudes (as well as their personal histories) during the previous twelve years. The directive also banned the employment of persons who had joined the NSDAP, the SA, and the SS before April 1, 1933. As interpreted by Maiholzer, the directive did not require the suspension of managing boards of normal insurance companies but only of reinsurance companies doing international business. It was clear, however, that the personnel policy of Allianz in Berlin had to take the directive into account even if laws in the American and other zones were not applicable to Berlin, just as laws in the Soviet zone of Germany were not applicable in Berlin. Denazification was in fact handled differently in the different zones, although the American model was the most important for the Western zones. On September 26, 1945, the military government in the American zone of Germany issued a new Law No. 8, which extended denazification to the entire economy, required the dismissal of all Party members from positions that involved more than ordinary labor, and made all enterprises liable for implementing the law. Lastly, a "Law for the Liberation from National Socialism and Militarism" issued for the American zone on March 5, 1946, set up five categories of persons: major offenders, offenders, lesser offenders, followers, and non-offenders or exonerated persons. The first three categories were subject to punishment: in the worst cases, imprisonment, confiscation of property, and prohibition from employment in responsible private or public positions; in other cases, fines. Persons in the second category, however, could be placed on probation. The burden of contesting placement in the first four categories fell on the individual, who might appeal the categorization to tribunals of Germans selected to deal with such cases.[11]

The anticipation that comparable legislation would soon come into effect in Berlin was realized on March 10, 1946, in the form of a Denazification Order of

---

[10] Maiholzer, "Die Berliner Allianz-Betriebe," pp. 163, 183–9, FHA.
[11] Zink, *United States in Germany*, pp. 162–3.

the Allied Control Council that required the dismissal of Party members insofar as their activity had been anything more than nominal. The types of activities that could make an employee liable to dismissal – such as violations of international law, mistreatment of foreign nationals in the areas occupied by Germany during the war, or accusations of having denounced opponents of the National Socialist regime – were in fact fairly substantial. In West Berlin as in West Germany, the accused had the right to appeal dismissal at a hearing.[12] As head of the Berlin Allianz offices, Maiholzer did not want the responsibility for deciding (along with one member of the employee group) on denazification appeals; he therefore secured Heß's permission to create a denazification commission composed of three representatives each from management and the employees to hear such cases. The commission held fifteen hearings between May 1946 and July 1949 and dealt with 60 cases. Such meetings could be summoned at the behest of the accused, management, the employees council, or a government agency in Berlin. Maiholzer participated in fourteen of the hearings, normally as chairman. The exception was on May 14, when Maiholzer's questionnaire and those of ten other Berlin managing board members – including that of Heß, who had never been a Party member – were discussed. No political reservations were expressed about any of them.[13]

The result of the 60 cases investigated by the commission was that 20 persons were dismissed or pensioned off, and in four cases the commission found that the individuals in question were genuine culprits. It would be a mistake, however, to think that these numbers tell the entire story (or even an accurate one) about the denazification problem in Berlin. On the one hand, many of those who knew they were vulnerable never asked for a hearing and simply gave up their jobs. On the other hand, in Maiholzer's view, many Allianz employees who appeared before government denazification commissions were unjustly charged and lost their positions because those commissions did not ask their employer (i.e., Allianz) about their behavior.[14]

It is to be noted that some of the major directors who had initially played an important role in postwar Berlin – Hans Goudefroy, Gerd Müller, Walther Mercker (who headed the Assets Division), and Werner Krause (who directed the Berlin branch) – did not come up for discussion in the Allianz commission. Goudefroy's case was not considered because he did not submit a questionnaire to this commission. He subsequently underwent denazification in Hamburg (where he directed the branch of Allianz) and was completely cleared, but he had already been permitted by authorities in Berlin-Zehlendorf to represent Heß on the basis of a variety of attestations by Maiholzer, members of the factory council, and other Allianz employees known to have opposed National Socialism. Heß wrote a strong letter on Goudefroy's behalf, pointing out that Goudefroy

[12] Maiholzer, "Die Berliner Allianz-Betriebe," pp. 204–9, FHA.
[13] Ibid., pp. 213–15.
[14] Ibid.

wanted to leave the Party in 1935 but was advised against it by Heß himself. As shown in Chapter 5, Goudefroy's account of his role in dealing with the insurance problems conncctcd with the Pogrom of November 1938 was, to say the least, a very skewed one, but there was no one around to challenge it.[15] Goudefroy was eventually to succeed Heß as general director in October 1948. Gerd Müller moved to Hannover and soon went to Stuttgart to assume the leadership of Allianz Leben in 1947. Although never a Party member, his activity as a military administrative councilor in France led to some inquiries, but he was also fully cleared.[16]

The case of Walther Mercker is interesting because he had been put on leave until his case could be clarified, which it had not been by the end of 1945 because the original certification given to him had to be supplied by another district office. Although it was anticipated that he would be adjudged as a person "not to be considered an NSDAP member," a decision was nonetheless made to keep him on leave "out of regard for the mood in the company." What this suggests is that there was considerable pressure from the employees to eliminate former Nazis and a tendency to be suspicious of premature exonerations. In the case of Mercker, the problem was eliminated (for Berlin, at least) by his transfer and the transfcr of his entire section to Hannover.[17]

Werner Krause's case is significant for rather different reasons. He had actually been dismissed on September 26 by the American military authorities for membership in the Party. Krause apparently knew what was coming and, after discussions with Erwin Weber (head of the employee representation at the branch), composed a lengthy letter describing his career. Krause, who had already reached retirement age, came from a well-to-do Berlin family with cultivated artistic and intellectual interests and had grown up in a milieu in which there was regular contact with Jewish artists and intellectuals. He found his originally intended career in the military too confining and, through the good offices of the Cologne banker Baron von Oppenheim, sought a position connected with horse racing (apparently one of his passions) or in commerce or industry; he became the general secretary of the Union-Klub of Berlin in 1919. In this capacity he later ran afoul of the Nazis because he was involved in disseminating an anti-Nazi brochure in Hoppegarten, the suburb of Berlin in which he lived, and in 1933 he found himself under pressure to leave his position. Hans Heß, who was head of the finance commission of the club, suggested that Krause resign voluntarily and take a position at Allianz. Thanks to his connections, he did splendidly as an insurance salesman and became head of the Berlin branch in 1940. This was a prominent position in the concern and the insurance business,

---

[15] See Chapter 5, p. 234.
[16] See the various letters of support, including that of Maiholzer and Scholber of July 6, 1945, and Heß of Aug. 6, 1945, Staatsarchiv Hamburg, 221-11, F 17350 (Dr. Hans Goudefroy). On Müller, see his Spruchkammerakte, Staatsarchiv Ludwigsburg, EL 902/20, AZ 3/11956.
[17] See Maiholzer, "Die Berliner Allianz-Betriebe," p. 199, FHA.

and the DAF pressured him to join the Party. He decided to join at this time, rather than run into trouble with the Party once again and possibly have the DAF (or President Amend of the RAA) insist on his dismissal on grounds of nonmembership and then dictate who should take his place. In his letter to Weber, Krause insisted that he joined in a purely formal sense, kept aloof from Party activities and demonstrations of support as much as possible, and also claimed contacts with members of the Resistance, especially State Secretary Erwin Planck, who kept him informed about the high military officers involved. Krause claimed that he knew of the July 20 plot over a week before it happened and that General Director Heß could confirm this. He also insisted that he stood up for a colleague married to a Jew who had been arrested for making what Krause described to the Gestapo as "incautious" remarks. This was found "interesting" by the Gestapo officials and was, of course, quite "incautious" of Krause.[18]

Krause's letter of testimony to Weber was remarkably detailed and precise, but also frank and blunt in recognizing that he was hardly alone in denying that he was really a Nazi while insisting he would have to be judged by his record. Convincing as his statement was, the most extraordinary supporting evidence Krause provided was that given by Günther Klein, who had directed the Warthegau branch in Posen. He and Krause had a great deal of social and business contact between 1940 and 1945, with Krause often Klein's hunting guest and the latter often visiting Krause's Berlin residence. They felt they could speak freely with one another in private and, as Klein reported:

We very often discussed political questions occasioned by the Polish evacuation in Posen in 1940, the persecution of the Jews in Litzmannstadt and later events. I was able to find complete agreement with Herr Krause in our views with respect to the condemnation of National Socialist methods, especially in the question of the Gestapo terror and the racial theories of the NSDAP.

Thus, "Herr Krause always expressed revulsion over the treatment of the Jews in general and especially in the former district of the Wartheland."[19] What makes this testimony notable is that Klein admitted that they both were aware of the crimes being committed in Poland. Indeed, the "later events" could only mean the Holocaust. This was not knowledge that Germans readily confessed to – either in August 1945 or later – and Klein could easily have rested with a recounting of Krause's good deeds in Berlin. It is rare evidence that at least a few civilians working in the East were revolted by the crimes being committed there. Whatever the case, Weber – writing on behalf of the employer representation at the Allianz – protested Krause's dismissal to the military commander in the district of Berlin-Schöneberg, pointing out that Krause was highly regarded by those who worked under him, had never behaved like a Nazi, and had indeed

---

[18] Krause an Weber, 17. Sept. 1945, FHA, S 17.13/163.
[19] Günther Klein, "Stellungnahme zu dem Antrag des Herrn Werner Krause ... zu seiner Zugehörigkeit zur NSDAP," 17. Aug. 1945, ibid.

been rather open about his distaste for the movement.[20] Apparently, the American military authorities had promised to review his case but had still not come up with a decision by the end of 1945. Allianz appeared very anxious to reemploy him and appealed to the anti-Fascist Committee in the community of Hoppegarten, where Krause lived, to consider his case as well. Ultimately, however, the matter was settled by a decision on Krause's part to retire.[21]

Berlin was in any case losing in importance and, as Goudefroy and Müller were to show, their future (and, indeed, that of Allianz) lay in the West. It was there rather than in Berlin that the most important denazification cases are to be found. To be sure, General Director Heß took personal charge of the central headquarters in Berlin and assumed authority over the various Berlin branches of the concern in February 1946, and Berlin remained the seat of the concern in a formal sense for the next few years. Berlin, however, had become an island inconveniently separated from the active reopened branches in the West. This was because its branches in the Soviet zone had been closed down and their assets taken over by public provincial insurance companies by the end of 1946. The East Berlin branches of Allianz continued to function until the currency reform of June 1948 and were then taken over as well. The actual business of Allianz in Berlin had thus been radically reduced, and the Berlin blockade that followed led to a formal decision to make Munich the seat of the concern in West Germany in 1949.

The Russian brand of "denazification" was ideologically based not on individual responsibility but on the proposition that capitalism was responsible for Nazism. It thus denied Allianz or the private insurance business any sort of future wherever possible. Within Berlin itself, the concern had to tread warily, as did the other private insurers, since both commercial and organizational activity on their part led to attacks from the Communist press charging that "Nazi organizations" were being revived by the "concerns" that allegedly stood behind them. For example, the effort to create a working community of private insurance companies in Berlin (under the leadership of Victoria, Gerling, and Allianz) was constantly attacked on such grounds.[22]

This did not mean, however, that the situation of the private insurance business in the ideologically more friendly West was an easy one, although it certainly was much more pleasant in the English than in the American zone. The Americans were particularly suspicious of German financial institutions, believing that the universal banks (with their combination of investment and commercial functions) and insurance companies – to whom they attributed a role in industrial finance comparable to that exercised in the United States – were an especially dangerous financial sector. The two were thus lumped together in this category, and special regulations were issued mandating suspension of leading persons in

[20] Weber an die Militärkommandantur, 26. Sept. 1945, ibid.
[21] Maiholzer, "Die Berliner Allianz-Betriebe," pp. 199–200, FHA.
[22] Ibid., pp. 148–50, 234–8, 264–82, FHA.

the larger concerns, immediate dismissal of certain categories (above all, Party members) among them, and the requirement that all company officials of rank fill out questionnaires. To be sure, the English and French dismissed many such persons as well. Nevertheless, the Americans tended to be quick to dismiss and slow to reinstate directors, and many more tribunal hearings were held in the American zone.[23] Even one so confident of exoneration (because of the strong support he was receiving) as Director Hans Parthier of Allianz Leben in Stuttgart faced over a year of uncertainty and unemployment. Dismissed in September 1945, he complained to a colleague in January 1946 that he still had not been reinstated,

despite the fact that I was only a nominal party member, that is so to speak, a follower because of my employment position .... In the American zone the leading persons are evaluated very strictly. Happily in my case a number of outstanding references have been assembled, also with regard to my political position and the company has petitioned for my reinstatement.[24]

Parthier was very experienced, and Allianz Leben needed his assistance badly. This was one of many instances in which denazification posed considerable difficulties in the reconstruction of the Allianz concern because it frequently prevented potential successors of the top leaders from taking immediate command. Another illustration was Alfred Haase, who was to become head of Frankfurter Versicherungs-AG in 1948 and head of the organization section in Munich in 1952, and to succeed Goudefroy as general director in 1962. In March 1947, at a time when Wiesbaden was being considered as a possible headquarters for Allianz (before the decision was finally made for Munich in 1949), Haase was slated to become head of the organization section. He was, however, undergoing denazification, although it seemed obvious that he would be fully exonerated since he had not been a Party member and had become an SA member only because his horseback riding association was asked to have its members join the SA Riding Association. Haase had served in the army from the beginning to the end of the war, when he became a prisoner of the Americans. He had excellent testimonials on his behalf, including one from the factory council and one from Allianz's former Jewish insurance agent Ludwig Pototzky, who was in London. Under these circumstances, Allianz petitioned for a speeding up of his case as

---

[23] See the manuscript, "Zur Entwicklung der Bayerische Versicherungsbank seit Kriegsausbruch 1. September 1939," FHA, S 17.13/177, pp. 8–9. The American requirements for the denazification in Württemberg-Baden were circulated by the Versicherungsausschuß für die amerikanische Zone in Württemberg-Baden, 26. Feb. 1946; this and related instructions are to be found in FHA, S 17.3/5. For the situation in Frankfurt, where the military authorities simply installed a Director Kettner to head the company, see the Niederschrift über die Abteilungsleitersitzung am 14. Mai 1945, FHA, S 17.18/124. For a comparison of the zones, see Zink, *United States in Germany*, pp. 15–167.

[24] Parthier an Hermann Hitzler, 7. Jan. 1946, HM, A0001-00056, Bd. 3; Parthier an Hitzler, 5. Okt. 1946, ibid., Bd. 6.

one of great importance to reconstruction of the concern. Apparently, however, it took until 1948 for the matter to be settled.[25]

As had been the case in Berlin, so in the West: denazification involved the middle management level and affected staffing. In Bavaria, which had the most insurance companies and personnel in the American zone, those subject to the law were screened at the company level while more important or complicated cases were reviewed by a screening committee for the Bavarian insurance business under the chairmanship of Director Georg Obermayer of Munich Re. The cases handled at the company level are interesting because of the light they shed on the more everyday circumstances that led to Party, SA, or SS membership among the less exalted (though by no means unimportant) members of the concern and also because they suggest how difficult was the task of establishing motives and meeting the confused goals of the denazification program. At Bayerische Versicherungsbank, no fewer than seventeen of the managerial personnel below the level of the managing board and its deputies had been dismissed in the summer of 1945, out of a total of 51 persons. Since three had retired, one had died, and one had not come back from the front, this meant that the dismissals had cut heavily into the company's officialdom.[26]

How complicated and laborious such denazification procedures could be is illustrated by the case of Michael Wispelsberger, who headed the fire insurance section of Bayerische Versicherungsbank. Wispelsberger was dismissed by the military government in July 1945 because of his Party membership. As he tried to explain in his effort to get reinstated, he had only joined the Party in 1938 (although his membership was backdated to 1937) and had done so because of his long-standing membership in the Munich Voluntary Fire Department, in whose development he had played a very important role and which he wanted to head in 1938 in order to ensure that it would not be given to an inexperienced Party person. Additionally, there had been constant agitation within the company emanating from new employees who had been brought into the company as part of the effort to reduce unemployment, and Wispelsberger felt joining was the only way to keep things under control and promote those who deserved promotion. There was no evidence of his ever having been a Party activist, although he had distinguished himself as a firefighter – though gaining distinction at one's work during the war was normally viewed as negative evidence by the occupation military government. In any case, he certainly was able to bring to bear strong support from his co-workers at Allianz, including a touching and probably spontaneous letter of support by a "non-Aryan" insurance adviser whose

---

[25] Schreiben Allianz an das Aufsichtsamt für Versicherung, Groß-Hessisches Finanzministerium, 26. März 1947; Aufsichtsamt an das Ministerium für politische Befreiung, 27. März 1947; Alfred Haase an die Spruchkammer Friedberg/Hessen, 24. März 1947, BAK, B 280/1707. On Pototzky, see Chapter 3, p. 135, and also pp. 504–5 in this chapter.

[26] See the lists in FHA, S 17.13/132. Five members of the managing board, including General Director Arendts, had also been dismissed.

job often involved doing things contrary to Wispelsberger's interests and who praised the latter for not, like so many others, taking advantage of the situation to eliminate a competitor. Finally, the management of Bayerische Versicherungs-bank was particularly anxious to get Wispelsberger back since the latter, himself 60 years old, had been replaced by a pensioner who could only remain for a lim-ited time and since younger replacements with the necessary expertise in the fire insurance branch were either sick or dead. Wispelsberger was reinstated with the approval of the American authorities in May 1946.[27]

The screening commission for the Bavarian insurance business (headed by Obermayer) usually dealt with higher-level cases, often referred to it by the in-dividual company screening committees, and was called on to judge not only the degree of activism of the suspects but also the motives of those who had joined the Party or other condemned organizations. He found the job quite ex-hausting, which is understandable since between February and the end of August 1946 they had to review some 399 cases and seriously consider 147. Final deci-sions were made in 84 cases; the remainder were referred to the tribunals. Out of every hundred cases, well over half could be classified as mere "followers." This does not mean that the commission was not diligent. At its May 14 meeting, for example, it could find no positive evidence on behalf of a health insurance ex-ecutive and deemed him "unworthy of professional employment." Similarly, it refused to overturn the classification of a Bayerische Versicherungsbank official because it had no positive evidence on his behalf. It did classify a second Bay-erische Versicherungsbank official as a follower who should be returned to his old position.[28]

More generally, denazification meant that some of the leading general di-rectors and directors of the Allianz concern and of Munich Re were summarily dismissed and faced investigation, hearings by tribunal, and potential penalties – among them Wilhelm Arendts at Bayerische Versicherungsbank, Alfred Wiede-mann in Frankfurt, Arno Eberhard from Allianz Leben in Stuttgart, Wilhelm Leicher from the Allianz branch in Stuttgart, and Karl Otto Meyer in Cologne. Finally, there were the cases at the very summit of the industry: Adolf Samwer, Alois Alzheimer, August von Finck, Eduard Hilgard, and Kurt Schmitt. Hence

---

[27] The relevant correspondence is to be found in FHA, S 17.13/140. Some other cases are to be found in FHA, S 17.13/133 and 138, although their ultimate disposition is unclear. Especially curious is the case of an insurance representative who had been a member of the SS between 1933 and 1935 and then married a non-Aryan woman in 1940, seemed to have enjoyed the protection of his military superiors, including General von Rundstedt, and ended up dismissed from the army as unworthy of service and returned to the company in 1942.

[28] See FHA, S 17.13/132 for the minutes of the meeting of Aug. 27, 1946, for the summary of ac-tivity; see the minutes of the May 14, 1946, meeting for the cases discussed. Another interesting case was that of General Director Tiedke's successor at Alte Leipziger, August Walz, who was re-instated because of a speech he gave appreciating Tiedke's services after taking over his job. See the minutes of Feb. 21, 1946, ibid.

the insurance leaders (with Allianz and Munich Re at the forefront) were forced, albeit certainly under more promising circumstances than in the East, to face a dual task. They had to exonerate themselves in denazification proceedings and also persuade the Western Allies that neither their enterprises nor the particular forms private capitalism had taken in Germany were responsible for Nazism and, indeed, to convince critics at home and abroad that German capitalism was antithetical to National Socialism. Ultimately the leaders of the German insurance business, and especially those coming from the Allianz and Munich Re concerns, were quite successful in these efforts. By studying their cases, one can gain some sense of the different ways in which Allianz leaders dealt with the Third Reich – or at least how they perceived their roles and actions.

There were, to be sure, rare individuals at the top of the German insurance business who could face neither the past nor the future, like Ernst Drumm, chairman of the supervisory board of Bayerische Rückversicherung AG. The major shareholder of this company was Swiss Re, and when one of the latter's directors visited Munich in July 1945, Drumm was in a foul mood, insisting that he was completely guiltless and knew nothing about the atrocities. He complained that the Swiss were leaving him in the lurch and found the lack of Swiss sympathy for the Germans an outrage. Drumm went on to insist that, if the Germans had the superiority in equipment enjoyed by the Americans, then the war would have ended differently. Indeed, he was not shy about saying that he wished that the Germans had won the war and, when reminded that this would have meant a continuation of the atrocities in the concentration camps, apparently did not think that a matter of consequence. His Swiss colleague felt differently and concluded that "despite his extraordinary intelligence, he continues to hold, without noticing it, the incomprehensible ideas of the Third Reich."[29] Nevertheless, Drumm had never been known as a Nazi and had tried to keep his Jewish General Director Simon Wertheimer until this became impossible in 1937.[30] Both his attitude and his end, therefore, came as something of a shock. In August, fearing imprisonment by the Allies in the wave of arrests of high-ranking executives then taking place, Drumm, who was 73 years old, committed suicide.

Drumm's ten-year-younger colleague in Munich, General Director Wilhelm Arendts of Bayerische Versicherungsbank, was obviously reaching the end of his career in any case and had spent most of the war in military service as a general staff officer with the rank of colonel. He had joined the Party in 1933, however, and was not only a plant leader of the Bayerische Versicherungsbank but also the treasurer of the Academy of German Law; he also held an appointed position in the DAF dealing with insurance. All this made him unacceptable to the American military government, which ordered his dismissal on August 4, 1945. The

[29] Vertraulicher Bericht, 1.–5. Juli 1945, SR, FA A7.3-03.
[30] Ausschuß Protokoll, 22. März 1937, SR; Ausschuß-Protokolle, Bd. XI, pp. 208–10; Ausschuß Protokoll, 24. Sept. 1945, SR; Ausschuß-Protokolle, Bd. XII, pp. 193f.

position was a crucial one because Bayerische Versicherungsbank was becoming a point of crystallization for the entire Allianz concern. The chief shareholders, Allianz and Munich Re, therefore acted rapidly and put Eberhard von Reininghaus, whose political credentials were satisfactory and whose person had indeed been protected by his position at Munich Re since 1938, into the leading director position at Bayerische Versicherungsbank. Von Reininghaus remained in this position until September 1946, when he returned to the rather leaderless Munich Re as chairman of the managing board, since both Schmitt and Alzheimer had been barred from service because of their denazification. Hans Dümmler then took over as chairman of the managing board of Bayerische Versicherungsbank.

Arendts, who intended to retire in any case, turned out to have much better political credentials than one would have thought. He was held in an American POW camp from September 7, 1945, to July 5, 1946, after which he began the process of trying to clear his name. Since he had held both a high position in the Bavarian business world and in the Army and since he belonged to a number of Nazi organizations aside from the Party, the public prosecutor placed him in category II as an offender. Arendts himself argued that he belonged in category V – that is, among the exonerated. In the Munich tribunal decision that finally came down on June 18, 1948, Arendts was both exonerated and praised for his role as a resister.[31] The tribunal accepted Arendts's explanation of his decision to join the Party. Although a member of the Bavarian People's Party before 1933 and a practicing Catholic, he had joined the Party for the sake of his company, which employed some 850 persons. He believed that "it was the obligation of all correct upstanding persons to join the Party in order to prevent the radical rowdies to run the government here." Having lived in Munich, he knew the kind of people running the Party but nevertheless "made the sacrifice," well knowing that he would be viewed as an enemy and that he was dealing with a particularly radical Nazi factory council. Arendts confessed to entertaining the hope that the Party might move in a constructive direction if it came into the "right hands," but he was rapidly disabused of this illusion. The tribunal also accepted Arendts's claim that his support of the regime in official speeches and in other activities was done for show. He was known to have protected Jews, half-Jews, and political opponents of the regime. The Nazi organization in Bayerische Versicherungsbank had formally complained to Gauleiter Adolf Wagner about Arendts's behavior in this respect and also about his Catholicism. All those who testified on his behalf were either known enemies of the regime or at least untainted. Given these facts, it was hard not to conclude that Arendts, his early illusions notwithstanding, was never a Nazi at heart and had used his power as general director to do what he could to mitigate Nazi abuses.

However, what really made the case for Arendts and saved him from being classified as a "follower" was that he was not simply aware of the Resistance

---

[31] The materials on Arendts's denazification are to be found in AM, Spruchkammerakten Wilhelm Arendts. See the lengthy final decision of June 18, 1948, with which the file begins.

but actually acted on its behalf once he went on active military duty in 1939. Arendts had planned a military career and was a staff officer in the First World War. He left the military after that war (because of lack of opportunity) but maintained his military connections, among them General Franz Halder, and served at a high rank when called up in 1939. Whereas Arendts only briefly mentioned his service in Poland, where he noted the dominating role of the Party but not his involvement with restructuring the insurance business there, he had a great deal to say about his service in France. This was with good reason, since he had been assigned to the headquarters in Paris, where he worked closely after the spring of 1942 with one of the chief conspirators, General Heinrich von Stülpnagel, and served as a liaison with other high-ranking officers willing to support or participate in a plot to overthrow Hitler. Stülpnagel was one of those convinced that Hitler had to be killed, and he informed Arendts rather precisely about the different attitudes of the military men with respect to taking action against the regime. Arendts thus also came to know who was not willing to participate in such a venture and who was willing to do so only after it succeeded, and the account he provided the tribunal is a remarkably precise and important source on this subject that deserves the attention of students of the Resistance and events of July 20. Stülpnagel also informed Arendts of the role to be played by the military staff in Paris in acting against the SS, Gestapo, and police in the event of an attempted assassination, and in September 1943 he assigned Arendts the task of keeping him informed about changes in the staff and the attitudes of persons newly assigned to it. Arendts's own role in the most crucial events was limited, however, by two factors that also probably saved his life: a bad heart, which compelled him to return to Germany for treatment in 1943, where he became involved in trying to recruit potential support in Bavaria (especially the popular Ritter von Epp, an old Nazi who was now having second thoughts); and then, after his return to duty, his reassignment to southern France, then under the command of General Johannes Blaskowitz, where Stülpnagel wanted him to assist if and when the plot succeeded. He thus "missed" the disastrous events of July 20 in Paris and, in the subsequent retreat of the German armies from the South, was able to prevent atrocities and undermine the scorched-earth tactics ordered in Berlin. Not only fellow German officers but also a French resistance officer were able to substantiate that he had saved the officer and his wife (along with eighteen French prisoners) from execution and had prevented the destruction of the Schneider Works in Le Creusot, one of France's greatest steelworks. Finally released from service in January 1945, Arendts was able to return to his position in Munich until he was arrested by the Americans.[32]

Arendts had obviously been in grave danger, and he was well aware of it. For this reason he had confided in two close friends from Munich Re, Kisskalt and

<hr />

[32] See his 15-page Niederschrift of March 28, 1948, in ibid. See also the statement on his behalf by Comte Bernard de Béarn of July 10, 1946, as well as letters of attestation by Generals Halder and Speidel and by the Bonn historian who had served in France, Max Braubach.

Director Walther Meuschel, so that they could explain the situation to his wife in case something happened to him. In addition to the aforementioned circumstances connected with his health and location on July 20, he attributed his good fortune to the destruction of incriminating evidence by the plotters in Paris, the self-interested dragging out of the army investigation in Paris, and the unenergetic handling of an investigation launched by the Munich Gestapo. Thus, given the impressive evidence in his favor and the repeated risks Arendts took, the tribunal in Munich felt justified in fully exonerating him. As the tribunal correctly pointed out, such full exonerations were rare, a quality that it chose to characterize as a demonstration of the "recognition of the new democratic state." In reality, the tribunals – thanks to the absurdities and contradictions of the denazification procedure – had turned into what one historian has called a "followers factory"[33] whereby the majority of those considered were more or less dumped into the least serious category of culprit, so that they were neither subject to significant penalty nor exonerated. The Arendts case, however, defied such homogenization, and from it the tribunal milked as much general significance as it could:

His collaboration in a decisive position in the preparations for the assassination also gives the outside world a picture of the difficulties of German life in the Hitler State, as it only can be judged by persons who were at this time in the midst of life in Germany as opponents [of the regime] and as soldiers. It is a refutation of German collective guilt and a demonstration that broad circles were active in trying to eliminate the regime at risk of their lives in order to prevent further shedding of blood and saving the honor of the German people and soldiers. If they did not succeed, this was not their fault.[34]

Although this may have put more freight on the Arendts case than was justifiable, the honoring of the men of July 20 was uncommon at this time and remained so for a number of years. From the perspective of this study, what is most exceptional is an aspect of Arendts's exoneration effort distinguishing it from that of his colleagues at Allianz and Munich Re. As devoted as he was to his work and his company, Arendts makes no mention whatever of his role or his desire to save the German insurance industry from the clutches of Schwede-Coburg and the publicly chartered or DAF companies. Rather, he described his acts of resistance in humane and political terms. Undoubtedly his religious engagement and the traditionalist sense of honor and responsibility played an important role in this attitude, but it reflected a markedly different self-understanding from that to be found in the other denazification cases now to be considered.

Needless to say, Arendts was a high-ranking officer with direct connection to many of the persons involved in the July 20 plot, and it can hardly be expected that other Allianz directors would have been in a position to compensate in the same way for their Party membership and public support of the regime and its works. This certainly was true of Arno Eberhard, the director of Allianz

---

[33] Niethammer, *Mitläuferfabrik*, Kap. 5.
[34] Decision of the Tribunal, June 18, 1948, AM, Spruchkammerakten Wilhelm Arendts.

Leben in Stuttgart, whom the tribunal there found to be a follower who was not really a convinced National Socialist or militarist. Apparently his speeches at plant assemblages were not considered true expressions of his convictions, and if the powerful testimony to his "Swabian" (and thus purportedly individualist and democratic) behavior is to be believed, then the speeches were of no account. Eberhard was able to provide a decent collection of attestations to the fact that he had given employment to known political opponents of the regime, Jews, and persons married to Jews, and the factory council confirmed that he did not support National Socialism. Apparently, he had also made rather impolitic comments in front of Party members opposing the war and criticizing the regime. He was placed in the follower category, fined 2,000 RM in October 1946, and charged for court costs.[35]

However, his explanations for applying in May 1933 for Party membership had certain peculiarities worth noting. On the one hand, he claimed that he was under great pressure from the company NSBO cell in Stuttgart, which warned that the directors should not be surprised if the movement took a radical turn if they did not join. Another consideration, according to Eberhard, was that the Stuttgart branch was constantly being threatened from Berlin with further centralization and losing its independent sales organization. The continued right of Stuttgart to have its own sales organization was finally confirmed in 1936, but Eberhard rather lamely asserted that this was the largest such organization in South Germany, that many jobs were at stake, and that joining the Party was viewed as giving the Stuttgart directors some leverage in appealing to political authorities if worse came to worst. On the other hand, it was precisely the central headquarters in Berlin to whom Eberhard attributed his decision to join the Party, a point reinforced by a letter of support from Schloeßmann on Eberhard's behalf.[36] Apparently, there had been much calling back and forth between the directors in Stuttgart and Berlin, as those in Stuttgart tried to figure out whether or not to join and what the directors in Berlin thought. According to Schloeßmann, who never joined the Party himself, the facts that Hindenburg had appointed Hitler chancellor and that Schmitt was contemplating becoming economics minister proved crucial in Eberhard's decision – along with the fact that Hitler received international recognition. Both Schloeßmann and Eberhard admitted that the directors in Berlin left the decision about joining the Party to individuals themselves, but Eberhard claimed in his statement for the tribunal that the Berlin directors suggested that one had to take appropriate account of the fact that Schmitt was taking over the RWM. According to Eberhard, the Berlin

---

[35] See Chapter 3, p. 113, for Eberhard's speeches. For the council statement of June 12, 1946, see the denazification proceedings held by the Stuttgart Tribunal, which handed down its judgment on Oct. 21, 1946, Staatsarchiv Ludwigsburg, EL 902/20, AZ 17/8068. Eberhard decided to retire for reasons of age.

[36] See Eberhard's "Gründe für meinen Beitritt zur Partei" and Schloeßmann an Eberhard, 8. Okt. 1945, ibid.

directors indicated that they were going to join the Party but then changed their minds without informing their colleagues in Stuttgart. The trouble with all this is that – while Schmitt and the Berlin offices certainly were advising the concern to take a positive attitude toward the regime – Schmitt himself was not asked by Göring to be economics minister until the end of June, yet Eberhard applied for membership in May. Amusingly, just as the blame for influencing directors to join the Party was attributed to Schmitt by Schloeßmann, so too was the increased criticism of the Party among Allianz directors, since Schmitt made them aware of his growing disaffection after assuming the post of economics minister. In the last analysis, the simplest explanation for Eberhard's joining the Party is that he got on the bandwagon for opportunistic reasons, along with a host of other businessmen, and certainly never was a Nazi by conviction. Apparently, he did contemplate leaving the Party later on and discussed the matter a number of times with Schloeßmann, but they both agreed, according to the latter, that staying in the Party was in the best interests of the company and also a way to prevent radical influences from gaining hold.

Compared to the painful efforts and gyrations of Eberhard in explaining his Party membership, the denazification of Wilhelm Leicher (the deputy director at Stuttgart since 1937) was a model of simplicity itself. He had joined the Party because, as he honestly admitted, he believed that one had to give the new political movement a chance to prove itself. Subsequently, he turned against the Party and could provide credible testimony that he had helped Jews and political opponents of the regime and had criticized the regime on various occasions. He was held to be a follower in July 1947, fined 1,000 RM, and went back to work. One has the impression that his denazification caused him disproportionate suffering, since he had been kept out of work since September 1945 and had considerable financial difficulties.[37]

The case of the head of the Cologne branch, Karl Otto Meyer, was another that, like many others, seemed to drag on – until 1948, in fact – although Meyer did not want to return to his old position because of his age and health and was quite content to be employed as an insurance representative. The denazification subcommittee of the Allianz branch in Cologne had already decided in December 1946 that employees would not understand Meyer's reappointment to a leading position but had no objection to his working as a representative. Their judgment of him was anything but flattering, which may have had something to do with the fact that he was known as a left-winger prior to 1933 and had then changed his political position. In their view, he was a "one hundred percent National Socialist." In contrast to the Eberhard case, Meyer's speeches as "plant leader" were taken seriously as aiding the National Socialist cause, although the committee did voice its doubts about the sincerity of his convictions at the time. In summary, according to the subcommittee, "it is questionable whether he was

[37] Spruchkammerakte Wilhelm Leicher, Staatsarchiv Ludwigsburg, E 902/20, AZ 6/14661.

a real convinced Nazi, and it is far more likely that the term 'time server' is on the mark in the case of M. In his case, one is dealing with one of the typical 'March fallen' who did not want to miss any advantages or wanted to 'be on the right side'."[38] At the same time, the subcommittee noted that Meyer had never put political pressure on non-Nazis, and Meyer himself was able to present an impressive array of testimonies to the help he gave to Jews and critics of the regime. The case was finally settled in 1948, when Meyer was put in the follower category. As a result, his assets were unblocked so that his bombed-out house could be restored. By this time he had reached 60, and General Director Heß instructed that Meyer's temporary pensioning since 1946 be made permanent and that his further services as a representative of Allianz be negotiated.[39]

Like Meyer, the Frankfurt branch head Alfred Wiedemann – who was generally regarded as one of the more formidable and important directors in the Allianz concern and, indeed, in the German insurance business in general – was characterized as a "time server." In his case, the phrase was used in the charge against him, which placed him in the offender category.[40] Wiedemann had joined the Party in May 1933, was a member of several other National Socialist organizations and of the Academy for German Law, and also held a variety of positions in regional economic and business organizations. In short, he was extremely prominent and was characterized as a "willing instrument of National Socialism, for whom every means was justified in order to have a good relationship with the NSDAP."

Wiedemann's lawyer strongly objected to these characterizations, especially the claim that he was a "time server," which his client considered an "insult." Wiedemann had a distinguished reputation in his field and did not need the Party to gain promotion, which most certainly was true, and his propriety during the Nazi period could be attested to by a variety of impeccable persons, among them Artur Lauinger (of the *Frankfurter Zeitung*), with whom Wiedemann maintained very close relations even though Lauinger was a Jew and under constant surveillance.[41] Wiedemann's goal all along was to have himself classified as a follower and, because of his age and health, he did not wish to return to a director position but rather to act as a consultant for the concern. He was in charge of the regional headquarters in Saxony and Silesia when he joined the Party in May 1933, and he did so in response to the general summons to join (coming from the Allianz headquarters in Berlin) and to the fact that some of the leading persons in the concern were taking this step. He would have had to join in any case if he wished to be a factory leader. Typically, he argued that he had never supported the Nazis but hoped that they would prove responsible.

---

38 Entnazifizierungs-Unterausschuß der Allianz an den Berufungsausschuß für Entnazifizierung des Stadtkreises Köln, 17. Dez. 1946, Nordrhein-Westfälisches Hauptstaatsarchiv, NW 1049/21108.
39 Mayer an Entnazifizierungs Hauptausschuß, 3. April 1948, ibid.
40 Klageschrift, 14. März 1947, HessHStA, Abt. 520-F, Nr. 248312 (Dr. Alfred Wiedemann).
41 See the letter of the law firm in question to the Großhessischer Staatsminister, April 1, 1947, ibid.

Whatever the case, his appointment to Frankfurt with the task of creating a single organization there in 1935 gave him a position of exceptional importance, and Wiedemann considered his Party membership not only a "service" to his concern but also to the entire German insurance business, which was threatened by the Party. Wiedemann claimed never to have believed in National Socialism and that his opposition took hold after the Röhm affair and increased when the war started. He credited himself with appointing non-Nazis to high positions in the company despite attacks from *Das Schwarze Korps* and insisted that he had no other motives in joining or staying in the Party than service to his profession.[42] Heß, who had been a friend of Wiedemann since their youth, came strongly to Wiedemann's defense, pointing out that they had both detested the Nazis and that he was initially very upset that Wiedemann had let others persuade him to join. He accepted Wiedemann's explanation, however, and believed his motives were honorable. Heß insisted that it was Wiedemann's talent and capability – not his membership in the Party – that were responsible for his promotion to the post in Frankfurt. Furthermore, according to Heß, Wiedemann had a close relationship with James Freudenburg and was certainly no anti-Semite. Heß also stated that he had informed Wiedemann about the plot against Hitler in 1944, claiming in a rather exaggerated way that he (Heß) was himself a participant in the plot. More convincingly, Heß argued that, given Wiedemann's prominent position, it would have been dangerous for him to leave the Party. It is hard not to conclude that Heß's defense of his old friend was somewhat embellished to make Wiedemann into a virtual resister.[43]

To be sure, Wiedemann was able to produce an impressive attestation to his rejection of anti-Semitism, revulsion at the November 1938 Pogrom, and assistance to opponents of the regime. The other side of the coin, however, was that it was precisely his prominence that made his example so important, and while the factory council in Frankfurt praised him for his being a model director – treating people equally without regard to their political position, and openly thanking James Freudenburg for his services – it also made a very telling comment about his political and personal performance: "In his being, Herr Dr. Wiedemann was no Nazi, even if externally in view of his position and the various honorary offices given him he became too obligated at public company rallies, from which he certainly should have abstained as a human being."[44] Thus, in the context of National Socialism, Wiedemann's ferocious professionalism became a vice rather than a virtue and came into conflict with his certainly strong ethical instincts. Although Wiedemann could clear himself of one of the charges levelled against him – firing persons who had been denounced for making anti-Nazi or antiwar comments – it was precisely his position that made it impossible for him

---

[42] Statement by Wiedemann, Sept. 25, 1946, ibid.
[43] Ibid.
[44] See the Betriebsrat statement, "Herr Dr. Wiedemann als Mensch in seinem Amt als Betriebsführer," 21. März 1946, ibid.

to avoid becoming implicated in serving the regime. In 1947, because of his "opportunistic attitude" and the fact that his turning away from National Socialism found no overt expression, he was placed in the category of "lesser offenders," obligated to pay 10,000 RM into the restitution funds plus court costs of 29,043 RM, and barred for two years from holding a high position in business, from performing work entailing responsibility or authority, and from working as a teacher, editor, writer, or radio commentator.[45] A year later, Wiedemann successfully asked for reduction of the two-year limitation on his activities and thus became eligible to act as a consultant for the Allianz concern.

In the case of Adolf Samwer, General Director of Karlsruher Leben, overweening ambition probably played a greater role than professionalism in explaining his behavior; this led him to formulate a lengthy and quite revealing self-defense. Known for his capacity and intelligence – but also for his cultivation of the Nazi bigwigs in Baden, his unscrupulous behavior as trustee for the Rhein und Mosel corporation, and the arrest of its former General Director André Mouchard – Samwer was not in very good standing with some of his colleagues. At the end of the war he had been almost immediately suspended from his position in Karlsruhe and expected to be dismissed, but in the meantime he had petitioned to be pensioned off because of his illness. The status of that request was uncertain, however, and Samwer was only 50 years old and anxious to return to the insurance business. This led him to turn to General Director Hermann Hitzler of Hamburg-Mannheimer, who assumed a position as leader of the insurance business in the English-controlled city. Samwer had heard that the British measures were "more reasonable" than those taken by the Americans in the South. He pointed out to Hitzler that

you know that I have done a great deal for the private insurance business and that it is just this work which I performed for the general good that brings me into the present difficulties. It is for these reasons that I believe also to be justified to turn in confidence to you, without wanting to be burdensome to you. One is today dependent on the understanding of leading colleagues if one does not want to be crushed.

Samwer had only joined the Party in 1936 (although his membership was backdated to May 1, 1933), and he claimed that Hitzler knew from their conversations that he was never a "convinced National Socialist."[46]

Whatever Hitzler may have known about Samwer's views, Samwer was anxious to provide him with as strong a case, and as much information, as possible; he thus appended an eighteen-page account of his career and another twelve-page explanation of his role as trustee of the Rhein und Mosel Company.[47] The

---

45 Spruch vom 6. Sept. 1947, ibid.
46 Samwer an Hitzler, 30. Aug. 1945, HM, A0001-00056, Bd. 2.
47 The two documents, "Ergänzende Mitteilungen" and "Aktennotiz: Meine Tätigkeit für die Rhein & Mosel Versicherungs-Gesellschaft-Straßburg. Niederschrift von Adolf Samwer," are appended to his letter to Hitzler, ibid., and are the basis of the discussion that follows.

first was composed to serve as an appendix to his questionnaire, which he had not yet actually filled out. The purpose of the second went unstated, but the obvious goal was to set down a self-defense for his actions in Alsace, either for his colleagues or in connection with the questionnaire. The main thrust of the first appendix was to insist that he was a businessman with a liberal commitment, like his father Karl Samwer, and had a similar commitment to private enterprise.[48] He was not a politician, had belonged to no political party, and had been a Rotarian for as long as that organization was not banned by the Nazis. When not engaged in his company's affairs, he was deeply involved in the struggle against the political instrumentalization of the publicly chartered companies; it could be demonstated that he was one of the chief opponents of Schwede-Coburg, Hans Goebbels, and Braß and that he provided some of the most important intellectual ammunition against the writings of Rath. What he defined as his idealistic engagement in this cause was well known to his friend and supporter Heß, whom he described as "a fanatic opponent of the Nazi regime." Although asked by the NSDAP district leader to join the Party in May 1933, and though he agreed to join because he liked the Party's anti-depression measures and the breaking of the "rigid" system of collective bargaining contracts, Samwer had refrained from pursuing the matter until 1936, when he found it politic to join and thus reduce his exposure to criticism. Insofar as his political attitudes were concerned, he boasted of helping out enemies of the regime – such as former SPD Landtag Deputy Alex Möller, who was a director of Karlsruher Leben (and would indeed replace Samwer and go on to a major career in the Federal Republic). He opposed the treatment of the Jews, and he claimed to have helped a number of them and to have found the Pogrom of November 1938 repugnant. Samwer constantly rejected appeals from the local authorities to give money to Julius Streicher's anti-Semitic and obscene *Der Stürmer*. Most interesting, however, is that Samwer is the only insurance director among those being considered who mentions the confiscation of Jewish property, which

I considered to be an injustice. If the Karlsruher could not place itself against government orders, I still tried to make difficulties in individual cases in carrying them out. I remember in this connection a mortgage case of 1945 in which the Reich tried to get us to renounce a personal debt liability so that the State could get hold of the property in question. I refused to do so.

What is significant about this remark is not that it reflects some extraordinary moment in the protection of Jewish assets. Rather, it supplies evidence that at least this insurance industry leader was prepared not only to comment on the issue but also to suggest that it was indeed possible to do something to undermine the process.

Although Samwer was willing to touch on the Jewish asset question, where he seemed to feel he had a clearer conscience, he studiously avoided any mention of

---

[48] See Chapter 4, p. 160.

his cultivation of Gauleiter Robert Wagner and Minister-President Walter Köhler in Baden, although this was widely known among his colleagues.[49] Samwer insisted that, insofar as he maintained contacts with the Party leadership in Baden, it was for the benefit of his company. At the same time, he willingly confessed to considerable cooperation with the social and educational programs of the DAF and was quite proud that it had designated Karlsruher a "model company." Indeed, his lengthy description of all the wonderful things done for his employees made it sound as if he were competing once again for DAF recognition. While Samwer had to admit to a positive attitude toward the "calm" brought by Germany's control of Europe from Norway to France, his wife was witness to his distress at the treatment of Czechoslovakia and the war against the Soviet Union, which he thought would lead to an "eastern Marne" – that is, a great offensive that would end in defeat, as had been the case in the First World War. He did admit to taking a more positive view of the regime prior to 1938, primarily because of the economic reconstruction he attributed to it. In sum, Samwer presented himself as an opponent of the persecution of the Jews and other designated opponents of National Socialism and as someone who cooperated with the regime only insofar as it promised economically positive results and promoted the well-being of Karlsruher and its employees. When turning to his role in the Rhein und Mosel affair and the arrest of Mouchard, however, Samwer claimed that he did all he could to benefit the company placed under his trusteeship and that Mouchard had presented him with forged documents claiming that Petain had confirmed his leadership of the company. Samwer argued that he had no choice but to report the situation to the authorities, and he noted that Mouchard was eventually released and held a high position in the Vichy regime without any opposition from himself.

There is no record of what Hitzler actually thought of all this self-defense, but he responded positively to Samwer as a person, pointing out that the insurance business needed active and energetic individuals while at the same time indicating that he could do nothing for him, since the British tended only to take care of their own subjects (except for persons coming from the Soviet zone) and rejected licensing persons from the American and French zones. It was indeed to be a long time before Samwer found a high position in the insurance business, although his colleagues at Allianz were trying to find a place for him at other companies. Thus, in August 1950, Allianz General Director Hans-Hermann Goudefroy was pessimistic about Samwer's chances. Ultimately, Samwer climbed back up the ladder in politics rather than in business, a rather surprising career for someone who claimed to be a businessman rather than a politician. He became a city councilman in Karlsruhe, a member of the Constitutional Parliamentary Assembly of Baden-Württemberg, and then a member of the Bundestag – first as a representative of the All-German Block/Refugee Party in 1953 and then as a

---

[49] See Chapter 8, pp. 337–8.

CDU/CSU deputy in 1955–1956. Unsurprisingly, he specialized in looking after the interests of the insurance industry. In 1957, with the help of Alzheimer, he became general director of the Deutsche Krankenversicherung AG in Cologne, Germany's largest private health insurance company. He died in an automobile accident in September 1958. Significantly, he viewed his appointment, which was intended to be transitional in any case because of his political career, as "rehabilitation" and was very grateful for it.[50]

Samwer undoubtedly did have some of the requisite qualities for replacing Hilgard, although his road back to the top levels of the insurance business appears to have been circuitous and limited. It suggests that, among leaders of the insurance business, there was a certain line in collaboration that was not to be crossed; Samwer had crossed it, and he had to work his way back into the good graces of his colleagues. A much sharper attitude was taken in the top echelons of Allianz toward Wilhelm Körner, a Party member before 1933, who assumed the position of deputy director of the machine insurance section of Allianz during the war. Körner seems to have been extremely proficient technically and a first-rate organizer, but he was also the National Socialist commissioner assigned to the direction of Allianz and regularly checked Heß's correspondence. When this last fact became known, Heß dismissed him from his executive position. He was utterly despised by the leading Allianz persons, especially Goudefroy, who would have nothing to do with him. In 1953, Munich Re hired him in order to build up their own machine reinsurance business abroad, but they had to assure Allianz that no contact or dealings between Allianz and Körner would be involved. Körner worked for Munich Re until 1964 and died in 1981.[51]

Hilgard, in contrast to Körner, was much admired for his loyalty and service to Allianz and the insurance industry. Nevertheless, Hilgard faced serious problems after the war. Although he had formally retired, Hilgard had played too prominent a role not to be called to account for his actions. Although he was later to find it somewhat discouraging that his retirement was announced by the management of Allianz without a word being said about his long years of service to the concern, his resignation may have proven very useful when the U.S. Army entered the Bavarian town of Feldkirchen and arrived at his estate of Irnberg on May 1. He was quite astonished to find that the American serving as translator (for the officers who came to his home) knew precisely who he was, and Hilgard thought the only thing that had saved him from immediate arrest was the information that he had already stepped down from the managing board of Allianz. Heß arrived at Irnberg a few days later, but the two men found it hard to fathom

---

[50] For Goudefroy's pessimism in 1950, when apparently an effort to place Samwer with Iduna-Germania was not working, see Müller an Heß, 9. Aug. 1950, FHA, B 1.3.1/27; for Samwer's subsequent employment, see Aktenvermerk Hitzler, Besprechung mit Herrn Samwer in Köln, 19. März 1957 and related correspondence, HM, E0001-00027, and the Nachruf in *Versicherungswirtschaft* 13 (1958), p. 651.

[51] Walther Meuschel, "Traumbuch," MR, D/6; FHA, AVK/53 (Wilhelm Körner).

what the future would bring, either for themselves or for Allianz. Their spirits seemed to pick up shortly afterward, however, as an effort was made to start up Allianz's business again in Bavaria at Bayerische Versicherungsbank, which had escaped the worst of the bombing, and they were soon joined by Schloeßmann with whom they discussed the problems of Allianz Leben.[52] Hilgard's engagement can be interpreted as a reflection of his loyalty to the concern and also the reasonable expectation that he would be given a position on the supervisory board if circumstances permitted. He believed in any case that the time had come for a new generation to take charge of the concern's boards of management.

He took a similar attitude with respect to reconstruction of insurance industry organizations. Travel and communication across Germany were, of course, quite difficult in the months following the war's end, and Hilgard was heartened by the news brought to him by the past and future executive director of the Association of Private Insurers (Edgar Gambke, who was effectively acting as a courier among the various large insurers) that organizational efforts were starting up again in Hamburg. Conditions for such activities appeared much better in the British occupation zone, where denazification was handled very pragmatically, and in late August Hilgard urged Hitzler to take charge, pointing out that "fundamentally, I am of the opinion that it is the youth – insofar as it is available and suitable – that must go to the front now ...." Hilgard certainly was glad to provide such assistance as he could, but, as he wrote Hitzler: "Everyone who knows the huge burden that has been upon my shoulders over the years will empathize with the fact that I do not have any more desire to step into the public limelight."[53] Hilgard urged that steps be taken in the direction of a preliminary organization and that a courier service be established to run between Hamburg, Cologne, Stuttgart, Frankfurt, and Munich so as to facilitate communication in the American and British zones. Hitzler did indeed help to create a preliminary organization and in September held a meeting among the insurers in Hamburg, but he continued to feel that Hilgard had the confidence of the insurance industry and should take a permanent chairmanship. However, as Hilgard explained in a moody letter of early November 1945, he felt bound to stay near his family because of the insecurity of his situation and also because every further activity on his part in the insurance field depended on the permission of the military authorities.[54] Indeed, Hilgard now entered the "gloomiest chapter" of his career, his denazification:

a time of the greatest personal disappointment and most painful renunciation. Shut out, indeed, thrust out of the circle for which I gave the best years of my life [and] still in the full possession of my mental and physical capacity, I had to stand idly by and observe how the severely injured house of Allianz was slowly brought back into order.[55]

---

[52] Hilgard, "Leben," FHA, NL 2/7, pp. 133–7.
[53] Hilgard an Hitzler, 25. Aug. 1945, HM, A0001-00056, Bd. 2.
[54] Hitzler an Hilgard, 8. Okt. 1945, Hilgard an Hitzler, 11. Nov. 1945, ibid., Bd. 3.
[55] Hilgard, "Leben," FHA, NL 2/7, p. 138.

Hilgard had first heard the term "denazification" from Baron Uexküll, who had visited him in Irnberg just after the capitulation and who, thanks to his connections, had already been at the American headquarters in Frankfurt, where he had stumbled upon the denazification office. Hilgard was deeply critical of the process – not only with respect to his own case but also more generally – and certainly many of his criticisms were well founded. Denazification varied from zone to zone, and in his view the American practice was especially problematic because it made Party membership the touchstone of whether or not to launch proceedings. It thereby overlooked the fact that some of the worst culprits were not Party members and operated in an excessively schematic way.[56] He was also highly critical of the staffing of the denazification tribunals, as exemplified in his own case by the first such tribunal to hear his case in Bad Aibling, whose chairman was subsequently arrested and sent to jail on moral charges, and by the prosecutor in the second tribunal in Rosenheim, who ended up in jail for embezzlement. In Hilgard's view, the presence of such "inferior material" as officers of the court made correct judgments – especially in cases like his – virtually impossible. That he had been classified as a major offender (i.e., placed in category I) undoubtedly reinforced such feelings, especially since he responded by asking to be placed in category V, that is, exonerated. Last but not least, he felt it improper that the tribunals could take up cases as the spirit moved them, so that one was not only kept on tenterhooks for a long time but, in his case, received a final judgment after the currency reform and thus was charged a fine in DM rather than RM.[57]

Hilgard's real animus, however, was for the case that had been made against him. He expressed his contempt in April 1946, when he wrote to General Director Hans Koenig of Schweizerische Rentenanstalt, asking if Koenig and other Swiss colleagues could bear witness on his behalf:

Things are going especially badly for me as you have perhaps already heard. I have, because I did battle for 12 long years with the Nazis and thereby risked my life and freedom more than once, been placed in the class of the especially guilty because of my leading economic position, and this is determining my prospects for the future.[58]

He continued to feel that way when, two years later, the tribunal classified him as a follower deserving of a significant financial penalty – despite the host of German and foreign (among them, Swiss) attestations to his anti-Nazi position and his struggle against the regime's threat to the insurance business as well as his efforts to treat his foreign colleagues decently in the occupied areas and his

---

[56] This was especially notorious in the case of military officers. Many actual war criminals in this category were not even Party members; see Niethammer, *Mitläuferfabrik,* esp. Ch. 5.

[57] Hilgard, "Leben," FHA, NL 2/7, pp. 138–40. See also the Klageschrift of Aug. 2, 1948, and Hilgard's response of Aug. 20, 1948, in FHA, NL 2/3.

[58] Hilgard an Generaldirektor H. Koenig, 5. April 1946, Nachlaß Heinrich Fehlmann, Privatbesitz.

alleged contribution to the Resistance through Jessen. Indeed, Hilgard's entire conception of what he had done between 1933 and 1945 was well summed up by his old ally in the Justice Ministry, Hans Thees, to whom he had offered a job at Allianz in 1942 if Thees found working in the increasingly Nazified ministry too difficult. Hilgard had urged him to stay on, however, just as he was staying on as head of the Reich Group – to prevent the worst. As Thees argued in his statement for the tribunal, "[t]he example of Hilgard is one of many that one had to carry on the fight against the Nazis not in submersion but rather in the lions' den."[59]

A major question in Hilgard's denazification, however, was whether or not he was one of the lions (albeit a tamer one) himself. It was none other than Schwede-Coburg who provided testimony against Hilgard along these lines, so that perhaps a more appropriate analogy would have been with the snake pit rather than the lions' den. Schwede-Coburg, like all the major figures involved in the insurance business, was interrogated by the American authorities in the summer of 1947 and was asked about the attitudes of Schmitt and Hilgard toward National Socialism. Schwede-Coburg's response was that Hilgard was just like Schmitt: "In economic questions, especially concerning insurance themes, we were often of different opinion; but insofar as the basic goals of National Socialism were concerned, Hilgard promoted these in a positive way." Originally, Schwede-Coburg said that "Hilgard promoted them with all his might," but then used the milder expression. Nevertheless, Schwede-Coburg flatly denied ever having denounced Hilgard to the Gestapo or SD:

According to my memory, he did not provide any reason for doing so, for Hilgard's position to the general political principles of the NSDAP was always positive. He emphasized this often enough when I on occasion was rather sharp with him in our disputes about insurance questions, when he always emphasized that he *also* was a good National Socialist even if he was of a different view on insurance questions.[60]

When Harald Mandt – who had worked closely with Hilgard in the Reich Group and who had become chairman of the presidium of the Association of the Insurance Business after the war – heard of this charge by Schwede-Coburg, he rallied to Hilgard's defense, insisting that Schwede-Coburg's claim was a "grotesque perversion of the truth"[61] and citing various examples of Hilgard's anti-Nazi position. A particularly strong attestation was provided by the Social Democratic

---

[59] Eidesstattliche Versicherung Hans Thees, 10. Juni 1946, FHA, NL 2/1, Anlage 9. Thees himself seems to have emerged politically unscathed from his service in the Justice Ministry, since he is to be found at a meeting of insurance supervisory officials in August 1948 as representative of the zone office for Hamburg, FHA, S 17.21/179.

[60] Verhör von Franz Schwede-Coburg, 24. Juni 1947, Amtsgericht Rosenheim, Spruchkammer Bad Aibling, Spruchkammerakten Eduard Hilgard.

[61] Eidesstattliche Erklärung Mandt, 14. Juli 1948, ibid.

general director of Karlsruher Lebensversicherung (and later Federal Minister of Finance) Alex Möller, who claimed to be a strong supporter of denazification but felt compelled to speak out in "the few cases, in which I could convince myself ... of the political cleanliness and compelling objective motives for the actions of a person ...."[62] In Möller's view, Hilgard had run the Reich Group in such a way as to preserve the private insurance business from the clutches of the Party and had managed through his skillful negotiating capacity to keep the holdings of the private insurance industry in Reich bonds down to a purportedly bearable level. He could only contain a politically powerful and ruthless character like Schwede-Coburg by letting the Reich Group appear as loyal as possible to the regime in an external sense. Möller praised him particularly for staying on in office at the behest of his colleagues despite all the miseries and difficulties of his job. In sum, Hilgard's show of support for the regime was pure tactics, and it was important not to allow appearance to be taken for reality in Hilgard's case.

It is difficult not to have the impression that Schwede-Coburg, whose potential for brutality and acts of revenge had become rather limited after 1945, was exercising his proclivities as best he could in responding to questions about Hilgard and Schmitt. Furthermore, Möller's was a particularly heavy-duty Persilschein, and the array of support Hilgard received on his behalf was impressive. At the same time, the minutes of the meeting in the Reich Air Ministry of November 12, 1938, gave Hilgard the appearance of having annoyed Göring and other Nazi leaders at the meeting, and his "Aha!" – in response to Göring's announcement that the money Hilgard was allegedly willing to pay to the Jews would instead go to the Finance Ministry – was interpreted in his favor. To this was added his support of Jessen, which in a sense linked the battle for private insurance with the larger cause of the Resistance.

Given these favorable factors, it is quite remarkable that the tribunal, however "inferior" the "material" of which it may have been composed in Hilgard's eyes, managed to produce so effective an affirmation of its basic lines of argument in supporting the judgment it handed down on October 28, 1948.[63] To begin with, the tribunal was sensitive to the fact that Hilgard's opposition to National Socialism was primarily grounded in differences with respect to political economy: "His struggle to maintain private insurance or industrial insurance in opposition to the nationalizing tendencies of the NSDAP runs like a red thread through all the statements of the witnesses." Certainly it was true that the socialization ideas of the NSDAP were really nothing more than a "Partyfication" of the insurance business, designed to give the Party control of insurance assets rather than to benefit the insured. It was not the business of the tribunal, however, to

---

[62] Alex Möller an den Vorsitzenden der Abwicklungsstelle der Spruchkammer Aibling bei der Spruchkammer Rosenheim, 25. Okt. 1948, ibid.

[63] A copy is to be found in ibid., as well as in FHA, NL 2/2. The quotations and discussions that follow come from it.

come to conclusions about the structure of the insurance business but rather to make a determination about Hilgard, who was manifestly successful in keeping the insurance business in private hands. Needless to say, this fight for the private insurance business in no way constituted a principled opposition to the regime itself.

The tribunal was prepared to give only limited credence to Schwede-Coburg's testimony and to accept the proposition that Hilgard was compelled to join the Party and demonstrate external loyalty. Nonetheless, his pro-regime and pro-Hitler speeches − even if, as he claimed, he did not write them himself − were statements for which he had to take responsibility and that did have an effect on those who heard them. While finding the testimony of Möller important, the most the tribunal would grant is that the speeches were made because of his position and were thus to be judged more mildly than would otherwise have been the case. Certainly Hilgard was no supporter of the brutal measures employed by the regime and its anti-Semitic policies. The favorable testimony of Scholber and others was accepted, as was evidence that Hilgard fought against putting any more insurance industry funds than was absolutely necessary into government bonds or into investment in war production, especially the Messerschmidt works. The tribunal refused, however, to treat the extra payment to Jessen as "an extraordinary anti-Fascist deed" and an act justifying Hilgard's exoneration. The payment was placed on the Allianz books, and the tribunal did not believe that even the National Socialist courts would have felt justified in charging Hilgard with supporting the July 20 plot on such a basis. Concerning Hilgard's behavior with respect to the Pogrom of November 9, 1938, the tribunal placed great weight on Hilgard's statement to Göring that the insurance industry wished to fulfill its obligations at the Air Ministry conference and also was impressed by Thees's testimony that Hilgard described the Pogrom as a public disturbance at a meeting in the Justice Ministry and thereby irritated the representatives of Göring and the Party. However, the tribunal members also took note of other information casually provided by Thees that between 80% and 85% of Germany's insurance business was private and only 15% was publicly chartered; they came to the conclusion that Hilgard was kept on by Göring as head of the Reich Group because of "the strong power of the private insurance industry." It thus seemed reasonable to conclude that

the defendant had to struggle against a certain circle of persons in the NSDAP. His struggle, however, was not absolutely against the totality of the National Socialist rule by force, even if he also was personally not a supporter .... If one is to form a just view of the defendant in his political attitude, then the tribunal must state that H., aside from the proclamations for which he takes responsibility, cannot be charged with a Nazi attitude. H. was not a typical Party person, but a man concerned solely with his professional and positional interests. He devoted himself fully to this work; he was an insurance expert and known as such and tirelessly active as a leader for these interests, especially the private insurance business .... He was a man of business and was not a supporter of a

National Socialist rule of force …. Hilgard had exclusively in an outstanding manner devoted himself to the interests of the private insurance business and fought against a 'Partyfication' of these institutions.

The tribunal thus found Hilgard to be a follower, fined him 1,000 DM, and ordered that he pay the costs of the proceedings. The latter were calculated on the basis of his estimated assets of 210,000 and so amounted to 11,500 DM.[64] Hilgard was extraordinarily angry about the decision. He considered the judgment unfair, but he found outrageous what was in effect a serious increase of his fine because the court costs had to be paid in the new currency. To make matters worse, his assets had been blocked so that the monies he had at Merck, Finck & Co. had depreciated and would be redeemed at the rate of 10 RM to 1 DM when he finally gained access to the accounts. Still, Hilgard had connections on which he could call. On the one hand, he could get a credit of 10,000 DM from Allianz. Naturally, he did not expect to pay it back, given that he had joined the Party and accepted the leadership of the Reich Group to aid the insurance business and Allianz. As it turned out, however, Allianz disappointed Hilgard and demanded every cent of the money back. On the other hand, it turned out that one of the state secretaries dealing with Hilgard's effort to have his court costs reduced was Camille Sachs, who was the son of a Jewish family in Würzburg who were neighbors of Hilgard and his wife when they were first married. Hilgard and Henry Sachs, Camille's father, had served in the army together, and Camille recognized the connection and helped to reduce the court costs to 3,001 DM. The alternative, as Sachs told Hilgard, was to reopen the case and try to be classified as "exonerated," but this was something for which Hilgard apparently had no stomach.[65] It is most unlikely, however, that the deplorable anti-Semitic argumentation employed by Hilgard and Goudefroy (in connection with Göring's demand for 20 million RM after the November Pogrom) was what stopped him. He had shed his speeches and writings of the past twelve years as if they were nothing more than distasteful and best forgotten by-products of his sacrifice for the German private insurance industry.

What really added insult to injury for Hilgard was that Georg Amend had also been classified as a follower by the tribunal in Munich but only had to pay 701 DM: a 200 DM fine and 501 DM in court costs.[66] Amend had presented himself as nothing more than an insurance official and expert who had always followed the laws and who "sharply condemned the crimes committed."[67]

---

[64] Hilgard, "Leben," FHA, NL 2/7, p. 140, claims that the amount was based on his peacetime income, but in his appeal to the Bayerisches Staatsministerium für Sonderaufgaben of Dec. 16, 1948, the amount stated is based on his net worth. See FHA, NL 2/12.

[65] Hilgard, "Leben," FHA, NL 2/7, pp. 143–5, and the documentation on the payment and Sachs's letter to Hilgard of Jan. 28, 1949, in FHA, NL 2/2.

[66] Hilgard thought Amend was fined only 50 DM. See his letter to the Bayerisches Staatsministerium für Sonderaufgaben, 16. Dez. 1948, ibid.

[67] See his questionnaire, AM, Spruchkammerakten Georg-Thomas Amend.

Amend, as it turned out, had not joined the Party until April 1933 and the SA until 1937. Hilgard may have been terribly exercised by the facts that Amend had worked for the Party treasurer for years, had won the Party Golden Badge of Honor (in 1943), would never have received the position as president of the RAA were it not for his Party connections, and had done everything in his power to squeeze money from the insurance business to support the war effort, but the reality was that there was very little left of Amend himself to squeeze. In 1948, when he returned home, he had spent almost three years in an internment camp, had a wife and two small children, had been bombed out, and had heart trouble.[68]

His experiences had not improved his character, however. On March 23, 1949, having found a job as an insurance mathematician and expert for the administrative division of the Bavarian Insurance Supervisory Authority, he wrote to Schmitt on stationery that not only sported his new titles but also presented himself as "President of the Reich Supervisory Office for Insurance, retired." Amend asked for an opportunity to see Schmitt – indeed, to visit him at Tiefenbrunn if possible – to tell him about his interrogation in the internment camp at Regensburg back in 1947. He claimed that his interrogators had tried as hard as possible to get him to denounce Schmitt, along with von Finck and Hilgard, for their Nazi connections. According to Amend, the Americans wanted Schmitt to "confirm" all kinds of "absurd combinations" as well as that the large growth of Allianz business – especially with Party organizations – after 1933 owed itself to Schmitt's connections with Göring and to the NSDAP treasurer Franz Xaver Schwarz. Amend assured Schmitt that he strongly contradicted such notions and "that such behavior would be beneath your dignity" and suggested that he might well have thereby done Allianz "a small service." Lastly, Amend also claimed that he had assured his skeptical interrogators that the Party was aware of Schmitt's anti-Nazi statements to Ambassador Dodd, as recorded in the latter's diary.[69]

But Amend was a liar. In his interrogation on July 7, 1947, Amend did indeed specifically attribute some of Allianz's contracts to Schmitt's connections with Hans Frank, Göring, and Schwarz. He also claimed that Schmitt had offered him the leadership of the Reich Group and a high position in the insurance business in 1940, which was absurd. Amend denied that he ever wanted to nationalize anything but hail and building insurance; he claimed that he had no differences with Schmitt on basic questions and that it was only Schwede-Coburg and Hans Goebbels who were lonely supporters of nationalization. Lastly, in complete contradiction to what he told Schmitt about the interrogation, Amend had denied ever hearing that Schmitt had made anti-Nazi comments to Dodd or knowing anything about the Dodd diaries.[70] There is no evidence that Schmitt ever answered Amend's 1949 letter or that he ever met him again to discuss what

---

[68] See his letter of Aug. 31, 1948, to the Spruchkammer München VIII, ibid.
[69] Amend an Schmitt, 23. März 1949, FHA, NL 1/17.
[70] Interrogation of Georg Amend, July 2, 1947, NA, RG 260, OMGUS, FINAD, 2/56/2.

was Amend's transparent effort to procure a job in the private insurance industry as a reward for his "services." It is also doubtful that Schmitt appreciated being written to by Amend as one "follower" to another "follower" who had also suffered the slings and arrows of an allegedly outrageous denazification.

Schmitt did indeed have a long, drawn-out denazification that lasted four years (between 1945 and 1949) and caused him great anguish before he was finally classified as a follower. He had been removed from all his positions and was not allowed to practice his profession beginning in the summer of 1945, and he was thus condemned to four years of professional idleness, which weighed heavily on him. Also, during most of this period, his assets were blocked except for a very limited allowance. While Schmitt could not pitifully claim anything comparable to Amend's three years of well-deserved internment, Schmitt had himself been interned twice for brief periods: from August 15 to September 1, 1945, in the internment camp at Moosburg, because he was in the category of those to be automatically arrested; and from November 11, 1946, to March 21, 1947, in the internment camp at Dachau. He was nearly arrested and interned again in connection with testimony he gave at the tribunal hearings on Hjalmar Schacht, but he managed to avoid it by putting up 50,000 RM in bail to guarantee that he would not flee. At the same time, he and his wife were quite fearful in 1947 – a year during which he, like Hilgard, underwent many American interrogations – that he would end up being tried in the so-called Wilhelmstraße successor trials at Nuremberg.[71]

The saga of Schmitt's denazification, however, was all played out in Bavaria, where he fought tooth and nail to be placed in the exonerated category after the public prosecutor charged him with being a major offender on June 27, 1946. His case was first heard by the tribunal in Starnberg, which – in a decision of September 17, 1947 – placed him in category III as a lesser offender and sentenced him to two years' probation, the loss of 15% of his assets, and an increase in the delivery requirements for agricultural products from his estate for two years. Schmitt contested the decision, and the appeals tribunal for Upper Bavaria rejected both the indictment of the public prosecutor and the decision of the Starnberg tribunal, declaring Schmitt to be in category V and thus exonerated on November 18, 1948. Schmitt was reported by General Director Hans Dümmler of Bayerische Versicherungsbank AG as having "absolutely beamed" at the news and "was especially happy to be able to hang up the house flag of Tiefenbrunn as an external sign of his 'seizure of power.'" Dümmler and his colleagues were also overjoyed that "again an Allianzer in the widest sense has, by all human measure, come out of the denazification machine."[72] The celebrations were premature,

---

[71] See the Spruch der Berufungskammer München, 27. Juni 1949, pp. 2–3 for the record of his incarcerations and hearings, AM, Spruchkammerakten Kurt Schmitt, Akten der Spruchkammer Starnberg, Teil 1. On his possible re-arrest, see Spruchkammer Stuttgart an Spurchkammer Starnberg, 20. März 1947 and related correspondence, ibid., Bl. 55–8. On his anxieties about being tried in Nuremberg, see Fritz Sarter an Schmitt, 24. Juli 1949, FHA, NL 1/17.

[72] Dümmler an Heß, 19. Nov. 1948, FHA, NL 3/7.

Kurt Schmitt and his lawyer, Oscar Maron, at the denazification tribunal in Starnberg, September 16, 1947.

however. On December 13, the general prosecutor formally protested the decision as being legally in error; the matter was then taken up by the supreme court of appeal, which rejected the ruling of the appeals tribunal exonerating Schmitt and on February 28, 1949, ordered a new hearing of the case. The appeals tribunal of Munich then heard the case and rendered its decision on June 27, 1949, declaring Schmitt a follower, fining him 1,500 DM, and ordering that he pay two thirds of the court costs (approximately 9,400 DM).

Schmitt, therefore, had almost succeeded in attaining full exoneration before ending up in the same category as a hard-boiled Nazi like Amend. This was, of course, testimony to the failure of the denazification program itself and the degree to which it had deteriorated by this time into a procedure that had lost its moral authority. This was well illustrated by Carl Goetz of Dresdner Bank, who wrote Schmitt to assure him about the overturning of his exoneration by telling him of a colleague who had recently written to him saying that "he feared being exonerated and was striving to be stamped a follower, since he probably has to go to South America soon, and there one is not much appreciated as one of the exonerated ...."[73] Nevertheless, Schmitt's near success in having himself totally exonerated was no mean achievement for a man who had considerable contact with Nazi leaders before they came to power, served as Reich Economics Minister, had worn his SS uniform on altogether too many occasions, maintained contact with the highest ranks of the Nazi leadership between 1933 and 1945, and remained one of the leading active figures in the German and European business world between 1935 and 1945.

Schmitt's achievement demonstrated the tenacity with which he fought to restore his honor, regain his position, and secure the control of his assets, which were blocked through most of this period. It was also bought at the price of constant preoccupation with his denazification between 1945 and 1949. His voluminous case, which includes not only the tribunal records but also the bulk of his personal papers, provides rich sources of information on his own self-understanding as well as that of the numerous persons – many of them quite important in their own right – who became involved in one way or another with Schmitt's case or corresponded with him about it. Although a full rendition of his case would be impossible here, certain aspects are highly relevant to this history and deserve consideration.

As in his dealings with the Nazis, so in his dealings with the denazification authorities: Schmitt oscillated between optimism about his persuasive powers and the rationality of his case and pessimism that he was faced with something totally incalculable. This is already evident in the way he dealt with his internment in Moosburg in the late summer of 1945. He had apparently been interned because of his rank as an SS Brigadeführer and placed in the civilian internment camp at Moosburg, although he had never been in the active service of the SS. The evidence on his treatment and the conditions of his confinement is rather contradictory. In an account he wrote for his own records on November 20, 1945,[74] he claimed that before being actually put in the camp he was able to speak to the two American officers in the camp administration and show them Ambassador Dodd's book with its positive remarks about himself. As a result, they interrogated him immediately and then lodged him in an administration building rather than the camp. He greatly appreciated this "honorable treatment," "since in this way I did not have to live together with the active Party people I had been avoiding for years, among them for example my own local group leader." He also thought the interrogation went very well and considered his interrogators very understanding, since one of them (a Lieutenant Levin) dismissed his honorary membership in the SS as something akin to being named to the Legion of Honor in France (!) and assured him that he had their complete confidence. The transcript of his interrogations was then sent on to

---

[73] Goetz an Schmitt, 3. März 1949, FHA, NL 1/17.
[74] Aktennote über meine Vernehmung, FHA, NL 1/94.

various American headquarters, including Frankfurt, after which he was personally brought to Bad Tölz on September 1 and was told he was a "free man." A
new round of interrogations began in late October and continued through early
December, and Schmitt was periodically reassured that things would be settled
soon.

There is a second, briefer account of Schmitt's incarceration in a report by
Director F. P. Zwicky of Swiss Re, who visited Schmitt on October 28. What
Schmitt told Zwicky about his confinement was not as "honorable" as Schmitt
described it in his personal records. Zwicky was told by Schmitt that he had
been placed in a barracks with SS and Gestapo people, had to sleep on the floor,
and received a very limited diet. Since he was worried about being arrested again
at the time of his interview with Zwicky and was pleading that his Swiss friends
write on his behalf, it is not impossible that Schmitt exaggerated the conditions
of his confinement to Zwicky in order to increase the sympathy of his Swiss colleagues. At the same time, there is good evidence that his actual release had
little to do with the good impression he supposedly created with the Americans or their alleged belief that honorary SS membership was like being in the
Legion of Honor. While it is not impossible that they did believe this and were
extremely stupid, it is far more likely that they were using a shrewd interrogation technique: there was nothing more apt to bring out Schmitt's effusiveness
than to tell him that he had done nothing wrong and that one had complete
confidence in him. The evidence indicates that Schmitt was actually released at
the behest of his wife, who apparently mobilized Schmitt's doctor and lawyer.
The former claimed that Schmitt suffered from "severe angina pectoris and violent psychic excitements and depressions." The latter, Paul Schulze zur Wiesche,
a Düsseldorf lawyer with anti-Nazi credentials whom the American authorities
were employing in an advisory role, argued that Schmitt's SS position was purely
honorary, that the published diaries of U.S. Ambassador Dodd demonstrated
that Schmitt never really was a Nazi, and that persons of known anti-Nazi conviction like Pastor Martin Niemöller would attest that Schmitt was an opponent
of the late regime. Schmitt, in any case, could be expected to accept the conditions of house arrest and would certainly not try to flee. As a result of these
efforts, Schmitt was released. It continued to be a difficult time for Schmitt; in
addition to receiving the shattering news of his son Klaus's death in November
after months of uncertainty, he was in constant fear of being arrested again and
having all his assets confiscated.[75]

---

[75] See the medical certification of Dr. Theodor Struppler, Aug. 17, 1945, and the statements by Paul
Schulze zur Wiesche of Aug. 20, 1948. The U.S. chief public safety officer, Lt. Col. John W. Quirk,
declared that he was willing to support the petition on Aug. 20. See FHA, NL 1/87. The formal
order of release was only signed on Sept. 25, 1945; see AM, Spruchkammerakten Kurt Schmitt,
Akten der Spruchkammer Starnberg, Teil 1, Bl. 7. For Schmitt's conditions in Moosburg, see the
report by F. P. Zwicky of Swiss Re of Oct. 30, 1945, after having visited Schmitt two days before,
SR, FA A7.3-03. For Schmitt's reaction to the news of Klaus's death, see his correspondence with
his daughter and son-in-law Carl Otto Pape of Nov. 20 and 28, 1945, FHA, NL 1/15.

Schmitt's chief activity now was working on his self-defense and above all gathering Persilscheine. Thus, he asked Director Zwicky of Swiss Re, who visited him on October 28, to mobilize as many as possible of Schmitt's Swiss colleagues and friends to attest to the anti-Nazi sentiments he expressed during his visits to Switzerland and to his opposition to rearmament while economics minister. While there was some doubt about the value of such letters, Schmitt was convinced that "spontaneous" letters would help if they were detailed enough and used the correct language. When some Swiss colleagues visited him again at Tiefenbrunn in early May 1946, Schmitt cut a rather sad picture. He had visibly aged and was terribly concerned that he had only 300 RM a month at his disposal, had lost the services of the administrator of his estate, and was unable to secure any income from his farming activities. He urged that his Swiss friends write to him personally, saying that they heard things were going badly and that he faced imprisonment and confiscation of his assets because he had served as Reich Minister. Schmitt suggested that the letters express regret about these circumstances since he had been an opponent of National Socialism and then provide concrete examples of things he had said that were anti-Nazi. Finally, he suggested that the letters conclude by urging him not to despair since the American justice system functioned well and would certainly do what was right.[76]

Schmitt was clearly mastering what might be called the politics of denazification, as he had once mastered conducting business politics in the Nazi regime. His classification as a chief offender certainly made matters much more difficult. In Schmitt's case, it seemed to be viewed as an "all or nothing" situation. Thus, Director Georg Obermayer of Munich Re, who was then chairing the earlier discussed denazification committee for the Bavarian insurance business, pointed out to Schmitt in mid-July that the Americans were well aware that Schmitt was no Nazi but that he would nevertheless have to go before a tribunal which could sentence him to 10–20 years imprisonment at hard labor and take his assets. The tribunals, Obermayer informed his Swiss colleagues, were composed of lay persons from the Starnberg area, many of whom were communists or socialists and regarded all capitalists as criminals anyway.[77] Schmitt thus continued to want as many recommendations as possible. He remained optimistic, and Zwicky reported back to his Swiss colleagues that "assuming his being cleared by the German People's Court he is being considered by the Americans as an adviser for German political and economic questions."[78]

This alternative between imprisonment at hard labor and a consultancy for the Americans was bizarre indeed, and it reflected the peculiarities of the denazification system: on the basis of formal criteria, individuals were placed in a

---

[76] Report, probably by Zwicky, May 7, 1946; Nachlaß Heinrich Fehlmann, Privatbesitz.

[77] While there certainly were some communists and socialists on the tribunals, the real problem was the frequent absence of qualified persons. See Niethammer, *Mitläuferfabrik*, pp. 386–411.

[78] Report of July 18, 1945, SR, FA A7.3-03.

specific category by the public prosecutor and then invited to prove they were as innocent as they claimed. At the same time, the stark alternative between condemnation and exculpation arose logically from the peculiarities of Schmitt's personality and position. Schmitt suffered terribly from his enforced inactivity, and he yearned to get back to reconstructing the insurance business as well as to play a role in promoting a united Europe that would prevent a repetition of the wars that had torn the continent apart. The idea of a united Europe was very much in the air during and immediately after the war – used by Germans to camouflage their imperialism, by collaborationists to legitimize themselves, and by various wings of the Resistance to promote a happier world to come. Schmitt began to set down his own ideas on this subject in September 1945 after coming back from internment. He believed that economic unity was the only rational way to solve the problems of reconstruction and overcome the hatreds left by the war, although he was well aware that Germany's misdeeds had made reconciliation very difficult. Nevertheless, he was convinced that there were many who lived through those years who recognized that the measures of the occupation government were not the sole reality and that "the behavior of many upright persons in all countries also prepared the groundwork for mutual understanding and collaboration." In a passage remarkable for its combination of fantasy and disingenuousness, Schmitt painted his picture of the past four and a half years in the warmest possible hues:

As a farmer in Upper Bavaria I saw during all the years of the war in the immediate and more distant surroundings thousands of foreign works and prisoners of war who moved about without any surveillance, who as industrious and reliable workers stood behind the plow, who shared the table with the German peasants and, in their free time, lived in completely natural, often in friendly relationship with the population. Tears often flowed when they took leave of one another. I also saw economic cooperation with one another, not "collaboration," not egotistical quest for profit at the expense of an exploited, raped country, but rather sympathetic mutual cooperation of people from various countries who in the last analysis found themselves in the same want and oppression and who wanted to honorably help one another. I have seen celebrations where members of the most different countries and tongues respected one another and made friends. If we promote this spirit, then it will be to the spiritual and economic advantage of all the peoples of all of Europe.[79]

Manifestly this was nonsense. Germany was not Tiefenbrunn, where Schmitt did indeed treat the French POWs and the Ukranian and Polish foreign workers on his estate just as he did his German workers, celebrated Christmas with them, gave them presents, and gave speeches expressing his hope that the war would be over soon and they would be able to return to their homes.[80] It certainly is true

---

[79] "Vereinigte Staaten von Europa," Tiefenbrunn, 11. Sept. 1945, FHA, NL 1/77.
[80] See the sworn statement of his chauffeur, Karl Rollbühler, Nov. 20, 1946, AM, Spruchkammerakten Kurt Schmitt, Akten der Spruchkammer Starnberg, Teil 1, Bl. 119.

that foreign workers in agriculture were often better off than their counterparts in industry, primarily because of access to food, and that some decent relationships did develop; it was also most likely that foreign employees in the insurance companies with which Schmitt was associated were treated well. Nonetheless, the workers, on the land and in the city, constituted forced labor. They were not in Germany for its bucolic attractions or to play the role of "guest workers." Indeed, the war economy functioned only because of forced labor, and this was a reality known to all Germans with eyes to see. To suggest that the Germans and their prisoners were locked in a common fate was, to say the least, a profound distortion of reality. Similarly, Schmitt seemed oblivious to the fact that it was absurd to dignify business relations founded on political and military hegemony as "economic cooperation." Schmitt was nevertheless convinced – and remained so two years later – that he had long been an ardent supporter of a united Europe. As he told Artur Lauinger, who had returned from England to resume his career as an economic journalist and serve as editor of the insurance industry's journal *Versicherungswirtschaft*, "if you study and follow the details of the spirit and practice of the so-called large risk association, then its ideal fulfillment in the area of insurance took place in the middle of the war surrounded by force and terror."[81]

If Schmitt was able to maintain such notions, and believe that he had something to contribute to the politics of reconstruction, and endure denazification confidently despite his bouts of anxiety, then it was not only because of his private fantasies but also because of an infectious personal conviction and because persons of considerable substance reinforced his self-image and were willing to bear witness on his behalf. A good illustration of both the positive impression Schmitt could make and his own self-understanding is an interview conducted with him by Harry Philippi, the public prosecutor of the district of Starnberg, on July 5, 1946. Philippi reported that

I did not have the impression of a guilty or incriminated man. Herr Dr. Schmitt provides every possible information without even being asked and openly answers every question. I came away with a very respectable impression of Schmitt himself and of the atmosphere of his house [and] of his wife who suffered from his appointment as Reich Minister; [I] had the impression of an outspoken anti-National Socialist. Dr. Kurt Schmitt gave me the impression of being an idealist optimist, who in his entire career, as is so often the case, perhaps had so much fortune precisely because he did not always engage in sober judgment on the basis of the real facts. He does not deny his part in the collective responsibility of the German people, but answers my question, whether he feels himself in any way guilty, negatively and this with an unmistakable sense of honesty with himself, in that he points out the conditions under which he became Reich Minister, that he turned down later offers of appointment and that he personally did everything he could do that

---

[81] Schmitt an Lauinger, 27. Nov. 1947, NL 1/14. For Lauinger's role as editor and adviser to the insurance industry in the postwar years, see the important correspondence with Gerd Müller of Allianz Leben in FHA, B 1.3.1/49.

the National Socialists at the minimum did not allow and actually forbade someone in his position.[82]

This self-perception was massively reinforced by Schmitt's supporters and friends, of whom he had many at home and abroad, and the collection of Persilscheine in his file was quite exceptional. He had, of course, solicited a great many of them himself, especially from his Swiss colleagues like Fehlmann and Koenig. But he also seems to have left an impressive trail of good will abroad, even in the occupied areas: the head of the French Minerve Insurance Company, Jean Béraud-Villars, wrote on his behalf, and President Gabriel Chéneaux de Leyritz of the Vichy Supervisory Office for Insurance actually came to testify for him. It is easy enough to dismiss some of the more general testimonies of friends and neighbors or from colleagues within the same concerns. It was standard fare to present such documents and in no way remarkable that Alzheimer and Hilgard should write for Schmitt or that he should write for them or that a host of persons should praise Schmitt for not being a Nazi and for making anti-Nazi comments – which is not to belittle the fact that he did make such comments.[83] Most notable in this respect was the repeatedly mentioned concern – on the part of those who worked at Tiefenbrunn or were personally connected with Schmitt – that he would end up a victim of his own effusiveness owing to his tendency to criticize the regime rather openly. There also could be no question about the fact that Schmitt had helped and employed Jews, half-Jews, persons married to Jews, and political opponents of the regime and that some of this simply could not be hidden from the Nazis.

Most impressive, however, were the detailed letters of support and engagement from persons whose testimony could certainly not be treated casually. One of these was Otto Jeidels, former manager of Berliner Handels-Gesellschaft, who had made a second distinguished career for himself in the United States and was a vice-president of the Bank of America in San Francisco when the war ended. The friendship between Schmitt and Jeidels was sincere and deep, and Jeidels began to help Schmitt out even before they could be in direct contact by mail. Writing to an American major he knew on August 5, 1945, he declared that

[n]othing would be more welcome to me than to be requested by the American authorities to testify about, and on behalf of, a man who stands high in my appraisal of character and human qualities and who has tried his best to assist the better elements of the population in an unforgettably dismal period of my former country and my own life.[84]

Again, at the end of 1945 he sought to make contact with Schmitt through Director Zwicky to assure him that he would be happy to give information to the

---

[82] Philippi, Niederschrift, 3. Juli 1946, AM, Spruchkammerakten Kurt Schmitt, Akten der Spruchkammer Starnberg, Teil 1, Bl. 18.

[83] There is an excellent discussion of the Persilscheine in Niethammer, *Mitläuferfabrik*, pp. 613–17, although a great deal more work could be done with them.

[84] Auszug aus einem Brief von Jeidels an Major Stewart Chaffee, 5. Aug. 1945, FHA, NL 1/73.

American authorities and that he considered Schmitt's willingness to become economics minister in 1933 an "almost heroic experiment for entirely unselfish reasons."[85] It was only in May 1946 that U.S.–German mail service resumed and Schmitt and Jeidels were able to exchange letters and look forward to a time – never to come, because of Jeidels's sudden death on a trip while in Bürgenstock, Switzerland – when he and his wife would visit the Schmitts at Tiefenbrunn.[86] Nevertheless, Jeidels produced a sworn statement on Schmitt's behalf based on their long relationship in Germany in which he described Schmitt as "what we in America would call a liberal, or perhaps best expressed, a progressive representative of the bourgeois *Mittelstand*." He claimed that Schmitt had warned the supervisory board of Allianz, of which Jeidels had been a member, of the dangers of National Socialism in the early 1930s and praised him for trying to tame the movement by taking the risk of becoming economics minister. He was above all appreciative of Schmitt's open friendship with himself, a Jew, when minister and after he left office, and he described their common efforts to regulate the affairs of the AEG and Dessauer Gas and to keep Party control at arm's length. Indeed, Jeidels saw himself and Schmitt as engaged in a common struggle before Jeidels found he had to leave Germany, concluding that "[h]ere is a man before whom I take off my hat in thankfulness and high esteem and to whom I would extend the hand of friendship any time if fate gives me the opportunity."[87]

Jeidels seemed to have no knowledge of Schmitt's contacts with Göring before 1933, but he must have been well aware of Schmitt's public support of the regime afterward. Jeidels was obviously prepared to discount such evidences of Schmitt's engagement and give more credence to what Schmitt said in private and the way he behaved in his business affairs. Schmitt received similarly strong support from Maximilian Eichbaum, who had established himself in Johannesburg, South Africa, and with whom Schmitt resumed correspondence as soon as possible. Eichbaum, to be sure, had no desire to return to Germany after all that had happened, but he remembered the protection and support he received from Schmitt and Heß with gratitude and said so. Artur Lauinger, with whom Schmitt corresponded about insurance questions throughout this period, was especially effusive; though he did have a personal debt to Schmitt for employing his son at a company associated with Munich Re in Argentina, Lauinger not only wrote and testified on his behalf but also sent a letter to State Secretary Camille Sachs in October 1948 – praising Schmitt for risking the wrath of the Nazi radicals as minister and for openly sending a signed and dedicated copy of his portrait to Lauinger, a Jew and Free Mason. As Schmitt had stood behind him in his most difficult hour, so now Lauinger felt impelled to do the same – especially since, in his view, Germany needed economic leaders like Schmitt who (as he had already

---

[85] Auszug aus einem Schreiben von Otto Jeidels an F. P. Zwicky, 19. Dez. 1945, ibid.

[86] The letters are to be found in FHA, NL 1/13 and 14.

[87] Otto Jeidels, Erklärung betreffend Herrn Dr. Kurt Schmitt, 4. Sept. 1946, AM, Spruchkammerakten Kurt Schmitt, Akten der Spruchkammer Starnberg, Teil 1, Bl. 39–44.

demonstrated in the Favag affair) had the experience and courage to act effectively in a crisis.[88]

What is extraordinary about Schmitt's correspondence with these Jewish colleagues driven into exile is the extent to which they shared what seemed to be a set of common values and agreement with Schmitt about his innocence. They did not reproach Schmitt for anything he had said or done and reinforced Schmitt's self-perception, as described by the prosecutor Philippi. There was only one exception: the banker Hans Arnhold, who dug a bit deeper into Schmitt's past and present attitudes. The two men had business dealings with one another in the Weimar Republic, and Arnhold had asked Schmitt to become finance minister on Chancellor Heinrich Brüning's behalf in 1931. When Schmitt (in his endless quest for testimonials but probably also with a genuine desire to resume old contacts and relationships) heard that Arnhold was alive and active in business in New York City, he wrote to him in late January 1948 cautiously asking if Arnhold remembered him and cared to let him know how he was or preferred to "draw a line" under the past. Schmitt told Arnhold that he was happy to learn that he was still active. It reminded him of his parting words to Jeidels in 1937: "we will envy you all yet."[89] Schmitt had used this deplorable expression of self-pity in his correspondence with Jeidels and Eichbaum,[90] but it was apparently only Arnhold who recognized or chose to recognize the self-centeredness behind it. He respected Schmitt enough to write to him but not enough to spare him deserved reproaches, however politely and modestly they were rendered:

I say that I am made somewhat melancholy by the remembrance of you. Today we know how much better it perhaps would have been if you had responded with a "yes" instead of with the words "it is too early," when I was commissioned in 1931 to contact you as to whether you would accept the position of Reich Finance Minister. Perhaps Germany would have been spared the fearful years about which you spoke if you had placed yourself at the disposal of the government then instead of only doing so under the Nazi regime in 1934. I know that you did so in the best faith and most complete love of the Fatherland, but it must be said that you made a mistake. Do not take it ill if I write this and add to it that there is no one who has not made mistakes, including myself, and perhaps I would have also made some if I had not been one of the persecuted. I say that I was also astonished. You quote your words to Dr. Otto Jeidels "we will envy you all some day," and believe that this case is now at hand. If you mean by that the peace that Dr. Jeidels has found in his quiet grave on the Bürgenstock far "from all partisan hate and favor," then you are right. But if you mean the fate of those driven from Germany, then you have a completely false picture. You only hear of the very few who have managed to gain a foothold here or in other parts of the world and believe that you can generalize their fate. Believe me, most of them, strewn over the entire world, fight hard from dawn to dusk for

[88] Lauinger an Sachs, 31. Aug. 1948, FHA, NL 1/80; Erklärung Eichbaum, 1. Sept. 1946, FHA, NL 1/74.

[89] Schmitt an Arnhold, 22. Jan. 1948, FHA, NL 1/16. For a published version of this exchange, see Feldman, "Existenzkämpfe," p. 5.

[90] Arnhold an Jeidels, 23. Juli 1946, Schmitt an Eichbaum, 29. Aug. 1946, FHA, NL 1/13.

their existence, and one hears daily about new misery on the part of many of those who once happily lived in Germany. I know that things are very, very bad for countless numbers in Germany, and I try myself to help old friends there; but I believe, that things still are much worse for the largest portion of the refugees. Quite aside from [this is] the unending misery that has overtaken many through the cruel death that was the fate of many relations left behind in Europe. The one thing that the refugees have to be sure is their freedom of thought, and that is worth a great deal.[91]

Schmitt replied to Arnhold in a chastened manner, recognizing that there were indeed greater sufferings than his own and, at the same time, recounting his experiences in the Third Reich. He claimed that he did not want the ministry under Brüning because he preferred staying at his job and because of the hopeless political situation. He had taken Göring's offer of the RWM with the best of intentions and ended up totally frustrated. He claimed to appreciate Arnhold's criticism, concluding that "to err is human. What I wanted and the views I represented cannot be condemned by any American."[92] The thrust of his remarks, however, remained his own unhappy experiences with denazification since the end of the war and a self-defense based on all he had done to prevent the worst and help others.

But could Americans (or, more importantly though left unmentioned, millions of Germans silenced by the Nazis) really not "condemn" what Schmitt wanted in 1933–1934 – the views he expressed as he guided himself and his concern toward a positive attitude and proactive policy with Hitler's regime, the speeches he gave as Reich Economics Minister lauding the new regime? The prosecutors who charged Schmitt made a regular point of noting that he was the member of a Cabinet that produced all sorts of repressive and discriminatory legislation. He may not have been prepared to accept there was a "Jewish question" in the economy, but he certainly did not object to there being such a "question" in law, the arts, and public life. As has been shown, he believed it to exist then and continued to see the role of Jews in these areas as a problem even after 1945. This, to be sure, did not stop him from hiring a Jewish lawyer, Oscar Maron, who had been involved in insurance and whom Schmitt believed knew his record and views.[93] The prosecutors also pointed out that legislation enacted under his aegis for organization of the economy installed the "leadership principle" and assumed suppression of the unions. As those who prosecuted Schmitt argued, the regime needed the services of precisely persons like himself – persons who would provide technical expertise, mold the instruments of the dictatorship, and give the Nazi government an aura of respectability when it was most vulnerable internationally.

Schmitt was willing to admit that he made "mistakes," and he was also quite willing to deal with the question of "guilt" in general terms. This was evidenced when one of his most outspoken defenders (and a strong critic of the

[91] Arnhold an Schmitt, 25. März 1948, FHA, NL 1/16.
[92] Schmitt an Arnhold, 1. April 1948, ibid.
[93] Schmitt an Günther Quandt, 21. Nov. 1947, FHA, NL 1/14.

denazification program), Martin Niemöller, gave a speech at the University of Erlangen on January 23, 1946. Niemöller took the position that the entire German people, even those like himself who had been in concentration camps, were responsible for the misery that had befallen Germany and thus had to choose the path of individual inner repentance and return to Christian values; he was jeered by students and placards accusing him of being an enemy of the Germans. Some members of the government were outraged and actually wanted to shut down the university, although the university rector – Schmitt's close friend and ardent supporter, Professor Theodor Süss, who had very close connections with the Bavarian government and the American military authorities – believed the entire matter would blow over despite the outrage in some quarters.[94] Schmitt agreed that it was wrong to punish misguided young people who did not understand what Niemöller was trying to say and took the liberty of writing to Niemöller and telling him that he had been misunderstood. What Niemöller was arguing, according to Schmitt, was that they all "more or less at the cost of ... spiritual values made concessions and were opportunists."[95] It reminded him of their talk years before in his Berlin garden, where Niemöller admitted that prior to 1934 he had hoped for a "strong man" to rule Germany but then drew the consequences of what had happened and decided to show his colors and take a stand, as was necessary for a man of the cloth – in contrast to a businessman, "where one correctly can win time and existence through evasion and concessions." Niemöller was arguing, in Schmitt's view, that the entire people were guilty of indifference and self-concern, so that they were so preoccupied with their own fate that they were indifferent to what was happening to the victims of the regime or the areas occupied by Germany until the bombs began to fall on themselves. Finally, in Schmitt's view, in addition to the passivity of most people, Germany's lack of democratic values – in comparison to countries like Switzerland and England – made it vulnerable to Nazi intolerance.

All this was as edifying as it was self-serving in that it placed Niemöller and Schmitt together in the great community of the sinful that was to find its way back into the fold through individual self-redemption. As far as one can tell, Niemöller in no way criticized Schmitt's interpretation and indeed showed complete sympathy with Schmitt's denazification travails. In January 1948, he expressed the hope that Schmitt's problems would come to an end and praised the criticism being launched by the churches against the continued "so called denazification": "There must finally at long last be an end to this entire method and attitude, if self-laceration is not to have the last word."[96] The secular counterpart

---

[94] On the incident, see Niethammer, *Mitläuferfabrik,* pp. 319–20; for Süss's response to Schmitt's inquiry about the matter of Feb. 15, 1946, and their extended correspondence, see FHA, NL 1/13.
[95] Schmitt an Niemöller, 19. Feb. 1946, FHA, NL 1/77.
[96] Niemöller an Schmitt, 14. Jan. 1948, FHA, NL 1/16. On the role of the churches as critics of denazification, see Norbert Frei, *Vergangenheitspolitik. Die Anfänge der Bundesrepublik und die NS-Vergangenheit* (Munich, 1996), pp. 137–59.

to this was Schmitt's close friend Süss, who put him into contact with Americans potentially interested in Schmitt's ideas as well as Bavarian Government officials, among them Ludwig Erhard (then the economics minister of Bavaria and future economics minister of the German Federal Republic), and who gave him strategic advice as to when it was best to push his cause and when it was best to wait until Bavarian government attitudes were more propitious. Süss's testimonial for Schmitt had many of the qualities of a laudatio for an honorary doctorate, containing among other things the absurd suggestion that one could almost believe that "the ideal characteristics of Abraham Lincoln served him as a model."[97] Even more absurd, however, was Süss's exculpation of Schmitt and suggestion that he had been passive in the early Nazi period until summoned and had then sacrificed himself for the purpose of trying to make the situation more bearable.

Given such support of both a spiritual and secular nature, it is therefore little wonder that Schmitt's proclivity toward a selective memory was regularly reinforced. Nevertheless, that memory was periodically jolted – not only by the public prosecutor, off whose necessarily adversarial position Schmitt and his lawyers could bounce a spirited defense, and not only by Arnhold's gentle reminders and reflections, but by unfriendly interrogators who pointedly questioned Schmitt about the when and wherefore of Schmitt's early contacts with Göring, for example. Most disturbing, however, were those whom Schmitt thought were personal allies but who remembered things he did not. One of these was the Allianz director Walter Eggerss, who insisted that Schmitt's first contacts with Göring were in the fall of 1930 and that Schmitt initially was enthused about National Socialism. Schmitt's response to this was to suggest to their common interrogator Emil Lang that Eggerss was most definitely mistaken and was perhaps suffering from senility, a claim that Lang brought to Eggerss's unappreciative attention. When Schmitt tried contacting Eggerss in late 1948 (through the latter's close friend Director Ernst-Justus Ruperti) to see if he could not persuade Eggerss that he had first met Göring in 1932 and had never been an enthusiastic Nazi, Eggerss responded that it would be shameful for him not to tell the truth and that, if summoned to another hearing, he would tell the truth again. As we have shown, Eggerss had indeed told the truth.[98]

Cruelest, however, were the blows that came from Schmitt's friend of thirty years, Hans Heß. Certainly Heß, from his first-hand knowledge, had provided a defense of Schmitt's motives for becoming minister and had testified about Schmitt's misery in that position, but both Hilgard and Schmitt felt that Heß's testimony in Starnberg lacked the conviction and passion one would have

[97] Statement by Süss, Jan. 2, 1946, FHA, NL 1/77. Süss had once taught at Antioch College in Ohio and this may have provided the background for such extraordinary analogies with American history. See his extensive correspondence with Schmitt in FHA, NL 1/13 and 16.

[98] See Chapter 1, pp. 51–6. See also Ruperti to Schmitt, Oct. 23, 1948, and Schmitt to Ruperti, Oct. 26, 1948, FHA, NL 1/16.

expected.[99] The friendship was badly frayed by the end of the war and wrecked soon after. Heß had already found Schmitt's self-pity and self-preoccupation insufferable in 1946. The personal losses of the Schmitts had certainly been terrible, but Heß reminded Schmitt that there were millions of others who were worse off. He was even more distressed by his "mimosa-like sensitivity" that had reached the point where "you treat every word that does not correspond with your memory or your position today as a personal affront."[100] Three years later the friendship was on the rocks, since Heß had become convinced by conversations with August von Finck that it was Schmitt who had been working to force him to retire, that Schmitt knew Heß had taken his 1944 trip to Switzerland for political reasons but had nevertheless supported von Finck's summons to Heß to return, and that Schmitt also supported the nonrenewal of Heß's contract for 1945. When Heß sought to remind Schmitt of this fact in personal conversation, Schmitt claimed not to remember. Heß then suggested to Schmitt that there were altogether too many things that Schmitt could not remember. As Heß told Goudefroy (his successor as general director of Allianz) in October 1949:

On this occasion I expressed many a bitter word about his general memory weakness of the Nazi period, although I had for years let his protestations which contradicted the truth silently pass because I knew the distress of his soul and did not want to increase it through my contradictions. So, among other things, I was a witness to an incident which had taken place years ago in Tiefenbrunn, when his cousin Bohl – we were three alone in a room together – in the course of conversation in his quiet manner one time let fall the remark: "Na, Kurt, but at the beginning you also were enthused!" The blood rushed to Schmitt's face; he sprang up with a fiery red visage, hissed at his cousin, and immediately left the room. And that in the presence of the old Heß, who daily experienced all the things that happened and kept them in his memory in all their details! In this conversation [with Schmitt] I recalled into memory all the experiences relating to *his* enthusiasm, and he did not have the courage to contest them.[101]

Whatever the complexities of the mutually painful conflict between Heß and Schmitt over the events of 1944, Heß had torn away the veil of Schmitt's selective memory and obfuscation about his real culpability. Schmitt regularly told his correspondents that it was important never again to follow "false prophets," and he hardly could be faulted for this sound message. As usual with Schmitt, however, it was an evasion of the deeper issue. The problem was not simply that he had followed a false prophet but that he had supped – better said lunched – with the devil and had, for a considerable time, done so with a rather short spoon. If anything he was a false prophet – or at least false apostle – himself. Kurt Schmitt was, after all, the most prominent insurance executive in Germany and exercised immense authority and influence – not only over his enterprises but over the entire field and in public life more generally. His proactive policy of identification

---

[99] Hilgard, "Leben," FHA, NL 2/7, p. 146.
[100] Heß an Schmitt, 6. Nov. 1946, FHA, NL 1/20.
[101] Schmitt an Goudefroy, 29. Okt. 1949, FHA, NL 1/19.

and support for the National Socialist regime in the crucial early phase of its establishment was a genuine contribution to its broader acceptance. To pass this off as a "political mistake" is to belittle the significance of politics.[102] The business mistakes of some insurance leaders ruined their enterprises, and Schmitt rightly condemned them, but it is really a more serious matter to make mistakes that contribute to the ruining of one's country. From this perspective, and however great the flaws of the denazification program and the terrible personal losses suffered by Schmitt, it was anything but unjust that he and some others suffered the humiliation of being forced to defend their pasts, of being unable to practice their professions while doing so, and to experience their accounts being blocked and their assets frozen.

Whether a personal understanding of the responsibility and guilt emerged from the entire experience is another question, and here the success rate was undoubtedly quite low, if existent at all. However valid some of the charges of the prosecutors may have been, those subjected to denazification came out convinced they were innocent. Matters were not helped by the homogenized manner in which the cases were terminated – so that, by 1949–1950, Hilgard, Schmitt, Kisskalt, August von Finck, and Alois Alzheimer had all been classified as followers and were getting back (or trying to get back) into the supervisory or managing boards. Even Amend felt he could try for a better job. Whether one was a self-seeking opportunist like von Finck or a cosmopolitan internationalist who, like Alzheimer, had behaved quite decently in the occupied areas, it was time to get back to business.[103] Furthermore, there was a business to go back to, which was also something of an achievement since by this time one had averted not only the worst possibilities inherent in denazification but also the danger presented by those advocating decartelization and socialization. Here, too, the insurance industry leaders had been compelled to stake out a position that involved their understanding not only of their personal role but also the role of their organizations in the National Socialist period.

Of the two concerns, Allianz and Munich Re, the latter appeared to be the most endangered. Alzheimer's internment, which lasted from September 14, 1946, until March 13, 1947, and his interrogations, which continued into the following year, were scarcely concerned with Alzheimer's Party membership or political views and much more concerned with his travels for Munich Re and his leadership of the economic group for reinsurance. Ironically, the American authorities shared some of the suspicions of the Party radicals and German military that the

---

[102] On the "right to make a political mistake" as the foundation of the early Federal Republic's way of dealing with the past, see Frei, *Vergangenheitspolitik,* p. 405.

[103] For von Finck's denazification, see AM, Spruchkammerakten August von Finck. Von Finck's case was settled in 1949, and he benefitted from one of the repeated Christmas amnesties. For Alzheimer's final denazification, which apparently took place in Hannover, see von Reininghaus an Alzheimer, 9. Feb. 1948, MR, B 22/36.

reinsurance companies were really in the business of spying, shifting around foreign exchange, and cloaking assets. To the Americans, Munich Re and its Swiss connections were out to corner the world reinsurance market and drive out the Americans. The Association for the Coverage of Large Risks was viewed with particular suspicion, thus vastly exaggerating its importance and success. More generally, of course, there was something to be suspicious about since Munich Re and other German insurers had been remarkably successful in establishing a special position for themselves with respect to foreign exchange and were most certainly involved in cloaking operations, which Alzheimer readily admitted. At the same time, they were obviously seeking to replace the British on the continent. Within this context, however, Alzheimer could make a reasonable case that he and his concern had behaved in a decent and civilized manner in the occupied countries in the West – neither the Americans nor the Germans seemed much concerned about Poland – and received strong support in this claim, especially from the Dutch insurer J. W. Gratama. The reality was that the reinsurance business was an international one and, whenever possible, tried to conduct business as usual.[104]

The American suspicion of the Swiss insurers and their German connections was well grounded, but it missed the essential principle on which their relations were based – namely, that theirs was a long-term relationship of mutual interest that transcended the vagaries of politics. Alzheimer's involvement in making a final transfer of funds for the Reichsbank account used to pay debts to Swiss insurers operating in Germany in early 1945 illustrated the collusion between the two insurance businesses. The tenacious and, by 1953, successful struggle of Hans Koenig in getting the funds in the Reichsbank drawing account (Girokonto I) released to the Swiss insurers – despite that it violated the February 1945 agreement between Switzerland and the United States to block such funds and have them turned over to the Allies – demonstrated, in Koenig's eyes, that contractual obligation had rightly triumphed over political considerations. One could only wish that the same principle had been followed with respect to Jewish insurance policies taken out with the branches of Swiss companies operating in Germany.[105]

Needless to say, the Americans were most suspicious of the German reinsurers, whose cloaking activities were regarded as a means of keeping money abroad to supply the Nazi regime with more resources. Actually, their chief concern, especially as the loss of the war became obvious, was to keep money abroad to maintain or later resume business. In anticipation that German accounts

---

[104] Report by Zwicky of Swiss Re, May 7, 1946; Nachlaß Heinrich Fehlmann, Privatbesitz; interrogation of Alois Alzheimer, July 17, 1947, NA, RG 260, OMGUS, FINAD, 2/56/1; Gratama an das Hauptquartier der III. Amerikanischen Armee, Bad Tölz, 7. Jan. 1946, MR, D/2.

[105] See Chapter 6, pp. 266–7, as well as Hans Koenig's unpublished "Der Kampf um das Girokonto I" (1954), BAR, E 6100 (B) 1981/96, Bd. 18.

and assets might be blocked, and as Allied blockage of German payment to its creditors in Switzerland and Sweden became more effective, Munich Re sought to ensure the payment of obligations abroad by depositing shares that could be used for such payment with friendly companies. This practice was to bring the concern and some of its directors considerable grief in 1946 when it was accused of failing to accurately report shares of the Pilot Insurance Company in the United States, in which it once had an interest, as well as in the El Fénix Company in Argentina and Plus Ultra in Spain. Because they were intended for use in payment of obligations, they were so reported on the forms provided by the American military authorities. As a result, Munich Re was charged on June 23, 1946, with deliberately falsifying the report and violating occupation authority orders. At the eleven-day trial ending with the rendering of a guilty judgment (except with respect to Plus Ultra) on August 8, the concern was fined 4 million RM. The directors who had signed the report, Franz Buchetmann and Willy Reichert, were sentenced to imprisonment for two and a half years; three others – Gustav Mattfeld, Georg Paul, and Hans Oldenburg – were sentenced to one and a half years with one year off because all were over 60 and not in good health. Since Schmitt and Alzheimer had, in this case, the good fortune to have been suspended from their positions and thus were not directly involved, they could not be formally charged; nonetheless, they were accused of being co-responsible by establishing the practices under which the allegedly deliberate effort to mislead the American authorities was carried out. The court ordered that they never be allowed to work for Munich Re again.[106]

The case was most peculiar in many respects, and it had been pushed by the legal division of the military authorities in Berlin rather than in Bavaria. Those charged were part of a rump managing board left over after the top leadership of the concern had been suspended, and they all had been reinstated by the American military authorities in Bavaria. The conditions under which those responsible had to write their assets report were extremely difficult because the Munich Re offices were occupied by the military authorities and only short-term access had been given to the materials. Reichert had not actually written the assets report but only signed it because he happened to be available. Franz Buchetmann, who did write the report, had been employed as insurance commissioner for Bavaria to the great satisfaction of American authorities before he was reinstated at Munich Re. The concern probably made a mistake in not pleading guilty to an unintentional error and negotiating clemency, and it was certainly a mistake to hire only one lawyer to face an American team of lawyers. There is strong evidence, however, that the chief purpose of the American prosecution of this case was political. For example, it insisted that the fine not be paid by a bank transfer but rather in cash, with a camera crew present to film the opening up of suitcases and turning over the money transported by hapless Munich Re

---

[106] The voluminous collection of documents relating to the case is to be found in MR, B 22/35 and 36.

employees in suitcases. The decision was widely held to be an error both in the insurance world and by the British authorities, and it was an embarrassment to the authorities in Bavaria. In August 1947, the military government court confirmed the judgment against Munich Re but cancelled the ban on Alzheimer and Schmitt working for the concern. The Munich Re did contemplate pursuing the case for full exoneration and employing a neutral audit that would include Director Zwicky of Swiss Re on its behalf, and it had also petitioned American Military Governor General Lucius D. Clay in this regard, but by late 1948 it decided to drop the matter. As General Director von Reininghaus wrote to a colleague, one could never be sure of full exoneration, the currency reform had made the fine paid "significantly less interesting," and those with whom they did business regarded the entire matter as a mistake and, indeed, judged it as "a politically motivated act of force of an era of the occupation."[107]

This, indeed, was how the Munich Re case was viewed from the very beginning, and it was immediately linked to other efforts – especially American – to attack the large concerns. As one insurance executive wrote in September 1946 after hearing about the "tragedy" from von Reininghaus: "I include this whole affair among the measures which are being taken against IG-Farben, the steel works and the like .... The sad thing about it is that general legal insecurity continues to mark our postwar period."[108] Kisskalt took the same view, noting that his own arrest and interrogation was first connected with his presence on the supervisory board of the Dresdner Bank and that the occupation authorities had even arrested bank directors and supervisory board members who were not Party members in order to see if the banks could be charged with war crimes. Afterward, the interrogation shifted to the insurance concerns, and he feared the Americans had the intention of destroying Munich Re just as they intended to break up IG Farben, the universal banks, and "everything large."[109] Kisskalt thought that a great deal of the blame in the case of insurance could be placed at the doorstep of Professor Alfred Manes, now at the University of Indiana, who had written an article in April 1945 calling for the breakup of Germany's "reinsurance cartel."[110]

Whether Manes had a long-standing animus against Munich Re (as the fretful Kisskalt suggested) was less to the point than how Munich Re and Allianz, who would be most threatened in any decartelization or socialization program, would prepare themselves and present their case so that they could confront such threats as they arose. It was important, therefore, to establish a self-exculpation

---

[107] Von Reininghaus an Adolphe Müller, 10. Nov. 1948, MR, B 22/36. This volume also contains the review of the military government court of Aug. 8, 1947, and correspondence with the Bavarian authorities, including Ludwig Erhard, and with the Bavarian military authorities about the case.

[108] Weinreich of Isar Lebensversicherungs-AG to Carl Otto Pape of Frankfurter Versicherungs-AG, Sept. 16, 1946, FHA, B 2.3.1/30.

[109] Kisskalt an Schmitt, 16. Dez. 1945, 29. Jan. und 20. Feb. 1946, FHA, NL 1/13.

[110] Alfred Manes, "Germany's Reinsurance Cartel," *Free World* 9, no. 4 (April 1945), p. 44. A copy is to be found in FHA, NL1/157 along with a lengthy unpublished rejoinder.

parallel to that developed in the denazifications. As in the past, so now did Munich Re and Allianz lead the way in trying to find a common position for the insurance business. In the case of Munich Re, which had been banned from selling reinsurance outside Germany by the occupation authorities and could only reestablish its position if the ban were lifted, the crucial point to make was that the concern was not part and parcel of Nazi Germany's imperialism and had played an internationalist role during the war. Walther Meuschel first tried his hand at what he sarcastically called "a history of reinsurance during the last thousand years," in tribute to the "Thousand Year Reich" that had just gone to the dogs, and produced a detailed argument that the reinsurance business had at once behaved properly and even protected the occupied areas from the worst potential exploitation – such as might have occurred, for example, if the direct insurers had a free hand both to enter these markets and to set whatever rates they wished. When Meuschel sent his piece around, Hilgard took umbrage at the suggestion contained in the essay that, insofar as there had been resistance on the part of the insurance industry, it had come from the reinsurers. He thought the direct insurers deserved some credit, above all those who paid attention to the problem in the Reich Group – by which he meant, of course, himself.[111] A more serious challenge came from the insurance expert Ludwig Arps, who bluntly suggested that it was a mistake to argue that the takeovers in the occupied areas were all forced upon the reinsurance companies by the regime. When challenged by Meuschel to support this claim, Arps produced some seventeen cases of involuntary takeover, six of which involved the Munich Re. One of these was Wiener Allianz, and this was obviously not an acquisition forced upon either Allianz or Munich Re but rather one forced on the Italians and Austria. As should be obvious, however, the interest here was not historical investigation and analysis but a self-generated Persilschein that would legitimize the restoration of the reinsurance business to its old status. It is significant that the reinsurers were confident they could call on the services of Lauinger toward this end. If there was a "restoration," then Lauinger was part of it. Unlike Manes, he had come "home" and was, probably deservedly, a more potent voice.[112]

The most formidable self-exculpation for the industry was provided by Hans Dümmler of Bayerische Versicherungsbank in the spring of 1946. Filled with detail about the struggle against the publicly chartered companies, the National Socialist control of investments, and the effort to be civilized in the occupied countries, the manuscript was a sober defense of the role of the private insurance industry in the Third Reich. Its fundamental message was stated in the conclusion:

---

[111] For Meuschel's essay and Hilgard's criticism of May 4, 1948, see MR, D/6. Alzheimer made a similar criticism and Meuschel agreed to make the necessary revisions.

[112] See Arps an Meuschel, 5. Jan. 1948, Rückversicherer Besprechung, 6. Jan. 1948, Aktennote Meuschel, 5. Feb. 1948, Meuschel an Arps, 6. Feb. 1948, Aktennote Weinreich, 6. Feb. 1948, Notiz Münch, 23. Feb. 1948, MR, E 4/15.

The presentation shows that the German private insurance business at home and abroad, insofar as its influence reached, defended itself in hard battles against the Party and limited itself to a moderate self-limitation abroad that restricted itself to pure professional business activity. It had thereby fought to make the claim, after the fall of National Socialism, to be promoted rather than destroyed by the democracy, whose principle bases in private insurance cannot be denied. It would be an irony of fate if it would be just that democracy that wanted to realize the National Socialist that will destroy it.[113]

The intention was to send the manuscript to the occupation authorities in the hope that it would influence them against socialization, and so, like the Meuschel manuscript, it was circulated for critical comment. Quite interesting in this regard were the comments of Director Hans Knoll of Kölnische Hagel Versicherungsgesellschaft, who certainly found the entire effort informative and laudable but nevertheless could not but help feeling that the manuscript made a great effort to push certain persons going through denazification into the background and to engage in an "all too zealous vindication" of them. He found it noteworthy that the Allianz group was scarcely mentioned, and while other persons were identified with their companies, Schmitt was only identified as an "experienced expert" or someone who was an insurance man and Hilgard was only once mentioned in connection with Allianz but regularly identified with the Reich Group. The head of the life insurance group was never even mentioned by name, although it happened to be Schloeßmann of Allianz Leben. Knoll also thought that the case would appear too apologetic because the profits made after 1933 were not mentioned, and someone was bound to discover not only the figures but also the praise given to the regime for cutting the crime rate.[114]

Such exercises in memory, however, were rapidly to fade in importance as the Cold War undermined the interest in decartelization and socialization and as currency reform created a foundation for recovery.[115] Breaking up the insurance concerns never had the urgency it had in industry or in banking for the Allies, where it was not very successful either, and socialization was not really a serious threat except perhaps in Hesse, where there was a strong movement for socialization. This was one of the reasons that Allianz decided in 1949 to set up its headquarters in the more friendly climes of Bavaria.[116] By 1950, Munich Re was again allowed to do business abroad. There had, to be sure, been disappointments. The Swiss authorities insisted that Union Rück be genuinely separated from Munich Re, as demanded by the Allies, while Schweizer National

[113] Hans Dümmler, *Die deutsche Versicherungswirtschaft und der Nationalsozialismus* (1946), p. 40, AXA, Bestand Kölnische Hagel Versicherungs-AG, Akte "Die Deutsche Versicherungswirtschaft und der Nationalsozialismus."

[114] Knoll an Karl Haus, 26. April 1946, ibid.

[115] See Eisenberg, *Drawing the Line*, pp. 139–51, 374–8.

[116] On the moderate attitude toward insurance decartelization, see the memorandum of Walter Lichtenstein (chief financial institutions branch) of July 15, 1946, NA, RG 260, 390/46/1/01/box 27. On the motives for moving to Munich, see the Aktenvermerk Lubowski, 20. Jan. 1949, BAK, B 280/1707.

did not keep to the promises made to Allianz leaders and never returned into the latter's fold; this made for ugly relations, lawsuits, and a settlement finally mediated by the Dutch insurer J. W. Gratama.[117] On the whole, however, the future looked bright, and business picked up after the currency reform. Thus, Allianz and Munich Re had survived the Third Reich, survived the occupation, and even survived the internecine quarrels of their old leaders. In addition to the broken friendship of Heß and Schmitt, there was an effort by August von Finck to become chairman of the supervisory board of both concerns, an effort that Alzheimer and Goudefroy found inappropriate and that led to a nasty public battle over shares, which gave them unwanted publicity. Otherwise, there was remarkable continuity. Heß yielded his general directorship to Goudefroy in late 1948 and became chairman of the supervisory board of Allianz until his retirement in 1954. Schmitt assumed the chairmanship of the supervisory board of Munich Re in 1949 but died unexpectedly the following year of a cancer. Hilgard joined the Allianz supervisory board and remained on it until 1960, when he retired at the age of 76. Alzheimer followed von Reininghaus, who died in 1950, as chairman of the board of management of Munich Re and remained in this position until 1968, after which he became chairman of the supervisory board until 1976. The continuity of personnel did much to ensure a continuity of attitude, above all the conviction that the German private insurance industry and its leaders and leading concerns had been among the victims of the National Socialist dictatorship.

This was a false perception, every bit as misguided as the "cognitive catastrophe" that had led the top leaders – especially Schmitt and Hilgard – to start doing business with Göring as early as 1930 and to assume a proactive posture toward the regime after it took power. They set the example that others followed, and if Heß was able to maintain his distance then it was in large part because he had colleagues who dirtied their hands and "covered" for him. When Goudefroy wanted to quit the Party in 1935, Heß would have none of it, just as Schmitt let Hilgard do the everyday business of dealing with the regime as head of the Reich Group. The performance of Hilgard and Goudefroy in connection with the Pogrom of November 1938 demonstrated the depths to which one had to sink when choosing to assume or remain in a leadership position. Whatever the particular mix of ambition, professionalism, and opportunism involved, "preventing the worst" became the all-absolving rationalization for their engagement. Although some of those discussed here did what they could to help Jews and others persecuted by the regime, they ultimately became participants – whether they wished or not – in the despoliation of their Jewish customers, and the insurance concern they served ended up doing business in Lodz and Auschwitz. Denazification, as practiced, focused the attention of business leaders on efforts to demonstrate that they were not "real Nazis" and were indeed opponents or

---

[117] See the correspondence in MR, A 2.19/109 and 121.

critics of National Socialism. The result was that these individuals – and their compatriots in other concerns and enterprises throughout Germany – emerged from the immediate postwar period with no clear consciousness of either the extent to which they had been implicated in the misdeeds of the regime or their moral responsibility.

ALLIANZ AND THE PROBLEMS OF RESTITUTION

This often repressed and clouded understanding of the business community's role in the National Socialist regime inevitably had consequences also for the way it dealt with restitution. The postwar management of Allianz was also compelled to confront and deal in some way with the claims and demands of the real victims of the Nazi regime – above all, its former Jewish employees, the former Jewish owners of various kinds of property in whose Aryanizations Allianz had been implicated, and its Jewish customers. As we have demonstrated, Nazi despoliation of the German Jews had been a complicated process in which legal and financial measures, intimidation, and force were all combined to tear asunder the network of citizenship rights and economic and social relations into which they had been embedded thanks to the liberal emancipatory legislation of the previous century. The task of "making good again" – what the Germans called *Wiedergutmachung,* the term used here when reference is made to legislation and practices encompassing both restitution and compensation – inevitably had to address the peculiarities of the shameful process of Jewish de-emancipation and exclusion under conditions that featured a host of complicating factors: forced emigration, murder, aging and natural death, physical destruction of assets through bombing, the financial constraints faced by Germany in its economic reconstruction, and the dilemmas of assigning responsibility.

Furthermore, *Wiedergutmachung* went through a number of phases and took some time to become uniform in its application. Initially, it was mandated by the Western Allies, with the Americans (as in the case of denazification) taking the lead. Subsequently, responsibility for *Wiedergutmachung* was transferred to the Germans and then assumed by the new German Federal Republic on the basis of a combination of international agreements and domestic legislation.[118] This is not the place to review this complicated history, but a brief description of the most relevant legislation and its applicability to the insurance industry is essential. The most important occupation authority legislation was American Military Law No. 52 of September 18, 1944, and its amendments of April 26

---

[118] The most important works are Goschler, *Wiedergutmachung,* and Herbst & Goschler, *Wiedergutmachung.* See also Jörg Fisch, *Reparationen nach dem Zweiten Weltkrieg* (Munich, 1992). An up-to-date and thoughtful account is that of Hans Günter Hockerts, "Wiedergutmachung in Deutschland. Eine historische Bilanz 1945–2000," *Vierteljahrshefte für Zeitgeschichte* 49 (2001), pp. 167–214.

and July 14, 1945, which enabled occupation authorities to seize and control not only the property and assets of Nazis and their organizations but also property wrongfully taken or acquired by duress, together with American Military Law No. 59 of November 10, 1947, which mandated the restitution or compensation of assets seized or transferred under duress by the National Socialist regime. Important portions of Law No. 59 were worked out with the minister presidents of the Länder, but it was ultimately decreed by the Americans after the German authorities (whose full support they had hoped to secure) protested the idea of being responsible for "heirless assets" and the provision for "strict liability" – that is, responsibility to make restitution if those holding the asset were aware (or should have been aware) that it had been confiscated from members of a persecuted group. This was of great importance, since it meant that a person or organization purchasing assets originally acquired by someone else could be held liable for restitution if they knew – or should have known – that the property had been acquired from a member of a persecuted group sometime between Hitler's seizure of power on January 30, 1933, and the unconditional surrender of Nazi Germany on May 8, 1945. Allianz or any other company would thus be responsible not only for the restitution or compensation of real property and shares it acquired directly from Jewish owners but also for such assets as it may have purchased from government authorities or banks. Article 2 of Law 59 also implicitly provided for compensation of life insurance assets, since it stipulated that "ascertainable assets" seized by the State to which a claimant had justified expectation were encompassed under the law. At the same time, however, article 89 declared that special regulations would be issued for the restoration of insurance, copyrights, and patents.[119]

Not only Law 59 but also certain features of its implementation served as a model for the later German legislation after the Federal Republic was established. Although the occupation authorities retained oversight powers and final adjudication rights under Law 59, the actual task of controlling property and implementing *Wiedergutmachung* was placed in the hands of German civil servants, and German restitution courts were set up to hear contested cases. Also, the law made provision for the representation of Jewish interests. Their rights of representation included Jewish assets that were unclaimed because of the death or disappearance of the owners or their heirs. Restitution for these could be made to Jewish organizations. These provisions were not lacking in complications. As in the case of denazification, turning the job over to the Germans inevitably produced conflicts of interest and sentiment, including cases where perpetrators and other dubious characters were placed in control of property to be restituted and where the court personnel were tainted. Furthermore, the

---

[119] There is a convenient compilation of the restitution legislation and international agreements in *Das Deutsche Bundesrecht*, 249. Lieferung – März 1968, Nr. II C 91; Law No. 59 appears as Anhang 4.

Jewish Restitution Successor Organization (JRSO), which had been established to represent the Jewish organizations involved in reparations questions,[120] was often overwhelmed by its tasks and sometimes had a conflict of interest with claimants who challenged its rights to distribute the heirless assets or German-Jewish assets to Jewish organizations outside Germany.[121] Lastly, the currency reform and the creation of the Deutschmark (DM) further complicated issues of restitution, since the reduction of most liquid assets to 10% of their worth led to hard feelings on the part of claimants; it also increased the amount of litigation and promoted delays in settlements.

After the founding of the German Federal Republic in 1949, the issue of reparation and restitution became the subject of a series of complicated negotiations between the German government, the Americans, Jewish organizations, and the State of Israel. The result was the Luxemburg Treaty of September 10, 1952, between the German Federal Republic and Israel under which the former, as the successor to the National Socialist regime, agreed to provide Israel 3 billion DM in goods over a period of 12–14 years, as well as another 450 million DM to be paid to the Jewish Material Claims against Germany. The Claims Conference, as it was called, was established in 1951 to assist in the negotiation of a global settlement with Germany; it became the legal heir of unclaimed Jewish assets and funds made available by the agreements with Germany to support hardship cases and Jewish institutions.[122] Under the First Hague Protocol to the Luxemburg Agreement, the German government agreed to pass a federal compensation law to provide compensation to individual victims or Jewish organizations making claims for loss of life, liberty, damage to health, property and income, educational opportunity, and assets. The law was hastily passed on October 1, 1953. It became the basis of more thoroughgoing and carefully crafted legislation in 1956–1957: the Federal Law for the Compensation of Victims of National Socialist Persecution (BEG) of June 29, 1956, which was made retroactive to October 1, 1953; and the Federal Restitution Law of July 19, 1957. This legislation laid out the categories of compensation as well as the procedures to be followed in implementing compensation.[123]

---

[120] On the JRSO and the other organizations involved, see Ronald W. Zweig, *German Reparations and the Jewish World. A History of the Claims Conference* (Boulder & London, 1987), pp. 1–30; for a list of the organizations, see App. 1, pp. 166–70.

[121] Ibid., p. 41.

[122] Ibid., pp. 15ff.

[123] These laws are to be found, respectively, in BGBl, 1953, I, pp. 387ff.; BGBl, 1956, I, pp. 559ff.; BGBl, 1957, I, pp. 734ff. They are conveniently compiled in *Rückerstattungsrecht. Bundesrückerstattungsgesetz vom 19.7.1957, Textausgabe mit Verweisen und Sachverzeichnis (Beck'sche Textausgaben), 5. neubearb. Aufl.* (Munich, 1970). There is a massive compilation of information in *Die Wiedergutmachung nationalsozialistischen Unrechts durch die Bundesrepublik Deutschland,* 6 vols., hrsg. vom Bundesminister der Finanzen in Zusammenarbeit mit Walter Schwarz (Munich, 1974–1987). See also the literature cited in note 4.

As has been shown earlier, direct claims against Allianz with respect to un-paid insurance were in the last analysis unlikely to play a major role in restitution claims against the company because of the massive cashing in of policies in the late 1930s.[124] Allianz's handling of claims of former business associates and employees – and of demands for restitution of property and securities in the "Aryanizations" of which it had been involved – were frequently more important and revealing of the attitudes of its postwar leadership. Broadly speaking, the management of claims after the war paralleled the concern's attitudes toward the claimants during the National Socialist regime. The greater the considera-tion and decency during the Nazi regime, the more likely these qualities would be exhibited in the postwar period. Similarly, indifference and callousness to-ward victims during the National Socialist regime continued when they or their heirs made their claims.

This should not be viewed as some kind of iron law, however, and the discus-sion that follows makes no pretense to completeness with respect to the Allianz concern – nor to be generalizable to other concerns or the restitution process in general. It deals with cases that have been found, no more and no less. System-atic work on restitution from a variety of perspectives remains to be undertaken, and the discussion here, while revealing much about restitution at Allianz, should serve also as a demonstration of how much work needs to be done by historians seeking to understand the political and legal – as well as the social and eco-nomic – dimensions of this process.

The Treatment of Former Employees and Business Associates

Turning first to Allianz's treatment of its former Jewish employees, it is evident from the available records that the greatest possible consideration was shown to Erika Freudenburg, the widow of Director James Freudenburg. As noted earlier, the company had been assiduous in protecting his pension until his deportation and murder in Auschwitz in 1942. His wife, who was not Jewish, continued to receive the pension he had provided for her until the end of the war, although it was subject to special deductions imposed by the government on the spouse of a Jew. The company then went on to pay her a respectable monthly 620 RM pen-sion (with an equivalent amount in DM after the currency reform) and raised it to 682 DM per month in 1955. This was possible because the Allianz pension fund successfully fought to pay its long-term members at a one-to-one ratio for RM to DM despite the currency reform. This was done on the basis of a con-tract with the members of 1925 that sought to reassure them, after the currency reform of 1923–1924, that they would not again be subjected to a devaluation of their pensions. Allianz promised full compensation to members of the pension fund and did so beginning in 1949 by supplementing its payments to cover the dif-ference between what they would have received under currency reform and what

---

[124] See Chapter 6, pp. 247–50.

they were entitled to under the 1925 guarantee. It was, of course, only proper to give Erika Freudenburg the full pension benefits her husband had assigned to her. At the same time, however, Allianz also supported her claim (made at the end of 1949) for compensation for losses her husband had incurred through his forced retirement. Although the full record of his compensation had been lost in air raids, Allianz nevertheless could – from the memory of Allianz managers who dealt with Freudenburg – attest that he would have been kept on between 1936 and 1943 with earnings between 80,000 RM and 100,000 RM a year. His estimated earnings, which were composed of salary and royalties, were calculated at 620,800 RM. This translated into 62,080 DM after the currency reform to be paid by the government compensation agencies.[125]

The case of the Magdeburg director Maximilian Eichbaum had been a happier one, and he could have taken up a managerial position at Allianz if he were willing to return to Germany. As noted earlier, he had a friendly correspondence with Schmitt and Heß after the war. While he petitioned in 1949 for restitution of his pension, whose payments had ceased in 1941 by government order, this seems to have been done for purely formal and legal reasons. In September 1949, he and Goudefroy reached an agreement under which Allianz compensated him for the money he had not received and also resumed pension payments until his death in 1958. Eichbaum received 77,700 DM for unpaid pensions, which was apparently in considerable excess of the 40,000 DM considered the maximum compensation for pension backpayments under the currency reform.[126] This by no means ended Allianz's engagement with the restitution of Eichbaum's assets, however, since Eichbaum not only renewed the general power of attorney (to represent his interests) that he had given Allianz when he left Germany in 1937 but also extended it in 1947 to cover his family as well. As his representative, Allianz became involved in trying to gain compensation for Eichbaum and his family for a variety of claims, the most difficult of which involved over 240,000 RM in securities, 57,600 of which had been used to pay the atonement tax and the remainder of which had been placed into an account in the name of his children (who were half-Jewish) at the Dresdner Bank but had been confiscated and sent to the Reichsbank and then sold to various private parties, firms, and banks. Allianz (more precisely, the legal section of its branch) successfully represented Eichbaum's claims for compensation due to damage done to his career and won a court case that brought 25,000 DM to Eichbaum's widow, Erna, in 1969. However, she did not live to receive the compensation granted her children for the

---

[125] See Erika Freudenburg an das Hessische Staatsministerium, 29. Dez. 1949, and other relevant documents in FHA, B 2.4.5/134. On the handling of the currency reform in the Allianz pension fund, see Maiholzer, "Die Berliner Allianz-Betriebe," pp. 216ff., FHA, and the material on the Allianz-Versorgungskasse in FHA, A 3.7.3. For the discussions concerning the Allianz pension regulation, see BAK, B 280/1696.

[126] See the correspondence for 1950–1953, WGÄ, 4 WGA 912/50 (Maximilian Eichbaum); for the September 27, 1949, agreement, see FHA, AZ 6/3.

securities in a complicated set of cases that dragged on before being brought to a successful conclusion in 1975 – that is, three years after her death. The value of the securities and the compensation demanded for the profit made from them by those, like Deutsche Bank, who held them after 1943 encouraged Erna Eichbaum and her children to press the case. Moreover, Allianz felt committed to placing its legal resources and personal efforts behind the family. Alfred Haase, who was chairman of the management board of Allianz in the late 1960s and who negotiated with Director Heinrich Ulrich of Deutsche Bank in an effort to settle the case, argued strongly to the latter in 1967 that the return on the shares for those who illegitimately held them had turned out to be far higher than originally thought, so that Erna Eichbaum was justified in refusing to settle prematurely and was understandably bitter about having been so far deprived of thirty years of returns on the securities. He was anxious to assist her so that "this unfortunate and tedious disagreement will finally be settled and not always time and again bring up the memory of the sad events of the past."[127] Allianz's willingness to employ its resources for so sustained a period in the case certainly was praiseworthy and deserves to be recorded.

At the same time, however, Freudenburg and Eichbaum were special cases, as they had been in the 1930s, and by no means typical. In some instances, the behavior of the concern toward its former Jewish employees could appear quite confusing and contradictory. Thus, in the case of Robert Sulzberger, a highly successful general agent for Allianz in Berlin between 1933 and 1938, the pension fund strongly urged the Allianz legal department to turn down his lawyer's demand that Sulzberger have his pension rights restored, among other things, on the grounds that Allianz "was obligated to pay Dr. Sulzberger from the perspective of collective guilt," presumably for the way the Germans had treated the Jews in the Nazi period.[128] Heß, as chairman of the supervisory board and previous general director, strongly supported this decision in the fall of 1951, asking that Sulzberger be reminded about how fairly he had been treated at the time of "his departure conditioned by the situation at that time" and that Heß had arranged for him to work for Schweizer National in Palestine. Allianz suggested that Sulzberger could turn to the public purse (i.e., the Senate of Berlin) for compensation for his pension loss. A year later, however, in November 1952, Allianz was happy to inform Sulzberger that permission had been received to put 6,000 DM in his blocked account at the Wiesbaden branch of the Süddeutsche Bank!

---

[127] Haase an Ulrich, 10. Okt. 1966 und 11. Aug. 1967, FHA, AZ 6/1, as well as FHA, AZ 6/2 and 3. Allianz did an extraordinary job of tracing the odyssey of the Allianz shares held by Eichbaum that were used to pay his atonement tax and to pay the costs of his emigration. The records showed that some of these even came into the hands of Kurt Schmitt; Merck, Finck & Co. and Süddeutsche Bank also held some, as did Bosch-Hilfe e.V., Bayerische Vereinsbank, and Deutsche Bank, as well as Metallgesellschaft. See Allianz Rechtsabteilung an die Vermögensverwaltung Allianz, 22. März 1967, and related documents, FHA, AZ 8.1/4.

[128] Allianz an Rechtsanwalt Hans Gumpert, 30. Nov. 1951, and Allianz Versorgungskasse an Allianz Rechtsabteilung, 29. Nov. 1951, FHA, O 1.4.2/24.

(One of the ugly ironies of the postwar situation was that exchange controls continued to exist – both under Allied occupation and in the Federal Republic – until 1953–1954 so that accounts of persons living abroad, including Jews receiving compensation, were blocked and thus required special permission for funds to be transferred outside the country.) In asking permission from the Bavarian State Bank to place the money in Sulzberger's account as a cash settlement agreed upon by Allianz and Sulzberger, Allianz expressly emphasized his extraordinarily successful work for the concern and that he had lost his membership in the pension fund when he had to leave because of the "increasing pressure of those who held power at the time on the Jews."[129] He had turned to Allianz for the settlement in question, and the concern had decided to agree because he had lost his membership in the pension fund and, given the circumstances in Israel, had not been in a position to build up new retirement savings.

How is one to explain the changes in tone and deed between 1951 and 1952? Since the record is incomplete, one must hypothesize, and the simplest answers are probably the best. On the one hand, Sulzberger must have explained his real situation directly to his former employers, who did indeed remember him as one of their star insurance agents. The Allianz leaders seem to have concluded that the "fairness" shown in 1938 did not eliminate the legacy of unfairness described to them by Sulzberger and that they had a moral obligation to compensate him for his exclusion from the pension fund. On the other hand, those managing the pension fund were extremely touchy about maintaining its rules and regulations and not setting precedents for the future, and they probably were doubly alarmed by the language of Sulzberger's lawyer with respect to the "collective guilt" of the concern. There is significant evidence that both the Allianz concern leadership and its pension fund leadership were exceedingly cautious in 1951 in dealing with claims and inquiries emanating from the U.S. Justice Department, to whom refugees from Germany who had become U.S. citizens often appealed for restitution on behalf of former employees and insurance agents of the concern.[130] It was, in any case, one thing to make an ad hoc settlement with Sulzberger, yet quite another to accept liability toward him and compensate him out of the pension fund. All this changed in the late 1950s and 1960s after the German *Wiedergutmachung* legislation had been passed and formulas had been devised under which pensioners and their immediate heirs had their rights reinstated. This made it possible to calculate both contributions to the fund and pension entitlements, so that pensions were paid out after previously unpaid contributions had been deducted.[131]

---

[129] Allianz an die Landeszentralbank Bayern, 4. Okt. 1952, Allianz an Sulzberger, 4. Nov. 1952, ibid.
[130] See Allianz Rechtsabteilung an die Allianz-Pensionsverwaltung, 27. Juli 1951, FHA, O 1.4.2/9.
[131] Files on such cases can be found in FHA, O 1.4.2/1 (Fritz Aronheim), O 1.4.2/3 (Sally Bieber), O 1.4.2/12 (Edith Hollander), and O 1.4.2/18 (Hilde Mosse). There are some interesting Allianz pension cases in WBG, Wiedergutmachungsakten, Ia1950 (Bernhard Selling) and Ia 5046 (Hans Heymann).

No such formulas could be found for the compensation of Allianz agents and representatives for the portfolios surrendered (from which Allianz had benefitted) and the settlements uncollected or confiscated owing to regulations of the National Socialist regime. This was well demonstrated by the case of Ludwig Pototzky, one of the owners of the firm of Pototzky & Co., which had sold insurance for Allianz in Berlin and Breslau. As discussed in Chapter 3, his two brothers in Breslau (Fritz and Hans) had given up their "Aryan" portfolio in 1937 in return for an annual pension of 3,000 RM each. Fearing Party interference a year later, Allianz did not "purchase" the portfolio managed by Ludwig Pototzky but instead initially promised him a yearly pension of 4,950 and subsequently agreed to his request for a settlement of 25,000 RM so that he could emigrate to London in 1939. In the end, he was only able to take 2,500 RM with him because of government impositions and controls.[132]

At the end of 1948, Pototzky petitioned for compensation from Allianz for his portfolio under Law No. 59. Allianz rejected his claim, arguing that no "ascertainable assets" were involved – that is, unpaid salaries, pensions, or royalties. The concern insisted that the pension originally promised to Pototzky was for commissions he would have received for managing the portfolio and not compensation for transfer of the portfolio itself; they also argued that rights to assets in Berlin still had not been regulated while assets in Breslau could not be compensated because the area was under Polish administration. Without prejudice to its position, Allianz was prepared to make a one-time payment to Pototzky of 1,000 English pounds from its sequestered assets in England if the British government would permit. It had hoped to make such a transfer to Pototzky in 1939, but the German Economics Ministry had refused to allow it at that time. Fundamentally, then, all Allianz would offer Pototzky was a sum in England over which it had no control anyway.[133]

After an effort to reach a compromise failed, Pototzky and his English solicitor Philipp Cromwell decided to take the case to the restitution courts in Bavaria, although Pototzky had Cromwell inform Allianz that he considered the litigation a necessary effort to settle a legal question and that he had no intention "of upsetting the friendly relations going back many years," a proposition with which Allianz agreed.[134] Pototzky was in fact more wounded than he pretended and, when he heard that Kurt Schmitt was head of the Allianz supervisory board, decided to write to him in May 1950 since he admired Schmitt for the position he had taken against the Nazi regime's anti-Semitic policies. He pointed out to Schmitt that the Pototzky brothers had suffered badly. Fritz had been thrown into a Gestapo prison in Norway in 1942 in such a manner that he died from head wounds. The 67-year-old Hans had made it to Palestine, where he was extremely unhappy. Only he, Ludwig, had succeeded in building up an insurance

---

[132] See Chapter 3, p. 135.
[133] Allianz an das Amt für Vermögenskontrolle und Wiedergutmachung, 19. Juli 1949, WGB, Ia 6059, Bl. 7–9.
[134] Cromwell an Allianz, 14. Nov. 1949, Allianz an Cromwell, 10. Dez. 1949, ibid. Bl. 15f.

agency in England, but it had been no easy task and he was over 60. Hence, he went on,

I am all the more so disappointed by the position of Allianz in its posture toward us .... Our contracts, which we concluded with Allianz in the transfer of our business were supposed to more or less provide us with security for the rest of our lives, and now every right is being contested so that I am forced to take recourse to the Restitution Chamber in Munich. The laws and court judgments are so clear that I have no doubt about a decision in my favor, but it is painful for me to sue Allianz which once – in a letter to us on the occasion of our 25th anniversary of working with Allianz and actually signed by you – maintained that: "The name Pototzky will always be assigned an outstanding place in the annals of the Allianz".[135]

Pototzky attributed some of his treatment to the fact that many of the old-timers were no longer in the top echelons and the newcomers did not understand the importance of the Pototzkys, and he praised Schmitt's son-in-law Carl Otto Pape, as well as Heß and Haase, for promising to use the services of Pototzky's London agency for reinsurance purposes. They, at least, had recognized that the Pototzkys had devoted themselves to Allianz and had, indeed, stayed on so long that, of the living Jewish associates of Allianz, they were the only ones who did not get a settlement in hard currency and were thus "subject to the hard fate of refugees without means." From Pototzky's perspective, he and his brothers had been forced to alienate their portfolios under compulsion and to do so for security and money they never received. He readily admitted that Allianz had also been forced to behave in this manner, but he nevertheless believed that "Allianz should itself undertake the act of ameliorating justice and should not leave it to the courts, even if the laws were not so clearly in my favor as they are."

Schmitt expressed shock at the fate of the Pototzkys and, while convinced that the men at Allianz were of good will, promised to pursue the matter further. As for Pototzky, he felt there was no choice but to battle the legal issues out in court and hope they would be resolved quickly and in a friendly manner; he also hoped that he could serve Allianz and Munich Re in London in the future.[136] In a decision of June 1951, the Restitution Chamber decided the basic issues in favor of Pototzky, declaring that an "ascertainable asset" was involved in the agreements of 1938–1939 and that Allianz was required to pay Pototzky both a yearly pension of 4,950 DM and 15,847 DM as an unpaid balance on the settlement. Further payment to the plaintiff for his losses were reserved for a final settlement.[137] This paved the way for negotiations leading to a 1952 agreement between Pototzky and Allianz in which the latter paid the former 60,000 DM plus 2,000 DM legal fees, in return for which Pototzky renounced all further claims as well as the monies granted under the June 1951 judgment.[138]

---

[135] Pototzky an Schmitt, 27. Mai 1950, FHA, NL 1/18.
[136] Schmitt an Pototzky, 19. Juni 1950, Pototzky an Schmitt, 16. Juni 1950, ibid.
[137] Teilbeschluß der Wiedergutmachungskammer, 4. Juni 1951, WGB, Ia 6059, Bl. 88–99.
[138] Vergleich, 8. März 1952, ibid., Bl. 93.

This appears to have been an amicable and fairly quick settlement. It contrasts with a similar claim made by another agent, Hans Grünebaum, whose 1936 contract was abruptly terminated in June 1938 under Nazi pressure even though it was supposed to run until 1941. He was given a year's commission of 35,000 RM as a settlement.[139] Grünebaum went to the United States and settled down in Chicago under the name of Harry H. Gray. In December 1948, he sued Allianz for 70,000 RM, which he considered to be the amount of commission he would have earned if the contract had not been broken by Allianz. As in the case of Pototzky, the concern contested the claim, arguing that no "ascertainable asset" was involved and also asserting that Grünebaum's portfolio was already seriously diminishing and would have diminished further if the contract had continued. Gray's case was clearly weaker than Pototzky's in that one could question how independent his agency actually was, but Gray was no less tenacious and apparently also sought to gain compensation through the U.S. Department of Justice by targeting Allianz assets in the United States. The case went through a number of courts, with an appeals court in Frankfurt deciding against Gray in 1952 and treating the 35,000 RM given by Allianz as an act of loyalty that was based on no legal obligation, because the plaintiff had not collected any premiums from his portfolio during the year for which he was being paid. Two years later, the 2nd Civil Court of the Superior Court in Frankfurt sent the case back to the lower court for reconsideration, and the case dragged on until April 1958, when a settlement was finally reached – although the exact nature of the settlement is unclear from the available records. It is not inconceivable that Allianz privately settled with Gray without surrendering its legal position but gaining the advantage of having Gray drop all claims in both Germany and the United States, the latter apparently being a matter of particular concern. The entire case reflected both the understandable bitterness felt by Gray as well as the tendency of Allianz to dig in its heels and contest such claims made against it. This attitude may have been reinforced by the position of the American military government, which (initially at least) viewed unrealized commissions as not being assets in the sense of Law No. 59.[140]

Because there is no full record of how many of Allianz's Jewish insurance agents and representatives contested settlements made during the Nazi period, it is difficult to draw satisfactory conclusions. Certainly the Franconian insurance agent Martin Lachmann, a subdirector of Allianz in Berlin, might have claimed to have had an "ascertainable asset" in his "Aryan" portfolio – of whose benefits he was suddenly deprived in 1938 in return for a pension worth a quarter of his previous income – but he and his wife were victims of the Holocaust. When their heirs, who lived in Sweden, tried to claim the pensions in 1950, they discovered

---

[139] See Chapter 3, p. 132.
[140] The records on the case can be found in the HessHStA, Wiedergutmachungsakten, FFm-6516 and BAK, B 215/1401. On possible claims against Allianz assets in the United States, see Allianz an die Allianz Pensionsverwaltung, 27. Juli 1951, FHA, O 1.4.2/9. On the U.S. military government position, see Aktennote of 21. Jan. 1949, FHA, AZ 8.1/2.

that rights to the pensions did not fall under the restitution legislation.[141] It is impossible to know if there were other such cases or how many there might be. One could imagine that Moritz Goldmann, an insurance agent from Magdeburg who gave up his agency and was promised a position in Berlin, only to end up with a paltry 5,000 RM settlement in 1938, might have been as bitter as Gray.[142] His lawyer did make inquiries in 1954 and was told that the Magdeburg branch had been confiscated by the Eastern zone authorities and that much of the documentation was lost in the bombing. Allianz did supply information from the memory of some of those who had worked in Magdeburg: the Goldmann agency made 8,000–9,000 RM. While noting that its files in Berlin had been destroyed, it did not mention the 1938 correspondence with Goldmann that happened to have been saved, but this is hardly surprising. The correspondence showed that Allianz was able to acquire his portfolio well below its worth and that it paid him a low settlement. Whatever the case, there is no record of Goldmann suing, and it is most unlikely he would have done so with much success under the existing legislation. Given the record presented here, however, the case certainly would have ended up in the courts, and Allianz might have been willing to come to a settlement.

Restitution and Compensation for "Aryanizations" of Real Estate and Securities

Allianz faced what were probably its most serious restitution problems in the area of "Aryanized" real estate, and the record often speaks poorly for the manner in which the concern dealt with claimants and even more negatively with respect to its attitude toward them. This is not to say that judging each individual case (an impossibility here) would be a simple matter. Most difficult, undoubtedly, are the cases of mortgage foreclosure and forced sale, especially when they took place in the early years of the National Socialist regime. Such events were hardly uncommon in the depression and were not ipso facto evidence of discrimination against Jews, especially if the price received by Allianz or any other mortgage holder for the sale of the property seemed reasonable.

Nevertheless, the handling of some of these cases by Allianz seems very disturbing today. A revealing illustration was the claim for restitution of a property in Frankfurt a.M. whose mortgage Allianz had foreclosed and which it auctioned off in 1935. The lawyers for the 70-year-old widow of the deceased Jewish owner Leo Levor, who had died a refugee in 1939, claimed that the forced sale was a consequence of the anti-Jewish discrimination, beginning with the boycott of April 1933 and above all because of his subsequent loss of business with the agricultural organizations with whom he dealt. As Hilde Levor told her lawyers, this loss of business made her husband "so nervous, that nothing else was left

---

[141] See Chapter 3, pp. 135–6, as well as WGÄ, 1 WGA 3745/50 (Ruth Ernestine Haas).
[142] On the Goldmann case, see Chapter 3, pp. 133–5.

to do than to leave the land that did not want us."[143] Allianz's position on the case was that the property was already indebted in 1932 and had been placed under its receivership in 1933, and that the owner was given further opportunity to straighten matters out without successfully doing so. Since the mortgage in question was part of the coverage for their insurance policies, they had no choice but to foreclose. Indeed, they were able to demonstrate that the Levors expressed gratitude to Allianz for showing forbearance despite their difficulties. The forced sale, therefore, was justified on a pure economic basis and, Allianz claimed, had nothing to do with Levor being a Jew. If Allianz had given credit to a Jew, then it could also collect debts from a Jew without being charged with discrimination. At the same time, Allianz also emphasized that both the restitution laws and the case law (i.e., the decisions handed down by restitution courts) placed the burden of demonstrating discrimination on the plaintiff rather than the defendant, and that it was important not to let the burden of proof be shifted, as often allegedly occurred. The concern instructed its lawyer in the case, Otto Dürichen of the Frankfurt office of Allianz Leben, to make use of decisions that required the plaintiff to show that actual intention to employ discriminatory legislation was at issue rather than the inability to pay debts. Furthermore, Allianz saw no reason to seek a settlement with Hilde Levor.[144]

Dürichen followed his instructions, but found the court very unhappy about Allianz's unwillingness to seek a settlement despite (what he considered to be) the sound arguments and legal precedents he had presented. In Dürichen's view, there was no justification for Allianz "to pay even so small a settlement sum" since Allianz had made a loss on the forced sale of the property by failing to collect what the Levors owed. As he went on to describe the situation, "the opposition constantly tried to place the present distress of his perhaps 75-year-old client, who even now must make a living by working, in the foreground. I responded to this by pointing to the present situation of the life insurance companies created by the adaptation to the new currency... etc."[145] Apparently, the court was more moved by the plight of Hilde Levor than by the travails of the insurance business. It demanded proof that Allianz had made a loss and also strongly urged some kind of payment to her, however small, the possibility of which Dürichen once again denied. Allianz went on to gather materials seeking to demonstrate that it made nothing but a loss on the property, a loss subsequently compounded by its total destruction in an air raid. The files do not indicate how this case turned out, but Allianz seemed confident in its case and totally resistent to a settlement. Such tenacity in dealing with claimants was by no means usual, but Allianz pursued at least one case where its legal position was much worse in order to satisfy the supervisory authority that it had not given in.

[143] Valentin Heckert an das Landgericht Frankfurt a.M., 3. Wiedergutmachungskammer, 24. Okt. 1952, FHA, S 17.16/75.

[144] Allianz Leben an Otto Dürichen, 20. April 1951, ibid., to which was appended a list of court decisions bearing on the case.

[145] Dürichen an Allianz Leben, 11. Mai 1951, ibid.

This suggests that the concern's attitude with respect to restitution cases was not always free of considerations of what might be said by regulators in the federal supervisory office for insurance, who had an obvious interest in reconstruction of the insurance industry as well as in preservation of existing coverage for insurance company policies.[146] Where Allianz did engage claimants in the courts, however, it was extremely sensitive to charges that it was in any way anti-Semitic in its treatment of Jewish mortgagees, insisting that the contrary had been the case.[147] Ironically, some of the evidence suggests that this was true; those in charge of dealing with Jewish mortgages at Allianz in the early 1930s may have been more sensitive to the plight of their Jewish clients than were their successors, who (as in the Levor case) bizarrely compared the postwar problems of their corporation with those of a Jewish refugee's aged widow.

Yet we have already seen that Allianz could make little claim to sensitivity in the Aryanizations of the late 1930s. The restitution courts were seemingly well aware of the brutality shown to the Jews in the late 1930s and tended to be less inclined to turn down plaintiffs whose properties had been alienated in 1937–1939. The evidence that Allianz took advantage of the anti-Semitic climate was also more compelling in the later period. The contrast is illustrated by two cases against Allianz handled by the Berlin lawyer Hans Friedberg. The first, brought by Manes and Cirl Tennenbaum, was for the restitution of a property on the Pariser Straße, which had been put into receivership in 1934 and then sold because of indebtedness. The property had been purchased by the Tennenbaums for paper marks in the inflation, but upkeep and costs thereafter led to chronic indebtedness even before 1933. Friedberg tried to argue that the eventual purchase of the property by Allianz in 1936 – from a person notorious for buying up Jewish properties – demonstrated that discrimination had played a role. However, Allianz's lawyers argued successfully that even non-Jews suffering from such chronic indebtedness would have lost their property under the circumstances, a conclusion reached also by the courts in 1953 and again in 1955. In the latter trial, the lawyer for the now widowed Cirl Tennenbaum tried to argue on the basis of a 1954 higher court decision in another case of forced sale that there was an entitlement to restitution because it was impossible for Jews to get credit in Nazi Germany. But the restitution court hearing the Tennenbaum case pointed out in its decision that the forced sale in question took place in 1939–1940 – that is, four years later, when conditions were dramatically more unfavorable for Jews – and thus there could be no question about the incapacity of the owner in that case to pay his debts.[148]

---

[146] Allianz Leben an Dr. Dürichen, 8. Mai 1951, ibid.

[147] Allianz Leben an die 3. Wiedergutmachungskammer beim Landgericht Frankfurt a.M., 7. Jan. 1952, ibid.

[148] See especially the Beschluß der öffentlichen Sitzung der 142. Zivilkammer des Landgerichts Berlin, 30. April 1953, and the Beschluß des 14. Zivilsenats des Kammergerichts in Berlin, 28. März 1955, WGÄ, 8 WGA 933/50 (Manes und Cirl Tennenbaum), Bl. 68–89, 104–24, and other relevant correspondence. Another case in which restitution was denied for the 1934 foreclosure

This distinction in time and circumstance may explain why Friedberg had more success against Allianz in the case of the forced sale of Adolf Wollenberg's properties (on the Kurfürstendamm and the Joachimsthaler Straße) in Berlin in February 1939 in response to his failure to pay 42,443 RM in interest. Allianz made familiar arguments that the indebtedness dated back to an earlier time and that it was forced to take action for economic reasons. Friedberg, representing Wollenberg and then his widow during the years 1950–1953, was able to show that Allianz's case for foreclosure specifically noted that the owner was a Jew, that his chances of making payment were doubtful because of his taxes, and that the property would be more profitable if it were in Aryan hands. In the end, Allianz agreed to a settlement and paid Wollenberg's widow 10,000 DM (and also covered court and other costs) in return for her renunciation of her property rights, whose estimated worth was 171,950 DM. It is likely that the settlement reflected the fact that encumbrances on the property, which were very high, would also have been taken into account and that Wollenberg's widow was living abroad and may have had no further interest in dealing with the property. The settlement was duly approved by the federal supervisory office for insurance.[149]

An even more interesting case of this type was that of Rebecca Halsband, who owned a property on Meinekestraße in Berlin which Allianz foreclosed on and then sold in November 1938. Allianz's initial response in April 1951 was to reject the claim and argue that Halsband had a long record of financial mismanagement that predated the National Socialist period. For reasons that are unclear from the restitution file but which, as in the Wollenberg case, may have had something to do with the Allianz's argument for foreclosure made in that most fateful year of 1938, Allianz changed its position and, in February 1954, agreed to pay Halsband 30,000 DM "in recognition of the special circumstances."[150] The overriding "special circumstance" in all these cases, of course, was the abnormal situation created by anti-Semitic discrimination and persecution that made what might have been normal economic activity suspect. Allianz may have had valid economic reasons for foreclosing on Wollenberg and Halsband – there is no reason, after all, to assume that all Jews are astute in the management of their finances. The Third Reich created circumstances, however, in which it was impossible for Jews either to succeed or to fail fairly. Thus, the Allianz lawyers and representatives in the late 1930s were so easily tempted to taint even their good cases with anti-Semitic content that they became defendants who were justifiably

---

and sale of a property in Berlin is that of a property on the Brandenburgische Straße in Berlin Wilmersdorf owned by Paul Mühlmann, then living in Haifa. See WGÄ, 7 WGA 2536/50 (Paul Mühlmann).

[149] Hans Friedberg an das Landgericht Berlin, 11. März 1953, Sitzung des Landgerichts Berlin, 23. März 1953; Bundesaufsichtsamt an den Vorstand von Allianz Leben, 18. April 1953, WGÄ, 6 WGA 2920/50 (Adolf Wollenberg), Bl. 69–70, 75–6, 89.

[150] See Allianz an die Wiedergutmachungsämter von Berlin, 11. April 1951 und 7. Feb. 1952, WGÄ, 11 WGA 405/51 (Rebecca Halsband), Bl. 10–12, 26. Marginal notations at the bottom of the 1951 letter suggest that Allianz was seeking out the documentation on the foreclosure. It is hard to imagine that in 1938 it would not have made reference to Halsband's "race."

liable to make at least some restitution a dozen or more years later. By capitalizing on the Jews as being poor risks, they became implicated in making them poor risks.

Such considerations produce a constant and perhaps unwarranted discomfiture in dealing with those restitution cases in which Allianz was involved yet emerged free and clear of all responsibility and liability to pay. It is important to bear in mind that Allianz was not called to account in cases like those just described if the properties in question were in the East. When Hugo Benjamin from Tel Aviv sought compensation for what he considered to be the undervaluation of his property in Breslau in a 1939 foreclosure by Allianz, he found that West Berlin courts were not competent to hear the case and that the restitution laws did not cover territories then considered under Polish occupation.[151] It is difficult to know what to make of the case of Leon Balaban, an engineer with a high position in the Berlin construction industry who lost his employment and then made a living – between 1933 and his emigration to Palestine in 1938 – by buying, renovating, and reselling real estate. The property in Berlin-Tempelhof that he sold to Allianz in 1935 was, he claimed, sold in order to finance his emigration and would not have been sold otherwise. His emigration had been delayed because he fell ill. Allianz contested his claim that the price had not been fair and pointed out that the money was used to purchase other properties as part of Balaban's business, a use which Balaban argued was made necessary in order to survive until he could emigrate. On the one hand, the account of Balaban's desperate efforts to make a living and find the means to emigrate after being thrown out of a profession in which he had prospered for 25 years hardly suggests that any action he took was motivated by normal economic decisions – those that would have been made under other political circumstances. He had been a very well-connected businessman, and this may have made it possible for him to conduct his real estate business despite the difficult situation. On the other hand, the claim that Allianz undercompensated him by paying only 238,000 RM instead of the 255,000 his lawyers claimed the property was worth is not very compelling, and it did not convince any of the courts to which it was taken – including the United States Court of Restitution Appeals of the Allied High Commission for Germany in 1953.[152]

Not all property restitution cases were as adversarial as those just described. In one case, at least, restitution actually led to a restoration of business relationships. Thus, Abraham Gorodecki, who had been in the real estate business and had sold off properties to Allianz in Berlin-Halensee in 1935, received them back and agreed to take out mortgages with Allianz to finance rebuilding of the totally

[151] See Allianz an Wiedergutmachungsämter von Berlin, 22. Sept. 1950, Beschluß der Wiedergutmachungsämter von Berlin, 30. Okt. 1951, as well as other relevant documents in WGÄ, 5 WGA 484/50 (Hugo Benjamin).
[152] The record of the lengthy case is to be found in WGÄ, 4 WGA 5004/50 (Leon Balaban). It is worth noting that this case demonstrates what a rich source restitution files can be for the historian of the social history of Jews in Germany in the 1930s.

destroyed structures.[153] There was anything but reconciliation, however, in the case of Ludwig Jansen, a Jewish businessman who had fled to Rio de Janeiro and whose house on the Kastanienallee in Berlin had been sold to Allianz in 1936. Jansen bought the property in 1927, and he built an especially attractive house for himself and his family and also one that would provide rental income. A large mortgage had been taken out with Karlsruher Leben, which belonged to the Allianz concern. From Allianz's standpoint, Jansen had received a fair price, especially since it had bought the property from a Jewish real estate agent and the sale was not made under duress. Jansen saw the matter differently, remembering that Director Maiholzer had told him that Jews should take what they could get under the cirumstances and that he subsequently had to flee the Gestapo, which was after him for trumped-up foreign exchange violations. In 1952, Allianz returned the property as part of a settlement with Jansen.[154]

Allianz was much more resistant, however, to accepting the claims of Jews whose properties had been purchased in connection with plans for creating the Runder Platz designated by Albert Speer for the new Allianz building. As shown earlier, Allianz was anything but the unwilling participant that its postwar claims would suggest in the realization of these megalomaniacal schemes. Contrary to Allianz's pretensions, the Jews whose properties were bought out in 1939–1940 received demonstrably less than others who were compelled to sell their properties under the laws governing the reconstruction of Berlin. Needless to say, the Jews in question also ended up not having free disposition over their funds. The family most affected by these losses – that of Richard and Walter Feige, whose heirs lived in the United States – made their restitution claims in 1949 and, after considerable effort, achieved substantial success in both a lower court and then in a decision by a higher court against Allianz's appeal in 1953. What is remarkable is the extent to which Allianz held to its claims with respect to the relative fairness of the price – despite the evidence presented by the concern itself regarding the prices paid to Aryan and Jewish property owners – and the even more extraordinary unwillingness to accept the Feige family's contention that Jews could not achieve a fair price under the circumstances.[155]

If anything, however, Allianz was even more tenacious in resisting the claims of another Jewish property owner forced to sell out, Walther Czempin, the son of the original owner, Alexander Czempin, a noted gynecologist who (as mentioned in Chapter 3) committed suicide at the age of 82 in order to avoid being deported.[156] In this case, which began in 1950 and lasted until 1961, Allianz actually mobilized the Senator for Finances, Special Assets and Buildings

[153] See Allianz an Abraham Gorodecki, 15. Mai 1950, WGÄ, 4 WGA 2475/50 (Abraham Gorodecki).
[154] See Chapter 3, pp. 144–5, and WGÄ, 5 WGA 4664/50 (Ludwig Jansen).
[155] See especially Allianz an das Kammergericht Berlin, 15. Zivilsenat, 7. Dez. 1953, Rechtsanwalt Joachim Bütner an das Kammergericht, 17. Dez. 1953, Beschluß des 15. Zivilsenats des Kammergerichts Berlin, 18. Dez. 1953, WGÄ, 6 WGA 264/51 (Berta Feige), Bl. 137–40, 141f., 150–8.
[156] See Chapter 3, p. 143.

of Berlin to argue in a lengthy memorandum that Czempin's claim should be rejected. Czempin's lawyer suggested that the Senator was not exactly a disinterested party, since Allianz had indicated that, if it lost, it would sue the City of Berlin for losses connected with the construction plans of its predecessor. Given the energy put into the matter by the Senator's office, this was quite plausible, and it suggests why the Czempin case proved so difficult and especially why the actual fairness of the payment made to the elder Czempin for his property was so difficult to contest by his son. Indeed, the Senator's office intervened repeatedly to argue for Allianz. In the end, the court urged a settlement on both parties in the form of a 20,000 DM payment by Allianz to Czempin in return for surrender of the Czempin claims, and this was accepted in November 1961.[157]

Allianz put up no such battle in the case of Kaufingerstraße 22 in Munich, which had been the property of the ill-fated Julius and Else Basch, who had hoped to join their son in the United States and instead ended up victims of the Holocaust.[158] The property was purchased by Allianz in 1940 from SA-Obersturmführer Hans Wegner, who had headed up the organization for the "Aryanization" of Jewish property in Munich, through the Baschs' appointed "representative," Hanns Stumfall, who acted as a "trustee" for Jews forced to sell their assets. Allianz paid 1,674,000 RM for this choice property in the center of Munich, which was well below its real worth; it paid a commission to Stumfall of 72,000 RM, along with 4,080 RM as a special fee for permission to buy Jewish property (under the decree for the mobilization of Jewish assets) and 410.25 RM in other fees. When Basch's son Ernest B. Ashton demanded restitution in 1949–1950, Allianz's initial response was to claim that the price it had paid was fair and that Stumfall was a legitimate agent for Basch. Allianz soon changed its tune in the face of documentation provided by Ashton's lawyers, a good move since evidence now available in the Moscow archives demonstrates that Allianz was totally aware of the duress under which the Baschs were selling their property and had actually used their detailed knowledge of the Baschs' tax debts to justify the money Allianz spent on the property to the RAA with the argument that the Baschs would have to give most of it to the government. Allianz thus settled with Ashton, paying 1.1 million DM in return for all rights to the property.

Allianz had now legitimately bought the property and all the rights and liabilities attached to it. Remarkably, Allianz then turned around and – in effect playing the role that could have been played by the deceased Baschs or by their son, had he chosen to retain any further connection with the sale of the property – proceeded to sue the government and the Nazi Party, whose sequestered assets were being used for restitution purposes, for the 72,000 RM paid Stumfall, the 4,080 RM paid in order to buy a Jewish property, and the 410.25 RM in other fees. Taking the position of Ashton seeking restitution for illegitimate costs in his compensation, Allianz now argued in effect that it had purchased

---

[157] See WGÄ, 1 WGA 2462/50, Bd. I–II (Walther Czempin).
[158] See Chapter 3, pp. 145–7.

The office block on Kaufingerstraße 22 (today, no. 28) was Aryanized in 1940 when Allianz purchased it. After 1945 this building became an object of restitution procedures.

Ashton's rights to seek compensation for these payments. Thus, the 4,080 RM fee under the decree for the mobilization of Jewish assets

is by its nature a remuneration for the fact that the racially persecuted had to pay for the fact that the authorities of the Reich took or decimated their assets. It is impossible that a fee which the Reich had instituted can be recognized as legal for the carrying out of measures which are today recognized as illegal and which the legislature has therefore ordered to be made good. If this activity of the Reich as such is condemned, then the remuneration for it must necessarily be regarded as a levy imposed by force.[159]

Allianz also laid claim to compensation for the commission Basch had paid to Stumfall, for Stumfall's retention of the commission had to be seen for what it really was: "In view of the machinations which the Nazi authorities employed to gain control of the assets of Herr Basch, one surely cannot speak seriously about there being a voluntary agreement from the side of Herr Basch." Indeed, Stumfall's very person and his known record militated against such an interpretation. His commission, therefore, was another compulsory and illegitimate fee aimed at despoiling Basch and so compensation for the legitimate owner of the property was likewise in order – and that owner, thanks to the settlement with Ashton, was Allianz.

Allianz had indeed travelled a rather long road from its response to Ashton's claims in the letter of April 1949 to the restitution authorities, when it had declared:

We contest that the seller at that time was in a situation of constraint. The Basch couple had presented themselves long before as being interested in selling, and had charged Herr Hanns Stumfall, an engineer and economic consultant to negotiate the sale of the property in question .... Also the power of attorney on the basis of which Herr Stumfall negotiated with us was granted by the Basch couple voluntarily and without any compulsion.[160]

Obviously, the perspective had changed when Allianz had "become" Basch or Ashton some seven years later, but the restitution court was not at all confused as to who was who in its deliberations in 1957. It heard testimony from Stumfall, who insisted that he was acting on behalf of Basch in a perfectly normal manner and that his commission was appropriate. The court then ruled that there was nothing discriminatory about Stumfall's commission and the charges in question since the buyer knew "that a Jewish asset was in question and that at that time special permissions were necessary."[161] If restitution often entailed a substantial gap between law and justice, in this case at least there was a welcome if curious confluence.

Such flickering moments of illumination – when those charged with dealing with restitution problems at Allianz were willing to recognize that they had been well aware that the assets coming into their hands were of Jewish origin and had been sold under constraint – were the exception rather than the rule. This was true not only with respect to real estate but also with respect to securities. One of the more protracted but telling cases dealing with securities was that of Peter Newman of New York City, who in November 1948 filed for restitution of

---

[159] Allianz an das Landgericht München I, Wiedergutmachungskammer, 18. Dez. 1956, WGB, Ia 919, Bd. 3.
[160] Allianz an die Wiedergutmachungsbehörde Bayern, 12. April 1949, ibid., Bd. 2.
[161] Sitzung der Wiedergutmachungskammer beim Landgericht München I, 12. Juli 1957, ibid., Bd. 3.

shares in Berlinische Lebensversicherungs Gesellschaft AG, a member of the Allianz concern. Peter was the son of Samuel Neumann, who owned a banking house and had died while still in Germany. Peter Newman, anxious to get out of Germany, found it necessary to transfer the shares to Merck, Finck & Co. in the spring of 1939, and the shares were sold to Allianz in August of that year. It was Newman's contention that anyone acquainted with the market at that time had to know that such a block of shares could only come from a Jewish portfolio, especially given the low price at which they were acquired. Furthermore, the shares of Berlinische Leben (as was not unusual in the case of insurance companies) could be purchased only with permission of the company, and the block of shares had been sizeable enough to merit a friendly visit to Samuel Neumann by the chairman of Berlinische Leben in the early 1930s.[162]

Allianz's response to the Newman claim was to declare – and, it must be said, with a disingenuousness that borders on the repulsive – that it certainly still held the shares that it had bought from Merck, Finck & Co. in Berlin and knew that they had been in the possession of the Neumanns, but that "the reason why these had been sold is unknown to us."[163] However, its chief argument against the Newman claim was that the shares in question, which had to bear a name and even if transferred were subject to approval by the corporation issuing the shares, could nevertheless be signed over to anyone. They were thus treatable (under the restitution laws and a variety of court decisions) as the equivalent of bearer certificates – that is, securities that could be bought and sold without being registered to a particular person – and therefore not subject to restitution. Newman kept on bringing the matter to court and losing, but the situation changed in February 1959 when the highest restitution court in Berlin ruled in Newman's favor, declaring that the shares in question were not a movable asset comparable to bearer certifications because approval had to be given by the company for their transfer. At this stage of the game, Allianz had no intention of going back to court. It certainly could not argue that Neumann would have sold the shares if the conditions created by National Socialism had not required it and the legal situation had not become "hopeless." Also, as the Allianz legal department argued, there were good "political reasons" for making a settlement with Newman: "the repeated justifiable public criticism concerning the drawn-out implementation of restitution in the Federal Republic."[164] Such considerations did not, however, lead to an initially acceptable offer of compensation to Newman by Allianz, which first valued the shares at 260% of the face amount even as they were selling on the market for 360%. After Newman's lawyer refused to accept the offer, Allianz agreed to the latter valuation,

---

[162] Peter Neuman an das zentrale Anmeldeamt, Bad Nauheim, 14. Nov. 1948; Peter Neuman an die Wiedergutmachungsämter von Berlin, 23. Juni 1952, WGÄ, 62 WGA 3397/51 (Peter Newmann, früher Neumann), Bl. 2–3, 20.

[163] Allianz an die Wiedergutmachungsämter, ibid., Bl. 6–7.

[164] Rechtsabteilung der Allianz an Allianz Vermögensverwaltung, 7. Juli 1959, FHA, AZ 8.1/2.

and in 1960 Newman received almost 59,000 DM instead of the 35,000 DM initially offered.[165]

While Newman had pursued his case quite aggressively, this was by no means true of other potential claimants on shares in Allianz's possession. Law 59 of the American military government had required Allianz to report all shares that might have belonged to Jews and been subject to restitution, and in May 1948 it had dutifully reported 598 shares of Allianz Leben that might possibly have been subject to restitution. No claims had been made on these shares until August 1955, when the organization designated to act in place of the Jewish Restitution Successor Organization (JRSO), the Hessian Trusteeship Administration GmbH in Wiesbaden, laid claim to the shares for purposes of restitution. As in the case of Newman, Allianz argued that the shares in question were like bearer certificates and were not subject to the legislation; Allianz also questioned whether it could be held responsible in certain cases where the provenance was unclear and where it was by no means certain the previous owner had been Jewish. There was no reason to presume that Kuno Feldmann or Otto Pieppel or someone with the name Blessing was Jewish. And even if an owner was clearly Jewish, as in the case of the banking house of Arnhold, shares bought in 1933 and then sold in 1934, or even shares that were traded by the bank in 1935–1937, could not be assumed to be distressed sales because the Arnhold Bank continued to both buy and sell shares at this time. Nevertheless, Hans Arnhold and his daughters Ellenmarie and Annamarie were claiming restitution. Allianz also questioned whether shares once held by the banking house of Mendelssohn & Co. in Berlin were also not traded in a normal manner. In negotiations with the Hessian Trusteeship Administration, the number of shares subject to possible restitution was reduced to 354. Aware that court decisions might prove unfavorable to their position, Allianz then offered to value the shares at the average quotation of 260 DM each, which would have amounted to 94,040 DM, and then settle for less than half this amount – namely, 46,020 DM. It would appear that the trusteeship administration was in the end prepared to accept 40,000 DM, but the federal supervisory office for insurance refused to approve the settlement on the grounds that the courts were still considering the shares in question to be bearer shares not subject to restitution. In reality, Allianz itself had little to lose since, under existing legislation, Allianz would then be substantially compensated for its settlement by the State of Bavaria, whose government (as shall be explained more fully) was guaranteeing the liabilities of the insurance companies. At the end of 1957, Allianz proposed a settlement of 20,000 DM and believed it would be possible to gain approval of the supervisory office for this sum, but the supervisory office contended that Allianz would only get 12,390 DM back from the Bavarian state and would thus lose 7,610 DM, which (in their view) constituted an unfair hardship for the concern. State guarantees of the insurance companies

---

[165] See the documentation in WGÄ, 62 WGA 3397/51 (Peter Newman, früher Neumann), Bl. 108–36.

had been based on the premise that they were technically bankrupt, which they had been at the end of the war. Thus, on the one hand, the Bavarian government was covering at least a portion of their restitution costs, while on the other it took the view that losses incurred by Allianz were unaffordable. This was not, in fact, the view held by Allianz, which thought that the amount in question could easily be absorbed. The supervisory office then gave permission for the settlement to go forward. What is one to make of this case? – aside from the fact that it was a good demonstration of how and why some of these restitution cases dragged on for as long as they did. To begin with, it took seven years before the trusteeship finally acted. It then proved difficult to determine in certain cases who was a Jew and who was not. Furthermore, in this instance, it could well be argued that some of the shares ended up in the Allianz portfolio through normal trading. Obviously, the lack of clarity about the legal situation served to diminish the settlement amount, but no less significant was that the federal supervisory office played a substantial role in reducing the settlement – even to the point where Allianz itself felt compelled to say that enough was enough.[166]

Matters were much simpler in other cases where the clear liability of Allianz was unquestionable. Thus, shares of Berliner Hagel-Assecuranz-Gesellschaft von 1832 belonging to the Mendelssohn family and purchased from Reichs-Kredit-Gesellschaft in 1938 obviously had to be restituted, since the name was known to Allianz and since the shares sold in 1938 were clearly alienated under duress. Simplest of all were the shares of Assecurantie Mij. De Nederlanden van 1845 which Allianz had bought in 1942 through Dresdner Bank. These shares were simply seized by the Allied military government in 1946, while other shares belonging to Dutch companies and citizens were handed over to the Dutch authorities.[167]

This is not to say that the various claims against German insurers by Germany's former enemies were that simple to settle, but once the Federal Republic had been established in 1949 and the emphasis was placed on reconstructing Germany and Europe, the settlement of insurance questions – as demonstrated by the record of negotiations in the archives – moved fairly rapidly. Not surprisingly, the British, who were most interested in getting the European economies and their own economy going again, led the way and even took the initiative. They were to be the driving force behind the London Debt Agreement of 1953, which dealt with prewar debts and, by giving priority to debt payment and reconstruction requirements, effectively protected German industry from reparations demands until the signing of a peace treaty.[168] The settling of insurance issues,

---

[166] The seemingly endless correspondence, running between 1955 and 1959, is to be found in FHA, AZ 8.1/1.

[167] See Allianz Vermögensabteilung an Rechtsabteilung der Allianz, 8. Feb. 1956, and other relevant documentation on the Mendelssohn case, FHA, AZ 8.1/3.

[168] On the London Debt Agreement, see Hermann J. Abs, *Entscheidungen 1949–1953. Die Entstehung des Londoner Schuldenabkommens*, 2. Aufl. (Mainz, 1991); Hans-Peter Schwarz (ed.),

however, antedated the larger agreement and demonstrated how, once again, insurance was given a special status in international arrangements from which the German insurance industry benefitted greatly. Thus, in March 1951 the British insurance leaders personally invited a number of leading German insurance executives (representing the Association of German Insurers) to privately discuss the question of settling prewar obligations between the insurance industries of the two countries. They took the view that the "international character of insurance" and the "inviolability of insurance contracts" required a settlement that would restore things to normal.[169] A formal agreement was reached in June that was very favorable to the Germans, enabling them to cover their obligations to their English counterparts by using the obligations of the latter to themselves. This was the beginning of a series of bilateral agreements in the 1950s between the German insurers and those of the countries occupied by Germany. The most important agreements certainly were with France in 1952, where so-called spoliation issues – that is, compensation to the French companies for the imposition of a German forced administration over their insurance companies, especially in Alsace-Lorraine, by German companies appointed as administrators – were subsumed under the general settlement of claims of a purely commercial nature. In short, no distinction was made between claims arising from the German occupation and prewar claims. In most cases, the assets of German insurers in these countries were, insofar as they had not been already used to compensate for assets taken during the war, released and thus available to cover the obligations of the German insurers. Normality in the international insurance business was thus restored by the end of the 1950s, a situation that obviously benefitted the German insurers, who were allowed to do international business again in 1954.[170]

Restitution to Customers: Property and Life Insurance

"Normality" also had important implications for the handling of insurance policies issued by German companies and held by persons living abroad. After the German hyperinflation of 1922–1923, there had been little enthusiasm on the

Die Wiederherstellung des deutschen Kredits. Das Londoner Schuldenabkommen (Stuttgart & Zürich, 1982); Christoph Buchheim, "Das Londoner Schuldenabkommen," in Ludolf Herbst (ed.), *Westdeutschland 1945–1955. Unterwerfung, Kontrolle, Integration* (Munich, 1986), pp. 219–27. For a good discussion on the relationship between the agreement and Wiedergutmachung, see Ulrich Herbert, "Nicht entschädigungsfähig? Die Wiedergutmachungsansprüche der Ausländer," in Herbst & Goschler, *Wiedergutmachung*, pp. 273–302.

[169] Niederschrift über die Besprechung am 4. Dez. 1951 betr. das Abkommen zwischen der deutschen und englischen Versicherungswirtschaft vom 5.–7. Juni 1951, GDV, RS/102.

[170] For the normalization of relations with France, see Politisches Archiv des Auswärtigen Amtes, B 86/89; with Belgium, the Netherlands, and Denmark, ibid., B 86/1045; with Austria, ibid., B 86/482 and 1045; with Great Britain, ibid., B 86/863; and for the restoration of the right to do business abroad, ibid., B 927.

part of foreigners about taking out German life insurance policies, so that most such policies held abroad were in the hands of emigrants. Their claims, according to accepted principles of international law, were considered part of the domestic German debt (i.e., what Germans and German entities owed to one another) and thus were subject to German legislation and regulations affecting such debt.[171] Therefore, turning to the final areas of restitution relevant to this study – namely, property insurance and above all life insurance – the question of insurance claims against German insurance companies had to be settled in accordance with German law.

Insofar as property insurance claims were at issue, the only significant area that came up with respect to restitution was the damage caused to Jewish assets during the Pogrom of November 1938. Allianz's position, as can be imagined, was that it had no liability since payment for damages caused through "domestic disturbances" was excluded from the insurance. The number of claims that poured in to the various insurers caused a considerable amount of worry, so that as early as the summer of 1947 the property insurers asked for a legal opinion from a major lawyer in Cologne, who affirmed in the strongest possible terms that the insurance conditions precluded coverage for such events. Just as the insurers in 1938 had argued that the payment of the 20 million RM demanded by Göring and the Finance Ministry threatened the existence of some of the insurance companies, so now, nine years later, their lawyer raised the same spectre:

Where such low instincts are set loose, where law and the consciousness of law are undermined, where the wild masses are let loose, there acts of force are unavoidable and damages incalculable. An insurance protection in such cases leads either to the collapse of the insurance companies or – if such a risk is included – burdens the insured with such high premiums that the conclusion of an insurance would be impossible. In the interest of the insured alone such a liability must be excluded.[172]

There were, nevertheless, certain peculiarities connected with the insurance situation of some of the victims of the Pogrom. One of them, Mali Fleischmann, whose father's home furnishings and possessions had been insured by Allianz, asserted that the company had used "the mood of the people" to refuse the payment claim and joined with her siblings in demanding compensation in 1948.[173] It is hard to imagine her making such a statement if it were not true, and in at least this case it would appear that Allianz used Goebbels's contention – that the Pogrom was an elemental outburst of the people against the Jews – not only in their efforts to escape payment to the government but also in claiming nonliability for the victims themselves. Then there was the Berlin shopowner Julius Schubert, who had made a claim and then suddenly received a notice on August

[171] See the negotiations with the Tripartite Commission in London, Oct. 21, 1952, GDV, RS/103.
[172] Gutachten Dr. Lenz, 22. Juli 1947, and Niederschrift über die Sitzung des Hauptausschusses der Arbeitsgemeinschaft Sachversicherung am 11. Juni 1947 in Köln, FHA, S 17.13/168.
[173] Mali Fleischmann an das Zentralmeldeamt, Bad Nauheim, 30. Nov. 1948, WGB, Ia 1688.

9, 1939, that he was receiving a payment of RM 3,850 – which, however, was being sent to the Reich Revenue Office. When his daughter and heir Gertrud Becker sought restitution from Allianz for the amount in question, Allianz contested the claim, pointing out that the fictitious payment made to Schubert was a consequence of the agreement reached between the insurance companies and the Reich, which relieved the companies of all obligation. Needless to say, the mystery of how they could be freed of all liability when they had no liability in the first place was never exactly explained, except by arguing that the companies had taken a stand on their nonliability but that the Reich had forced them to make some kind of payment anyway.[174] While one of the three courts that heard the case and decided against Becker made note of the fact that the payment could be deducted from a portion of the atonement tax, both Allianz and the courts took the position that there was never any liability on the part of the insurers and that the payment, on the one hand, was made without any claim for liability being recognized and, on the other, provided relief from all future claims against the companies. Gertrud Becker, who was living in Brooklyn, New York, had not found any of this convincing from the very start, and she had a particular animus against Allianz – claiming that its leadership (and especially Hilgard) had promoted the Nazi system and had consorted "especially with Göring and other worthies of this kind" already in 1933. She charged that even in that year Jews had been barred from entering the headquarters of Allianz and insisted that Allianz was one of the chief culprits in bringing about the Third Reich. It was they who had helped bring to power the "lunatics or criminals, who dragged down beautiful Germany and a large portion of the world into mass misery and misfortune."[175] She considered it scandalous that someone like Hilgard should still have a high position in the company, and she demanded that her claims should therefore be granted and what she considered the purely formal arguments of Allianz rejected. In any case, she intended to fight on for principled reasons and to demonstrate for all to see how restitution for the Jews was being handled in Germany.

Manifestly, this was not a very compelling legal argument, and the real test of the adequacy of restitution would be the success of her claims not against Allianz but rather against the government. One suspects, however, that the emotions reflected by her remarks were widespread and help to explain the insistence of many Jewish claimants on taking their cases from court to court. As has been shown, the performance of Hilgard and other Allianz leaders in the Pogrom was often morally deplorable, but this did not make it actionable. It is thus hard to fault the basic position of Allianz and the other insurers that, in view of the Nuremberg Trial evidence on the Pogrom, the responsibility for the damages lay with the Reich and its successor state – namely, the German Federal Republic.

---

[174] Allianz an den Magistrat von Groß-Berlin, Wiedergutmachungsamt, 31. Aug. 1950, FHA, S 17.13/168.
[175] Gertrud Becker an das Wiedergutmachungsamt Berlin, 29. Okt. 1950, ibid.

It was thus proper for Allianz to urge its former clients, like the aforementioned Fleischmann family, to seek recompense from that quarter under the Law for the Compensation of National Socialist Injustice of August 12, 1949, rather than the American Restitution Law (Law No. 52).[176]

This position received important confirmation in the key decision of the 2nd Civil Senate of the Federal Supreme Court of April 23, 1952, discussed earlier in this study,[177] which upheld the standpoint of the insurers and placed full responsibility on the government. It is important to note that it was an argument also accepted by the director of the JRSO, Ernst Katzenstein, who visited the Allianz offices on September 3, 1958, to discuss the claims that the JRSO intended to bring against the government on behalf of those who had suffered losses in the Pogrom. He pointed out that there was no intention of making claims against the insurers "since the JRSO is clear about the fact that the employment of the domestic unrest clause was justified."[178] Katzenstein believed, however, that the Reich should also restitute the payments it received from the insurers in the compromise worked out in 1939, although it remained unclear exactly what those arrangements were, and he wanted to know if Hilgard – whose testimony at Nuremberg had obviously been very important – was still alive. Indeed, the JRSO representative went so far as to suggest that the insurance companies join with it in suing the government for the "unjustly paid damage compensations" but agreed with the Allianz executive involved that it was not a paying proposition because compensation would have to be converted into DM. Whether a conversation between Katzenstein and Hilgard ever took place is unknown to this author, but Hilgard's position could not have been any different from that of Allianz, which told Katzenstein they had argued that domestic unrest was the issue but that

those in power at the time would not let this objection hold with the claim that it was not a matter of domestic disturbance, but of an "outburst of the people's rage against the agitation of international Jewry" .... Göring declared in unmistakable terms to the then head of the Reich Group for Insurance that there was to be no negotiation at all over the reason for the claims but there was only the question of what sum the insurance industry was in a position to spend.[179]

The result was the compromise under which the insurers were to act as if they were paying some portion of claims made by the Jews. What was left out of all this – assuming anyone involved at the time remembered (or cared to remember) what had actually happened – was that the originally much higher sums

---

[176] See Rechtsabteilung an die Generaldirektion, E.D.-Abteilung, 24. Nov. 1949, ibid., and Allianz an Justizrat Carl Drescher, 12. Dez. 1949, as well as Drescher an die Wiedergutmachungsbehörde I, Oberbayern, 17. Jan. 1950, withdrawing the Fleischmann complaint against Allianz, WGB, Ia 1688.

[177] See Chapter 5, pp. 228–9, as well as *Entscheidungen des Bundesgerichtshofes in Zivilsachen* 6 (1952), pp. 28–35.

[178] Aktennotiz, Betr. Pogromschäden aus dem Jahre 1938, FHA, S 17.13/169.

[179] Allianz an JRSO, 12. Aug. 1953, ibid.

demanded by Göring had been reduced to 1.3 million, and that this had been accomplished using arguments concerning the Pogrom by Hilgard and Goude-froy that were replications of those used by Goebbels and other perpetrators of the Pogrom. Now, thanks to Hilgard's and Goudefroy's liberation, they could speak freely of the Pogrom as being a domestic disorder once again.

As can be imagined, the most important claims made against Allianz and the other big insurance companies pertained to life insurance policies. At least for the period prior to the currency reform of June 1948, this problem must be viewed in part from the perspective of the financial and physical condition of the life insurance industry in 1945. This was succinctly described by the head of the insurance section of the OMGUS finance division for Württemberg-Baden in September 1945:

> When the Finance Division first began operations ... it was found that the insurance business of Württemberg/Baden was paralyzed. The major assets of most companies were Reich bonds and the Reich was non-existent. Most buildings had been bombed and records lost. Premiums, interest and dividends could not be collected and new policies were not being written. Also many policyholders moved and left no forwarding addresses.[180]

The greatest problem insofar as reconstruction of the industry was concerned was the overwhelming amount of state paper held by the companies. At the end of June 1946, such holdings for Allianz Leben amounted to 1,159,000,000 RM, which was much greater than their holdings of 93,067,000 RM in real property and 674,000,000 RM in mortgages.[181] Under Allied regulations, the Reich bonds could neither be cashed in nor sold on the exchanges, and they were simply liquidated in the currency reform of 1948. Fundamentally, then, they were nothing but fictitious coverage, and this – combined with the other immediate postwar circumstances – created a high degree of uncertainty. As a consequence and with Allied approval, the life insurance industry decided in February 1946 that it could not pay full value on insurance policies but chose instead to pay only 40% on the policies of those who died before the capitulation on May 8, 1945, and full payment to the beneficiaries of those who died after that date. The motive for this arrangement, whose basic unfairness was fully recognized by the insurers, was that it would promote confidence in the industry among the living – the full number and cost of the deceased still being uncertain – and thereby encourage them to pay their premiums.[182] These payment restrictions were eased in October 1946 and then eliminated in March 1947, although a levy was imposed by the insurance companies on payments in order

---

[180] Report by George R. Cooper, NA, RG 260, OMGUS, OMG WB, Admin. Div., 12/16–3/3.

[181] "Erhebung über den Versicherungsbestand und die Liquiditätslage der Lebensversicherungsun-ternehmungen," Hauptstaatsarchiv Stuttgart, EA5/002 L1, Bd. 181.

[182] Bericht über die Sitzung des Bankausschusses-Unterausschusses Versicherungen vom 12. März 1946, ibid., EA1/104, Bd. 236.

to make them possible despite loss of the premiums and interest suffered by the companies.[183]

Ultimately, the future of the industry depended upon general economic conditions and above all a currency reform, which would restore confidence more generally and for which the insurance companies prepared and calculated assiduously well before it took place. The leaders of the insurance industry – of which Gerd Müller of Allianz Leben was among the most outstanding in his capacity to define the situation and the possibilities with rigor and impeccable logic – were well aware that the government would need a healthy insurance industry, and Müller was explicit about the importance of the insurance industry for the encouragement of savings and the generation of tax revenues. It could and would claim special treatment and be in a position to transform the liabilities of yesterday into claims against the state and thereby, although technically bankrupt, enjoy a virtual state guarantee of survival as stability was being restored. Indeed, the insurance companies had an entitlement to make "equalization demands" of the government as compensation for the damages they suffered because of the war and especially because of the total loss of value of the Reich bonds. It was only by such means that coverage requirements could be met.[184]

Thus, a fundamental aspect of this insurance industry reconstruction effort (albeit one that was typical for the private economy as a whole) was, as much as possible, to shed past burdens and shift responsibilities to the government for the disasters of the past. The management of insurance claims emanating from Jewish policyholders – who had been compelled to make their policies premium-free and/or repurchase their policies or who had their policies confiscated under the 11th Decree – was part and parcel of this more general tendency. This does not mean that there was anything sinister involved or that the German Federal Republic, as the legal successor to the National Socialist regime, should not have taken responsibility for the compensation of such policies. As we shall see, however, Allianz and the insurance industry organizations played a major and direct role in structuring the manner in which the compensation of confiscated Jewish insurance assets was effectuated. On the one hand, the response of Allianz to the claims of Jewish policyholders inevitably promoted the self-exculpation process. On the other, the form taken by the compensation procedure no less

---

[183] A useful source of information on the reconstruction problems is "Verband der Lebensversicherungsunternehmen e.V., Geschäftsbericht 1938–1948, Teile I–III." An account of the changing policies toward policy payment is to be found in Teil II, pp. 26–8. The copy used here is from Staatsarchiv Bremen, 3-V6-12/348.

[184] Verband der Lebensversicherungsunternehmen e.V., Geschäftsbericht 1938–1948, Teil III, p. 18, Staatsarchiv Bremen, 3-V6-12/348; Gerd Müller an Rechtsanwalt Wehl, Württ.-Badisches Finanzministerium, 10. Juni 1947, and his memorandum, "Die Behandlung der Lebensversicherung in der Finanzreform," Hauptstaatsarchiv Stuttgart, EA5/002 L1, Bd. 181. The slow process of postwar financial reconstruction is well described in Arps, *Wechselvolle Zeiten,* pp. 166–98. On the currency reform and equalization demands, see Deutsche Bundesbank (ed.), *Fünfzig Jahre Deutsche Mark. Notenbank und Währung in Deutschland seit 1948* (Munich, 1998), pp. 130f.

inevitably veiled the extent to which the relationship between insurer and policy-holder had been compromised by the confiscation of Jewish insurance assets. The management of the compensation of Jewish insurance assets, however rational and justified it may appear in the context of the time, necessarily served to block or attenuate any serious reflection on the implications of what had happened with respect to business ethics and the social responsibility of business. The Jewish policyholders had, after all, been stakeholders in the much vaunted "community of risk" who had been cast out. How (assuming it was at all possible to do so) and on what terms was one to "make good" the damage done to them?

If the question is put in this way, then even the simplest and most straightforward problem in the payment of Jewish insurance assets (i.e., the payment of an insurance policy due to death or because the policy came to term) was not without its problematic aspects. Take, for example, the case of Otto Jeidels, who had taken out a 100,000-RM life insurance policy in 1931 and died in 1947. Apparently, the policy had not been reported to the financial authorities under the 11th Implementation Decree to the Reich Citizenship Law. Possibly this was because Jeidels was known already to be an American citizen and thus could not be classified as a German Jew living abroad, but it is also possible that those in charge at Allianz chose to "overlook" the policy. In any case, Allianz Leben paid out 8,161.94 DM to his widow Gertrud Jeidels in 1949 – that is, at the ratio defined by the June 1948 currency reform of 10 RM for 1 DM. It would appear that the actual DM payment was reduced to cover unpaid premiums and pay the so-called war levy, a 10% charge imposed on all insurance payments and designed to spread the costs of payments for those killed in the war. Gertrud Jeidels had maintained personal contact with Kurt Schmitt after her husband's death and visited him on the occasion of a trip to Germany in 1950, where, as Schmitt reported in a letter to Gerd Müller of Allianz Leben, "she also brought up the life insurance of her husband, which, if I correctly understood her – was paid out by Allianz at 10 : 1. She asked me whether as an American and one of the persecuted she did not have a claim to 1 : 1."[185] Schmitt promised to look into the matter, pointing out to Müller that Jeidels had been an important supervisory board member and adviser to Allianz as well as a prominent banker in Germany and the United States and that his death was a loss to Germany. Müller responded by observing that the status of RM claims by citizens of the victorious powers had not yet been regulated, so that Gertrud Jeidels's question was "premature."[186] However, in reality the Allies, especially the Americans, were the guardians of currency reform and took the position that hardships would be alleviated in the projected law on the equalization of burdens. Mrs. Jeidels's heir was, in fact, a beneficiary of this law since Jeidels had an entitlement under the "Old Savers' Law" passed in 1953, which sought to give special compensation to persons who

---

[185] Schmitt an Gerd Müller, 13. Sept. 1950, FHA, NL 1/18.
[186] Müller an Schmitt, 22. Sept. 1950, ibid.

had savings prior to 1939 and had suffered unfairly from the currency reform. As a result, in 1955 he received a credit slip from Allianz entitling him to draw 4,200 DM from the Burden Equalization Fund along with an expression of Allianz's regret that more was not being granted for life insurance policies.[187]

Underlying Gertrud Jeidels's question about the conversion rate for the assets of the persecuted under the currency reform was a more fundamental question: Why should Jews (or any other persecuted group or persons) be in any way financial victims of Hitler's war in the calculation of their restitution? Thus, another German-Jewish refugee-turned-American-citizen was furious when he received only 2,502.14 DM in 1949 on the 20-year 30,000-RM life insurance policy he had taken out in 1928. The policy had apparently escaped confiscation, possibly because the policyholder was not recognized to be Jewish, and dividends had apparently covered the premiums until late 1944, which now left almost 500 DM to be deducted from the final 3,000-DM payout. He promptly made a claim for restitution: "Insofar as the problem of the 'restitution' of the paid life insurance contributions is concerned, payment in depreciated money is really no 'restitution' but rather an avoidance of real restitution. Therefore I hereby petition that the repayment value be brought into a reasonable relation to the true sense of a 'life insurance' policy."[188] Allianz's position was that its payment was in conformity to the currency law and that the policyholder had the choice of either accepting the payment or refusing it and waiting for a regulation of his rights in the future. It is interesting that the policyholder himself could not define a reasonable relation between the expectations he held in 1928 and those he was entitled to hold in 1948. Needless to say, currency reforms are notoriously unfavorable to those holding liquid assets. Indeed, while the Americans demanded restitution to Jews, they also demanded German reconstruction, and this particular policyholder also complained bitterly about the breakdown of American–Soviet relations and his inability to be compensated for assets in the East. He even went so far as to demand payment from Marshall Plan Funds being used to reconstruct Germany! As was often the case with Jews at this time, there was a good deal of resentment at the rebuilding of Germany so soon after the war and a strong sense that everything was being forgotten because of the change in the international situation. Restitution in the context of German reconstruction and the Cold War necessarily implied that compensation of German-Jewish assets be an integral part of the postwar financial and economic scenario: lost real value and destruction resulting from the war launched by those who had oppressed and despoiled the Jews.

A variety of claims were made against Allianz by Jews (or on behalf of deceased Jews) for restitution of insurance policies that had been repurchased and/or made

---

[187] For the Jeidels policy see AZLB, A 104788.
[188] Ernst E. Englehart [originally Engelhardt], MD, an das Zentralmeldeamt, Bad Nauheim, 9. Jan. 1949, and Allianz Leben an das Amtsgericht Stuttgart, 1. Nov. 1949, Hauptstaatsarchiv Stuttgart, EA5/002 R10, Bd. 272. Actually, it was not Englehart but his wife who was Jewish, and he and his family left Germany for this reason.

premium-free during the National Socialist period, as well as for policies whose repurchase value had been confiscated under the 11th Implementation Decree of the Reich Citizenship Law of November 1941. Allianz rejected these claims, and its position was regularly upheld in the courts. In some cases, neither Allianz nor the claimants had evidence of the policies or sufficient information about their history. Most basically, however, Allianz (and other insurers) took the position – forcefully expressed in an Allianz letter to Ministerial Director Richard Ringelmann of the Bavarian Finance Ministry on April 23, 1949 – that

it was a matter of indifference as to what the reasons are that insurance policies expire, whether through unilateral action of the policyholder or through termination by the insurer because of non-payment of premiums, or through interventions on the part of the authorities (11th Implementation Decree of the Reich Citizenship Law). The fact is, in any case, that these policies no longer exist and that the insurance companies, which had in no way contributed to the dissolution of these contracts, are not in the position to restore them again on their own authority. This position has also been taken by the military governments and the Länder in the American and French zones. As a consequence, the Länder have been summoned to issue compensation laws according to which the persecuted should be given compensation for their claims insofar as they cannot be made good according to the Restitution Law.[189]

This letter was written at a time when the disposition of such cases by the restitution courts was anything but certain. Allianz faced a suit by the heirs of a Jewish policyholder who had repurchased his policies (which fell due in 1941–1942) in 1939 and had instructed Allianz to place the money in his blocked account. In this case, the claimants were not asking Allianz for the money already paid – they were presumably planning to sue the government for that – but rather for the difference between what had already been paid and the full value of the policies when they came to term, minus the premiums that would have been paid under normal circumstances. Quite aside from the fact that this could have been a costly precedent in the case of large policies, it was a potentially dangerous precedent since it opened up the possibility that all policies that were repurchased or confiscated could be liable to at least partial resurrection. From the standpoint of the insurers, it was essential to establish the principle that they had no liability whatever toward the policyholders, that the liability lay with the public authorities, and that paragraph 89 of the restitution law (Law 59), which provided for special legislation to deal with insurance, be implemented in a way that confirmed the insurers' position. Turning to Ringelmann for his advice in this matter was especially relevant because he was considered by Allianz as the "father" of the *Wiedergutmachung* law passed by the Council of Länder and subsequently approved by the American authorities in the summer of 1949. Allianz won its case in a decision of the Stuttgart Restitution Chamber of June 1, 1949, but the appeal to Ringelmann is interesting since he tended to take a hard line

---

[189] Allianz an Ministerialdirektor Ringelmann, 23. April 1949, BAK, B 280/1706, and Bayerisches Hauptstaatsarchiv, MF 71778.

on *Wiedergutmachung* for financial reasons and undoubtedly could be counted upon to be sympathetic to the Allianz position.[190]

Nevertheless, the complicated problem of *Wiedergutmachung* for the insured remained to be solved, and both the conceptual approach to such *Wiedergutmachung* and the mode of implementation were of obvious concern to the insurers. The most fully developed and important statement of their position was made by Gerhard Frels of Gothaer Leben, deputy chairman of the Association of Life Insurance Companies, whose various zonal branches were allowed to join together to form an association for all the Western zones in June 1948. He was also the chairman of the association's committee for legal and legislative questions and served as its most important spokesman on *Wiedergutmachung* questions.[191] In an article of January 1950, Frels laid down the basic position of the insurance industry toward the issue of *Wiedergutmachung,* which is especially notable for the way in which it brought together the self-understanding of the industry about its role in the National Socialist period, its financial condition as a result of National Socialist rule and the wiping out of a substantial portion of its paper assets in the currency reform, and the primacy of reconstruction considerations. Frels was quite insistent that policyholders deserved and had to receive a restoration of their rights and assets, and that this needed to be done as rapidly as possible. At the same time,

the financial burdens of this *Wiedergutmachung,* however, ought not to be placed on the shoulders of the insurance companies. Otherwise, one injustice would replace another, for the German life insurers are not to blame for the persecutory measures under which many of their policyholders had to suffer. They abhorred these measures and did nothing by themselves to promote them. But they could just as little ward them off any more than the entire German people could prevent the terroristic measures of the Nazi regime. *Wiedergutmachung* with respect to life insurance must ... be carried out at the expense of the State (the Länder or the Federation). One must also consider in this regard that the life insurance companies, which have delivered to the Länder from the assets of these companies an estimated two billion DM in debtor's gain, have been left with no means for *Wiedergutmachung* purposes. Such means must therefore also be provided to them subsequently if they are burdened with *Wiedergutmachung* obligations, and this would lead to a raising of the equalization demands to be provided them. By means of this laborious and costly detour the end result would still be a burdening of the State with *Wiedergutmachung* costs. This detour can and must be avoided.[192]

The basic principle under which policyholders would receive justice was laid down in the *Wiedergutmachung* laws accepted by the Western occupation powers, above all in section 37 of the Bavarian law in August 1949, which became the

---

[190] The court decision is in BAK, B 280/1706. On Ringelmann, see Goschler, *Wiedergutmachung,* pp. 138ff.

[191] "Verband der Lebensversicherungsunternehmen e.V., Geschäftsbericht 1938–1948," Teil III, pp. 5–9, Staatsarchiv Bremen, 3-V6-12/348.

[192] Gerhard Frels, "Wiedergutmachung nationalsozialistischen Unrechts in der Lebensversicherung," in *Versicherungsrecht* 1 (1950), pp. 1–3, 60–1, quote on p. 1.

model not only for the other Western zones but also for the federal compensation legislation of 1953 and 1956. Under this law, "*Wiedergutmachung* is constituted by the restoration at the expense of the State of the legal situation which would have existed if the damaging event had not occurred."[193] The amount of compensation was limited to 10,000 DM, and the insurance companies were obligated to provide information to claimants and collaborate in the restoration of their entitlements. Yet implementing the quoted principle was no simple matter, and it provided the insurers and their organizations with considerable opportunity to shape the rules and regulations governing compensation; indeed, the Association of Life Insurers drew up a draft for the implementation of section 37 in 1949. In March 1950, the coordination bureau of the Interministerial Working Group for *Wiedergutmachung* and Compensation Questions of the German Federal Republic set up a committee to work on these questions and was also charged to do so in consultation with the Association of German Life Insurers.[194] It moved very slowly, however, in part because its chairman (Ministerial Director Heiland of the Baden Finance Ministry) was appointed to the Federal Constitutional Court, so that numerous technical questions continued to remain open at the end of 1951. Initially, for example, the insurance companies thought that government compensation could be used not simply to restore insurance rights as some sort of useful fiction but actually to enable the claimant to choose to revive the policy on a DM basis. That is, assuming the policy had not come to term, the former policyholder would become a policyholder once again by using compensation monies to pay the premiums and keep the policy going. Ultimately, the opening of such an option was considered too complicated, but it is illustrative of the technical issues that had to be faced. A more basic problem, as the insurance organizations justifiably argued, was the need for regulation of the matter at the federal level, so that there would be uniformity and consistency of practice. The difficulty here was that all issues of restitution and compensation remained a special reserve of the occupation powers even after the establishment of the Federal Republic, so that the West German government had first to develop the basic principles under which it would regulate these questions and then secure Allied agreement.[195] Ultimately, this came about in the wake of the Luxemburg Agreement between Germany and Israel in 1952 and the Federal Compensation Laws of 1953 and 1956, all of which explains why most of the compensation for insurance assets dates from the late 1950s and early 1960s.

The provisions for the compensation of lost insurance assets were contained in sections 127–133 of the Federal Compensation Law (BEG), which in its provisions leaned very heavily on the basic principles (just discussed) that were developed in 1949–1950.[196] The insurance companies were freed of all responsibility

---

[193] Quoted in ibid., p. 2.
[194] Koordinierungsbüro an das Finanzministerium Württemberg-Baden, 4. Aug. 1950, Hauptstaatsarchiv Stuttgart, EA5/002 R10, Bd. 272.
[195] Frels, *Wiedergutmachung,* pp. 60f.
[196] See the excellent discussion of Detlef Kaulbach, "Versicherungsschäden außerhalb der Sozialversicherung (§§127–133 BEG)," in *Die Wiedergutmachung nationalsozialistischen Unrechts durch*

for the compensation of policies, but were responsible for helping to find the policies of claimants and, most importantly, were assigned the task of calculating the entitlement of the claimants. This was done on a special form designed by the federal supervisory office for insurance.[197] Under this legislation, the German government recognized that Jews who ceased paying premiums, had made their policies premium-free, or had repurchased their policies in the Nazi regime had done so under duress and deserved compensation – just as did those whose policies were confiscated by government order under the 11th Decree of the Reich Citizenship Law. The point of departure for all compensation was that one started with the full value of the policy and what its present worth would be if the Third Reich had never existed. Then, a distinction was made between those who had received the repurchase value of their policies (whether directly or in a blocked account) and those who had their repurchase value confiscated by the authorities. The value of the policies of those in the first category was calculated by deducting the repurchase value they had received and/or monies they had borrowed on the policies and by deducting unpaid premiums after due credit was given for dividends that would have been received. The fictitious premiums owing before 1948 were calculated at 10% of their RM value, since the RM had been reduced under the currency reform, while those owing after 1948 were calculated in DM. The compensation given was the remaining cash value with the RM portion reduced by 90% (because of the currency reform) plus the Old Saver's entitlement. In those cases where the repurchase value was paid out directly by the insurer to agencies of the Nazi government, the policy was treated in terms of its full face value and there was no deduction of repurchase value at the time of confiscation. Whatever was then owed in RM was reduced to 10% (i.e., converted into DM) and to this was added the Old Saver's entitlement.

Clearly, those who had been subject to direct confiscation were very much favored by this arrangement, while those who had experienced either no confiscation or indirect confiscation were likely to receive pathetically little. Thus, a doctor who had taken out a 20-year policy in 1925 for 25,000 RM and who repurchased it in 1938 for 14,571 RM – 12,000 of which he needed to pay the Reich Flight Tax – ended up receiving 339.20 DM in 1956. This was because the repurchase value he had received in 1938 was deducted from the value of the policy as having been paid out already. The fact that the Nazis got most of the value he had received was irrelevant from the standpoint of the insurer, although the policyholder had every right to claim compensation from the government for the Reich Flight Tax and probably did. Even more extreme was the case of a widow whose husband had taken out a 20-year 10,000–gold mark policy in

die Bundesrepublik Deutschland, hrsg. vom Bundesminister der Finanzen in Zusammenarbeit mit Walter Schwarz, Bd. 5: Hans Giessler u.a., *Das Bundesentschädigungsgesetz. Zweiter Teil (§§51 bis 171 BEG)* (Munich, 1983), pp. 321–35.

[197] A copy is to be found in ibid., pp. 334f. For the discussion that follows, see also the report of Rudolf Gerlach in J. D. Bindenagel (ed.), *Washington Conference on Holocaust-Era Assets. November 30–December 3, 1998. Proceedings* (Washington, D.C., 1999), pp. 623–7.

1925 – subject to mandatory conversion into RM in 1938 – and had repurchased his policy in 1939 for 5,308.30 RM. She applied for compensation in 1956 and, when all the calculations were done, received 10 DM. The 10,000 RM less the money received in 1939 had left a policy worth 4691.70 RM, or 469.17 DM before premium deductions, which ate up most of the remaining value.[198]

To understand – in concrete terms – how so much could be reduced to so little and what this meant to a policyholder, it is useful to consider an actual case that demonstrates the odyssey of a German-Jewish life insurance policy from its purchase in 1925 to its final payment in 1960. The 20-year policy for 50,000 gold marks was taken out by the then 30-year-old engineer. At the time, the policy was redeemable either in RM or dollars and was reinsured by a foreign reinsurer. Despite this, the policyholder decided to convert his policy into RM after 1934, presumably because the dollar's devaluation (and his desire to take advantage of Allianz's 1:1 conversion offer) left him with little choice. In 1937, he and his wife emigrated, putting the repurchase value of their insurance (then amounting to 16,981.61 RM) into a blocked account, which was subsequently confiscated in 1943. They first went to France, where they had to go underground, and then ended up in the United States. In November 1948, the policyholder sent a lengthy demand for compensation to the U.S. military government under Law No. 59 asking not only for the worth of his insurance but also for the dollar value of the insurance on the day the policy fell due, March 1, 1945. The policyholder felt entitled to such compensation because he had been deprived of the security that the policy was intended to provide and had "only been able to live his life under unworthy and wretched circumstances." He was demanding compensation from both Allianz and the legal successor to the Reich Treasury. Allianz responded to this claim in 1950 by arguing that the RM conversion of the policy had been voluntary and that it had effectively paid off the policy, so that the responsibility lay with the government. The case dragged on until 1960, when the policyholder's widow finally collected 494.39 DM under the Compensation Law of 1956. The calculation was as follows.[199]

Value of policy:	50,000.00 RM	
Repurchase value paid in 1937		16,981.51 RM
Unpaid premiums on balance		25,071.30 RM
War levy		3,000.00 RM
Total deductions		45,052.81 RM
Balance:	4,947.19 RM = 494.72 DM	

That the widow of this engineer could collect only 494 DM on a 50,000-RM policy while the daughter of a businessman could collect 371 DM on a 25-year 10,000-RM policy, also originally denominated in gold marks and taken out in 1925, demonstrated the relative advantage for assets compensated as a consequence of direct confiscation. In this complicated and tragic case, the businessman in question – who had apparently been allowed to continue as a wholesaler

---

[198] AZLB, F 234080 and F 236446.
[199] AZLB, F 235163. The discrepancy in the pfennig is due to the rounding off of the figures.

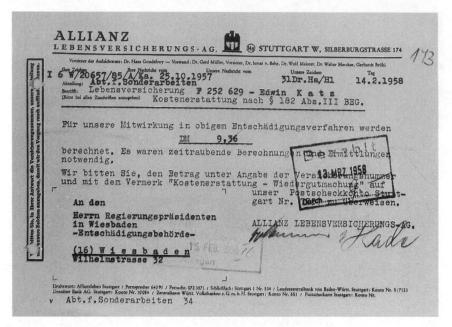

For offering services in restitution procedures, Allianz Leben charges the Wiesbaden Restitution Office an amount according to the official flat rate, February 14, 1958.

dealing in old paper as late as 1940 – wrote Allianz in April 1940 asking about making his policy premium-free with the intention of later repurchasing it when he would emigrate. Allianz warned him that this would significantly reduce the value of his policy, so the policyholder did nothing except to make a prepayment on the policy – that is, a credit on future repurchase – of 727.50 RM. He and his wife were deported in October 1940; after sending him a number of premium bills and warnings, Allianz learned that he had been "deported with his family to an unknown place." The policy was then made premium-free and set at a value of 5,298 RM on the death of the insured or on April 1, 1950. In early 1943, Allianz reported the existence of the policy to the revenue office in accordance with the 11th Implementation Decree of the Reich Citizenship Law, and it subsequently paid the value of the policy to the Mannheim revenue office's bureau for the Administration of Assets of Jews and Enemies of the Reich. A decade later, in 1953, the daughter of the policyholder made inquiries at Allianz. After being informed that the policy had been cancelled owing to nonpayment of premiums, she told the company that the premiums had not been paid because her parents had been killed in 1942. In October 1957, the restitution value of the policy was calculated and the daughter received 371.67 DM.[200]

The calculations in these cases, as in all insurance restitution cases, were done by the insurance company involved, which under the law was allowed to charge

[200] AZLB, F 235590.

3, 6, or 9 DM, the last amount being asked in cases involving "time consuming calculations and investigations."²⁰¹ Perhaps such language was a formulaic requirement needed to justify charging the very nominal 9 DM rather than 3 DM or 6 DM in simpler cases, but it is hard not to find it jarring today – and the reflection of an underlying attitude of irritation over an unwanted distraction. This said, it is important not to let the distressingly low sums paid in such "restoration" of insurance rights – with all its fictions and complications – lead to overdrawn negative conclusions, and this for two reasons. First, however little one received for insurance policies repurchased by the policyholder, such payment in no way precluded making substantial claims for compensation of monies used to pay the Reich Flight Tax, the atonement tax, and other costs involved in dealing with and escaping from the Nazi authorities. Second, life insurance was a relatively small and marginal part of *Wiedergutmachung* and hence is no basis for drawing large-scale conclusions about a unique effort, however flawed, to recognize and (insofar as possible) make some recompense for the despoliation perpetrated by the National Socialist regime. True, a prominent Jewish lawyer who sought refuge in Honduras in 1939 may in 1956 have received only 105.67 DM for his 10,000-RM life insurance policy. The more important question in judging *Wiedergutmachung,* however, is what he received for his claims for the destruction of his valuable home furnishings and art works by SA thugs in the November Pogrom, his incarceration in Dachau, the loss of his lucrative career – estimated by him to be worth 500,000 RM – and the sale of his possessions at prices far below their real value. There were also the costs of obtaining visas and passage for himself and his family, as well as suitable tropical clothing. Moreover, the gold discount bank did not allow him to take more than 1,447 RM (or 6%) of the 24,128 RM remaining to him so that he might begin a new life in a far-away country – to which he would never have dreamed of emigrating had he not been told by the camp commandant at Dachau that the purpose of his incarceration (and also of his fellow Jews) was to persuade them to leave Germany and that they would not survive a second stay in Dachau. The insurance file in question does not reveal how many of these claims were compensated nor how much this individual received for all his claims, and much more research needs to be done before a proper evaluation of the postwar compensation effort can be made.²⁰²

Life insurance looms large in this study for obvious reasons, but the purpose of the discussion is not to determine whether more could or should have been paid or whether some other formula should have been found for insurance compensation; rather, our purpose is to explore the mentality and attitude of the

---

²⁰¹ The law in question was the 4. Durchführungsverordnung zum BEG vom 15. März 1957 (BGBl, 1957, I, p. 281). For an illustration, see Allianz an den Regierungspräsidenten in Kassel, 21. Juni 1961, and other relevant documents in HessHStA, Abt. 518/14011.

²⁰² AZLB, F 257045. The case is especially interesting because of the detailed accounts and estimates of losses contained in the claim (made by this former corporate lawyer in 1949), which happens to be included in the insurance file.

businessmen who dealt with the problem in the postwar years. That was a mentality of putting behind them all they had been doing in the National Socialist period and all the ugly things that had happened. While Allianz employees were filling out the tedious compensation forms, the concern was prospering once again, and no one was celebrating this more in public than Artur Lauinger. In an article of May 1956, he reported that Allianz Leben had raised its capital shares from 5.25 to 12.25 million DM, that it was paying an 8% dividend (which reflected its steady and moderate policy in this regard), and that – despite Germany's shrunken size – its life insurance portfolio had almost attained the value of 1938 while its premium intake exceeded that of 1938. The growth of large insurance policies was especially notable. At the same time, costs had been reduced thanks to rationalization measures. In other articles, Lauinger was no less enthusiastic about the development of Allianz and Munich Re, and he particularly celebrated the return of the latter to international markets after 1954. He was what he had always been, a critical but strong supporter of a private German insurance industry as part of a liberal and cosmopolitan international insurance business: "The German insurance business abroad and with the outside world had a very significant volume before the war, and it demonstrated itself to be a strong source of foreign exchange. The return to normal relations can be greeted on all sides."[203] Indeed, the Third Reich appeared as an ugly and almost irrelevant intermezzo in more ways than one. Thus, when Lauinger received the Commander's Cross of the Order of Merit at the end of 1952, Hilgard rushed to congratulate him: "Whoever like myself could observe over the decades what you have done for the German insurance business as an incorruptible journalist knows how much you have earned this decoration." Lauinger was happy to hear from Hilgard and shared the latter's desire to get together again and, "as in the old days, talk not only about the German insurance business but also about the world in which we live and which has changed so much."[204] Lauinger probably never knew, and Hilgard had either repressed or forgotten, how enraged the latter had been at the former in 1935 and how Hilgard had threatened to use the fact that Lauinger was a Jew to silence him.[205] In any case, it was easy enough and certainly more pleasant to skip over the recent past and concentrate on such previous achievements as the handling of the Favag affair and on the current positive situation of the insurance business.

There are limits, however, to adaptation and forgetting, and they were certainly reached when Allianz celebrated its centenary in 1990. Neither General Director Wolfgang Schieren nor the invited speaker on the occasion, the

---

[203] Lauinger an die Wirtschaftsredaktion der Frankfurter Neuen Presse, 3. Feb. 1959, his article entitled "Wieder Fremdwährungsversicherungen," and his articles on Allianz Leben, Allianz, and Munich Re of 1956, Institut für Stadtgeschichte Frankfurt am Main, S 1/48 (Nachlaß Lauinger), Nr. 22.

[204] Hilgard an Lauinger, 4. Jan. 1953, and Lauinger an Hilgard, 23. Jan. 1953, ibid.

[205] See Chapter 4, pp. 166–7.

prominent journalist and Hitler biographer Joachim Fest, gave even a suggestion that Allianz might in any way have been implicated in the Third Reich. Schieren did, to be sure, mention that Heß had replaced Schmitt in 1933, but the reason for Schmitt's departure was simply left unmentioned. As for the Second World War, it had "initially destroyed all hopes" and then cut deeply into Allianz's personnel and leadership and caused losses of domestic and international markets as well as of valuable physical assets. The speech given by Fest was primarily a broad historical overview stressing the follies of utopianism, as demonstrated especially by the recent collapse of communism. Allianz did also commission a history for the occasion in which the Nazi period received some coverage but in which the weight of interpretation was given to efforts by Heß and others to help Jews and contacts with the Resistance. The book, of course, was intended to cover a century, but it is a very different interpretation of Allianz in the Third Reich from that presented here and, in this author's opinion, must be viewed as a lost opportunity to deal with this part of Allianz's past.[206]

The opportunity would arise again under most unexpected circumstances. Seven years later, Allianz and some of its subsidiaries – along with a host of other companies, some non-German – were forced to confront the past as a result of a class action filed against them in the State of New York for refusing to pay Jewish life insurance policyholders or their heirs. Along with this came revelations about Allianz's involvement in the insuring of concentration camp factories.[207] Whether ignorance is ever bliss is an arguable point, but it certainly had ceased to be so in 1997. It must also be said – to the credit of the present leadership of Allianz – that some of its members had been very unhappy about the superficial treatment of the concern's role in the Third Reich as described in the commissioned history of 1990. The effort to correct that situation led to the commissioning of this book, which is one of a number of such studies requested by German concerns and companies who have decided to open their archives and support independent scholarly research into what is also inevitably a most unhappy chapter in their histories. Perhaps this could only be done by a generation of managers who were too young to have been involved with the Third Reich and whose education and development took place in the much more liberal and cosmopolitan context of Germany in the last few decades. Certainly "globalization" and doing business in the United States has been a powerful influence on the willingness of German and other business enterprises to face the past, and it is hard to imagine that the opening up of archives and the confronting of various compensation issues would have taken place as they have absent the peculiarities of American tort law and the American regulatory and political

---

[206] *100 Jahre Allianz. Festansprachen 9. März 1990* (Munich, 1990), esp. pp. 28–9 and 59–95; Borscheid, *100 Jahre Allianz*, esp. pp. 105–33. Here I find myself in complete agreement with the remarks of Arno Surminski in his useful overview, *Versicherung unterm Hakenkreuz* (Berlin, 1999), esp. pp. 260–7.

[207] See "Das 'Wagnis Auschwitz'," *Der Spiegel*, Heft 23 (June 1997), pp. 50–63.

system. Recent revelations about the past of prominent German historians and other professionals, who faced no lawsuits and are anything but "globalized," have also demonstrated that Germany's business enterprises are not alone in the slowness with which they confront the past – as well as in the need for a measure of external and public pressure to force them to do so.

Historians can no more evade the public controversies involved in this study than can businessmen. It would be improper to conclude this study without saying something about the issue to which it owes its existence: the question of unpaid Jewish insurance policies.[208] For reasons involving the manner in which German Jews were despoiled and the way in which restitution was organized, it is most unlikely that significant life insurance assets remain unpaid. Allianz and other German insurance companies had no interest in hiding them, since the bill would be paid by the government anyway. Obviously, every effort should be made to satisfy unmet claims that are justified, but the search for unpaid policies should be subject to cost–benefit considerations – above all, in consideration of the needs of surviving victims of National Socialism in Eastern Europe. Also, insurance assets were differently treated in different national venues, and it is important not to lump together truly unpaid insurance assets in the former communist countries once held by Italian (or even German) companies, whose holdings were nationalized, with the policies of German or former German citizens held by German (or non-German) companies operating in Germany.

It is understandable that lawyers concentrate on what is actionable rather than on what is simply awful. The latter seems to be the province of the historian and, as this study has tried to show, Allianz and its leaders were implicated in various ways in the evils of the Nazi regime. There were certainly much worse companies and businessmen, but the Allianz of today has at least been proactive and taken a leading role in facing the moral issues involved and in dealing with the social responsibilities arising from them. Restitution and compensation must nevertheless come to their inevitable closure, but the history discussed here – and in other studies dealing with the National Socialist period – should remain open to future correction and reflection and thus to inclusion as part of both corporate and general history.

This is not to say that the events of 1933–45 can or should be "historicized." The twelve-year reign of National Socialism was and hopefully will remain a unique descent into barbarism by a highly advanced industrial society. The most depressing finding of this book is that the German business community, of which the insurance business was a vital member, not only failed to defend civilized values but all too often actively engaged in their destruction. This began even before the National Socialists came to power, when Schmitt and Hilgard

---

[208] For my general views on this subject see Gerald D. Feldman, "Unternehmensgeschichte im Dritten Reich und die Verwantwortung der Historiker. Raubgold und Versicherungen, Arisierung und Zwangsarbeit," in Norbert Frei, Dirk van Laak, & Michael Stolleis (eds.), *Geschichte vor Gericht. Historiker, Richter und die Suche nach Gerechtigkeit* (Munich, 2000), pp. 103–29.

lunched with Göring and then assumed a proactive posture toward the National Socialist regime after it came to power. In doing so, they set the tone for the Allianz Concern and for the insurance industry generally, as well as for the business community. Schmitt's acceptance of the position of Reich Economics Minister was an act of national and international import that sent a signal that the business community could and would work with the regime. Similarly, Hilgard's assumption of the leadership of the Reich Group, his adoption of Nazi language and principles in his public performances, his willingness to violate basic principles of liberal economics in accepting state direction of the economy, and his participation in the imperialist ambitions of the Third Reich during the war involved a great deal more than "preventing the worst." Perhaps that is the way he felt after a hard day of running from ministry to ministry and dealing with people like Schwede-Coburg, and it certainly was the way he felt after 1945, but the truth is that Hilgard's was an extraordinarily skillful effort to conduct interest-group politics under the stressful conditions of National Socialist rule and that this effort had little or no moral content.

The leadership of Allianz were not not rabid anti-Semites, but they were sufficiently anti-Semitic to approve of early National Socialist measures and then to put up relatively little resistance as the regime increased its persecution of the Jews. As the events surrounding the Pogrom of November 1938 demonstrated, little remained of business ethics when it came to the treatment of Jews, and thus the way was paved for active participation in the despoliation of Jews, including Jews who worked for the concern, in the "Aryanization" process. Various acts of genuine decency and of assistance to Jews on the part of Allianz executives (such as Hans Heß) and officials notwithstanding, Nazi Germany had turned anti-Semitism into a national and international endeavor in which Allianz became a participant. Its role in Lodz and in insuring SS factories was the end result of a process that began at Restaurant Hiller.

Of course, those who lunched with Göring did not want – and could not have imagined – what National Socialism would bring, but they also failed to acknowledge their engagement and responsibility after it had all taken place. The pretension of Allianz (and of the German business community generally) after 1945 that they were "victims" of National Socialism was truly appalling, and it infected the postwar restitution effort as well. There is, of course, no reason why corporations and businessmen should be better than the society of which they are a part, and there was nothing particularly unique about their attitudes in postwar Germany. They are certainly not the last group in German society that needs to own up to its past. Nevertheless, capitalist institutions and those who guide them do have a special responsibility in societies organized on the basis of private property and liberal economic principles. This was a responsibility that they not only failed to meet but also betrayed under National Socialism. As this book has tried to show, the question was not merely a matter of survival in a totalitarian state, since this survival involved a mixture of willing participation and spineless conformism, of narrow professionalism and self-interested pursuit of profit, and, above all, of opportunism. It would be unhistorical and unrealistic to expect businessmen to have been resistance leaders, and Wilhelm Arendts became one only as a high officer in the German military, but as his case (and those of Hans Heß and Johannes Tiedke) demonstrated, it was possible to set limits to one's engagement with the regime. Of course, more than such distancing was needed, since what was totally lacking was a commitment to democratic values.

Bibliography

Archives

The following is not a complete list of the archives visited but rather a list of those in which at least some material of relevance to this study was found.

Algemeen Rijksarchief, Den Haag, Nederlandsche Beheeres Institut
Allianz Elementar Versicherungs-AG, Archiv, Vienna (AZ Wien)
Allianz Lebensversicherungs-AG, Archiv, Berlin (AZLB)
Altbankarchiv der Dresdner Bank, Berlin
Amtsgericht München, Registratur S, Munich (AM)
Amtsgericht Rosenheim, Spruchkammer Bad Aibling, Rosenheim
Archiv générales des Royaumes, Brussels
Archives Nationales, Paris (AN)
Archiwum Głownej Komisji Badania Zbrodni przeciwo Narodowi Polskiemu – Instytut Pamię ci Narodowej (Archiv der Hauptkommission zur Untersuchung der Verbrechen am polnischen Volk – Institut des nationalen Gedenkens), Warsaw
Archiwum Państwowe w Łodzi (Staatsarchiv Lodz), Lodz (APL)
Archiwum Państwowe w Poznaniu (Staatsarchiv Posen), Posen (APP)
Archiwum Państwowe w Wrocławiu (Staatsarchiv Breslau), Wroclaw
AXA Colonia Konzern AG, Historisches Archiv, Cologne (AXA)
Banca Commerciale Italiana, Archiv, Milan (BCI)
Basler Lebens-Versicherungs-Gesellschaft, Archiv, Basel
Bayerisches Hauptstaatsarchiv, Munich
Bundesarchiv Berlin (BAB)
Bundesarchiv Koblenz (BAK)
Bundesarchiv-Militärarchiv, Freiburg i.Br.
Centr Chranenijsa Istoriko-Dokumental'nych Kollekcii (Zentrum für die Aufbewahrung historisch-dokumentarischer Sammlungen – "Sonderarchiv Moskau"), Moscow (SM)
Centre de Recherches et d'Etudes Historiques De la Seconde Guerre Mondiale, Brussels (CREH)
Centre des Archives Economiques et Financières, Savigny-Le-Temple
Centre des Archives du Monde Travail, Roubaix
Firmenhistorisches Archiv der Allianz AG, Munich (FHA)
Geheimes Staatsarchiv Preußischer Kulturbesitz, Berlin
Gesamtverband der deutschen Versicherungswirtschaft e.V., Archiv, Berlin (GDV)
Hamburg-Mannheimer Versicherungs-Gruppe, Unternehmensarchiv, Hamburg (HM)
Hauptstaatsarchiv Stuttgart
Hauptstaatsarchiv Weimar
Hessisches Hauptstaatsarchiv, Wiesbaden (HessHStA)
Historický ústav Armády Česke republiky (Militärhistorisches Archiv), Prague
Historisches Archiv der Deutschen Bank, Frankfurt a.M. (HADB)
Historisches Archiv der Dresdner Bank, Frankfurt a.M.

Institut für Stadtgeschichte, Frankfurt a.M.
Institut für Zeitgeschichte, Munich (IfZ)
Leo Baeck Institute, New York
Ministère des Finances, Office des Sequestres (Sequesterarchiv), Brussels (MdF)
Ministerie van Justitie, Centraal Archief Bijzondere Rechtspleging, The Hague (CABR)
Münchener Rückversicherungs-Gesellschaft Aktiengesellschaft, Historisches Archiv, Munich (MR)
Nachlaß Dr. Heinrich Fehlmann, Privatbesitz
Nachlaß Johannes Tiedke, Privatbesitz
Niedersächsisches Hauptstaatsarchiv, Hannover
Nordrhein-Westfälisches Hauptstaatsarchiv, Düsseldorf
Oberfinanzdirektion Berlin
Österreichisches Staatsarchiv – Archiv der Republik, Vienna (ÖStA-AdR)
Politisches Archiv des Auswärtigen Amtes, Bonn
Rijksinstituut voor Orlogsdocumentatie, Amsterdam (RIOD)
Schweizerische Rückversicherungs-Gesellschaft, Archiv, Zurich (SR)
Schweizerisches Bundesarchiv, Bern (BAR)
Staatsarchiv Bremen
Staatsarchiv Hamburg
Staatsarchiv Ludwigsburg
Staatsarchiv München
Stadt- und Landesarchiv Wien
Stadtarchiv Leipzig
Stadtarchiv München
Stadtgeschichtliches Institut der Stadt Bühl
Statni Ustredni Archiv v Praze (Zentrales Staatsarchiv), Prague
U.S. National Archives, Washington, D.C. (NA)
Wiedergutmachungsämter von Berlin (WGÄ)
Wiedergutmachungsbehörde Bayern, Ansbach (WGB)

Periodicals, Official Publications, and Documentary Collections

Akten der Reichskanzlei. Weimarer Republik. Die Kabinette Brüning I und II, bearbeitet von
   Tilman Koops, Bd. 3: 10. Oktober 1931 bis 30. Mai 1932 (Boppard am Rhein, 1990).
Akten der Reichskanzlei. Regierung Hitler 1933–1938, hrsg. von Konrad Repgen & Hans Booms,
   bearb. von Karl-Heinz Minuth, 2 vols. (Boppard am Rhein, 1983).
Akten zur Deutschen Auswärtigen Politik 1918–1945, Serie D (1937–1941), Bd. V: Polen, Südost-
   europa, Lateinamerika, Klein- und Mittelstaaten. Juni 1937–März 1939 (Baden-Baden, 1953).
Allianz-Adler.
Allianz-Zeitung.
Assecuranz-Compass. Internationales Jahrbuch für Versicherungswesen 47 (1939).
Bindenagel, J. D. (ed.), *Washington Conference on Holocaust-Era Assets. November 30–December*
   3, 1998. Proceedings (Washington, D.C., 1999).
Bundesgesetzblatt.
Deutschland-Berichte der Sozialdemokratischen Partei Deutschlands (Sopade) 1934–1940, 1934
   (Frankfurt a.M., 1980).
Enderle-Burcel, Gertrude (ed.), *Christlich-Ständisch-Autoritär. Mandatare im Ständestaat 1934–*
   1938. Biographisches Handbuch der Mitglieder des Staatsrates, Bundeskulturrates, Bundeswirt-
   schaftsrates und Länderrates sowie des Bundestages (Vienna, 1991).
Entscheidungen des Bundesgerichtshofes in Zivilsachen, Bd. VI–VII (1951–1952).
Gaertringen, Friedrich Freiherr Hiller von (ed.), *Die Hassell-Tagebücher 1938–1944. Ulrich von*
   Hassell. Aufzeichnungen vom andern Deutschland (Berlin, 1988).
Independent Commission of Experts Switzerland – Second World War (Bergier Commission),
   Switzerland and Gold Transactions in the Second World War. Interim Report (Bern, 1998).

Junz, Helen B., "Report on the Pre-War Wealth Position of the Jewish Population in Nazi-Occupied Countries, Germany, and Austria," in Independent Committee of Eminent Persons, *The Volcker Commission: The Report on Dormant Accounts of Victims of Nazi Persecution in Swiss Banks* (Bern, 1999).

Ministerialblatt für die Preußische innere Verwaltung.

Neumanns Zeitschrift für Versicherungswesen.

Der Prozeß gegen die Hauptkriegsverbrecher vor dem Internationalen Militärtribunal. Nürnberg 14. November–1. Oktober 1946, Bd. 28 (Nuremberg, 1948) [International Military Tribunal at Nuremberg].

Les Rapports de la Mission d'étude sur la spoilation des Juifs de France (Matteoli Report), ⟨http://www.ladocfrancaise.gouv.fr⟩.

Reichsgesetzblatt.

Rosenkranz, Robert, *Die Versicherungswirtschaft im Protektorat Böhmen und Mähren, im Sudetenland und in der Slowakischen Republik* (Prague, 1941).

Rückerstattungsrecht. Bundesrückerstattungsgesetz vom 19.7.1957, Textausgabe mit Verweisen und Sachverzeichnis (Beck'sche Textausgaben), 5. neubearb. Aufl. (Munich, 1970).

Das Schwarze Korps.

Second World War. Final Report of the Second World War Assets Contact Group: Theft and Restoration of Rights (Amsterdam, 2000).

Die Tagebücher von Joseph Goebbels, hrsg. von Elke Fröhlich, Teil I: Aufzeichnungen 1923–1941, Bd. 6: August 1938–Juni 1939, bearb. von Jana Richter (Munich, 1998).

Die Tagebücher von Joseph Goebbels, hrsg. von Elke Fröhlich, Teil II: Diktate 1941–1945, Bd. 13: Juli–September 1944, bearb. von Jana Richter (Munich, 1995).

Unhabhängige Expertenkommission Schweiz – Zweiter Weltkrieg, *Die Schweiz und die Goldtransaktionen im Zweiten Weltkrieg. Zwischenbericht* (Bern, 1998) [Bergier Commission].

Veröffentlichungen des Reichsaufsichtsamts für Privatversicherung (Leipzig, 1901ff.).

Völkischer Beobachter.

Walk, Joseph (ed.), *Das Sonderrecht für die Juden im NS-Staat. Eine Sammlung der gesetzlichen Maßnahmen und Richtlinien – Inhalt und Bedeutung, 2. ed.* (Heidelberg, 1996).

Die Wiedergutmachung nationalsozialistischen Unrechts durch die Bundesrepublik Deutschland, 6 Bde., hrsg. vom Bundesminister der Finanzen in Zusammenarbeit mit Walter Schwarz (Munich, 1974–1987).

Zusammengefaßter Geschäftsbericht über die Tätigkeit des Reichsaufsichtsamtes für Privatversicherung 1939 bis 1945 [Veröffentlichungen des Bundesaufsichtsamtes für das Versicherungs- und Bausparwesen, Sonderheft 3] (Berlin, 1955).

Secondary Literature

50 Jahre Allianz. Eine Chronik in Bildern (Berlin, 1940).

100 Jahre Allianz. Festansprachen 9. März 1990 (Munich, 1990).

Aalders, Gerard, *Geraubt! Die Enteignung jüdischen Besitzes im Zweiten Weltkrieg* (Cologne, 2000).

Aalders, Gerard, "Three Ways of German Economic Penetration in the Netherlands: Cloaking, Capital Interlocking and 'Aryanization'," in Overy et al., *Die "Neuordnung" Europas*, pp. 273–98.

Abs, Hermann J., *Entscheidungen 1949–1953. Die Entstehung des Londoner Schuldenabkommens*, 2 Aufl. (Mainz, 1991).

Ackerl, Isabella, "Der Phönix-Skandal," in Ludwig Jedlicka & Rudolf Neck (eds.), *Das Juliabkommen von 1936. Vorgeschichte, Hintergründe und Folgen. Protokoll des Symposiums in Wien am 10. und 11. Juni 1976* (Vienna, 1977), pp. 241–79.

Adler, Hans Günther, *Der verwaltete Mensch. Studien zur Deportation der Juden aus Deutschland* (Tübingen, 1974).

Arps, Ludwig, *Auf sicheren Pfeilern. Deutsche Versicherungswirtschaft vor 1914* (Göttingen, 1965).

Arps, Ludwig, *Wechselvolle Zeiten. 75 Jahre Allianz Versicherung 1890–1965* (Munich, 1965).

Arps, Ludwig, "Kurt Schmitt und Hans Heß," in Ludwig Arps, *Deutsche Versicherungsunternehmer* (Karlsruhe, 1968), pp. 165–79.

Arps, Ludwig, *Durch unruhige Zeiten. Deutsche Versicherungswirtschaft seit 1914, Bd. 1: Erster Weltkrieg und Inflation, Bd. 2: Von den zwanziger Jahren zum Zweiten Weltkrieg* (Karlsruhe, 1970 & 1976).

Augustinovic, Werner, & Moll, Martin, "Gunter d'Alquen – Protagonist des SS-Staates," in Ronald Smelser & Enrico Syring (eds.), *Die SS: Elite unter dem Totenkopf. 30 Lebensläufe* (Paderborn, 2000), pp. 100–18.

Bähr, Johannes, *Der Goldhandel der Dresdner Bank im Zweiten Weltkrieg. Ein Bericht des Hannah-Arendt-Instituts* (Leipzig, 1999).

Bajohr, Frank, *"Arisierung" in Hamburg. Die Verdrängung der jüdischen Unternehmer 1933–1945* [Hamburger Beiträge zur Sozial- und Zeitgeschichte. Bd. 35] (Hamburg, 1997).

Barkai, Avraham, " 'Schicksalsjahr 1938'. Kontinuität und Verschärfung der wirtschaftlichen Ausplünderung der deutschen Juden," in Pehle, *Der Judenpogrom 1938*, pp. 94–117.

Bazyler, Michael J., "Nuremberg in America: Litigating the Holocaust in United States Courts," *University of Richmond Law Review* 34 (2000), pp. 1–283.

Benz, Wolfgang, "Der Rückfall in die Barbarei. Bericht über den Pogrom," in Pehle, *Der Judenpogrom 1938*, pp. 13–51.

Benz, Wolfgang, Graml, Hermann, & Weiß, Hermann (eds.), *Enzyklopädie des Nationalsozialismus* (Munich, 1997).

Benz, Wolfgang, Houwink ten Cate, Johannes, & Otto, Gerhard (eds.), *Die Bürokratie der Okkupation. Strukturen der Herrschaft und Verwaltung im besetzten Europa* (Berlin, 1998).

Berghahn, Volker, *The Americanisation of West German Industry 1945–1973* (Cambridge, 1985).

Bernhardt, Heike, *Anstaltspsychiatrie und "Euthanasie" in Pommern 1933–1945. Die Krankenmorde an Kindern und Erwachsenen am Beispiel der Landesheilanstalt Ueckermünde* (Frankfurt a.M., 1994).

Boelcke, Willi, *Die deutsche Wirtschaft 1930–1945. Interna des Reichswirtschaftsministeriums* (Düsseldorf, 1983).

Böhle, Ingo, "Die Volksfürsorge Lebensversicherungs-AG im 'Dritten Reich'," Magisterarbeit Universität Hamburg (Hamburg, 1996).

Böhle, Ingo, "Die Volksfürsorge Lebensversicherungs AG – ein Unternehmen der Deutschen Arbeitsfront (DAF) im 'Dritten Reich'," *Zeitschrift für Unternehmensgeschichte* 45 (2000), pp. 49–78.

Böhret, Carl, *Aktionen gegen die "kalte Sozialisierung" 1926–1930. Ein Beitrag zum Wirken ökonomischer Einflußverbände in der Weimarer Republik* [Schriften zur Wirtschafts- und Sozialgeschichte, Bd. 3] (Berlin, 1966).

Borscheid, Peter, *100 Jahre Allianz* (Munich, 1990).

Botur, André, *Privatversicherung im Dritten Reich. Zur Schadensabwicklung nach der Reichskristallnacht unter dem Einfluß nationalsozialistischer Rassen- und Versicherungspolitik* [Berliner Juristische Universitätsschriften, Zivilrecht, Bd. 6] (Berlin, 1995).

Broszat, Martin, *Der Staat Hitlers Grundlegung und Entwicklung seiner inneren Verfassung* (Munich, 1969).

Broszat, Martin, et al. (eds.), *Deutschlands Weg in die Diktatur* (Berlin, 1983).

Browning, Christopher, *Nazi Policy, Jewish Workers, German Killers* (Cambridge & New York, 2000).

Buchheim, Christoph, "Das Londoner Schuldenabkommen," in Ludolf Herbst (ed.), *Westdeutschland 1945–1955. Unterwerfung, Kontrolle, Integration* (Munich, 1986), pp. 219–27.

Burrin, Philippe, *France under the Germans. Collaboration and Compromise* (New York, 1996).

Chandler, Alfred D., *Scale and Scope. The Dynamics of Industrial Capitalism* (Cambridge, 1990).

Corni, Gustavo, & Gies, Horst, *Brot. Butter. Kanonen. Die Ernährungswirtschaft unter der Diktatur Hitlers* (Berlin, 1997).

Deutsche Bundesbank (ed.), *Fünfzig Jahre Deutsche Mark. Notenbank und Währung in Deutschland seit 1948* (Munich, 1998).

Dingell, Jeanne, "Die Haupttreuhandstelle Ost, Treuhandstelle Posen: Staatliche Raubzüge. Deutsche Kolonialisierungsbestrebungen und deren Auswirkung auf das warthländische Geschäftsleben im Zweiten Weltkrieg," unpublished lecture presented to the "Arbeitskreis zur Rolle der Unternehmen im Nationalsozialismus" der Gesellschaft für Unternehmensgeschichte, Frankfurt a.M. (January 2000), ⟨http://www.unternehmensgeschichte.de⟩.

Dirks, Christian, "Die 'Juni-Aktion' 1938 in Berlin," in Beate Meyer & Hermann Simon (eds.), *Juden in Berlin 1938–1945. Begleitband zu der gleichnamigen Ausstellung in der Stiftung "Neue Synagoge Berlin – Centrum Judaicum." Mai bis August 2000* (Berlin, 2000), pp. 33–41.

Dodd, William E., Jr., & Dodd, Martha, *Ambassador Dodd's Diary, 1933–1938* (London, 1942).

Eggenkämper, Barbara, "Die Vision vom 'aktenlosen Büro.' Von der Lochkarte zum Computer," in Burkhart Lauterbach (ed.), *Großstadtmenschen. Die Welt der Angestellten* (Frankfurt a.M., 1995), pp. 229–48.

Eggenkämper, Barbara, Rappl, Marian, & Reichel, Anna, "Der Bestand Reichswirtschaftsministerium im 'Zentrum für die Aufbewahrung historisch-dokumentarischer Sammlungen' ('Sonderarchiv') in Moskau," *Zeitschrift für Unternehmensgeschichte* 43 (1998), pp. 227–36.

Eichholtz, Dietrich, "Institutionen und Praxis der deutschen Wirtschaftspolitik im NS-besetzten Europa," in Overy et al., *Die "Neuordnung" Europas*, pp. 29–62.

Eichholtz, Dietrich (ed.), *Krieg und Wirtschaft. Studien zur deutschen Wirtschaftsgeschichte 1939–1945* (Berlin, 1999).

Eisenberg, Carolyn, *Drawing the Line. The American Decision to Divide Germany 1944–1949* (New York, 1996).

Etmektsoglou, Gabriella, "Changes in the Civilian Economy as a Factor in the Radicalization of Popular Opposition in Greece, 1941–1949," in Overy et al., *Die "Neuordnung" Europas*, pp. 193–240.

Farquharson, John E., *The Plough and the Swastika. The NSDAP and Agriculture in Germany 1928–1945* (London & Beverly Hills, 1976).

Faulstich, Heinz, *Hungersterben in der Psychiatrie 1914–1949. Mit einer Topographie der NS-Psychiatrie* (Freiburg i.Br., 1998).

Feldman, Gerald D., "Industrialists, Bankers and the Problem of Unemployment in the Weimar Republic," *Central European History* 25 (1992), pp. 76–96.

Feldman, Gerald D., "The Deutsche Bank from the First World War to the World Economic Crisis, 1914–1933," in Gall et al., *The Deutsche Bank*, pp. 130–276.

Feldman, Gerald D., "Politische Kultur und Wirtschaft in der Weimarer Zeit," *Zeitschrift für Unternehmensgeschichte* 43 (1998), pp. 3–18.

Feldman, Gerald D., "Existenzkämpfe," in *Der Tagesspiegel, 6. Nov. 1998, Sonderbeilage über die American Academy Berlin*, p. 5.

Feldman, Gerald D., "Nazi Confiscation of Insurance Policy Assets" and "Compensation and Restitution: Special Issues," in Bindenagel, *Washington Conference on Holocaust-Era Assets*, pp. 579–83, 599–604.

Feldman, Gerald D., "Unternehmensgeschichte im Dritten Reich und die Verantwortung der Historiker. Raubgold und Versicherungen, Arisierung und Zwangsarbeit," in Norbert Frei, Dirk van Laak, & Michael Stolleis (eds.), *Geschichte vor Gericht. Historiker, Richter und die Suche nach Gerechtigkeit* (Munich, 2000), pp. 103–29.

Feldman, Gerald D., "Insurance Company Collapses in the World Economic Crisis: The Frankfurter Allgemeine Versicherungs-AG (Favag) and the Austrian Phönix," in Harold James (ed.), *The Interwar Depression in an International Context* (Munich, 2001).

Fest, Joachim, *Albert Speer. Eine Biographie* (Berlin, 1999).

Fisch, Jörg, *Reparationen nach dem Zweiten Weltkrieg* (Munich, 1992).

Földi, Tamás, "Insurance Claims in a Historical Context with Special Regard to the Holocaust in Hungary," in Bindenagel, *Washington Conference on Holocaust-Era Assets*, pp. 629–48.

Förster, Michael, *Jurist im Dienst des Unrechts: Leben und Werk des ehemaligen Staatssekretärs im Reichsjustizministerium, Franz Schlegelberger, 1876–1970* (Berlin, 1995).

Frei, Norbert, *Vergangenheitspolitik. Die Anfänge der Bundesrepublik und die NS-Vergangenheit* (Munich, 1996).

Frels, Gerhard, "*Wiedergutmachung* nationalsozialistischen Unrechts in der Lebensversicherung," *Versicherungsrecht* I (1950), pp. 1–3, 60–1.

Friedlander, Saul, *Nazi Germany and the Jews: Vol. 1: the Years of Persecution 1933–1939* (New York, 1998).

Gaede, Herbert, *Schwede-Coburg. Ein Lebensbild des Gauleiters und Oberpräsidenten von Pommern* (Berlin, 1939).

Gall, Lothar, et al., *The Deutsche Bank 1870–1995* (London, 1995).

Genschel, Helmut, *Die Verdrängung der Juden aus der Wirtschaft im Dritten Reich* [Göttinger Bausteine zur Geschichtswissenschaft, Bd. 38] (Göttingen, 1966).

Gerlach, Christian, *Kalkulierte Morde. Die deutsche Wirtschafts- und Vernichtungspolitik in Weißrußland 1941 bis 1944* (Hamburg, 1999).

Gimbel, John, *The American Occupation of Germany. Politics and the Military, 1945–1949* (Stanford, 1968).

Goschler, Constantin, *Wiedergutmachung. Westdeutschland und die Verfolgten des Nationalsozialismus (1945–1954)* [Quellen und Darstellungen zur Zeitgeschichte, Bd. 34] (Munich, 1992).

Graml, Hermann, *Reichskristallnacht. Antisemitismus und Judenverfolgung im Dritten Reich* (Munich, 1988).

Harrison, Ted, " 'Alter Kämpfer' im Widerstand. Graf Helldorf, die NS-Bewegung und die Opposition gegen Hitler," *Vierteljahrshefte für Zeitgeschichte* 45 (1997), pp. 385–423.

Hayes, Peter, "Big Business and 'Aryanization' in Germany, 1933–1939," *Jahrbuch für Antisemitismusforschung* 3 (1992), pp. 254–81.

Hayes, Peter, "State Policy and Corporate Involvement in the Holocaust," in Michael Berenbaum & Abraham J. Pecks (eds.), *The Holocaust and History: The Known, the Unknown, the Disputed, and the Reexamined* (Bloomington, Ind., 1998), pp. 197–218.

Hensel, Rudolf, *Amerika. Aus Tagebuchblättern einer Reise* (Berlin, 1928).

Herbert, Ulrich, *Fremdarbeiter. Politik und Praxis des "Ausländer-Einsatzes" in der Kriegswirtschaft des Dritten Reiches* (Berlin & Bonn, 1985).

Herbert, Ulrich, Orth, Karin, & Dieckmann, Christoph (eds.), *Die nationalsozialistischen Konzentrationslager. Entwicklung und Struktur*, 2 vols. (Göttingen, 1998).

Herbst, Ludolf, & Goschler, Constantin (eds.), *Wiedergutmachung in der Bundesrepublik Deutschland* (Munich, 1989).

Hilberg, Raul, *The Destruction of the European Jews,* 3 vols. (New York, 1985).

Hildebrand, Klaus, "Monokratie oder Polykratie? Hitlers Herrschaft und das Dritte Reich," in Gerhard Hirschfeld & Lothar Kettenacker (eds.), *Der "Führerstaat": Mythos und Politik. Studien zur Struktur und Politik des Dritten Reiches* (Stuttgart, 1981), pp. 73–97.

Hockerts, Hans Günter, "Wiedergutmachung in Deutschland. Eine historische Bilanz 1945–2000," *Vierteljahrshefte für Zeitgeschichte* 49 (2001), pp. 167–214.

Houwink ten Cate, Johannes, & Otto, Gerhard (eds.), *Das organisierte Chaos. "Ämterdarwinismus" und "Gesinnungsethik". Determinanten nationalsozialistischer Besatzungsherrschaft* (Berlin 1999).

James, Harold, "The Deutsche Bank and the Dictatorship," in Gall et al., *The Deutsche Bank,* pp. 277–356.

Jelinek, Tomas, "Insurance in the Nazi Occupied Czech Lands: Preliminary Findings," in Bindenagel, *Washington Conference on Holocaust-Era Assets,* pp. 605–21.

Jelinek, Tomas, "Insurance in the Nazi Occupied Czech Lands," (http://www.hrad.cz/kpr/holocaust/pojistky_uk.html).

Kaulbach, Detlef, "Versicherungsschäden außerhalb der Sozialversicherung (§§127–133 BEG)," in *Die Wiedergutmachung nationalsozialistischen Unrechts durch die Bundesrepublik Deutschland. Hrsg. vom Bundesminister der Finanzen in Zusammenarbeit mit Walter Schwarz, Bd. 5: Hans*

Giessler u.a., *Das Bundesentschädigungsgesetz. Zweiter Teil (§§51 bis 171 BEG)* (Munich, 1983), pp. 321–35.

Kershaw, Ian, *Hitler. 1889–1936, Hubris* (New York, 1999).

Kisch, Wilhelm, *Fünfzig Jahre Allianz. Ein Beitrag zur Geschichte der Deutschen Privatversicherung* (Munich 1940).

Klee, Ernst, *"Euthanasie" im NS-Staat. Die "Vernichtung lebensunwerten Lebens"* (Frankfurt a.M., 1985).

Klemperer, Viktor, *LTI. Notizbuch eines Philologen* (Leipzig, 1975).

Knebusch, Roland, "Als Versicherungs-Generaldirektor im Dritten Reich" (Letter to the Editor), *Frankfurter Allgemeine Zeitung*, 17. Nov. 1998.

Köbel, Heinrich, "Der nebenberufliche Vertreter im Versicherungsgewerbe," *Neumanns Zeitschrift für Versicherungswesen* 56 (1933), pp. 832f.

Kracauer, Siegfried, *Die Angestellten. Aus dem neuesten Deutschland* (Frankfurt a.M., 1930); republished as *Die Angestellten. Eine Schrift vom Ende der Weimarer Republik* (Allensbach & Bonn, 1959).

Ladwig-Winters, Simone, *Anwalt ohne Recht. Das Schicksal jüdischer Rechtsanwälte in Berlin nach 1933* (Berlin, 1998).

Lauinger, Artur, *Das öffentliche Gewissen. Erfahrungen und Erlebnisse eines Redakteurs der Frankfurter Zeitung* (Frankfurt a.M., 1958).

Lecroix-Riz, Annie, *Industriels et Banquiers sous l'Occupation. La Collaboration économique avec le Reich et Vichy* (Paris, 1999).

Loewy, Hanno, & Schoenberner, Gerhard (eds.), *"Unser einziger Weg ist Arbeit." Das Ghetto Lodz 1940–1944* (Vienna, 1990).

Longerich, Peter, *Politik der Vernichtung. Eine Gesamtdarstellung der nationalsozialistischen Judenverfolgung* (Munich & Zurich, 1998).

Lösener, Bernhard, "Als Rassereferent im Reichsministerium des Innern," *Vierteljahrshefte für Zeitgeschichte* 9 (1961), pp. 264–313.

Lotz, Wolfgang, *Die Deutsche Reichspost 1933–1945. Eine politische Verwaltungsgeschichte, Bd. 1: 1933–1939* (Berlin, 1999).

Lumans, Valids O., *Himmler's Auxiliaries. The Volksdeutsche Mittelstelle and the German National Minorities of Europe, 1933–1945* (Chapel Hill & London, 1993).

Manes, Alfred (ed.), *Versicherungslexikon. Ein Nachschlagewerk für alle Wissensgebiete der gesamten Individual- und Sozial-Versicherung*, 3. Auflage (Berlin, 1930).

Mason, Tim, *Sozialpolitik im Dritten Reich. Arbeiterklasse und Volksgemeinschaft* (Opladen, 1977).

Mehl, Stefan, *Das Reichsfinanzministerium und die Verfolgung der Deutschen Juden 1933–1943* [Berliner Arbeitshefte und Berichte zur Sozialwissenschaftlichen Forschung, Nr. 38] (Berlin, 1990).

Moeller, Robert G., "War Stories: The Search for a Usable Past in the Federal Republic of Germany," *American Historical Review* 101 (1996), pp. 1008–48.

Mommsen, Hans, *Alternative zu Hitler. Studien zur Geschichte des deutschen Widerstandes* (Munich, 2000).

Mommsen, Hans, & Grieger, Manfred, *Das Volkswagenwerk und seine Arbeiter im Dritten Reich* (Düsseldorf, 1996).

Mußgnug, Dorothee, *Die Reichsfluchtsteuer 1931–1953* [Schriften zur Rechtsgeschichte. Heft 60] (Berlin, 1993).

Naasner, Walter, *Neue Machtzentren in der deutschen Kriegswirtschaft 1942–1945. Die Wirtschaftsorganisation der SS, das Amt des Generalbevollmächtigten für den Arbeitseinsatz und das Reichsministerium für Bewaffnung und Munition/Reichsministerium für Rüstung und Kriegsproduktion im nationalsozialistischen Herrschaftssystem* [Schriften des Bundesarchivs, Bd. 45] (Boppard am Rhein, 1994).

Naimark, Norman, *The Russians in Germany. A History of the Soviet Zone of Occupation, 1945– 1949* (Cambridge, Mass., & London, 1995).

Nicholls, Anthony, J., *Freedom with Responsibility. The Social Market Economy in Germany 1918–1963* (Oxford, 1994).

Niethammer, Lutz, *Die Mitläuferfabrik. Die Entnazifizierung am Beispiel Bayerns*, 2. Aufl. (Berlin & Bonn, 1982).

Nolan, Mary, *Visions of Modernity. American Business and the Modernization of Germany* (Oxford & New York, 1994).

Overy, Richard J., *War and Economy in the Third Reich* (Oxford, 1994).

Overy, Richard J., "The Economy of the German 'New Order'," in Overy et al., *Die "Neuordnung" Europas*, pp. 11–28.

Overy, Richard J., "The Four-Year Plan" [Arbeitspapier des "Arbeitskreises zur Rolle von Unternehmern und Unternehmen im Nationalsozialismus" der Gesellschaft für Unternehmensgeschichte in Frankfurt a.M.] (Frankfurt a.M., 2000).

Overy, Richard J., Otto, Gerhard, & Houwink ten Cate, Johannes (eds.), *Die "Neuordnung Europas." NS-Wirtschaftspolitik in den besetzten Gebieten* (Berlin, 1997).

Paul, Gerhard, "Josef Bürckel. Der rote Gauleiter," in Ronald Smelser, Enrico Syring, & Rainer Zitelmann (eds.), *Die braune Elite II. 21 weitere biographische Skizzen* (Darmstadt, 1993), pp. 51–65.

Pehle, Walter H. (ed.), *Der Judenpogrom 1938. Von der "Reichskristallnacht" zum Völkermord* (Frankfurt a.M., 1988).

Pierenkemper, Toni, "Was kann eine moderne Unternehmensgeschichte leisten? Und was sollte sie tunlichst vermeiden," *Zeitschrift für Unternehmensgeschichte* 44 (1999), pp. 15–31.

Pierenkemper, Toni, "Sechs Thesen zum gegenwärtigen Stand der deutschen Unternehmensgeschichtsschreibung. Eine Entgegnung auf Manfred Pohl," *Zeitschrift für Unternehmensgeschichte* 45 (2000), pp. 158–66.

Pohl, Dieter, "Die großen Zwangsarbeiterlager der SS- und Polizeiführer für Juden im Generalgouvernement 1942–1945," in Ulrich Herbert et al., *Die nationalsozialistischen Konzentrationslager*, vol. I, pp. 415–38.

Pohl, Manfred, "Zwischen Weihrauch und Wissenschaft? Zum Standort der modernen Unternehmensgeschichte. Eine Replik auf Toni Pierenkemper," *Zeitschrift für Unternehmensgeschichte* 44 (1999), pp. 150–63.

Rappl, Marian, "'Arisierungen' in Munich. Die Verdrängung der jüdischen Gewerbetreibenden aus dem Wirtschaftsleben der Stadt 1933–1939," *Zeitschrift für bayerische Landesgeschichte* 63 (2000), pp. 123–84.

Rauh-Kühne, Cornelia, "Die Entnazifizierung und die deutsche Gesellschaft," *Archiv für Sozialgeschichte* 35 (1995), pp. 35–70.

Roloff, Marita, & Mosser, Alois, *Wiener Allianz. Gegründet 1860* (Vienna, 1991).

Scholder, Klaus (ed.), *Die Mittwochs-Gesellschaft: Protokolle aus dem geistigen Deutschland 1932 bis 1944* (Berlin, 1982).

Schulte, Jan Erik, "Das SS-Unternehmen 'Deutsche Ausrüstungswerke GmbH'," in Herbert et al., *Die nationalsozialistischen Konzentrationslager*, vol. II, pp. 558–83.

Schwarz, Hans-Peter (ed.), *Die Wiederherstellung des deutschen Kredits. Das Londoner Schuldenabkommen* (Stuttgart & Zurich, 1982).

Sereny, Gita, *Albert Speer: His Battle with Truth* (New York, 1995).

Silverman, Dan P., *Hitler's Economy. Nazi Work Creation Programs, 1933–1936* (Cambridge, Mass., 1998).

Sipos, Péter, "Hungary in the German Sphere of Interest," in Overy et al., *Die "Neuordnung" Europas*, pp. 241–56.

Smelser, Ronald, *Robert Ley. Hitler's Labor Front Leader* (New York & London, 1988).

Speer, Albert, *Inside the Third Reich. Memoirs* (New York, 1970).

Speier, Hans, *German White-Collar Workers and the Rise of Hitler* (New Haven & London, 1986).

Steinberg, Jonathan, *The Deutsche Bank and Its Gold Transactions during the Second World War* (Munich, 1999).

Sundhausen, Holm, "Improvisierte Ausbeutung. Der Balkan unter deutscher Okkupation," in Houwink ten Cate & Otto, *Das organisierte Chaos,* pp. 55–76.

Surminski, Arno, *Versicherung unterm Hakenkreuz* (Berlin, 1999).

Teichova, Alice, "Instruments of Economic Control and Exploitation: The German Occupation of Bohemia and Moravia," in Overy et al., *Die "Neuordnung" Europas,* pp. 83–108.

Thuer, Hans, "Die 'Österreichische Versicherungs-AG' und 'Deutscher Ring Österreichische Lebensversicherung AG' der Deutschen Arbeitsfront (1936–1945)," in Wolfgang Rohrbach (ed.), *Versicherungsgeschichte Österreichs, Bd. 3: Das Zeitalter des modernen Versicherungswesens* (Vienna, 1988).

Turner, Henry A., Jr., *German Big Business and the Rise of Hitler* (New York, 1985).

Turner, Henry A., Jr. (ed.), *Hitler aus nächster Nähe. Aufzeichnungen eines Vertrauten 1929–1932* (Frankfurt a.M., 1978); translated as *Hitler – Memoirs of a Confidant, 1929–1932* (New Haven, 1985).

Tyrell, Albrecht, "Gottfried Feder – Der gescheiterte Programmatiker," in Ronald Smelser & Rainer Zitelmann (eds.), *Die braune Elite I. 22 biographische Skizzen* (Darmstadt, 1989), pp. 28–40.

Ueberschär, Gerd R., *Die Deutsche Reichspost 1933–1945. Eine politische Verwaltungsgeschichte, Bd. 2: 1939–1945* (Berlin, 1999).

Vogelsang, Reinhard, *Der Freundeskreis Himmler* (Göttingen, 1972).

"Das 'Wagnis Auschwitz'," *Der Spiegel* 23 (June 2, 1997), pp. 50–63.

Walter, Dirk, *Antisemitische Kriminalität und Gewalt. Judenfeindschaft in der Weimarer Republik* (Bonn, 1999).

Wandel, Eckhard, *Hans Schäffer. Steuermann in wirtschaftlichen und politischen Krisen* (Stuttgart, 1974).

Wandel, Eckhard, *Banken und Versicherungen im 19. und 20. Jahrhundert* [Enzyklopädie Deutscher Geschichte, Bd. 45] (Munich, 1998).

Weiß, Hermann (ed.), *Biographisches Lexikon zum Dritten Reich* (Frankfurt a.M., 1998).

Weiß, Volker, "Ist das, was wir machen, auch gerecht? Zum Gedächtnis an Generaldirektor Johannes Tiedke 1881–1947" (Oberursel, 1995) (unpublished manuscript).

Werner, Andreas, "SA und NSDAP. 'Wehrverband', 'Parteitruppe' oder 'Revolutionsarmee'? Studien zur Geschichte der SA und der NSDAP 1920–1933," Phil. Diss. (Erlangen, 1964).

Wiesen, Jonathan, "Overcoming Nazism: Big Business and the Politics of Memory," *Central European History* 29 (1996), pp. 201–26.

Wiesen, Jonathan, *West German Industry and the Challenge of the Nazi Past* (Chapel Hill, 2001).

Wren, Christopher S., "Insurers Swindled Jews, Nazi Files Show," *New York Times* (May 16, 1998), p. 3.

Ziegler, Dieter, "Die Verdrängung der Juden aus der Dresdner Bank 1933–1938," *Vierteljahrshefte für Zeitgeschichte* 47 (1999), pp. 187–216.

Zink, Harold, *The United States in Germany 1944–1945* (Princeton, 1957).

Zweig, Ronald W., *German Reparations and the Jewish World. A History of the Claims Conference* (Boulder & London, 1987).

Index